B. Woodcroft

Historic index of patents applied for and patents granted

B. Woodcroft

Historic index of patents applied for and patents granted

ISBN/EAN: 9783741170348

Manufactured in Europe, USA, Canada, Australia, Japa

Cover: Foto ©knipser5 / pixelio.de

Manufactured and distributed by brebook publishing software
(www.brebook.com)

B. Woodcroft

Historic index of patents applied for and patents granted

SUBJECT-MATTER INDEX

OF

PATENTS APPLIED FOR AND PATENTS GRANTED

For the Year 1865.

15 & 16 VICTORIÆ, Cap. 83. Sec. XXXII.

SUBJECT-MATTER INDEX

OF

PATENTS APPLIED FOR AND PATENTS GRANTED,

For the Year 1865.

Printed and Published by Order of the Honourable the Commissioners of Patents

UNDER THE

ACT of 15 & 16 VICTORIÆ, Cap. 83. Sec. XXXIII.

BY BENNET WOODCROFT,

CLERK OF THE COMMISSIONERS OF PATENTS.

LONDON:
PRINTED BY GEORGE EDWARD EYRE AND WILLIAM SPOTTISWOODE,
PRINTERS TO THE QUEEN'S MOST EXCELLENT MAJESTY.
PUBLISHED AT THE OFFICE OF THE COMMISSIONERS
OF PATENTS FOR INVENTIONS,
SOUTHAMPTON BUILDINGS, HOLBORN.

1867.

	Page
Saccharometers — (see thermometers)	427
Marking for herbs and safes — (see upholstery)	445
Marks and bags — (see bags)	30
Mad irons, smoothing irons — (see mangling)	272
Saddles for horses, saddle-trees — (see harness)	194
Safes and strong boxes — (see locks)	224
Safes for shop windows — (see show-cases)	378
Safety nets for arresting the fall of heavy bodies — (see accidents)	1
Safety plugs — (see gauges)	180
Safety valve regulators — (see valves)	437
Saggers used in potteries — (see earthenware)	130
Sails for mills; windmill sails — (see air engines)	8
Sails for ships, ships' rigging — (see ships' rigging)	374
Salt and saltpetre	366
Salts and oxides of metals — (see metallic salts)	269
Salts of alumina and potash — (see alkalies)	24
Sand and glass paper and cloths — (see grinding, sharpening)	168
Sandals or shoes — (see boots)	36
Sashes and windows — (see windows)	469
Satchels and bags — (see bags)	30
Satin white — (see painting)	291
Saucepans — (see cooking)	99
Sawyers and rope — (see plates)	316
Sausages — (see preserving food)	320
Saw-mills — (see lamps)	221
Saving fuel — (see smoke)	347
Saving life and property at sea — (see lamps)	68
Sawing machines, saws and saw-mills — (see cutting)	102
Scabbards or sheaths for swords and daggers — (see bayonets)	32
Scaffolding and ladders — (see building)	54
Scale or rust, preventing formation of — (see oxidation)	289
Scales and arbo for knives — (see knives)	219
Scales or rules for measuring — (see measuring length)	256
Scarfs and shawls — (see petticoats)	301
Scarfs for gentlemen — (see shirts)	375
Scarlet colours — (see dyes)	124
Scattering guano and artificial manures — (see sowing)	391
Scenic effects — (see dramatic effects)	127
Scent and smelling bottles — (see hair-dressing)	196
Scissors and shears — (see knives)	219
Scouring and cleaning fabrics, yarns, &c. — (see washing)	445
Scouring stones, marble and slate — (see stone)	418
Scrapers for roads — (see paving)	289
Scraps of leather — (see leather)	226
Screens, strainers and sieves — (see sifting)	374
Screens or blinds, flower-cases — (see window-blinds)	468
Screw drivers, screw-wrenches, screw-stocks — (see wire)	441
Screw grills or heckle frames — (see spinning)	383
Screw jacks — (see boats)	284
Screw propellers — (see propelling)	381
Screws and screw blanks — (see nails)	276
Scribbling and carding fibrous substances — (see spinning)	383
Scrolls and frets — (see mouldings)	274

	Page
Scrotal and abdominal bandages — (see surgery)	423
Scratching fibrous substances — (see spinning)	383
Scythes — (see reaping)	362
Sea-going vessels — (see ship-building)	369
Sea walls — (see docks)	117
Sea-weeds and plants — (see plants)	315
Seating and lining carriages — (see carriages)	62
Seatings for valves — (see valves)	437
Seats and fittings for ships and boats — (see ship-building)	369
Seats of water-closets — (see watercloset)	447
Securing artificial teeth in the mouth — (see dentistry)	113
Securing buttons to fabrics — (see wearing apparel)	452
Securing corks or stoppers in bottles — (see bottles)	42
Securing doors when shut — (see doors)	119
Securing envelopes — (see envelopes)	137
Securing labels and invoices — (see stamps)	403
Securing rails to sleepers — (see railways)	352
Securing safes and strong rooms — (see locks)	224
Securing the ends of hoops in packing bales — (see presses)	322
Securing tubes in tube plates — (see steam-boilers)	405
Seed and manure drills — (see sowing)	391
Seed crushing — (see grinding corn)	165
Seeds and rice, cleaning and dressing — (see thrashing)	429
Segmental grates for furnaces — (see furnaces)	164
Self-acting alarms — (see signals)	380
Self-acting boiler-feeders — (see steam-boilers)	411
Self-acting temples for looms — (see weaving)	460
Self-generating motive-power — (see motive-power)	273
Self-supplying pens — (see pens)	300
Separating and sorting — (see sifting)	374
Separating fibres from fabrics — (see rags)	351
Separating metals; smelting — (see metals)	269
Separating serobbins from grain — (see grinding corn)	165
Serpents or fireworks — (see rockets)	363
Setting and distributing printing type — (see printing)	336
Sewage and manure — (see manure)	233
Sewers — (see drains)	121
Sewing and embroidering	366
Shackles or couplings for railway carriages — (see railways)	356
Shackles or links for chains — (see chains)	76
Shades and blinds for windows — (see window-blinds)	468
Shades for lamps — (see lamps)	221
Shaft sinking — (see mining)	260
Shafting; shafts and axles — (see axles)	26
Shafts for hoists — (see hoists)	209
Shafts for ventilation — (see ventilation)	441
Shale oils — (see oils of tar)	294
Shampooing by machinery — (see hair-dressing)	196
Shampooing horses — (see horses)	198
Shanks for buttons — (see buttons)	69
Shaping and trimming boots and shoes — (see boots)	36
Shaping hat and bonnet blocks — (see hats)	200

SYNOPSIS.

SUBJECT-MATTER INDEX

OF

PATENTS APPLIED FOR AND PATENTS GRANTED,

For the Year 1865.

Subject-matter of Patent.	Number of Patent.	Date.	Name of Patentee.
ACCIDENTS (*Prevention of*).			
Improved apparatus for preventing the explosion of steam-boilers.	808	3rd Feb. 1865	John Westerby.
Improvements in the miner's safety lamp	859	8th Feb. 1865	Richard Clarke Thorp. Philip Young.
Hydraulic presses	417	14th Feb. 1865	George Whitton.
An improved means of securing the safety of railway passengers.	454	17th Feb. 1865	Coleman Defries.
Arrangements or apparatus to be applied to vehicles drawn by horses to restrain and prevent them from running away.	680	2nd March 1865	Peter Rotherell.
Revolving fire-arms (*Communicated by Sébastien Amédée Noël and François Garvey.*)	859	9th March 1865	William Clark.
Improvements in the construction of railway plant to ensure the safety of passengers' lives in the event of accident or collision	688	11th March 1865	Charles Middleton Kennol. Nathaniel Symons.
Stoves or fire-places, ash-pans and fenders (*fender or dress protector.*)	699	23rd March 1865	James Clifford Morgan.
Gun locks	858	24th March 1865	Daniel Arnold.
An improved safety tackle for raising and lowering heavy weights.	937	3rd April 1865	Pierre Joseph Jannet.
Improvements in or applicable to boilers furnished with pipes for the circulation of water for domestic purposes.	974	6th April 1865	John Brown.
Couplings for railway carriages, waggons, trucks and other vehicles.	1035	11th April 1865	Josiah Dadley.
Lamps for burning petroleum, naphtha or other mineral oils	1040	12th April 1865	Charles Bourbon. Josef Kindtner. William Caffou.
An improved safety apparatus for steam-boilers	1066	15th April 1865	John Minton Courtauld.
Construction of ships or vessels or cars to float on water.	1083	18th April 1865	William Holder.
Means of covering railway trucks, vans, and other carriages.	1090	19th April 1865	William Riddell.
Apparatus for preventing explosions in steam-boilers.	1096	20th April 1865	John Hocking the younger.

A

Subject-matter of Patent.	Number of Patent.	Date.	Name of Patentee.

Subject-matter of Patent.	Number of Patent.	Date.	Name of Patentee.
ACCIDENTS—*continued.*			
Improvements in apparatus and equipments used by persons employed under water, part of the improvements being also applicable for the use of persons employed where noxious gases or vapours prevail.	1840	12th July 1865	Auguste Denayrouse.
Ventilators - - - - - - - *(for preventing accidents by fire.)*	1896	18th July 1865	John Paul Baugh Le Patourel.
An improved apparatus for producing sound for signals, calls and alarms, adapted to use on vessels, railway trains, buoys, reefs, lighthouses and in other places of danger. *(Communicated by The Incorporated Marine Signal Company.)*	1898	20th July 1865	John Harkness Wray.
Apparatus for cleaning windows - - -	1907	21st July 1865	Charles Gardner.
Apparatus for preventing accidents on railways -	1945	26th July 1865	Jean Jacques Namual Wrah. Alexandre Alphonse Mathieu.
Manufacture of anti-flammable starch - -	1946	26th July 1865	Tobiah Pepper.
Apparatus to be used in swimming - - - *(or for saving life.) (Communicated by Jean Baptiste Victor Chestel.)*	1982	31st July 1865	William Clark.
Improvements in the construction of railway carriages, and in railway breaks and signals, part of which is applicable to marine purposes -	2005	2nd Aug. 1865	William Henry Petitjean. Edward McNally.
Railway electrical signal apparatus - -	2016	3rd Aug. 1865	William Henry Preece
Improvements in the makings of metallic and other bedsteads, sofas, couches and other like articles, which said improvements may also be applied to the seats of chairs, railway carriages and other articles. *(Communicated by Thomas Tannington.)*	2036	5th Aug. 1865	Henry Oerring.
A self-acting coupling for railway carriages and wagons - - - - - -	2037	5th Aug. 1865	Thomas Smith. John Brook.
Improvements in preparing and treating gunpowder in order to render the same unexplosive and to protect it from damp.	2057	8th Aug. 1865	James Gale, jun'.
Apparatus for giving immediate warning of undue heat, whether occasioned by fire, spontaneous combustion or any other causes, of leakage in ships, and of the sudden irruption of water, and of the accumulation of choke damp in mines.	2064	9th Aug. 1865	Charles West.
A combination of improved method, apparatus and receptacles for storing, preserving, transferring and discharging certain fluids, for sanitary and protective purposes. *(Communicated by Henry Pixlus.)*	2096	14th Aug. 1865	Robert Alexander William Westley.
Improved safety couplings for railway carriages -	2159	22nd Aug. 1865	Frederick Charles Bryan Robinson.
Tanks and other receptacles for obtaining and transporting petroleum, naphtha and other oils and liquids, to prevent wastage by fire or filtration or evaporation, or hazard of life.	2195	25th Aug. 1865	George Washington Howard.
Machinery or apparatus for disengaging runaway horses from carriages and stopping them, so as to prevent accidents.	2214	29th Aug. 1865	Robert Thomas Holmes.
Improved steam-heating apparatus - - *(Communicated by Henry Bulkley.)*	2255	1st Sept. 1865	Alfred Vincent Newton.

Subject-matter of Patent.	Number of Patent.	Date.	Name of Patentee.
ACCIDENTS—*continued.*			
Improved apparatus for promptly disconnecting horses from carriages and other vehicles.	2271	4th Sept. 1865	Pierre Marrand.
Apparatus for preventing incrustation in steam-boilers, and for preventing explosion of such boilers, heating the feed water, and consuming smoke	2272	4th Sept. 1865	James Howard, William Stafford, William Porter McCallum.
Life rafts and surf boats (Communicated by Edward Livingston Perry.)	2273	4th Sept. 1865	Alfred Vincent Newton.
An improved method of fixing and unfixing the tubes of steam-boilers. (Communicated by Daniel McDowell.)	2284	6th Sept. 1865	Samuel Soutar.
Apparatus connected with safes for protecting valuables from fire	2318	9th Sept. 1865	Adolf Erik Nordenskiold, John William Smith.
An improved stirrup latch bar	2320	11th Sept. 1865	Samuel Davis.
An improved safety valve for steam-boilers	2322	11th Sept. 1865	Henry Hackett, Thomas Wrigley, Edmund Pearson.
Safety lamps for use in mines and other localities (Communicated by André Jean Olivier.)	2370	16th Sept. 1865	Leo H Adries Bonneville.
An improved construction of projectile (Communicated by Orario Lugo.)	2381	18th Sept. 1865	Alfred Vincent Newton.
Safety apparatus for cages and hoists	2383	19th Sept. 1865	John Charton Broadbent.
Improvements in railways and in the wheels for railways (Communicated by Alexander Shelton.)	2409	21st Sept. 1865	Alfred Vincent Newton.
Breech-loading fire-arms (Communicated by Samuel Norris.)	2452	25th Sept. 1865	Alexander Prince.
Life rafts	2510	30th Sept. 1865	John Witherden Hurn.
A new or improved double-acting safety stirrup bar	2704	21th Oct. 1865	William Johns.
Fire-arms (Communicated by Emile Delle-Noce.)	2800	31st Oct. 1865	Charles Chartrway.
Apparatus for effecting communications between the passengers, guard and engine drivers in railway trains, and for giving notice to engine drivers in cases of accidents. (Communicated by Samuel Carewallis Amesbury.)	2845	4th Nov. 1865	Henry Radcliffe.
Making amalgams or alloys of metals (preventing explosive action.) (Communicated by Henry Wurtz.)	2903	11th Nov. 1865	William Edward Newton.
Safety apparatus for the prevention of accidents upon railways, by working signals or alarms in order to attract the attention of the guard or driver of the train. (Communicated by Pierre François Rocke.)	2930	14th Nov. 1865	William Edward Newton.
An improved safety net to arrest the fall of persons or heavy bodies under circumstances of danger.	2969	18th Nov. 1865	Léon Edouard Lamreury.
An improved nautical safety apparatus	3045	24th Nov. 1865	François Mola.
Apparatus for increasing the safety of railway passengers and trains, signalling and forming a communication externally and internally between all parts of such trains, lighting, warming and securing the doors of the carriages, and indicating therein and at the stations the names of the places at which the train stops.	3069	29th Nov. 1865	Richard Howarth.

Subject-matter of Patent.	Number of Patent.	Date.	Name of Patentee.
ACCIDENTS—continued.			
Improved means of preventing water-pipes from bursting. (Communicated by John Brown.)	8088	1st Dec. 1865	Longdon McMurdo Rogers.
Apparatus for raising, lowering and moving heavy bodies, and for transmitting and arresting motion for various purposes. (preventing accidents.)	8099	2nd Dec. 1865	Thomas Aldridge Weston.
Apparatus applicable for fire-escapes and builders' scaffolds.	8128	5th Dec. 1865	Edward Vagg.
Construction and arrangement of railway carriages, for the purpose of obviating or diminishing the bad consequences of collisions of or accidents to railway trains	8844	14th Dec. 1865	{ Henry Negretti. Joseph Warren Zambra.
Boilers or apparatus for generating steam . . (arising from explosions.) (Communicated by Julien Belleville.)	8869	18th Dec. 1865	Richard Archibald Brooman.
ACIDS AND VINEGAR.			
An improved method of treating apatite and other mineral phosphates. (obtaining phosphoric acid.) (Communicated by Mr. John Oliver.)	8	2nd Jan. 1865	Montague Richard Leverson.
Treating the pitch obtained in or resulting from the distillation of palm oil and other fats in candle making. (obtaining fatty acids.)	9	2nd Jan. 1865	Robert Irvine.
Filtering apparatus . . . (vinegar, &c.)	249	28th Jan. 1865	Victor Burg.
Manufacture of benzoic acid . . .	393	30th Jan. 1865	{ François Alexandre Laurent. John Combelas.
Improvements in the manufacture of citric and tartaric acids, and in the manufacture and treatment of citrate and tartrate of lime and analogous basic compounds, and in apparatus employed therefor.	507	4th Feb. 1865	Frederic Row.
Extracting turpentine and tar from resinous wood. (and acetic acid.)	403	13th Feb. 1865	Jean Antoine Pastorelly.
Manufacture of oxalic acid - . .	449	16th Feb. 1865	{ François Alexandre Laurent. John Casterias. Nicolas Basset.
Obtaining sulphurous acid	729	14th March 1865	Astley Paston Price.
Manufacture of soluble and available superphosphates of lime, by the application of phosphoric acid and acid phosphates. (Communicated by Lucien Henri Blanchard and Théodore Chaffin.)	1161	25th April 1865	William Clark.
Improvements in brewing, distillation, the production of vinegar, and the extract of malt and other grain.	1865	5th May 1865	Solomon Bennett.

Subject-matter of Patents.	Number of Patent.	Date.	Names of Patentees.
ACIDS, &c.—continued.			
Obtaining certain compounds of nitrogen and of sulphur. (sulphurous and sulphuric acid.)	1385	19th May 1865	Thomas Richardson. Martin Diederich Rucker.
A new method of manufacturing oil from fatty matters or the residuum arising from the distillation of fatty matters, the manufacture of stearic acid, soap, and purification of oils. (Communicated by Pierre René Brevmant.)	1456	27th May 1865	Richard Archibald Brooman.
Improvements in the manufacture of naphthalic acid and chloroxynaphthalic acid, and in dyeing and printing.	1605	13th July 1865	François Alexandre Laurent. John Carthelas.
Obtaining jellies, syrups, drinks and other products from the tree Arbutus Unedo, known as the Arbutus. (enlarger.)	1649	20th June 1865	Philippe Mingaud.
Improvements in distilling and rectifying, and in the apparatus employed therein, parts of which improvements are applicable to steam generators. (distillation of acids.)	1662	20th June 1865	Evariste Vignier.
Treatment of hydrocarbon or paraffin oils	2008	3rd Aug. 1865	John William Perkins.
Obtaining spirits of turpentine, rosin, pitch, tar, pyroligneous acid and other products from wood. (Communicated by Albert Hamilton Emery.)	2247	31st Aug. 1865	William Edward Newton.
Manufacture of oxalic acid	2314	9th Sept. 1865	John Carthelas. Nicolas Bessrt.
Apparatus used for calcining and roasting copper and other ores and substances containing sulphur (obtaining sulphuric acid.)	2350	14th Sept. 1865	Thomas Bell. Thomas Leslie Gregson Bell.
Improvements in obtaining and applying sulphurous acid and in apparatus used therein.	2453	24th Sept. 1865	Reen Reure.
Apparatus for decomposing and superheating liquids, vapours, and gases. (Communicated by Gustave Renard and Amedée Lipman.)	2535	3rd Oct. 1865	Richard Archibald Brooman.
Improvements in the manufacture of chromium or ammonia and chromic acid, and in the preparation of nitrates of lime and baryta. (Communicated by Félix Debaut.)	2702	19th Oct. 1865	William Clark.
ADVERTISING.			
A novel and improved means of advertising	31	5th Jan. 1865	George Howels Davies. John William Jones.
Protecting letters, numerals, and ornamental designs on glass.	1111	21st April 1865	David Nisbon Buckman.
Improvements in the manufacture and application of devices and representations to tombstones, and in other public or exposed situations, for various purposes. (for representations of goods for advertising.)	1130	22nd April 1865	Alfred Grainger. Charles Mitchel Girdler.

Subject-matter of Patent.	Number of Patent.	Date.	Name of Patentee.
AERATING; AËRATED LIQUIDS; MINERAL WATERS; CARBONIC ACID GAS.			
Preparing and keeping aërated beverages - -	59	5th Jan.	1865	Thomas Pickford.
Certain improvements in the manufacture of magnesium and its compounds. (for making carbonic acid gas.)	450	17th Feb.	1865	John Osborne Christian, F.C.S. John Charlton. Henry Charlton.
Improvements in surface condensers for steam-engines, and in feeding boilers therefrom. (aerating the water.)	1669	21st June	1865	Charles Talbot Porter.
An improved machine for the manufacture of aërated waters.	1774	5th July	1865	William Saunders Parfitt.
Means of obtaining or producing oxygen applicable to various useful purposes. (for aërating water.)	1780	6th July	1865	Hermann Brigel.
Improving draught beer, ale, porter, and cider -	1781	6th July	1865	Thomas Symes Pridmore.
An improved portable pocket gas generator or gasogene.	1795	7th July	1865	Augustin François Morelle.
An improved portable chamber or receptacle to contain aërated liquids, and the apparatus connected therewith by which the flow of such liquid is regulated and measured.	1928	25th July	1865	Max Benjamin Schumann.
Apparatus for supplying carbonic acid gas to casks and other vessels from which beer, wine and other fermented liquors are drawn.	2167	25th Aug.	1865	Charles Adolphus Watkins.
Improved means of securing corks in the necks of bottles.	2233	30th Aug.	1865	William Henry Postlethwaite Gore.
Arrangement and fittings of certain apparatuses for extinguishing fires. (carbonic acid gas.)	2373	16th Sept.	1865	François Carlier.
An improved method of making effervescing drinks	2377	19th Sept.	1865	Oliver Weldon Jeyes.
Certain improvements in the production and uses of carbonic acid gas.	2660	16th Oct.	1865	Albert Julius Mott.
An improved manufacture of aërated waters -	3304	12th Dec.	1865	Robert Hinman.
AËRIAL MACHINES; BALLOONS.			
Navigable balloons - - - -	930	1st April	1865	Paul Haenlein.
A new apparatus or mechanism for flying through the air.	1037	12th April	1865	Gustave Wilhelm Rothlieb.
Rotatory aërial wings - - - -	1073	17th April	1865	James John Matthewson. Heinrich Louis Rudolph Nehlev.
Fire-engines and hydraulic machines - - (or aërial machines, inflating balloons, &c.)	1958	24th July	1865	Leon Paul Laroche.
Improvements in the construction of flying toys, also applicable to other purposes. (applicable to parachutes.) (Communicated by Charles Edmond François Coulariev.)	2208	24th Aug.	1865	Henri Adrien Bonneville.
Apparatus for aërial navigation - - - (Communicated by Salomon Andrews.)	3253	19th Dec.	1865	William Clark.

Subject-matter of Patent.	Number of Patent.	Date.	Name of Patentee.
AIR, GAS AND WIND ENGINES AND MILLS; PNEUMATIC MOTIVE-POWER.			
Motive-power and means of communication between passengers while travelling, and appliances connected therewith.	55	7th Jan. 1865	George Bell Galloway.
Regulating and working the valves of steam and other engines.	82	11th Jan. 1865	John Frederick Spencer.
Steam-engines - - - - (or gas-engines.)	168	19th Jan. 1865	William Cleveland Hicks.
Obtaining motive-power - - -	391	6th Feb. 1865	John Isaac Watts.
Steam engines - - - -	468	14th Feb. 1865	James Grafton Jones.
Obtaining motive-power from aëriform fluids and from liquids.	501	22nd Feb. 1865	Matthew Piers Watt Boulton.
Machinery for obtaining motive-power from ammoniacal gas. (Communicated by Joseph Flemdria.)	611	4th March 1865	Richard Archibald Brosman.
Motive-power engines - - - (Communicated by Auguste Gevin.)	651	8th March 1865	William Clark.
Gas engines - - - -	731	15th March 1865	Hugh Smith.
An elementary power engine or a new or improved compressed air engine, for imparting power and motion to all kinds of machinery.	818	23rd March 1865	Anthony Bernhard, Baron Von Rathen.
Obtaining motive-power from aëriform fluids and from liquids.	827	23rd March 1865	Matthew Piers Watt Boulton.
Improvements in obtaining motive-power, parts of which improvements are applicable to the compressing of air and gases.	840	24th March 1865	Valentine Baker.
An improvement in engines worked by heated air or gases.	905	31st March 1865	John Pinchbeck.
Navigable balloons - - - -	930	1st April 1865	Paul Haenlein.
Means or apparatus for obtaining motive-power by the aid of steam, gas or other fluids. (Communicated by Joseph Perrignon, Marie Joseph Denis Farcot, Jean Joseph Leon Farcot, Michel Basile Abel Farcot, Joseph Etienne Abel Chêtron, and Emmanuel Denis Farcot.)	940	4th April 1865	William Brookes.
Apparatus employed to actuate the valves of engines worked by steam, air or other fluid.	962	6th April 1865	James Grafton Jones.
Certain improvements in gas engines - -	986	6th April 1865	Pierre Hugon.
Certain improvements in gas-ammoniacal engines -	1074	17th April 1865	Louis de St. Céran.
Machinery for obtaining motive-power - -	1601	10th May 1865	William Joseph Rice.
An improved metallic stuffing box - -	1555	7th June 1865	Victor Dutarre.
Calorie or heated air engines - - - (Communicated by Cyrus W. Baldwin and Walter Davis Richards.)	1568	8th June 1865	Samuel Blatchford Tucker.
Means and apparatus for generating motive-power - (Communicated by Jules Gros.)	1656	28th June 1865	William Clark.
Obtaining motive-power - - - (Communicated by Monsieur Charles Tellier.)	1832	11th July 1865	Hector Auguste Dufresd.
Certain improvements in the method of obtaining motive-power and in apparatus connected therewith.	1910	22nd July 1865	Edmund Perré.

Subject-matter of Patent.	Number of Patent.	Date.	Name of Patentee.
AIR ENGINES, &c.—*continued*.			
Obtaining motive-power when heated air or aëriform fluid is employed.	1815	22nd July 1865	Matthew Piers Watt Boulton.
Means of and apparatus for treating animal and vegetable fibrous materials, which apparatus is also applicable to various useful purposes. (*gears for gas engines*.)	1858	27th July 1865	Henry Sherwood.
An improved water meter, which may be employed as a water, steam or gas engine. (*Communicated by Henry Isham*.)	1866	29th July 1865	William Edward Newton.
Applying and utilising water power - - (*for working air engines*.)	1867	29th July 1865	Valentine Baker.
Obtaining motive-power by heat - - -	1909	1st Aug. 1865	Matthew Piers Watt Boulton.
Improvements in generating steam and in heating steam and vaporiform fluids.	2051	7th Aug. 1865	Matthew Piers Watt Boulton.
Apparatus for obtaining and applying motive-power to various useful purposes - - -	2080	11th Aug. 1865	William Thomas Cole. Henry Frank Swift, Augusto Souten.
Improved machinery or apparatus for obtaining motive-power by expansion of air. (*Communicated by Abraham David Cherfils*.)	2600	9th Oct. 1865	William Edward Gedge.
Caloric or hot-air engines - - - - (*Communicated by Guillaume Reistria*.)	2675	17th Oct. 1865	Richard Archibald Brooman.
New or improved cranes and apparatus for destroying ships and such like floating bodies, parts of which said apparatus are also applicable to saving life and property at sea. (*gas-engine*.) (*Communicated by Monsieur Stanislas Sorel*.)	2756	26th Oct. 1865	Hector Augusto Dufrené.
Improvements in obtaining motive-power and in apparatus employed therein.	3014	24th Nov. 1865	Jules Wunthier.
Producing and applying rotating motion by means of an apparatus to be worked by fluids, steam, compressed air, or by water or by gas.	3270	19th Dec. 1865	John Wright Carr.
Improvements in propellers for ships and vessels, parts of which are applicable to windmill sails and fan blowers - - - -	3295	29th Dec. 1865	Frederick Lamb Hancock. Charles Lamb Hancock.
Obtaining and employing continuous lengths of tanned leather for various useful purposes - (*for making mill sails*.)	3334	23rd Dec. 1865	George Hurn. Daniel Hurn.
Improvements in obtaining motive-power, and in apparatus employed therein. (*from abroad*.) (*Communicated by Jean Frot*.)	3358	29th Dec. 1865	Richard Archibald Brooman.

See also "GOVERNORS."

Subject-matter of Patent.	Number of Patent.	Date.	Name of Patentee.

AIR SUPPLYING, BLOWING, EXHAUSTING ; DRAFT AND VENTILATION.

I.—Supplying Air to Furnaces, Stoves, Lamps, &c.; Exhausting and Regulating Draft; Tuyeres; Dampers; Chimney Wind Guards; Heating Blast.

Lamps for burning the vapour of volatile fluids	41	6th Jan. 1865	John Clarke Bayley. Daniel Campbell.
Improvements in furnaces, ash-pits and flues for the consumption of smoke and noxious products of combustion, and in the apparatus or means connected therewith.	51	6th Jan. 1865	James Robertson.
Improvements in puddling, heating, and other reverberatory furnaces used in the manufacture of iron and steel and for other purposes, which improvements may also be applied to steam-boiler furnaces.	173	24th Jan. 1865	John Hewes.
Petroleum and coal oil burners and glasses	201	23rd Jan. 1865	Michael Alexander Dietz.
Furnaces for melting metals and smelting ores	209	24th Jan. 1865	William Woodward, Robert Woodward, John Woodward, Adam Woodward, jun'.
Lanterns for burning hydrocarbon fluids	254	24th Jan. 1865	Alexander Septimus Macrae.
Construction of caps or pots for the chimneys of dwelling houses and public buildings.	264	30th Jan. 1865	George Carter.
Improvements in effecting the combustion of fuel in the furnaces of steam-boilers and the fire-places of stoves, and of gas in gas-burners, and in apparatus connected therewith.	311	4th Feb. 1865	Frank Clarke Hills.
Improvements in furnaces for smelting iron ores, commonly called blast furnaces, also in cupolas used in foundries, for rendering down or melting iron or other metals.	374	10th Feb. 1865	Evan Leigh.
Improvements in furnaces and boilers and parts connected with them, for generating steam and heating fluids, and also for improved apparatus for reducing and shutting off steam and regulating the speed of steam-engines.	395	11th Feb. 1865	John Case.
Cupolas and blast furnaces	397	11th Feb. 1865	Henry Houldsworth Grierson. John Merricar Rigby.
Fire-places	407	13th Feb. 1865	Edward Brown Wilson.
Improved apparatus for supplying with a constant and regular pressure air to burners for consuming or burning hydrocarbons for illuminating purposes.	409	13th Feb. 1865	Edward John Cowling Welch.
Furnaces for smelting or reducing ores and for melting metals	411	14th Feb. 1865	Herbert John Walduck. Edward Barton.
An improved blowing apparatus	427	15th Feb. 1865	Samuel Richards Freeman. Abraham Grundy.
An improvement in the utilization of the waste gases of blast furnaces.	476	20th Feb. 1865	Joseph Cliff.

Subject-matter of Patent.	Number of Patent.	Date.	Name of Patentee.

Air Supplying, &c.—continued.

An improved atmospheric pressure lamp for the burning of benzole, paraffin, naphtha or other volatile oils, which lamp may be used for all the purposes for which lamps are usually required, either for lighting, cooking, heating or other purposes. (Partly communicated by John Joseph Riddle.)	569	24th Feb. 1865	William Bell Dalston.
Smoke consuming apparatus . . .	684	2nd March 1865	{ Samuel Hopkinson. Edwin Hopkinson.
Water tuyere for blast furnaces . . (Partly communicated by Mr. Norris Best.)	729	15th March 1865	Nathaniel Neal Solly.
Apparatus for smoke vents or chimneys . .	794	15th March 1865	Thomas Kennedy.
Apparatus for blowing smiths' and other fires	795	16th March 1865	{ James Coulson. Philip Billington.
Argand gas-burners	809	22nd March 1865	William Morvant Baker.
Stoves or fire-places, ash-pans, and fenders	828	23rd March 1865	James Clifford Morgan.
Apparatus for obtaining light . .	841	24th March 1865	Giacomo Felice Marchisio.
Improvements in the manufacture or preparation of materials for and in their application to lighting and heating purposes, also in apparatus used for the same. (Communicated by Auguste de Peyrousy.)	855	25th March 1865	William Clark.
Certain improvements in gas-burners . .	876	28th March 1865	François Adolphe Mocquard.
Furnaces or apparatus for heating the blast for furnaces used in smelting iron, and for other furnaces.	891	29th March 1865	John Player.
Means or method of curing or preventing smoky chimneys.	911	31st March 1865	Benjamin Greenwood.
Apparatus applicable to furnaces for smelting ores and melting metals	942	3rd April 1865	{ Henry Brook. John Eastwood. George Brook, jun'.
An improved rabble or hoe used in puddling iron .	966	5th April 1865	George Walter Dyson.
Fire-places and flues and apparatus connected therewith.	989	7th April 1865	Edward Welch.
A new method of applying suction and blast, and the apparatus employed therein. (Communicated by Fritz Alexandre Trutad de Beaurepaire.)	1028	11th April 1865	Richard Archibald Brooman.
Smoke consuming furnaces . . . (Communicated by Etienne Souret and Eugene de Flercy.)	1169	25th April 1865	Richard Archibald Brooman.
Improvements in drying malt and grain, and in the machinery or apparatus connected therewith.	1297	10th May 1865	John Forbes.
Gas-burners and chimneys . . . . (Communicated by William Brew.)	1334	13th May 1865	William Clark.
Ovens or kilns for the manufacture of coke	1435	25th May 1865	John Gjers.
Cupola and other blast furnaces . .	1445	26th May 1865	Richard Canham.
Means and apparatus employed for preventing downward draft in chimneys, facilitating the escape of smoke therefrom, and for ventilating apartments or buildings . . .	1471	29th May 1865	{ Edward Myers. James Nicalari.
An improved burner for gas and other lighting apparatus.	1494	31st May 1865	Hypolite Mosier.

Subject-matter of Patent.	Number of Patent.	Date.	Name of Patentee.
AIR SUPPLYING, &c. —*continued.*			
Foundry cupolas	1498	31st May 1865	Thomas Summerson.
Caloric or heated air engines (*Communicated by Cyrus W. Baldwin and Walter Davis Richards.*)	1553	8th June 1865	Samuel Blatchford Tucker.
Lamp burners and parts connected therewith (*Communicated by Rufus Spaulding Merrill and William Lincoln.*)	1631	16th June 1865	John Henry Johnson.
An improved method of and apparatus for burning liquid hydrocarbons, and the employment thereof for heating purposes. (*Communicated by Alexandre Schpakofsky and Nicolas Stange.*)	1711	27th June 1865	Richard Archibald Brooman.
Means and apparatus for increasing the mechanical power of steam.	1820	10th July 1865	William Alexander Lyttle.
Lamps	1872	15th July 1865	Anson Henry Platt.
Construction and working of furnaces for puddling, balling, heating and melting metals.	1882	19th July 1865	David Caddick.
Fire-engines and hydraulic machines (*blow pipes of forges.*)	1953	24th July 1865	Leon Paul Laroche.
Locomotive and other tubular boilers	1990	1st Aug. 1865	Louis Emile Constant Martin.
Wick holders or burners for lamps	2024	4th Aug. 1865	{ Emil Wild. Wilhelm Wessel.
Lamps for burning paraffin oil and other volatile oils.	2042	7th Aug. 1865	Abraham Follet Osler.
Manufacture of candles (*Communicated by Charles Gauthier.*)	2088	11th Aug. 1865	John Henry Johnson.
Improvements in carburetting coal gas and manufacturing artificial gas, and in the machinery or apparatus employed therein.	2095	12th Aug. 1865	Henry Woodward.
Improvements in and connected with the manufacture of copper.	2100	14th Aug. 1865	James Thomas Lorkey.
Furnaces to be used in the manufacture of glass and iron and steel, and for other like purposes. (*Communicated by Henning Bortius.*)	2108	15th Aug. 1865	John Frederick Bortius.
Blacksmiths' bellows, more especially those used in portable forges.	2152	21st Aug. 1865	John Bowden.
Steam-boiler and other furnaces	2158	22nd Aug. 1865	John Lockwood.
A new and useful steam blower or blast apparatus for furnaces. (*Communicated by John Allen Bassett.*)	2245	31st Aug. 1865	Oliver Bennett.
Means of and apparatus for consuming smoke in furnaces.	2392	19th Sept. 1865	Charles Worssam.
Improvements in and applicable to furnaces for the consumption of smoke.	2405	21st Sept. 1865	William Watkin.
Apparatus for ventilating and for preventing down draught in flues.	2467	26th Sept. 1865	John Hilliar.
Apparatus for lighting and heating suitable for sick rooms and carriages, and applicable also as holders for matches, watches and other necessary articles. (*Communicated by François René Menaud and Charles Louis Marie Menaud.*)	2515	30th Sept. 1865	John Henry Johnson.
Blast furnaces	2526	2nd Oct. 1865	Silas Covell Salisbury.

Subject-matter of Patent.	Number of Patent.	Date.	Name of Patentee.
AIR SUPPLYING, &c.—continued.			
Improvements in apparatus for the regulation of the up and down currents of air, and for the prevention and cure of smoky chimneys.	2509	10th Oct. 1865	William Cooke.
Paraffine lamps	2516	10th Oct. 1865	Daniel Galafent.
Improvements in steam-boilers and other apparatus applicable to the heating and evaporation of liquids, parts of which improvements are applicable also to other purposes	2551	16th Oct. 1865	Francis Wise, Edward Field, Enoch Harrison Aydon.
Treatment of copper ores in the manufacture of copper. (Communicated by Frédéric le Clerc.)	2562	16th Oct. 1865	William Clark.
A new or improved steam consuming apparatus, or an apparatus intended to make available as fuel all or part of the steam actually evolving from engines into the atmosphere, and also to absorb the smoke resulting from the combustion.	2576	17th Oct. 1865	François George Nicardo.
Furnaces	2592	17th Oct. 1865	William Boardmore.
Hydrocarbon lamps. (Communicated by Dr. Moritz Herzog and David Leopold Cohn.)	2742	24th Oct. 1865	William Snell.
Lanterns for burning coal oil, petroleum and other hydrocarbon fluids. (equalizing admission of air.) (Communicated by William Westlake.)	2809	1st Nov. 1865	Edwin Addison Phillips.
An improved apparatus for increasing draught in and preventing or curing smoky chimneys, and economizing heat. (Communicated by François Perrochon.)	2823	2nd Nov. 1865	William Edward Gedge.
Improvements in the manufacture of iron and steel, and in apparatus employed in such manufactures.	2835	3rd Nov. 1865	Henry Bessemer.
Improvements in forges and in apparatus for lubricating parts thereof, which apparatus is also applicable for lubricating other moving parts of machinery. (Communicated by Claude Henri Turyo, &c°.)	2879	8th Nov. 1865	William Edward Gedge.
Furnaces for heating the blast for blast furnaces	2897	10th Nov. 1865	Thomas Whitwell.
Gas stoves	2935	14th Nov. 1865	Samuel Lawrence Gill.
Cooking apparatus (arranging dampers.)	2971	18th Nov. 1865	Samuel Hazard Huntly.
Apparatus for condensing exhaust steam, and heating air by the heat abstracted in effecting the condensation of such steam. (for supplying oxygen to boiler furnaces.) (Communicated by Addison Calvin Fletcher.)	2999	21st Nov. 1865	Alfred Vincent Newton.
Apparatus for obtaining artificial light from volatile liquids or fluids	2998	22nd Nov. 1865	William Webb, Samuel Marland.
Furnaces	3025	25th Nov. 1865	William Alexander Lyttle.
Means or apparatus for economizing and inducing more perfect combustion of fuel in furnaces.	3062	29th Nov. 1865	Thomas Lancaster.
Furnaces (supplying with a current of hot air.)	3095	2nd Dec. 1865	Edward Brown Wilson.
Improvements in puddling, heating, and other reverberatory furnaces used in the manufacture of iron and steel, and for other purposes.	3130	6th Dec. 1865	Thomas Lewis Nicklin.

Subject-matter of Patent.	Number of Patent.	Date.	Name of Patentee.

AIR SUPPLYING, &c.—continued.

An improved mode of applying the compression of air for ventilating purposes, and the compression of any gas for conveying along elastic fluids in conveying pipes .   .   .   . (increasing draft of fire-places.)

3153 — 14th Dec. 1865 — { Pierron de Mondésir. Paul Lehmite. Augustin Jullienne.

Improvements in locomotive engines and in the means employed for generating steam therein. — 3168 — 9th Dec. 1865 — Robert Francis Fairlie.

Construction of fire-places and furnaces .   . — 3247 — 15th Dec. 1865 — George Warring.

Improvements applicable to steam-boilers, iron, steel, retort and other furnaces. — 3339 — 26th Dec. 1865 — Joshua Fisher.

II.—Supplying Air in Cleansing, Threshing and Dressing Grain and Seeds.

Machinery or apparatus for cleaning and decorticating grain. — 115 — 13th Jan. 1865 — Wilson Agar.

An improvement in the construction of mills for grinding and pulverizing grain and other substances. — 211 — 25th Jan. 1865 — Anthony Stevenson.

Improvements in the means of decorticating grain and other seeds, and in apparatus for the same. (Communicated by Gustave Latoste, Christophe Ours Ballot and Clément Montcalle.) — 551 — 24th Feb. 1865 — William Clark.

An improved fan or exhaust for threshing machines (Communicated by Hyppolyte Hallé and Auguste Hallé.) — 1241 — 3rd May 1865 — William Edward Gedge.

Flour mills .   .   .   .   .   . (Communicated by Charles Simon Olivier Martineau, Narcisse Justine and Nicolas François Demet-Préfront.) — 1345 — 15th May 1865 — Henri Adrien Bonneville.

Improvements in drying grass, hay and other substances, and in the machinery for effecting the same .   .   .   .   .   . (forcing heated air through.) — 1969 — 2nd July 1865 — { Baldwin Latham. Robert Campbell.

Machinery or apparatus for hulling and winnowing grain. (Communicated by Friedrich Hrachel and Wilhelm Serk.) — 2300 — 7th Sept. 1865 — William Lloyd Wise.

Improvements in grinding wheat and other grain, and in apparatus for drying and improving the condition of damp wheat or other grain. — 2485 — 24th Sept. 1865 — Benjamin Wren.

An improved mode of ventilating millstones (Communicated by Alexandre Désiré Lespagny.) — 2924 — 13th Nov. 1865 — Henry Edward Newton.

Apparatus employed in grinding corn and other substances capable of being ground by millstones. — 3126 — 5th Dec. 1865 — Edward Alfred Cowper.

Machinery for drying and bleaching grain and other materials. — 3276 — 19th Dec. 1865 — William Cremy.

Subject-matter of Patent.	Number of Patent.	Date.	Name of Patentee.
AIR SUPPLYING, &c.—continued.			
XII.—Admitting, Forcing, and Exhausting Air for Manufacturing and other Purposes; Air Pumps, Bellows, Fans and other Blowers; Forcing Gas through melted Metal, &c			
An improved jacket or protector for metallic and other vessels and structures containing solid substances, liquids or gases, to prevent radiation of heat from or communication of heat to such vessels and structures (air or gas jackets.)	4	2nd Jan.	1865	Edward Bevan, Abel Fleming.
Fan blowers	23	4th Jan.	1865	Wilson Ayre.
A new system of boiling grain sugar in vacuo	42	6th Jan.	1865	Jules Lebaudy.
Locomotive engines (Communicated by Auguste De Bergue.)	48	6th Jan.	1865	Charles De Bergue.
Construction of vacuum pans	57	7th Jan.	1865	Edward Hames, Conrad William Finzel.
Improvements in machinery used for condensing atmospheric air, and in machinery worked by compressed air, employed in getting coal, stone and minerals.	90	11th Jan.	1865	James Grafton Jones.
Furnaces (Communicated by Dominique Chicolo.)	103	12th Jan.	1865	Michael Henry.
Applying power to the working of ships' windlasses, winches, capstans, pumps and other ships' gear.	242	27th Jan.	1865	Handel Moore.
An improved system of drying wool, cotton and other fibrous materials, and in the machinery or apparatus connected therewith. (Communicated by Carl Bru and Louis Boettcher.)	255	28th Jan.	1865	Edward Thomas Hughes.
A new or improved method or process and apparatus for obtaining the concentrated extract of hops, and for preserving the same from deterioration. (Communicated by George Perry, Walter Wells, Charles Brown, John Mulford, and John Maximilian Webb.)	309	4th Feb.	1865	Joseph Rideal Webb.
An improved combustion pump (Communicated by Thomas John Linton.)	314	4th Feb.	1865	William Clark.
Improvements applicable to air cushions, mattresses, portable baths and other like air inflated articles.	317	4th Feb.	1865	Arthur Henry Robinson.
Improvements in the ventilation of pressing irons heated by gas, and for preventing the condensation of the vapour in the tubes or flues leading therefrom.	350	7th Feb.	1865	Samuel Egan Rouer.
Looms for weaving	377	10th Feb.	1865	Rowland Gibson Hamud.
Apparatus for communicating between the passengers, guard and engine driver of a railway train.	378	10th Feb.	1865	Arthur Cordy Edwards.
Case hardening or converting partially into steel articles of wrought or malleable iron. (Partly communicated by Anthony Leonard Fleury.)	393	11th Feb.	1865	Edwin Henry Newby.
Machinery and tools for making collars, cuffs, wristbands and other articles of dress, also adapted for cutting metal blanks	399	13th Feb.	1865	David Barr, William Henry Page, James Clements Newry.
Waterproofing skins, hides and leather	413	14th Feb.	1865	George Haston.
Apparatus for extracting liquid from solid substances (Communicated by Lyman Smith.)	489	21st Feb.	1865	William Edward Newton.

Subject-matter of Patent.	Number of Patent.	Date	Name of Patentee.
AIR SUPPLYING, &c.—*continued.*			
Machinery or apparatus for working or cutting coal or minerals, and for compressing or exhausting air to be employed therein, or for other purposes, some parts of which apparatus are also applicable to upright shafts, and other parts for regulating the flow or discharge of steam or other elastic fluids.	1208	29th April 1865	William Latham.
Improving and strengthening shields of steel, iron or other material for ships, fortifications and other constructions.	1228	2nd May 1865	Thomas Hay Campbell.
A mode of obtaining decortions and apparatus for carrying the same into effect. (*Communicated by Benjamin Green Martin.*)	1237	2nd May 1865	Francis Wise.
Machines for drying and stretching woollen and other textile fabrics. (*Communicated by Joseph Sprague Weaver.*)	1253	3rd May 1865	George Tomlinson Bomfield.
Manufacture of iron and steel - - - (*forcing air through.*)	1310	11th May 1865	Joseph Bennett.
An improvement in stoppers and flasks, bottles and other similar vessels.	1320	12th May 1865	Spencer Thomas Garrett.
An improved method of testing railway and other springs - - - - -	1574	18th May 1865	Joseph Mitchell. George Tilfourd.
An improvement in atmospheric forging hammers -	1380	19th May 1865	Edward Augustus Raymond.
Apparatus for raising oil and other liquids from deep wells. (*Communicated by Francis Stebbins Pease.*)	1392	20th May 1865	William Edward Newton.
A new and improved mode of making and venting cores and parts of moulds, to be used in the casting of iron or other metal. (*Communicated by Joseph Harrison, junior.*)	1434	25th May 1865	John Henry Johnson.
A new or improved machine for obtaining motive-power and other useful purposes. (*for exhausting or condensing air.*)	1468	29th May 1865	Henry Mowley.
A new or improved method of obtaining motive-power, together with certain machinery or apparatus for applying the same - - -	1504	1st June 1865	David Hancock. Frederick Barnes.
Furnaces used in the manufacture of welded iron tubes.	1517	2nd June 1865	Thomas Pritchard.
Turbines - - - - - -	1534	5th June 1865	Thomas Gentle. Joseph Allmark.
An improved break applicable to various descriptions of steam-engines and also to railway purposes. (*Communicated by Eugene Dutheil.*)	1542	6th June 1865	Frederick Tothampro.
An improved method of and machinery for cutting and excavating rock for railway tunnels and other purposes. (*Communicated by Thales Lindsley.*)	1557	12th June 1865	George Hazeltine.
An improved force dispeller or spring buffing apparatus. (*containing air.*)	1599	13th June 1865	William Jeffrey Hopkins.
Sizing machines for sizing yarns, beams or warps to be woven - - - - -	1729	29th June 1865	David Mercer. Thomas Mercer. Jonathan Mercer. Joseph Mercer.

Subject-matter of Patent.	Number of Patent.	Date.		Name of Patentee.
AIR SUPPLYING, &c.—*continued.*				
An improved mode of pressing and moulding clay, sand or cement for making bricks, and for other purposes. (*Communicated by John Steele.*)	1745	1st July	1865	William Robert Lake.
Improvements in the conversion of wrought or malleable iron into steel, and in the means or apparatus employed therein (*passing gas over red hot iron.*)	1776	5th July	1865	{ John Johnson. John Farmcriey Dickson.
Improved machinery for boring rocks and hard substances.	1778	5th July	1865	George Low.
Improvements in harmoniums, organs or other musical instruments, a part of which invention is applicable to turning over the leaves of music.	1783	6th July	1865	James Henry Smith.
An improved manufacture of coffins and air-tight receptacles.	1804	7th July	1865	Joseph George.
Fountains	1823	10th July	1865	Frederick Taylor.
A new and improved mode of elevating ships or boats in the water, to enable them to pass over mud bars, shallows and the like, and for raising sunken vessels and docks.	1838	13th July	1865	Thomas Cato M'Kean.
Apparatus for the locomotion of trains on railways, by atmospheric pressure.	1852	14th July	1865	William Podmore Bayliss.
Looms for weaving (*worked by pneumatic power.*)	1870	19th July	1865	Mark Knowles.
An improved apparatus for producing sound for signals, calls and alarms, adapted to use on vessels, railway trains, buoys, reefs, lighthouses and in other places of danger. (*Communicated by The Incorporated Marine Signal Company.*)	1886	20th July	1865	John Harkness Wray.
Apparatus for burning combustible and volatile liquids for generating steam and similar purposes. (*Communicated by Patrick Hayes.*)	1968	26th July	1865	George Tomlinson Bousfield.
Improvements in drying grass, hay and other substances, and in the machinery for effecting the same (*revolving fan for forcing currents of air.*)	1963	29th July	1865	{ Baldwin Latham. Robert Campbell.
Applying and utilising water power (*for compressing air.*)	1967	29th July	1865	Valentine Baker.
Means or apparatus for stopping or retarding railway carriages	1969	29th July	1865	{ John Swinburne. James Laming.
Improvements in the manufacture of hoops and tyres, and in the machinery employed therein. (*applying heated air to hoops.*)	1975	31st July	1865	John Ramsbottom.
Improvements in the construction of railway carriages and in railway breaks and signals, part of which is applicable to marine purposes	2008	2nd Aug.	1865	{ William Henry Pcitjean. Edward McNally.
Improvements in brewing and distilling, also in drying yeast, and in the apparatus employed.	2019	4th Aug.	1865	Patrick Robertson.
Means of and mechanism for obtaining motive-power.	2020	4th Aug.	1865	Adderley Sleigh.
Apparatus applicable as a motive-power engine, or pumping fluid meter. (*Communicated by Francis Bernard de Kermann.*)	2021	4th Aug.	1865	William Clark.

Subject-matter of Patent.	Number of Patent.	Date.	Name of Patentee.

Air Supplying, &c.—continued.

Subject-matter of Patent.	Number of Patent.	Date.	Name of Patentee.
Machinery for moulding hollow articles in earth, clay and other like materials.	2094	11th Aug. 1865	Robert Williams Armstrong.
Improvements in carburetting coal gas and manufacturing artificial gas, and in the machinery or apparatus employed therein.	2096	12th Aug. 1865	Henry Woodward.
Blacksmiths' bellows, more especially those used in portable forges.	2152	21st Aug. 1865	John Bowden.
Improvements in the manufacture of steel, iron and metal suitable for bearings, and in apparatus for the same.	2176	24th Aug. 1866	William Colburne Cambridge.
Improvements in apparatus by means of which certain liquids, common air and certain elastic fluids are made available in the production of light, and their quantity regulated and measured, parts of which improvements are applicable for other purposes. (applying air for organs.)	2184	25th Aug. 1865	Edwin Augustus Curley.
Dyeing and printing woollen or silk fabrics and yarns	2301	28th Aug. 1865	Alfred Paraf.
Obtaining spirits of turpentine, resin, pitch, tar, pyroligneous acid and other products from wood. (using partial vacuum.) (Communicated by Albert Hamilton Emery.)	2347	31st Aug. 1865	William Edward Newton.
Meters or apparatus for measuring water or other fluids, partly applicable for exhausting air or other gases.	2359	1st Sept. 1865	Charles Horsley.
Vent pegs for casks or vessels from which beer or other liquid is drawn off from time to time.	2366	15th Sept. 1865	Robert Mann Lowne.
Construction of gas meters - - - -	2372	16th Sept. 1865	William Esson.
Improvements in the machinery or apparatus, and in the processes for the treatment and manufacture of sugar. (vacuum pans.)	2386	19th Sept. 1865	John Fletcher.
Improvements in the manufacture of bricks, blocks, flue covers and tiles, and in the machinery and apparatus employed therefor.	2397	19th Sept. 1865	James Gillespie.
Adaptation of elastic material to articles requiring a bellows arrangement, or a partially rigid and partially expansible arrangement.	2425	22nd Sept. 1865	Matthew Cartwright.
Improvements in generating illuminating gas, and in the machinery or apparatus employed therein. (Communicated by Freeman Allington Pond, Mark Staples Richardson, and Edmund Alonzo Morss.)	2426	23rd Sept. 1865	John Henry Johnson.
Improved apparatus for generating illuminating gas (Communicated by John Irwin.)	2429	23rd Sept. 1865	Alfred Vincent Newton.
Manufacture of cast iron, malleable iron, and steel -	2456	26th Sept. 1865	Nicholas Korshnoff.
An improved mode of decarbonising retorts - (Communicated by George Washington Edge.)	2465	26th Sept. 1865	Alfred Vincent Newton.
Centrifugal pumps and fans - - - -	2489	24th Sept. 1865	Arthur Rigg, Jun.
Atmospheric hulling apparatus - - -	2520	2nd Oct. 1865	Thomas Williams.
Pneumatic ways for the transmission of letters, merchandise and passengers. (Communicated by Elias Portuous Needham.)	2537	3rd Oct. 1865	William Edward Newton.
Improvements in apparatus and means for extinguishing fires, part of such improvements being applicable for other purposes.	2550	5th Oct. 1865	William Henry Phillips.

Subject-matter of Patent.	Number of Patent.	Date.	Name of Patentee.

AIR SUPPLYING, &c.—continued.

Subject-matter of Patent.	Number of Patent.	Date.	Name of Patentee.
Improvements in evaporating and distilling liquids, and in the apparatus employed therein.	2480	7th Oct. 1865	Tomkin Campbell.
Improvements in apparatus for the regulation of the up and down currents of air, and for the prevention and cure of smoky chimneys.	2501	10th Oct. 1865	William Cooke.
Improvements in submarine electric telegraph cables, and in apparatus connected therewith. (admitting air to maintain a part of cable.)	2505	10th Oct. 1865	François Thierry Hubert.
Heating calender bowls and other cylinders or rollers (supplying air to bowls, &c.)	2536	12th Oct. 1865	William Mather.
An improved mode of treating or preparing casks and other vessels, to make them tight and suitable for containing hydrocarbon and other fluids.	2544	13th Oct. 1865	George Marshall.]
Apparatus for applying carbonic and other gases to iron and other metals in a molten state.	2557	14th Oct. 1865	James Cartmell Ridley.
The improvement of the means of and apparatus for laying submarine electrical telegraphic wires, lines, cables or other contrivances of a like sort.	2570	16th Oct. 1865	Reinhold Edward Kaalbach.
Improvements in desiccating the leaves and flowers of plants and other vegetable substances, and in the apparatus to be employed therein. (Communicated by Benjamin Dickinson.)	2703	30th Oct. 1865	Allan Lewin McGavin.
Construction of pumps for raising or forcing water or other liquids or fluids . . .	2745	24th Oct. 1865	Hyde Bateman. Edward Gooch Garrard.
Arrangements or apparatus for drying peat .	2804	2nd Nov. 1865	Murdoch Campbell. Algernon Charles Plumptre Coote. John Charles Augustus Henry Wolfram.
Improvements in generating and applying certain gases, and in apparatus to be employed therein. (blue paper.)	2833	2nd Nov. 1865	James Webster.
Machinery for transmitting and receiving signals. (Communicated by Count Ambjörn Pietro Sparre.)	2841	3rd Nov. 1865	Alexander Horace Brandon.
Looms for weaving . . . . (pneumatic loom.)	2843	3rd Nov. 1865	Arthur Heald.
Means of preventing vessels from sinking, which means are also applicable for raising sunken vessels.	2851	4th Nov. 1865	Thomas Page.
An improved truck or barrow for wheeling and tipping coke, coal or other substances. (admitting air for cooling.)	2848	4th Nov. 1865	William Brett.
Preserving meat and other articles for food . .	2919	13th Nov. 1865	Wilson Fox.
Purifying or refining iron	2929	14th Nov. 1865	John Dixon.
An improvement in the process for making butter .	2936	15th Nov. 1865	Henry Clifton.
Improvements in preserving animal and vegetable substances, and in means or apparatus employed therein. (producing a vacuum.)	2962	16th Nov. 1865	Richard Jones.
Apparatus for condensing exhaust steam, and heating air by the heat abstracted in effecting the condensation of such steam. (Communicated by Addison Colvin Fletcher.)	2996	21st Nov. 1865	Alfred Vincent Newton.
Apparatus for signalling on railways . . (operating by compressed air.)	3032	25th Nov. 1865	Charles Frederick Whitworth.

Subject-matter of Patent.	Number of Patent	Date.	Name of Patentee.
AIR SUPPLYING, &c.—continued.			
An improved mode of applying the compression of air for ventilating purposes, and the compression of any gas for hurrying along elastic fluids in conveying pipes	3153	8th Dec. 1865	Pierron de Mondésir. Paul Lebaire. Augustin Jallieme.
An improved mode of preserving animal and vegetable substances. (Communicated by Francis Stabler.)	3172	9th Dec. 1865	Alfred Vincent Newton.
Improvements in constructing atmospheric railways and carriages, and in working the same, parts of which are applicable to exhausting and condensing air for other purposes.	3173	9th Dec. 1865	Alexander Doull.
Machinery for opening and cleaning cotton and other fibrous substances	3233	14th Dec. 1865	Thomas Ridley Hetherington. Samuel Thornton.
Improvements in propellers for ships and vessels, parts of which are applicable to windmill sails and fan blowers	3296	20th Dec. 1865	Frederick Lamb Hancock. Charles Lamb Hancock.
An improved method of and apparatus for preserving, purifying, mixing, separating, cooling, airating, roasting and otherwise treating grain, corn and various other matters	3344	27th Dec. 1865	Gaston Charles Auge. Marquis D'Auty.
Improvements in distilling and in relieving distilled and other liquids from gases mechanically mixed therewith. (air discharging apparatus.)	3351	27th Dec. 1865	Norman Willis Wheeler.
Means of feeding meal to the boiling reel in flouring mills.	3385	30th Dec. 1865	William Fraser Cochrane.
XV.—Ventilation Supplying and Purifying Air for Buildings, Mines, Ships, Carriages, &c.			
Construction of railway carriages (and ventilating.)	96	11th Jan. 1865	Rock Chidley.
An improved machine for raising and carrying earth, mud, stones or other similar solid or liquid materials for dredging, ventilating or winnowing grain, or other analogous purposes.	176	20th Jan. 1865	Louis Balma.
Boots and shoes	190	23rd Jan. 1865	John Eadie.
Improvements in armour-plated and other ships or vessels, also applicable to fortifications generally. (tubes for ventilation.)	806	2nd Feb. 1865	Julius Saunders Jeffreys.
A new method for removing or destroying the momentum of heavy bodies by means of an elastic machine or machinery, so as to prevent injury and damage from concussion, applicable to ship cables, ship and fort armour, railway trains, tenders to penheads and floating piers, gangways, breakwaters and other similar structures, also as a motive power. (moving pistons.) (Communicated by William Graham McIvor.)	321	6th Feb. 1865	Clements Roberts Markham.
Apparatus for ventilating horticultural and other buildings.	322	6th Feb. 1865	Charles Beard.
Improvements in ventilating blinds or screens, and in means of ventilating ships and vessels.	439	16th Feb. 1865	Charles Langley.

Subject-matter of Patent.	Number of Patent.	Date.	Name of Patentee.
AIR SUPPLYING, &c.—continued.			
Improvements in treating sewage and in arranging apparatus in sewers and culverts to facilitate the ventilation of such structures.	481	16th Feb. 1865	Richard Smith.
Apparatus for ventilating hats - - -	498	22nd Feb. 1865	John Carter.
Improvements in ships of war, partly applicable to ships designed for the merchant service. (*Communicated by Augustus Wöller.*)	509	23rd Feb. 1865	George Haseltine.
Apparatus for heating and cooling atmospheric air and other aëriform bodies, and for heating ovens, and for heating and ventilating buildings.	636	7th March 1865	Loftus Perkins.
Furnaces and fire-places - - -	692	11th March 1865	Edward Brown Wilson.
Improvements in securing low and uniform temperatures, applicable to public and private buildings, also to refrigerators, coolers and condensers, and to ships and other vessels, and in the apparatus employed therein. (*Communicated by Daniel Somes.*)	718	14th March 1865	Alfred Vincent Newton.
Improved means of ventilation by the use of perforated tubular cornices and centre-pieces.	813	23rd March 1865	Thomas Harvey Saunders.
Ventilating blinds - - - -	879	29th March 1865	Henry Welchman King.
Improved apparatus for collecting or receiving pulverized dirt or dust.	909	31st March 1865	Elias Leak.
An improved hat ventilator - - -	951	5th April 1865	Robert Stanley.
Improvements in machinery or apparatus for drilling or boring rocks and other hard substances, in tunnelling, mining and other like operations, parts of which improvements are also applicable to the ventilating of the workings in mines and similar places. (*Communicated by Herman Haupt.*)	961	6th April 1865	John Henry Johnson.
Fire-places and flues and apparatus connected therewith.	969	7th April 1865	Edward Welch.
Improvements in apparatus for lighting and ventilating ships, part of which is also applicable for producing fresh water at sea.	996	7th April 1865	Henry Edmonds.
Means and apparatus employed for preventing downward draft in chimnies, facilitating the escape of smoke therefrom, and for ventilating apartments or buildings - - -	1471	29th May 1865	{ Edward Myers. James Stodart.
An improved method of and machinery for cutting and excavating rock for railway tunnels and other purposes. (*Communicated by Thales Lindsley.*)	1587	12th June 1865	George Haseltine.
Method of constructing partitions, walls, floors and roofs of buildings.	1588	13th June 1865	John James Bodmer.
Improvements in ventilating railway carriages and in the apparatus to be employed therefor.	1648	19th June 1865	William Clay.
Improved sanitary apparatus or arrangements for preventing noxious exhalations such as arise when coating or treating iron or other articles.	1690	24th June 1865	{ Matthew Andrew Muir. James McIlwham.
Improvements in tubular structures, rendering them specially applicable for ships' masts and building purposes.	1755	3rd July 1865	Edward Deane.
'*shafts for ventilation.*)			

Subject-matter of Patent.	Number of Patent.	Date.	Name of Patentee.
AIR SUPPLYING, &c.—continued.			
Means of obtaining or producing oxygen applicable to various useful purposes. (for purifying air in ships, mines, &c.)	1780	6th July 1865	Hermann Beigel.
A diving apparatus for submarine purposes	1837	12th July 1865	Thomas Cato M'Kean.
Improvements in apparatus and equipments used by persons employed under water, part of the improvements being also applicable for the use of persons employed where noxious gases or vapours prevail.	1840	13th July 1865	Auguste Denayrouze.
Ventilators - - - - -	1886	14th July 1865	John Paul Baugh Le Patourel.
Fire-engines and hydraulic machines (or concentrated ventilators.)	1963	29th July 1865	Leon Paul Laroche.
Roofing-tiles and slabs - - - (securing ventilation.)	1991	1st Aug. 1865	Frederick Ransome.
Ventilators - - - - -	2111	15th Aug. 1865	James Billings.
Punkahs - - - - -	2148	19th Aug. 1865	John Edwin Marsh.
An improved arrangement of apparatus and materials to be employed for effecting the deodorizing of the noxious gases arising from sewers and drains, and for the more effectual ventilation and inspection of such sewers and drains.	2451	25th Sept. 1865	Edward Brooke the younger.
Apparatus for ventilating and for preventing down draught in flues.	2487	26th Sept. 1865	John Hilliar.
A new or improved ventilating spring mattress	2511	30th Sept. 1865	Joseph Edwin Townshend.
Certain improvements in window fittings -	2603	10th Oct. 1865	William Cooke.
An improved ventilating apparatus for use in steamboats, vessels and other places requiring to be ventilated.	2609	10th Oct. 1865	John Garrison Woodward.
Trapping and ventilating sewers - -	2614	10th Oct. 1865	Richard Abell.
Greenhouses - - - - -	2654	18th Oct. 1865	Thomas Hungate Preston Dennis.
Ventilators for windows and other like openings -	2799	31st Oct. 1865	David Blair White.
Improvements in apparatus for obtaining fresh water from salt and impure water, also applicable for ventilating purposes.	2943	17th Nov. 1865	Samuel Hazard Huntly.
Apparatus for preventing draughts of air between the floor and the lower part of doors.	3050	29th Nov. 1865	Louis Desiré Carbonnier.
An improved mode of applying the compression of air for ventilating purpose, and the compression of any gas for hurrying along elastic fluids in conveying pipes - -	3155	8th Dec. 1865	Farron de Mondésir, Paul Lebaiter, Augustin Jullienne.
Improvements in constructing atmospheric railways and carriages, and in working the same, parts of which are applicable to exhausting and condensing air for other purposes. (for ventilation.)	3173	9th Dec. 1865	Alexander Doull.
An improved mode of and apparatus for purifying and deodorising impure air, whether in buildings, ships, mines or sewers, which improvement is also applicable for ventilating purposes -	3287	20th Dec. 1865	Joseph John Harrison, Edward Harrison.
A new and improved apparatus for cooling and purifying air in rooms or compartments, and ventilating the same. (Communicated by Axel Sturre Lyman.)	3292	20th Dec. 1865	William Clark.

Subject-matter of Patent.	Number of Patent.	Date.	Name of Patentee.
AIR SUPPLYING, &c.—continued.			
Pipes, tabular columns and hollow structures, for masts, oars, sheer legs, life boats and ordinary boats, for water, gas and waste water pipes, and for other similar constructions where great strength is required. *(shafts for ventilation.)*	3314	22nd Dec. 1865	Edward Deane.
ALKALIES; ALKALINE AND EARTHY SALTS; SALTS OF ALUMINA; BARYTA, IODINE AND COMPOUNDS.			
An improved method of treating apatite and other mineral phosphates. *(obtaining sulphate and biphosphate of lime.)* (Communicated by Mr. John Oliver.)	3	2nd Jan. 1865	Montagua Rinhard Leverson.
Improvements in the manufacture of oxygen gas and in treating and economising the residual products of the said manufacture — — *(obtaining caustic soda.)*	5	2nd Jan. 1865	{ John Frederick Parker. Joseph Tanner.
Treating phosphates of lime and salts of potass and soda in order to fit them for agricultural uses. (Communicated by Georges Ville.)	140	17th Jan. 1865	Richard Archibald Brooman.
Treating spent or used lyes resulting from the preparation of fibrous substances used in the manufacture of paper stock. *(recovering alkali.)*	297	2nd Feb. 1865	Thomas Routledge.
Preparation of superphosphate of lime — — (Communicated by Robert Barnhill Potts.)	330	4th Feb. 1865	William Edward Newton.
A new or improved insulating material for telegraphic and other purposes, together with an improvement in protecting telegraph wires, especially applicable to submarine and subterranean telegraphs. *(asbestos.)* (Communicated by Jules Brakmann.)	362	9th Feb. 1865	William Alfred Marshall.
Certain improvements in the manufacture of magnesium and its compounds — — —	456	17th Feb. 1865	{ John Osborne Christian, F.C.S. John Charlton. Henry Charlton.
Obtaining sulphates and carbonates of potash and soda.	490	17th Feb. 1865	Charles Frederick Claus.
Treatment and utilisation of certain products obtained in the manufacture of paper or of paper stock — — — — —	522	25th Feb. 1865	{ Thomas Routledge. Thomas Richardson.
Treatment of certain products obtained in the smelting of iron — — — — — *(collecting ammoniacal products.)*	580	2nd March 1865	{ Thomas Horton. David Simpson Price.
An improvement in carburetting gas, also in the preparation of hydrocarbons for carburetting gas, and improved methods of treating alkali which has been used to purify coal oils, shale oils, petroleum and other mineral oils.	596	3rd March 1865	William Renwick Bowditch.

Subject-matter of Patent.	Number of Patent.	Date.	Name of Patentee.
ALKALIES, &c.—continued.			
An improved process of and apparatus for making caustic liquor or caustic less.	989	6th March 1865	Thomas Nicholson.
Preparation of hyposulphite of lime	766	18th March 1865	James Cochran Stevenson.
Treating the waste liquors obtained in bleaching certain vegetable substances.	797	22nd March 1865	Harold Potter.
Apparatus employed in the concentration of all solutions where quick or speedy concentration or evaporation is required. (*manufacture of soda, &c.*)	873	24th March 1865	William Walsh.
Improvements in the preparation or treatment of sea weed and in obtaining products therefrom -	877	29th March 1865	Richard Young. Charles Finlay Oliphant Glassford, F.C.S.
Manufacture of sulphate of alumina	900	30th March 1865	Alexander Angus Croll.
Manufacture of soda and potash	1011	4th April 1865	Andrew George Hunter.
Manufacture of soluble and assimilable superphosphates of lime, by the application of phosphoric acid and acid phosphates. (*Communicated by Lavien Henri Blanchard and Théodore Chollot.*)	1161	25th April 1865	William Clark.
Obtaining certain compounds of nitrogen and of sulphur (*ammonia and compounds.*)	1386	10th May 1865	Thomas Richardson. Martin Diederich Rücker.
Apparatus for washing or purifying coal gas, and for producing ammoniacal water therefrom.	1389	19th May 1865	William Davey.
Certain improvements in the manufacture and production of chromate and bichromate of potash employed in dyeing and printing woven fabrics.	1679	10th June 1865	Joseph Mayer Dentith.
Obtaining sulphates and carbonates of potash and soda.	1786	6th July 1865	Charles Frederick Claus.
An improved process of preparing sea weeds and other vegetable substances for the production of artificial guano, felt, alkaline salts and iodine.	1877	19th July 1865	Donald M'Crummen.
Certain improvements in the manufacture of superphosphate of lime from guano. (*Communicated by Gustave Adolph Liebig.*)	1790	6th July 1865	Alfred Vincent Newton.
Treating ammoniacal liquors for purifying gas and other purposes.	1818	10th July 1865	George Thomas Livesey.
Manufacture of soda and carbonate of soda	1914	22nd July 1865	Joseph Pierre Gillard.
Improvements in the manufacture of carbonate of ammonia, and in the utilisation of the product obtained in such manufacture. (*Communicated by Dr. Hugo Krahein.*)	1933	25th July 1865	Astley Paston Price.
Certain improvements in the manufacture of sal-ammoniac	1939	26th July 1865	William Richards. Joseph Richards.
Improvements in the manufacture of compounds of silica and in the production of silicated alkaline inks, colours and dyes.	2267	2nd Sept. 1865	Henry Ellis.
An improved process of and apparatus for making caustic liquor or caustic lime.	2289	6th Sept. 1865	Thomas Nicholson.
Treating soda waste to obtain sulphur therefrom	2442	23rd Sept. 1865	Max Schaffarr.
An improved preparation or composition for coating, covering or coloring walls and other surfaces or parts of buildings, and for forming mouldings, cornices and other decorative parts of houses. (*preparing carbonate of lime.*)	2638	12th Oct. 1865	William Barrick.

Subject-matter of Patent.	Number of Patent.	Date.	Name of Patentee.

Alkalies, &c.—continued.

Subject-matter of Patent.	Number of Patent.	Date.	Name of Patentee.
Improvements in the manufacture of chromates of ammonia and chromic acid, and in the preparation of nitrates of lime and baryta. (Communicated by Félix Dehons.)	2702	19th Oct. 1865	William Clark.
Improvements in the method of and apparatus for utilising the liquors used in the treatment of straw or other fibrous materials for the manufacture of paper, which improvements are also applicable to the evaporation of liquids generally. (recovering the alkalies.) (Communicated by Eugene Porion.)	2726	21st Oct. 1865	James Wright.
Manufacture of caustic soda - - -	2801	31st Oct. 1865	George Robinson.
Treatment and deodorization of sewage water (preparing lime compounds.)	2808	31st Oct. 1865	Henry Young Darracott Scott.
Improvements in the process of treating materials for the manufacture of paper and other similar textile fabrics, and in apparatus for the same. (and recovering alkali.) (Communicated by Robert Henham Collyer.)	3067	29th Nov. 1865	Charles Stuart Bakey.
Improvements in the mode of applying mineral soda to the scouring and lubrication of textile matters and machinery, and in the manufacture of soap.	3107	4th Dec. 1865	Leopold Joseph Bouchart.
Improvements in the manufacture of soda and in the apparatus employed in the said manufacture. (Communicated by Alphonse Lourent.)	3340	26th Dec. 1865	Michael Henry.

Anchors; Mooring Anchors.

Subject-matter of Patent.	Number of Patent.	Date.	Name of Patentee.
Mooring anchors - - - - -	420	14th Feb. 1865	John Trotman.
Anchors - - - - -	3004	22nd Nov. 1865	Samuel Hunter.

Axles, Shafts, Bearings, Journals, Axle-boxes, Packings for Axles; Lubricating Axles, &c.

Subject-matter of Patent.	Number of Patent.	Date.	Name of Patentee.
An improved method of and apparatus for lubricating the axles or journals of coal or ironstone waggons or tubs, or of other carriages or railery used upon tramways or railways, for carrying mineral or other material - - -	6	2nd Jan. 1865	Joseph Smith, jun'. John Williamson.
Bearings for general mechanical purposes, and the application of fluid metallin in lieu of oleaginous or other lubricants to prevent friction - -	109	13th Jan. 1865	Frederick George Mulholland. Thomas Dugard.
Packing for steam joints, stuffing boxes, pistons and the like.	217	26th Jan. 1865	William Paton.
Steam-engines - - - - -	839	7th Feb. 1865	Charles Langley.

Subject-matter of Patent.	Number of Patent.	Date.	Name of Patentee.
AXLES, &c.—continued.			
Case hardening, or converting partially into steel, articles of wrought or malleable iron. (surfaces of shafts and axles.) (Partly communicated by Anthony Leonard Fleury.)	590	11th Feb. 1865	Edwin Henry Newby.
Bogie trucks used for supporting railway locomotive engines, carriages and waggons.	606	13th Feb. 1865	William Adams.
Apparatus for rinsing and drying by centrifugal force. ('Communicated by Félix Meunier and Auguste Bassuet.)	804	4th March 1865	Henri Adrien Bonneville.
An improved packing for piston and other rods - (Communicated by William Bolivar Davis.)	847	8th March 1865	Francis Wise.
An improved rotary spader or digging machine for tilling land. (Communicated by Cicero Comstock.)	871	10th March 1865	Edwin Addison Phillips.
An improved agricultural implement - -	878	10th March 1865	George Wright.
Preparing lubricating compounds - - (for axles and bearings.)	907	27th March 1865	William West.
File cutting machinery - - - - ('Communicated by Alfred Ford.)	928	29th March 1865	William Brunton.
Improvements in machinery or apparatus for drilling or boring rocks and other hard substances, in tunnelling, mining and other like operations, parts of which improvements are also applicable to the ventilating of the workings in mines and similar places. (Communicated by Herman Haupt.)	981	6th April 1865	John Henry Johnson.
Improvements in carriage and other wheels, and in connecting or fixing the said wheels to their axle boxes.	1084	11th April 1865	Stephen Wright.
Apparatus for lubricating spindles, shafts or other frictional surfaces. (Communicated by William Francis Rippon.)	1080	13th April 1865	James Rippon.
An improved packing for steam cylinders, stuffing boxes and closed vessels containing water, air or gases, and for other similar purposes. (Communicated by Frederic Henry Briskoques and Ernest Frederic Wertwein the younger.)	1112	21st April 1865	Edward Thomas Hughes.
Wheels and the manner of applying the same to railway carriages for passengers' and goods' traffic, as also the leading wheels for locomotives.	1114	21st April 1865	William Day.
Digging machinery - - - -	1124	22nd April 1865	Orsmed Coffern Evans.
Machinery for preparing and spinning cotton and other fibrous substances.	1125	22nd April 1865	Edward Lord.
Improvements in motive-power machinery for cultivating land, part of which improvements is applicable to driving machinery generally	1134	22nd April 1865	James Howard. Edward Tenney Bousfield.
Certain improvements in apparatus for lubricating frictional surfaces, and in the lubricant to be employed therewith.	1175	27th April 1865	Joseph Wilson Lowther.
Improvements in the manufacture of pig iron or foundry metal, and in making and treating castings of such metal. (for machine framing.)	1206	1st May 1865	Henry Bessemer.

Subject-matter of Patent.	Number of Patent.	Date.	Name of Patentee.
AXLES, &c.—continued.			
Apparatus for receiving the thrust of screw propeller and other revolving shafts (applicable for footstep bearings.)	1234	3rd May 1865	Edward Thornton Band, John Brough Fyfe.
Improved apparatus for cutting, turning and smoothing metal pipes, and the surfaces of bolts, rods or spindles (shafts.)	1311	11th May 1865	George Monatford, Edward Worroll.
A new or improved spring apparatus to be applied to the bearings of the axles of pulleys or drums used in collieries	1343	15th May 1865	George Elliot, Samuel Bailey Coxon.
A new or improved method of obtaining motive-power, together with certain machinery or apparatus for applying the same	1504	1st June 1865	David Hancock, Frederick Barnes.
An improved metallic stuffing box	1588	7th June 1865	Victor Deterne.
Locomotive engines and railway carriages (segmental bearings.)	1646	19th June 1865	George Smith the younger.
Improvements in the preparation of amalgams of quicksilver or mercury, and in the application of such amalgams to various purposes in the arts. (for lubricating bearings.) (Communicated by Henry Worts.)	1710	28th June 1865	William Edward Newton.
Axles for carriages	1762	4th July 1865	Stephen Wright.
Improvements in steam carriages and in adapting wheels for common roads to railways. (Communicated by Joseph Alphanse Loubat.)	1621	10th July 1865	Richard Archibald Brotman.
An improvement in the mode of uniting different metals, such as iron and copper or alloys, to form compound metallic castings. (adapted to shafts.)	1885	19th July 1865	George Nimmo.
Construction of valves for steam and other engines (bearings or seats.) (Communicated by Thomas Skrimton Davis.)	1913	22nd July 1865	William Edward Newton.
Conical plug steam valves (bearing surface.) (Communicated by John Wesley Cerhart.)	1960	24th July 1865	William Edward Newton.
Construction of axle-boxes and bearings (Communicated by Edouard Challet.)	2028	4th Aug. 1865	Henri Adrien Bonneville.
Improvements in and applicable to railway carriages to enable passengers to pass from one compartment to another, and to give signals on trains in motion.	2066	11th Aug. 1865	Thomas English Stephens.
Machinery for lubricating the axles of colliery and other similar waggons or trucks.	2080	12th Aug. 1865	James Knowles.
Preparing lubricating compounds	2116	16th Aug. 1865	William West.
Improvements in the manufacture of steel, iron and metal suitable for bearings, and in apparatus for the same.	2175	24th Aug. 1865	William Colburn Cambridge.
Treating, working or manipulating cast steel, for the manufacture of wheel tires, armour plates or other articles requiring great hardness and tensile strength. (axles, shafts, &c.)	2277	5th Sept. 1865	Julian Orand.
Apparatus for lubricating shafts and other running surfaces.	2288	6th Sept. 1865	William Mycock.

Subject-matter of Patent.	Number of Patent.	Date.	Name of Patentee.
AXLES, &c.—continued.			
Improvements in locomotive engines, parts of which improvements are also applicable to railway carriages. (Friction gearing.)	2370	14th Sept. 1865	Russel Aitken.
Tools for securing tubes in tube plates, and for other purposes where concentrated power or adjustment is necessary. (for tightening bearing surfaces of shafts.)	2455	26th Sept. 1865	Richard Taylor Nelson Howry.
Machinery for shaping metal and other substances. (railway axles.)	2562	5th Oct. 1865	Hesketh Hughes.
Railway carriages and locomotives. (Communicated by Henry Gifford.)	2621	11th Oct. 1865	Michael Henry.
Carriages propelled by manual power	2622	11th Oct. 1865	Thomas Du Bouley.
Certain improvements in machinery or apparatus for preparing and spinning cotton and other fibrous substances. (bearings for spindles.)	2651	14th Oct. 1865	Godfrey Anthony Erasco.
Improvements in machinery or apparatus known as "roving," "intermediate," "slubbing" and "throstle" frames and "doublers," and also in winding machines used for preparing, spinning and winding cotton, wool, flax, silk and other fibrous substances. (collars or bearings.)	2713	20th Oct. 1865	William Sumner.
Obtaining sliding surfaces by the interposition and revolution of a liquid or gaseous fluid between the frictional surfaces. (axles or bearings.)	2729	21st Oct. 1865	Louis Dominique Girard.
An improved axle-box for supplying oil to the journals of railway vehicles. (Communicated by Prosper Pint and Edmund Pint.)	2757	23rd Oct. 1865	William Edward Gedge.
Machinery for rolling shafts and axles (Communicated by Thomas Cowper.)	2904	11th Nov. 1865	Alfred Vincent Newton.
Crank axles of locomotives for railroads (Communicated by Dyer Williams.)	2908	11th Nov. 1865	William Robert Lake.
Means of connecting drums or pulleys with their shafts or drivers. (Communicated by Lemuel Homer Olmsted.)	2953	14th Nov. 1865	William Clark.
Apparatus for signalling on railways (bearings with india-rubber packings.)	3089	25th Nov. 1865	Charles Frederick Whitworth.
Shaft couplings (Communicated by Louis Hollenbeck.)	3044	27th Nov. 1865	William Robert Lake.
Apparatus for increasing the safety of railway passengers and trains, signalling and forming a communication externally and internally between all parts of such trains, lighting, warming and securing the doors of the carriages, and indicating therein and at the stations the names of the places at which the train stops. (coupling shafts and gas pipes.)	3068	29th Nov. 1865	Richard Howarth.
Improvements in the manufacture and treatment of railway bars, tyres and axles; also in the construction of furnaces, machinery and apparatus connected therewith.	3084	1st Dec. 1865	Thomas Weatherburn Dodds.
Apparatus for raising, lowering and moving heavy bodies, and for transmitting and arresting motion for various purposes. (adapting the coupling to shafts.)	3088	2nd Dec. 1865	Thomas Aldridge Weston.

Subject-matter of Patent.	Number of Patent.	Date.	Name of Patentee.
AXLES, &c.—continued.			
Improvements in reaping and mowing machines, part of which is applicable to machinery in general. (lubricating bearings.)	3142	6th Dec. 1865	Adam Carlisle Bamlett.
Naves and axletree boxes of carriage wheels - -	3210	12th Dec. 1865	Levi Lemon Sovereign.
Improvements in the bearings of certain wheels and pulleys applicable to various kinds of machinery.	3231	14th Dec. 1865	William Winter.
Improvements in the manufacture of axles for carriages and spindles for various purposes, and in machinery to be employed in the said manufacture, part of which improvements in machinery may also be applied to other purposes - - - - - - -	3330	20th Dec. 1866	Elias Lowe. Joseph Constant Lowe. John Lowe. John Rettell. Thomas Rettell. Charles Vernon.
Improvements applicable to the lubrication of machinery.	3342	27th Dec. 1865	Joshua Ren.
Duplex steam-engines - - - - (construction of brasses.)	3350	27th Dec. 1865	Norman Willis Wheeler.
Machinery for boring, turning, and shaping articles of metal - - - - - - (crank axles, bushes and bearings.)	3362	29th Dec. 1865	William Harrison. Thomas Walker.
For Bearing Springs, see "SPRINGS."			
BAGS, BASKETS, SACKS, HOLDERS AND FASTENINGS.			
Mail and despatch bags and bags for other similar uses. (Communicated by Thomas James Claxton.)	725	15th March 1865	George Tomlinson Bousfield.
Improved apparatus for securing the frames carrying the fittings in travelling bags.	816	23rd March 1865	Louis Augustus Laime.
Manufacture of flook fabrics - - - (for travelling bags.) (Communicated by The American Waterproof Cloth Company.)	1216	1st May 1865	William Edward Newton.
An improved manufacture of waterproof fabric - (for travelling bags.) (Communicated by The American Waterproof Cloth Company.)	1219	1st May 1865	William Edward Newton.
Manufacture of carpets and other terry and cut pile fabrics. (for travelling bags.) (Communicated by The American Waterproof Cloth Company.)	1499	31st May 1865	William Edward Newton.
Ornamental frames and baskets to contain flowers and other articles.	1806	7th July 1866	William Goulding.
Construction of travelling and other bags - -	2031	2nd Aug. 1866	Heiman Frankenburg.
Construction of sewing-machines particularly adapted for sewing sacks and bags - -	2067	9th Aug. 1865	Barnabas Ram. Edward Gandell the younger.
Machinery or apparatus for the manufacture of paper bags. (Communicated by Delamore Clark.)	2116	16th Aug. 1865	John Henry Johnson.

Subject-matter of Patent.	Number of Patent.	Date.	Name of Patentee.
Bags, &c.—continued.			
Locks for trunks, bags, dressing-cases and other like articles. (Communicated by Nicolas Chrétien Goysaud.)	2360	15th Sept. 1865	Richard Archibald Brooman.
Improved machinery for the manufacture of bags and envelopes made of paper or other fibrous materials, or woven or textile fabrics, either separately or combined.	2420	22nd Sept. 1865	Henry Rankin.
Adaptation of elastic material to articles requiring a bellows arrangement, or a partially rigid and partially expandible arrangement. (for travelling bags.)	2423	22nd Sept. 1865	Matthew Cartwright.
An improvement in clasps or fastenings . . (for bags.)	2525	2nd Oct. 1865	Frederic Jenner.
Improvements in satchels and in the manufacture of the gussets of leather satchels, bags and purses, and of the gussets of other articles made of leather.	2707	20th Oct. 1865	Frederick Thompson.
An improved fastening for travelling bags and other similar receptacles. (Communicated by Auguste Schubros.)	2814	1st Nov. 1865	Louis Pfeiffer.
Frames and fastenings of carpet and other bags -	2950	4th Nov. 1865	{ John King. Alfred Watson.
Machinery for cutting paper - . . . . (making bags.)	3189	11th Dec. 1865	Thomas Corbauld Usher.
Preparation of glue or gelatine so as to render it insoluble in water, and applicable by the admixture of other substances to various purposes for which common glue or gelatine cannot now be used. (a material for baskets.) (Communicated by Henry Worts.)	3293	23rd Dec. 1865	William Edward Newton.
Obtaining and employing continuous lengths of tanned leather for various useful purposes (for game and meat bags, travelling bags, bands for hampers, &c.)	3334	23rd Dec. 1865	{ George Horn. Daniel Horn.
Baths and Basins; Bathing Appliances.			
Improvements applicable to air cushions, mattresses, portable baths and other like air inflated articles.	317	4th Feb. 1865	Arthur Henry Robinson.
A new or improved combined garment - - (bathing dress.)	423	14th Feb. 1865	Robert Pasco Barrett.
Apparatus for supplying regulated or measured quantities of water and other fluids. (to wash basins.)	707	13th March 1865	Robert Gordon Rattray.
Fire-places and flues and apparatus connected therewith. (flues for heating baths.)	989	7th April 1865	Edward Welch.
Manufacture and application of glass and other vitreous compositions . . . . (for wash basins.)	1290	1st May 1865	{ Arthur Howard Emerson. Robert Fowler.

Subject-matter of Patent.	Number of Patent.	Date.	Name of Patentee.
BATHS, &c.—continued.			
Driving apparatus for hair brushing and shampooing by machinery . . }	1490	31st May 1865	{ Thomas Appleton Brown. John Knight.
An improved combination of materials for the manufacture of carpets, floor cloth, felt, wall paper, fire-proof flexible roofing, ship and boat building, and for other similar purposes (overshot and bath mats.)	1775	5th July 1865	{ John Longbottom. Abram Longbottom.
Apparatus to be used in swimming - (or bathing.) (Communicated by Jean Baptiste Victor Chastel.)	1992	31st July 1865	William Clark.
Improvements in ice houses and in glaciaria or skating places, and in baths.	2292	6th Sept. 1865	Augustus William Parker.
A new revolving cover for dishes, bowls and other vessels requiring a movable cover. (for basins.) (Communicated by Julius Rhodes Pomeroy.)	2591	3rd Oct. 1865	Charles Pomeroy Button.
Apparatus for administering injections and douches to the human body.	2555	5th Oct. 1865	William Robert Barker.
An improved overflow for basins, sinks and baths -	2637	12th Oct. 1865	Hugh Houston Craigie.
Bath apparatus - - - - (Communicated by Aloys Bisagnes.)	2749	25th Oct. 1865	William Clark.
Manufacture of tanks, baths, mangers and other vessels.	3129	5th Dec. 1865	Edward Hendy.
Construction of door mats, flesh and bath brushes made principally of India-rubber.	3216	13th Dec. 1865	George Barber.
BAYONETS, DAGGERS, SWORD-HANDLES, SCABBARDS.			
A combined key and weapon of defence - (Communicated by Théodore de Bonrousse de Laffore.)	552	27th Feb. 1865	Richard Archibald Brooman.
Improvements in breech-loading fire-arms, and in cartridges and bayonets for breech-loading fire-arms. (Communicated by Charles Roches.)	1360	16th May 1865	Richard Archibald Brooman.
Means of securing the handles of table knives and forks and other similar articles.	2671	16th Oct. 1865	Thomas M'Grah.
BELLS; ACTUATING BELLS.			
Fog and storm signals, buoys and spindles - (automatically ringing a bell.) (Communicated by William Smith Sampson.)	125	14th Jan. 1865	Theodore Bourne.
Apparatus or bell alarms to facilitate the communication between passengers and guards of railway trains, which said apparatus is equally applicable to apartments and other similar purposes.	545	27th Feb. 1865	Ferdinand Dancart.

Subject-matter of Patent.	Number of Patent.	Date.	Name of Patentee.
BELLS, &c.,—continued.			
Improved apparatus for the protection of houses and property from burglars, parts of the invention being applicable for other purposes.	619	6th March 1865	Cromwell Fleetwood Varley.
Apparatus for making communications from one part of a building to another.	1143	24th April 1865	John Joseph Parker.
An improved system of telegraphic communication on railways, parts of which invention are also applicable to other telegraphic purposes.	1543	5th June 1865	Alice Isabel Lacon Gordon.
An improved indicator for electric bells and a new battery manipulator combined, for ringing electric bells and other signals.	2421	22nd Sept. 1865	Walker Mawley.
Apparatus for increasing the safety of railway passengers and trains, signalling and forming a communication externally and internally between all parts of such trains, lighting, warming and securing the doors of the carriages, and indicating therein and at the stations the names of the places at which the train stops. (*spring bell-ringing instrument.*)	3068	29th Nov. 1865	Richard Howarth.
Obtaining and employing continuous lengths of tanned leather for various useful purposes - (*for bell-pulls and ropes.*)	3324	23rd Dec. 1865	{ George Hare. Daniel Hare.
BELTS, BRACES, GIRTHS AND BANDS.			
An improved belt for ladies' wear - - -	17	3rd Jan. 1865	Louis Goldberg.
Manufacture of driving bands or belts for machinery and other purposes - - -	300	3rd Feb. 1865	{ George Hare. Daniel Hare.
Improvements in the construction of life belts, swimming belts, jackets and buoys, and in the employment and utilisation of certain materials in the manufacture of the same.	841	7th Feb. 1865	Charles Kilburn.
A new or improved apparatus for supporting and steadying the arm in rifle shooting.	1014	14th April 1865	Jean Baptist Hausman.
Improvements applicable to capes, paletôts, overcoats and other such like garments.	1128	22nd April 1865	John Emary.
A new or improved fastening for fastening articles of dress, which said fastening is also applicable to the joining of belts and bands, and to other like purposes.	1186	26th April 1865	Charles William Heaven.
Fasteners for driving bands, straps, belts, harness or other such like purposes - - - -	1322	1st May 1865	{ Joseph Felix Allender. Thomas Frederick Cashin.
Apparatus for elongating and contracting waist and other belts, which apparatus is also applicable for other purposes - - -	2224	29th Aug. 1865	{ George Frederick White. Harvey Chamberlain.
Manufacture of bands, belts or straps for harness, for driving machinery or for other purposes.	2618	11th Oct. 1865	James Crutchett.
Fasteners for driving bands, straps, belts, harness or other such like purposes - - - -	2502	31st Oct. 1865	{ Thomas Frederick Cashin. Joseph Felix Allender.
A new or improved elastic belt or band truss -	3037	24th Nov. 1865	Charles Reader.

Subject-matter of Patent.	Number of Patent.	Date.	Name of Patentee.
BELTS, &c. — *continued.*			
Improvements in the manufacture or production of stays, corsets and bodices and other similar articles of dress, and in the fastenings for same. (*applicable to belts.*)	3078	30th Nov. 1865	Stephen Dixon.
Manufacture of leather driving belts	3148	7th Dec. 1865	Clarke Dschesne Hitchcock. John Shimmen.
Obtaining and employing continuous lengths of tanned leather for various useful purposes (*for garters.*)	3334	23rd Dec. 1865	George Hurn. Daniel Hurn.
BLEACHING AND DECOLOURISING.			
Machinery or apparatus to be employed in the bleaching and dyeing of hanks or skeins of yarns and threads.	710	14th March 1865	Longis Gautet.
Treating the waste liquors obtained in bleaching certain vegetable substances.	797	22nd March 1865	Harold Putter.
Washing or steeping and bleaching textile or fibrous materials. (*Communicated by Messieurs. Negret, Orioli and Predet.*)	1144	24th April 1865	William Clark.
Machinery for stretching cotton and other fabrics or materials. (*applied to bleachers' mangles.*)	1317	12th May 1865	James Henfwd.
Improvements in the raising, lifting or drawing and forcing of water and other liquids, and in the apparatus and means employed therefor (*for bleach works.*)	1996	2nd Aug. 1865	James M'Ewan. William Neilson.
Machinery used in washing, bleaching and dyeing yarns and textile fabrics in the hank	2118	16th Aug. 1865	John Smith. William Schofield.
An improved liquid composition for cleansing, scouring and bleaching textile animal, mineral and vegetable substances	2440	23rd Sept. 1865	Gustave Emile Rolland. Emile Léon Rolland.
Machinery and apparatus for bleaching, steeping, clearing and washing fibrous and other materials, yarns and fabrics	2501	29th Sept. 1865	William Schofield. John Smith.
Bleaching feathers (*Communicated by Adolphe Pierre Viel and Cherie Pierre Duflot.*)	2997	20th Nov. 1865	William Clark.
Dyeing, printing and other operations based on chemical reactions. (*discharging or decolouring.*) (*Communicated by Mathias Paraf-Javal.*)	3110	4th Dec. 1865	Richard Archibald Brooman.
Machinery for drying and bleaching grain and other materials. (*see "THRASHING."*)	3270	19th Dec. 1865	William Crossy.

Subject-matter of Patent.	Number of Patent.	Date.	Name of Patentee.
BOBBINS AND COP-TUBES.			
Spools or bobbins to be used in certain frames for preparing fibrous materials for spinning.	1187	22nd April 1865	Joshua Henry Wilson.
Machinery or apparatus for spinning, doubling or twining cotton and other fibrous materials	1551	6th June 1865	Alfred Pemberton. Alfred William Pemberton.
Certain improvements in machinery or apparatus for turning and cutting wood and other substances to be employed in the manufacture of spools or bobbins or other similar articles.	1773	5th July 1865	John Braithwaite.
Improvements in sewing-machines and in winders for sewing-machines	2165	23rd Aug. 1865	Henry Wilks. George Rice.
Bobbins or spools used in spinning and winding yarns and threads. (Communicated by Charles Reynolds.)	2388	16th Sept. 1865	Jebiel Keeler Hoyt.
Bobbin holders (see "SPINNING.")	2406	21st Sept. 1865	John Goulding.

BONES, IVORY AND HORN; CARBONIZING BONES.			
Improvements in extracting and purifying fats and other products from bones and other animal substances, and in apparatus for the same.	93	11th Jan. 1865	Alfred George Lock.
New or improved compositions in imitation of ivory and woods, to be employed in the manufacture of umbrella tips, umbrella and walking stick handles and other useful and ornamental purposes	1622	23rd June 1865	Michael Dietrich Rosenthal. Solomon Gradenwitz.
Apparatus employed in grinding corn and other substances capable of being ground by mill-stones. (steam-drum,)	3129	5th Dec. 1865	Edward Alfred Cowper.
New or improved compositions in imitation of ivory and wood, to be employed in the manufacture of umbrella tips, umbrella and walking-stick handles and other useful and ornamental purposes	3310	22nd Dec. 1865	Michael Dietrich Rosenthal. Solomon Gradenwitz.
Preparation of glue or gelatine so as to render it insoluble in water, and applicable by the admixture of other substances to various purposes for which common glue or gelatine cannot now be used. (applicable to ivory, horn, bone, &c.) (Communicated by Henry Werts.)	3325	23rd Dec. 1865	William Edward Newton.

Subject-matter of Patent.	Number of Patent.	Date.	Name of Patentee.
BOOKS, ALBUMS, PORTFOLIOS, BOOK COVERS, BOOK SLIDES OR HOLDERS; BOOK-BINDING.			
A new or improved machine for trimming or cutting the edges of books, magazines and such like articles	324	6th Feb. 1865	William Henry Latham, Frederic Cartwright Ward Latham.
A chemical combustible substance and apparatus to which it is applicable. (An apparatus for bookbinders.) (Communicated by François Stolov.)	477	20th Feb. 1865	William Edward Gedge.
Manufacture of letter clips, bookmarkers, paper knives and clips for suspending stationery, drapery and pictures, and for other such like purposes	962	3rd April 1865	Thomas Corbett, Robert Harrington.
Adaptation of elastic material to articles requiring a bellows arrangement, or a partially rigid and partially expansible arrangement. (for pocket books.)	2482	22nd Sept. 1865	Matthew Cartwright.
Portfolios and paper files (Communicated by Henry Tillinghast Simon.)	2468	26th Sept. 1865	George Tomlinson Bousfield.
An improvement in clasps or fastenings (for albums and books.)	2525	2nd Oct. 1865	Frederic Jenner.
An improved fastening for books, portfolios, despatch boxes and other similar articles	2654	16th Oct. 1865	Joseph Orvis, Thomas Gear.
Manufacture of embossed wood (for book covers.) (Communicated by Henry May and Henry Taylor Blake.)	2895	10th Nov. 1865	Alfred Vincent Newton.
Portfolios, writing desks, writing cases and other similar apparatus.	2918	13th Nov. 1865	John Stephens.
Locks or catches for portmonnaies, portfolios or other articles	2939	15th Nov. 1865	George Chambers, George Gregory.
A covering or cap for protecting the ends of maps, drawings, rolls of paper and other materials that are capable of being rolled up.	3175	9th Dec. 1865	Saint George Howard Davies-Usys.
BOOTS, SHOES, LEGGINGS, SKATES; CLEANING BOOTS.			
Machinery for shaping and trimming the heels of boots and shoes. (Communicated by Charles Helms.)	49	6th Jan. 1865	George Hawkins.
Manufacture of boots, shoes, saddlery, harness and other articles. (Communicated by Toussaint Landrin.)	169	19th Jan. 1865	William Clark.
Boots and shoes	190	23rd Jan. 1865	John Fadie.
Improvements in the manufacture of boots and shoes, and in apparatus therefor.	291	2nd Feb. 1865	Andrew Murray.
Fastenings for stay-busks, leggings, gaiters and other similar articles.	349	7th Feb. 1865	George Twigg.

Subject matter of Patent.	Number of Patent.	Date.	Name of Patentee.
Boots, &c.—continued.			
Manufacture of boots, shoes and other coverings for the feet	391	10th Feb. 1865	George Colon. James Archibald Jaques. John Americus Fanshawe.
Case hardening, or converting partially into steel, articles of wrought or malleable iron. (shoe irons.) (Partly communicated by Anthony Leonard Fleury.)	393	11th Feb. 1865	Edwin Henry Newby.
Waterproofing skins, hides and leather . . (for boots and shoes.)	413	14th Feb. 1865	George Harton.
An improved system of manufacturing clog soles, patten boards and similar articles by machinery.	416	14th Feb. 1865	Robert John Joure.
Manufacture of boots, shoes and other like coverings for the feet. (Communicated by Alexandre Loverd.)	443	16th Feb. 1865	Richard Archibald Brennan.
Machinery for sewing or uniting leather and other hard substances, particularly applicable to the manufacture of boots and shoes.	464	21st Feb. 1865	Charles Paulet.
Gaiters, spatterdashes and other similar articles .	569	1st March 1865	Jean Baptiste Toussaint.
Manufacture of shoes and other coverings for the feet	637	7th March 1865	Alexandre Eugene Adolphe Aubert. Gustave Eugene Michel Gerard.
An improved system of closing spatterdashes, applicable also to boots, portemonnaies and other similar articles.	668	9th March 1865	Emile Carchon.
An improvement in heels for boots, shoes and other like articles.	710	14th March 1865	George Evans.
Manufacture of boots and shoes . .	784	21st March 1865	Daniel Gourley.
Socks, soles or feet protectors, to be used loose in boots and shoes, or affixed thereto . .	806	31st March 1865	John Poole. Thomas Brown.
An improved flexible spring valve for boots and shoes.	1034	11th April 1865	Benjamin William Leslie Nicoll.
Elastic binders for boots and shoes . . (Communicated by Daniel Franklin Packer.)	1060	12th April 1865	William Edward Newton.
A new or improved shoe or sandal for facilitating the art of swimming.	1145	24th April 1865	Aaron Atkins.
Manufacture of flock fabrics . . . (for shoes and shoe linings.) (Communicated by The American Waterproof Cloth Company.)	1216	1st May 1865	William Edward Newton.
Manufacture of boots and shoes . . (Communicated by William Emerson Baker.)	1318	12th May 1865	George Haseltine.
Improvements in vessels for containing blacking, polishing oils and other similar materials, and in apparatus connected therewith.	1397	12th May 1865	Thomas Davis.
Machinery for manufacturing clog and patten soles	1551	16th May 1865	Walter Brown.
Skates . . . . (Communicated by August Muller.)	1700	24th June 1865	Wilhelm Bever.
Manufacture of boxes suitable among other uses for containing paste blacking and other cheap marketable articles. (Communicated by Edwin Price.)	1709	6th July 1865	Alfred Vincent Newton.
Instruments used in cutting the soles of boots and shoes.	1808	18th July 1865	John Pusey West.

Subject-matter of Patent.	Number of Patent.	Date.	Name of Patentee.

Boots, &c.—continued.

Subject-matter of Patent.	Number of Patent.	Date.	Name of Patentee.
Protecting crinoline steel, stay-busks, springs for leggings or gaiters and other similar fastenings	1885	19th July 1865	William Edwards.
An improved mode of lacing boots, shoes and other articles united by laces. (Communicated by Van Wagener.)	1931	25th July 1865	John Henry Johnson.
An improved fastening for leggings or other articles	2194	17th Aug. 1865	Frederick John Jones.
Applying elastic material to boots, shoes and such like coverings for the feet - - -	2132	18th Aug. 1865	{ Matthew Cartwright. Augustus Dale.
Improvements in boots and other coverings for the feet, which improvements are applicable also to trunks and other articles, for the purpose of strengthening, preserving or protecting them. (Communicated by Jared Nichols and Mowr Petter.)	2133	16th Aug. 1865	Phineas Lawrence.
Skates - - - - - (Communicated by James Greenwood.)	2180	25th Aug. 1865	Joseph Ingall Barber.
Construction of skates - - - (Communicated by James Leonard Plimpton.)	2190	25th Aug. 1865	Alfred Vincent Newton.
An improved roller skate - - -	2241	29th Aug. 1865	Washington Parker Gregg.
Brushes - - - - - } (for wiping shoes.)	2226	30th Aug. 1865	{ George Smith. Charles Ritchie.
Construction of boots and shoes - -	2359	13th Sept. 1865	James Dunbar.
Manufacture of boots and shoes - -	2410	21st Sept. 1865	Henry Hibling.
Adaptation of elastic material to articles requiring a bellows arrangement, or a partially rigid and partially expansible arrangement. (for gaiters.)	2432	22nd Sept. 1865	Matthew Cartwright.
Socks for boots and shoes - - -	2423	22nd Sept. 1865	{ Charles White. Thomas White.
An improvement in the manufacture of waterproof soles for boots and shoes.	2449	25th Sept. 1865	John Wiggins Coburn.
Manufacture of knickerbockers and such like coverings for the legs.	2460	26th Sept. 1865	William Ambler.
Elastic fronts, sides and backs for boots and shoes	2640	13th Oct. 1865	Matthew Cartwright.
Construction and mode of fixing skates to the boots or shoes of the wearer.	2642	13th Oct. 1865	William May.
An improved mode of uniting pieces of leather, more especially adapted to the manufacture of boots and shoes. (Communicated by John Chipman Hoadley.)	2750	25th Oct. 1865	George Haseltine.
Improvements in roller skates, and in the rollers to be used therewith and for other purposes.	2770	27th Oct. 1865	Robert Bell Samson.
Machinery employed in the manufacture of boots and shoes.	2785	28th Oct. 1865	Claudius Erskine Goodman.
Improved knickerbockers or leggings - -	2788	30th Oct. 1865	Jabez Stanley.
Skates - - - - - - (Communicated by Owen Wilson Taft.)	2790	30th Oct. 1865	Frederick Tolhausen.
Means and apparatus for finishing the soles of boots and shoes.	2901	6th Nov. 1865	Robert Finde.
Manufacture of boots and shoes - - -	2977	8th Nov. 1865	Charles Mole.
Certain improvements in the manufacture of socks or inner soles for boots and shoes.	2910	11th Nov. 1865	David Adam Jones.

Subject-matter of Patent.	Number of Patent.	Date.	Name of Patentee.

BOOTS, &c.—continued.

Subject-matter of Patent.	Number of Patent.	Date.	Name of Patentee.
Machinery for cutting and rounding boot and shoe soles of leather and other analogous substances. (Communicated by John Gillingham Felt.)	2916	13th Nov. 1865	Nathaniel Henry Felt.
Lasting-boots and shoes	3019	24th Nov. 1865	George Morrison.
Improvements in sewing-machines and in sewing or embroidering. (sewing leather.)	3079	1st Dec. 1865	Isaac Merritt Singer.
Improved arrangement of the parts in sewing-machines, for using wax thread for sewing on the soles of boots and shoes.	8170	9th Dec. 1865	William Jackson.
Utilising scraps or small pieces of leather (waste in boot making.)	3263	19th Dec. 1865	{ John Farmerley Dickson. { John Barn.
Improvements in the manufacture of boots and shoes for rendering them waterproof.	3270	19th Dec. 1865	James Bolton.
Foot protectors	3318	19th Dec. 1865	Augustus Henry Thurgur.
Obtaining and employing continuous lengths of tanned leather for various useful purposes (for boots or shoes.)	3384	23rd Dec. 1865	{ George Horn. { Daniel Horn.
Manufacture of boots and shoes	3371	29th Dec. 1865	John Hall.

BORING, DRILLING, RIFLING AND PUNCHING; GIMLETS, AUGERS AND BRACE-BITS.

Subject-matter of Patent.	Number of Patent.	Date.	Name of Patentee.
Drilling apparatus for hand or steam power, adaptable also as a vice and for lifting purposes	18	3rd Jan. 1865	{ George Hodgson. { James Pitt.
Apparatus for transmitting and converting reciprocating motion into rotary motion, applicable to various useful purposes. (actuating drills.)	145	17th Jan. 1865	William John Cunningham.
Improvements in certain sewing-machine shuttles, and in the mode of and tools for manufacturing the same.	162	19th Jan. 1865	George Francis Bradbury.
Improvements in fire-arms and in ammunition for the same. (rifling barrels.)	198	21st Jan. 1865	Jacob Snider, jun'.
Improvements in preparing for fixing and in fixing plates or sheets of metal, such as are used for roofing and other similar purposes.	272	26th Jan. 1865	George Dibley.
Action and arrangement of drilling machines, turning lathes and other machine tools in which a variable speed is required.	341	27th Jan. 1865	John Combe.
Machinery and tools for making collars, cuffs, wristbands and other articles of dress, also adapted for cutting metal blanks. (piercing the holes.)	809	13th Feb. 1865	{ David Barr, { William Henry Page. { James Clement Newey.
Apparatus for operating engineers' and carpenters' tools by hand or other power. (for drilling, boring, slotting, punching, &c.) (Communicated by Henry Wiaaw.)	600	3rd March 1865	James Spence.

Subject-matter of Patent.	Number of Patent.	Date.	Name of Patentee.
Boring, &c.—*continued.*			
Machinery for cutting, punching, raising, clamping or drawing through sheet metal, by means of tools and dies.	796	22nd March 1865	George Forster.
Improvements in machinery or apparatus for drilling or boring rocks and other hard substances in tunnelling, mining and other like operations, parts of which improvements are also applicable to the ventilating of the workings in mines and similar places. (*Communicated by Herman Haupt.*)	981	6th April 1865	John Henry Johnson.
An improved hand drilling machine . -	1015	8th April 1865	Joseph White.
Improvements in boring or excavating and blasting rocks and minerals, and in the treatment of the tools employed therein.	1192	28th April 1865	Julian Bernard.
Machinery for drilling boiler and other plates of metal, and for rivetting them together.	1891	10th May 1865	Daniel Adamson.
Improvements in power looms for weaving and in apparatus connected therewith. (*punching holes in metal cylinders.*)	1807	11th May 1865	William Jamieson.
Improvements in the mode of rifling muzzle-loading cannon, and in projectiles for the same. (*Communicated by John Seigel.*)	1339	13th May 1865	William Spruce.
Machinery for the manufacture of hinges - - (*Punching the strips.*) (*Communicated by Jean Baptiste Esvard and Jean Pierre Boyer.*)	1335	13th May 1865	William Clark.
Certain improvements in the manufacture of gun barrels and ordnance - - - - }	1341	15th May 1865	{ William Deakin. John Bagnall Johnson.
Machinery or tools for cutting metals or other materials.	1671	9th June 1865	William Wilson Hulse.
An improved method of and machinery for cutting and excavating rock for railway tunnels and other purposes. (*Communicated by Thales Lindsley.*)	1587	12th June 1865	George Hawkins.
Hammers and other machines actuated by steam or other fluid or vapour - - - } (*machines for punching.*)	1607	14th June 1865	{ Benjamin Massey. Stephen Massey.
Portable punching apparatus - -	1708	26th June 1865	John Medhurst.
Heating chisels, knives, plane irons, gouges, augers, steels, shears, scythes and saws.	1715	27th June 1865	William Brooks.
Machinery or apparatus for cutting, punching and broding sheet metal. (*Communicated by Nathan Harper.*)	1798	29th June 1865	Robert Henry Lesson.
Improved machinery for boring rocks and hard substances.	1778	5th July 1865	George Law.
Improvements in the manufacture of hoops and tyres, and in the machinery employed therein. (*perforating discs.*)	1975	31st July 1865	John Ramsbottom.
Apparatus for cutting scales for knives and forming metal webs for knives.	1936	1st Aug. 1865	William Singleton.
An improved combination drill brace - -	2019	9th Aug. 1865	{ Edward Davis. Richard Hobbs Taunton.
Improvements in the manufacture of tubes for gun barrels and other purposes, parts of which improvements are also applicable to the manufacture of rods or bars, and to the rifling of ordnance and fire-arms.	2351	14th Sept. 1865	Gustavus Palmer Harding.

Subject-matter of Patent.	Number of Patent.	Date.	Name of Patentee.
Boats, &c.—continued.			
An improved form of rifling for fire-arms and ordnance.	2354	14th Sept. 1865	Wilmot Burrows Edward Ellis.
A new or improved method of and apparatus for securing or fastening metal plates to beams, rafters and other places, for roofing and other purposes.	2384	19th Sept. 1865	Robert Fox.
Machinery for making casks, barrels and other wooden vessels of capacity. (boring bung holes.)	8426	22nd Sept. 1865	James Davidson.
Improvements in the manufacture of horse-shoes, and in the machinery used for such manufacture. (Communicated by Léon Chrysostóme Viré and Pierre Michel Sidat.)	8433	23rd Sept. 1865	George Davies.
Tools for securing tubes in tube plates, and for other purposes where concentrated power or adjustment is necessary. (for working punches, adjusting cutters, &c.)	2455	26th Sept. 1865	Richard Taylor Nelson Howry.
Improvements in rifling fire-arms, and in missiles or projectiles used in such, and in the machinery for the production of these improvements.	2465	24th Sept. 1865	William Ellis Metford.
Improved self-centering and tightening chucks for drilling machines, lathes and other machines in which chucks are used. (Communicated by John Edwin Earle.)	2491	28th Sept. 1865	Edward Thomas Hughes.
Improvements in connections for and in stopping pipes used for conveying water and gas and for other like purposes, and in preventing leakages in the said pipes, and in apparatus employed therein. (and drilling.)	2508	29th Sept. 1865	Charles Forster Cotterill.
Instruments for punching or perforating leather and other materials.	2556	6th Oct. 1865	{ Edward Marsland. Peter Williams.
Improvements in submarine electric telegraph cables, and in apparatus connected therewith. (punching press for perforating gutta percha.)	2606	10th Oct. 1865	François Thierry Hubert.
Manufacture of tyres for railway wheels. (punching.)	2654	14th Oct. 1866	{ William James Armitage. Fairfax Woolfe. John Hodgson.
Improvements in the construction of braces for bits, applicable also to stocks, handles or holders for holding tools and other articles to which stocks, handles or holders are applied.	2735	23rd Oct. 1865	John Orvin.
Improvements in the manufacture of wheels for railway carriages, and in the machinery to be employed therein. (drilling machines.)	2771	27th Oct. 1865	Thomas Greenwood.
Improvements in tools and apparatus employed in blasting, boring and cutting rock, stone and other hard substances, and in the means employed for making such tools.	2774	27th Oct. 1865	Julius Bernard.
Machinery for mortising, tenoning and boring hard or soft woods and drilling iron.	2890	2nd Nov. 1865	James Curtis.
An improved bit for boring mortices in wood or other material.	2857	6th Nov. 1865	William Tighe Hamilton.
Fire-arms and projectiles. (rifling barrels.)	2902	11th Nov. 1865	Charles William Jones.

Subject-matter of Patent.	Number of Patent.	Date.	Name of Patentee.
BORING, &c.—continued.			
Machinery or apparatus for stamping or impressing railway or other tickets. (perforating.)	3005	22nd Nov. 1865	Alfred Lancefield.
An improved screwing and tapping machine -	3166	9th Dec. 1865	Emile Watters.
Machinery for boring rock and other mineral - (Communicated by Carl Sacks.)	3216	13th Dec. 1865	Frederick Bernard Darring.
Improvements in the furniture of door locks and latches, and in the means used in applying the same. (apparatus for cutting holes.)	3290	20th Dec. 1865	John Martin.
An improvement in envelopes - - - (perforating.)	3331	23rd Dec. 1865	Frederic Jeaner.
Improvements in the construction and manufacture of steel crossings for railways, and in the moulds for casting the same, all or part of which said improvements in moulds are applicable for casting other articles. (casting punch blocks.)	3339	23rd Dec. 1865	Francis William Webb.
Machinery for boring, turning and shaping articles of metal - - - - - - - -	3369	29th Dec. 1865	{ William Harrison. Thomas Walker.
BOTTLES AND JARS; STOPPERS, CAPSULES AND CORKS; STOPPERING, CLOSING AND OPENING BOTTLES AND JARS; CORKSCREWS; BOTTLE-HOLDERS.			
Stoppers for bottles, jars, vessels and tubes, also for ordnance and fire-arms.	27	4th Jan. 1865	Nathan Thompson.
Preparing and keeping aërated beverages -	39	5th Jan. 1865	Thomas Pickford.
Improved means of closing the mouths of bottles or other vessels - - - - -	132	16th Jan. 1865	{ Henry James Rogers. Jonathan Mather Scholefield.
An improved apparatus for containing and dispensing stouts and other liquids.	194	23rd Jan. 1865	Edward Atkinson.
Corkscrews - - - - - -	263	1st Feb. 1865	Joseph Royer.
Stoppering bottles or other similar vessels, and measuring quantities therefrom.	414	14th Feb. 1865	William Conway Hine.
An improved method of stopping bottles -	464	18th Feb. 1865	John James Chidley.
Manufacture of ornamented articles of glass - (decanters, wine glasses, &c.)	497	22nd Feb. 1865	Thomas George Webb.
An improvement in air-tight jars for preserving eggs and fruits and such like articles of food.	546	27th Feb. 1865	George Kennedy Geyelin.
Stopping bottles - - - - - (Communicated by Henry Bateman Goodyear.)	606	4th March 1865	John Henry Johnson.
Cork cutting machinery - - - - (Communicated by François Perret.)	636	7th March 1865	William Clark.
Stoppers for closing bottles and for other like purposes.	646	8th March 1865	George Ireland.

PATENTS APPLIED FOR AND PATENTS GRANTED.   43

Subject-matter of Patent.	Number of Patent.	Date.	Name of Patentee.
Bottles, &c.—continued.			
Improvements in stoppers for bottles, jars or other vessels, the same being applicable to fire-arms and ordnance.	814	23rd March 1865	Charles Henry Crown.
Protective labels for bottles, jars and other similar vessels.	853	25th March 1865	William Potts.
An improvement or improvements in ornamenting articles made of glass. (decanters and drinking vessels.)	858	24th March 1865	Joseph Williams.
Vessels or apparatus for melting sealing wax, glue or other substances. (for sealing bottles.) (Communicated by Frederick Kükmann.)	931	3rd April 1865	William Bünger.
An improved implement for removing corks from the interior of bottles and other vessels. (Communicated by Francis Daniel Pastorius and John Jackson.)	1131	27nd April 1865	George Haseltine.
Improved apparatus for pouring and decanting liquids.	1146	25th April 1865	Nicholas Sihly.
Manufacture and application of glass and other vitreous compositions. (making bottles.)	1290	1st May 1865	{ Arthur Howard Emerson. Robert Fowler. }
An improvement in stoppers and flasks, bottles and other similar vessels.	1290	12th May 1865	Spencer Thomas Garrett.
Improvements in vessels for containing blacking, polishing oils and other similar materials, and in apparatus connected therewith.	1397	12th May 1865	Thomas Davis.
Vessels or receptacles for containing oil and other liquids.	1550	16th May 1865	Ernad Svenders.
An improved method of securing corks or stoppers in bottles. (Communicated by Gustave Bandgure.)	1575	18th May 1865	Richard Archibald Brooman.
An improved bottle stopper. (Communicated by John Matthews.)	1466	29th May 1865	William Fettle.
Corks or bungs for closing bottles and other receptacles for liquids. (Communicated by Adolphe Jacquenum.)	1689	5th June 1865	John Henry Johnson.
Improvements in the construction of the necks of bottles and other vessels, and in means for closing or covering the mouths of such bottles or vessels.	1870	9th June 1865	Howard Busby Fox.
Improvements in envelopes or wrappers for covering, packing and protecting bottles, jars or other fragile articles, and in apparatus for manufacturing the same.	1660	20th June 1865	George Clark.
A new and improved food or fluid regulator for feeding bottle and other tubes.	1727	24th June 1865	William Botham.
An improved combination of materials for the manufacture of carpets, floor cloth, felt, wall paper, fire-proof flexible roofing, ship and boat building and for other similar purposes. (stoppers for bottles.)	1775	5th July 1865	{ John Longbottom. Abram Longbottom. }
Ornamental tables and table stands, such as cruet frames, liqueur frames, flower, egg and other stands.	1885	25th July 1865	{ Louis Pètre. Edward Samuel Tucker. }
Manufacture of capsules.	2008	12th Aug. 1865	William Betts.

Subject-matter of Patent.	Number of Patent.	Date.	Name of Patentee.
BOTTLES, &c.—continued.			
An improvement in the manufacture of metallic capsules.	2195	17th Aug. 1865	Eugene Rimmel.
Packing-cases or boxes for holding or packing bottles or bottled liquids.	2141	14th Aug. 1865	John Hope.
Apparatus for stopping bottles - - -	2150	19th Aug. 1865	James Battle Austin.
An improvement in syphons - - - (for bottles, jars, &c.)	2168	23rd Aug. 1865	Lippmann Jacob Levinsohn.
Apparatus for supplying carbonic acid gas to casks and other vessels from which beer, wine and other fermented liquors are drawn. (constructing corks or stoppers.)	2157	25th Aug. 1865	Charles Adolphus Watkins.
Improved means of securing corks in the necks of bottles.	2253	30th Aug. 1865	William Henry Postlethwaite Gare.
Apparatus for stopping bottles - - -	2246	31st Aug. 1865	William Thomas Brad.
Machinery for cutting and shaping cork, with apparatus for registering the manufacture.	2383	20th Sept. 1865	Leon Villette.
Construction of vessels for preserving food and liquids.	2475	27th Sept. 1865	Louis Henri Gillet.
Manufacture of sweet and smelling bottles - -	2599	9th Oct. 1865	Thomas Miln.
Improvements in tompions for ordnance and small arms, and in stoppers for bottles and other vessels. (Communicated by George Richard Hildmer.)	2650	13th Oct. 1865	William Edward Newton.
Manufacture of chemical toys known as Pharaoh's serpents. (and capsules for same.)	2694	18th Oct. 1865	Thomas King.
Packing and labelling bottles, jars and other fragile articles.	2775	24th Oct. 1865	George Clark.
A new or improved machine for drawing corks from bottles.	2844	4th Nov. 1865	Henry John Sanders.
A new or improved bottle fountain for pocket and other purposes.	2847	4th Nov. 1865	Jean Nadal.
A combination of improved method, apparatus and receptacles for storing, preserving, transferring and discharging certain fluids, for sanitary and protective purposes - - - (Communicated by Henry Pinkus.)	2908	11th Aug. 1865	Robert Alexander William Westley.
An improved trap or liquid sealing to the covers of cisterns, pans, jars, tubs and other vessels or chambers - - - -	2988	20th Nov. 1865	George Putland Hemming. Henry Coyle.
Cork cutting machines - - - (Communicated by George Hommer and Alfred Buss.)	3033	25th Nov. 1865	John Henry Johnson.
BOXES, TRUNKS, PORTMANTEAUS, LETTER-BOXES, WORK-BOXES, DRESSING-CASES, CANISTERS.			
An improved ornamental flower box - - (see "HORTICULTURE.")	126	14th Jan. 1865	George Calver.
Fire and thief proof safes, chests and strong room doors.	543	27th Feb. 1865	Walter Henry Tucker.

Subj.-matter of Patent.	Number of Patent.	Date.	Name of Patentee.
BOXES, &c.—continued.			
Improvements in the construction of joints for boxes, drawers and other like articles, and for planks and timbers, and in machinery to be used in the preparation of such joints.	840	7th March 1865	Henry William Wimshurst.
An improved system of closing spittardashes, applicable also to boxes, portemonnaies and other similar articles.	858	9th March 1865	Emile Carchon.
Fire and burglar proof safes, chests, doors and iron rooms.	895	11th March 1865	John Tann.
Manufacture of jewelry cases and other similar cases.	808	22nd March 1865	John James Carter.
An improvement in the construction of cartridge and other boxes. (Communicated by Robert Augustus Chesebrough.)	902	30th March 1865	Alfred Vincent Newton.
Improved means of preventing the leakage of barrels, and of rendering packages and fabrics impervious to air and gases. (Communicated by Lewis Francis and Cyrus Lowrel.)	912	31st March 1865	Alfred Vincent Newton.
Manufacture of a compound or material to be used as a substitute for india-rubber. (for lining boxes.) (Communicated by Henry Larivenbery and Emile Gruzier.)	1059	15th April 1865	William Clark.
Manufacture and application of glass and other vitreous compositions - - - - (for boxes.)	1290	1st May 1865	{ Arthur Howard Emerson. Robert Fowler.
Certain improvements in hydraulic presses for packing cotton and other materials or substances, and in the boxes for containing the same - -	1290	9th May 1865	{ Edward Taylor Bellhouse. William John Dorning.
Manufacture of boxes suitable among other uses for containing paste blacking and other cheap marketable articles. (Communicated by Edwin Price.)	1789	6th July 1865	Alfred Vincent Newton.
An improved manufacture of coffins and air-tight receptacles.	1804	7th July 1865	Joseph George.
The use and application of paper, printed or otherwise ornamented with water colors, for covering floors and other analogous purposes as a substitute for carpets and oil cloths, and of an improved coating or varnish to be applied to the same to protect its surface from injury and wear. (and for covering trunks.)	1878	19th July 1865	Aaron Henry Platt.
Construction of travelling and other bags - -	2001	2nd Aug. 1865	Heiman Frankenburg.
Certain improvements in the mode of firing safes, boxes or other depositories for the protection of papers or other materials from fire.	2061	11th Aug. 1865	Peter Carlman Kjellberg.
Improvements in knots and other coverings for the feet, which improvements are applicable also to trunks and other articles, for the purpose of strengthening, preserving or protecting them. (Communicated by Jacob Nichols and Moers Petter.)	2123	19th Aug. 1865	Phineas Lawrence.
Packing cases or boxes for holding or packing bottles or bottled liquids.	2141	19th Aug. 1865	John Hope.
Construction of iron safes, strong boxes and other receptacles.	2294	7th Sept. 1865	John Matthias Hart.

Subject-matter of Patent.	Number of Patent.	Date.	Name of Patentee.
BOXES, &c.—continued.			
Locks for trunks, bags, dressing-cases and other like articles. (Communicated by Nicolas Chrétien Goynand.)	2290	15th Sept. 1865	Richard Archibald Brooman.
Adaptation of elastic material to articles requiring a bellows arrangement, or a partially rigid and partially expansible arrangement. (for portmanteaus.)	2423	22nd Sept. 1865	Matthew Cartwright.
Construction of vessels for preserving food and liquids.	2478	27th Sept. 1865	Louis Henri Gillet.
An improved fastening for books, portfolios, despatch boxes and other similar articles	2664	16th Oct. 1865	{ Joseph Orrin. Thomas Geer.
Manufacture of embossed wood (for boxes.) (Communicated by Henry May and Henry Taylor Blake.)	2895	10th Nov. 1865	Alfred Vincent Newton.
Portfolios, writing desks, writing cases and other similar apparatus.	2918	13th Nov. 1865	John Stephens.
Manufacture of boxes or receptacles for merchandise. (Communicated by François Barthélemy Loubtchenkoff.)	3006	22nd Nov. 1865	John Henry Johnson.
Shields for trunks or packages (Communicated by Alford Hoses and Henry Alonzo Hoses.)	3022	24th Nov. 1865	William Edward Newton.
Waterproof linings of cases, boxes and apparatus in which articles are desired to be packed waterproof.	3201	11th Dec. 1865	John Jones.
Boxes or cases for needles	3309	22nd Dec. 1865	Richard Newhall.
Improvements in the manufacture of safes, and in apparatus connected therewith. (and chests, deed boxes, &c.)	3321	23rd Dec. 1865	Samuel Chatwood.
Obtaining and employing continuous lengths of tanned leather for various useful purposes (requ. for chests, portmanteaus, &c.)	3334	23rd Dec. 1865	{ George Ham. Daniel Ham.

BREAD, BISCUITS AND PASTRY ; KNEADING-MACHINES; BAKERS' OVENS.

A new method for removing or destroying the momentum of heavy bodies by means of an elastic machine or machines, so as to prevent injury and damage from concussion, applicable to ship cables, ship and fort armour, railway trains, fenders to pierheads and floating piers, gangways, breakwaters and other similar structures, also as a motive power. (working bread making apparatus.) (Communicated by William Graham M'Ivor.)	321	6th Feb. 1865	Clements Roberts Markham.
Certain improvements in the manufacture of magnesium and its compounds (making gas for aërating bread.)	456	17th Feb. 1865	{ John Osborne Christian, F.C.S. John Charlton. Henry Charlton.

Subject-matter of Patent.	Number of Patent.	Date.	Name of Patentee.

BREAD, &c.—continued.

Subject-matter of Patent.	Number of Patent.	Date.	Name of Patentee.
Machinery or apparatus for kneading or working dough. (Communicated by Jean Joseph Etienne Lenoir.)	449	21st Feb. 1865	John Henry Johnson.
Machinery or apparatus for baking biscuits	556	27th Feb. 1865	George Thomas Ellwick.
Fire-places and flues and apparatus connected therewith. (for baking ovens.)	989	7th April 1865	Edward Welch.
Baking of bread, biscuits and other farinaceous articles.	1108	20th April 1865	John Yeldham Betts.
Ovens for baking bread	1446	15th May 1865	John Danglish.
Improvements in coke and charcoal ovens and in the manufacture of coke, parts of which are applicable to bread, biscuit and pastry ovens.	2477	27th Sept. 1865	William Morgam.
Apparatus for impressing designs upon biscuits made by machinery.	2506	29th Sept. 1865	George Gillett.
Manufacture of lozenges, cakes and other similar articles from plastic substances.	2534	3rd Oct. 1865	Charles James Tinker.
Treatment of flour and the manufacture of bread	2973	18th Nov. 1865	John Crawford Walker.
Machinery or apparatus for cutting bread	3261	15th Dec. 1865	Henry Charles Litchfield.
Boilers or apparatus for generating steam (for baking.) (Communicated by Julien Belleville.)	3366	18th Dec. 1865	Richard Archibald Brooman.
Machinery for raising or forming articles of sheet metal. (ovens cake dishes.) (Communicated by Mellen Bray.)	3318	22nd Dec. 1865	George Tomlinson Bousfield.

BREAKS, SKIDS AND BUFFERS FOR CARRIAGES AND RAILWAYS.

Subject-matter of Patent.	Number of Patent.	Date.	Name of Patentee.
Method of and apparatus for applying electro-magnetism as a break power to railway and other carriages and machines	101	12th Jan. 1865	Frederic Barnes. David Hancock. Edward Cowpe.
Improvements in furnaces and boilers and parts connected with them, for generating steam and heating fluids, and also for improved apparatus for reducing and shutting off steam and regulating the speed of steam-engines.	386	11th Feb. 1865	John Cam.
Machinery for stopping railway trains (Communicated by Candido Rarelli.)	487	22nd Feb. 1865	Eugenio Jevarra.
Construction of buffers for railway carriages	513	23rd Feb. 1865	William Rowe.
An improved means of securing and protecting the india-rubber rings of buffer springs of railway carriages, which invention is also applicable to air-pump and valve castings and lids faced with india-rubber.	639	6th March 1865	William John Oliver.
Railway breaks (Communicated by Charles Louis Joseph Félix Jacquet.)	745	17th March 1865	Henri Adrien Bonneville.
Improved mechanical arrangements for stopping or retarding railway carriages, waggons and trucks.	1031	10th April 1865	George Voigt.

Subject-matter of Patent.	Number of Patent	Date.	Name of Patentee.
BREAKS, &c.—continued.			
Certain improvements in brakes for railway carriages.	1431	25th May 1865	Jules Xavier Joseph Barbuis.
An improved break applicable to various descriptions of steam-engines and also to railway purposes. (Communicated by Eugène Dutheil.)	1542	8th June 1865	Frederick Tolhausen.
An improved force dispeller or spring buffing apparatus.	1599	13th June 1865	William Jeffrey Hopkins.
An improved self-acting break for four-wheeled carriages.	1604	13th June 1865	James Griffiths.
Drags for carriages - - - -	1680	23rd June 1865	Archibald Edward Dobbs, B.A.
An improved apparatus for stopping railway trains	1684	23rd June 1865	William Jeremiah Murphy.
Means of and apparatus for retarding the velocity of the wheels of railway and other carriages when in motion.	1710	27th June 1865	Henry Shaw.
Means applied for arresting and stopping the motion of locomotive engines, trains, carriages and other rolling stock of railways.	1736	30th June 1865	Patrick Denis Finnigan.
Improvements in railway carriages, which improvements are intended to neutralise the destructive effects arising from the collision of trains.	1746	30th June 1865	Louis Faure.
Locomotive engines - - - - (Communicated by Auguste De Bergue.)	1754	3rd July 1865	Charles De Bergue.
Apparatus for stopping and retarding railway carriages and locomotive engines.	1759	3rd July 1865	Joseph Navrana.
An improved break for retarding the progress of wheel carriages. (Communicated by François Piatti.)	1810	8th July 1865	William Edward Newton.
Apparatus for retarding the progress of railway carriages and trains.	1964	29th July 1865	William King.
An improved break for railway and other wheeled carriages.	1969	24th July 1865	Robert Brightmore Mitchell.
Means or apparatus for stopping or retarding railway carriages - - - -	1989	29th July 1865	{ John Swinburne. James Lansing.
Improvements in the construction of railway carriages and in railway breaks and signals, part of which is applicable to marine purposes -	2006	2nd Aug. 1865	{ William Henry Pettican. Edward McNally.
Improved means or apparatus for retarding or stopping railway carriages and trains.	2045	7th Aug. 1865	John Mend.
Apparatus or mechanism for stopping or retarding railway trains.	2154	21st Aug. 1865	William Shakespear.
A new or improved method of and apparatus for applying electro-magnetism as a break power on railways - - - - -	2255	31st Aug. 1865	{ Edward Cowpe. David Hancock.
An improved hydraulic break for railway and other purposes.	2337	12th Sept. 1865	William Jeremiah Murphy.
Railway breaks - - - - (Communicated by Eugène Étienne Berthomieux, Jean Massien and Louis Lacerdieu.)	2375	18th Sept. 1865	Michael Henry.
Railway carriages and other vehicles - - (operating the breaks.) (Communicated by Henry Hudson Trower.)	2394	20th Sept. 1865	John Henry Johnson.

Subject-matter of Patent.	Number of Patent.	Date.	Name of Patentee.
BREAKS, &c.—continued.			
Atmospheric buffing apparatus	2590	2nd Oct. 1865	Thomas Williams.
Brakes for carriages and other vehicles	2601	5th Oct. 1865	Archibald Richard Shaw.
Mechanical arrangements for stopping or retarding railway carriages, waggons and trucks.	2606	9th Oct. 1865	George Voight.
Certain improvements in breaks for carts, wagons and other vehicles.	2617	11th Oct. 1865	Thomas Warburton.
Carriages propelled by manual power	2623	11th Oct. 1865	Thomas Du Rouley.
Improvements in common road carriages and in breaks for the same.	2687	18th Oct. 1865	James Rock the younger.
An improved arrangement of buffing and drawing apparatus for railway carriages	2840	3rd Nov. 1865	George Wilson. William Kitching Hydes.
Breaks	2927	11th Nov. 1865	Joseph Williamson. James Lindley. James Colman.
An improved arrangement of mechanism for stopping or retarding railway carriages, waggons, trucks or other rail or tram road vehicles	2948	15th Nov. 1865	Louis Alexis Velu. François Eugène Fouré. Louis Eugène Alphonse Fouré.
An improved drag for carriages	3227	11th Dec. 1865	Archibald Edward Dobbs, M.A.
Breaks or apparatus for stopping or retarding railway trains.	3356	30th Dec. 1865	David William Thomas.

BREWING, FERMENTING, MANUFACTURING AND TREATING BEER, WINE, &c.; YEAST; TREATING MALT AND HOPS.

An improved jacket or protector for metallic and other vessels and structures containing solid substances, liquids or gases, to prevent radiation of heat from or communication of heat to such vessels and structures. (for wine coolers.)	4	2nd Jan. 1865	Edward Bevan. Abel Fenning.
Filtering apparatus. (wine, beer, &c.)	249	24th Jan. 1865	Victor Durg.
A new or improved method or process and apparatus for obtaining the concentrated extract of hops, and for preserving the same from deterioration. (Communicated by George Perry, Walter Wells, Charles Brown, John Molford and John Mermillion Webb.)	306	4th Feb. 1865	Joseph Rideal Webb.
Improvements in mashing machines and in apparatus connected therewith.	481	21st Feb. 1865	Robert Willson.
Improvements in securing low and uniform temperatures, applicable to public and private buildings, also to refrigerators, coolers and condensers, and to ships and other vessels, and in the apparatus employed therein. (cooling apparatus for breweries.) (Communicated by Daniel Sinner.)	719	14th March 1865	Alfred Vincent Newton.

D

Subject-matter of Patent.	Number of Patent.	Date.	Name of Patentee.
BREWING, &c.—continued.			
An improved composition for clarifying and fining beer and other fermented liquors.	790	22nd March 1865	William Juby Coleman.
Certain improvements in non-conducting composition for preventing the radiation or transmission of heat or cold. (for brewers.)	804	27th March 1865	Ferdinand Le Roy.
Machinery or apparatus employed in breweries and distilleries.	1204	29th April 1865	Francis Gregory.
A mode of obtaining decoctions and apparatus for carrying the same into effect. (from hops.) (Communicated by Benjamin Green Martin.)	1297	2nd May 1865	Francis Wise.
An improved refrigerator and condenser - -	1349	4th May 1865	Josiah Hampton.
Improvements in brewing, distillation, the production of vinegar and the extract of malt and other grain.	1363	6th May 1865	Solomon Bennett.
Improvements in drying malt and grain, and in the machinery or apparatus connected therewith.	1397	10th May 1865	John Forbes.
Obtaining jellies, syrups, drinks and other products from the tree Arbutus Unedo, known as the Arbutus. (wines and liquors.)	1649	30th June 1865	Philippe Minguard.
Improvements in distilling and rectifying, and in the apparatus employed therein, parts of which improvements are applicable to steam generators.	1662	20th June 1865	Evariste Vignier.
An improved brewers' and distillers' refrigerator or apparatus for cooling liquids, condensing steam or other vapours.	1700	26th June 1865	Morris Ashby.
Improving draught beer, ale, porter and cider -	1781	6th July 1865	Thomas Symes Pridmore.
Improvements in drying grain, hay and other substances, and in the machinery for effecting the same - - - - - - - (malt.)	1863	29th July 1865	{ Baldwin Latham, Robert Campbell.
Means or apparatus for promoting the combustion of fuel in furnaces of steam-boilers, dyers' or brewers' pans and other furnaces, whereby smoke is prevented and fuel economised - -	1979	31st July 1865	{ Benjamin Robinson, Joseph Varley.
Improvements in the raising, lifting or drawing and forcing of water and other liquids, and in the apparatus and means employed therefor (for brewers.)	1999	2nd Aug. 1865	{ James M'Ewan, William Neilson.
Improvements in brewing and distilling, also in drying yeast, and in the apparatus employed.	2019	4th Aug. 1865	Patrick Robertson.
A combination of improved method, apparatus and receptacles for storing, preserving, transferring and discharging certain fluids, for sanitary and protective purposes. (Communicated by Henry Pinkus.)	2096	14th Aug. 1865	Robert Alexander William Westley.
Improvements in cisterns or chambers for the steeping of grain in the manufacture of malt, which improvements are also applicable to other chambers or enclosures.	2422	24th Sept. 1865	Charles Edmund Davis.
Certain improvements in the production and uses of carburetted coal gas. (preserving fermented liquors.)	2680	16th Oct. 1865	Albert Julius Mott.

Subject matter of Patent.	Number of Patent.	Date.	Name of Patentee.
BREWING, &c.—continued.			
Treating brewers' grains in order to render them more suitable for the food of animals.	3996	10th Nov. 1865	Edward John Davis.
A new kind of unfermented and uninterminating malt liquor, which shall keep sound for any period of time.	8047	25th Nov. 1865	Charles Henry Newman.
Fining, purifying and mellowing spirituous liquors by combining therewith other substances, for the production of a new spirituous or vinous compound therefrom.	8071	30th Nov. 1865	William Thompson.
Improvements in the treatment of grain and in the process of malting, and in the apparatus employed therein.	8097	1st Dec. 1865	William Rowland Taylor.
A new and improved compound to be employed as a drinking beverage. (Communicated by Edward Davis.)	8303	12th Dec. 1865	Joachim Kaspary.

BRICKS, TILES AND BUILDING BLOCKS.

Machinery or apparatus for the manufacture of compressed bricks.	77	10th Jan. 1865	Humphrey Chamberlain.
Machinery for compressing coal dust and other materials &c for burning, also clay into bricks, tiles, pipes and other like articles.	230	28th Jan. 1865	William Smith.
Improvements in fixing front screen awnings and netting for protecting well-fruit trees, in fixing trellis for training fruit and other trees to walls, and in bricks therefor.	287	1st Feb. 1865	Charles Anthony Wheeler.
An improvement in the manufacture of artificial stone for building and other purposes.	441	16th Feb. 1865	William Kirrage.
An improved preparation or treatment of clay for the manufacture of bricks . . .	458	17th Feb. 1865	Richard Hill. Robert Tushingham.
Machinery for making and pressing bricks . .	480	21st Feb. 1865	Charles William Homer.
Improved machinery or apparatus for securing stones, marbles, slates and bricks . .	636	11th March 1865	Jonas Hird. Joshua Walker.
Portable or fixed machines for the manufacture of bricks and tiles, whether plain or for ornamental purposes . . .	767	18th March 1865	Charles William Spark. Thomas Spurreon Cross. William Adkins.
Improvements in the manufacture of bricks and in the apparatus employed therein . . .	939	3rd April 1865	Alfred Lockwood. Alfred Lockwood, jun'.
Bricks	1698	29th June 1865	Thomas Lewis Jewett.
Improvements in the manufacture of gas retorts and other articles made of fire-clay, and in furnaces for burning the same, and for other purposes. (making fire-door tiles.)	1787	30th June 1865	William Schofield.
An improved mode of pressing and moulding clay, sand or cement, for making bricks and for other purposes. (Communicated by John Steele.)	1745	1st July 1865	William Robert Lake.
Roofing tiles and slabs	1991	1st Aug. 1865	Frederick Ransome.
Paints or preparations for coating surfaces . . (coating bricks.)	2015	3rd Aug. 1865	Ernest Leslie Ransome.

52 SUBJECT-MATTER INDEX OF

Subject-matter of Patent.	Number of Patent.	Date.	Name of Patentee.

BRICKS, &c.—continued.

Manufacture of bricks and blocks for building and other purposes	2068	9th Aug. 1865	James William Sumner, Clement Augustus Scott.
Manufacture of terra-cotta or vitreous stone	2071	10th Aug. 1865	Mark Henry Blanchard.
Certain improvements in machinery for making bricks. (Communicated by Egbert Cox Bradford and James Henry Revick.)	2149	19th Aug. 1865	William Edward Newton.
An improved method of ornamenting the surface of tiles.	2378	14th Sept. 1865	Henry Venables.
Improvements in the manufacture of bricks, blocks, flue covers and tiles, and in the machinery and apparatus employed therefor.	2392	19th Sept. 1865	James Gillespie.
Machinery used in the manufacture of bricks and tiles.	2396	20th Sept. 1865	William Porter.
Manufacture of bricks and other analogous materials	2571	6th Oct. 1865	Victor Jean Baptiste Germain.
Tiles for roofing	2693	14th Oct. 1865	John Taylor, jun'.
Machinery for screening, tempering and moulding clays and earths into bricks, tiles and other articles.	2728	21st Oct. 1865	Isaac Roberts.
Manufacture of bricks and artificial stone and marble.	2867	7th Nov. 1865	David Barker.
Improvements in the manufacture of bricks for building and other purposes, and in apparatus therefor.	2916	13th Nov. 1865	Edwin Guthrie.
Manufacture of bricks or building blocks	2967	17th Nov. 1865	Louis Gonzague Speyser.
A new or improved cement or composition, applicable to the agglomeration or moulding of various materials, and to other useful and decorative purposes. (blocks for constructive purposes.) (Communicated by Stanislas Sorel and Emile Justin Menier.)	3119	5th Dec. 1865	Richard Archibald Brooman.
Machinery for the manufacture of bricks	3125	5th Dec. 1865	Peter Rawden.
Improved machinery for compressing and solidifying coal, clay and other amalgous substances.	3242	14th Dec. 1865	Henry George Fairburn.
Preparation of glue or gelatine so as to render it insoluble in water, and applicable by the admixture of other substances to various purposes for which common glue or gelatine cannot now be used. (for not proofing bricks.) (Communicated by Henry Wurtz.)	3285	23rd Dec. 1865	William Edward Newton.

BRIDGES, VIADUCTS AND AQUEDUCTS.

Improvements in the permanent way of railways and in tramline plates to be used therein, the same being applicable to the construction of ballasted buildings, bridges and other like structures, also in the machinery or apparatus for producing such improved plates.	164	19th Jan. 1865	Robert Mallet.

Subject-matter of Patent.	Number of Patent.	Date.	Name of Patentee.
BRIDGES, &c.—continued.			
Improvements in the construction of roadways, pavements and iron girders specially applicable for the purpose of constructing roads, pavements, bridges and all description of buildings.	335	7th Feb. 1865	Constantine Henderson.
Improvements in buoys, beacons, floats or pontoons, which improvements are also applicable to floating bodies generally - -	387	11th Feb. 1865	{ Charles Atherton, Amherst Hawker Renton.
An improved blowing apparatus - - (for bridge builders.)	437	15th Feb. 1865	{ Samuel Richards Freeman, Abraham Grundy.
Improvements in the construction of beams or supports applicable to the building of bridges, viaducts, roofs, arches and ships, and in instruments to be used therein.	578	1st March 1865	William Edward Kocha.
Construction of bridges - - - -	633	7th March 1865	Edward William Young.
Construction of bridges and arches - -	688	29th March 1865	Frederick Allen Leigh.
Improvements in casing iron girders and in apparatus therefor. (for railway bridges.)	1304	11th May 1865	James Goodwin.
Manufacture of iron piers or erections, applicable more especially for carrying bridges at high elevations, or available for river legs and lighthouses.	1539	5th June 1865	Charles De Bergue.
Construction of roadways, floorings or other surfaces (for bridges.)	1639	17th June 1865	Thomas Russell Crampton.
Construction of suspended bridges, roads, aqueducts or other way.	1768	4th July 1865	Sylvain Benjamin Labourel.
Construction of sliding or rolling bridges - -	1834	26th July 1865	Michael Kearney.
Manufacture of iron and steel - - - (rolling girders.) Communicated by Martin Dieudonné Heuveux.)	1984	29th July 1865	Ephraim Nabel.
An improved system of constructing cast and other iron bridges, viaducts and other similar structures. (Communicated by William Carvill Teasdale.)	3320	30th Aug. 1865	William Brookes.
A new and improved cramp - - - (for viaducts, railway bridges, &c.)	3863	7th Nov. 1865	{ Thomas Grann, James O'Donoghue.
Bridges and viaducts - - - -	3248	15th Dec. 1865	Charles De Bergue.
Constructing and securing floating structures (or pier of a bridge.)	5365	16th Dec. 1865	{ Charles Liddell, Robert Stirling Newall.

BRUSHES AND BROOMS.			
Improvements in brushes for brushing the hair, which improvements are also applicable to brushes for other purposes.	61	7th Jan. 1865	Theophilus Harris.
Improvements in the construction of brushes used for brushing the human or other hair, and in the apparatus or means connected therewith.	234	25th Jan. 1865	Casimir Roques.
Machinery or apparatus for brushing the hair -	343	7th Feb. 1865	John Butler Watters.
Brushes or brooms - - - - -	764	16th March 1865	James Vero.

Subject-matter of Patent.	Number of Patent.	Date.	Name of Patentee.
BRUSHES, &c.—continued.			
An improved application of rotary brushes, and in the mechanism and apparatus connected therewith.	920	1st April 1865	John Drinkwater.
An improved application of rotary brushes to the grooming or cleaning of horses and other quadrupeds.	1029	12th April 1865	John Haworth.
Improvements in door and other mats, part of which is also applicable to brushes and brooms, and in producing card or tooth surfaces employed in operating on various fibrous substances.	1223	9th May 1865	Thomas Jefferson Mayall.
Brooms or brushes	1452	30th May 1865	William Martin.
Manufacture of mats, matting and brushes	1759	3rd July 1865	George Hurn, Daniel Hurn.
An improved arrangement of machinery for brushing hair	2026	8th Aug. 1865	Samuel Middleton.
Brushes	2230	9th Aug. 1865	George Smith, Charles Ritchie.
Hair brushing machinery or apparatus	2276	5th Sept. 1865	Joseph Neal, Francis Ford.
Brooms or brushes for sweeping and dusting	2368	19th Sept. 1865	George Smith, Charles Ritchie.
Machinery for brushing hair	2417	22nd Sept. 1865	Frederick Thomas Bramwreth. John Henry Bramdreth.
Apparatus for polishing and brushing	2615	14th Oct. 1865	James Lamb Hancock.
Improvements in brushes for hair dressing and other uses, also in brooms and apparatus for cleaning, preparing, painting, coating and smoothing surfaces	3085	30th Nov. 1865	George Smith, Charles Ritchie.
Hair brushing apparatus	3004	21st Nov. 1865	George Smith, George Smith, jun., Charles William Smith.
Certain improvements in the manufacture of brushes	3090	29th Nov. 1865	James Stoban, Thomas Gray.
Construction of shoe mats, desk and bath brushes made principally of india-rubber.	3216	13th Dec. 1865	George Barber.
Preparation of glue or gelatine so as to render it insoluble in water, and applicable by the admixture of other substances to various purposes for which common glue or gelatine cannot now be used. *(for stiffening fibres for brushes, &c.) (Communicated by Henry Norts.)*	3325	23rd Dec. 1865	William Edward Newton.

BUILDINGS, PLASTERING, FLOORING AND ROOFING; WALLS, CEILINGS AND COR-NICES; TENTS; LADDERS.

Construction of public houses and other houses of entertainment.	1	2nd Jan. 1865	William Muir.
Construction of roofs or coverings of buildings	129	14th Jan. 1865	Félix Clovis Fourgeon.

Subject-matter of Patent.	Number of Patent.	Date.	Name of Patentee.
BUILDING, &c.—continued.			
Improvements in the permanent way of railways and in breaked plates to be used therein, the same being applicable to the construction of fireproof buildings, bridges and other like structures, also in the machinery or apparatus for producing such improved plates.	184	19th Jan. 1865	Robert Mallet.
An improved machine for raising and carrying earth, sand, stones or other similar solid or liquid materials for dredging, ventilating, or winnowing grain, or other analogous purposes.	174	20th Jan. 1865	Lewis Balcom.
Mode of working hydraulic lifts - - -	180	20th Jan. 1865	William Clay.
Ground vineries or glass ridges for the cultivation of grapes or other fruit.	204	24th Jan. 1865	Charles Tennant Wells.
Improvements in preparing for fixing and in fixing plates or sheets of metal, such as are used for roofing and other similar purposes.	222	26th Jan. 1865	George Dibley.
Improvements in the construction of roadways, pavements and iron girders especially applicable for the purpose of constructing roads, pavements, bridges and all descriptions of buildings.	325	7th Feb. 1865	Constantine Henderson.
An improvement in the manufacture of artificial stone for building and other purposes. (for copings, window sills, &c.)	441	16th Feb. 1865	William Kirrage.
Iron safes and strong rooms - - - -	450	17th Feb. 1865	James Ferguson.
New or improved indicating apparatus for the protection of railway passengers, buildings, rooms, safes and other objects - - - (see "SIGNALS.")	472	18th Feb. 1865	Leicester William Glen Rowe. Adolphe Bash.
Iron safes and strong rooms - - - -	490	22nd Feb. 1865	George Nathaniel Shore.
Improved portable frames and joints for tables and other articles, applicable also for building purposes and the like.	542	27th Feb. 1865	Charles Whiting.
Fire and thief proof safes, chests and strong room doors.	543	27th Feb. 1865	Walter Henry Tucker.
Improvements in the construction of beams or supports applicable to the building of bridges, viaducts, roofs, arches and ships, and in instruments to be used therein.	579	1st March 1865	William Edward Kochs.
An improvement in fitting sliding partitions in stables and other buildings.	610	4th March 1865	Louis Le Chevalier Cuttam.
Bolts for connecting sheets of zinc and other metals employed for covering roofs and other enclosures.	662	9th March 1865	Rowland George Fisher.
Fire and burglar proof safes, chests, doors and iron rooms.	696	11th March 1865	John Tann.
An improvement in securing safes and strong rooms.	702	13th March 1865	Henry Hill.
Construction of walls, houses and other buildings -	822	23rd March 1865	Joseph Tall.
Construction of bridges and arches - - -	869	25th March 1865	Frederick Allen Leigh.
Improvements in the treatment of meal and the dressing of flour, and the machinery and apparatus employed therein. (constructing grinding mills)	896	30th March 1865	William Nevory.
An improved safety tackle for raising and lowering heavy weights. (in building.)	937	3rd April 1865	Pierre Joseph Jamet.

Subject-matter of Patent.	Number of Patent.	Date.	Name of Patentee.
BUILDING, &c.—continued.			
A new or improved method of and apparatus for securing or fastening metal plates to beams, rafters and other places, for roofing and other purposes.	2384	19th Sept. 1865	Robert Fox.
Improvements in the construction of safes, strong rooms and other similar depositories, and in the locks thereof - - - - -	2457	26th Sept. 1865	Claude Parigot. Antoine Grivel the younger.
Improvements in fittings for stables, cow sheds and piggeries, and in effluvium traps for stables and other places.	2459	28th Sept. 1865	Edward Cottam.
Means employed for fixing sheet metal for roofing and other purposes.	2542	2nd Oct. 1865	James William Tylor.
Construction of fireproof floors for buildings	2570	6th Oct. 1865	John Cunningham.
Construction of wrought-iron girders -	2593	7th Oct. 1865	Julius Homan.
Constructing fireproof floors and ceilings -	2594	7th Oct. 1865	Julius Homan.
Certain improvements in window fittings -	2608	10th Oct. 1865	William Cooke.
A new composition of india-rubber mastic or cement, made in a more or less fluid state according to the use to be made of it, and the process or contrivance for applying the same. (coating walls and floors to prevent damp.)	2630	12th Oct. 1865	Auguste Aimé Leronard.
An improved preparation or composition for coating, covering or colouring walls and other surfaces or parts of buildings, and for forming mouldings, cornices and other decorative parts of houses.	2635	12th Oct. 1865	William Barwick.
Tiles for roofing - - - - -	2596	14th Oct. 1865	John Taylor, junr.
Construction of roadways, floorings and other surfaces.	2758	26th Oct. 1865	Thomas Russell Crampton.
An improved safety net to arrest the fall of persons or heavy bodies under circumstances of danger. (for use in house building.)	2969	14th Nov. 1865	Léon Edmond Lauretny.
A new or improved cement or composition, applicable to the agglomeration or moulding of various materials, and to other useful and decorative purposes. (for inlaid flooring ; to preserve from damp, &c.) (Communicated by Stanislas Sorel and Emile Justin Mesnir.)	3119	5th Dec. 1865	Richard Archibald Brooman.
Apparatus applicable for fire-escapes and builders' scaffolds.	3128	5th Dec. 1865	Edward Vagg.
Improvements in the construction of safes, strong rooms and other similar depositories, and in the locks thereof.	3160	9th Dec. 1865	Antoine Grivel the younger.
Constructing the treads of steps or stairs -	3308	21st Dec. 1865	George Hawksley.
Pipes, tubular columns and hollow structures, for masts, cans, shear legs, life boats and ordinary boats, for water, gas and waste water pipes, and for other similar constructions where great strength is required. (for towers of observation.)	6314	27nd Dec. 1865	Edward Deane.
Improvements in the manufactory of safes and in apparatus connected therewith. (and strong rooms.)	3342	22rd Dec. 1865	Samuel Chatwood.
Improvements in safes and in protecting the locks and bolts of safes, and other locks and bolts - (applicable to a strong room.)	3334	22rd Dec. 1865	Joseph Groves. George Robinson the younger.

Subject-matter of Patent.	Number of Patent.	Date.	Name of Patentee.
BUILDING, &c.—continued.			
Obtaining and employing continuous lengths of tanned leather for various useful purposes (for traes or marquees, ladder ropes, &c.) For ventilating buildings, see " VENTILATION." For warming buildings, see " HEATING." For lighting buildings, see " LAMPS."	3234	23rd Dec. 1865	George Hurn. Daniel Hurn.
BUOYS, SWIMMING BELTS, DRESSES AND APPARATUS ; BUOYING AND DIVING ; PRESERVING LIFE AND PROPERTY IN CASE OF SHIPWRECK ; MARINE LIGHTS.			
Fog and storm signals, buoys and spindles (Communicated by William Smith Sampson.)	125	14th Jan. 1865	Theodore Bourne.
Improvements in the construction of life belts, swimming belts, jackets and buoys, and in the employment and utilization of certain materials in the manufacture of the same.	341	7th Feb. 1865	Charles Kilburn.
Protecting wooden surfaces from the fouling and injury to which they are ordinarily liable in sea water (buoys.)	888	9th Feb. 1865	John Cornelius Cragie Halkett.
Improvements in buoys, beacons, floats or pontoons, which improvements are also applicable to floating bodies generally	887	11th Feb. 1865	Charles Atherton. Amherst Hawkes Ranton.
An improvement in paints or compositions used for coating iron or wooden vessels and other structures exposed to the action of sea water. (buoys, &c.)	871	28th March 1865	John Cornelius Craigie Halkett.
Means' and apparatus employed for illuminating lighthouses.	945	4th April 1865	John Richardson Wigham.
A new or improved shoe or sandal for facilitating the art of swimming.	1145	24th April 1865	Aaron Atkins.
An improved composition for coating iron or other vessels, and for other similar purposes. (buoys, &c.)	1278	9th May 1865	John Cornelius Craigie Halkett.
Manufacture of iron piers or erections, applicable more especially for carrying bridges at high elevations, or available for other legs and lighthouses.	1538	5th June 1865	Charles De Bergue.
Producing a light applicable to photographic purposes, to lighthouses and to other illuminations.	1653	20th June 1865	Prospero Castrucia.
A new or improved apparatus for producing the magnesium light. (for lighthouses.)	1606	24rd June 1865	Charles Ross Bamber.
Improvements in tubular structures rendering them specially applicable for ships' masts and building purposes. (for lighthouses.)	1788	3rd July 1865	Edward Deane.
Means of obtaining or producing oxygen applicable to various useful purposes. (for generating light for lighthouses.)	1790	6th July 1865	Hermann Beigel.

Subject-matter of Patent.	Number of Patent.	Date.	Name of Patentee.
BOOTS, &c.—continued.			
A diving apparatus for submarine purposes - -	1837	12th July 1865	Thomas Cato M'Kern.
A new and improved mode of elevating ships or boats in the water, to enable them to pass over sand bars, shallows and the like, and for raising sunken vessels and docks.	1838	12th July 1865	Thomas Cato M'Kern.
Improvements in apparatus and equipments used by persons employed under water, part of the improvements being also applicable for the use of persons employed where noxious gases or vapours prevail.	1840	12th July 1865	Auguste Denayrouze.
Apparatus to be used in swimming - - (Communicated by Jean Baptiste Victor Chastel.)	1953	31st July 1865	William Clark.
Floating lights, beacons, floating batteries and other vessels.	2173	24th Aug. 1865	John Mordy.
The improvement of the means of and apparatus for laying submarine electrical telegraphic wires, lines, cables or other contrivances of a like sort.	2570	16th Oct. 1865	Reinhold Edward Kamlach.
New or improved means and apparatus for destroying ships and such like floating bodies, parts of which said apparatus are also applicable to saving life and property at sea. (Communicated by Monsieur Stanislas Sorel.)	2758	26th Oct. 1865	Hector Augustus Dufrené.
Raising sunken vessels - - - -	2764	26th Oct. 1865	Thomas Page.
Means of preventing vessels from sinking, which means are also applicable for raising sunken vessels.	2851	4th Nov. 1865	Thomas Page.
An improved nautical safety apparatus - -	3043	27th Nov. 1865	François Mols.
Producing an oxy-hydro-magnesian light, applicable to photographic purposes, to lighthouses and to other illuminations. (Communicated by Prospero Carleraris.)	3248	15th Dec. 1865	Thomas Parker.
Constructing and mooring floating structures -	3265	18th Dec. 1865	Charles Liddell. Robert Stirling Newall.
Pipes, tubular columns and hollow structures, for masts, oars, shear legs, life boats and ordinary boats, for water, gas and waste water pipes, and for other similar constructions where great strength is required. (for lighthouses.)	3314	22nd Dec. 1865	Edward Deane.
Obtaining and employing continuous lengths of tanned leather for various useful purposes. (tackle for life buoys.) For life boats see "SHIP BUILDING."	3334	23rd Dec. 1865	George Hurn. Daniel Hurn.
BUTTONS, BUCKLES, STUDS, SLEEVE-LINKS AND OTHER DRESS FASTENINGS.			
Improvements in sleeve-links, which improvements are also applicable to other dress fastenings and ornaments.	130	14th Jan. 1865	William Henry Richards.
Apparatus for securing studs in shirt fronts and similar garments.	178	20th Jan. 1865	Charles Searle.

Subject-matter of Patent.	Number of Patent	Date.	Name of Patentee.
BUTTONS, &c.—*continued.*			
Fastenings for stay-busks, leggings, gaiters and other similar articles.	849	7th Feb. 1865	George Twigg.
Manufacture of buttons . . . . (Communicated by Joseph Edward Mittler, senior.)	594	2nd March 1865	William Clark.
An improved system of closing spatterdashes, applicable also to boots, portemonnaies and other similar articles.	656	9th March 1865	Emile Carebon.
Machinery for cutting, punching, raising, shaping or drawing through sheet metal, by means of tools and dies. (shells for buttons.)	786	22nd March 1865	George Farmer.
Fastenings for pins, buttons and other articles with metallic backs.	861	24th March 1865	Isac Louis Pulvermacher.
Fastenings for sleeve-links, solitaires and other like purposes.	847	4th April 1865	Henry Jenkins.
Improvements in buttons and in devices for securing the same to fabrics. (Communicated by Willoughby Hain Reed.)	1007	8th April 1865	George Davies.
Elastic binders for boots and shoes . . (Communicated by Daniel Franklin Peeler.)	1060	12th April 1865	William Edward Newton.
Manufacture of buttons	1110	21st April 1865	{ Thomas Greaves. John Skirrow Wright.
A new or improved fastening for fastening articles of dress, which said fastening is also applicable to the joining of belts and bands and to other like purposes.	1168	26th April 1865	Charles William Heaven.
An improved manufacture of buttons . .	1199	29th April 1865	George Augustus Huddart.
An improvement in buttons and means of attaching the same.	1294	10th May 1865	Herbert William Hart.
An improved arrangement for fastening shirts, collars and other articles of wearing-apparel, by which the ordinary button or stud is dispensed with.	1618	15th June 1865	Stanislaus Helcman.
An improved description of stud for fastening shirts, cuffs, waistcoats and other articles of wearing-apparel.	1618	15th June 1865	Stanislaus Helcman.
An improved shank for buttons, studs and solitaires.	1930	25th July 1865	Henry Wright.
Certain improvements in the manufacture of linen buttons.	2066	9th Aug. 1865	William Aston.
Machines for making eyelets . . . (Communicated by James Lewis Harriss and Theodore Lazerne Payne.)	2079	10th Aug. 1865	William Edward Newton.
Fastenings for sleeve-links, solitaires, brooches and other articles of jewellery . . .	2108	15th Aug. 1865	{ Reuben Cornelius Lilly. James Sunderland.
An improved fastening for leggings or other articles	2184	17th Aug. 1865	Frederick John Jones.
Manufacture of buttons	2140	19th Aug. 1865	{ Charles Edkins. James Newman. Thomas Greaves.
An improvement in clasps or fastenings . .	2525	2nd Oct. 1865	Frederic Jenner.
Certain new and useful improvements in shirt collars and bosoms . . . . (Communicated by Celius Edgar Richards.)	2627	12th Oct. 1865	{ Vernon Augustus Messinger. Virgil Jackson Messinger.

Subject-matter of Patent.	Number of Patent.	Date.	Name of Patentee.
BUTTONS, &c.—continued.			
Certain improved methods of manufacturing or arranging the spring bolts and attendant parts of sleeve-links, and other like articles where the means of a portable connection are required	2686	16th Oct. 1865	John Reading. Samuel Alfred Reading. George Edward Reading. Frederick Francis Reading.
Improvements in buttons and in attaching buttons to garments or fabrics.	2763	25th Oct. 1865	George Augustus Hudart.
Fasteners for driving bands, straps, belts, harness or other such like purposes (buckles.)	2802	31st Oct. 1865	Thomas Frederick Cashin. Joseph Felix Allender.
An improved composition for enamel, paint, varnish, cement or plaster. (for buttons.) (Communicated by William Berney Wallias.)	3042	27th Nov. 1865	William Robert Lake.
Improvements in fastenings for waistband buckles, applicable also for other similar purposes.	3132	6th Dec. 1865	Joseph Walker.
An improvement in buttons and studs for fastening garments.	3190	8th Dec. 1865	Florian Dahis.
Improvements in buttons and in the method of attaching buttons and ornaments to garments and other articles. (Communicated by Frederic Ingersoll Palmer.)	3184	8th Dec. 1865	George Tomlinson Bousfield.
Preparation of glue or gelatine so as to render it insoluble in water, and applicable by the admixture of other substances to various purposes for which common glue or gelatine cannot now be used. (for buttons.) (Communicated by Henry Wurtz.)	3395	23rd Dec. 1865	William Edward Newton.
CALCULATING, TEACHING.			
Instruments or apparatus for teaching and transposing music. (Communicated by Ferdinand Bellow.)	103	13th Jan. 1865	Richard Archibald Brooman.
Numbering machines	625	6th March 1865	Thomas Craig. David Carlaw.
Dissected maps and charts (for teaching.) (Communicated by François Auguste Lauririaque.)	1107	20th April 1865	Henri Adrien Bonneville.
Means or apparatus to aid in the teaching of arithmetic.	3147	7th Dec. 1865	William Grosvenor.
Improved means of assisting the teaching and study of musical notation.	3196	11th Dec. 1865	Alexander Victor Martinos Marie.
CANDLES; CANDLE AND LAMP WICKS.			
Treating the pitch obtained in or resulting from the distillation of palm oil and other fats, in candle making.	9	2nd Jan. 1865	Robert Irvine.

Subject-matter of Patent.	Number of Patent.	Date.	Name of Patentee.
CANDLES, &c.—continued.			
A new or improved machine for cutting or forming the tips or points of candles and for other like purposes.	674	10th March 1865	John Lyon Field.
Treating fats and fatty matters for the manufacture of candles. (Communicated by Emile Dangiville and Victor Baliat.)	817	23rd March 1865	Richard Archibald Brooman.
An improved method of treating fatty matters	852	29th March 1865	Samuel Childs, jun'.
Mechanism applicable to frame filling machines for wooden matches, vestas and vesuvians.	1003	4th April 1865	Henry Joseph Smallek.
Manufacture of paraffin candles. (Communicated by Augustin Etienne Pirton.)	1286	9th May 1865	John Henry Johnson.
Ornamenting candles	1289	10th May 1865	Peter Brush. Robert Irvine.
Manufacture of candles. (Communicated by Charles Gualtier.)	2085	11th Aug. 1865	John Henry Johnson.
Improvements in the manufacture of night lights and in apparatus employed therein	2387	15th Sept. 1865	Frederick Meyer. Joseph William Freestone.
Manufacture of candles and other illuminating bodies from peat and petroleum.	2580	7th Oct. 1865	Thomas Vincent Lee.
Purification and preparation of animal and vegetable wax, stearine, oleruomorti, paraffin and other solid, waxy or fatty substances. (for candles and tapers.)	2766	27th Oct. 1865	Scipio Soquelin.
An improvement in the manufacture of friction matches and tapers.	3002	22nd Nov. 1865	Samuel Alexander Bell.
Cups or sockets applied to candles and other lights (see "LAMPS.") (Communicated by Charles St. Cumbury.)	3187	9th Dec. 1865	William Clark.
CARD-CASES.			
Cases or receptacles for matches, stamps, cards and other articles	1121	21st April 1865	George Betjemann. George William Betjemann. John Betjemann.
An improved apparatus for carrying securely railway and other tickets, so as to afford a ready inspection thereof.	2229	31st Aug. 1865	Matthew Woodfield.
CARRIAGES, OMNIBUSES, WAGGONS, CARTS, TRUCKS, VELOCIPEDES.			
Improvements in perambulators, a part or parts of which improvements may also be applied to other wheel carriages.	14	3rd Jan. 1865	Henry Lloyd.

Subject-matter of Patent.	Number of Patent.	Date.	Name of Patentee.
CARRIAGES, &c.—*continued.*			
Improvements in locomotive engines and in the springs of railway carriages.	85	5th Jan.	1865	James Edwards Wilson.
Construction of railway carriages	96	11th Jan.	1865	Rock Chidley.
An improved machine for raising and carrying earth, mud, stones or other similar solid or liquid materials for dredging, ventilating, or winnowing grain, or other analogous purposes. (*including carts.*)	174	20th Jan.	1865	Louis Balms.
Apparatus for taking up and delivering mails and other parcels in railway trains while in motion. (*Communicated by Julius Euphas Curér.*)	177	20th Jan.	1865	William Clark.
Improved carriage step arrangements	189	21st Jan.	1865	Henry Arnold Dobson.
Improved apparatus for transmitting letter bags and parcels to and from railway trains whilst in motion. (*Communicated by Charles Louis Ferdinand Versailles-Laflèbie.*)	197	21st Jan.	1865	Charles Deaton Abel.
Construction of carriages	213	24th Jan.	1865	Stephen Leedham Fuller. Arthur Fuller. Charles Martin.
Improved apparatus for adjusting the weight of railway carriages and engines. (*Communicated by Johann Heinrich Eberhardt.*)	216	24th Jan.	1865	Otto Günnell.
Improvements in the manufacture of ordnance and other like castings and in the apparatus employed therein, also in carriages or moulds for the same. (*Communicated by William Jones.*)	385	2nd Feb.	1865	John Henry Johnson.
A new method for removing or destroying the momentum of heavy bodies by means of an electric machine or machines, so as to prevent injury and damage from concussion, applicable to ship cables, ship and fort armour, railway trains, tenders to perbrade and floating piers, gangways, breakwaters and other similar structures, also as a motive-power. (*carting produce, manure, &c.*) (*Communicated by William Graham M'Iver.*)	332	6th Feb.	1865	Clements Roberts Markham.
Bogie trucks used for supporting railway locomotive engines, carriages and waggons.	404	13th Feb.	1865	William Adams.
An improved machine for clearing, sweeping and removing the refuse from highways, streets and roads or ways, applicable also for removing the leaves of cut grass and other refuse from lawns and other grass lands and walks. (*cart.*)	444	16th Feb.	1865	Henry John Pickard.
An improved means of securing the safety of railway passengers.	454	17th Feb.	1865	Coleman Defries.
Improvements in ships of war, partly applicable to ships designed for the merchant service. (*gun carriage.*) (*Communicated by Augustus Waller.*)	509	23rd Feb.	1865	George Haseltine.
Permanent way and rolling stock of railways	520	24th Feb.	1865	John Kennedy Donald.
Construction of a portable vehicle for teaching children to walk and giving assistance to invalids.	537	25th Feb.	1865	John Askew.
Apparatus for coupling and uncoupling railway waggons or carriages.	608	4th March 1865	Daniel Morris. Joseph Morris. James Morris.

Subject-matter of Patent.	Number of Patent.	Date.	Name of Patentee.
CARRIAGES, &C.—*continued.*			
Improvements in carriage ways and in carriages for the same.	661	9th March 1865	William Henry James.
Certain improvements in venetian blinds for carriages, and which said improvements are also applicable to certain blinds or screens for other purposes.	676	10th March 1865	Thomas Startin.
Apparatus for enabling the passengers in a railway train to communicate with the guard.	679	10th March 1865	Albert Westhead.
Improvements in the construction of railway plant to ensure the safety of passengers' lives in the event of accident or collision - - -	688	11th March 1865	Charles Middleton Kernot. Nathaniel Symons.
Machinery or apparatus for rolling, shaping or forging metals. (*carriage springs.*)	701	13th March 1865	Robert Marsden.
Locomotive engines and carriages for common roads and tramways, and also for agricultural and other purposes.	780	20th March 1865	Alexander Richard Mackenzie.
Improvements in the construction of railway carriages, to facilitate the passage of the guard or other person from end to end of the train whilst it is travelling - - - - -	866	27th March 1865	John Calvin Thompson. John James Malbourne Green.
A new or improved arrangement of mechanism for propelling waggons in connection with railway bolas.	895	30th March 1865	George Greenish.
Improvements in the construction of locomotive engines and railway carriages, for facilitating their passage round curves - - - (*Communicated by George John Horner.*)	918	31st March 1865	George Robert Stephenson. George Henry Phipps.
An improved application of steam power to locomotion on ordinary roads. (*Communicated by Alfred Trilleadeau.*)	1002	8th April 1865	William Edward Gedge.
Means for communicating between the passengers and guards of railway trains, or between two or more different situations. (*Communicated by Thomas Hunt.*)	1030	11th April 1865	John Henry Johnson.
Couplings for railway carriages, waggons, trucks and other vehicles.	1035	11th April 1865	Josiah Dudley.
Apparatus for signalling on railway trains -	1068	13th April 1865	Albert Westhead.
Apparatus for covering railway tracks or ruas and other carriages - - - - -	1075	17th April 1865	Edward Morgan. George Henry Morgan.
Means of communicating and signalling between the passengers, guards and drivers of railway trains.	1076	17th April 1865	George William Garrard.
Means of covering railway tracks, vans and other carriages.	1090	19th April 1865	William Riddell.
"Pulleys" used by brewers and others for lifting and lowering weights into and out of cars, waggons or trucks.	1091	19th April 1865	Fredric William Gilbert.
Apparatus for communicating and signalling between passengers, guards and drivers of railway trains, by day or by night.	1097	20th April 1865	David Hancock. Thomas Evans.
Wheels and the manner of applying the same to railway carriages for passengers' and goods' traffic, as also the leading wheels for locomotives.	1114	21st April 1865	William Day.
Invalid carriages - - - - - (*Communicated by Auguste Quilroot.*)	1120	21st April 1865	Henry Edward Newton.

Subject-matter of Patent.	Number of Patent.	Date.	Name of Patentee.
CARRIAGES, &c.—continued.			
Fire-escapes and portable ladders - - -	1164	26th April 1865	Thomas Dixon Whitehead.
An improved manufacture of waterproof fabric - (for car seating.) (Communicated by The American Waterproof Cloth Company.)	1219	1st May 1865	William Edward Newton.
An improved carriage step - - - -	1290	10th May 1865	Stephen Leedham Fuller. Arthur Fuller. Charles Martin.
A new mail catching apparatus for bags or packages, without stopping the express trains or others.	1388	16th May 1865	André Chavanne.
An improved method of testing railway and other springs - - - - - -	1374	16th May 1965	Joseph Mitchell. George Tilleard.
Mass-motive carriages - - - -	1069	19th May 1865	George Reed.
Apparatus for increasing the safety of railway passengers and trains, signalling, lighting and forming a communication between all parts of such trains, also for securing the carriage doors.	1472	31st May 1865	Richard Howarth.
Construction of vans, waggons or carts employed for transporting furniture and other goods, on common roads and railways.	1496	31st May 1865	Frederick Hazeldine.
An improved system of telegraphic communication on railways, parts of which invention are also applicable to other telegraphic purposes.	1543	5th June 1865	Alice Isabel Lucas Gordon.
Improved arrangements for opening and shutting carriage windows - - - -	1613	14th June 1865	Sidney Courtauld. Charles Wilkins Atkinson.
Improvements in lamps for railway and other carriages, and in connecting lamps to carriages, a part of which improvements may also be applied to handles for carriages - - -	1637	17th June 1865	Walter Howes. William Hurley.
Locomotive engines and railway carriages - -	1648	19th June 1865	George Smith the younger.
Improvements in or applicable to railway and other carriage windows.	1718	24th June 1865	John Kay Farnworth.
Improvements in railway carriages, which improvements are intended to neutralise the destructive effects arising from the collision of trains.	1746	30th June 1865	Louis Faure.
Carriages - - - - -	1787	4th July 1865	Josiah Harrington.
Improvements in locomotive engines and in springs of railway carriages.	1789	4th July 1865	James Edwards Wilson.
An improved combination of materials for the manufacture of carpets, floor cloth, felt, wall paper, fireproof flexible roofing, ship and boat building and for other similar purposes - (lining for carriages.)	1776	6th July 1865	John Longbottom. Abram Longbottom.
Carriages for breech-loading ordnance - -	1801	7th July 1865	Fisher Alexander Wilson.
Improvements in steam carriages and in adopting wheels for common roads to railways. (Communicated by Joseph Alphonse Lambert.)	1881	10th July 1865	Richard Archibald Brooman.
Construction of springs for railroad and other carriages.	1860	15th July 1865	John Crawford Walker.
Construction of railway carriages - - -	1924	22nd July 1865	John Rigg.
Construction of omnibuses - - -	1951	27th July 1865	Alexander Cheffins.
Improvements in the construction of atmospheric railways and carriages, and in working the same.	1687	1st Aug. 1865	Alexander Doull.

E

Subject-matter of Patent.	Number of Patent.	Date.	Name of Patentee.
CARRIAGES, &c.—*continued.*			
Improvements in the construction of railway carriages and in railway breaks and signals, part of which is applicable to marine purposes	2006	2nd Aug. 1865	{ William Henry Petitjean. Edward M'Nally. }
A self-acting coupling for railway carriages and wagons	2007	5th Aug. 1865	{ Thomas Smith. John Brook. }
An improved mode of and apparatus for facilitating the transportation and delivery of letters, newspapers and other freight. (*Communicated by Alfred Ely Brook.*)	2049	7th Aug. 1865	Alfred Vincent Newton.
Couplings or fastenings of railway carriages or trucks.	2082	11th Aug. 1865	Richard Douglas Morgan.
Improvements in and applicable to railway carriages, to enable passengers to pass from one compartment to another and to give signals on trains in motion.	2089	11th Aug. 1865	Thomas English Stephens.
Improved safety couplings for railway carriages	2159	22nd Aug. 1865	Frederick Charles Bryan Robinson.
Construction of vans, waggons or carts employed for transporting furniture and other goods on common roads and railways.	2192	26th Aug. 1865	Frederick Huntefeur.
The improvement of the permanent way of railways and carriages for the same.	2227	28th Aug. 1865	James Cole Green.
An improved mode of retaining and preventing the vibration of sliding windows used in dwellings and in railway and other vehicles, and for an improved apparatus for effecting the said purposes	2232	30th Aug. 1865	{ Thomas Wrigley. Marcus Brown Westhead. }
Traction engines and other vehicles	2234	30th Aug. 1865	Samuel Lawrence James.
Applying springs to two-wheeled carriages, to prevent the unpleasant jolting motion of the draught animal attached thereto being communicated to the body of the vehicle.	2242	31st Aug. 1865	William George.
Improvements in the means of fixing or attaching the bobbins of winding and other machines on to their spindles, which improvements are also applicable to other similar or analogous purposes, and to the detaching of railway carriages from trains whilst in motion.	2250	31st Aug. 1865	John Ward.
A new shackle or coupling for connecting railway carriages, wagons and other vehicles used on railroads, whereby going between the carriages, wagons or other vehicles, to couple or uncouple, is rendered totally unnecessary	2288	4th Sept. 1865	{ Samuel Rickards Freeman. Abraham Grundy. }
Apparatus used in opening and closing carriage and other windows.	2319	9th Sept. 1865	John Pennington.
A locomotive cat	2344	13th Sept. 1865	Joseph Page Woodbury.
Improvements in locomotive engines, parts of which improvements are also applicable to railway carriages.	2375	14th Sept. 1865	Samuel Aitken.
Sun shades or canopies for perambulators and other wheeled carriages.	2389	19th Sept. 1865	Henry Lloyd.
Railway carriages and other vehicles (*Communicated by Henry Hudson Tresar.*)	2394	20th Sept. 1865	John Henry Johnson.
An improved apparatus or mechanism for locking and unlocking railway carriage doors, and for making signals with reference thereto.	2442	23rd Sept. 1865	John Hawkins Simpson.

Subject-matter of Patent.	Number of Patent.	Date.	Name of Patentee.
CARRIAGES, &c.—continued.			
Improvements in the construction of railway plant to ensure the safety of passengers' lives in the event of accident or collision . . .	2485	25th Sept. 1865	{ Charles Middleton Kernot. Nathaniel Symons.
Construction of gun carriages - - -	2569	6th Oct. 1865	George Wightwick Rendel.
Construction of railway carriages, waggons and trucks, and other road vehicles.	2591	7th Oct. 1865	Henry Griffith Craig.
Railway carriages and locomotives - - (Communicated by Henry Gifford.)	2621	11th Oct. 1865	Michael Henry.
Carriages propelled by manual power - -	2623	11th Oct. 1865	Thomas Du Boulay.
An improved barrow for use by builders and contractors, and also for general purposes.	2659	14th Oct. 1865	Robert Stephens.
Improvements in common road carriages and in breaks for the same.	2697	18th Oct. 1865	James Rock the younger.
Apparatus for raising and lowering the windows of railway and other carriages and other windows.	2919	1st Nov. 1865	John Kay Farnworth.
An improved truck or barrow for wheeling and tipping coke, coal or other substances.	2948	4th Nov. 1865	William Brett.
Formation of railway carriages - - -	2959	6th Nov. 1865	{ Braham Sims. Robert Burns.
Railway steam-engines and carriages - -	3029	14th Nov. 1865	Joseph Alphonse Lenbat.
Gun carriages . - - - -	3070	20th Nov. 1865	{ Thomas Bridges Heathorn. Joseph Henry George Wells.
Apparatus for increasing the safety of railway passengers and trains, signalling and forming a communication externally and internally between all parts of each train, lighting, warming and securing the doors of the carriages, and indicating therein and at the stations the names of the places at which the train stops.	3089	29th Nov. 1865	Richard Howarth.
Carriages and railway trucks on and with which they run.	3100	2nd Dec. 1865	Adolphe Nicole.
Hoods, aprons and dashers of carriages and other vehicles.	3150	7th Dec. 1865	George Fitzjames Rowell.
Improvements in constructing atmospheric railways and carriages, and in working the same, parts of which are applicable to exhausting and condensing air for other purposes.	3178	9th Dec. 1865	Alexander Doull.
Construction and arrangement of railway carriages, for the purpose of obviating or diminishing the bad consequences of collisions of or accidents to railway trains . - - -	3244	14th Dec. 1865	{ Henry Negretti. Joseph Warren Zambra.
A new or improved method of and apparatus or machinery for applying water or other fluid as a motive-power - . - - (constructing a carriage.)	3328	23rd Dec. 1865	{ Edmund Dwyer. Henry Moss.
Obtaining and employing continuous lengths of tanned leather for various useful purposes (ropes for drays, carts, carriage trimmings, &c.)	3334	27th Dec. 1865	{ George Hurn. Daniel Hurn.

See also "AXLES."
See also "HORSES."
See also "WHEELS FOR CARRIAGES."
For ventilating carriages, see "VENTILATION."
For warming carriages, see "HEATING."
For lighting carriages, see "LAMPS."

Subject-matter of Patent.	Number of Patent.	Date.	Name of Patentee.
CARTRIDGES AND CASES; GUN WADS.			
Improvements in fire-arms and in ammunition for the same.	188	21st Jan. 1866	Jacob Snider, jun'.
Breech-loading fire-arms and cartridges (Communicated by Charles Claude Etienne Minié.)	253	24th Jan. 1865	William Clark.
An improvement in cartridge boxes for breech-loading fire-arms.	254	24th Jan. 1865	Erastus Blakeslee.
Certain Improvements in revolving fire-arms and cartridges for the same.	309	4th Feb. 1865	Stephen Wells Wood.
An improvement in the manufacture of patched balls for fire-arms.	367	9th Feb. 1865	Milo Peck.
Improvements in breech-loading fire-arms and in cartridges for breech-loading fire-arms.	421	14th Feb. 1865	Johann Von der Poppenburg.
Cartridges (Communicated by Charles Edward Snider.)	429	14th Feb. 1865	Benjamin Thompson.
An improvement in cartridges for breech-loading guns.	518	21th Feb. 1865	Charles William Lancaster.
Improvements in breech-loading fire-arms and in cartridges for breech-loading fire-arms. (Partly communicated by William Montgomery Storm.)	709	14th March 1865	Francis Augustus Bracudlin.
Improvements in the construction of fire-arms and in cartridges for the same.	800	22nd March 1865	Alfred Pierre Treachen.
An improvement in the construction of cartridge and other boxes. (Communicated by Robert Augustus Chesebrough.)	802	30th March 1865	Alfred Vincent Newton.
Projectiles and cartridges for central fire breech-loading fire-arms and ordnance.	932	3rd April 1865	Johann von der Poppenburg.
Improvements in fire-arms, and in cartridges to be used therewith and with other fire-arms.	1046	12th April 1865	Thomas Jefferson Mayall.
An improved apparatus for charging and closing cartridge cases. (Communicated by Thomas James Thackeray.)	1183	27th April 1865	Richard Archibald Brooman.
Improvements in boring or excavating and blasting rocks and minerals, and in the treatment of the tools employed therein.	1192	28th April 1865	Julian Bernard.
Breech-loading fire-arms and cartridges	1280	9th May 1865	John Charles Cosybrarr.
Manufacture of gun-cotton cartridges for cannon and small arms.	1300	10th May 1865	Julian John Blvy.
Improvements in breech-loading fire-arms, and in cartridges for breech-loading fire-arms.	1308	11th May 1865	Joseph Rock Cooper.
Apparatus to be used with breech-loading fire-arms and ordnance.	1385	16th May 1865	Pierre Camille Lafont.
Improvements in breech-loading fire-arms, and in cartridges and bayonets for breech-loading fire-arms. (Communicated by Charles Forbes.)	1386	16th May 1865	Richard Archibald Brooman.
Improvements in breech-loading fire-arms and ordnance, and in cartridges for breech-loading fire-arms.	1439	24th May 1865	Thomas Wilson.
An improved method of loading and turning over the shells of cartridges, and in the machine used for the same.	1468	27th May 1865	George Gibson Bussey.
Improvements in breech-loading fire-arms and in metallic cartridge cases for the same. (Communicated by James Ingersoll Day.)	1546	6th June 1865	George Haseltine.

Subject-matter of Patent.	Number of Patent.	Date.	Name of Patentee.

CARTRIDGES, &c.—continued.

Subject-matter of Patent.	Number of Patent.	Date.	Name of Patentee.
Improvements in breech-loading fire-arms and in cartridges to be used therewith. (Communicated by Pierre Didier Jardinier.)	1750	1st July 1865	William Edward Newton.
Improvements in portable charge holders for breech-loading guns, whether single or double barrelled, as also in the means of manufacturing the said holders and in exploding the charge.	1868	20th July 1865	Charles Rosson.
Improvements in fire-arms and in cartridges for the same.	1889	29th July 1865	William Tranter.
Improvements in breech-loading fire-arms and in the charges and projectiles to be used therewith.	1894	29th July 1865	William Le Penotière.
Construction of needle cartridges	1906	31st July 1865	James Warren Bolarton.
Improvements in breech-loading fire-arms and in revolving fire-arms, and in cartridges.	2030	4th Aug. 1865	Thomas William Webley.
Improvements in revolving fire-arms, in projectiles and cartridges.	2108	15th Aug. 1865	James Broun.
Breech-loading fire-arms and cartridges	2345	13th Sept. 1865	Frederic Walker Prince.
Improvements in breech-loading fire-arms and in cartridges to be used therewith. (Communicated by Hiram Berdan.)	2438	23rd Sept. 1865	William Edward Newton.
Cartridges	2478	27th Sept. 1865	James Broun.
Improvements in breech-loading guns and in projectiles and cartridges.	2512	30th Sept. 1865	Edward Lindner.
Cartridges for breech-loading fire-arms	2542	4th Oct. 1865	{ Joseph Jones. Frederick James Jones.
Cartridges for certain kinds of breech-loading fire-arms.	2629	12th Oct. 1865	Jasper Henry Selwyn.
Sabots for projectiles	2632	12th Oct. 1865	Henry Handly Williams.
Preparing the ammunition or charges for rifled ordnance and rifled fire-arms.	2858	4th Nov. 1865	Joseph Whitworth.
Cartridges	2906	11th Nov. 1865	John Miller.
Improvements in breech-loading guns, and in cartridges for breech-loading guns.	2991	20th Nov. 1865	Charles Witney.
Improvements in breech-loading fire-arms, and in cartridges for breech-loading fire-arms.	3176	9th Dec. 1865	Thomas Wilson.
Central fire breech-loading cartridge	6151	9th Dec. 1865	William Thomas Eley.
An improved blasting powder (for cartridges.) (Communicated by Bernhard August Schäffer and Christian Friedrich Badralery.)	3206	12th Dec. 1865	Arnold Badralery.
Improvements in breech-loading fire-arms and in ammunition for the same.	6340	15th Dec. 1865	James Aston.
Breech-loading fire-arms and rotating breech cylinder pistols, and cartridges to be used therewith. (Communicated by Silas Crispin.)	3288	16th Dec. 1865	Alfred Vincent Newton.
Cartridges for breech-loading fire-arms (Communicated by Caleb Huse,)	6304	21st Dec. 1865	William Edward Newton.
Improvements in breech loading fire-arms, and in cartridges for breech loading fire-arms.	3337	26th Dec. 1865	Charles Reeves.
Improvements in breech loading fire-arms, and in cartridges for the same.	3345	27th Dec. 1865	William Castle Dodge.
Apparatus for closing charged cartridge cases	3379	30th Dec. 1865	George Hawksley.

Subject-matter of Patent.	Number of Patent.	Date.	Name of Patentee.
CASKS AND BARRELS; CASK-STANDS; BUNGS.			
Machinery or apparatus for forming certain parts of metallic casks and drums.	337	6th Feb. 1865	George Duncan.
Apparatus for lifting and tilting casks containing liquids.	446	16th Feb. 1865	Charles Octavius Staunton.
Improvements in treating certain hydrocarbon oils and in vessels for containing the same. (lining casks with glue and treacle.)	564	24th Feb. 1865	John Fordred.
Improved arrangements and apparatus for drawing off liquors or liquids from casks and other vessels, without the aid of pumps.	761	18th March 1865	Joseph Walls.
Constructing gasometers, tanks, casks and similar vessels.	781	21st March 1865	Charles Hill Pennycook.
Casks or vessels for storing petroleum and hydrocarbons.	834	24th March 1865	John Bailey Brown.
Improved means of preventing the leakage of barrels, and of rendering packages and fabrics impervious to air and gases. (Communicated by Lewis Francis and Cyrus Lentrel.)	913	31st March 1865	Alfred Vincent Newton.
Manufacture of a compound or material to be used as a substitute for india-rubber. (for lining barrels.) (Communicated by Henry Lacouderey and Emile Ursuier.)	1068	15th April 1865	William Clark.
Machinery or apparatus for cutting cylindrical or conical articles. (lamps.)	1347	4th May 1865	George Redrup.
Nullagrus, stands or supports for barrels, casks or other similar vessels	1289	13th May 1865	{ Thomas Parkinson. William Snodgrass.
Apparatus for setting up casks or barrels . .	1704	4th July 1865	{ William Clapperton. Abram Lyle.
An improved combination of materials for the manufacture of carpets, floor cloth, felt, wall paper, fireproof flexible roofing, ship and boat building and for other similar purposes. (lamps.)	1775	5th July 1865	{ John Longbottom. Abram Longbottom.
An improved portable chamber or receptacle to contain aërated liquids, and the apparatus connected therewith by which the flow of such liquid is regulated and measured.	1925	25th July 1865	Max Benjamin Schumann.
An improved process for applying airproof solutions to the interior of casks and barrels. (for holding volatile liquids.) (Communicated by Edward Dekuns Woodruff.)	1967	28th July 1865	William Edward Newton.
A combination of improved method, apparatus and receptacles for storing, preserving, transferring and discharging certain fluids, for sanitary and protective purposes. (Communicated by Henry Pinho.)	2096	14th Aug. 1865	Robert Alexander William Westley.
An improvement in syphons . . . . (for casks, &c.)	2169	23rd Aug. 1865	Lippmann Jacob Levinsohn.
Apparatus for supplying carbonic acid gas to casks and other vessels from which beer, wine and other fermented liquors are drawn.	2187	25th Aug. 1865	Charles Adolphus Watkins.

Subject-matter of Patent.	Number of Patent.	Date.	Name of Patentee.

Casks, &c.—continued.

Vent pegs for casks or vessels from which beer or other liquid is drawn off from time to time.	2266	15th Sept. 1865	Robert Mann Lowne.
Machinery for making casks, barrels and other wooden vessels of capacity.	2426	22nd Sept. 1865	James Davidson.
Construction of casks to be used more especially for the transport of oil.	2500	29th Sept. 1865	Johann Heinrich Pinckross.
An improved mode of treating or preparing casks and other vessels, to make them tight and suitable for containing hydrocarbon and other fluids.	2644	13th Oct. 1865	George Marshall.
Improved apparatus for facilitating the treating or preparing of casks and other vessels, to make them tight and suitable for containing hydrocarbon and other fluids.	3081	29th Nov. 1865	George Marshall.
Preparation of glue or gelatine so as to render it insoluble in water, and applicable by the admixture of other substances to various purposes for which common glue or gelatine cannot now be used. (for lining barrels, firkins, &c.) (Communicated by Henry Warts.)	3328	23rd Dec. 1865	William Edward Newton.

Casting and Moulding Metals; Manufacture of Castings.

Improvements in the manufacture of metallic bedsteads, which improvements are also applicable to the manufacture of other metallic articles.	58	7th Jan. 1865	James Atkins.
A new or improved process or method of treating articles of cast iron and of cast iron mixed with other metals.	192	23rd Jan. 1865	Perceval Moses Parsons.
Improvements in the manufacture of ordnance and other like castings and in the apparatus employed therein, also in carriages or moulds for the same. (Communicated by William Jones.)	295	2nd Feb. 1865	John Henry Johnson.
An improved mode of making metal pipes	356	8th Feb. 1865	William Anderson.
An improved "core" to be employed in the casting of metallic pipes or tubes.	587	2nd March 1865	David Hartley.
Casting steel railway-wheel tyres	614	4th March 1865	Joseph Whitley.
Manufacture of crucibles and pots in which metals or other substances may be melted.	630	6th March 1865	George Nimmo.
Improvements in the manufacture of railway-wheel tyres, and in the implements or tools employed in such manufacture.	665	9th March 1865	William Daniel Allen.
Improvements in the manufacture of metallic bedsteads, which improvements are also applicable to the manufacture of other metallic articles.	699	13th March 1865	James Atkins.
Casting ingots of steel and malleable iron	661	27th March 1865	Carl Johan Lanrutz Loffler.
Manufacture of steel tires for railway wheels	878	24th March 1865	Francis William Webb.

Subject-matter of Patent.	Number of Patent	Date.	Name of Patentee.
CASTING METALS, &c.—continued.			
Machinery or apparatus for cutting scrolls, frets and filigree work.	920	1st April 1865	James Kynman.
Manufacture of ploughshares, socks, or points for ploughs, cultivators or scarifurrows and other implements used in the cultivation of the land where these points are used or required -	996	7th April 1865	William Gray. Edward Gray. John Gray.
Manufacture of malleable iron sheaves and bushes for pulley blocks .	1085	19th April 1865	Joseph Gardner. Richard Lee. George Henry Wain. Samuel Hargrove. Charles Hargrove. Samuel Hargrove, jun.
Casting and working so-called "Bessemer steel" ingots .	1100	20th April 1865	Thomas Hampton. James Abbott.
Machinery for moulding and making cores for moulding or casting metals.	1122	21st April 1865	Richard Canham.
Making moulds for casting pipes and other articles of various sizes.	1200	1st May 1865	David Yoolow Stewart.
Improvements in the manufacture of pig iron or foundry metal, and in making and treating castings of such metals.	1209	1st May 1865	Henry Scurmer.
Certain improvements in the manufacture of "moulds" for metallic castings having a cylindrical form.	1296	10th May 1865	David Hartley.
Improvements in casting iron girders and in apparatus therefor.	1304	11th May 1865	James Goodwin.
Improvements in the manufacture of crossings for the permanent way of railways, and also in tyres for wheels.	1396	20th May 1865	Joseph Armstrong.
Apparatus for making cores and moulds for casting -	1409	25th May 1865	David Law. James Braunt.
A new and improved mode of making and casting cores and parts of moulds to be used in the casting of iron or other metal. (Communicated by Joseph Harrison, junior.)	1434	25th May 1865	John Henry Johnson.
An improved method of and apparatus for moulding wheels.	1468	30th May 1865	Luke Martin.
Foundry cupolas -	1498	31st May 1865	Thomas Summerson.
An improved system of wheels for railway carriages	1683	20th June 1865	Emile Dupont.
Manufacturing gun barrels and tubes of cast steel and homogeneous iron.	1738	30th June 1865	Henry Powell Tipper.
An improvement or improvements in the manufacture of the handles of something iron or and irons, which said improvements or improvements may also be applied to the manufacture of the handles of various other articles. (moulding.)	1798	7th July 1865	Thomas Sheldon.
Manufacture of cast steel - (Communicated by Charles Peuvert.)	1813	8th July 1865	Richard Archibald Brennan.
An improved process for obtaining oxygen (used in preparing moulds for casting.) (Communicated by Monsieur Charles Tellier.)	1835	11th July 1865	Hector Auguste Dufrene.
Apparatus employed in the manufacture of tin and terne plates -	1843	12th July 1865	John Naugulers. Joseph Piper.
Improvements in ingot moulds and in casting metals.	1849	14th July 1865	John Clayton.

Subject-matter of Patent.	Number of Patent.	Date.	Name of Patentee.
CASTING METALS, &c.—continued.			
An improvement in the mode of uniting different metals, such as iron and copper or alloys, to form compound metallic castings.	1686	19th July 1865	George Nimmo.
Improvements in the manufacture of hoops and tyres, and in the machinery employed therein.	1878	31st July 1865	John Ramsbottom.
Burglar proof safes - - - - -	2008	2nd Aug. 1865	Herbert Allman.
Railway chairs - - - - -	2099	14th Aug. 1865	William Frederick Henson.
Moulds for casting metallic pipes, retorts and other articles.	2218	29th Aug. 1865	George Robinson.
Manufacture of cast steel or other metallic tubes -	2241	31st Aug. 1865	William Henry Brown.
Improvements in the manufacture of metallic safes and strong rooms, and in apparatus connected therewith.	2266	2nd Sept. 1865	Samuel Chatwood.
Improvements in founding or casting metals, and in moulds used for the same.	2401	29th Sept. 1865	Daniel Spink.
Improvements in the construction of steam generators, applicable also to the construction of condensers, the heating of water generally, and to the warming of buildings. (Communicated by Joseph Harrison, junior, and Thomas Ladert.)	2610	17th Oct. 1865	John Henry Johnson.
Apparatus for raising liquids - - -	2632	12th Oct. 1865	Jean Urein Bazin.
Apparatus for moulding toothed or other wheels or pullies or portions of circles, for casting.	2751	25th Oct. 1865	George Lamb Scott.
Certain improvements in apparatus employed in the manufacture and production of metallic pipes, tubes or other similar hollow castings. (moulds and cores.) (Communicated by Alfred Bertach.)	2804	31st Oct. 1865	Arthur Denhardes.
Casting hoops of steel suitable for making tyres -	2889	8th Nov. 1865	William Daniel Allen.
Stoves for drying moulds - - - -	2945	15th Nov. 1865	Henry Cochrane.
Machinery for the manufacture of moulds for casting metallic wheels.	2959	17th Nov. 1865	Thomas Joseph Perry.
An improvement in the manufacture of steel castings. - - - - - - -	2970	18th Nov. 1865	George Taylor. John Ferrar.
Cotton gins - - - - - -	2994	20th Nov. 1865	William James Burgess.
Improvements in casting iron and steel and in apparatus employed for this purpose.	6010	24th Nov. 1865	Joseph Whitworth.
Moulding for casting steel, iron and other metals -	3030	25th Nov. 1865	Frederick Trochast. William Hall.
Improvements in the manufacture of safes and in apparatus connected therewith.	3351	23rd Dec. 1865	Samuel Chatwood.
Improvements in the construction and manufacture of steel crossings for railways, and in the moulds for casting the same, all or part of which said improvements in moulds are applicable for casting other articles.	3392	23rd Dec. 1865	Francis William Webb.

Subject-matter of Patent.	Number of Patent.	Date.	Name of Patentee.
CASTING AND MOULDING PLASTIC MATERIALS ; MANUFACTURE OF MOULDED ARTICLES ; PLASTIC COMPOSITIONS ; MOULDING FUEL.			
Improvements in the treatment of carbonaceous minerals and in apparatus for preparing agglomerated fuel.	40	6th Jan. 1865	Joseph Emile Vigoulois.
Photo-sculpture and apparatus to be employed therein.	218	26th Jan. 1865	David Gay.
Machinery for compressing coal dust and other materials fit for burning, also clay into bricks, tiles, pipes and other like articles.	220	26th Jan. 1865	William Smith.
An improvement in the manufacture of artificial stone for building and other purposes.	441	16th Feb. 1865	William Kirrage.
Manufacture of crucibles and pots in which metals or other substances may be melted.	630	6th March 1865	George Nimmo.
Manufacture of jewelry cases and other similar cases.	809	27nd March 1865	John James Carter.
Process of preparing kaolin or china clay and other clays, for potters' use, and for expelling water from other earthy deposits. (Communicated by Joseph Muir.)	806	22nd March 1865	James Wright.
Construction of walls, houses and other buildings. (moulding cornices.)	822	23rd March 1865	Joseph Tall.
Manufacture and application of glass and other vitreous compositions - - - -	1020	1st May 1865	{ Arthur Howard Emerson. Robert Fowler.
Manufacture of slabs, bearers and other articles of artificial stone where great strength is required.	1037	13th May 1865	Frederick Ransome.
Superseding the unsightly chimney pots now in use.	1400	22nd May 1865	Robert Harwell.
Manufacture of artificial fuel applicable chiefly to the kindling of fires.	1438	25th May 1865	Henry Gibbs.
Improvements in ornamenting japanned surfaces and in machinery or apparatus for that purpose. (moulding the rollers.)	1464	27th May 1865	Leonard Brierly.
Method of constructing partitions, walls, floors and roofs of buildings.	1598	13th June 1865	John James Bodmer.
A new or improved artificial fuel - - -	1600	13th June 1865	Charles James Collins.
Improved machinery for compressing and solidifying coal and other analogous substances.	1608	14th June 1865	Henry George Fairburn.
New or improved compositions in imitation of ivory and woods, to be employed in the manufacture of umbrella tips, umbrella and walking stick handles and other useful and ornamental purposes - - - - - -	1682	23rd June 1865	Michael Dietrich Roenthal. Solomon Gradenwitz.
Clay tobacco pipes - - - - -	1683	23rd June 1865	Lesley White.
An improved composition for the manufacture of printers' rollers.	1694	24th June 1865	Frederic Gervasie David.
An improved pulping and compressing machine for the treatment of peat as a fuel, and gas for illuminating purposes - - -	1705	26th June 1865	{ Charles Worman. George Evans.

Subject-matter of Patent.	Number of Patent.	Date.	Name of Patentee.
CASTING PLASTIC, &c.—continued.			
An improved mode of combining and forming small coal or coal dust into lumps, blocks or otherwise, to be employed for the purposes of fuel.	1718	29th June 1865	Henry George Fairburn.
Improvements in the manufacture of gas retorts and other articles made of fire-clay, and in furnaces for burning the same and for other purposes.	1737	30th June 1865	William Schofield.
An improved mode of pressing and moulding clay, sand or cement, for making bricks and for other purposes. (Communicated by John Stevis.)	1746	1st July 1865	William Robert Lake.
An improved combination of materials for the manufacture of carpets, floor cloth, felt, wall paper, fire-proof flexible roofing, ship and boat building and for other similar purposes.	1775	5th July 1865	{ John Longbottom, Abram Longbottom.
Manufacture of bricks and blocks for building and other purposes.	2058	9th Aug. 1865	{ James William Sumner, Clement Augustus Krout.
Manufacture of terra-cotta or vitreous stone.	2071	10th Aug. 1865	Mark Henry Blanchard.
Machinery for moulding hollow articles, in earth, clay and other like materials.	2084	11th Aug. 1865	Robert Williams Armstrong.
Manufacture of the straw of rye and other straws and grasses into fibre, and utilising the refuse. (pulp for moulding.)	2171	23rd Aug. 1865	Edward Henry Craderk Monckton.
Method of and apparatus for treating peat and other plastic materials.	2219	29th Aug. 1865	{ Hull Terrell. Thomas Dos.
An improved method of ornamenting the surfaces of tiles.	2376	18th Sept. 1865	Henry Venables.
Improvements in moulding crucibles and other hollow articles of plastic materials, and in apparatus employed therein. (Communicated by Samuel Maynard.)	2454	26th Sept. 1865	Richard Archibald Brooman.
Machinery for comparing and preparing peat for fuel. (Communicated by Nathaniel Prothingham Potter.)	2459	26th Sept. 1865	George Tomlinson Bonsfield.
Improvements in submarine electric telegraph cables and in apparatus connected therewith. (moulding gutta percha for cables.)	2505	10th Oct. 1865	François Thierry Habert.
A new composition of indian-rubber mastic or cement, made in a more or less fluid state according to the use to be made of it, and the process or contrivance for applying the same.	2630	12th Oct. 1865	Auguste Aimé Leramard.
An improved preparation or composition for coating, covering or coloring walls and other surfaces or parts of buildings, and for forming mouldings, cornices and other decorative parts of houses.	2639	12th Oct. 1865	William Berwick.
Purification and preparation of animal and vegetable wax, stearine, spermaceti, paraffine and other solid, waxy or fatty substances.	2769	27th Oct. 1865	Scipion Requelin.
Manufacture of embossed wood. (Communicated by Henry Mey and Henry Taylor Blake.)	2896	10th Nov. 1865	Alfred Vincent Newton.
Improvements in the manufacture of air-tight coffins and in the mode of ornamenting or finishing the same, as also in the application of a material or composition not hitherto used in their production. (paper pulp moulded.)	3014	24th Nov. 1865	{ Henry John Cox. William Leach.

Subject-matter of Patent.	Number of Patent.	Date.	Name of Patentee.
CASTING PLASTIC, &c.—*continued.*			
An improved system of pavement to supersede the macadamised system used in the main streets of large cities and causeways subject to a great circulation of vehicles. (*making moulded flagstones.*)	3035	25th Nov. 1865	Theophilus Berren.
Dyeing, printing and other operations based on chemical reactions. (*preventing cracks in works of plaster.*) (*Communicated by Mathias Paraf-Javal.*)	3110	4th Dec. 1865	Richard Archibald Brooman.
A new or improved cement or composition, applicable to the agglomeration or moulding of various materials, and to other useful and decorative purposes. (*Communicated by Stanislas Sorel and Emile Justin Menier.*)	3119	5th Dec. 1865	Richard Archibald Brooman.
An improved method of and apparatus for making mortars, bowls, spill pots, jelly cans, galvanic troughs and other similar articles . . .	3150	8th Dec. 1865	{ William Boulton. { Joseph Worthington.
Improvements in preparing compounds of xyloidine or gun cotton, and in the apparatus employed.	3163	8th Dec. 1865	Alexander Parkes.
Improved machinery for compressing and solidifying coal, clay and other analogous substances.	3242	14th Dec. 1865	Henry George Fairburn.
Preparation of glue or gelatine so as to render it insoluble in water, and applicable by the admixture of other substances to various purposes for which common glue or gelatine cannot now be used. (*for moulding or copying medals.*) (*Communicated by Henry Wurts.*)	3396	23rd Dec. 1865	William Edward Newton.

See also " BOTTLES."
See also " BRICKS."
See also " EARTHENWARE."
For moulding sugar, see " SUGAR."

CEMENT AND PLASTER.

An improvement in the construction of mills for grinding and pulverizing grain and other substances. (*cement.*)	211	25th Jan. 1865	Anthony Harrison.
Improvements in mortar mills, applicable also to grinding other substances.	252	28th Jan. 1865	John Raines.
Certain improvements in non-conducting composition for preventing the radiation or transmission of heat or cold. (*substitute for cement.*)	864	27th March 1865	Ferdinand Le Roy.
Certain improvements in the manufacture of lime - (*Communicated by Monsieur Louis Poulet.*)	1467	29th May 1865	Peter Armand Le Comte De Fontaine Moreau.
A new or improved self-acting apparatus for distributing the feeding materials in high furnaces. (*such as limestone.*) (*Communicated by Emile Langen.*)	1783	29th June 1866	Alexander Prince.

Subject-matter of Patent.	Number of Patent.	Date.	Name of Patentee.
CEMENT, &c.—continued.			
A new composition suitable for use as paint and protective coating. (Communicated by William Potter.)	2163	22nd Aug. 1865	John Gilbert Avery.
Manufacture of cement - - - -	2505	29th Sept. 1865	Joseph Duke.
A new composition of indian-rubber mastic or cement, made in a more or less fluid state according to the use to be made of it, and the process or contrivance for applying the same.	2630	12th Oct. 1865	Auguste Aimé Leremed.
An improved preparation or composition for coating, covering or colouring walls and other surfaces or parts of buildings, and for forming mouldings, cornices and other decorative parts of houses.	2639	12th Oct. 1865	William Barwick.
Constructing and mounting or hanging millstones	2692	18th Oct. 1865	William Henry Parker.
An improved non-conducting composition for preventing the radiation or transmission of heat or cold.	2853	4th Nov. 1865	James Thyr.
A new and improved cement - - - -	2963	7th Nov. 1865	{ Thomas Gruson. James O'Donoghue.
An improved composition for enamel, paint, varnish, cement or plaster. (Communicated by William Barney Watkins.)	3048	27th Nov. 1865	William Robert Lake.
Dyeing, printing and other operations based on chemical reactions. (making plaster, cement, &c.) (Communicated by Mathias Peruf-Jorel.)	3110	4th Dec. 1865	Richard Archibald Brooman.
A new or improved cement or composition, applicable to the agglomeration or moulding of various materials, and to other useful and decorative purposes. (Communicated by Stanislas Sorel and Emile Justin Mercier.)	3119	5th Dec. 1865	Richard Archibald Brooman.
Apparatus employed in grinding corn and other substances capable of being ground by millstones. (cement.)	3126	5th Dec. 1865	Edward Alfred Cowper.
CEMENTED AND FLOCKED FABRICS ; ADHERING ORNAMENTS AND DEPOSITING METAL ON FABRICS.			
Vulcanising compounds and vulcanised fabrics - (coating fabrics with flock.) (Communicated by Simon Strouse.)	176	20th Jan. 1865	Benjamin Franklin Stevens.
Manufacture of flock fabrics - - - (Communicated by The American Waterproof Cloth Company.)	1215	1st May 1865	William Edward Newton.
An improved manufacture of waterproof fabric - (Communicated by The American Waterproof Cloth Company.)	1219	1st May 1865	William Edward Newton.
Improvements in the manufacture of hose and other flexible tubing, which improvements are also applicable in uniting surfaces of india-rubber, gutta percha or of compounds thereof, to each other, or to woven or other fabric or material for other purposes.	1309	11th May 1865	Thomas Jefferson Mayall.

Subject-matter of Patent.	Number of Patent.	Date.	Name of Patentee.
CEMENTED FABRICS, &c.—*continued.*			
Ornamentation of fabrics and leather · · · (creating artificial flowers, &c.) (Communicated by Miss Nathalie Kulb.)	1389	19th May 1865	William Clark.
Apparatus for the manufacture of impressed gold and similar paper hangings · · · -	1899	22nd May 1865	{ John Wyke. { James Rew.
Manufacture of carpets and other terry and cut pile fabrics. (Communicated by The American Waterproof Cloth Company.)	1490	31st May 1865	William Edward Newton.
Certain new and useful improvements in the construction of hats. (Communicated by Elias Rosenzweig.)	1971	31st July 1865	Thomas Drew Stetson.
Manufacture and ornamenting of carpets, rugs and other fabrics. (creating or sewing on designs.)	2191	25th Aug. 1865	Lemuel Clayton.
Ornamentation of fringes and trimmings · ·	2230	5th Sept. 1865	Thomas Bird Bailey.
Improvements in the manufacture of trimmings and in the machinery employed therein,	3320	23rd Dec. 1865	William Smith.
Improvements in floor cloths and similar compositions fabrics, in the manufacture of such fabrics, and in machinery employed therein · · -	3370	29th Dec. 1865	{ John Howard Kidd. { James Chadwick Mather.
CHAINS; CHAIN CABLES; HOOKS, HOOPS, RINGS.			
Mode of making or forming the links of iron or steel chains, chain cables, shackles, couplings or parts of the same, and for machinery to be used therein.	423	14th Feb. 1865	George Homfray.
Improvements in cast steel or other metal chains for cables and for other purposes, and in machinery or apparatus for manufacturing the same.	431	15th Feb. 1865	William Henry Brown.
Manufacture of chain cables · · : ·	594	24th Feb. 1865	John Sturbridge.
Certain improvements in the method of securing the extremities of bands or hoops used in packing bales, and in the means employed for such purposes. (Communicated by Edward Taylor Bellhouse.)	662	9th March 1865	William John Dorning.
Manufacture of ornamental metallic chains ·	843	25th March 1865	Edwin Wolverson.
Manufacture of cornice pole and other rings ·	977	6th April 1865	Charles Horton Williams.
Mode of making or forming the links of iron or steel chains and chain cables, and for machinery to be used therein.	1004	8th April 1865	Alfred Homfray.
An improved chain or iron-cable shackle · ·	1086	11th April 1865	Robert Turner.
Shackles or links for connecting chain cables and other chains.	1250	4th May 1865	William Roberts.
Machines for testing the strength of chains and cables and for other like purposes.	1347	15th May 1865	James Tangye.
Machinery employed in the manufacture of hoops and tyres.	1425	25th May 1865	John Ramsbottom.

Subject-matter of Patent.	Number of Patent.	Date.	Name of Patentee.

CHAINS, &c.—continued.

Subject-matter of Patent.	Number of Patent.	Date.	Name of Patentee.
A new or improved apparatus for the purpose of stopping and easing strains on ships' cables when in use.	1608	14th June 1865	Charles de Vendeuvre.
Manufacture of chains, bracelets, necklaces and other articles of jewelry.	1794	7th July 1865	Pierre Matharin Charles Réusd.
Improvements in the manufacture of hoops and tyres, and in the machinery employed therein.	1975	31st July 1865	John Ramsbottom.
Manufacture of swivels - - - -	2284	12th Sept. 1865	Joseph Welch.
Manufacture of chains, bracelets, necklaces and other analogous articles.	2497	28th Sept. 1865	Carlo Giuliano.
Apparatus for raising liquids - - - (chains for pumps.)	2639	12th Oct. 1865	Jean Urain Bastier.
Casting hoops of steel suitable for making tyres -	2860	8th Nov. 1865	William Daniel Allen.
Manufacture of gold and other ornamental chains -	3070	30th Nov. 1865	{ John Hollands. Edward Richard Hollands. Thomas Hollands.
A new or improved swivel snap - - } (for harness chains.)	3090	2nd Dec. 1865	{ Emile Morin. Roman Schwring.
Improvements in apparatus for mixing materials, which is also applicable for smoothing, finishing, rounding or polishing articles of metal or other material. (smoothing chains.)	3243	14th Dec. 1865	William Robinson.

CHARCOAL, COKE, CARBON, MOULDERS' BLACKING, LAMP-BLACK.

Subject-matter of Patent.	Number of Patent.	Date.	Name of Patentee.
Apparatus for charging and drawing gas retorts } and for other purposes - - - }	148	17th Jan. 1866	{ Sealy James Best. James John Holden.
An improvement in the construction of mills for grinding and pulverising grain and other substances. (charcoal.)	211	25th Jan. 1865	Anthony Stevenson.
Process and apparatus for producing oil and coke from coal and slack.	600	22nd Feb. 1865	James Nicholas.
Apparatus for cooling animal and other charcoal -	780	15th March 1865	John Frederick Brinjes.
Apparatus for the distillation of coal and peat, and such other substances as are or may be used for the manufacture of solid and liquid volatile hydrocarbons, or for the manufacture of the said hydrocarbons and coke.	796	22nd March 1865	William Mattieu Williams.
Apparatus employed in the reburning of animal charcoal.	1106	29th April 1865	Thomas White.
Manufacture and reburning or revivification of animal charcoal.	1290	13th May 1865	George Henry Ogston.
Preparation of materials to be used as substitutes } for animal charcoal - - - }	1409	22nd May 1865	{ Richard Müller. Arthur Thomas Weld. John Follott Powell.
Ovens or kilns for the manufacture of coke - -	1435	25th May 1865	John Glew.

Subject-matter of Patent.	Number of Patent.	Date.	Name of Patentee.
CHARCOAL, &c.—continued.			
Manufacture of artificial fuel - - -	1547	6th June 1865	David Barker.
A new material to be used in the purification of heating and lighting gases.	1591	12th June 1865	John Thomas.
Means or method of applying mineral oils for generating steam and heat. (substitute for coke.) (Partly communicated by Alexandre Sapis.)	1929	25th July 1865	Wladislaus Zbyszewski.
Improvements in coke ovens and in the manufacture of coke.	2013	3rd Aug. 1865	William Morgans.
Obtaining spirits of turpentine, rosin, pitch, tar, pyroligneous acid and other products from wood. (obtaining charcoal.) (Communicated by Albert Hamilton Emery.)	2247	31st Aug. 1865	William Edward Newton.
Manufacture of materials for decolorising sugar and other saccharine and liquid matters. (Communicated by Chrétien Jean Gaude.)	2408	21st Sept. 1865	William Clark.
Improvements in coke and charcoal ovens and in the manufacture of coke, parts of which are applicable to bread, biscuit and pastry ovens.	2477	27th Sept 1865	William Morgans.
Means and apparatus to be employed in the manufacture of sugar. (Partly communicated by Aimnion Hippolyte Loplay.)	2608	10th Oct. 1865	Jean Adolphe Léon.
An improvement in treating animal charcoal -	2670	17th Oct. 1865	Edward Beanes.
Improvements in the distillation of coal and shale, and in the apparatus employed therein.	2795	30th Oct. 1865	Edward Meldrum.
An improved truck or barrow for wheeling and tipping coke, coal or other substances.	2848	4th Nov. 1865	William Brett.
An improved method of utilising the waste heat of coke ovens. (Communicated by Antoine Barbier-Perroton.)	3048	24th Nov. 1865	William Edward Gedge.
Revivifying, deodorising and calcining animal and vegetable charcoal and other matters.	3372	29th Dec. 1865	William Coranch.
CHEQUES AND BANKERS' BILLS.			
An improved preparation for the prevention of forgery of bank cheques, bills and other documents.	2101	14th Aug. 1865	{ John Callender Dale. Richard Samuel Dale.

Subject-matter of Patent.	Number of Patent.	Date.	Name of Patentee
CHLORINE AND CHLORIDES.			
An improved process for obtaining oxygen . (Communicated by Monsieur Charles Tellier.)	1838	11th July 1865	Hector Auguste Dufrené.
Treatment of hydrocarbon or paraffin oils .	2006	3rd Aug. 1865	John William Perkins.
Manufacture of bichloride of carbon, and chloride of sulphur.	3259	15th Dec. 1865	Richard Ransford.
CHURNS ; MAKING CHEESE AND BUTTER.			
A new method for removing or destroying the momentum of heavy bodies by means of an elastic teaching or machines, so as to prevent injury and damage from concussion, applicable to ship cables, ship and fort armour, railway trains, tenders to pierheads, and floating piers, gangways, breakwaters and other similar structures, also as a motive-power. (driving churning apparatus.) (Communicated by William Graham M'Iver.)	321	6th Feb. 1865	Clements Roberts Markham.
Certain improvements in churns - - - (Communicated by Howard Tilden.)	1298	10th May 1865	William Edward Broderick.
An improved apparatus for separating the whey from the curd in the manufacture of cheese.	1535	5th June 1865	Philip Coombes.
Treatment of condensing pans employed in the condensation of milk. (Communicated by Samuel Perry.)	1545	5th June 1865	Charles Howard Wansbrough.
A new or improved table or support to be employed in the dressing and finishing of cheese.	1782	29th June 1865	William Percival.
Construction of washing-machines and churns .	2472	27th Sept. 1865	John Taylor.
An improvement in the process for making butter .	2936	15th Nov. 1865	Henry Clifton.
CISTERNS, RESERVOIRS, TANKS AND BUCKETS.			
An improved machine for raising and carrying earth, mud, stones or other similar solid or liquid materials for dredging, ventilating, or winnowing grain or other analogous purposes. (cleansing reservoirs.)	174	20th Jan. 1865	Louis Balme.
Improvements in the means and apparatus employed for treating timber with antiseptic or preservative fluids, also applicable to other purposes. (constructing tanks.)	734	16th March 1865	Samuel Bagster Boulton.
Constructing gasometers, tanks, casks and similar vessels.	781	21st March 1865	Charles Hill Pennycook.

F

Subject-matter of Patent.	Number of Patent.	Date.	Name of Patentee.
CISTERNS, &c.—*continued.*			
Apparatus for storing petroleum and other inflammable liquids of less specific gravity than water. (*Communicated by Félix Birard and Pierre Labarre.*)	1027	11th April 1865	Richard Archibald Brooman.
Construction of reservoirs for containing and storing petroleum and other oils. (*Communicated by Paul Jacurenco.*)	1549	6th June 1865	Richard Archibald Brooman.
Apparatus for the decantation and raising of petroleum and other oils. (*reservoirs for storing.*)	1724	28th June 1865	Paul Jacurenco.
Fountains	1828	10th July 1865	Frederick Taylor.
Construction or arrangement of sluices or dams .	1870	14th July 1865	Timothy Ward Wood.
A new or improved apparatus for supplying disinfecting liquids to waterclosets, urinals and other places requiring the same.	1879	19th July 1865	Charles Nicholas.
An improved portable chamber or receptacle to contain aërated liquids, and the apparatus connected therewith by which the flow of such liquid is regulated and measured.	1923	25th July 1865	Max Benjamin Schumann.
Applying and utilising water power . . (*storing water tanks.*)	1957	29th July 1865	Valentine Baker.
A combination of improved method, apparatus and receptacles for storing, preserving, transferring and discharging certain fluids, for sanitary and protective purposes. (*Communicated by Henry Pinkus.*)	2096	14th Aug. 1865	Robert Alexander William Westley.
Tanks and other receptacles for obtaining and transporting petroleum, naphtha and other oils and liquids, to prevent wastage by fire or filtration or evaporation, or hazard of fire.	2165	25th Aug. 1865	George Washington Howard.
Improvements in the construction of lids or covers for saucepans and other cooking utensils, part of which improvements is also applicable to the lids or covers of housemaids' pails.	2249	31st Aug. 1865	John Ward.
A new and improved machine for the collecting and diffusing of water or other fluids.	2419	22nd Sept. 1865	Charles Wyatt Orford.
Improvements in cisterns or chambers for the steeping of grain in the manufacture of malt, which improvements are also applicable to other chambers or enclosures.	2422	24th Sept. 1865	Charles Edmund Davis.
A certain composition having anti-corrosive and anti-fouling properties, for the preservation of and keeping clean the bottoms of iron vessels, and also for the preservation of iron submerged and iron structures exposed to the action of the atmosphere or water . . . (*preserving water tanks.*)	2553	14th Oct. 1865	William Jardine Combe Mac Millan. James Mason. John Vickers Scarborough.
An improved apparatus for regulating the supply of water to tanks, water butts or cisterns, applicable also to other purposes .	2710	20th Oct. 1865	Richard Pell. Davy Hammond.
Improvements in supplying cattle with food and water on railways, and in the apparatus or means connected therewith.	2909	11th Nov. 1865	William Reid.
An improved trap or liquid sealing to the covers of cisterns, pans, jars, tubs and other vessels or chambers	2968	20th Nov. 1865	George Portland Hemming. Henry Coyle.

Subject-matter of Patent.	Number of Patent.	Date	Name of Patentee.
CISTERNS, &c.—*continued.*			
Construction of metal tanks and cisterns - -	3109	4th Dec. 1865	{ Frederick Braby, Alfred Moore.
Manufacture of tanks, baths, mangers and other vessels.	8129	5th Dec. 1865	Edward Headly.
Improvements in locomotive engines and in the means employed for generating steam therein. (*water heaters.*)	3188	9th Dec. 1865	Robert Francis Fairlie.
Preparation of glue or gelatine so as to render it insoluble in water, and applicable by the admixture of other substances to various purposes for which common glue or gelatine cannot now be used. (*for oilproofing tanks.*) (*Communicated by Henry Warts.*)	3325	23rd Dec. 1865	William Edward Newton.
CLOCKS, WATCHES AND OTHER TIME-KEEPERS; WATCH KEYS, CHAINS AND GUARDS.			
Construction of escapements for watches and other time-keepers.	55	6th Jan. 1865	George Raymond.
Construction of watches - - - - (*Communicated by Eugène Deracke.*)	157	19th Jan. 1865	Charles Denton Abel.
Certain improvements in the manufacture of pencil cases. (*combined with watch keys.*)	326	3rd Feb. 1865	William Vale.
Application to clocks and alarms of a circular escapement in place of the ordinary balance wheel. (*Communicated by Joseph Génévrier.*)	469	16th Feb. 1865	Pierre Eugène Bidaux.
Keyless watches - - - - -	726	15th March 1865	Henry Chevah.
Differential wheel gearing - - - (*for clock work.*)	744	17th March 1865	John Standfield.
Manufacture of ornamental metallic chains -	843	25th March 1865	Edwin Wolveram.
Photographic cameras - - - -	1009	8th April 1865	Victor Albert Prout.
An improved method of forming tapered rods and bits. (*for clock work.*) (*Communicated by Crozet Auguste Deracke.*)	1016	10th April 1865	Richard Archibald Brooman.
Watches - - - - - -	1032	11th April 1865	Lawrence Barnett Phillips.
Motors and apparatus for regulating the power and velocity of machinery or apparatus in motion. (*registering time.*)	1230	2nd May 1865	Charles William Siemens.
Clocks and time-pieces - - - -	1415	23rd May 1865	Herman Adler.
Construction of keyless watches - -	1470	29th May 1865	Henri Son.
Electro-magnetic clocks and other time-keepers - (*Communicated by Jean Theodore Scholle.*)	1516	2nd June 1865	Richard Archibald Brooman.
Watches and other time-keepers - - (*Communicated by Felix Broisé Bonnatid.*)	1650	16th June 1865	Richard Archibald Brooman.
Regulating or controlling the power employed in actuating sewing and other machines of a light nature. (*watchmakers' lathes.*)	1835	11th July 1865	Benjamin Fothergill.

Subject-matter of Patent.	Number of Patent.	Date.	Names of Patentees.
CLOCKS, &c.—continued.			
An improved method of winding up watches and other time-keepers. (Communicated by Robert Thrower, senior, and Robert Thrower, junior.)	2274	4th Sept. 1865	Richard Archibald Brooman.
Improvements in watches, and in the method of and apparatus for winding up fusee watches and pocket chronometers, and setting the hands, without a key.	2330	11th Sept. 1865	David Keys.
Manufacture of swivels · · · ·	2334	12th Sept. 1865	Joseph Webb.
Apparatus for lighting and heating, suitable for sick rooms and nurseries, and applicable also as holders for matches, watches and other necessary articles. (Communicated by François Réaf Méraud and Charles Louis Morin Méraud.)	2516	30th Sept. 1865	John Henry Johnson.
Manufacture of scent and smelling bottles (containing watch dial and movements.)	2599	9th Oct. 1865	Thomas Miles.
Means of renewing the teeth of worn out files (used in watch making.)	2887	4th Nov. 1865	Joseph Bernard Oscar Lazzara.
An improved instrument or apparatus for measuring intervals of time. (See " MUSICAL INSTRUMENTS.")	2899	11th Nov. 1865	Henry Carnegie Curden.
Improved mechanism for winding keyless watches.	3280	14th Dec. 1865	August Goye.
Obtaining motive-power applicable to various useful purposes. (electric clocks.)	3290	16th Dec. 1865	Ceril Loftus Wellesley Reade.
Obtaining and employing continuous lengths of tanned leather for various useful purposes. (for clock lines.)	3334	23rd Dec. 1865	{ George Hurn. Daniel Hurn.

COATING, COVERING, PLATING, SHEATHING.			
I.—Coating, Plating, Plating and Facing Metallic Surfaces with Metals or other Substances.			
Improvements in lining the sides and bottoms of puddling furnaces and other furnaces employed in the manufacture of iron or steel, and in mending, repairing and fettling the sides and bottoms of the said puddling and other said furnaces.	224	26th Jan. 1865	Robert Murbet
Improvements in rail and tramways, in laying electric telegraph wires, and in compositions for insulating the same. (Communicated by Jean Armand Emile Lainabre.)	283	31st Jan. 1865	Richard Archibald Brooman.
A new or improved method or process and apparatus for obtaining the concentrated extract of hops, and for preserving the same from deterioration. (lining the vacuum pans with stearine.) (Communicated by George Percy, Walter Wells, Charles Brown, John Mafford and John Maximilian Webb.)	308	4th Feb. 1865	Joseph Rideal Webb.

Subject-matter of Patent.	Number of Patent.	Date.	Name of Patentee.
COATING, &c.—*continued.*			
A new or improved insulating material for telegraphic and other purposes, together with an improvement in protecting telegraph wires, especially applicable to submarine and subterranous telegraphs. (*Communicated by Jules Errismann.*)	862	9th Feb. 1865	William Alfred Marshall.
Treating products obtained when coating iron with zinc.	469	14th Feb. 1865	James Graham.
Musical instruments in the nature of organs in which reeds are employed. (*lining the pipes.*)	879	1st March 1865	Augustine Thomas Godfrey.
Improvements in covered steel for crinoline skirts, and in the machinery for covering and uniting the same. (*Communicated by Oliver Rogers Burnham.*)	568	2nd March 1865	William Sparks Thomson.
An improved means of securing and protecting the india-rubber rings of buffer springs of railway carriages, which invention is also applicable to air pump and valve seatings, and lids faced with india-rubber.	588	6th March 1865	William John Oliver.
Bolts for connecting sheets of zinc and other metals employed for covering roofs and other enclosures.	662	9th March 1865	Rowland George Fisher.
Locks for safes, strong rooms and other purposes -	778	24th March 1865	Samuel Chatwood.
Certain improvements in non-conducting composition for preventing the radiation or transmission of heat or cold. (*for coating boilers, cylinders, pipes, &c.*)	864	27th March 1865	Ferdinand Le Roy.
An improvement in paints or compositions used for coating iron or wooden vessels, and other structures exposed to the action of sea water.	871	28th March 1865	John Cornelius Craigie Halkett.
Certain improvements in machinery or apparatus used in carding cotton or other fibrous substances	887	29th March 1865	{ Evan Leigh. / Frederick Allen Leigh.
Improvements in the construction of submarine telegraph cables, and in the mode of submerging or laying them in the water. (*Communicated by Jean Lucien Arman.*)	1081	11th April 1865	William Edward Newton.
Manufacture of tin and terne plates - -	1061	14th April 1865	John Jones Jenkins.
Paints or compositions for coating and preserving metallic and other substances from oxidation and decay	1154	25th April 1865	{ John Nuthall Brown. / Thomas Deykin Clare.
An improved composition for coating iron or other vessels, and for other similar purposes.	1278	9th May 1865	John Cornelius Craigie Halkett.
Manufacture of parkesine or compounds of pyroxyline, and also solutions of pyroxyline known as collodion. (*for coating wire.*)	1818	11th May 1865	Alexander Parkes.
Certain improvements in the formation and construction of metallic vessels, chambers or hollow cylinders used in hydraulic apparatus, cannon or heavy guns, and for like purposes.	1608	1st June 1865	Herbert Altman.
Improved sanitary apparatus or arrangements for preventing noxious exhalations such as arise when coating or treating iron or other articles -	1690	24th June 1865	{ Matthew Andrew Muir. / James M'Ilwham.

Subject-matter of Patent.	Number of Patent.	Date.	Name of Patentee.
COATING, &c.—continued.			
Improvements in the preparation of amalgams of quicksilver or mercury, and in the application of such amalgams to various purposes in the arts. (coating iron surfaces.) (Communicated by Henry Hurts.)	1719	24th June 1865	William Edward Newton.
Improvements in the manufacture of certain kinds of metallic tubes and rods, and in ornamenting metallic tubes and rods.	1749	1st July 1865	James Atkins.
Apparatus employed in the manufacture of tin and terne plates	1843	12th July 1865	{ John Saunders. Joseph Piper.
Protecting crinoline steel, stay busks, springs for leggings or gaiters and other similar fastenings.	1883	19th July 1865	William Edwards.
Manufacture of pots and crucibles wherein metals and other materials may be heated or melted.	1884	19th July 1865	George Nimmo.
Improvements in the mode or method of preparing materials for, and in the manufacture of submarine telegraphic cables, the same being generally applicable for other purposes.	2025	4th Aug. 1865	Frederick George Mulholland.
Construction of submarine telegraph cables - -	2068	11th Aug. 1865	Henry Robert Guy.
Certain improvements in looms for weaving .	2091	12th Aug. 1865	William Bullough.
Improvements in the preparation or production of spongy metals, and in their applications. (for being steam generators.) (Communicated by François Drivet.)	2108	15th Aug. 1865	John Henry Johnson.
Improvements in the construction of electric telegraph cables and in the preparation of telegraph wires.	2161	22nd Aug. 1865	Charles Marsden.
Improvements in constructing and insulating telegraphic conductors, and in apparatus connected therewith.	2352	12th Sept. 1865	John Macintosh.
Manufacturing wire conductors for electro-telegraphic purposes.	2416	22nd Sept. 1865	William Boggett.
Compositions used for coating metallic surfaces .	2460	27th Sept. 1865	{ John Boffey. Charles William Smith.
Preparation of iron, steel and alloyed metals, for electro-plating.	2521	2nd Oct. 1865	Thomas Allan.
Coating iron and steel with gold, silver, platinum or copper.	2562	7th Oct. 1865	Jacob Bayton Thompson.
Improvements in the construction of steam generators, applicable also to the construction of condensers, the heating of water generally and to the warming of buildings. (Communicated by Joseph Harrison, junior, and Thomas Loders.)	2610	10th Oct. 1865	John Henry Johnson.
Improvements in the construction and working of electric telegraphs, and in apparatus connected therewith, partly applicable to other purposes. (electro-deposition of metals.)	2709	26th Oct. 1865	Henry Wilde.
Plating or combining gold, platinum and other metals or their alloys.	2842	3rd Nov. 1865	Edward John Neithwood.
An improved non-conducting composition for preventing the radiation or transmission of heat or cold. (for coating boilers, &c.)	2853	4th Nov. 1865	James Thys.

Subject-matter of Patent.	Number of Patent.	Date.	Name of Patentee.
COATING, &c.—*continued.*			
Making amalgams or alloys of metals (coating metals with fused metals.) (Communicated by Henry Wurtz.)	2903	11th Nov. 1865	William Edward Newton.
Improvements in the construction of and in the method of laying submarine electric cables. (coating copper wire with gold.)	2945	18th Nov. 1865	John De La Haye.
An improved composition for enamel, paint, varnish, cement or plaster. (for coating metal.) (Communicated by William Barney Watkins.)	3049	27th Nov. 1865	William Robert Lake.
A new or improved method of preventing the escape of heat from steam cylinders (covering pistons with wood.)	3051	29th Nov. 1865	{ William Simons. Andrew Brown.
Improvements in steam-boilers and in the furnaces and grates thereof, the same improvements in furnaces and grates being also applicable to other furnaces and to stoves. (covering and lining mixing chambers.) (Communicated by Robert Winslow Davis, Daniel Davis and Henry Shreden Anable.)	3141	6th Dec. 1865	William Edward Newton.
Construction of wire conductors for electro-telegraphic purposes.	3180	9th Dec. 1865	William Boggett.
Improvements in coating metals and in apparatus to be used for this purpose.	3185	9th Dec. 1865	Edmund Norwood.
Improvements in the manufacture of steel and purified iron, and in the apparatus employed therein. (lining the furnace with clay plates.) (Communicated by Antoine Golp-Carolot.)	5300	21st Dec. 1865	Henri Adrien Bonneville.
Improvements in caps employed in spinning, and in the manufacture thereof. (electro-brassing.)	3313	23rd Dec. 1865	Edward Clifton.
Preparation of glue or gelatine so as to render it insoluble in water, and applicable by the admixture of other substances to various purposes for which common glue or gelatine cannot now be used. (for coating wire.) (Communicated by Henry Wurtz.)	3315	23rd Dec. 1865	William Edward Newton.
Manufacture of electric conductors insulated with india-rubber.	3347	27th Dec. 1865	Hugh Adams Silver.
Improvements in breech-loading fire-arms, and in cartridges for the same. (coating metallic cartridge cases with tin.)	3348	27th Dec. 1865	William Castle Dodge.
Construction of telegraphic cables or conductors	3387	29th Dec. 1865	Cromwell Fleetwood Varley.
II.—Coating, Plating, Lining and Facing Glass, Wood, Stone, Plastic Materials, Textile Fabrics, &c.			
Coverings of telegraphic conductors and cables	66	12th Jan. 1865	John Fuller.
Vulcanising compounds and vulcanised fabrics. (coating fabrics with cork.) (Communicated by Simon Stevens.)	178	20th Jan. 1865	Benjamin Franklin Stevens.

Subject-matter of Patent.	Number of Patent.	Date.	Name of Patentee.
Coating, &c.—*continued.*			
Protecting wooden surfaces from the fouling and injury to which they are ordinarily liable in sea water.	369	9th Feb. 1865	John Cornelius Craigie Halkett.
Manufacture of mirrors - (*Communicated by Lewis Paul Anpenard.*)	554	27th Feb. 1865	George Haseltine.
Improvements in treating certain hydrocarbon oils and in vessels for containing the same. (*lining casks with glue and treacle.*)	564	28th Feb. 1865	John Fordred.
Improvements in floor cloth and in machinery for the manufacture of floor cloth -	766	18th March 1865	{ John Howard Kidd. James Chadwick Mather.
Improvements in the manufacture of looking-glasses or mirrors, and in apparatus employed therein. (*Communicated by The Society Randal Cromwell, Alfred Townsaw and Edward Dodd.*)	798	21st March 1865	John Henry Johnson.
An improvement in paints or compositions used for coating iron or wooden vessels, and other structures exposed to the action of sea water.	871	24th March 1865	John Cornelius Craigie Halkett.
Improved means of preventing the leakage of barrels, and of rendering packages and fabrics impervious to air and gases. (*Communicated by Lewis Francis and Cyrus Lambert.*)	919	31st March 1865	Alfred Vincent Newton.
Manufacture of flexible tubing or hose - (*Communicated by David Knight Harris and Thomas Lyons Reed.*)	959	4th April 1865	George Tomlinson Bousfield.
Manufacture of a compound or material to be used as a substitute for india-rubber. (*Communicated by Henry Larroudery and Emile Oranier.*)	1088	15th April 1865	William Clark.
Protecting letters, numerals and ornamental designs on glass.	1111	21st April 1865	David Simeon Bachman.
Improvements in taking impressions from the grain of wood, and in transferring the same on to various surfaces - (*preparing the wood with a coating.*)	1117	21st April 1865	{ William Scarrat. William Dean.
Improvements in photographing upon wood, and in the preparation of wood, canvas, silk, glass and other substances, for the purpose of receiving and retaining impressions.	1174	26th April 1865	William Henry Smith.
Manufacture and application of glass and other vitreous compositions - (*for lining articles.*)	1290	1st May 1865	{ Arthur Howard Emerson. Robert Fowler.
An improved composition to be employed in the manufacture of bonnets and hats. (*for coating or remoulding.*)	1442	25th May 1865	Jeffery Eustace.
Staining and graining woods -	1651	14th July 1865	{ John Morrough Murphy. James Morrough Murphy.
Flexible gas tubing - (*Communicated by Henry Reilton.*)	1861	15th July 1865	William Robert Lake.
Paints or preparations for coating surfaces -	2015	3rd Aug. 1865	Ernest Leslie Ransome.
Looms for weaving - (*coating the picker spindles.*)	2073	10th Aug. 1865	{ John Ingham. Henry Ingham. James Broadley.

Subject-matter of Patent.	Number of Patent.	Date.	Name of Patentee.
COATING, &c.—continued.			
An improved method or process for ornamenting walls and other surfaces of buildings. (covering with veneers.) (Communicated by Carl Friedrich Günther.)	2188	18th Aug. 1865	George Howard.
Submarine electric telegraph cables	2209	24th Aug. 1865	Stopford Thomas Jones.
Improvements in the manufacture of rope, cordage, yarn, wire rope, and other such like twisted and plaited fabrics, and in the machinery employed therein (covering telegraph cables.)	2198	30th Aug. 1865	Thomas Cope. William Guest.
Improvements in covering submarine telegraph cables, and in the machinery and means employed for paying out or hauling in the same.	2330	11th Sept. 1865	Samuel Inkpen.
Improved means for rendering leather more durable and flexible	2357	15th Sept. 1865	Louis Gustave Bouriac. Louis Bombail.
Certain improvements in telegraphic cables	2509	30th Sept. 1865	James Austin Mee.
Construction of submarine telegraph cables (Communicated by Claude Ernest Laml de Norre.)	2530	3rd Oct. 1865	Henri Adrien Bonneville.
Improvements in submarine electric telegraph cables and in apparatus connected therewith. (protective covering for gutta percha.)	2606	10th Oct. 1865	François Thierry Hubert.
A new composition of indian-rubber mastic or cement, made in a more or less fluid state according to the use to be made of it, and the process or contrivance for applying the same.	2620	12th Oct. 1865	Auguste Aimé Levoseard.
An improved preparation or composition for coating, covering or coloring walls and other surfaces or parts of buildings, and for forming mouldings, cornices and other decorative parts of houses.	2629	12th Oct. 1865	William Berwick.
An improved mode of treating or preparing casks and other vessels, to make them tight and suitable for containing hydrocarbons and other fluids.	2644	13th Oct. 1865	George Marshall.
Improvements in the manufacture of bricks for building and other purposes, and in apparatus therefor. (facing bricks.)	2913	13th Nov. 1865	Edwin Guthrie.
An improved composition for enamel, paint, varnish, cement or plaster. (for coating earthenware.) (Communicated by William Barney Watkins.)	3042	27th Nov. 1865	William Robert Lake.
Improved apparatus for facilitating the treating or preparing of casks and other vessels, to make them tight and suitable for containing hydrocarbon and other fluids. (coating with glue.)	3061	29th Nov. 1865	George Marshall.
A new or improved cement or composition, applicable to the agglomeration or ennobling of various materials, and to other useful and decorative purposes. (for coating walls.) (Communicated by Stanislas Sorel and Emile Justin Menier.)	3119	5th Dec. 1865	Richard Archibald Brooman.
Waterproof linings of cases, boxes, and apparatus in which articles are desired to be packed waterproof.	3201	11th Dec. 1865	John Jones.

Subject-matter of Patent.	Number of Patent.	Date.	Name of Patentee.

COATING, &c.—continued.

Preparation of glue or gelatine so as to render it insoluble in water, and applicable by the admixture of other substances to various purposes for which common glue or gelatine cannot now be used.
(*for Sizing barrels, coating leather, &c.*)
(*Communicated by Henry Wurts.*) — 3325 — 23rd Dec. 1865 — William Edward Newton.

Improvements in floor cloths and similar composition fabrics, in the manufacture of such fabrics, and in machinery employed therein — 3370 — 29th Dec. 1865 — John Howard Kidd. James Chadwick Mather.

Coverings for floors - - - - -
(*Communicated by Antoine Perrin and Achille Bandouin.*) — 3384 — 30th Dec. 1865 — John Henry Johnson.

III.—Coating, Sheathing and Facing Ships: Compositions for the Purpose.

Coating the bottoms and sides of ships and other submerged structures, to prevent fouling and decay. — 284 — 1st Feb. 1865 — John Moysey.

Construction of armour-plated ships, forts and other like structures. — 308 — 1st Feb. 1865 — John Hughes.

Improvements in armour-plated ships, forts, gun carriages and works of defence, and in fastenings to be employed therein. — 292 — 2nd Feb. 1865 — Charles Langley.

An improved varnish for preserving wood, and for protecting iron ships and other metal work from oxydation and from fouling.
(*Communicated by Adolphe Guibert.*) — 315 — 4th Feb. 1865 — Richard Archibald Brooman.

Protecting wooden surfaces from the fouling and injury to which they are ordinarily liable to sea water. — 363 — 9th Feb. 1865 — John Cornelius Craigie Halkett.

Construction of armour-plated ships - -
(*Communicated by Charles Oris Holyoke.*) — 438 — 15th Feb. 1865 — George Tomlinson Bousfield.

Armour plates for vessels of war and for other similar purposes. — 455 — 17th Feb. 1865 — John Brown.

Improvements in ships of war, partly applicable to ships designed for the merchant service.
(*Communicated by Augustus Walker.*) — 509 — 23rd Feb. 1865 — George Haseltine.

Improvements in coatings for the prevention of the fouling to which iron and other ships and structures are ordinarily liable in sea water. — 624 — 6th March 1865 — Francis Cruikshank.

Improvements in coating the bottoms of iron ships and other surfaces, to prevent oxidation, the adhesion of marine animals and plants, and in compositions to be therein employed. — 681 — 10th March 1865 — Richard Percy Roberts.

An improvement in paints or compositions used for coating iron or wooden vessels, and other structures exposed to the action of sea water. — 871 — 28th March 1865 — John Cornelius Craigie Halkett.

Protecting iron ships and other submerged structures from oxidation and corrosion. — 970 — 5th April 1865 — Edward Ritherdon.

An improved composition for preventing the fouling of ships and other vessels.
(*Communicated by William Bolivar Davis.*) — 1008 — 8th April 1865 — George Davis.

Subject-matter of Patent.	Number of Patent.	Date.	Name of Patentee.
COATING, &c.—continued.			
Improvements in the construction of ships of war and floating batteries, part of which improvements are applicable to land fortifications.	1107	20th April 1865	Henry Cardwell.
Securing or fastening wooden planking to iron frames in ships or vessels, and also to the outside of iron ships.	1108	25th April 1865	William Husband.
Improving and strengthening shields of steel, iron or other material, for ships, fortifications and other constructions.	1226	2nd May 1865	Thomas Hay Campbell.
An improved composition for coating iron or other vessels, and for other similar purposes.	1278	9th May 1865	John Cornelius Craigie Halkett.
Composition and manufacture of paints applicable to iron and other ships' bottoms, and for other general purposes.	1469	31st May 1865	Thomas Spencer.
Sheathing or coating the bottoms of ships or vessels.	1567	10th June 1865	Barnet Holsmon Cohen.
Sheathing iron ships - - - -	1612	14th June 1865	William Robinson Mulkey.
Preparation of paints - - - -	1807	7th July 1865	George Fentiman.
Constructing ships and vessels - - -	1817	8th July 1865	Christopher Oswald Papengouth.
An improved composition for coating ships' bottoms, and the surfaces of other vessels or structures which are exposed to the action of sea water - - - - - - -	1943	26th July 1865	{ Frederick Pulman. Richard Gimman.
An improved composition for coating the bottoms of iron and wooden ships, by which the same are preserved from fouling and the iron from corrosion, whether internally or externally, by sea or other water or moisture, which is applicable to iron of any kind exposed to the action of moisture.	1966	1st Aug. 1865	William La Penotière.
Iron knees and riders for ships' fastenings, and iron frames for wood and iron ships.	2010	3rd Aug. 1865	Peter Cato.
A new or improved composition for coating iron or wooden ships' bottoms.	2120	16th Aug. 1865	Samuel Parry.
Treating, working or manipulating cast steel for the manufacture of wheel tires, armour plates or other articles requiring great hardness and tensile strength.	2277	5th Sept. 1865	Julien Graad.
Improvements in cleansing and coating the bottoms of ships and other submerged surfaces, to prevent oxidation and the adhesion of marine animals and plants, also in compositions to be employed for these purposes.	2316	9th Sept. 1865	Richard Perry Roberts.
A new composition of indian-rubber mastic or cement, made in a more or less fluid state according to the use to be made of it, and the process or contrivance for applying the same. (*coating hulls of ships.*)	2630	13th Oct. 1865	Auguste Aimé Lennard.
A certain composition having anti-corrosive and anti-fouling properties, for the preservation of and keeping clean the bottoms of iron vessels, and also for the preservation of iron submerged and iron structures exposed to the action of the atmosphere or water - - - -	2653	14th Oct. 1865	{ William Jenkins Combe Mac Millan. James Mason. John Vickers Scarborough.

Subject-matter of Patent.	Number of Patent.	Date.	Name of Patentee.
COATING, &c.—*continued.*			
An improved coating for covering the bottoms of iron and steel ships and other navigable vessels and marine works, to prevent oxidation and the adhesion of animal and vegetable matter thereto.	2791	30th Oct. 1865	Robert Doyne Dwyer.
An improved method of sheathing iron vessels	2832	2nd Nov. 1865	Edwin Clark.
A new and improved cement . . . } (*for lining iron vessels.*)	2863	7th Nov. 1865	{ Thomas Graces. { James O'Donoghue.
Protecting the bottoms and sides of ships and other structures exposed to the action of sea water.	3000	22nd Nov. 1865	Cowper Phipps Coles.
Planking or sheathing iron ships and iron framed ships.	3012	23rd Nov. 1865	William Robinson Mulley.
Means of applying copper or alloys of copper to the bottoms and sides of navigable vessels built of iron, steel or homogeneous metal.	6339	26th Dec. 1866	William Francis Drane.
IV.—Covering Rollers.			
Improvements in wringing machines, parts of which are applicable to the construction of rollers. (*Communicated by Stephen Wiley and Henry Holly.*)	922	1st April 1865	Henry Lewis.
An improved metallic preparation or composition for cleaning, sharpening, burnishing and grinding articles of cutlery, edge tools or cutting instruments, and for grinding the cards or rollers of carding-engines and the surfaces of cylinders, and covering rollers for various kinds of woollen and cotton machinery.	1054	13th April 1865	George Mountford.
Manufacture of a compound or material to be used as a substitute for india-rubber. (*Communicated by Henry Lavavasseur and Emile Grenier.*)	1069	15th April 1865	William Clark.
Digging machinery	1124	22nd April 1865	Ormrod Coffern Evans.
An improvement in the drawing and other rollers used in preparing and spinning cotton and other fibrous materials and textile manufactures. (*Communicated by Amos Ashum Taylor.*)	1439	25th May 1865	William Edward Newton.
Covers for rollers used in spinning cotton . .	1901	21st July 1865	{ George Taylor. { Joseph Crossley.
An improved covering for rollers or cylinders .	2167	22nd Aug. 1865	James Alfred Turner.
Manufacture of covers applicable to drawing or printing rollers and as endless blankets . }	2716	20th Oct. 1865	{ Manuel Leopold Jonas { Lavater. { John Kershaw.
A new or improved method of preventing the escape of heat from steam cylinders . . } (*lining with wool.*)	3051	29th Nov. 1865	{ William Kenozos { Andrew Brown.
"Top rollers" employed in the manufacture of fibrous substances.	3078	30th Nov. 1865	John Kerfoot.

Subject-matter of Patent.	Number of Patent.	Date.	Name of Patentee.
COFFEE AND COCOA ; COFFEE-POTS AND TEA URNS.			
Machinery or apparatus for cleaning rice, coffee and other grains or seeds having an outer hull or inner pellicle. (Communicated by Nathaniel Overne and Walter Clement Key.)	64	9th Jan. 1865	John Henry Johnson.
A chemical combustible substance and apparatus to which it is applicable. (heating tea urns, coffee-pots, &c.) (Communicated by François Stoler.)	477	20th Feb. 1865	William Edward Gedge.
A new or improved material to be used in combination with or as a substitute for coffee. (Communicated by René Charles Jules Provet and Maximilien Louis Joseph Chollet.)	979	6th April 1865	Martin Dinny.
A mode of obtaining decoctions and apparatus for carrying the same into effect. (Communicated by Benjamin Green Martin.)	1227	2nd May 1865	Francis Wise.
Means and apparatus for firing and curing tea. (Communicated by Thomas Walters.)	1584	13th June 1865	Albert Robinson.
An improved self-acting apparatus for obtaining a circulation of volatile liquids. (infusing coffee, tea, &c.) (Communicated by Mesurs Françisque Mennot and Auguste Jaquin.)	1816	8th July 1865	Hector Auguste Dufrené.
Tea and coffee pots and urns	1980	27th July 1865	Thomas Brown.
Improvements in desiccating the leaves and flowers of plants and other vegetable substances, and in the apparatus to be employed therein. (leaves of the tea plant.) (Communicated by Benjamin Dickinson.)	2708	20th Oct. 1865	Allan Lowrie M'Gavin.
Improvements in treating or curing the tea leaf and in apparatus employed therein.	2866	4th Nov. 1865	Frederick Campbell.
An improved manufacture of caramel. (for colouring coffee.) (Communicated by Thaddeus Hyatt.)	2950	16th Nov. 1865	Alfred Vincent Newton.
An improvement in the roasting of coffee. (Communicated by Thaddeus Hyatt.)	2951	16th Nov. 1865	Alfred Vincent Newton.
Handles of tea and coffee pots and other similar articles.	3066	25th Nov. 1865	James Thompson.
An improved machine for dressing, sifting, cleaning and polishing fruit, coffee, grain and other matter, parts of which are applicable to coffee sifting, roasting, cooking and cleaning, and other purposes.	3183	6th Dec. 1865	Edwin Whele.
Apparatus for screening grain, seed, rice, tea and other materials.	3329	14th Dec. 1865	Henry William Miller.

Subject-matter of Patent.	Number of Patent.	Date.	Name of Patentee.
COFFINS, TOMBSTONES, MONUMENTAL TABLETS.			
Improvements in the manufacture and application of devices and representations to tombstones, and in other public or exposed situations, for various purposes - - - - - -	1180	22nd April 1865	{ Alfred Grainger. Charles Mitchel Girdler.
Manufacture and application of glass and other vitreous compositions - - - - (for coffins, monumental tablets, &c.)	1220	1st May 1865	{ Arthur Howard Emerson. Robert Fowler.
An improved manufacture of coffins and air-tight receptacles.	1804	7th July 1865	Joseph George.
Certain military improvements in coffins - -	2459	26th Sept. 1865	John Hargreaves.
Coffins - - - - - - - (Communicated by Josef Franz Mayr.)	2496	24th Sept. 1865	Samuel Dunn.
Improvements in the manufacture of air-tight coffins and in the mode of ornamenting or finishing the same, as also in the application of a material or composition not hitherto used in their production - - - - -	3014	24th Nov. 1865	{ Henry John Cox. William Leech.
A new or improved cement or composition, applicable to the agglomeration or moulding of various materials, and to other useful and decorative purposes. (requiring monumental sculpture.) (Communicated by Stanislas Sorel and Emile Justin Menier.)	3119	5th Dec. 1865	Richard Archibald Brooman.
COINS AND MEDALS.			
Tools for securing tubes in tube plates, and for other purposes where concentrated power or adjustment is necessary. (for moving dies for stamping medals or coins.)	2455	26th Sept. 1865	Richard Taylor Nelson Howry.
COMBS.			
Improved machinery or apparatus for shaping the elastic dents of expanding and contracting combs.	189	21st Jan. 1865	Matthew Robinson.
Manufacture of a compound or material to be used as a substitute for india-rubber. (Communicated by Henry Lorrenberry and Emile Grenier.)	1068	15th April 1865	William Clark.
Preparation of glue or gelatine so as to render it insoluble in water, and applicable by the admixture of other substances to various purposes for which common glue or gelatine cannot now be used. (for combs.) (Communicated by Henry Werts.)	3396	23rd Dec. 1865	William Edward Newton.

Subject-matter of Patent.	Number of Patent.	Date.	Name of Patentee.
COMPASSES ; MEASURING ANGLES ; SURVEYING AND LEVELLING ; MATHEMATICAL AND ASTRONOMICAL INSTRUMENTS.			
Theodolites	70	9th Jan. 1865	Bartholomew Parker Bidder.
A new or improved topograph - - - -	84	11th Jan. 1865	Auguste Frederic Leudy.
Ship and other compasses - . . .	128	14th Jan. 1865	John Lilley.
Mathematical compasses for ascertaining the utmost correctness of the contents and square of any circle.	235	27th Jan. 1865	Johann Ernst Friedrich Lüdcke.
Compasses or apparatus for registering the course steered by a vessel during any given period.	787	21st March 1865	William Arthur.
Improved apparatus for ascertaining the state of sewers, tunnels, drifts or other subterranean work, part of which apparatus is applicable to levelling purposes.	849	25th March 1865	Richard Williams Barnes.
Straight line dividing engines and tools for regulating distances. (for marking scales, rules, &c.)	1245	4th May 1865	William Ford Stanley.
Ship and other compasses - - - -	1251	4th May 1865	John Lilley.
An improved apparatus for adjusting levels and other instruments. (Communicated by Carl Johann Reinhart Jahns.)	2085	9th Aug. 1865	Arnold Dudenberg.
Mounting telescopes and microscopes - (and arranging them for measuring angles.)	2075	10th Aug. 1865	Carl Johann Reinhart Jahns.
An improved apparatus for illustrating astronomical phenomena. (tellurians.)	2189	14th Aug. 1865	Joseph Lionel Nalsh.
An improved apparatus for and method of ascertaining the state of sewers, tunnels, drifts or other subterranean works, without descending thereinto, by means of the natural, artificial or magnesium light, part of which apparatus is applicable to levelling purposes.	2446	25th Sept. 1865	Richard William Barnes.
Improvements in rules for measuring, and in other instruments or articles requiring to be adjusted or disposed at various angles.	2513	10th Oct. 1865	Arthur Nicholls.
Certain improvements in the manufacture of compasses, callipers and dividers - - . }	3089	1st Dec. 1865	{ Isaac John Handley. Charles Wilkins.
Astronomical instruments - - - (Communicated by George Davidson.)	3316	22nd Dec. 1865	William Edward Newton.
Preparation of glue or gelatine so as to render it insoluble in water, and applicable by the admixture of other substances to various purposes for which common glue or gelatine cannot now be used. (for mathematical instruments.) (Communicated by Henry Wurtz.)	3328	23rd Dec. 1865	William Edward Newton.
Construction of levels and theodolites - -	3339	23rd Dec. 1865	John Coope Haddan.

Subject-matter of Patent.	Number of Patent.	Date.	Name of Patentee.
CONDENSING, COOLING, FREEZING.			
An improved jacket or protector for metallic and other vessels and structures containing solid substances, liquids or gases, to prevent radiation of heat from or communication of heat to such vessels and structures - - - - (for its safer and wiser makers.)	4	2nd Jan. 1866	{ Edward Bevan. Abel Fleming.
Improvements in machinery used for condensing atmospheric air, and in machinery worked by compressed air, employed in getting coal, stone and minerals.	96	11th Jan. 1865	James Grafton Jones.
Apparatus called ice safes - - - -	230	26th Jan. 1865	Charles Falch.
Condensation and refrigeration of vapours and fluids.	573	1st March 1865	George Harman Barth.
An improved process and apparatus for impregnating wood with chemical solutions. (Communicated by Ernest Bazin and Jules Hémery.)	590	2nd March 1865	William Edward Newton.
Apparatus for heating and cooling atmospheric air and other aëriform bodies, and for heating ovens, and for heating and ventilating buildings.	636	7th March 1865	Loftus Perkins.
Process and apparatus for refrigerating or freezing liquids.	691	11th March 1865	James Henderson.
Improvements in securing low and uniform temperatures, applicable to public and private buildings, also to refrigerators, coolers and condensers, and to ships and other vessels, and in the apparatus employed therein. (Communicated by Daniel Somrs.)	718	14th March 1865	Alfred Vincent Newton.
Apparatus for distilling oils and other liquids from coal and other substances. (Communicated by William George Washington Jasper.)	727	15th March 1865	William Edward Newton.
Apparatus for cooling animal and other charcoal -	730	16th March 1865	John Frederick Bringée.
Certain improvements in non-conducting composition for preventing the radiation or transmission of heat or cold.	864	27th March 1865	Ferdinand Le Roy.
Improvements in the treatment of meal and the dressing of flour, and the machinery and apparatus employed therein. (cooling the meal.)	896	30th March 1865	William Savory.
Improvements in apparatus for lighting and ventilating ships, part of which is also applicable for producing fresh water at sea.	998	7th April 1865	Henry Edmonds.
Improvements in steam generators applicable also to condensers or coolers. (Communicated by Thomas Laders.)	1029	11th April 1865	John Henry Johnson.
Certain improvements in gas-ammoniacal engines -	1074	17th April 1865	Louis de St. Céran.
Casting and working so-called "Bessemer steel" ingots " - - - - - - -	1100	20th April 1865	{ Thomas Hampton. James Abbott.
Improvements in the fitting of surface condenser tubes, and in the tools to be used therein, and in the means of retarding corrosion in steam boilers. (Communicated by William Judson.)	1153	22nd April 1865	Alfred Vincent Newton.

Subject-matter of Patent.	Number of Patent.	Date.	Name of Patentee.
CONDENSING, &c.—continued.			
Washing or steeping and bleaching textile or fibrous materials. (Communicated by Messieurs Neyret, Oriol and Fredet.)	1144	20th April 1865	William Clark.
Apparatus for disintegrating vegetable and animal substances.	1168	26th April 1865	François Dominique Pierre Jacques Cabanon.
An improved apparatus for condensing steam and feeding boilers with the product therefrom.	1180	27th April 1865	Anthony Francis.
Apparatus employed in the returning of animal charcoal.	1198	29th April 1865	Thomas White.
Machinery or apparatus employed in breweries and distilleries.	1904	29th April 1865	Francis Gregory.
An improved refrigerator and condenser.	1249	4th May 1865	Josiah Hampton.
Improvements in or applicable to marine condensing steam-engines.	1263	4th May 1865	Thomas Wood.
Flour mills (cooling the stones.) (Communicated by Charles Simon Olivier Mattieron, Norrisse Justine and Nicolas François Danot-Prévost.)	1848	15th May 1865	Henri Adrien Bonneville.
An improved apparatus for freezing, icing and cooling liquids. (Communicated by Henry Nicholas Dallemayne.)	1406	22nd May 1865	John Henry Johnson.
Treatment of condensing pans employed in the condensation of milk. (Communicated by Samuel Percy.)	1548	5th June 1865	Charles Howard Wansbrough.
Caloric or heated air engines. (Communicated by Cyrus W. Baldwin and Walter Davis Richards.)	1565	14th June 1865	Samuel Blatchford Tucker.
Improvements in surface condensers for steam-engines, and in feeding boilers therefrom.	1669	21st June 1865	Charles Talbot Porter.
Surface condensers. (Communicated by Allan Crocker Stimers.)	1677	22nd June 1865	William Edward Newton.
An improved brewers' and distillers' refrigerator or apparatus for cooling liquids, condensing steam or other vapours.	1700	26th June 1865	Morris Ashby.
An improved combination of materials for the manufacture of carpets, floor cloth, felt, wall paper, fireproof flexible roofing, ship and boat building and for other similar purposes. (See ditto.)	1776	4th July 1865	John Loughbottom. Abram Loughbottom.
Ventilators (for cooling air.)	1860	10th July 1865	John Paul Haugh Le Patourel.
An improved apparatus for cooling liquids and cooling or condensing vapours or gases.	1875	19th July 1865	Thomas Metcalf. Henry Metcalf. Thomas Clayton.
Condensing apparatus for steam-engines.	1897	20th July 1865	Morgan Lawrence Parry.
Improvements in brewing and distilling, also in drying yeast, and in the apparatus employed.	2019	4th Aug. 1865	Patrick Robertson.
Apparatus for regulating the passage or flow of steam, water and other fluids.	2043	7th Aug. 1865	Adrienne Anastasie Foubert.
Improvements in and connected with the manufacture of copper.	2100	14th Aug. 1865	James Thomas Larkey.

Subject-matter of Patent.	Number of Patent.	Date.	Name of Patentee.
CONDENSING &c.—continued.			
Construction of apparatus for distilling and rectifying alcohols. (Communicated by François Désiré Savalle.)	2203	24th Aug. 1865	Henri Adrien Bonneville.
Improvements in condensing and utilising sulphurous smokes and vapours, and in apparatus to be used for that purpose.	2216	29th Aug. 1865	Adolf Gurlt.
Ice safes	2244	31st Aug. 1865	Henry Clarke Ash.
Improvements in ice houses and in glaciaria or skating places, and in baths.	2292	6th Sept. 1865	Augustus William Parker.
Cooling bacon-curing rooms or chambers - -	2326	12th Sept. 1865	Robert Andrew Boyd.
Improvements in cooling, heating and evaporating, and in apparatus employed therein.	2361	15th Sept. 1865	Walter Blundell.
A new method of and apparatus for condensing the steam of steam-engines.	2376	18th Sept. 1865	Francesco Daina.
Improvements in coke and charcoal ovens and in the manufacture of coke, parts of which are applicable to bread, biscuit and pastry ovens.	2477	27th Sept. 1865	William Morgans.
Improvements in obtaining and applying sulphurous acid and in apparatus used therein. (for refrigeration.)	2485	29th Sept. 1865	Rees Reece.
Apparatus for heating, evaporating and cooling liquids	2494	29th Sept. 1865	{ Isaac Smith. William Fothergill Batho.
Improvements in the construction of steam generators, applicable also to the construction of condensers, the heating of water generally, and to the warming of buildings. (Communicated by Joseph Harrison, junior, and Thomas Laidern.)	2610	10th Oct. 1865	John Henry Johnson.
A new or improved steam consuming apparatus, or an apparatus intended to make available as fuel all or part of the steam actually evolving from engines into the atmosphere, and also to absorb the smoke resulting from the combustion.	2676	17th Oct. 1865	François Georges Ricardo.
An improved truck or barrow for wheeling and tipping coke, coal or other substances. (cooling.)	2846	4th Nov. 1865	William Brett.
An improved non-conducting composition for preventing the radiation or transmission of heat or cold.	2853	4th Nov. 1865	James Thys.
Preservation of meat and the concentration of its juices.	2892	10th Nov. 1865	Theophilus Redwood.
Improvements in apparatus for obtaining fresh water from salt and impure water, also applicable for ventilating purposes.	2953	17th Nov. 1865	Samuel Hazard Huntly.
Apparatus for condensing exhaust steam, and heating air by the heat abstracted in effecting the condensation of such steam. (Communicated by Addison Calvin Fletcher.)	2996	21st Nov. 1865	Alfred Vincent Newton.
Apparatus for distilling oils and condensing oily vapours.	3101	2nd Dec. 1865	Thomas Newton Bennis.
An improved machine for dressing, sifting, cleaning and polishing fruit, coffee, grain and other matter, parts of which are applicable to coffee sifting, roasting, cooling and cleaning, and other purposes.	3162	6th Dec. 1865	Edwin Whole.

Subject-matter of Patent.	Number of Patent.	Date.	Name of Patentee.
CONDENSERS, &c.—continued.			
Improvements in constructing atmospheric railways and carriages, and in working the same, parts of which are applicable to exhausting and condensing air for other purposes.	3173	9th Dec. 1865	Alexander Doull.
A new and improved apparatus for cooling and purifying air in rooms or compartments, and ventilating the same. (Communicated by Axel Storrs Lyman.)	3222	20th Dec. 1865	William Clark.
An improved method of and apparatus for preserving, purifying, mixing, separating, cooling, aerating, roasting and otherwise treating grain, ores and various other matters.	3344	27th Dec. 1865	Gaston Charles Ange, Marquis D'Aussy.
Improvements in distilling and in relieving distilled and other liquids from gases mechanically mixed therewith. (and refrigerating.)	3351	27th Dec. 1865	Norman Willis Wheeler.
CONFECTIONERY, LOZENGES, LIQUORICE CAKES.			
A new kind of pearled or ornamented confectionery	1819	10th July 1865	Henry Schooling.
Improvements in the manufacture of pomfret cakes, rolls and pipes, and of lozenges, and in apparatus to be used in the manufacture of such articles - - - - - -	2143	19th Aug. 1865	William Wood. James William Wood.
Manufacture of lozenges, cakes and other similar articles, from plastic substances.	2554	3rd Oct. 1865	Charles James Tinker.
Manufacture of scent and smelling bottles - (containing lozenges.)	2569	9th Oct. 1865	Thomas Miles.
Machinery for the manufacture of lozenges, wafers or pastilles of pasty materials. (Communicated by Monsieur Joseph Jules Derriey.)	2730	21st Oct. 1865	Hector Auguste Dufresul.
COOKING AND APPARATUS USED IN COOKING.			
An improved method of cooking and apparatus to be employed therein.	150	18th Jan. 1865	Stephen Ballard.
An improved atmospheric pressure lamp for the burning of benzole, paraffin, naphtha or other volatile oils, which lamp may be used for all the purposes for which lamps are usually required, either for lighting, cooking, heating or other purposes. (Partly communicated by John Joseph Riddle.)	543	24th Feb. 1865	William Bell Dalston.
An improved cooking utensil - - -	1041	12th April 1865	Frederic Pelham Warren.
Jacks used when roasting and baking - -	1108	20th April 1865	William Robinson.
Apparatus used when boiling milk - -	1510	2nd June 1865	George Kent. William Hayward West.

Subject-matter of Patent.	Number of Patent.	Date.	Name of Patentee.
COOKING, &c.—continued.			
An improvement or improvements in the manufacture of the handles of smoothing irons or sad irons, which said improvement or improvements may also be applied to the manufacture of the handles of various other articles. (handles of tea kettles.)	1786	7th July 1865	Thomas Sheldon.
An improved apparatus for cooking, a portion of the same being applicable for washing and ironing.	1917	22nd July 1865	William Wapshare.
Construction of cooking stoves and ranges	1944	26th July 1865	William Barton.
Sheet metal handles for spoons, saucepans and other utensils for culinary purposes.	2226	30th Aug. 1865	James Falkous.
The manufacture of boilers and tea kettle bottoms, and every other description of die-struck hollow ware.	2237	31st Aug. 1865	Michael Judge.
Improvements in the construction of lids or covers for saucepans and other cooking utensils, part of which improvements is also applicable to the lids or covers of housemaids' pails.	2249	31st Aug. 1865	John Ward.
Treating certain descriptions of vegetables in the process of cooking or boiling the same	2744	24th Oct. 1865	{ Matthew Thomas Cooper Nash, Charles John Nash.
Improvements in generating and applying certain gases, and in apparatus to be employed therein. (and for cooking.)	2833	2nd Nov. 1865	James Webster.
Cooking apparatus	2971	18th Nov. 1865	Samuel Hazard Huntly.
Construction of kitchen stoves and cooking ranges	3144	6th Dec. 1865	George Fitzjames Buswell.
Apparatus for cooking by steam (Communicated by Francis Milliken.)	3182	8th Dec. 1865	George Tomlinson Bousfield.
Boilers or apparatus for generating steam (for boiling.) (Communicated by Julien Belleville.)	3399	18th Dec. 1865	Richard Archibald Brooman.
Improved apparatus for burning combustible vapour (such as that from naphtha or coal oil) for heating, cooking and lighting purposes. (Communicated by James Stratton.)	3417	22nd Dec. 1865	George Davies.
COPYING, TRACING, DRAWING AND WRITING.			
Improvements in pencil holders and pen holders, and in holders for crayons and other marking, writing or drawing materials.	339	4th Feb. 1865	William Edward Wiley.
Improvements in ornamenting china and earthenware, and in preparing materials to be employed therefor. (crayons.)	438	15th Feb. 1865	Francis Joseph Emery.
Improvements in reproducing or producing copies of writings, drawings, music and other characters, and in preparing originals to be transmitted by electric telegraph. (Communicated by Jacques Paul Landrigot.)	1487	27th May 1865	Richard Archibald Brooman.

Subject-matter of Patent.	Number of Patent.	Date.	Name of Patentee.

COPYING, &c.—continued.

Subject-matter of Patent.	Number of Patent.	Date.	Name of Patentee.
Copying presses - - - - -	1694	15th June 1865	Phineas Lawrence. George Jefferys.
An improved automaton toy figure (Communicated by Pierre Galilbert.)	1788	6th July 1865	William Edward Gedge.
Improvements in copying letters, plans and other manuscripts, and in the apparatus and substances employed therein. (Communicated by Edward Casper.)	1846	14th July 1865	Henri Adrien Bonneville.
An improved drawing instrument - - - (Communicated by Mr. Garvin de Marolin.)	1864	14th July 1865	George Clark.
Copying-presses for copying letters and other written documents.	2186	25th Aug. 1865	George Owen.
Engraving on metal - - - (Communicated by Narcisse Guillot and Pierre Héritier.)	2596	19th Sept. 1865	Richard Archibald Brooman.
Portfolios, writing desks, writing cases and other similar apparatus.	2818	13th Nov. 1865	John Stephens.
Application of photography to the obtaining of printed proofs or impressions or engravings -	2964	17th Nov. 1865	Edward Bullock. James Bullock.
An improved piece of furniture convertible into a seat with back on either side, a seat with desk on either side, or a seat with table on either side.	8067	29th Nov. 1865	Thomas Laurie.
A covering or cap for protecting the ends of maps, drawings, rolls of paper and other materials that are capable of being rolled up.	3175	9th Dec. 1865	Saint George Howels Davies-Gwyn.
An improved ruler - - - (Communicated by George Sckremm.)	3188	11th Dec. 1865	James Theodore Griffin.
Preparation of glue or gelatine so as to render it insoluble in water, and applicable by the admixture of other substances to various purposes for which common glue or gelatine cannot now be used. (for copying models, for rulers, &c.) (Communicated by Henry Wurtz.)	3386	23rd Dec. 1865	William Edward Newton.
Apparatus for damping and gumming labels, stamps, envelopes and sheets of paper - - (for copying letters.)	3543	27th Dec. 1865	Joseph Benn. George Oswald Lachman.

CORK; CORKS AND BUNGS.

Subject-matter of Patent.	Number of Patent.	Date.	Name of Patentee.
Improvements in the construction of life belts, swimming belts, jackets and buoys, and in the employment and utilization of certain materials in the manufacture of the same.	341	7th Feb. 1865	Charles Milburn.
Cork cutting machinery - - - (Communicated by François Perrot.)	638	7th March 1865	William Clark.
Apparatus for shaping corks - - -	1068	15th April 1865	John M'Dowall.
Machinery or apparatus for cutting cylindrical or conical articles. (bungs.)	1247	4th May 1865	George Bishop.

Subject-matter of Patent.	Number of Patent.	Date.	Name of Patentee.
CORK, &c.—continued.			
Corks or bungs for closing bottles and other receptacles for liquids. (Communicated by Adolphe Jacquemon.)	1559	5th June 1865	John Henry Johnson.
An improved combination of materials for the manufacture of carpets, floor cloth, felt, wall paper, fireproof flexible roofing, ship and boat building and for other similar purposes (bungs.)	1775	5th July 1865	{ John Longbottom. Abram Longbottom.
Machinery for cutting and shaping cork, with apparatus for registering the manufacture.	2393	20th Sept. 1865	Leon Villette.
Cork cutting machines (Communicated by George Hammer and Alfred Buss.)	3033	23th Nov. 1865	John Henry Johnson.
CUTTING, SAWING, PLANING.			
2.—Cutting, Sawing, Planing, &c., Metal, Stone, Wood, Cork and Slate.			
An improvement in machines for cutting match splints, tooth picks and similar articles.	74	10th Jan. 1865	Jonathan Clark Brown.
An improved apparatus for cutting iron gas or other pipes. (Communicated by Jules Chartier.)	86	11th Jan. 1865	William Edward Gedge.
Machinery or apparatus for planing and moulding or otherwise shaping wood.	143	17th Jan. 1865	{ John Robinson. John Smith.
An improved system of manufacturing clog soles, patten boards and similar articles by machinery.	416	14th Feb. 1865	Robert John Joass.
Mode of making or forming the links of iron or steel chains, chain cables, shackles, couplings or parts of the same, and for machinery to be used therein.	423	14th Feb. 1865	George Humfrey.
Armour plates for vessels of war and for other similar purposes. (grooving.)	455	17th Feb. 1865	John Brown.
Machinery for sawing wood	523	24th Feb. 1865	Samuel William Worssam.
Apparatus for operating engineers' and carpenters' tools by hand or other power. (for planing.) (Communicated by Henry Winser.)	600	3rd March 1865	James Spence.
Cork cutting machinery (Communicated by François Perret.)	636	7th March 1865	William Clark.
Machinery or apparatus for cutting and shaping metals, making nails, rivets and similar articles.	644	8th March 1865	{ Joseph Wadsworth. James Wadsworth.
A new or improved machine for dressing and rounding the inner surfaces of fellows.	794	22nd March 1865	Hiram Smith Jacobs.
Machinery for cutting, punching, raising, shaping or drawing through sheet metal, by means of tools and dies.	795	22nd March 1865	George Farmer.
Machinery or apparatus for cutting or shaping the threads of screws or worms.	855	24th March 1865	Joseph Green.
Machines for planing and shaping metals	856	27th March 1865	John Todd.

Subject-matter of Patent.	Number of Patent.	Date.	Name of Patentee.
CUTTING, &c.—continued.			
Certain improvements in the manufacture of hoop or narrow strip iron.	1083	13th April 1865	Thomas Bennett.
Apparatus for shaping corks - - -	1085	15th April 1865	John M'Dowall.
Machinery for cutting and dressing stones and other hard substances. (*Communicated by Gustavus Cuppers.*)	1093	19th April 1865	Maurice Vogl.
Casting and working so-called " Bessemer steel ingots " - - - - - -	1100	20th April 1865	{ Thomas Hampton. James Abbott.
Improvements in the fitting of surface condenser tubes, and in the tools to be used therein, and in the means of retarding corrosion in steam-boilers. (*Communicated by William Judson.*)	1153	22nd April 1865	Alfred Vincent Newton.
An improved cigar cutter - - - -	1139	24th April 1865	Henry Charles Batcher.
Machinery for cutting or shaping meats, spars and other beams and articles of wood.	1179	27th April 1865	Samuel Harvey.
Machinery or apparatus for cutting cylindrical or conical articles.	1247	4th May 1865	George Redrup.
Improvements in means or apparatus for fixing or tightening the ends of boiler and other tubes, and in cutting the ends or other parts of such tubes.	1282	9th May 1865	Ralph Hart Tweddell.
Improved apparatus for cutting, turning and smoothing metal pipes, and the surfaces of bolts, rods or spindles - - - -	1311	11th May 1865	{ George Mountford. Edward Worrell.
Construction of saw mills - - - -	1340	15th May 1865	George Ennis.
Machinery for manufacturing clog and patten soles	1351	16th May 1865	Walter Brown.
Machinery applicable to the cutting off the upper parts of piles - - - - - -	1408	22nd May 1865	{ George Forness. James Slater.
Certain improvements in apparatus for cutting or forming screws, which is also applicable for cutting pipes or tubes.	1411	23rd May 1865	Edward M'Nally.
Machinery employed in the manufacture of hoops and tyres. (*making grooves on roughing rolls.*)	1425	25th May 1865	John Ramsbottom.
Sewing-machines - - - - -	1452	27th May 1865	Charles Fraser.
Improvements in making cast-steel railway tires, and in apparatus therefor.	1456	27th May 1865	John Martin Rowan.
Improved machinery or apparatus for cutting off wooden piles below water.	1474	29th May 1865	Charles Henry Murray.
Circular saws commonly called drunken saws -	1476	29th May 1865	William Tighe Hamilton.
Tube cutters and screw stocks - - -	1587	3rd June 1865	Charles Taylor.
Machinery or tools for cutting metals or other materials.	1671	9th June 1865	William Wilson Hulse.
Hammers and other machines actuated by steam or other fluid or vapour - - - - (*machines for cutting.*)	1607	14th June 1865	{ Benjamin Massey. Stephen Massey.
Machinery for cutting dovetails for joiners' work -	1671	21st June 1865	William Roberts.
Heating chisels, knives, plane irons, gouges, augers, steels, shears, scythes and saws.	1715	27th June 1865	William Brooks.
Machinery or apparatus for cutting, punching and bending sheet metal. (*Communicated by Nathan Harper.*)	1729	29th June 1865	Robert Henry Lacas.

Subject-matter of Patent.	Number of Patent.	Date.	Name of Patentee.
CUTTING, &c.—*continued.*			
Improvements in portable charge holders for breech loading guns, whether single or double barrelled, as also in the means of manufacturing the said holders and in replacing the charge.	1828	20th July 1865	Charles Reeves.
Machinery for planing metals - (*Communicated by William Sellers.*)	1942	26th July 1865	William Edward Newton.
Apparatus for cutting scales for knives and forming metal webs for knives.	1988	1st Aug. 1865	William Singleton.
A new portable machine or apparatus for the cutting of screw threads on pipe or on solid materials, and for the cutting of pipes asunder.	2055	9th Aug. 1865	Thomas Goode Messenger.
Friction matches, lucifer matches, and matches for relighting, called taper matches.	2153	21st Aug. 1865	Gideon G. Dennis.
Saws for sawing and cutting marble and other analogous substances.	2168	25th Aug. 1865	Edward Henry Woodward.
An improved combination drill brace (*cutting off the ends of tubes.*)	2212	24th Aug. 1865	Edward Davies, Richard Hobbs Taunton.
Apparatus for sawing curved designs -	2262	2nd Sept. 1865	John Elverson.
Improved machinery for cutting stone (*Communicated by George Jeffords Wardwell.*)	2363	15th Sept. 1865	Alfred Vincent Newton.
Machinery for cutting and shaping cork, with apparatus for registering the manufacture.	2393	20th Sept. 1865	Leon Villette.
Machinery for making casks, barrels and other wooden vessels of capacity. (*mounting the ends.*)	2436	22nd Sept. 1865	James Davidson.
Bench stops or abutments used for planing wood and other operations.	2539	3rd Oct. 1865	Joseph Heydon.
Machinery or apparatus for the manufacture of wooden spills.	2577	6th Oct. 1865	Thomas Macbin.
Machinery for cutting screws -	2658	14th Oct. 1865	Joseph Taggez.
Machinery for the manufacture of fish hooks	2678	17th Oct. 1865	Albert Fenton.
Improvements in block matches and in machinery for making the same	2690	18th Oct. 1865	James Whitford Trueman, Henry Lovi.
Reeds for weaving cotton-nut, jute and other fibres - (*cut from metal.*)	2691	18th Oct. 1865	Thomas Catchpole.
Machinery or apparatus for moulding or cutting moulds, and planing wood and other similar materials -	2711	20th Oct. 1865	William Blackett Haigh, William Bissell.
Apparatus for splitting and preparing cane -	2717	20th Oct. 1865	Rémy Bienay.
Mortising machines -	2761	21st Oct. 1865	William Parwes.
Improvements in tools and apparatus employed in blasting, boring and cutting rock, stone and other hard substances, and in the means employed for making such tools.	2774	27th Oct. 1865	Julius Bernard.
Apparatus for producing accelerated motion for driving purposes - (*for planing machines.*)	2779	28th Oct. 1865	John Hawthorn Kitson, John Kirby.
Manufacture of spikes -	2806	31st Oct. 1865	Moses Bayliss.
Machinery for mortising, tenoning and boring hard or soft woods, and drilling iron.	2820	2nd Nov. 1865	James Curtis.
An improved bit for boring mortices in wood or other material.	2857	6th Nov. 1865	William Tighe Hamilton.
Means of renewing the teeth of worn out files - (*for cutting new teeth.*)	2897	8th Nov. 1865	Joseph Bernard Oscar Laama.

Subject-matter of Patent.	Number of Patent.	Date.	Name of Patentee.
CUTTING, &c.—continued.			
Machines for fret cutting or sawing	3000	10th Nov. 1865	William Middleton.
An improved apparatus for cutting tenons	3011	13th Nov. 1865	William Tighe Hamilton.
Certain improvements in cutting or dividing timber, and in the machinery or apparatus connected therewith.	3023	13th Nov. 1865	John Jex Long.
Machinery for cutting or shearing sheet iron and other metallic sheets or plates	3069	21st Nov. 1865	Richard Walters. Thomas Edwin Meem Walters.
Cork cutting machines (Communicated by George Hammer and Alfred Bate.)	3033	25th Nov. 1865	John Henry Johnson.
A combined adjustable spanner, tube cutter and pipe wrench. (Communicated by Henry Hitchings Baragwanath and Martin Van Winkle.)	3036	27th Nov. 1865	John Phillips Baragwanath.
Machinery for cutting mouldings in wood (Communicated by John Bartlett Winslow.)	3040	27th Nov. 1865	William Edward Newton.
Improved machinery for manufacturing sewing-machine needles (cutting wire into lengths.) (Partly communicated by Joseph Thorne.)	3143	6th Dec. 1865	Naham Salomon. William John Lawrence Davids.
Machinery or tools for cutting wood or other substances.	3188	9th Dec. 1865	William Wilson Hulse.
An improved construction of tool for cutting tubes. (Communicated by David Mercer Nichols.)	3214	12th Dec. 1865	Alfred Vincent Newton.
Machinery for grinding pit frame, crosscut, mill, carpenters' hand back and other saws, and other like metal surfaces where great truth and accuracy is required	3223	13th Dec. 1865	George Atkin. Edwin Atkin. Alfred Aaron Atkin.
For cutting dye woods, see "Dyes." For cutting files, see "Files and Rasps." For cutting screws, see "Nails."			
D.—Cutting Paper, India-rubber and Tobacco; Cutting and Splitting Leather and Cloth.			
Machinery for the manufacture of "cavendish," "negrohead" and other tobaccos.	60	9th Jan. 1865	William Davies.
Machinery for pressing and cutting tobacco (Communicated by William Woodman Hane.)	122	14th Jan. 1865	Alfred Vincent Newton.
Certain improvements in looms and apparatus for weaving velvet-pile and terry-faced fabrics, and a certain mode of producing designs on such like fabrics. (cutting.)	155	16th Jan. 1865	Joseph Burch.
A new or improved machine for trimming or cutting the edges of books, magazines and such like articles	334	6th Feb. 1865	William Henry Latham. Frederic Cartwright Ward Latham.
Machinery and tools for making collars, cuffs, wristbands and other articles of dress, also adapted for cutting metal blanks	399	13th Feb. 1865	David Harr. William Henry Page. James Clement Newry.
An improved apparatus for shearing and barling all sorts of woven fabrics. (Communicated by Calixte Hippolyte Jean Pierre Denaye and Jean Compagnie.)	517	24th Feb. 1865	William Edward Gedge.

Subject-matter of Patent.	Number of Patent.	Date.	Name of Patentee.
CUTTING, &c.—*continued.*			
Paper and cloth-lined paper collars for ladies and gentlemen.	656	24th Feb. 1865	Solomon Falkly Coy.
Certain improvements in apparatus for cutting paper, pasteboard and similar substances.	657	28th Feb. 1866	Mark Mason.
Improvements in machinery employed in the manufacture of paper, part of which is applicable to drying cylinders for other purposes.	681	2nd March 1865	James Park.
Improvements in cutting sheets of India-rubber and like materials into strips or threads, and in machinery or apparatus for the purpose.	686	9th March 1865	Benoni Collins.
An improved machine for cutting button-holes (*Communicated by George Rehfus.*)	687	11th March 1865	Julius Garelly.
Apparatus for cutting pasteboard and other like boards. (*Communicated by Elizur Ely Clarke.*)	786	21st March 1865	William Clark.
Manufacture of letter slips, book markers, paper knives and clips for suspending stationery, drapery and pictures, and for other such like purposes	935	3rd April 1865	{ Thomas Corbett. Robert Harrington.
Dissected maps and charts (*Communicated by François Auguste Lamerisque.*)	1197	24th April 1865	Henri Adrien Bonneville.
An improved cigar cutter	1129	24th April 1865	Henry Charles Batcher.
Certain improvements in mechanism or apparatus for making and cutting cardboard.	1366	17th May 1866	William Haigh.
Apparatus for "lap" and "surface shaving," the splitting and levelling of leather and other like substances, in sheets and strips.	1635	17th June 1865	Henry Evrard Clifton.
Machinery for cutting fustian and like fabrics	1814	8th July 1865	{ Benoni Collins. John Butterfield.
Instruments used in cutting the soles of boots and shoes.	1888	14th July 1865	John Pusey Wirt.
Improvements in the manufacture of velvets, plushes and other pile fabrics, and in the machinery or apparatus connected therewith. (*cutting and operating the pile.*)	1937	26th July 1865	Jules Bélizard, the younger.
Machinery or apparatus for cutting the edges of paper hangings.	1985	29th July 1865	Alfred Augustus Larmuth.
Improvements in reducing vegetable fibre to pulp, and in machinery employed therein.	2002	2nd Aug. 1865	William Wharton Burdon.
Machinery for manufacturing cigars (*Communicated by John Prentice.*)	2052	4th Aug. 1865	Alfred Vincent Newton.
Printing machines	2086	8th Aug. 1865	William Rock.
Improved machinery or apparatus for reducing the thickness of parts of calf skins or of other skins or hides. (*Communicated by Adolphe Bel.*)	2190	14th Aug. 1865	William Edward Gedge.
Improvements in the manufacture of velvet and in the apparatus employed therein. (*cutting after dyeing.*) (*Communicated by Messieurs Freisz-Brustard, fils jeune.*)	2204	29th Aug. 1865	Henri Adrien Bonneville.
Improvements in cutting the terry or loops of "fustians," cords and similar fabrics, which are also applicable to cutting velvets.	2251	31st Aug. 1865	James Leslie.

Subject-matter of Patent.	Number of Patent.	Date.	Name of Patentee.
CUTTING, &c.—continued.			
Machines for splitting, shaving and paring hides, skins and leather.	2262	6th Sept. 1865	Henry Harrison Doty.
Apparatus for cutting tobacco	2359	15th Sept. 1865	Edward Thornton Reed.
Manufacture of lozenges, cakes and other similar articles, from plastic substances.	2534	3rd Oct. 1865	Charles James Tinker.
Means or apparatus for cutting or shearing the nap or pile of nap or pile fabrics	2547	4th Oct. 1865	William Blakey Storks. James Whitwam. William Blakey.
Improvements in submarine electric telegraph cables and in apparatus connected therewith. (cutting gutta-percha for cables.)	2606	10th Oct. 1865	François Thierry Hubert.
Process of and machinery for preparing flax, hemp, jute, china grass and other analogous vegetable fibres for spinning. (cutting and mixing.)	2728	21st Oct. 1865	James Hill Dickson.
Machinery for cutting and rounding boot and shoe soles of leather and other analogous substances. (Communicated by John Gillingham Felt.)	2916	13th Nov. 1865	Nathaniel Henry Felt.
An improved leather shaving machine	3118	5th Dec. 1865	William Samuel Clederoy.
Machinery for cutting paper	3169	11th Dec. 1865	Thomas Carfield Ushry.
Machinery for splitting leather, shins and other similar articles. (Communicated by Scovil Brown Noyes.)	3277	19th Dec. 1865	George Tomlinson Bousfield.
For cutting roots, &c., see "FOOD FOR CATTLE." For cutting sugar, see "SUGAR." For cutting rags for paper-making, see "PAPER." For rasping dye-woods, see "DYES."			
CYLINDERS, ROLLERS, DRUMS; COVERING ROLLERS.			
Apparatus for hulling grain and for reducing granular substances.	63	5th Jan. 1865	Gustav Adolph Buchholz.
Machinery for opening and carding cotton and other fibrous materials. (rubbing rollers.)	90	11th Jan. 1865	Robert Tempest.
Manufacturing ordnance and gun barrels of cast-steel or of homogeneous iron	212	25th Jan. 1865	John Marshall. Henry Mills.
Improvements in the manufacture of ordnance and other like castings and in the apparatus employed therein, also in carriages or moulds for the same. (cylinders of hydraulic pressure.) (Communicated by William James.)	296	2nd Feb. 1865	John Henry Johnson.
Mills for grinding wheat and other grain (teeth of grinding cylinder.)	333	6th Feb. 1865	William Pickford Wilkins.
An improved composition as a substitute for leather or other similar materials (for cotton gin rollers.)	468	14th Feb. 1865	Christopher Brakell. William Hochl. William Günther.

Subject-matter of Patent.	Number of Patent.	Date.	Name of Patentee.
**CYLINDERS, &c.—*continued.* **			
Certain improvements in mechanism or apparatus for lubricating the cylinders of "slashing" and "taping" machines, such machinery being employed in the sizing of cotton and other yarns.	468	18th Feb. 1865	Thomas Ogden.
Circular box looms (*card cylinders.*)	469	22nd Feb. 1865	John Keighley. Richard Shepherd.
Cotton gins (*Communicated by François Durand.*)	531	24th Feb. 1865	Edmond Paul Henri Gondouin.
Improvements in machinery employed in the manufacture of paper, part of which is applicable to drying cylinders for other purposes.	561	2nd March 1865	James Park.
Machinery for scutching and refining flax and other vegetable substances.	627	6th March 1865	Andrew Potts.
Cotton gins	673	10th March 1865	Evan Leigh.
Machinery for preparing flax, hemp and other fibrous materials requiring like treatment	680	10th March 1865	Joseph Nasmyth. Nasmyth McKibourn.
Machinery or apparatus for rolling, shaping or forging metals. (*formation of rolls.*)	701	12th March 1865	Robert Marsden.
Machinery or apparatus to be employed in the bleaching and dyeing of hanks or skeins of yarns and threads. (*construction of rollers.*)	718	14th March 1865	Longin Cazteri.
Certain improvements in a non-conducting composition for preventing the radiation or transmission of heat, or cold. (*for coating cylinders.*)	864	27th March 1865	Ferdinand Le Roy.
File cutting machinery (*Communicated by Alfred Ford.*)	888	29th March 1865	William Browhes.
Improvements in the treatment of wool and the dressing of flour, and the machinery and apparatus employed therein.	898	30th March 1865	William Harcury.
An improved manufacture of inking rollers (*Communicated by Lewis Francis and Cyrus Lautrel.*)	914	31st March 1865	Alfred Vincent Newton.
Improvements in wringing machines, parts of which are applicable to the construction of rollers. (*Communicated by Stephen Wing and Henry Holly.*)	922	1st April 1865	Henry Lewis.
Improved apparatus for reducing wheat and other straw.	968	6th April 1865	Richard Garrett, jun'.
Machinery for cutting files	1018	9th April 1865	Thomas Turton.
Printing machinery	1026	11th April 1865	David Payne.
An improved metallic preparation or composition for cleaning, sharpening, burnishing and grinding articles of cutlery, edge tools or cutting instruments, and for grinding the cards or rollers of carding engines and the surfaces of cylinders, and covering rollers for various kinds of woollen and cotton machinery.	1054	13th April 1865	George Mountsford.
Certain improvements in looms for weaving	1081	13th April 1865	Christopher Tarner. Thomas Ravn.
Manufacture of a compound or material to be used as a substitute for india-rubber. (*Communicated by Henry Lamerabrg and Emile Ormier.*)	1088	15th April 1865	William Clark.

Subject-matter of Patent.	Number of Patent.	Date.	Name of Patentee.
CYLINDERS, &c.—*continued.*			
Machines for setting or minsing emst, oart and other substances.	1077	17th April 1865	Albert Ward Hale.
Cushions for steam cylinders (Communicated by Henry Johnson.)	1079	14th April 1865	Frederick Collier Bakewell.
Manufacture of tin and terne plates	1081	14th April 1865	John James Jenkins.
An improved machine for straightening, bending, curving and circling beams, bars and plates of iron or other metals.	1082	18th April 1865	John Todd.
Construction of ships or vessels or cars to float on water.	1083	18th April 1865	William Bedder.
Certain improvements in looms for weaving	1086	19th April 1865	James Edward Hyde Andrew.
Machinery for carding cotton and other fibrous substances and for doubling yarns	1094	20th April 1865	James Hall. William Dunkerley. Samuel Schofield.
An improved packing for steam cylinders, stuffing boxes and closed vessels containing water, air or gases, and for other similar purposes. (Communicated by Frederic Henry Brislmann and Ernest Frederic Warkwitz the younger.)	1113	21st April 1865	Edward Thomas Hughes.
Improvements in taking impressions from the grain of wood, and in transferring the same on to various surfaces	1117	21st April 1865	William Scarratt. William Dean.
Engines, machinery and implements employed in ploughing and tilling land.	1120	21st April 1865	Collinson Hall.
Digging machinery	1124	22nd April 1865	Ormrod Coffren Evam.
Machinery for preparing and spinning cotton and other fibrous substances.	1126	22nd April 1865	Edward Lord.
Improvements in motive-power machinery for cultivating land, part of which improvements is applicable to driving machinery generally	1154	22nd April 1865	James Howard. Edward Tenney Bousfield.
Improved means or apparatus for printing felts, floor cloths, carpets and woven fabrics.	1156	25th April 1865	John Wilkinson the younger.
Improvements in steering ships or vessels, and in the machinery or apparatus connected therewith.	1157	25th April 1865	William Elder.
Improvements in the manufacture of waterproof fabrics and in apparatus to be employed therein	1160	25th April 1865	John Collins Wickham. Auguste Edward Deiss.
Improvements applicable to rollers of machinery for preparing and spinning fibrous substances, which improvements are also applicable to other rollers which are pressed towards each other.	1160	25th April 1865	William Oxley.
Machinery for cutting or shaping masts, spars and other beams and articles of wood.	1170	27th April 1865	Samuel Harvey.
Furnaces used for smelting and melting iron and other metals.	1189	27th April 1865	William Balh.
Apparatus employed in the reburning of animal charcoal.	1198	29th April 1865	Thomas White.
Machinery or apparatus for working or cutting coal or minerals, and for compressing or exhausting air to be employed therein or for other purposes, some parts of which apparatus are also applicable to upright shafts, and other parts for regulating the flow or discharge of steam or other elastic fluids.	1208	29th April 1865	William Lashham.

Subject-matter of Patent.	Number of Patent.	Date.	Name of Patentee.
CYLINDERS, &c.—continued.			
Steam-engines (Communicated by Ebenezer Donford.)	1284	6th May 1865	William Edward Newton.
Certain improvements in hydraulic presses for packing cotton and other materials or substances, and in the boxes for containing the same	1290	9th May 1865	Edward Taylor Bellhouse. William John Dorning.
Improvements in power looms for weaving and in apparatus connected therewith.	1307	11th May 1865	William Jamieson.
An improvement in the drawing and other rollers used in preparing and spinning cotton and other fibrous materials and textile manufactures. (Communicated by Amos Askam Taylor.)	1439	25th May 1865	William Edward Newton.
Improvements in ornamenting japanned surfaces and in machinery or apparatus for that purpose. (Forming the rollers.)	1464	27th May 1865	Leonard Brierley.
Instruments or apparatus for rimming the interior of tubes or hollow cylinders, gas chimneys and other hollow articles.	1479	30th May 1865	James Hare the younger.
Certain improvements in the formation and construction of metallic vessels, chambers or hollow cylinders used in hydraulic apparatus, cannon or heavy guns, and for like purposes.	1506	1st June 1865	Herbert Allman.
Machinery or apparatus for bending and straightening angle iron, T iron and other iron bars.	1532	5th June 1865	Charles De Bergue.
Caloric or heated air engines (Communicated by Cyrus W. Baldwin and Walter Davis Richards.)	1563	8th June 1865	Samuel Blatchford Tucker.
Spinning of cotton and other fibrous materials	1574	9th June 1865	Julius De Hemptinne.
Apparatus for printing wool, worsted or other fibrous materials.	1580	10th June 1865	John Henderson.
An improved machine for rutting or curving collars and cuffs.	1589	12th June 1865	George Knight.
Improvements in the manufacture or shaping of iron intended for the shoes of horses and other animals, and in machinery employed therein. (Communicated by Hector Edward Bastien.)	1629	16th June 1865	Richard Archibald Brooman.
An improved composition for the manufacture of printers' rollers.	1694	24th June 1865	Frederic Germain David.
Machines for making paper board	1756	3rd July 1865	John Franklin James.
An improved combination of materials for the manufacture of carpets, floor cloth, felt, wall paper, fireproof flexible roofing, ship and boat building and for other similar purposes. (printing and spinning rollers.)	1775	5th July 1865	John Longbottom. Abram Longbottom.
Mandrils for rollers such as are used for printing or embossing	1850	11th July 1865	David Fulton. John Fulton.
Processes and machinery for producing fibres suitable for being spun, from rags or remnants of woven or other textile fabrics made of silk, wool, cotton or other fibrous materials.	1881	19th July 1865	Henry Ernest Gülcher.
Apparatus for propelling vessels	1890	20th July 1865	Cortland Herbert Simpson.
Covers for rollers used in spinning cotton	1901	21st July 1865	George Taylor. Joseph Crowley.
Manufacture of iron and steel (rollers for rolling.) (Communicated by Martin Diosdado and Henraux.)	1904	27th July 1865	Ephraim Sabel.

Subject-matter of Patent.	Number of Patent.	Date.	Name of Patentee.
CYLINDERS, &c.—continued.			
Machinery to be used in the manufacture of plate or sheet iron and steel. (Communicated by Martin Diredume! Henneur.)	2012	3rd Aug. 1865	Ephraim Babri.
Apparatus applicable as a motive-power engine, a pump or fluid meter. (Communicated by Francis Bernard de Kerunware.)	2021	4th Aug. 1865	William Clark.
Machinery or apparatus for sizing, drying and braiming yarns of cotton or other fibrous substances - - - - - -	2023	4th Aug. 1865	John Gaskroger. John Dodgeon.
Machinery or apparatus for washing wool and other fibrous materials.	2039	5th Aug. 1865	John Petrie, jun'.
Printing machines - - - - -	2056	8th Aug. 1865	William Rock.
Machinery for moulding hollow articles, in earth, clay and other like materials.	2084	11th Aug. 1865	Robert Williams Armstrong.
An improved covering for rollers or cylinders	2157	22nd Aug. 1865	James Alfred Turser.
Steam hammers - - - - -	2174	24th Aug. 1865	David Davies.
Construction of hydrostatic presses - - -	2206	6th Sept. 1865	John Werms. William Werms.
Magnetic telegraphs - - - - (roller.) Communicated by Robert Kirk Boyle and Onisyppe Topliuber.)	2356	14th Sept. 1865	William Clark.
Apparatus for lubricating machinery - - - (cylinders.) (Communicated by Joseph Bouillon.)	2429	23rd Sept. 1865	Henri Adrien Bonneville.
Presses worked by steam and hydraulic power - } (steam cylinder.)	2447	25th Sept. 1865	William Routledge. Frederick Francis Ont nunnhey.
Machinery or apparatus for preparing and spinning cotton and other fibrous materials.	2476	27th Sept. 1865	William Tatham.
Compositions used for coating metallic surfaces - } (steam cylinders.)	2480	27th Sept. 1865	John Bodey. Clarke William Smith.
Apparatus for grinding cards of carding-engines -	2518	30th Sept. 1865	Samuel Faulkner.
Improvements in the manufacture of short iron or steel cylinders for boilers and similar articles, and in the apparatus relating thereto. (Communicated by Benoit Bausiard.)	2529	3rd Oct. 1865	Henri Adrien Bonneville.
Machinery for shaping metal and other substances - (constructing the rolls.)	2553	5th Oct. 1865	Hesketh Hughes.
Apparatus for propelling vessels - - - (Communicated by Clésanthe St. Coumbury.)	2601	9th Oct. 1865	William Clark.
Improvements in submarine electric telegraph cables and in apparatuses connected therewith.	2606	10th Oct. 1865	François Thierry Hubert.
Double or single action pumps - - - (Communicated by Clésude Gavin.)	2623	11th Oct. 1865	William Edward Gedge.
Heating calender bowls and other cylinders or rollers.	2638	13th Oct. 1865	William Mather.
Machinery employed for crushing, amalgamating and washing gold quartz and other materials or matters containing gold or other metal. (Communicated by James Hart.)	2643	13th Oct. 1865	William Halse Gatty Jones.
Certain improvements in machinery or apparatus for preparing and spinning cotton and other fibrous substances.	2651	14th Oct. 1865	Godfrey Anthony Ermen.

Subject-matter of Patent.	Number of Patent	Date.	Name of Patentee.
CYLINDERS, &c.—continued.			
Improvements in steam-boilers and other apparatus applicable to the heating and evaporation of liquids, parts of which improvements are applicable also to other purposes	2661	16th Oct. 1865	Francis Wise. Edward Field. Enoch Harrison Aydon.
Machinery for weaving the covering of blind-cord and other tubular fabrics. (Communicated by Isaac Emerson Palmer.)	2661	17th Oct. 1866	Henry Edward Newton.
Rollers for washing yarns and fabrics and for other purposes	2666	16th Oct. 1865	William Schofield. John Smith.
A new or improved sifter for sifting cinders, slack and gravel, and for other like purposes.	2669	18th Oct. 1865	Charles Henry Cope.
Manufacture of covers applicable to drawing or printing rollers and as endless blankets	2716	20th Oct. 1865	Manuel Leopold Jonas Lavater. John Kershaw.
An improved method of hanging or suspending blinds from blind rollers, and improvements in the manufacture of such rollers.	2762	21st Oct. 1865	Samuel Parkes Matthews.
Improvements in roller skates, and in the rollers to be used therewith and for other purposes.	2770	27th Oct. 1865	Robert Bell Sasson.
Generating steam in combined vertical cylinders	2776	28th Oct. 1865	Thomas Brown Jordan.
Certain new or improved machinery for the manufacture of nails. (rolls.)	2789	30th Oct. 1866	William Whittle.
Apparatus for grinding and pointing the cards on carding engines. (grinding rollers.)	2972	9th Nov. 1865	Robert Swires.
Certain improvements in mechanism or apparatus to be employed for lubricating the cylinders of steam-engines, or other similar frictional surfaces	2961	9th Nov. 1865	Neville Beard. John Maiden.
A new or improved method of preventing the escape of heat from steam cylinders	3051	24th Nov. 1865	William Simons. Andrew Brown.
An improved apparatus for stretching and rolling fabrics for dyeing. (stretching roller.) (Communicated by Messieurs Jules Weber and Victor Jacques.)	6069	29th Nov. 1865	Hector Auguste Dufresné.
"Top rollers" employed in the manufacture of fibrous substances.	3075	30th Nov. 1865	John Kerfoot.
Manufacture of metal tubes (grooved rolls.)	3117	5th Dec. 1865	Philip Albert Muntz.
Steam-engines (Communicated by George Brader Whiting and Thomas Fitch Rowland.)	3506	22nd Dec. 1865	William Clark.
Preparation of glue or gelatine so as to render it insoluble in water, and applicable by the admixture of other substances to various purposes for which common glue or gelatine cannot now be used. (for printers' inking rollers.) (Communicated by Henry Warts.)	6226	23rd Dec. 1865	William Edward Newton.
Improvements in the manufacture of axles for carriages and spindles for various purposes, and in machinery to be employed in the said manufacture, part of which improvements in machinery may also be applied to other purposes (constructing rolls.)	3336	26th Dec. 1865	Elias Lones. Joseph Constant Lones. John Lones. John Brettell. Thomas Brettell. Charles Vernon.

Subject-matter of Patent.	Number of Patent.	Date.	Name of Patentee.
CYLINDERS, &c.—continued.			
An improved method of and apparatus for preserving, purifying, mixing, separating, cooling, aërating, roasting and otherwise treating grain, corn and various other matters. (cylinders or drums.)	8344	27th Dec. 1865	Gaston Charles Ange Marquis D'Auxy.
Apparatus for expanding or keeping fabrics straight in passing into, " through " or out of any machine, or over, under or upon rollers	3375	29th Dec. 1865	{ William Edleston. John Schofield.
DENTISTRY; ARTIFICIAL TEETH, TOOTH-PICKS.			
An improvement in machines for cutting match splints, tooth-picks and similar articles.	74	10th Jan. 1866	Jonathan Clark Brown.
A new or improved tooth powder	301	3rd Feb. 1865	Benjamin Lewis Mosely.
An improved instrument for concentrating light, applicable to dental, surgical and other operations	591	2nd March 1865	Charles Rahn.
Apparatus to facilitate dental operations	708	13th March 1865	William Donald Napier.
A new or improved receptacle for tooth powder, and for conveying the same from such receptacle to the tooth brush, so as to economise the use of the powder and to prevent the escape of the perfume with which it may be scented.	2470	27th Sept. 1865	Archer Farr.
Securing artificial teeth in the mouth	3098	2nd Dec. 1865	George Ash.
Apparatus for regulating heat obtained by the combustion of gas. (for vulcanising india-rubber for dentists.)	3263	14th Dec. 1865	Henry Planck.
DESTROYING INSECTS; TRAPS FOR VERMIN, RABBITS, &c.; GAME NETS.			
Vermin and other traps	812	4th Feb. 1865	Robert Sibley Baker.
Vermin traps	959	3rd April 1865	George Kennedy Geyelin.
Traps used for catching rabbits and other animals	1575	18th May 1865	Richard Toomer Birt.
Vermin traps	1886	19th July 1865	James Miles.
An improved apparatus for scattering lime, guano or other artificial manure, either in a dry or liquid state, or for scattering disinfectants. (or destroying turnip flies.)	2846	4th Nov. 1865	Alexander Jemmett.
Obtaining and employing continuous lengths of tanned leather for various useful purposes (for game nets.)	3234	23rd Dec. 1865	{ George Horn. Daniel Horn.

Subject-matter of Patent.	Number of Patent.	Date.	Name of Patentee.
DISINFECTING, DEODORIZING, PERFUMING.			
Impregnating air for hygienic or therapeutic purposes with the vapours or emanations arising from tar, creosote or other suitable liquid antiseptic or antiputrid substances, or disseminating in the air for the said purposes suitable pulverized substances.	112	13th Jan. 1865	Antoine Joseph Sav.
An improved apparatus for containing and dispersing scents and other liquids.	194	23rd Jan. 1865	Edward Atkinson.
Improvements in treating sewage and in arranging apparatus in sewers and culverts to facilitate the ventilation of such structures.	451	16th Feb. 1865	Richard Smith.
A new apparatus for ejecting and spreading liquids and powder.	1044	12th April 1865	Gaspard Alfred Montenot.
Utilizing the stalks, smells and waste of tobacco for certain purposes. (fumigating greenhouses.)	1644	13th July 1865	George Clayton Collyer. Charles Lewis Roberts.
Ventilators (for diffusing disinfectants.)	1698	18th July 1865	John Paul Bough Le Patourel.
A new or improved apparatus for supplying disinfecting liquids to water-closets, urinals and other places requiring the same.	1679	19th July 1865	Charles Nicholas.
A combination of improved method, apparatus and receptacles for storing, preserving, transferring, and discharging certain fluids, for sanitary and protective purposes. (Communicated by Henry Pinkus.)	2096	14th Aug. 1865	Robert Alexander William Westley.
Improvements in apparatus by means of which certain liquids, common air, and certain elastic fluids are made available in the production of light, and their quantity regulated and measured, parts of which improvements are applicable for other purposes. (impregnating the air with disinfectants.)	2184	25th Aug. 1865	Edwin Augustus Curley.
An improved apparatus for the distribution of perfumes, disinfecting or other fluids.	2240	13th Sept. 1865	James Dunbar. James William Butler.
An improved arrangement of apparatus and materials to be employed for effecting the deodorising of the noxious gases arising from sewers and drains, and for the more effectual ventilation and inspection of such sewers and drains.	2461	25th Sept. 1865	Edward Brooke the younger.
Trapping and ventilating sewers	2514	10th Oct. 1865	Richard Ahsil.
The utilisation of town sewage for agricultural purposes, and also to prevent the pollution of rivers and streams, and the machinery and apparatus for effecting the same.	2520	12th Oct. 1865	John Linton.
An improved preparation or composition for coating, covering or coloring walls and other surfaces or parts of buildings, and for forming mouldings, cornices and other decorative parts of houses. (disinfectant.)	2539	12th Oct. 1865	William Darwick.
Manufacture of chemical toys known as Pharaoh's serpents. (perfuming.)	2594	18th Oct. 1865	Thomas King.
Treatment and decolorization of sewage water	2608	31st Oct. 1865	Henry Young Darracott Scott.

Subject-matter of Patent.	Number of Patent.	Date.	Name of Patentee.
DISINFECTING, &c.—continued.			
An improved apparatus for scattering lime, guano or other artificial manures, either in a dry or liquid state, or for scattering disinfectants.	2846	4th Nov. 1865	Alexander Jennett.
Improvements in disinfecting stables and cattle sheds, and in the apparatus employed therein.	3075	30th Nov. 1865	John Gamgee.
Manufacture of disinfectants	3115	4th Dec. 1865	John Thomlinson.
An improved mode of and apparatus for purifying and deodorising impure air, whether in buildings, ships, mines or sewers, which improvement is also applicable for ventilating purposes.	3237	20th Dec. 1865	{ Joseph John Harrison. Edward Harrison.
A new and improved apparatus for cooling and purifying air in rooms or compartments, and ventilating the same. (Communicated by Axel Storrs Lyman.)	3293	20th Dec. 1865	William Clark.
Compounds for deodorising and disinfecting .	3355	24th Dec. 1865	{ Edward Vincent Gardner. Louis Ash Israel. Henry Ash Israel, jun'.
Revivifying, decolorising and calcining animal and vegetable charcoal and other matters.	3372	29th Dec. 1865	William Cormack.

DISTILLING AND RECTIFYING.

1.—Alcoholic Distillation, Manufacture of Spirituous Liquors.

Subject-matter of Patent.	Number of Patent.	Date.	Name of Patentee.
Improvements in the rectification of alcohol, and in the apparatus to be employed therein. (Communicated by Adrienne Anastasie Foubert.)	250	28th Jan. 1865	William Edward Newton.
Condensation and refrigeration of vapours and fluids. (in distilling.)	572	1st March 1865	George Harman Barth.
Apparatus for distilling, purifying and storing spirituous liquors.	574	1st March 1865	Carl Johan Falkman.
Improvements in securing low and uniform temperature, applicable to public and private buildings, also to refrigerators, coolers and condensers, and to ships and other vessels, and in the apparatus employed therein. (cooling apparatus for distilleries.) (Communicated by Daniel Somes.)	719	14th March 1865	Alfred Vincent Newton.
Machinery or apparatus employed in brewing and distilleries.	1204	29th April 1865	Francis Gregory.
Improvements in brewing, distillation, the production of vinegar, and the extract of malt and other grain.	1349	5th May 1865	Solomon Barrett.
Apparatus for measuring spirits . . . (Communicated by John Hutchings Cox, John Murphy and William Murphy.)	1372	6th May 1865	John Henry Johnson.
Improvements in drying malt and grain, and in the machinery or apparatus connected therewith.	1397	10th May 1865	John Forbes.
Improvements in distilling and rectifying, and in the apparatus employed therein, parts of which improvements are applicable to steam generators.	1582	20th June 1865	Evariste Vignier.

Subject-matter of Patent.	Number of Patent.	Date.	Name of Patentee.
DISTILLING, &c.—*continued*.			
An improved brewers' and distillers' refrigerator or apparatus for cooling liquids, condensing steam or other vapours.	1700	26th June 1865	Morris Ashby.
Improvements in the raising, lifting or drawing and forcing of water and other liquids, and in the apparatus and means employed therefor (*for distilleries*.)	1996	2nd Aug. 1865	James McEwan. William Neilson.
Improvements in brewing and distilling, also in drying yeast, and in the apparatus employed.	2019	4th Aug. 1865	Patrick Robertson.
Apparatus for regulating the passage or flow of steam, water and other fluids.	2043	7th Aug. 1865	Adrienne Anastasie Fonbert.
An improved construction of spirit meter - (*Communicated by Edward Payne.*)	2193	26th Aug. 1865	John Fullock Heazey.
Construction of apparatus for distilling and rectifying alcohols. (*Communicated by François Désiré Savalle.*)	2208	24th Aug. 1865	Henri Adrien Bonneville.
Improvements in evaporating and distilling liquids, and in the apparatus employed therein.	2590	7th Oct. 1866	Tomlin Campbell.
An improved manufacture of caramel - (*for colouring brandy.*) (*Communicated by Thaddeus Hyatt.*)	2960	16th Nov. 1865	Alfred Vincent Newton.
Treatment of spirituous liquors -	2962	17th Nov. 1865	Patrick Joseph Fallon.
Fining, purifying and mellowing spirituous liquors by combining therewith other substances, for the production of a new spirituous or vinous compound therefrom.	3071	30th Nov. 1865	William Thompson.
Improvements in distilling and in relieving distilled and other liquids from gases mechanically mixed therewith. (*See "* FILTERING.*"*) For distilling water, see "FILTERING."	3351	27th Dec. 1865	Norman Willis Wheeler.
II.—Bituminous, Resinous, and Oleaginous Distillation.			
Apparatus for distilling petroleum and other volatile liquids and for making gas. (*Communicated by George Hughes Sinclair Duffus.*)	447	16th Feb. 1865	William Edward Newton.
Certain improvements in the manufacture of magnesium and its compounds - (*useful in distilling for water.*)	456	17th Feb. 1865	John Osborne Christian, F.C.S. John Charlton. Henry Charlton.
Improvements in distilling bituminous substances and in apparatus employed therein.	571	1st March 1865	James Young.
Apparatus for distilling oils and other liquids from coal and other substances. (*Communicated by William George Washington Jasper.*)	787	15th March 1865	William Edward Newton.
Apparatus for the distillation of coal and peat, and such other substances as are or may be used for the manufacture of solid and liquid volatile hydrocarbons, or for the manufacture of the said hydrocarbons and coke.	796	22nd March 1865	William Mattieu Williams.
Improvements in distilling hydrocarbons from coals, shale and other minerals.	1078	17th April 1866	Joseph Dungea.

Subject-matter of Patent.	Number of Patent.	Date.	Name of Patentee.
DISTILLING, &c.,—continued.			
Apparatus used in distilling hydrocarbons -	1361	16th May 1865	George Walton.
Distilling apparatus - - - -	1363	21th May 1865	John Ambrose Coffey.
An improved method and apparatus for distilling coal shale and other carbonaceous substances. (Communicated by John Howarth.)	1553	7th June 1865	James Howarth, M.D.
Treatment of hydrocarbon or paraffin oils -	2009	3rd Aug. 1865	John William Perkins.
Stills for the distillation of petroleum and other oily substances.	2040	5th Aug. 1865	Adolph Millochau.
Obtaining spirits of turpentine, rosin, pitch, tar, pyroligneous acid and other products from wood. (Communicated by Albert Hamilton Emery.)	2347	31st Aug. 1865	William Edward Newton.
Apparatus for extracting oil from coal shale and other minerals.	2544	4th Oct. 1865	Allan Craig.
Improvements in the distillation of coal and shale, and in the apparatus employed thereon.	2703	30th Oct. 1865	Edward Meldrum.
Manufacture or purification of hydrocarburets, and especially of petroleum oils used for lighting purposes. (Communicated by Doctor Pierre Gédéon Barry and Chevalier Barthélemy Drysle.)	2945	15th Nov. 1865	William Clark.
Apparatus for the production of hydrocarbon or other vapours, parts of which apparatus are also applicable to measuring gaseous or fluid matter.	2972	14th Nov. 1865	Frederick Wilkins.
Apparatus for distilling oils and condensing oily vapours.	3101	2nd Dec. 1865	Thomas Newton Barnin.
Obtaining oil and other products from bituminous shale - - - - - }	3296	20th Dec. 1865	{ John Watson. { John Player.
Treating hydrocarbon oils - - - -	3345	27th Dec. 1865	James Young, jun'.
See also "GAS."			
DOCKS, HARBOURS, BREAKWATERS, PIERS, LANDING-STAGES, CANALS, SEA-WALLS, SUBMARINE WORKS, WEIRS.			
An improved machine for raising and carrying earth, mud, stones or other similar solid or liquid materials for dredging, ventilating, or winnowing grain, or other analogous purposes.	174	20th Jan. 1865	Louis Balme.
A new method for removing or destroying the momentum of heavy bodies by means of an elastic machine or machines, so as to prevent injury and damage from concussion, applicable to ship cables, ship and fort armour, railway trains, tenders to pier heads, and floating piers, gangways, breakwaters and other similar structures, also as a motive power. (Communicated by William Graham M'Ivor.)	331	6th Feb. 1865	Clement Robert Markham.
Protecting wooden surfaces from the fouling and injury to which they are ordinarily liable in sea water. (piers, breakwaters, &c.)	363	9th Feb. 1865	John Cornelius Craigie Halkett.

Subject-matter of Patent.	Number of Patent.	Date.	Name of Patentee.
DOCKS, &c.—*continued.*			
Formation of embankments, sea-walls, breakwaters and other similar constructions. (*Communicated by Frederic Gherr.*)	220	10th Feb. 1865	William Edward Newton.
Improvements in driving piles and in apparatus therefor - - - - - (*for harbours, piers, docks, wharves, &c.*)	567	3rd March 1865	{ David Manwell, James Manwell.
Dredgers - - - - -	538	24th March 1865	{ William Simons, Andrew Brown.
An improvement in paints or compositions used for coating iron or wooden vessels, and other structures exposed to the action of sea-water. (*piers, piles, &c.*)	871	24th March 1865	John Cornelius Craigie Halkett.
An improved composition for preventing the fouling of ships and other vessels. (*Communicated by William Baker Davis.*)	1006	4th April 1865	George Davies.
An improved mode of and apparatus for deepening the bottom or bed of rivers, canals, harbours or other similar places.	1017	10th April 1865	Charles François Gbrerbrant.
Construction of ships or vessels or cars to float on water.	1063	14th April 1865	William Hedder.
An improved composition for coating iron or other vessels, and for other similar purposes. (*piers, &c.*)	1278	9th May 1865	John Cornelius Craigie Halkett.
Manufacture of iron plate or erections, applicable more especially for carrying bridges at high elevations, or available for sheer legs and light-houses.	1533	5th June 1865	Charles De Fergue.
Method of constructing partitions, walls, floors and roofs of buildings.	1598	13th June 1865	John James Bodmer.
Floating docks - - - -	1682	24th June 1865	George Turton.
A new and improved mode of elevating ships or boats in the water, to enable them to pass over sand bars, shallows and the like, and for raising sunken vessels and docks.	1825	12th July 1865	Thomas Cato M'Kern.
Applying and utilising water power - - (*pumping docks.*)	1967	29th July 1865	Valentine Baker.
Improvements in the raising, lifting or drawing and forcing of water and other liquids, and in the apparatus and means employed therefor. (*from docks.*)	1996	2nd Aug. 1865	{ James M'Ewan, William Nellson.
An improved apparatus to facilitate the cleansing and examination of the bottoms of ships and other submerged structures.	2162	22nd Aug. 1865	Dennis Owen Jones.
Caissons for closing the entrances of docks and canals.	2364	15th Sept. 1865	Henry Law.
Floating dry docks - - -	2407	19th Sept. 1865	Edwin Clark.
New or improved means and apparatus for destroying ships and such like floating bodies, parts of which said apparatus are also applicable to saving life and property at sea. (*defending harbours.*) (*Communicated by Monsieur Stanislas Sorel.*)	2755	26th Oct. 1865	Hector Auguste Dubreul.
A new and improved cement - -} (*for breakwaters.*)	2863	7th Nov. 1865	{ Thomas Oraeon, James O'Donoghue.

Subject-matter of Patent.	Number of Patent.	Date.	Name of Patentee.

Docks, &c.—continued.

| Improvements in the hulls and tackle of navigable vessels, and in the gear for propelling the same by wind and steam or other motive-power engine, and clearing the same from water, and in apparatus connected therewith, to enable the said vessels to be converted in floating graving docks, or lifts for raising vessels and other submerged or partially submerged heavy bodies to or above the surface of the water. | 3091 | 25th Nov. 1865 | John Ferrar. |

Doors and Gates; Door Furniture.

Fastenings for doors, windows, drawers and other like purposes - - - -	399	9th Feb. 1865	George Edward Meek, William Howes Howes.
Fire and thief proof safes, chests and strong room doors.	548	27th Feb. 1865	Walter Henry Tucker.
Improved iron doors especially adapted for use in ordinary buildings.	660	9th March 1865	Joseph Thomas Harris.
Construction of fastenings or bolts for window sashes and other purposes.	672	10th March 1865	William Smith.
Fire and burglar proof safes, chests, doors and iron rooms.	696	11th March 1865	John Tann.
An improvement in securing safes and strong rooms	702	13th March 1865	Henry Hill.
Certain improvements in the fastenings to be employed in metallic "safes" or other similar depositories - - - -	803	31st March 1865	William Milner, Daniel Rowlinson Ratcliff.
Construction of safes or depositories intended to contain valuable property.	804	31st March 1865	Thomas Cook.
Improvements in locks, and in fixing knobs and spindles to doors and latches.	946	4th April 1865	Richard Nobbs.
Securing the doors of safes and other doors -	948	4th April 1865	George Carr Thompson.
Door locks and latches - - - -	1043	12th April 1865	John Walker.
Bolting and locking arrangements for safe and other doors.	1045	13th April 1865	John Matthias Hart.
Iron safes and strong rooms - - -	1056	13th April 1865	John Chubb, Robert Gomer.
Indicators and fastenings for water-closets and other purposes.	1096	20th April 1865	Henry Kindon Taylor.
Invalid carriages - - - - - (Communicated by Auguste Quitsow.)	1130	21st April 1865	Henry Edward Newton.
Locks and lock furniture	1194	29th April 1865	Walter Henry Tucker.
An improved system of telegraphic communication on railways, parts of which invention are also applicable to other telegraphic purposes.	1543	5th June 1865	Alice Isabel Lucas Gordon.
Fastenings for doors, windows, drawers and other like purposes	1578	9th June 1865	George Edward Meek, William Howes Howes.
Improved means or apparatus to be applied to doors and windows for the purpose of supporting or maintaining them in any required position when open, and in securing them when shut.	1581	10th June 1865	Arthur Hamilton Gilmour.

Subject-matter of Patent.	Number of Patent.	Date.	Names of Patentees.
DOORS, &c.—continued.			
Preventing the forcing or wedging open iron safes, iron doors and strong rooms - - -	1557	20th June 1865	James Parrish. Charles Thatcher. Thomas Glascock.
Construction of safes or strong receptacles for the protection of property.	1911	22nd July 1865	William Diaper.
Improved mechanical arrangements or fastenings applicable to the doors and cases of safes and strong rooms, for the purpose of preventing the opening thereof by wedges or levers - -	1986	2nd Aug. 1865	Thomas Andrew. James Whiley Taylor.
Improvements in the construction of railway carriages and in railway breaks and signals, part of which is applicable to marine purposes - -	2005	2nd Aug. 1865	William Henry Petitjean. Edward McNally.
Burglar proof safes - - - - -	2006	2nd Aug. 1865	Herbert Allman.
An improved mode of retaining and preventing the vibration of sliding windows used in dwellings and in railway and other vehicles, and for an improved apparatus for effecting the said purposes - - - - - (or vibration of doors.)	2232	30th Aug. 1865	Thomas Wrigley. Marcus Brown Westhead.
Improvements in the manufacture of metallic safes and strong rooms, and in apparatus connected therewith.	2285	2nd Sept. 1865	Samuel Chatwood.
An improved apparatus or mechanism for locking and unlocking railway carriage doors, and for making signals with reference thereto.	2449	23rd Sept. 1865	John Hawkins Simpson.
Fasteners for doors - - - - -	2559	6th Oct. 1865	Charles Fitz-Gerald.
Improvements in rules for measuring, and in other instruments or articles requiring to be adjusted or disposed at various angles. (doors.)	2613	10th Oct. 1865	Arthur Nicholls.
A new self-adjusting apparatus for railway signals, applicable also to other purposes. (working level crossing gates.)	2715	20th Oct. 1865	George Nassell.
Improved means or apparatus to be applied to doors and windows, for the purpose of supporting or maintaining them in any required position when open, and in securing them when shut.	2819	1st Nov. 1865	Arthur Hamilton Gilmore.
Improvements in the construction of door locks, latches and such like fastenings, and in knob and handle spindles and furniture used therewith.	2859	9th Nov. 1865	Benjamin Pitt.
Manufacture of embossed wood - - - (for panel ornaments.) (Communicated by Henry May and Henry Taylor Blake.)	2895	10th Nov. 1865	Alfred Vincent Newton.
Door springs - - - - - -	2917	13th Nov. 1865	William Williams.
Fastenings for safe doors and other doors and lids, and for other like purposes.	2979	20th Nov. 1865	Joseph Beverley Fenby.
Apparatus for preventing draughts of air between the floor and the lower part of doors.	3050	28th Nov. 1865	Louis Desiré Carbonnier.
Apparatus for increasing the safety of railway passengers and trains, signalling and forming a communication externally and internally between all parts of such trains, lighting, warming and securing the doors of the carriages, and indicating therein and at the stations the names of the places at which the train stops.	3068	29th Nov. 1865	Richard Howarth.

Subject-matter of Patent.	Number of Patent.	Date.	Name of Patentee.
DOORS, &c.—continued.			
Certain improvements in the manufacture of knobs for doors, cupboards, ash-pans, and for other like purposes.	3091	1st Dec. 1865	John Wilson.
A new or improved method of and apparatus for locking and unlocking gates, turnstiles and stiles, on railway crossings.	3158	6th Dec. 1865	George Daws.
Improvements in the construction of safes, strong rooms and other similar depositories, and in the locks thereof.	3189	9th Dec. 1865	Antoine Grivel, the younger.
Improvements in the furniture of door locks and latches, and in the means used in applying the same.	3290	20th Dec. 1865	John Martin.
Improvements in the manufacture of safes and in apparatus connected therewith. (doors.)	3321	23rd Dec. 1865	Samuel Chatwood.
Improvements in safes and in protecting the locks and bolts of safes, and other locks and bolts (applicable to warehouse doors.)	3324	23rd Dec. 1865	Joseph Groves. George Robinson, the younger.
Preparation of glue or gelatine so as to render it insoluble in water, and applicable by the admixture of other substances, to various purposes for which common glue or gelatine cannot now be used. (for door knobs.) (Communicated by Henry Werts.)	3325	23rd Dec. 1865	William Edward Newton.

DRAINS, SEWERS, GUTTERS; DRAIN PIPES AND TILES; DRAINING; STENCH TRAPS.			
An improved machine for raising and carrying earth, mud, stones or other similar solid or liquid materials for dredging, ventilating, or winnowing grain, or other analogous purposes. (for draining.)	174	20th Jan. 1865	Louis Balma.
Working ships' pumps	303	3rd Feb. 1865	Matthew Blank.
An improvement in the manufacture of artificial stone for building and other purposes. (for sinks.)	441	16th Feb. 1865	William Kitrage.
Improvements in treating sewage and in arranging apparatus in sewers and culverts to facilitate the ventilation of such structures.	451	16th Feb. 1865	Richard Smith.
Traps to prevent the uprising of noxious gases in sewers, drains, sinks, shafts and other passages for fumes and other matter.	698	13th March 1865	John Bragg.
Improved apparatus for ascertaining the state of sewers, tunnels, drifts or other subterranean work, part of which apparatus is applicable to levelling purposes.	849	25th March 1865	Richard William Barnes.
Improvements in steam-engines, relating to valve motions, governors and drain pipes	1195	29th April 1865	Andrew Wyllie. John McFarlane Gray.
Manufacture and application of glass and other vitreous compositions (for sinks.)	1230	1st May 1865	Arthur Howard Emerson. Robert Fowler.

Subject-matter of Patent.	Number of Patent.	Date.	Name of Patentee.
DRAINS, &c.—*continued.*			
Apparatus for trenching and laying drain pipes for draining land.	1396	27th May 1865	William Eddington, jun'.
Method of constructing partitions, walls, floors and roofs of buildings.	1599	13th June 1865	John James Bodmer.
An improvement in ejectors for discharging bilge water and for other purposes. (*Communicated by Nathan Leffingwell Chappell and Blair Lorillard.*)	1981	31st July 1865	Alfred Vincent Newton.
Improvements in the raising, lifting or drawing and forcing of water and other liquids, and in the apparatus and means employed therefor. (*from marshes, sewerage, pools, &c.*)	1999	2nd Aug. 1865	{ James McEwan. William Nailson.
An improved gully or stench trap for the prevention of the escape of noxious effluvia from drains or sewers, and for preventing the ingress of mud or other solid matters into the same.	2167	23rd Aug. 1865	John Newton.
An improved stench-trap and sink-pipe protector -	2220	29th Aug. 1865	William Henry Gummer.
An improved apparatus for and method of ascertaining the state of sewers, tunnels, drifts, or other subterranean works, without descending thereinto, by means of the natural, artificial, or magnesium light, part of which apparatus is applicable to levelling purposes.	2446	25th Sept. 1865	Richard William Barors.
An improved arrangement of apparatus and materials to be employed for effecting the deodorising of the noxious gases arising from sewers and drains, and for the more effectual ventilation and inspection of such sewers and drains.	2451	25th Sept. 1865	Edward Brooks, the younger.
Improvements in fittings for stables, cowsheds, and piggeries, and in effluvium traps for stables and other places.	2499	28th Sept. 1865	Edward Cottam.
Trapping and ventilating sewers - - -	2614	10th Oct. 1865	Richard Abell.
The utilization of town sewage for agricultural purposes, and also to prevent the pollution of rivers and streams, and the machinery and apparatus for effecting the same.	2629	12th Oct. 1865	John Linton.
An improved overflow for basins, sinks and baths -	2637	12th Oct. 1865	Hugh Henreton Craigie.
Construction of pumps for raising water and other liquids. (*for collieries.*)	2946	15th Nov. 1865	William Easton.
An improvement in ejectors for discharging bilge water and for other purposes. (*Communicated by Nathan Leffingwell Chappell.*)	3001	22nd Nov. 1865	Alfred Vincent Newton.
A new or improved cement or composition, applicable to the agglomeration or moulding of various materials, and to other useful and decorative purposes. (*making waterproof.*) (*Communicated by Stanislas Sorel and Emile Justin Menier.*)	3119	5th Dec. 1865	Richard Archibald Brooman.
An improved mode of applying the compression of air for ventilating purposes, and the compression of any gas for hurrying along elastic fluids in conveying pipes. (*purifying sewer pits.*)	3163	8th Dec. 1865	{ Firmin de Mondésir. Paul Lehaitre. Augustin Jullienne.

Subject-matter of Patent.	Number of Patent.	Date.	Name of Patentee.
DRAINS, &c.—continued.			
An improved mode of and apparatus for purifying and deodorising impure air, whether in buildings, ships, mines or sewers, which improvement is also applicable for ventilating purposes	3287	20th Dec. 1865	Joseph John Harrison. Edward Harrison.
DRAMATIC AND SCENIC EFFECTS, ILLUSORY EXHIBITIONS, STAGE SCENERY.			
Improved machinery for working all stage scenery in theatres.	181	16th Jan. 1865	Walter Edwin.
A new or improved apparatus for illusory exhibitions	182	26th Jan. 1865	John Henry Pepper. Thomas William Tobin.
Philosophical examination into the alleged spirit manifestations, consisting of a lamp and a close room.	1145	24th April 1865	Owen Greenliffe Warren.
A new or improved method of obtaining or producing optical illusions.	1568	12th June 1865	Gaetan Bonelli.
A new or improved apparatus for illusory exhibitions	1983	1st Aug. 1865	Thomas William Tobin. Coleord Steadam.
Apparatus for illusory exhibitions	3189	6th Dec. 1865	John Henry Pepper. Thomas William Tobin.
A novel optical arrangement by which a new trestle effect is produced.	3294	20th Dec. 1865	Walter Kerr.
DRYING AND STRETCHING; EXPRESSING MOISTURE.			
Manufacturing paper (Communicated by Jules Joseph Maxey.)	15	3rd Jan. 1865	Léopold D'Aubréville.
Apparatus for drying paper in sheets	195	23rd Jan. 1865	Alfred Sheldon.
Filtering apparatuses (and draining or drying.)	249	28th Jan. 1865	Victor Bury.
An improved system of drying wool, cotton and other fibrous materials, and in the machinery or apparatus connected therewith. (Communicated by Carl Brx and Louis Bartteher.)	255	29th Jan. 1865	Edward Thomas Hughes.
An improved clothes fastener, that may also be used as a letter clip. (violet drying.)	388	31st Jan. 1865	James William Gill.
Machinery for washing and drying wool and other fibrous materials	351	1st Feb. 1865	John McNaught. William McNaught, jun'.
Improvements in treating or manufacturing peat for fuel, and in apparatus for the same.	319	4th Feb. 1865	Robert Morellet Alloway.
Apparatus for extracting liquid from solid substances. (See "PRESSES.") (Communicated by Lyman Smith.)	486	21st Feb. 1865	William Edward Newton.

Subject-matter of Patent.	Number of Patent.	Date.	Name of Patentee.
DYEING, &c.—continued.			
Boilers for heating water and delivering it at an equal temperature to any number of flow pipes, and also for the generation of steam. (heating drying rooms.)	449	22nd Feb. 1865	Joseph Hulley.
Manufacture or treatment of floor cloths - -	548	27th Feb. 1865	Michael Barker Nairn.
Improvements in machinery employed in the manufacture of paper, part of which is applicable to drying cylinders for other purposes.	561	2nd March 1865	James Park.
Drying apparatus - - - - - (Communicated by Félix Moumon and Auguste Racinet.)	603	4th March 1865	Henri Adrien Bonneville.
Apparatus for rinsing and drying by centrifugal force. (Communicated by Félix Moumon and Auguste Racinet.)	604	4th March 1865	Henri Adrien Bonneville.
Improvements in drying and sorting coals, peat and mineral ores, in separating extraneous matters therefrom, and in apparatus used in these processes.	716	14th March 1865	Ferdinand Henry Warlich.
Process of preparing kaolin or china clay and other clays for potters' use, and for expelling water from other earthy deposits. (Communicated by Joseph Muir.)	806	22nd March 1865	James Wright.
Improvements in the preparation or treatment of ores used in obtaining products therefrom -	877	28th March 1865	{ Richard Young. Charles Finlay Oliphant Glassford, F.C.N.
Certain improvements in machinery or apparatus for drying "warps" of cotton and other fibrous substances - - - - - -	889	29th March 1865	{ Richard Holroyd. Joseph Holroyd Bolton.
Improved apparatus for expressing liquids from pulpy and semi-fluid substances. (Communicated by Louis Pierre Robert de Massy.)	968	4th April 1865	William Edward Newton.
Fire places and flues and apparatus connected therewith. (flues for drying sheds.)	989	7th April 1865	Edward Welch.
Certain improvements in dyeing or printing upon the fabric known as " mil cloth."	1008	9th April 1865	James Isherwood.
Clamps for stretching frames and other purposes -	1089	12th April 1865	Henry Brideon.
Treating wool in order to cleanse it from burrs, seeds and other foreign matters - -	1042	12th April 1865	{ Henry Sikes. George Jarmain.
Constructing portable hot rooms or chambers for drying cloths and other articles.	1185	24th April 1865	Welburn Williamson.
Improvements in the manufacture of water-proof fabrics, and in apparatus to be employed therein	1189	25th April 1865	{ John Collins Wickham. Auguste Edward Delae.
Dyeing yarns - - - - - - (and stretching yarns whilst dyeing.)	1193	25th April 1865	{ Robert Ferris. John Murray. Adam Wilson.
Machines for drying and stretching woollen and other textile fabrics. (Communicated by Joseph Sprague Winsor.)	1253	3rd May 1865	George Tomlinson Bousfield.
Means and apparatus used for stretching woven fabrics and other materials. (Communicated by Jules Ducommun.)	1258	3rd May 1865	William Clark.
Improvements in drying malt and grain, and in the machinery or apparatus connected therewith.	1297	10th May 1865	John Forbes.

Subject-matter of Patent.	Number of Patent.	Date.	Name of Patentee.

DYEING, &c.—continued.

Subject-matter of Patent.	Number of Patent.	Date.	Name of Patentee.
Machinery or apparatus for stretching and drying textile fabrics, part or parts of which said apparatus are also applicable to other machines wherein fabrics are required to be distended	1290	16th May 1865	James Worrall. Thomas Hughes.
An improved mode of desiccating eggs and apparatus for effecting the same.	1632	16th June 1865	Charles Augustus Lamont.
Sizing machines for sizing yarns, beams or warps to be woven	1729	29th June 1865	David Mercer. Thomas Mercer. Jonathan Mercer. Joseph Mercer.
Machinery for the manufacture of paper board and paper.	1787	6th July 1865	John Franklin Jones.
Machinery for washing, wringing, mangling and drying domestic clothes or other fabrics and fibrous substances	1827	10th July 1865	Henry Fearnley. Christopher Smith.
Improvements in drying grass, hay and other substances, and in the machinery for effecting the same	1963	29th July 1865	Baldwin Latham. Robert Campbell.
Machinery or apparatus for sizing, drying, and beaming yarns of cotton or other fibrous substances	2023	4th Aug. 1865	John Goskroger. John Dodgwon.
An improved mode of and apparatus for drying timber, grain and other marketable products. (Communicated by Henry Balling.)	2127	17th Aug. 1865	Alfred Vincent Newton.
Method of and apparatus for treating peat and other plastic materials (drying apparatus.)	2219	29th Aug. 1865	Hull Terrell. Thomas Don.
Preparing peat or turf for fire lights and fuel, and for machinery to be employed therein.	2436	23rd Sep. 1865	Thomas Vincent Law.
Improvements in grinding wheat and other grain, and in apparatus for drying and improving the condition of damp wheat or other grain.	2485	28th Sep. 1865	Benjamin Wren.
Improved machinery for feeding fibrous substances to preparing, carding and other machinery for working wool and other filamentous substances. (drying machines.) (Communicated by Alexandre Devs.)	2517	30th Sep. 1865	William Edward Newton.
Preparation of meat for food (drying meat.)	2677	17th Oct. 1865	Arthur Hill Hassall, M.D.
Machinery for hanging fabrics in stoves or chambers	2686	18th Oct. 1865	William Schofield. John Smith.
Improvements in desiccating the leaves and flowers of plants and other vegetable substances, and in the apparatus to be employed therein. (Communicated by Benjamin Dobinson.)	2708	20th Oct. 1865	Allan Lawrie M'Garie.
Certain improvements in apparatus employed in the manufacture and production of metallic pipes, tubes or other similar hollow castings. (Communicated by Alfred Bertsch.)	2824	31st Oct. 1865	Arthur Deslandes.
Arrangements or apparatus for drying peat	2864	2nd Nov. 1865	Murdoch Campbell. Algernon Charles Plumptre Conte. John Charles Augustus Henry Wolfram.
Stoves for drying moulds	2945	16th Nov. 1865	Henry Cochrane.
An improvement in the manufacture of friction matches and tapers.	3003	22nd Nov. 1865	Samuel Alexander Bell.

Subject-matter of Patent.	Number of Patent.	Date.	Name of Patentee.
DYEING, &c.—continued.			
An improved apparatus for stretching and rolling fabrics for dyeing. (Communicated by Messieurs Jules B'cker and Victor Jacquet.)	3059	29th Nov. 1865	Hector Auguste Dufrené.
Construction of fire-places and furnaces (with curves or drying chambers.)	3347	15th Dec. 1865	George Warriner.
Boilers or apparatus for generating steam (for drying.) (Communicated by Julien Belleville.)	3369	18th Dec. 1865	Richard Archibald Brooman.
Machinery for drying and bleaching grain and other materials.	3378	19th Dec. 1865	William Cressy.
DYEING TEXTILE FABRICS, YARNS AND MATERIALS; FIXING COLOURS; MORDANTS.			
Dyeing leather	169	19th Jan. 1865	{ Theo Labrousse. John Kelly.
Coloring hempy wool and hair	237	26th Jan. 1865	Henry William Ripley.
Dying the herbs and straw used in the manufacture of straw hats and artificial flowers, or other fancy articles.	443	16th Feb. 1865	Emile Carchon.
An improved method of treating yarns or threads previously to the processes of dyeing or dressing.	490	22nd Feb. 1865	James Mallison.
An improved process and apparatus for dyeing and preparing cotton, worsted and silk warps.	617	4th March 1865	Abraham Akeroyd.
Machinery or apparatus to be employed in the bleaching and dyeing of hanks or skeins of yarns and threads.	718	14th March 1865	Longin Gentant.
Preparing, fixing and mordanting cloth and yarns	769	18th March 1865	Thomas Kenyon the younger.
Dyeing and printing cotton or linen fabrics or yarns.	806	22nd March 1865	Alfred Paraf.
Certain improvements in machinery or apparatus for drying "warps" of cotton and other fibrous substances (after dyeing.)	889	29th March 1865	{ Richard Holroyd. Joseph Holroyd Bolton.
Certain improvements in dyeing or printing upon the fabric known as "sail cloth."	1008	8th April 1865	James Isherwood.
Means of ornamenting linen cuffs and collars	1010	8th April 1865	Joseph Debnam.
Dyeing yarns	1199	29th April 1865	{ Robert Farra. John Murray. Adam Wilson.
Manufacture of flock fabrics (dyeing, &c.) (Communicated by the American Waterproof Cloth Company.)	1218	1st May 1865	William Edward Newton.
An improved manufacture of waterproof fabric (Communicated by the American Waterproof Cloth Company.)	1219	1st May 1865	William Edward Newton.

Subject-matter of Patent.	Number of Patent.	Date.	Name of Patentee.
Dyeing, &c.—continued.			
A new or improved machine or apparatus for tying or winding strings or threads upon a certain part or parts of hanks of cotton, silk, linen, thread, worsted, merino or other yarn, previous to dyeing the same.	1948	4th May 1865	Frederick Caldwell.
Machinery for stretching cotton and other fabrics or materials.	1317	12th May 1865	James Hasford.
Dyeing and sizing cotton, silk, woollen and other yarns - - - - - -	1418	23rd May 1865	{ Isaac Holt. William Holt. James Holt. Joseph Maude.
Applying coal-tar colors to cotton and linen -	1438	26th May 1865	Robert Maxwell.
Certain improvements in the manufacture and production of chromate and bichromate of potash employed in dyeing and printing woven fabrics.	1679	10th June 1865	Joseph Meyer Dentith.
Apparatus for printing wool, worsted or other fibrous materials.	1580	10th June 1865	John Henderson.
Improvements in the manufacture of naphthalic acid and chloroxynaphthalic acid, and in dyeing and printing - - - -	1605	13th July 1865	{ François Alexandre Laurent. John Casthelaz.
An improved self-acting apparatus for obtaining a circulation of volatile liquids. (infusing colours.) (Communicated by Messieurs Francisque Massol and Auguste Jaquin.)	1616	8th July 1865	Hector Auguste Dufresnl.
An improved system of manufacturing salts, sulphates and acetates of chrome, and of applying them as mordants in dyeing and printing textile substances both animal and vegetable.	1606	21st July 1865	Jean Henri Chaudet.
Preparation and application of certain colouring matters - - - - - -	1947	27th July 1865	{ Pierre Alexis. Francisque Robexal.
Means or apparatus for promoting the combustion of fuel in furnaces of steam-boilers, dyers' or brewers' pans and other furnaces, whereby smoke is prevented and fuel economised -	1972	31st July 1865	{ Benjamin Robinson. Joseph Varley.
Printing and dyeing yarns and fabrics of cotton or other vegetable materials - - -	2053	7th Aug. 1865	{ James Buchanan, jun'. Robert Boyd.
Printing-machines - - - -	2056	8th Aug. 1865	William Reck.
Production of violet colours from magenta for dyeing and printing.	2070	9th Aug. 1865	Ludwig Schad.
Machinery used in washing, bleaching, and dyeing yarns and textile fabrics in the hank -	2118	16th Aug. 1865	{ John Smith. William Schofield.
An improvement in dyeing and preparing hemp and other fibres for the manufacture of yarns and fabrics.	2129	18th Aug. 1865	George Hedgecombe Smith.
Dyeing and printing woollen or silk fabrics and yarns.	2201	24th Aug. 1865	Alfred Paraf.
Improvements in the manufacture of velvet and in the apparatus employed therein. (dyeing before cutting.) (Communicated by Messieurs Praine-Brossard, fils frères.)	2204	24th Aug. 1865	Henri Adrien Bonneville.
Dyeing and fixing colours in fibres, yarns and fabrics. (Communicated by Auguste Jeanselle.)	2206	24th Aug. 1865	Henri Adrien Bonneville.

Subject-matter of Patent.	Number of Patent.	Date.	Name of Patentee.
DYEING, &c.—continued.			
Dyeing and printing fabrics and yarns, and animal or mixed animal and vegetable substances.	2297	11th Sept. 1865	John Lightfoot.
Improvements in the manufacture of coloring matter, and in the application thereof to dyeing and printing.	2424	22nd Sept. 1865	Alexander Siebolts.
Dyeing	2506	29th Sept. 1865	{ John De Wewrices, jun. Alexandre Verschaffelt.
Printing or impressing and dyeing fabrics and tissues. (Communicated by Félix Dehant.)	2701	19th Oct. 1865	William Clark.
Improvements in the manufacture of chromates of ammonia and chromic acid, and in the preparation of nitrates of lime and baryta. (from residues of dye-works.) (Communicated by Félix Dehant.)	2702	19th Oct. 1865	William Clark.
Printing and dyeing textile fabrics and yarns	2859	6th Nov. 1865	Alfred Paraf.
Means of producing from remollins blue and violet colouring matters. (and applying.) (Communicated by Prosper Monnet.)	2894	10th Nov. 1865	Edward Thomas Hughes.
Bleaching feathers . . . . . (and dyeing.) (Communicated by Adolphe Pierre Viol and Claire Pierre Dufat.)	2957	20th Nov. 1865	William Clark.
An improved apparatus for stretching and rolling fabrics for dyeing. (Communicated by Messieurs Jules Webre and Victor Jacquet.)	3059	29th Nov. 1865	Hector Auguste Dufresne.
Treatment of matter for dyeing and printing .	3069	30th Nov. 1865	Alexander Campbell Duncan.
Dyeing, printing and other operations based on chemical reactions. (Communicated by Mathieu Paraf-Javal.)	3110	4th Dec. 1865	Richard Archibald Brooman.
Dyeing and printing	3250	19th Dec. 1865	Louis Durand.
Improvements in the manufacture of yarns, string and paper, and in the preparation of dyes, and in dyeing fabrics, by the application of vegetable substances not hitherto used for such purposes.	3316	23nd Dec. 1865	John Alexander Cooper.
See also " DYES."			
DYES AND PRINTING-COLOURS.			
Filtering apparatus . . . . . (extracts of dye woods.)	249	28th Jan. 1865	Victor Berg.
Certain improvements in the treatment of madder and the products obtained therefrom. (Communicated by Monsieur Jules Persoz.)	588	25th Feb. 1865	Peter Armand Le Comte de Fontaine-Moreau.
Preparing certain colouring matters for dyeing and printing. (Communicated by Ivan Levinstein.)	705	13th March 1865	Francis Wise.
Preparation of hydrated oxide of chromium (Communicated by Charles Kratner.)	788	21st March 1865	Richard Archibald Brooman.

Subject-matter of Patent.	Number of Patent.	Date.	Name of Patentee.
DYES, &c.—continued.			
Obtaining violet coloring matters	1098	28th April 1865	{ Ernest Smith. Christian Surberg.
Calico and linen printing	1420	24th May 1865	{ John Dale. Alfred Paraf.
Means of producing from rosaniline blue and violet colouring matters soluble in water. (Communicated by Prosper Monnet.)	1566	12th June 1865	Edward Thomas Hughes.
Obtaining jellies, syrups, drinks and other products, from the tree Arbutus Unedo, known as the Arbutus. (violet and green colours.)	1649	20th June 1865	Philippe Mingand.
Production of pigments suitable for printing upon paper and woven fabrics	1766	4th July 1865	{ John Dale. Richard Samuel Dale.
An improved system of manufacturing salts, sulphates and acetates of chrome, and of applying them as mordants, in dyeing and printing textile substances both animal and vegetable.	1905	21st July 1865	Jean Henri Chaudet.
Preparation and application of certain colouring matters	1947	27th July 1865	{ Pierre Alexis. Francisco Hoborul.
Apparatus for filtering vegas and other liquid solutions	2022	4th Aug. 1865	{ Jean Adolphe Leon. George Trummond. John Kinnick.
Printing and dyeing yarns and fabrics of cotton or other vegetable materials	2062	8th Aug. 1866	{ James Buchanan, jun'. Robert Hoyd.
Production of violet colours from magenta, for dyeing and printing.	2070	9th Aug. 1865	Ludwig Schad.
Manufacture of violet dye-stuffs	2194	26th Aug. 1865	James Alfred Wanklyn.
Improvements in the manufacture of compounds of silica and in the production of silicated alkaline inks, colours and dyes.	2287	2nd Sept. 1865	Henry Ellis.
Preparing certain coloring matters	2235	12th Sept. 1865	John Holliday.
Improvements in the manufacture of coloring matter, and in the application thereof to dyeing and printing.	2424	22nd Sept. 1865	Alexandre Schultz.
Preparing red and violet colouring matters for dyeing and printing silk, wool, cotton and other textile vegetable and mineral substances. (Communicated by Philibert Cacvalier.)	2556	3rd Oct. 1865	Richard Archibald Brooman.
Preparing violet, blue and red coloring matters	2564	6th Oct. 1865	James Holliday.
Improvements in the manufacture of chromates of ammonia and chromic acid, and in the preparation of nitrates of lime and baryta. (from residues in manufacture of aniline.) (Communicated by Félix Delmal.)	2703	19th Oct. 1865	William Clark.
Manufacture of coloring matter for dyeing and printing.	2885	2nd Nov. 1865	Ludwig Schad.
Means of producing from rosaniline blue and violet colouring matters. (Communicated by Prosper Monnet.)	2894	10th Nov. 1865	Edward Thomas Hughes.
Treatment of matter for dyeing and printing	3089	30th Nov. 1865	Alexander Campbell Duncan.
Dyeing, printing and other operations based on chemical reactions. (mixing colours.) (Communicated by Mathieu Paraf-Javal.)	3110	7th Dec. 1865	Richard Archibald Brooman.

Subject-matter of Patent.	Number of Patent.	Date.	Name of Patentee.
DYES, &c.—*continued.*			
A new coloring matter for producing scarlet colors upon woven fabrics and yarns	3111	4th Dec. 1865	Alfred Paraf. Richard Samuel Dale.
Improvements in the manufacture of yarns, string and paper, and in the preparation of dyes, and in dyeing fabrics, by the application of vegetable substances not hitherto used for such purposes.	3318	22nd Dec. 1865	John Alexander Cooper.
Manufacture of aniline green (*Communicated by Charles Lauth.*)	3374	29th Dec. 1865	Edward Joseph Hughes.
EARTHENWARE AND PORCELAIN; POTTERY KILNS; POTTERS' GLAZES; CERAMIC WARES; TERRA COTTA.			
Certain improvements in rendering soundless furniture and other articles for domestic purposes. (*china and pottery.*)	196	23rd Jan. 1865	Adolphe Drevelle.
Filtering apparatus (*for ceramic slips.*)	249	24th Jan. 1865	Victor Basy.
A new mode of placing china, stone and earthenware, in saggers, ovens and kilns, or other receptacles for firing the same.	276	1st Feb. 1865	James Meakin.
Improvements in ornamenting china and earthenware, and in preparing materials to be employed therefor.	435	15th Feb. 1865	Francis Joseph Emery.
An improved method and machinery for the manufacture of various articles in pottery, earthenware or porcelain, by mechanical process. (*Communicated by Edme Mercier.*)	459	17th Feb. 1865	William Edward Gedge.
Process of preparing kaolin or china clay and other clays, for potters' use, and for expelling water from other earthy deposits. (*Communicated by Joseph Muir.*)	805	22nd March 1865	James Wright.
Improvements in taking impressions from the grain of wood, and in transferring the same on to various surfaces (*such as articles made in clay.*)	1117	21st April 1865	William Scarratt. William Dean.
Improvements in the manufacture and application of devices and representations to tombstones, and in other public or exposed situations, for various purposes (*ornamenting porcelain.*)	1180	22nd April 1865	Alfred Grainger. Charles Mitchel Girdler.
Improvements in photographing upon wood, and in the preparation of wood, canvas, silk, glass and other substances, for the purpose of receiving and retaining impressions.	1174	26th April 1865	William Henry Smith.
Production of portraits or likenesses on certain materials, by means of photography (*producing likenesses on ceramic ware.*)	1194	27th April 1865	Alfred Grainger. Charles Mitchel Girdler.
Improvements in the treatment of clays and other materials with which they are mixed when used in the manufacture of china, porcelain, earthenware and other like wares, and in ornamenting or decorating china, porcelain, earthenware and other like wares.	1414	23rd May 1865	Alexander Hett.

Subject-matter of Patent.	Number of Patent.	Date.	Name of Patentee.
EARTHENWARE, &c.—continued.			
A new or improved compound spherical rest for ornamental turning lathes. (or for engraving pottery.)	1441	25th May 1865	Thomas Hallam Hoblyn.
Kilns for firing porcelain and other ware (Communicated by François Durand.)	1543	10th June 1865	Richard Archibald Brooman.
An improved method of and apparatus for manufacturing pottery. (Communicated by Georges Gros.)	1627	16th June 1865	William Edward Gedge.
Manufacture of terra-cotta or vitreous stone	2071	10th Aug. 1865	Mark Henry Blanchard.
Machinery for moulding hollow articles, in earth, clay and other like materials.	2061	11th Aug. 1865	Robert William Armstrong.
Preparing the surfaces of paper, leather, woven and other fabrics and substances, for receiving photographic pictures, engravings, lithographs and prints, and for rendering such substances fire and water proof. (enamelling earthenware.) (Communicated by William Gibson.)	2891	9th Nov. 1865	William Edward Newton.
Machinery or apparatus for making pottery, earthenware or ceramic articles.	3015	24th Nov. 1865	George Wardle Turner.
An improved composition for enamel, paint, varnish, cement or plaster. (for coating earthenware.) (Communicated by William Barney Watkins.)	3042	27th Nov. 1865	William Robert Lake.
An improved method of and apparatus for making mortars, bowls, spill pots, jelly cans, galvanic troughs and other similar articles (from pulverised clay.)	3159	8th Dec. 1865	William Boulton. Joseph Worthington.
Improved machinery for compressing and solidifying coal, clay and other analogous substances.	3343	14th Dec. 1865	Henry George Fairburn.
ELECTRICITY, GALVANISM AND MAGNETISM, AND THEIR APPLICATION.			
Electro-magnets and their application to telegraphic and other purposes. (Communicated by Charles Frédéric Cartier.)	22	4th Jan. 1866	William Clark.
Apparatus used in train signalling on railways	52	6th Jan. 1865	Edward Tyer.
Method of and apparatus for applying electro-magnetism as a break power to railway and other carriages and machines	101	12th Jan. 1865	Frederic Barron. David Hancork. Edward Cowper.
A new electric pile	208	24th Jan. 1865	Jules Rivière. Hilarion Antoine Bernard Huguet.
The application of hydro-electricity to steam for the purpose of increasing its expansion and power, and the machinery or apparatus connected therewith, and also the application of galvano or frictional electricity for the same purpose	273	31st Jan. 1865	Joseph Fletcher. Daniel Hamer.
The improved use of magnets in overbalancing weights.	441	18th Feb. 1865	Thomas Philip Twygaskis.

Subject-matter of Patent.	Number of Patent.	Date.	Name of Patentee.
ELECTRICITY, &c.—continued.			
Improvements in the manufacture of iron and in articles made thereof.	470	18th Feb. 1865	William Robinson.
New or improved indicating apparatus for the protection of railway passengers, buildings, rooms, safes and other objects	472	18th Feb. 1865	Leicester William Glen Rowe. Adolphe Baab.
Construction of electro-magnetic apparatus for railway signalling and other purposes	488	22nd Feb. 1865	Charles Vincent Walker. Alfred Owen Walker.
An improved process and apparatus for impregnating wood with chemical solutions. (Communicated by Ernest Baria and Jules Héaury.)	590	2nd March 1865	William Edward Newton.
Improved apparatus for the protection of houses and property from burglars, parts of the invention being applicable for other purposes.	612	6th March 1865	Cromwell Fleetwood Varley.
Electric telegraphs (Communicated by Gaetano Bonelli.)	679	10th March 1865	Harry Whiteside Cook.
Electric piles and apparatus (Communicated by Pierre Etienne Lequeme.)	782	15th March 1865	William Clark.
Engraving on metal (Communicated by Narcisse Guillot and Pierre Heritier.)	807	22nd March 1865	Richard Archibald Brooman.
Improved means of communication between the passengers, guard and engine driver of a railway train, part of which said improvements is also applicable for the prevention or detection of burglary.	847	25th March 1865	Alice Isabel Lucan Gordon.
Improvements in certain electric telegraphs, part of which invention is applicable to other purposes.	960	5th April 1865	Adam Millar.
Conducting electricity for communicating or transmitting signals and alarms in the event of burglary, fire, railway accidents and other purposes	975	6th April 1865	John Samuel Watson. Albert Harwood.
An improved mode of pointing or tapering the ends of metallic rods or wires, applicable to the manufacture of pins, needles and other articles where points or tapered ends are required. (Communicated by Henry Camdroy.)	979	6th April 1865	Edwin Henry Newby.
Electro-magnetic engines	1012	8th April 1865	Siegmund Moore.
Improvements in and apparatus for communicating intelligence by means of electricity	1088	19th April 1865	Ralph Augustine Jones. Joseph Hedges.
Improvements in the construction of ships of war and floating batteries, part of which improvements are applicable to land fortifications.	1107	20th April 1865	Henry Cardwell.
Rotary magneto-electric machines (Communicated by Mr. Henry Brandon.)	1362	18th May 1865	Theodore Fanchwas.
Production and application of electricity	1412	23rd May 1865	Henry Wilds.
Improvements in the treatment of clays and other materials with which they are mixed when used in the manufacture of china, porcelain, earthenware and other like wares, and in ornamenting or decorating china, porcelain, earthenware and other like wares.	1414	23rd May 1865	Alexander Hett.
Certain improvements applicable to spinning, weaving and knitting machines. (stopping by electricity.) (Communicated by Charles Arthur Radiguet and Jean Adolphe Lartre.)	1460	25th May 1865	William Edward Newton.

Subject-matter of Patent.	Number of Patent.	Date.	Name of Patentee.
ELECTRICITY, &c.—continued.			
Improvements in reproducing or producing copies of writings, drawings, music and other characters, and in preparing originals to be transmitted by electric telegraph. (Communicated by Jacques Paul Landrigot.)	1487	27th May 1865	Richard Archibald Brooman.
Electro-magnetic clocks and other time-keepers (Communicated by Jean Theodore Scholte.)	1518	2nd June 1865	Richard Archibald Brooman.
An improved system of telegraphic communication on railways, parts of which invention are also applicable to other telegraphic purposes.	1543	5th June 1865	Alice Isabel Lucas Gordon.
Improved means of conducting electric currents through railway trains, and of actuating signals or alarums therein.	1609	14th June 1865	Andrew Edmund Bew.
Apparatus for preventing collisions and other accidents on railways. (Communicated by Espbar Visrvoti.)	1631	16th June 1865	William Clark.
Improvements in the preparation of amalgams of quicksilver or mercury, and in the application of such amalgams to various purposes in the arts. (preparing plates of voltaic batteries.) (Communicated by Henry Wurtz.)	1719	29th June 1865	William Edward Newton.
Fire-arms	1805	7th July 1865	{ Robert Green. John William Heinke. }
An improved method of obtaining induced currents of electricity from magnets and induction coils. (Communicated by Jerome Kidder.)	1979	31st July 1865	Alfred Vincent Newton.
Obtaining motive-power by heat (igniting mixtures by electricity.)	1892	1st Aug. 1865	Matthew Piers Watt Boulton.
Railway electrical signal apparatus	2016	3rd Aug. 1865	William Henry Preece.
Improvements in the mode or method of preparing materials for, and in the manufacture of submarine telegraphic cables, the same being generally applicable for other purposes.	2025	4th Aug. 1865	Frederick George Mulholland.
Electric telegraphic apparatus (Communicated by Louis Breguet.)	2047	7th Aug. 1865	Louis John Crossley.
Improvements in the preparation or production of spongy metals, and in their applications. (for electric batteries.) (Communicated by François Drivet.)	2106	15th Aug. 1865	John Henry Johnson.
Constructing constant galvanic batteries for giving a signal or alarm in case of fire, and any other telegraphic purposes	2144	19th Aug. 1865	{ John Samuel Watson. Albert Horwood. Charles Bright. }
A new or improved method of and apparatus for applying electro-magnetism as a break power on railways	2235	31st Aug. 1865	{ Edward Coope. David Hancock. }
An improved indicator for electric bells, and a new battery manipulator combined, for ringing electric bells and other signals.	2431	22nd Sept. 1865	Walter Mowley.
An improved mode of generating steam (by electric currents.)	2604	10th Oct. 1865	John Sturgeon.
Improvements in submarine electric telegraph cables and in apparatus connected therewith.	2605	10th Oct. 1865	François Thierry Hubert.
Submarine telegraphy	2612	10th Oct. 1865	John Fletcher Wiles.

Subject-matter of Patent.	Number of Patent.	Date.	Name of Patentee.
ELECTRICITY, &c.—*continued.*			
Improvements in steam-boilers and other apparatus applicable to the heating and evaporation of liquids, parts of which improvements are applicable also to other purposes - - - (*passing a galvanic current through boilers to prevent corrosion.*)	2561	16th Oct. 1865	Francis Wise. Edward Field. Enoch Harrison Aydon.
The improvement of the means of and apparatus for laying submarine electrical telegraphic wires, lines, cables or other contrivances of a like sort.	2570	16th Oct. 1865	Reinhold Edward Kaulbach.
Improvements in the manufacture of chromates of ammonia and chromic acid, and in the preparation of nitrates of lime and baryta. (*from residues from electric batteries.*) (*Communicated by Felix Dehaut.*)	2702	19th Oct. 1865	William Clark.
Improvements in the construction and working of electric telegraphs, and in apparatus connected therewith, partly applicable to other purposes.	2782	26th Oct. 1865	Henry Wilde.
Manufacture of copper from copper ore - -	2838	3rd Nov. 1865	James Bulkey Elkington.
Apparatus for effecting communications between the passengers, guard and engine drivers in railway trains, and for giving notice to engine drivers in cases of accidents. (*Communicated by Samuel Cornwallis Amesbury.*)	2845	4th Nov. 1865	Henry Radcliffe.
A new appliance of an electro-magnetic apparatus to increase the adherence of locomotive engine wheels to the rails.	2977	20th Nov. 1865	Angelo Vercovall.
Apparatus for signalling on railways - - -	3038	25th Nov. 1865	Charles Frederick Whitworth.
Improvements in the applications of electricity for the testing and discharge of torpedo mines, either on land or at sea, and in the apparatus connected therewith. (*Partly communicated by Matthew Fontaine Maury.*)	3154	4th Dec. 1865	Nathaniel John Holmes.
An improved method of and apparatus for making mortars, bowls, spill pots, jelly cans, galvanic troughs and other similar articles - -	3169	6th Dec. 1865	William Boulton. Joseph Worthington.
Obtaining motive power applicable to various useful purposes. (*by magnetism.*)	3290	16th Dec. 1865	Cecil Loftus Wellesley Reade.
Electro-magnetic engines - - - - (*Communicated by Lohan Clarke Stuart.*)	3291	19th Dec. 1865	Alfred Vincent Newton.
Improvements in caps employed in spinning, and in the manufacture thereof.	3325	23rd Dec. 1865	Edward Clifton.
Manufacture of electric conductors insulated with india-rubber.	3347	27th Dec. 1865	Hugh Adams Silver.

For electric telegraphs, see "TELEGRAPHS."
For magnetic compasses, see "COMPASSES."
See also "Electro-plating."

Subject-matter of Patent.	Number of Patent.	Date.	Name of Patentee.
ELECTRO-PLATING AND GALVANISING; DEPOSITING METAL BY ELECTRICITY.			
Treating products obtained when coating iron with zinc.	409	14th Feb. 1865	James Graham.
Improvements in the preparation of amalgams of quicksilver or mercury, and in the application of such amalgams to various purposes in the arts. (Communicated by Henry Wurtz.)	1710	29th June 1865	William Edward Newton.
Preparation of iron, steel and alloyed metals, for electro-plating.	2521	2nd Oct. 1865	Thomas Allan.
Coating iron and steel with gold, silver, platinum or copper.	2593	7th Oct. 1865	Jacob Baynes Thompson.
Improvements in the construction and working of electric telegraphs, and in apparatus connected therewith, partly applicable to other purposes. (electro-deposition of metals.)	2782	26th Oct. 1865	Henry Wilde.
Improvements in caps employed in spinning, and in the manufacture thereof, (electro-brazing.)	5323	23rd Dec. 1865	Edward Clifton.
EMBOSSING; PRODUCING RAISED PATTERNS.			
Improvements in producing and finishing photographs and photographic transparencies on paper and other suitable substances, and in the machinery employed therein. (producing imitation cameos.)	58	7th Jan. 1865	{ Barraclough Wright Bentley. William Henry Bailey.
Fly or embossing presses	208	24th Jan. 1865	James Bailey.
Manufacture of paper hangings	522	6th Feb. 1865	John Booth.
Engraving on metal (in relief.) (Communicated by Narcisse Gaillot and Pierre Heritier.)	607	22nd March 1865	Richard Archibald Brooman.
An improved manufacture of waterproof fabric (Communicated by The American Waterproof Cloth Company.)	1210	1st May 1865	William Edward Newton.
Improvements in embossing presses to facilitate the operation of relief coloring on envelopes, note paper and other similar articles of stationery.	1234	2nd May 1865	Rest Fenner.
Mandrils for rollers such as are used for printing or embossing	1850	14th July 1865	{ David Fulton. John Fulton.
Certain improvements in envelope machines (Communicated by Thomas Vraise Weymoth, Henry Clay Bevin and George Jones.)	1886	20th July 1865	Alfred Vincent Newton.
Ornamenting and enforcing veneers and other articles of wood.	2279	5th Sept. 1865	Thomas Thompson Ponsonby.
An improved method of ornamenting the surfaces of tiles.	2878	14th Sept. 1865	Henry Vrumbier.
Engraving on metal (Communicated by Narcisse Gaillot and Pierre Heritier.)	2388	19th Sept. 1865	Richard Archibald Brooman.

Subject-matter of Patent.	Number of Patent.	Date.	Name of Patentee.
EMBOSSING, &c.—continued.			
Manufacture of embossed wood . . . (Communicated by Henry May and Henry Taylor Blake.)	2896	10th Nov. 1865	Alfred Vincent Newton.
Apparatus for embossing	3063	29th Nov. 1865	John Erskine Brown.
ENAMELLING, ENAMELS.			
Manufacture of enamelled glass to render it more useful in photographic art.	19	3rd Jan. 1865	William George Helsby.
An improved composition to be employed in the manufacture of bonnets and hats. (for enamelling.)	1443	25th May 1865	Jeffery Kostner.
Preparing the surfaces of paper, leather, woven and other fabrics and substances, for receiving photographic pictures, engravings, lithographs and prints, and for rendering such substances fire and water proof. (enamelling.) (Communicated by William Gibson.)	2891	9th Nov. 1865	William Edward Newton.
An improved composition for enamel, paint, varnish, cement or plaster. (Communicated by William Barney Watkins.)	3042	27th Nov. 1865	William Robert Lake.
Photographic surfaces and the compositions and process for preparing the same. (opal picture enamel.)	3180	11th Dec. 1865	Victor Moreau Griswold.
ENGRAVING AND ETCHING ; PRODUCING SUNK DEVICES.			
Engraving upon crystal and silicious substances . (Communicated by Charles Raphael Maréchal and Cyprien Marie Tessié du Motay.)	86	11th Jan. 1865	Richard Archibald Brooman.
Engraving on metal . . . . . (Communicated by Narcisse Guillot and Pierre Herisier.)	807	22nd March 1865	Richard Archibald Brooman.
A new or improved compound spherical rest for ornamental turning lathes. (or for engraving glass.)	1441	25th May 1865	Thomas Hallam Hoblyn.
A new or improved method of producing a photographic image on the surface of copper or other metal plates. (for engraving or etching.)	1984	1st Aug. 1865	Francis Ross Wells.
Engraving on metal . . . . . (Communicated by Narcisse Guillot and Pierre Herisier.)	2388	19th Sept. 1865	Richard Archibald Brooman.

Subject-matter of Patent.	Number of Patent.	Date.	Name of Patentee.
ENVELOPES.			
Apparatus for folding envelopes . . .	479	20th Feb. 1865	John Davidson Nichol.
An improved fastener for envelopes . . .	495	22nd Feb. 1865	Herbert Penmore Rilston.
Improvements in embossing presses to facilitate the operation of relief coloring on envelopes, note paper and other similar articles of stationery.	1224	2nd May 1865	Reid Fennet.
An improvement in the manufacture of envelopes -	1416	23rd May 1865	Henry Gibbs.
Means of securing envelopes for enclosing letters and other papers.	1858	14th July 1865	Stevens Tripp.
Certain improvements in envelope machines (Communicated by Thomas Vrazie Haymoth, Henry Clay Bevin and George James.)	1898	20th July 1865	Alfred Vincent Newton.
Improved machinery for the manufacture of bags and envelopes made of paper or other fibrous materials or woven or textile fabrics, either separately or combined.	2420	22nd Sept. 1865	Henry Rankin.
Securing or fastening envelopes . . .	2430	23rd Sept. 1865	The Honourable Jane Elizabeth Turbot.
An improved apparatus for bordering paper and envelopes.	2441	23rd Sept. 1865	Joseph Parkins.
Improvements in envelopes and in the construction thereof.	2794	30th Oct. 1865	Robert Girdwood.
Envelopes	3207	12th Dec. 1865	Henry Yate Thompson.
Envelopes -	3301	21st Dec. 1865	Vincent Pétément-Van-Leuf.
An improvement in envelopes . . .	3331	23rd Dec. 1865	Frederic Jenner.
Apparatus for damping and gumming labels, stamps, envelopes and sheets of paper - . }	3343	27th Dec. 1865	Joseph Benn. George Oswald Luckman.
EXCAVATING AND DREDGING; TUNNELS AND EMBANKMENTS.			
An improved machine for raising and carrying earth, sand, stones or other similar solid or liquid materials for dredging, ventilating, or winnowing grain, or other analogous purposes.	174	20th Jan. 1865	Louis Bahzu.
Formation of embankments, sea walls, break waters and other similar constructions. (Communicated by Frederic Glover.)	380	10th Feb. 1865	William Edward Newton.
Apparatus for propulsion by atmospheric pressure -	599	3rd March 1865	Sir John Scott Lillie, Knight.
Dredgers	779	24th March 1865	William Simons. Andrew Brown.
Improved apparatus for ascertaining the state of sewers, tunnels, drifts or other subterranean work, part of which apparatus is applicable to levelling purposes.	849	25th March 1865	Richard William Barnes.

Subject-matter of Patent.	Number of Patent.	Date.	Name of Patentee.
EXCAVATING, &c.—continued.			
Improvements in machinery or apparatus for drilling or boring rocks and other hard substances, in tunnelling, mining and other like operations, parts of which improvements are also applicable to the ventilating of the workings in mines and similar places. (Communicated by Herman Houpt.)	981	6th April 1865	John Henry Johnson.
An improved mode of and apparatus for deepening the bottom or bed of rivers, canals, harbours or other similar places.	1017	10th April 1865	Charles François Ghevrbrand.
Constructing of ships or vessels or cars to float on water.	1083	18th April 1865	William Bedder.
Improvements in boring or excavating and blasting rocks and minerals, and in the treatment of the tools employed therein.	1102	24th April 1865	Julius Bernard.
An improved method of and machinery for cutting and excavating rock for railway tunnels and other purposes. (Communicated by Tholes Lindsley.)	1587	12th June 1865	George Hazeltine.
Improved machinery for boring rocks and hard substances.	1770	5th July 1865	George Low.
Improvements in the raising, lifting or drawing and forcing of water and other liquids, and in the apparatus and means employed therefor (impure water from rivers.)	1996	2nd Aug. 1865	James M'Ewan. William Neilson.
Machinery for excavating earth	2408	21st Sept. 1865	John Bostock Hulme.
An improved apparatus for and method of ascertaining the state of sewers, tunnels, drifts or other subterranean works, without descending thereinto, by means of the natural, artificial or magnesium light, part of which apparatus is applicable to levelling purposes.	2446	25th Sept. 1865	Richard William Barnes.
Improved machinery for cutting tunnels and sinking shafts	2940	15th Nov. 1865	Alexander Allison. Henry Hoskins.
A new or improved cement or composition, applicable to the agglomeration or moulding of various materials, and to other useful and decorative purposes. (sheets of embankments.) (Communicated by Stanislas Sorel and Emile Justin Mraire.)	3110	5th Dec. 1865	Richard Archibald Brooman.
An improved mode of applying the compression of air for ventilating purpose, and the compression of any gas for hurrying along elastic fluids in conveying pipes (ventilating tunnels.)	3133	8th Dec. 1865	Pierron de Mondésir. Paul Lehaitre. Augustin Jullienne.
Improvements in constructing atmospheric railways and carriages, and in working the same, parts of which are applicable to exhausting and condensing air for other purposes. (constructing tunnels.)	3178	9th Dec. 1865	Alexander Doull.
Machinery for boring rock and other mineral (Communicated by Carl Sachs.)	3218	12th Dec. 1865	Frederick Bernard Dorring.

Subject-matter of Patent.	Number of Patent.	Date.	Name of Patentee.

Extracts and Decoctions.

Subject-matter of Patent.	Number of Patent.	Date.	Name of Patentee.
Filtering apparatus - - - - (extracts or decoctions.)	849	24th Jan. 1865	Victor Burg.
A new or improved method or process and apparatus for obtaining the concentrated extract of hops, and for preserving the same from deterioration. (Communicated by George Percy, Walter Wells, Charles Brown, John Mulford and John Maximilien Webb.)	306	4th Feb. 1865	Joseph Rideal Webb.
Apparatus for extracting liquid from solid substances. (Communicated by Lyman Smith.)	480	21st Feb. 1865	William Edward Newton.
A mode of obtaining decoctions and apparatus for carrying the same into effect. (Communicated by Benjamin Green Martin.)	1227	2nd May 1865	Francis Wise.
Improvements in brewing, distillation, the production of vinegar, and the extract of malt and other grain.	1263	5th May 1865	Solomon Bennett.
Improvements in tanning and in the preparation of extracts to be used therein. (Communicated by Edward Druid Cole.)	2291	30th Aug. 1865	John Henry Johnson.

Fabrics; Elastic Fabrics.

Subject-matter of Patent.	Number of Patent.	Date.	Name of Patentee.
Vulcanising compounds and vulcanised fabrics - (Communicated by Simon Stevens.)	176	20th Jan. 1865	Benjamin Franklin Stevens.
An improved manufacture of barège stuffs - (Communicated by Edmund Dirom.)	440	16th Feb. 1865	William Edward Gedge.
Certain improvements in scarfs and in the manufacture of the same. (Communicated by Leon de Meure Parivete.)	491	22nd Feb. 1865	Isaac Parivete.
Improvements in the manufacture of textile fabrics and in the machinery or apparatus employed therefor. (see "Weaving.")	562	24th Feb. 1865	David Chalmers.
An improved method of treating, cleaning or preparing painted or other canvas, tarpaulins and dirty cotton waste, so as to render the same suitable to be used for household and other purposes for which they may be applicable. (for towels, knife-cloths, dusters, &c.)	782	17th March 1865	William Maurice Williams.
Machinery or apparatus employed in the manufacture of cloth and other fabrics - - - (see "Weaving.")	801	23rd March 1865	Joseph Lees. Moses Mellor.
A new or improved method of conditioning or preparing fibres, threads and fabrics, and apparatus to be employed therein. (Communicated by Stanislas Vigouroux.)	1100	26th April 1865	Richard Archibald Brooman.
Manufacture of a certain description of woven fabric called "turkish towelling."	1271	9th May 1865	James Gorton.
An improved woven fabric - - - } (towelling.)	1316	12th May 1865	Thomas Smith. Henry James.

Subject-matter of Patent.	Number of Patent.	Date.	Name of Patentee.
FABRICS, &c.—*continued.*			
Ornamentation of fabrics and leather - . (*Communicated by Miss Nathalie Kolb.*)	1889	19th May 1865	William Clark.
Improvements in the manufacture of textile fabrics and in the machinery or apparatus connected therewith. (*see* "WEAVING.") (*Communicated by David Chalmers.*)	2117	16th Aug. 1865	Flora McDougall Chalmers,
Improvements in the manufacture of velvet and in the apparatus employed therein. (*see* "DYEING.") (*Communicated by Messieurs Fraisse-Brossard fils jeunes.*)	2204	24th Aug. 1865	Henri Adrien Bonneville.
Improvements in certain knitted fabrics and in the means for producing the same.	2718	21st Oct. 1865	Thomas Webb.
Manufacture of endless cloths - . - .	2966	17th Nov. 1865	James Heywood Whitehead.
Manufacture of shawls and similar ornamental weavings.	3145	6th Dec. 1865	William Houghton Clabburn.
Manufacture of bed quilts, table and toilet covers -	3255	16th Dec. 1865	{ Thomas Jones. Joseph Buckley.
Improvements in the manufacture of trimmings and in the machinery employed therein. (*for textile fabrics.*)	3320	23rd Dec. 1865	William Smith.
Obtaining and employing continuous lengths of tanned leather for various useful purposes - } (*for counterpanes or quilts.*)	3334	23rd Dec. 1866	{ George Horn. Daniel Horn.
FEATHERS ; ARTIFICIAL FEATHERS AND FLOWERS.			
Dying the herbs and straw used in the manufacture of straw hats and artificial flowers, or other fancy articles.	463	18th Feb. 1865	Emile Carchon.
Improved contrivances to facilitate the arrangement of flowers and leaves. (*and artificial flowers.*)	1167	29th April 1865	Thomas Charles March.
A new manufacture of or improvement in ornaments for personal wear.	1779	5th July 1865	Harry Emanuel.
Dyeing and printing fabrics and yarns, and animal or mixed animal and vegetable substances.	2327	11th Sept. 1865	John Lightfoot.
Purification and preparation of animal and vegetable wax, stearine, spermaceti, paraffine and other solid, waxy or fatty substances. (*for flowers.*)	2788	27th Oct. 1865	Scipion Saquella.
Bleaching feathers - . . . - . (*Communicated by Adolphe Pierre Viol and Cléoire Pierre Deflot.*)	2957	20th Nov. 1865	William Clark.
Obtaining and employing continuous lengths of tanned leather for various useful purposes - } (*for flowers, &c.*)	3334	23rd Dec. 1865	{ George Horn. Daniel Horn.

Subject-matter of Patent.	Number of Patent.	Date.	Name of Patentee.
FENCES AND RAILWAYS.			
Certain improvements in standards for strained wire or rod fencing.	76	10th Jan. 1865	William Baylis.
New or improved machinery for the manufacture of wire and other netting. (*Communicated by Edmund Paul Henri Gandanie.*)	390	8th Feb. 1865	Richard Archibald Brooman.
Constructing strained wire fences - - -	582	2nd March 1865	Robert Johnson.
Improvements in the manufacture of metallic bedsteads, which improvements are also applicable to the manufacture of other metallic articles. (*railing and baluster bars.*)	689	13th March 1865	James Atkins.
An improved socket for fencing and telegraph posts	775	20th March 1865	Arthur Giraud Browning.
Ornamental fences and baskets to contain flowers and other articles.	1806	7th July 1865	William Goulding.
Manufacture of bricks and other analogous materials. (*for balustrades, &c.*)	2571	6th Oct. 1865	Victor Jean Baptiste Germain.
Hurdles for fencing or dividing grass and other lands and for other like purposes.	2629	12th Oct. 1865	Robert Longdon.
A new composition of India-rubber mastic or cement, made in a more or less fluid state according to the use to be made of it, and the process or contrivance for applying the same. (*coating fences.*)	2680	12th Oct. 1865	Auguste Aimé Lavocard.
FIBRES (*Obtaining from Plants, Recovering from Manufactured Goods, Separating, Cleaning, Packing.*)			
Machinery for ginning cotton - - -	44	6th Jan. 1865	{ Benjamin Dobson. William Slater. Robert Halliwell.
Machinery for opening and carding cotton and other fibrous materials. (*separating fibres.*)	80	11th Jan. 1866	Robert Tempest.
Machinery or apparatus for ginning and cleaning cotton and other fibrous materials - - (*Partly communicated by Albert Westfeld.*)	191	23rd Jan. 1865	{ Christopher Brakell. William Hoehl. William Günther.
Machinery for threshing, beating, and dressing flax	221	25th Jan. 1865	William Creasy.
Cotton gins - - - - - -	249	28th Jan. 1865	{ Benjamin Dobson. William Slater.
Machinery or apparatus for washing wool and other fibrous materials.	251	24th Jan. 1865	John Petrie, jun'.
An improved system of drying wool, cotton and other fibrous materials, and in the machinery or apparatus connected therewith. (*Communicated by Carl Bro and Lewis Bentticher.*)	255	28th Jan. 1865	Edward Thomas Hughes.
Apparatus for breaking and scutching flax or similar fibrous materials.	377	1st Feb. 1865	John Gray.

Subject-matter of Patent.	Number of Patent.	Date.	Name of Patentee.
FIBRES, &c.—continued.			
Machinery for washing and drying wool and other fibrous materials - - - -	281	1st Feb. 1865	{ John M'Naught. { William M'Naught, jun'.,
Machinery for breaking the stems of and preparing flax, hemp and other fibrous substances. (Communicated by Auguste Henri Lorroz.)	336	7th Feb. 1865	Henry Bernoulli Barlow.
Separating wool from refuse mixed fabrics and materials.	511	23rd Feb. 1865	Samuel Neville.
Cotton gins - - - - - (Communicated by François Durand.)	531	24th Feb. 1865	Edmund Paul Henri Gondowin.
Application and utilization of certain materials suitable for the manufacture of paper. (Communicated by Joachim John Monteiro.)	706	13th March 1865	John Webb.
Apparatus for washing wool, hair and other fibres -	808	22nd March 1865	George Edmund Doulethorpe.
Presses for cotton and wool - - - -	846	25th March 1865	William Miller.
Cotton gins - - - - -	851	25th March 1865	William Richardson.
Separating fibre from vegetable materials containing the same. (Communicated by Antonio Menocci.)	956	4th April 1865	George Tomlinson Bousfield.
Treating wool in order to cleanse it from burrs, seeds and other foreign matters - -	1042	12th April 1865	{ Henry Sikes. { George Jarmain.
Apparatus for disintegrating vegetable and animal substances.	1168	26th April 1865	François Dominique Pierre Jacques Cabasson.
A new or improved method of conditioning or preparing fibres, threads and fabrics, and apparatus to be employed therein. (Communicated by Stanislas Vigoureux.)	1169	26th April 1865	Richard Archibald Brooman.
Hydraulic presses for compressing cotton and other substances - - - - -	1234	5th May 1865	{ George Peel, jun'. { Isaac Mason.
Certain improvements in hydraulic presses for packing cotton and other materials or substances, and in the boxes for containing the same	1300	9th May 1865	{ Edward Taylor Bellhouse. { William John Dorning.
Presses used for pressing cotton, wool, hay and fibrous materials.	1423	24th May 1865	George Ashcroft.
Machinery for separating or sorting fibres and filaments of different lengths, and forming them into a lap or fleece. (see "Spinning.") (Communicated by Charles Simon.)	1430	24th May 1865	Richard Archibald Brooman.
Improvements in treating fibrous materials and textile fabrics, and in producing soap. (Communicated by Leon Pasquier and Alphonsine Julie Dumont.)	1443	25th May 1865	Michael Henry.
Machinery or apparatus for washing wool and other fibrous materials.	1500	31st May 1865	John Petrie, jun'.
An improvement in the preparation of vegetable fibre for the manufacture of paper.	1624	17th June 1865	William Bellhouse.
Manufacture of hats and other felted goods and fabrics. (Communicated by Edwin Dodd M'Cracken, James M'Cracken, Charles Edward M'Cracken, John Adams Southmayd and Robert Warner Southmayd.)	1707	26th June 1865	William Edward Newton.

Subject-matter of Patent.	Number of Patent	Date.	Name of Patentee.
FIBRES, &c.—*continued.*			
Cotton gins - - - - - (Communicated by Frederick Tabor Ackland, Henry George Mitchell and Mustapha Mustapha.)	1714	27th June 1865	John Henry Johnson.
Treating and preparing flax for scutching - -	1823	10th July 1865	George Firmin.
Means or apparatus for opening and straightening wool, cotton and other fibres.	1885	16th July 1865	Joshua Thornton.
Processes and machinery for producing fibres suitable for being spun, from rags or remnants of woven or other textile fabrics made of silk, wool, cotton or other fibrous materials.	1931	19th July 1865	Henry Ernest Gillet.
An improved cotton press - - - -	1916	22nd July 1865	Samuel Boyd.
Means of and apparatus for treating animal and vegetable fibrous materials, which apparatus is also applicable to various useful purposes.	1962	27th July 1865	Henry Sherwood.
Improvements in drying grass, hay and other substances, and in the machinery for effecting the same - - - - - - (flax, hemp, cotton, wool, hair, &c.)	1969	29th July 1865	{ Baldwin Latham. { Robert Campbell.
Improvements in reducing vegetable fibre to pulp, and in machinery employed therein. (are " RAGS.")	2002	2nd Aug. 1865	William Wharton Bardon.
Machinery or apparatus for washing wool and other fibrous materials.	2039	5th Aug. 1865	John Petrie, jun'.
Process of and machinery for cleaning china grass and flax, and removing therefrom the resinous and woody matters that adhere to the useful fibres of the plant.	2078	10th Aug. 1865	Joseph Farro.
Treating of china grass or other vegetable fibrous substances }	2114	16th Aug. 1865	{ John Ingham. { John Culpan.
Manufacture of the straw of rye and other straws and grasses, into fibre, and utilizing the refuse.	2171	23rd Aug. 1865	Edward Henry Cradock Monckton.
Mode of treating the roots of the lucerne plant, for the purpose of manufacturing paper, pasteboard, fabrics and ropes therefrom. (extracting the fibres.) (Communicated by John Peter Comisade.)	2593	2nd Oct. 1865	Charles Denton Abel.
Cotton presses - - - - - (Communicated by Samuel Boyd.)	2723	21st Oct. 1865	Clotworthy Boyd.
Process of and machinery for preparing flax, hemp, jute, china grass and other analogous vegetable fibres for spinning.	2726	21st Oct. 1865	James Hill Dickson.
Improvements in machinery for compressing cotton, wool and other materials, for the economy of transit, which said improvements more particularly relate to the more expeditious filling of the box of the press and fastenings for bales.	2837	3rd Nov. 1865	James Jennings M'Comb.
Treating vegetable fibres used in the manufacture of paper and other similar substances made from pulp. (Communicated by Louis Horst.)	2882	8th Nov. 1865	Godfrey Anthony Ermen.
An improved machine for taking off the fibre from cotton seed and cleaning it.	2956	17th Nov. 1865	William Henry Cope.
Cotton gins - - - - -	3024	20th Nov. 1865	William James Burgess.

Subject-matter of Patent.	Number of Patent.	Date.	Name of Patentee.
FIBRES, &c.— continued.			
Improvements in machinery employed where weaving hair, and in preparing and treating hair for weaving. (Communicated by Charles Bradley.)	3066	29th Nov. 1865	George Tomlinson Bonsfield.
Improvements in the process of treating materials for the manufacture of paper and other similar textile fabrics, and in apparatus for the same. (Communicated by Robert Henham Collyer.)	3067	29th Nov. 1865	Charles Stuart Baker.
Improvements in the mode of applying mineral soda to the scouring and lubrication of textile matters and machinery, and in the manufacture of soap. (silk cocoons, wool, &c.)	3107	4th Dec. 1865	Leopold Joseph Bombart.
An improved method in the production of fibre from various fibrous plants and animal products.	3112	4th Dec. 1865	James Stuart.
Machinery for opening and cleaning cotton and other fibrous substances.	3120	5th Dec. 1865	Samuel Wright Wilkinson.
Machinery or apparatus for cleaning and ginning cotton and other fibrous substances.	3137	6th Dec. 1865	George Macdonald.
A new or improved method of preparing cuaurto, alpha or mogador grasses or other similar vegetable substances, for spinning, weaving, and for substitution for hair and for other fibres now in use	3150	8th Dec. 1865	Oliver Maggs. George Hedgecombe South.
Machinery for opening and cleaning cotton and other fibrous substances . . .	3223	14th Dec. 1865	Thomas Ridley Hetherington. Samuel Thornton.
Improved apparatus for manufacturing paper pulp	3245	14th Dec. 1865	William Alfred West.
Improvements in the manufacture of yarns, string and paper, and in the preparation of dyes, and in dyeing fabrics, by the application of vegetable substances not hitherto used for such purposes.	3316	22nd Dec. 1865	John Alexander Cooper.
Machinery used in tearing silk and other fabrics and rags . . .	3356	28th Dec. 1865	Sidney Collins. Charles Collins.
Means or apparatus for extracting wool from cotton and other vegetable substances contained in mixed fabrics . . .	3378	30th Dec. 1865	Arthur Knowles. James Knowles. Joshua Barraclough.
See also " SPINNING (Opening)."			
FILES AND CLIPS; FORCEPS.			
An "improved clothes fastener" that may also be used as a letter clip.	268	31st Jan. 1865	James William Gill.
Certain improved means for holding, attaching or suspending fancy articles as exposed in bazaars, show rooms or shop windows, for sale, as well as the providing of means for portably fixing or holding the price ticket to such articles, a modification of which arrangement is also applicable for holding and filing papers, or other purposes	505	23rd Feb. 1865	William Westbury. Thomas Wathen.

Subject-matter of Patent.	Number of Patent.	Date.	Name of Patentee.
FILES, &c.—continued.			
Manufacture of letter clips, book markers, paper knives, and clips for suspending stationery, drapery and pictures, and for other such like purposes	935	3rd April 1865	{ Thomas Corbett. Robert Harrington
Letter clips or paper holders . . .	1254	16th May 1865	Henry Edwin Dixon.
Files or holders for holding letters and cards, and for other like purposes.	2097	14th Aug. 1865	Frederick Bampton.
Portfolios and paper files . . . . (Communicated by Henry Tillinghast Sisson.)	2468	28th Sept. 1865	George Tomlinson Bousfield.
FILES AND RASPS.			
Manufacture of files . . . . (Communicated by Moses Griffin Crane.)	418	14th Feb. 1865	William Boxer Newbery
An improved machine for shaping file or other "blanks" by means of dies fitted into vibrating jaws.	619	4th March 1865	Thomas Turton.
Improvements in steam hammers applicable to the manufacture of files, to welding steel of common machinery and to other purposes.	641	7th March 1865	James Dodge.
Machinery or apparatus for rolling, shaping or forging metals. (blanks for files.)	701	13th March 1865	Robert Marsden.
Heating preparatory to and for the purpose of hardening or tempering of knives, files, tools and all other descriptions of cutlery or hardware usually subject to the process of hardening or tempering.	747	17th March 1865	Henry Wetherred.
File cutting machinery . . . . (Communicated by Alfred Weed.)	885	29th March 1865	William Brookes.
Machinery for cutting files . . .	1015	8th April 1865	Thomas Turton.
Heating files and file blanks . . .	1080	10th April 1865	William Brooks.
File cutting machines	1172	26th April 1865	James Dodge.
Certain improvements in machinery or apparatus for rolling or shaping metallic articles of irregular form, such as "file-blanks" and similar articles.	1190	29th April 1866	Edward McNally.
Machinery for cutting files . . . (Communicated by William Van Andre.)	1762	6th July 1865	William Clark.
File cutting machines	2546	4th Oct. 1865	John Dodge.
Means of renewing the teeth of worn out files .	2897	8th Nov. 1865	Joseph Bernard Oscar Lassen.
Machinery for cutting files . . . (Communicated by Aaron Chambers.)	3188	8th Dec. 1865	George Tomlinson Bousfield.

Subject-matter of Patent.	Number of Patent.	Date.	Name of Patentee.
FILTERING, PURIFYING AND CLARIFYING LIQUIDS; FILTERS; DISTILLING WATER, SOFTENING WATER.			
Filtering apparatuses	249	24th Jan. 1865	Victor Barg.
Filters	467	18th Feb. 1865	Richard Archibald Brooman.
(*Communicated by Gabriel Planche.*)			
Manufacture of Ink	888	24th March 1865	William Edward Newton.
(*Communicated by Josiah Vincent Lavers.*)			
Certain improvements in non-conducting composition for preventing the radiation or transmission of heat or cold. (*for coating charcoal filters.*)	904	27th March 1865	Ferdinand Le Roy.
An improved process for purifying water	1248	3rd May 1865	Carl Gustav Lenk.
Preparation of materials to be used as substitutes for animal charcoal (*for filtering water.*)	1409	22nd May 1865	Richard Müller. Arthur Thomas Weld. John Folliott Powell.
Purifying paraffine	1686	12th June 1865	John Edgar Poynter.
Improvements in distilling and rectifying, and in the apparatus employed therein, parts of which improvements are applicable to steam generators.	1682	20th June 1865	Evariste Vignier.
Preventing the incrustation of steam-boilers (*filtering the feed water.*) (*Communicated by Charles James Eames.*)	1784	29th June 1865	William Edward Newton.
An improvement in refining petroleum and other hydrocarbon oils. (*Communicated by Robert Augustus Chesebrough.*)	1980	31st July 1865	Alfred Vincent Newton.
Treatment of hydrocarbon or paraffin oils	2002	3rd Aug. 1865	John William Perkins.
Apparatus for filtering sugar and other liquid solutions	2023	4th Aug. 1865	Jean Adolphe Leon. George Trealmond. John Kissock.
Purifying water	2415	21st Sept. 1865	Alfred Bird.
An improved liquid compound for purifying sea and other waters. (*Communicated by Léandre Danjou.*)	2646	13th Oct. 1865	Richard Archibald Brooman.
Improvements in steam-boilers and other apparatus applicable to the heating and evaporation of liquids, parts of which improvements are applicable also to other purposes. (*extracting salt from water.*)	2661	14th Oct. 1865	Francis Wise. Edward Field. Enoch Harrison Aydon.
An improved process for purifying and preserving water.	2674	17th Oct. 1865	Carl Gustav Lenk.
Improvements in apparatus for obtaining fresh water from salt and impure water, also applicable for ventilating purposes.	2968	17th Nov. 1865	Samuel Hazard Huntly.
Improvements in distilling and in relieving distilled and other liquids from gases mechanically mixed therewith. (*obtaining pure water from salt water.*)	3351	27th Dec. 1865	Norman Willie Wheeler.

Subject-matter of Patent.	Number of Patent.	Date.	Name of Patentee.
FINISHING, DRESSING, SINGEING, SHEARING, FOLDING AND PRESSING WOVEN FABRICS, YARNS, &c.			
Apparatus for ironing and dressing woollen and other tissues. (Communicated by André Egron.)	148	18th Jan. 1865	François Paul Henri Cabasse.
Facing woollen cloth and other textile fabrics	178	20th Jan. 1865	{ John Snell, William Renton.
Machinery or apparatus for folding fabrics on to cardboards, for the purpose of hot pressing.	578	1st Feb. 1865	Arthur Freeman.
Improvements in the ventilation of pressing irons heated by gas, and for preventing the condensation of the vapour in the tubes or flues leading therefrom.	630	7th Feb. 1865	Samuel Egan Rosser.
An improved winder and arrangement for winding and putting up velvet and other ribands	689	11th Feb. 1865	{ Theodor Aston Yorknures. Morits Aston Yorknures.
An improved apparatus for shearing and burling all sorts of woven fabrics. (Communicated by Colorin Hippolyte Jean Pierre Demage and Jean Cominyeur.)	817	24th Feb. 1865	William Edward Gedge.
Certain improvements in machinism or apparatus for "blacking," rolling and measuring calico, linen, flannel or other woven fabrics	838	25th Feb. 1865	{ Thomas Bromfield, Thomas Edwin Jones. John Ashton.
Machinery or apparatus to be employed in the bleaching and dyeing of hanks or skeins of yarns and threads. (and finishing.)	718	11th March 1865	Longin Gautert.
Apparatus used in the winding and rewinding of silk and other fabrics.	921	1st April 1865	William Kiltey.
Improvements in wringing-machines, parts of which are applicable to the construction of rollers. (Communicated by Stephen Wing and Henry Holly.)	922	1st April 1865	Henry Lewis.
Certain improvements in dyeing or printing upon the fabric known as "oil cloth."	1006	8th April 1865	James Isherwood.
Machinery for finishing yarns or threads	1012	10th April 1865	{ Robert Ferguson, Walter Ralston.
Clamps for stretching frames and other purposes	1039	12th April 1865	Henry Brinlos.
Machinery for folding fabrics for pressing	1067	13th April 1865	William Nunkunan Yates.
Machinery for folding and carding lace or light fabrics.	1286	3rd May 1865	Thomas Wright Rae.
Means and apparatus used for stretching woven fabrics and other materials. (Communicated by Jules Durmontus.)	1289	3rd May 1865	William Clark.
Improvements in treating fibrous materials and textile fabrics, and in producing soap. (Communicated by Leon Pasqueur and Alphonsine Julie Demond.)	1442	25th May 1865	Michael Henry.
An improved plain or graduated gophering or puffing and pressing machine (blonde art, &c.)	1444	26th May 1865	{ Charles Cotton, Francis Anderson, Daniel Hunter.
Improved machinery for raising the pile of woven or other fabrics. (Communicated by Pierre Noe d'Argence.)	1514	1st June 1865	William Edward Newton.

a 2

Subject-matter of Patent.	Number of Patent.	Date.	Name of Patentee.
FINISHING, &c.—continued.			
Circular pressing machines for finishing woven fabrics.	1717	24th June 1865	William Ingham.
Machinery for cutting fustian and like fabrics	1814	8th July 1865	{ Benoni Collins. { John Butterfield.
Machinery or apparatus for folding fabrics on to cardboards or metallic plates, for the purpose of hot pressing	1909	21st July 1865	{ William Sprakman Yates. { Arthur Freeman.
Means or apparatus for cutting or shearing the nap or pile of nap or pile fabrics *(producing patterns.)*	2547	4th Oct. 1865	William Blakey Stocks. James Whitwam. William Blakey.
Machinery for folding fabrics and inserting cardboard or other substances between the folds.	2550	5th Oct. 1865	Richard Tonge.
Apparatus for steeping or treating paper pulp and other matters subjected to the action of alkalies. *(fabrics.)* *(Communicated by Messrs. Neyret, Orioli and Fredet.)*	2574	6th Oct. 1865	William Clark.
Apparatus for mangling and calendering	2597	9th Oct. 1865	Robert Walmsley.
Heating calender bowls and other cylinders or rollers.	2636	12th Oct. 1865	William Mather.
Apparatus for finishing textile fabrics	2647	13th Oct. 1865	{ William Robertson. { James Guthrie Urchar.
Improvements in calendering and finishing woven fabrics, and in apparatus employed therein.	2789	27th Oct. 1865	Edwin Heywood.
Dressing lace or other fabrics	2927	2nd Nov. 1865	William Ebenezer Dobson.
Machinery for measuring woollen and other cloths	2969	6th Nov. 1865	William Hebdon.
An improved apparatus for shrinking cotton, woollen and other textile fabrics.	3020	21th Nov. 1865	Samuel Colley Salter.
An improved apparatus for stretching and rolling fabrics for dyeing. *(Communicated by Messieurs Jules Weber and Victor Jacquet.)*	3055	29th Nov. 1865	Hector Auguste Duferot.
Improvements in machinery employed when wearing hair, and in preparing and treating hair for weaving. *(shearing or finishing when woven.)* *(Communicated by Charles Bradley.)*	3066	29th Nov. 1865	George Tomlinson Bonsfield.
Improvements in the mode of applying mineral soda to the scouring and lubrication of textile matters and machinery, and in the manufacture of soap.	3107	4th Dec. 1865	Leopold Joseph Bomhart.
A new or improved press for pressing shawls, clothes, table linen, and various other fabrics, manufactured articles and substances requiring pressure.	3184	5th Dec. 1865	William Bryan Masters.
Apparatus to be employed in stiffening fabrics	3209	12th Dec. 1865	Robert Howarth.
The conversion of the refuse of starch and gummaline into useful gummaline. *(used for dressing laces.)*	3253	18th Dec. 1865	William Ebenezer Dobson.
Preparation of glue or gelatine so as to render it insoluble in water, and applicable by the admixture of other substances to various purposes for which common glue or gelatine cannot now be used. *(for stiffening textile fabrics.)* *(Communicated by Henry Wurtz.)*	3325	23rd Dec. 1865	William Edward Newton.

Subject-matter of Patent.	Number of Patent	Date.	Name of Patentee
FINISHING, &c.—*continued.*			
Apparatus for expanding or keeping fabrics straight in passing into, "through" or out of any machine, or over, under or upon rollers - See also "DYEING."	3378	29th Dec. 1865	{ William Edleston. John Schofield.
FIRE-ARMS, GUNS, ORDNANCE, GUN CARRIAGES, TARGETS, RIFLE PRACTICE.			
Stoppers for bottles, jars, vessels and tubes, also for ordnance and fire-arms.	37	4th Jan. 1865	Nathan Thompson.
An improved method of constructing ordnance or cannon of wrought iron.	54	6th Jan. 1865	Horatio Ames.
Improvement in breech-loading fire-arms (Communicated by Wilhelm Gerhardt.)	70	10th Jan. 1865	{ Adolphe Meyer. Moritz Meyer.
Breech-loading fire-arms - - - -	106	12th Jan. 1865	George Henry Daw.
Breech-loading fire-arms - - - -	134	14th Jan. 1865	William Ansell.
Breech-loading fire-arms - - - (Communicated by Walter Fitzgerald.)	138	16th Jan. 1865	George Tomlinson Bousfield.
Breech-loading fire-arms - - - -	139	16th Jan. 1865	James Simeon Edge the elder.
Breech-loading fire-arms - - - (Communicated by Philo Remington, Samuel Remington and Eliphalet Remington.)	152	18th Jan. 1865	William Edward Newton.
Improvements in fire-arms and in ammunition for the same.	188	21st Jan. 1865	Jacob Snider, junior.
Manufacturing ordnance and gun barrels of cast steel or of homogeneous iron - - -	213	24th Jan. 1865	{ John Marshall. Henry Mills.
Breech-loading fire-arms - - - -	247	26th Jan. 1865	{ Samuel Trulock. Richard Trulock. William Trulock.
Breech-loading fire-arms and cartridges - (Communicated by Charles Claude Etienne Minié.)	253	26th Jan. 1865	William Clark.
Improvements in breech-loading guns and in priming and capping the same - -	288	30th Jan. 1865	{ Cecil Henry Russell. Joseph Needham.
Improvements in armour-plated ships, forts, gun carriages and works of defence, and in fastenings to be employed therein.	392	2nd Feb. 1865	Charles Langley.
Improvements in the manufacture of ordnance and other like castings and in the apparatus employed therein, also in carriages or moulds for the same. (Communicated by William Jones.)	395	2nd Feb. 1865	John Henry Johnson.
Breech-loading fire-arms - - - -	299	3rd Feb. 1865	Thomas Joyce.
Certain improvements in revolving fire-arms and cartridges for the same.	308	4th Feb. 1865	Stephen Webb Wood.
Breech-loading fire-arms - - - -	358	8th Feb. 1865	Edward Lindner.
Locks for fire-arms - - - -	368	9th Feb. 1865	John Parker Lindsay.
Certain improvements in breech-loading ordnance -	372	10th Feb. 1865	Alfred Krupp.
Improvements in breech-loading fire-arms and in cartridges for breech-loading fire-arms.	423	14th Feb. 1865	Johann Von der Poppenburg.

Subject-matter of Patent.	Number of Patent.	Date.	Name of Patentee.
FIRE-ARMS, &c.—*continued.*			
Breech-loading fire-arms - - - -	494	14th Feb. 1865	James Purdey.
Fire-arms - - - - - (Communicated by Charles Edward Snider.)	495	14th Feb. 1865	Benjamin Thompson.
Breech-loading fire-arms - - - -	506	23rd Feb. 1865	William Henry Aubin.
Improvements in ships of war, partly applicable to ships designed for the merchant service. (gun carriage.) (Communicated by Augustus Walker.)	509	23rd Feb. 1865	George Haseltine.
Cap carriers for fire-arms - - - -	519	24th Feb. 1865	Henry Everard Clifton. Saul Myers. Abraham Hoffnung.
A magazine repeating and breech-loading rifle - (Communicated by Joshua Gray.)	540	25th Feb. 1865	Edward Henry Eldredge.
Rocket guns and rocket harpoons and apparatus to be used therewith, for the capture of whales and other purposes - - - - -	583	27th Feb. 1865	Thomas Welcome Roys. Gustavus Adolphus Lilliendahl.
Breech-loading fire-arms - - - - (Communicated by John Webster Cochran.)	642	8th March 1865	Frederick Tolhausen.
Revolving fire-arms - - - - (Communicated by Sebastien Amédée Noel and François Gevary.)	650	9th March 1865	William Clark.
Improvements in breech-loading fire-arms and in cartridges for breech-loading fire-arms. (Partly communicated by William Montgomery Storm.)	708	14th March 1865	Francis Augustus Beaendolin.
Breech-loading fire-arms - - - -	711	14th March 1865	Richard Archibald Brooman.
Breech-loading fire-arms - - - -	772	20th March 1865	John Thomas Cook. John Thomas Cook the younger.
Improvements in vessels of war and in ordnance -	783	21st March 1865	William Vincent Greene.
Fire-arms - - - - -	790	21st March 1865	Richard Jordan Gatling.
Improvements in the construction of fire-arms and in cartridges for the same.	800	22nd March 1865	Alfred Pierre Tronchon.
Improvements in stoppers for bottles, jars or other vessels, the same being applicable to fire-arms and ordnance.	814	23rd March 1865	Charles Henry Crown.
Gun locks - - - - -	838	24th March 1865	Daniel Arnold.
Improvements in fire-arms and in apparatus for extracting cartridges and cartridge cases therefrom.	969	5th April 1865	Charles William Lancaster.
Breech-loading fire-arms - - - -	987	7th April 1865	Andrew Muir.
A new or improved apparatus for supporting and steadying the arm in rifle shooting.	1014	8th April 1865	Jean Baptiste Hussman.
Improvements in fire-arms, and in cartridges to be used therewith and with other fire-arms.	1046	12th April 1865	Thomas Jefferson Mayall.
Breech-loading fire-arms - - - -	1071	17th April 1865	Alexander Henry.
Breech-loading fire-arms - - - - (Communicated by Henry Oliver Peabody.)	1092	19th April 1865	George Tomlinson Bousfield.
Certain improvements in breech-loading fire-arms - (Communicated by Monsieur Marie Joseph Eugene du Liège de Psychameis.)	1158	24th April 1865	Peter Armand Le Comte de Fontaine Moreau.
Breech-loading needle guns for military and other purposes.	1146	24th April 1865	John Frederik Christian Carle.

Subject-matter of Patent.	Number of Patent.	Date.	Name of Patentee.
FIRE-ARMS, &c.—*continued.*			
Improvements in breech-loading fire-arms and ordnance, and in projectiles.	1177	27th April 1865	James Carr.
Breech-loading guns - - - -	1197	29th April 1865	Lewis Wells Broadwell.
Fire-arms - - - - - -	1207	1st May 1865	Emile Della-Noce.
Improvements in the manufacture of pig iron or foundry metal, and in making and treating castings of such metals. (*for founding guns.*)	1208	1st May 1865	Henry Bessemer.
An improvement in igniting the fuzes of shells - (*Communicated by Thomas Taylor.*)	1211	1st May 1865	John Blackie, jun'.
Breech-loading fire-arms - - - -	1276	9th May 1865	{ Stephen Law. Joseph Law.
Breech-loading fire-arms and cartridges - -	1289	9th May 1865	John Charles Conybeare.
Breech-loading fire-arms - - - -	1293	10th May 1865	Patrick O'Hagan.
Improvements in breech-loading fire-arms, and in cartridges for breech-loading fire-arms.	1308	11th May 1865	Joseph Rock Cooper.
Improvements in breech-loading fire-arms and ordnance, and in apparatus connected therewith.	1328	13th May 1865	Thomas Craig.
Improvements in the mode of rifling muzzle-loading cannon, and in projectiles for the same. (*Communicated by John Seipel.*)	1332	13th May 1865	William Spence.
Certain improvements in the manufacture of gun barrels and ordnance - - - - }	1341	15th May 1865	{ William Deakin. John Bagnall Johnson.
Apparatus to be used with breech-loading fire-arms and ordnance. (or "CARTRIDGES.")	1346	16th May 1865	Pierre Camille Lafont.
Improvements in breech-loading fire-arms, and in cartridges and bayonets for breech-loading fire-arms. (*Communicated by Charles Rocius.*)	1349	16th May 1865	Richard Archibald Brooman.
Breech-loading fire-arms - - - -	1392	19th May 1865	Samuel Ehrill.
A new kind of casing intended to protect the stock and lock of fire-arms, with guiding caps to take aim.	1403	22nd May 1865	André Gustave Bigorie.
Fire-arms - - - - - -	1433	25th May 1865	Edward Paton.
Improvements in breech-loading fire-arms and ordnance, and in cartridges for breech-loading fire-arms.	1436	25th May 1865	Thomas Wilson.
Improvements in breech-loading fire-arms and in sights for rifles.	1461	27th May 1865	Thomas Bissell.
Certain improvements in the formation and construction of metallic vessels, chambers or hollow cylinders used in hydraulic apparatus, cannon or heavy guns, and for like purposes.	1506	1st June 1865	Herbert Allman.
Breech-loading fire-arms - - - -	1525	3rd June 1865	Alfred Lancaster.
Improvements in breech-loading fire-arms and in metallic cartridge cases for the same. (*Communicated by James Ingersoll Day.*)	1545	6th June 1865	George Haseltine.
Central fire breech-loading fire-arms - -	1602	8th June 1865	Joseph Rock Cooper.
Improvements applicable to breech-loading fire-arms	1651	20th June 1865	Abraham Colley.
Manufacturing gun barrels and tubes of cast steel and homogeneous iron.	1728	30th June 1865	Henry Powell Tipper.

Subject-matter of Patent.	Number of Patent.	Date.	Name of Patentee.
FIRE-ARMS, &c.—*continued.*			
Improvements in breech-loading fire-arms and in cartridges to be used therewith. (Communicated by Pierre Didier Jardinier.)	1760	1st July 1865	William Edward Newton.
An improved method of training guns - - -	1789	7th July 1865	Henry Duncan Preston Cunningham.
Carriages for breech-loading ordnance - -	1801	7th July 1865	Fischer Alexander Wilson.
Fire-arms - - - - - - -	1806	7th July 1865	{ Robert Green. { John William Heinke.
Improvements in portable charge holders for breech-loading guns, whether single or double barrelled, as also in the means of manufacturing the said holders and in exploding the charge.	1888	20th July 1865	Charles Roman.
Improvements in fire-arms and in cartridges for the same.	1889	24th July 1865	William Tranter.
Improvements in breech-loading fire-arms and in the charges and projectiles to be used therewith.	1894	29th July 1865	William La Penotière.
An improved method of working guns - -	2014	3rd Aug. 1865	Henry Duncan Preston Cunningham.
Revolver pistols - - - - - - (Communicated by Pierre Drieux and Claude Joseph Sirou.)	2027	4th Aug. 1865	Henri Adrien Bonneville.
Improvements in breech-loading fire-arms and in revolving fire-arms, and in cartridges.	2030	4th Aug. 1865	Thomas William Webley.
An improvement in gun wipers - - - (Communicated by Hiram Berdan, Charles Lawrence Perkins and Walter Hoyes Barns.)	2031	4th Aug. 1865	Alfred Vincent Newton.
Fire-arms - - - - - - -	2060	7th Aug. 1865	William Castle Dodge.
Breech-loading fire-arms - - - -	2068	9th Aug. 1865	{ Stephen Law. { Joseph Law.
Improvements in revolving fire-arms, in projectiles and cartridges.	2108	15th Aug. 1865	James Brown.
Breech-loading fire-arms - - - -	2161	19th Aug. 1865	William Soper.
Improvements in the manufacture of steel iron and metal suitable for bearings, and in apparatus for the same. (gun metal.)	2175	24th Aug. 1865	William Colbourne Cambridge.
Breech-loading revolvers - - - -	2210	24th Aug. 1865	Prosper Fulain.
Improvements in the construction of fire-arms, such improvements being also applicable to the alteration and adaptation of parts of existing fire-arms.	2275	5th Sept. 1865	Jacob Snider, junior.
Treating, working or manipulating cast steel, for the manufacture of wheel tires, armour plates or other articles requiring great hardness and tensile strength. (except for ordnance.)	2277	5th Sept. 1865	Julius Grand.
Mounting and working guns in ships, forts and batteries.	2306	8th Sept. 1865	John Walker.
Breech-loading fire-arms and cartridges - -	2345	13th Sept. 1865	Frederic Waller Prince.
Improvements in the manufacture of tubes for gun barrels and other purposes, parts of which improvements are also applicable to the manufacture of rods or bars, and to the rifling of ordnance and fire-arms.	2351	14th Sept. 1865	Gustavus Palmer Harding.

Subject-matter of Patent.	Number of Patent.	Date.	Name of Patentee.
FIRE-ARMS, &c.—continued.			
An improved form of rifling for fire-arms and ordnance.	2254	14th Sept. 1865	Wilmot Burrows Edward Ellis.
An improved construction of projectile - - . (and firing.) (Communicated by Orazio Lago.)	2291	16th Sept. 1866	Alfred Vincent Newton.
Improvements in breech-loading fire-arms and in cartridges to be used therewith. (Communicated by Hiram Berdan.)	2436	23rd Sept. 1865	William Edward Newton.
Breech-loading fire-arms - - - . (Communicated by Samuel Norris.)	2452	25th Sept. 1865	Alexander Prince.
Fire-arms and ordnance - - - - - . (Communicated by Anthony Arthur Varas.)	2468	26th Sept. 1865	William Edward Newton.
Improvements in rifling fire-arms and in missiles or projectiles used in such, and in the machinery for the production of these improvements.	2488	24th Sept. 1865	William Ellis Metford.
Improvements in breech-loading guns and in projectiles and cartridges.	2512	30th Sept. 1865	Edward Lindner.
Breech-loading fire-arms - - - .	2552	5th Oct. 1865	{ John Miller, Bethel Burton.
Construction of gun carriages - - - .	2560	6th Oct. 1865	George Wightwick Rendel.
Breech-loading fire-arms - - - . (Partly communicated by Albert Rohde.)	2645	13th Oct. 1865	Henry Hedley Williams.
Improvements in tompions for ordnance and small arms, and in stoppers for bottles and other vessels. (Communicated by George Richard Wilmot.)	2650	13th Oct. 1865	William Edward Newton.
Improvements in central-fire breech-loading fire-arms, and in ammunition for the same - }	2709	20th Oct. 1865	{ Joseph Nordham. George Henry Nordham.
Construction of gun locks for the discharging central-fire cartridges as used in breech-loading fire-arms.	2743	24th Oct. 1865	Frederick Hargrave Gray.
Breech-loading fire-arms - - - .	2762	25th Oct. 1865	William Middleditch Scott.
Breech-loading fire-arms - - - . (Communicated by Cyprien Chabot and George Joseph Richardson.)	2772	27th Oct. 1865	William Edward Newton.
Manufacture of ordnance whole or in parts -	2795	30th Oct. 1865	{ William Deakin. John Bagnall Johnson.
Fire-arms - - - - - - . (Communicated by Emile Delis-Nore.)	2800	31st Oct. 1865	Charles Chataway.
Apparatus for working, pointing and checking the recoil of cannon or ordnance. (Communicated by John Ericsson.)	2849	7th Nov. 1865	William Edward Newton.
Fire-arms and projectiles - - - - .	2902	11th Nov. 1865	Charles William Jones.
Breech-loading fire-arms - - - - .	2956	17th Nov. 1865	Joseph Rock Cooper.
Gun carriages - - - - - .	2976	20th Nov. 1865	{ Thomas Bridges Heathorn. Joseph Henry George Wells.
Improvements in breech-loading guns, and in cartridges for breech-loading guns.	2981	20th Nov. 1865	Charles Witney.
Certain new and useful improvements in breech-loading and repeating fire-arms. (Communicated by Albert Ball.)	3012	23rd Nov. 1865	Ebenezer Goodnow Lamsod.

Subject-matter of Patent.	Number of Patent.	Date.	Name of Patentee.
FIRE-ARMS, &c.—continued.			
Improvements in casting iron and steel and in apparatus employed for this purpose. (ordnance.)	3016	24th Nov. 1865	Joseph Whitworth.
Mounting ordnance	3021	21th Nov. 1865	Robert Mallet.
Certain improvements in breech-loading fire-arms	3082	1st Dec. 1865	William Pringle.
Construction of breech-loading fire-arms	3112	4th Dec. 1865	Edwin Charles Hodges.
Breech-loading fire-arms (Communicated by Philo Remington, Samuel Remington and Eliphalet Remington.)	3131	7th Dec. 1865	Samuel Norris.
Machinery for rolling gun barrels and other articles	3155	8th Dec. 1865	Thomas Claridge.
Improvements in breech-loading fire-arms, and in cartridges for breech-loading fire-arms.	3176	9th Dec. 1865	Thomas Wilson.
An improved method of and apparatus for the working of breech-loading guns.	3197	11th Dec. 1865	William Jeremiah Murphy.
Improvements in breech-loading fire-arms and in ammunition for the same.	3249	15th Dec. 1865	James Aston.
Breech-loading fire-arms and rotating breech cylinder pistols, and cartridges to be used therewith. (Communicated by Silas Crispin.)	3258	16th Dec. 1865	Alfred Vincent Newton.
Repeating fire-arms (Communicated by Oliver Fisher Winchester.)	3284	19th Dec. 1865	William Clark.
Improvements in the manufacture of metal tubes for gun barrels and other purposes, and in machinery or apparatus employed therein.	3329	25th Dec. 1865	Thomas Ricketts.
Improvements in the manufacture of steel and purified iron, and in the apparatus employed therein. (making copper.) (Communicated by Antoine Galy-Cazalat.)	3300	21st Dec. 1865	Henri Adrien Bonneville.
Improvements in breech-loading fire-arms, and in cartridges for breech-loading fire-arms.	3337	26th Dec. 1865	Charles Reeves.
Improvements in breech-loading fire-arms, and in cartridges for the same.	3348	27th Dec. 1865	William Castle Dodge.

For ammunition, see "CARTRIDGES."
" "GUNPOWDER."
" "SHOT."

FIRE-ENGINES; FIRE-ESCAPES; EXTINGUISHING FIRES.

Locomotive engines and carriages for common roads and tramways, and also for agricultural and other purposes.	780	20th March 1865	Alexander Richard Mackenzie.
Fire-escapes and portable ladders	1104	25th April 1865	Thomas Dixon Whitehead.
An improved self-acting apparatus for and means of extinguishing fires	1279	9th May 1865	Joe Green Hey. Valentine Savory.
Fire-engines	1404	22nd May 1865	James Shand.

Subject-matter of Patent.	Number of Patent.	Date.	Name of Patentee.
FIRE-ENGINES, &c.—continued.			
A new preparation for subduing and extinguishing fire. (Communicated by Gustav Zeisler.)	1480	26th May 1865	Charles Benjamin Spaeth.
An improved fire-escape, applicable also to raising loads from mines and other purposes. (Communicated by Xavier Philippart.)	1606	21st June 1865	William Edward Gedge.
Means of and apparatus for raising water for agricultural and other useful and ornamental purposes. (in case of fire.) (Communicated by Jean Louis Celestin Ackard.)	1616	22nd July 1865	William Edward Gedge.
Fire-engines and hydraulic machines - -	1683	24th July 1865	Leon Paul Laroche.
Self-acting apparatus for extinguishing fire and sounding fire alarms - - - -	2100	15th Aug. 1865	{ William Oldfield Wilson. Joseph Wilson.
Arrangement and fittings of certain apparatuses for extinguishing fires.	2373	16th Sept. 1865	François Carlier.
Improvements in apparatus and means for extinguishing fires, part of such improvements being applicable for other purposes.	2559	5th Oct. 1865	William Henry Phillips.
Certain improvements in telegraphic communication for the purpose of indicating danger. (giving alarm at fire-engine stations.)	2584	7th Oct. 1865	Charles Hanson Mellor.
Double or single action pumps - - - (Communicated by Claude Genin.)	2622	11th Oct. 1865	William Edward Gedge.
An improved mode of extinguishing fires in warehouses, offices, dwelling houses, theatres, ships and other buildings or structures.	2854	4th Nov. 1865	James Charles Edington.
An improved safety net to arrest the fall of persons or heavy bodies under circumstances of danger. (in case of fire)	2969	18th Nov. 1865	Léon Edouard Laurency.
Apparatus applicable for fire-escapes and builders' scaffolds.	3148	5th Dec. 1865	Edward Vagg.
Boilers or apparatus for generating steam - - (for fire-engines.) (Communicated by Julien Belleville.)	3369	16th Dec. 1865	Richard Archibald Brooman.
Pumps - - - - - - - } (for fire-engines.)	3330	23rd Dec. 1865	{ Henry Davis Hoskold. William Blanch Brain.
Obtaining and employing continuous lengths of tanned leather for various useful purposes (ropes for fire-escapes.) }	3534	23rd Dec. 1865	{ George Huro. Daniel Huro.

FIRE-PLACES, GRATES AND STOVES; FENDERS AND FIRE GUARDS.

Means of and apparatus for generating steam and heat. (portable stove.)	83	5th Jan. 1865	John Malsbury Kirby.
Improvements in effecting the combustion of fuel in the furnaces of steam-boilers and the fire-places of stoves, and of gas in gas-burners, and in apparatus connected therewith.	611	4th Feb. 1865	Frank Clarke Hills.

Subject-matter of Patent.	Number of Patent.	Date.	Name of Patentee.
FIRE-PLACES, &c.—continued.			
Fire-places - - - - - -	407	13th Feb. 1865	Edward Brown Wilson.
Furnaces and fire-places - - - -	693	11th March 1865	Edward Brown Wilson.
Improvements in the manufacture of metallic bedsteads, which improvements are also applicable to the manufacture of other metallic articles. (crinoline guards.)	698	13th March 1865	James Atkins.
Stoves or fire-places, ash pans and fenders - - (fender or dress protector.)	826	23rd March 1865	James Clifford Morgan.
Construction of kitchen ranges having their fire-places enclosed.	876	24th March 1865	Frederick Thomas.
Kitchen ranges - - - - -	940	3rd April 1865	Frederick Brown.
Fire-places and flues and apparatus connected therewith.	969	7th April 1865	Edward Welch.
Construction of and mode of supplying fuel to fire-grates, stoves and the furnaces of locomotive and other steam-boilers.	1259	5th May 1865	Charles Lamport.
Furnace fire-grates - - - - -	1270	9th May 1865	James Buchanan.
Manufacture of wire gauze dish covers, plate covers, window blinds, fire guards, and meat safes - - - - - -	1401	22nd May 1865	David Powis. Henry Brittain the younger.
Improvements applicable to furnace bars and fire grates.	1678	21st June 1865	Samuel Godfrey.
An improved method of and apparatus for burning liquid hydrocarbons, and the employment thereof for heating purposes. (Communicated by Alexandre Schpakofsky and Nicolas Stamps.)	1711	27th June 1865	Richard Archibald Brooman.
The use and application of paper, printed or otherwise ornamented with water colors, for covering floors and other analogous purposes, as a substitute for carpets and oil cloths, and of an improved coating or varnish to be applied to the same, to protect its surface from injury and wear. (and for covering fuel boxes.)	1878	19th July 1865	Anson Henry Platt.
Construction of cooking stoves and ranges -	1944	26th July 1865	William Barton.
Method of heating the ovens and boilers of kitchen ranges or cooking stoves.	2176	24th Aug. 1865	Frederick Thomas.
Improvements in apparatus by means of which certain liquids, common air and certain elastic fluids are made available in the production of light, and their quantity regulated and measured, parts of which improvements are applicable for other purposes. (preserving uniform temperature in stoves.)	2184	25th Aug. 1865	Edwin Augustus Corley.
An improved fire-place with turning grate -	2296	7th Sept. 1865	Abel Duvernois.
An improved method of and apparatus for separating ashes from cinders.	2607	16th Oct. 1865	James Lamb Hancock.
Gas stoves - - - - - -	2936	14th Nov. 1865	Samuel Lawrence Gill.
Stoves for drying moulds - - - - (see " FURNACES.")	2943	15th Nov. 1865	Henry Cochrane.
Cooking apparatus - - - - -	2971	18th Nov. 1865	Samuel Hazard Huntly.
Certain improvements in the manufacture of knobs for doors, cupboards, ash-pans, and for other like purposes.	3091	1st Dec. 1865	John Wilson.

Subject-matter of Patent.	Number of Patent.	Date	Name of Patentee.
FIRE-PLACES, &c.—continued.			
A new and improved fire pot and retort for stoves, ranges and furnaces in which steam is generated and superheated.	3140	6th Dec. 1865	William Ennis.
Improvements in steam-boilers and in the furnaces and grates thereof, the same improvements in furnaces and grates being also applicable to other furnaces and to stoves. (Communicated by Robert Winslow Davis, Daniel Davis and Henry Sheldon Anable.)	3141	6th Dec. 1865	William Edward Newton.
Construction of kitchen stoves and cooking ranges	3144	6th Dec. 1865	George Fitzjames Russell.
Construction of fire-places and furnaces . .	3247	16th Dec. 1865	George Warriner.
Fire-places, furnaces and stoves . . .	3337	23rd Dec. 1865	Julius Jeffreys.
FISHING; FISHING NETS, FISH HOOKS, HARPOONS.			
An improvement in fish hooks . . .	429	15th Feb. 1865	William Ashton Hackett.
Rocket guns and rocket harpoons and apparatus to be used therewith, for the capture of whales and other purposes	550	27th Feb. 1865	Thomas Welcome Roys. Gustavus Adolphus Lilieodahl.
Machinery for the manufacture of fish hooks	2673	17th Oct. 1865	Albert Fenárc.
Fish hooks	3177	9th Dec. 1865	Charles Baylis.
Obtaining and employing continuous lengths of tanned leather for various useful purposes (note for fishing and for aviaries.)	3334	23rd Dec. 1865	George Hurn. Daniel Hurn.
FLUES AND CHIMNEYS; CHIMNEY TOPS; CURING SMOKY CHIMNEYS; CHIMNEY WIND GUARDS.			
Certain improvements in the construction of tubular boilers, and in the means for cleaning the tubes of such boilers	37	5th Jan. 1865	James Chapman Amos. William Anderson.
Improvements in furnaces, ash-pits and fires, for the consumption of smoke and noxious products of combustion, and in the apparatus or means connected therewith.	51	6th Jan. 1865	James Robertson.
Motive-power and means of communication between passengers while travelling, and appliances connected therewith.	55	7th Jan. 1865	George Bell Galloway.
Improvements in furnace flues for the consumption of smoke.	94	11th Jan. 1865	Abraham Cooper.
Boilers for generating steam	115	13th Jan. 1865	Richard Lewis.
Improvements in steam generators or steam-boilers and furnaces, part of which is also applicable to other heat generating apparatus.	242	27th Jan. 1865	Joseph Twibill.

SUBJECT-MATTER INDEX OF

Subject-matter of Patent.	Number of Patent.	Date.	Name of Patentee.
FLUE, &c.—continued.			
Means of and apparatus for treating animal and vegetable fibrous materials, which apparatus is also applicable to various useful purposes. (*preventing deposition of carbon in boiler tubes.*)	1868	27th July 1865	Henry Sherwood.
Improvements in and connected with the manufacture of copper.	2100	14th Aug. 1865	James Thomas Lockey.
Improvements in boilers and furnaces, and in cleansing the flues thereof - - -	2291	6th Sept. 1865	Edward Green, Edward Green (the younger.
A locomotive car - - - - - - (*smoke and exhaust pipe.*)	2344	13th Sept. 1865	Joseph Page Woodbury.
Improved apparatus for cleaning the tubes of steam-boilers. (*Communicated by Daniel M'Dowell.*)	2346	13th Sept. 1865	Samuel Bolitar.
Improvements in the manufacture of bricks, blocks, flue covers and tiles, and in the machinery and apparatus employed therefor.	2392	19th Sept. 1865	James Gillespie.
Apparatus for ventilating and for preventing down draught in flues.	2457	26th Sept. 1865	John Hillier.
Improvements in coke and charcoal ovens and in the manufacture of coke, parts of which are applicable to bread, biscuit and pastry ovens.	2477	27th Sept. 1865	William Morgans.
Collecting or drawing off the gases from blast furnaces - - - - -	2507	29th Sept. 1865	John Addenbrooke, George Addenbrooke, Philip Anthony Millward.
Improvements in apparatus for the regulation of the up and down currents of air, and for the prevention and cure of smoky chimneys.	2602	10th Oct. 1865	William Cooke.
An improved ventilating apparatus for use in steam boats, vessels and other places requiring to be ventilated.	2609	10th Oct. 1865	John Garrison Woodward.
Improvements in the construction of steam generators, applicable also to the construction of condensers, the heating of water generally, and to the warming of buildings. (*Communicated by Joseph Harrison, jun., and Thomas Landers.*)	2610	10th Oct. 1865	John Henry Johnson.
Improvements in steam-boilers and other apparatus applicable to the heating and evaporation of liquids, parts of which improvements are applicable also to other purposes - - -	2681	16th Oct. 1865	Francis Wise, Edward Field, Enoch Harrison Aydon.
An improved apparatus for forming or repairing the mouths of boiler and other tubes. (*Communicated by Edward Clark.*)	2697	19th Oct. 1865	George Berridy Ghiselin.
Construction of furnaces and boilers for the consumption of smoke - - -	2746	24th Oct. 1865	Charles Matthews, Henry Booth Southwick, John Frereday.
An improved mode of and apparatus for cleaning the tubes of steam-boilers. (*Communicated by Abraham Byrom.*)	2761	26th Oct. 1865	George Davies.
An improved apparatus for increasing draught in and preventing or curing smoky chimneys, and economising heat. (*Communicated by François Perrachon.*)	2822	2nd Nov. 1865	William Edward Gedge.
Stoves for drying moulds - - - (*formation of flues.*)	2942	15th Nov. 1865	Henry Cochrane.

Subject-matter of Patent.	Number of Patent.	Date.	Name of Patentee.
FLUES, &c.—continued.			
Cooking apparatus	2971	18th Nov. 1865	Samuel Hazard Huntly.
An improved chimney cowl *(Communicated by Victor Etienne Antoine Berne and Irma Victorine Carabin.)*	3083	29th Nov. 1865	Henry Edward Newton.
Improvements in steam-boilers and in the furnaces and grates thereof, the same improvements in furnaces and grates being also applicable to other furnaces and to stoves. *(Communicated by Robert Winslow Davis, Daniel Davis and Henry Sheldon .Isable.)*	3141	6th Dec. 1865	William Edward Newton.
An improved mode of applying the compression of air for ventilating purpose, and the compression of any gas for burrying along elastic fluids in conveying pipes *(increasing draft of chimneys.)*	3183	8th Dec. 1865	Pierron de Mondésir. Paul Lebarbre. Augustin Jullimane.
Improvements in steam-boilers and in apparatus adapted for cleaning the flues of boilers.	3194	9th Dec. 1865	Norman Willis Wheeler.
Boilers or apparatus for generating steam *(preservation of the tubes.)* *(Communicated by Julien Belleville.)*	3269	16th Dec. 1865	Richard Archibald Brooman.
Pipes, tubular columns and hollow structures, for masts, cars, shear legs, life boats and ordinary boats, for water, gas and waste water pipes, and for other similar constructions where great strength is required. *(passages for smoke.)*	3314	22nd Dec. 1865	Edward Deane.
FOOD FOR CATTLE ; FODDER-CUTTING ; CHAFF-CUTTING ; ROOT-PULPING.			
Manufacture of oil cake and food for animals	282	1st Feb. 1865	George Julius Vertue.
Improved machinery for cutting, sifting, separating, bruising, braising and preparing straw and other vegetable fibrous substances to be employed in the manufacture of various kinds of paper, and also for preparing food for cattle	340	7th Feb. 1865	John Carnes. William Simpson.
Machinery or apparatus for preparing and supplying food for cattle.	927	1st April 1865	Robert Willacy.
Apparatus applicable to machines for cutting hay, straw and such like substances	984	3rd April 1865	Richard Robert Riches. Charles James Watts.
Improved apparatus for reducing wheat and other straw. *(as cattle food.)*	986	6th April 1865	Richard Garrett, jun'.
Machines for cutting hay, straw and other vegetable substances	1601	1st June 1865	Francis Richmond. Henry Chandler. James Gadsby Richmond.
Apparatus for cutting hay, straw and other vegetable material.	1712	27th June 1865	James Spratt.
Improvements in food for horses and in the preparation of the same.	1829	10th July 1865	Robert Hinson.
Preparation and preservation of food for animals	1857	15th July 1865	Richard Vine Tosoo.

Subject-matter of Patent.	Number of Patent.	Date.	Name of Patentee.
FOOD FOR CATTLE, &c.—continued.			
Applying and utilising water power (driving chaff cutters.)	1867	29th July 1865	Valentine Baker.
Machinery or apparatus for preparing and supplying food for cattle.	2516	30th Sept. 1865	Robert Willacy.
Treating brewers' grains in order to render them more suitable for the food of animals.	2899	10th Nov. 1865	Edward John Davis.
An improved apparatus for apportioning the fodder of horses, cattle and other domestic animals.	3257	14th Dec. 1865	Jacques Masson.
FORTIFICATIONS, BATTERIES, SHIPS OF WAR, GUN-BOATS, ARMOUR PLATED SHIPS.			
Construction of armour-plated ships, forts, and other like structures.	286	1st Feb. 1865	John Hughes.
Improvements in armour plated ships, forts, gun carriages and works of defence, and in fastenings to be employed therein.	292	2nd Feb. 1865	Charles Langley.
Improvements in armour plated and other ships or vessels, also applicable to fortifications generally.	296	2nd Feb. 1865	Julius Saunders Jeffreys.
A new method for removing or destroying the momentum of heavy bodies by means of an elastic machine or machines, so as to prevent injury and damage from concussion, applicable to ship cables, ship and fort armour, railway trains, tenders to piers-heads and floating piers, gangways, breakwaters and other similar structures, also as a motive-power. (Communicated by William Graham M'Ivor.)	321	6th Feb. 1865	Clemente Roberts Markham.
Construction of armour plated ships. (Communicated by Charles Otis Halpole.)	438	15th Feb. 1865	George Tomlinson Bousfield.
Armour plates for vessels of war and for other similar purposes.	455	17th Feb. 1865	John Brown.
Improvements in ships of war, partly applicable to ships designed for the merchant service. (Communicated by Augustus Walker.)	509	23rd Feb. 1865	George Haseltine.
Improvements in vessels of war and in ordnance	783	21st March 1865	William Vincent Greuer.
Improvements in the construction of ships of war and floating batteries, part of which improvements are applicable to land fortifications.	1107	20th April 1865	Henry Caudwell.
Improvements in iron fortifications, such improvements being applicable to the construction and protection of ships and floating batteries.	1209	1st May 1865	George Johnson.
Improving and strengthening shields of steel, iron or iron or other material, for ships, fortifications and other constructions.	1235	2nd May 1865	Thomas Hay Campbell.
Sheathing iron ships	1618	14th June 1865	William Robinson Mulley.
Floating lights, beacons, floating batteries and other vessels.	2170	24th Aug. 1865	John Mondy.

Subject-matter of Patent.	Number of Patent.	Date.	Name of Patentee.
FORTIFICATIONS, &c.—continued.			
Treating, working or manipulating cast steel, for the manufacture of wheel tires, armour plates, or other articles requiring great hardness and tensile strength.	2277	5th Sept. 1866	Julius Grund.
Mounting and working guns in ships, forts and batteries.	2300	8th Sept. 1865	John Walker.
New or improved means and apparatus for destroying ships and such like floating bodies, parts of which said apparatus are also applicable to saving life and property at sea. (Communicated by Monsieur Stanislas Sorel.)	2758	26th Oct. 1865	Hector Auguste Dufresne.
FUEL; TREATING COAL; PREPARING FIRE-WOOD; FIRE-LIGHTERS.			
Improvements in the treatment of carbonaceous minerals and in apparatus for preparing agglomerated fuel.	40	6th Jan. 1865	Joseph Emile Vigoulette.
Artificial fuel - - - - -	81	10th Jan. 1865	{ Daniel Colladont. Frederick Pontifex. }
Machinery for compressing coal dust and other materials fit for burning, also clay into bricks, tiles, pipes and other like articles.	220	26th Jan. 1865	William Smith.
Improvements in treating or manufacturing peat for fuel and in apparatus for the same.	319	4th Feb. 1865	Robert Marcellet Alloway.
A chemical combustible substance and apparatus to which it is applicable. (Communicated by François Stoher.)	477	20th Feb. 1865	William Edward Gedge.
Improvements in drying and sorting coals, peat and mineral ores, in separating extraneous matters therefrom, and in apparatus used in these processes.	715	14th March 1865	Ferdinand Henry Wastlich.
New or improved apparatus for separating or sorting and washing ores, minerals, coal, emery, and other substances in a granular or pulverulent state. (Communicated by Charles Prieger and Theodor Heudt.)	963	5th April 1865	Henry Simon.
Improvements in the manufacture of iron, and in preparing fuel to be used in the manufacture and melting of iron - - -	1153	25th April 1865	{ John Northall Brown. Thomas Deykin Clare. }
Manufacture of artificial fuel applicable chiefly to the kindling of fires.	1438	25th May 1865	Henry Gibbs.
Manufacture of artificial fuel - - -	1547	6th June 1865	David Barker.
A new or improved artificial fuel - - -	1600	13th June 1865	Charles James Collins.
Improved machinery for compressing and solidifying coal and other analogous substances.	1606	14th June 1865	Henry George Fairburn.
An improved pulping and compressing machine, for the treatment of peat as a fuel, and gas for illuminating purposes - - -	1702	26th June 1865	{ Charles Wormann. George Evans. }
An improved mode of combining and forming small coal or coal dust into lumps, blocks or otherwise, to be employed for the purposes of fuel.	1710	29th June 1865	Henry George Fairburn.

Subject-matter of Patent.	Number of Patent.	Date.	Name of Patentee.
FUEL, &c.—continued.			
A new or improved method of dissolving pitch (Communicated by François Colestin Armelin.)	1770	4th July 1865	Richard Archibald Brooman.
Means or method of applying mineral oils for generating steam and heat. (for fuel.) (Partly communicated by Alexandre Sapis.)	1999	25th July 1865	Wladislaus Zbyszewski.
Apparatus for burning combustible and volatile liquids for generating steam and similar purposes. (Communicated by Patrick Hoyer.)	1938	26th July 1865	George Tomlinson Bousfield.
Method of and apparatus for treating peat and other plastic materials (for fuel.)	2219	25th Aug. 1865	{ Hull Terrell. Thomas Ikin.
Separation of sulphide of iron from coal and carbonaceous matter.	2252	1st Sept. 1865	Thomas Louse.
Means and apparatus applicable to the lighting and reviving of fires.	2329	11th Sept. 1865	Charles James Webb.
Preparing peat or turf for fire lights and fuel, and for machinery to be employed therein.	2438	23rd Sept. 1865	Thomas Vincent Lee.
Machinery for tempering and preparing peat for fuel. (Communicated by Nathaniel Frothingham Potter.)	2469	26th Sept. 1865	George Tomlinson Bousfield.
Caloric or hot air engines (Communicated by Guillaume Reiciris.)	2675	17th Oct. 1865	Richard Archibald Brooman.
A new or improved steam economising apparatus, or an apparatus intended to make available as fuel all or part of the steam actually evolving from engines into the atmosphere, and also to absorb the smoke resulting from the combustion.	2676	17th Oct. 1865	François Georges Ricardo.
Improved machinery for compressing and solidifying coal, clay and other analogous substances.	3243	14th Dec. 1865	Henry George Fairburn.

See also "CHARCOAL."

FULLING AND FELTING; FELTED FABRICS; FLOCK, WADDING.

Improved means or apparatus for printing felts, floor cloths, carpets and woven fabrics.	1155	25th April 1865	John Wilkinson the younger.
Manufacture of flock fabrics (Communicated by The American Waterproof Cloth Company.)	1216	1st May 1865	William Edward Newton.
Improved machinery for fulling fur hats or felt hats (Communicated by Onesippe Sibès.)	1214	12th May 1865	Etienne Lucien Girard.
Manufacture of hats and other felted goods and fabrics. (Communicated by Edwin Dodd M'Cracken, James M'Cracken, Charles Edward M'Cracken, John Adams Southmoyd and Robert Warner Southmoyd.)	1707	26th June 1865	William Edward Newton.
An improved combination of materials for the manufacture of carpets, floor cloth, felt, wall paper, fireproof flexible roofing, ship and boat building, and for other similar purposes	1776	5th July 1865	{ John Longbottom. Alexan Longbottom.

Subject-matter of Patent.	Number of Patent.	Date.	Name of Patentee.
FULLING, &c.—continued.			
An improved process of preparing sea weeds and other vegetable substances for the production of artificial grass, felt, alkaline salts and iodine.	1877	19th July 1865	Donald M'Cromara.
Improvements in the mode of applying mineral soda to the scouring and lubrication of textile matters and machinery, and in the manufacture of soap. (*fulling cloth*.)	3107	4th Dec. 1865	Leopold Joseph Bouchet.
Means or apparatus for the fulling, scouring and cleansing of woollen yarns and cloths	3201	13th Dec. 1865	Benjamin Parvin. William Priestley.
Certain improvements in the manufacture of felt	3298	14th Dec. 1865	Harry Prowse.
FURNACES AND FIRE-BOXES; SUPPLYING FURNACES WITH FUEL.			
An improved jacket or protector for metallic and other vessels and structures containing solid substances, liquids or gases, to prevent radiation of heat from or communication of heat to such vessels and structures (*for blast furnaces.*)	4	2nd Jan. 1865	Edward Bevan. Abel Fleming.
Improvements in furnaces, ash-pits and flues, for the consumption of smoke and noxious products of combustion, and in the apparatus or means connected therewith.	51	6th Jan. 1865	James Robertson.
Motive-power and means of communication between passengers while travelling, and appliances connected therewith.	55	7th Jan. 1865	George Bell Galloway.
Improvements in furnace flues for the consumption of smoke.	94	11th Jan. 1865	Abraham Cooper.
Furnaces (*Communicated by Dominique Chiesia.*)	105	12th Jan. 1865	Michael Henry.
Furnaces	110	13th Jan. 1865	William Smith Longridge. James Mash.
Apparatus for charging and drawing gas retorts and for other purposes (*charging boiler furnaces.*)	142	17th Jan. 1865	Nealy James Best. James John Holden.
Improvements in puddling, heating and other reverberatory furnaces used in the manufacture of iron and steel and for other purposes, which improvements may also be applied to steam-boiler furnaces.	178	20th Jan. 1865	John Hewm.
Furnaces for melting metals and smelting ores	209	24th Jan. 1865	William Woodward. Robert Woodward. John Woodward. Adam Woodward, jun.
Improvements in lining the sides and bottoms of puddling furnaces and other furnaces employed in the manufacture of iron or steel, and in mending, repairing and fettling the sides and bottoms of the said puddling and other said furnaces.	224	26th Jan. 1865	Robert Menhet.
Furnaces	240	27th Jan. 1865	Charles de Bergue.

Subject-matter of Patent.	Number of Patent.	Date.	Name of Patentee.
**FURNACES, &c.—*continued.*			
Improvements in steam generators or steam-boilers and furnaces, part of which is also applicable to other heat generating apparatus.	343	27th Jan. 1865	Joseph Tribbil.
Improvements in effecting the combustion of fuel in the furnaces of steam-boilers and the fire-places of stoves, and of gas in gas burners, and in apparatus connected therewith.	311	4th Feb. 1865	Frank Clarke Hills.
Improvements in furnaces for smelting iron ores, commonly called blast furnaces, also in cupolas used in foundries, for rendering down or melting iron or other metals.	374	10th Feb. 1865	Evan Leigh.
Case hardening or converting partially into steel, articles of wrought or malleable iron. (*Partly communicated by Anthony Leonard Fleury.*)	333	11th Feb. 1865	Edwin Henry Nrwly.
Improvements in furnaces and boilers and parts connected with them, for generating steam and heating fluids, and also for improved apparatus for reducing and shutting off steam and regulating the speed of steam-engines.	396	11th Feb. 1865	John Cass.
Cupolas and blast furnaces	397	11th Feb. 1865	{ Henry Houldsworth Grimm. John Macriear Rigby. }
Furnaces for smelting or reducing ores and for melting metals . . . . . }	411	14th Feb. 1865	{ Herbert John Waldack. Edward Barton. }
An improved blowing apparatus . . .	427	15th Feb. 1865	{ Samuel Richards Freeman. Abraham Grundy. }
Furnaces . . . . . (*for boilers, &c.*)	443	16th Feb. 1865	Edward Brown Wilson.
Apparatus for distilling petroleum and other volatile liquids and for making gas. (*Communicated by George Hughes Sinclair Duffus.*)	447	16th Feb. 1865	William Edward Newton.
Improvements in puddling furnaces and in apparatus connected therewith.	473	18th Feb. 1865	John Gay Newton Alleyne.
A chemical combustible substance and apparatus to which it is applicable. (*for furnaces, chafing dishes, &c.*) (*Communicated by François Stoler.*)	477	20th Feb. 1865	William Edward Gedge.
An improvement in the utilisation of the waste gases of blast furnaces.	478	20th Feb. 1865	Joseph Cliff.
Boilers for heating water and delivering it at an equal temperature to any number of flow pipes, and also for the generation of steam.	493	22nd Feb. 1865	Jasper Hulley.
Method of and apparatus for generating heat . .	516	24th Feb. 1865	{ Joseph Jacob. Rudolph Filzinger. }
Smoke consuming apparatus . . .	554	2nd March 1865	{ Samuel Hopkinson. Edwin Hopkinson. }
Tubular boilers . . . . . (*Communicated by Louis Felix Meunier.*)	624	7th March 1865	Richard Archibald Brooman.
Improvements in converting cast iron or pig iron into wrought iron or steel, and in machinery employed therein.	648	14th March 1865	Morgan Morgans.
Stoves for heating air supplied to blast furnaces .	650	8th March 1865	Richard Howson.
An improved manufacture of iron forgings .	654	8th March 1865	William Clay.

Subject-matter of Patent.	Number of Patent.	Date.	Name of Patentee.
FURNACES, &c.—continued.			
An improvement in the construction of hot air stoves for blast furnaces.	680	9th March 1865	Joseph Cliff.
Steam-boilers and the furnaces thereof - -	685	11th March 1865	{ Edward Brown Wilson. / James Howden.
Manufacture of iron and steel - - -	689	11th March 1865	James Henderson.
Furnaces and fire-places - - - -	692	11th March 1865	Edward Brown Wilson.
Puddling, heating and other furnaces - -	700	13th March 1865	Joseph Wright.
Water tuyeres for blast furnaces - - (Partly communicated by Mr. Norris Brett.)	723	15th March 1865	Nathaniel Neal Solly.
Apparatus for blowing smiths' and other fires -	755	18th March 1865	{ James Cookson. / Philip Billington.
Improvements in the manufacture of looking glasses or mirrors, and in apparatus employed therein. (Communicated by The Society Randal Cromwell, Alfred Tavernier and Edouard Dodé.)	789	21st March 1865	John Henry Johnson.
Improvements in the construction of furnaces for the consumption of smoke - -	862	27th March 1865	{ Charles Marthews. / John Fereday. -
Furnaces or apparatus for heating the blast for furnaces used in smelting iron and for other furnaces.	891	29th March 1865	John Player.
A new or improved mode of rapidly reducing, cementing and melting iron and other ores, also iron slag or cinders, dross and scales or crust, to produce directly therefrom steel or malleable or cast iron. (Communicated by Jean Baptiste Hoison.)	899	30th March 1865	William Brookes.
Steam-boilers - - - -	908	31st March 1865	{ John Swarbrick. / David Swarbrick. / Benjamin Swarbrick. / Ormerod Swarbrick.
Apparatus applicable to furnaces for smelting ores and melting metals - - -	942	3rd April 1865	{ Henry Brook. / John Eastwood. / George Brook, jun'.
An improved rabble or bar used in puddling iron -	969	5th April 1865	George Walter Dyson.
Steam-boilers, steam-boiler tubes, sides of steam-boilers' flues and furnaces.	989	7th April 1865	George Rydill.
A new method of applying suction and blast, and the apparatus employed therein. (Communicated by Felix Alexandre Trutad du Beauregard.)	1029	11th April 1865	Richard Archibald Brooman.
Improvements in steam generators applicable also to condensers or coolers. (Communicated by Thomas Leaders.)	1039	11th April 1865	John Henry Johnson.
Arrangement of furnaces used for puddling and reheating iron, the generation of steam and other similar purposes.	1064	13th April 1865	William Beardmore.
Smoke consuming furnaces (Communicated by Etienne Sauvet and Eugene de Flavy.)	1152	25th April 1865	Richard Archibald Brooman.
Apparatus for disintegrating vegetable and animal substances.	1168	26th April 1865	François Dominique Pierre Jacques Cabasson.
Furnaces used for smelting and melting iron and other metals.	1183	27th April 1865	William Balk.
Furnaces - - - - -	1188	27th April 1865	Dundas Simpson.

Subject-matter of Patent.	Number of Patent.	Date.	Name of Patentee.
FURNACES, &c.—*continued.*			
Means and apparatus for puddling iron -	1321	1st May 1865	Thomas Frederick Unshin, Joseph Felix Allender.
Improvements in steam generators and engines, and in apparatus for feeding steam generators. (*Communicated by George Bailey Brayton.*)	1340	3rd May 1865	John Henry Johnson.
Construction of and mode of supplying fuel to fire grates, stoves and the furnaces of locomotive and other steam-boilers.	1359	5th May 1865	Charles Lamport.
Furnace fire-grates - - - -	1370	8th May 1865	James Buchanan.
Furnaces of steam-boilers - - - -	1372	10th May 1865	Thomas Holden, John Newroom, James Akeroyd.
Cupola and other blast furnaces - - -	1448	26th May 1865	Richard Casham.
Construction of furnaces or fire-places - (*Communicated by Louis Philip Cohen.*)	1451	26th May 1865	Mylius Cohen.
Improvements in the manufacture of steel, and in furnaces used in such manufacture. (*Communicated by Jules Poulie.*)	1460	27th May 1865	Louis Moutz.
Construction of furnaces - - - - (*for steam-boilers.*)	1469	29th May 1865	Peter Young.
Foundry cupolas - - - -	1498	31st May 1865	Thomas Summerson.
An improved economic boiler for hot water apparatus, applicable for the heating of hothouses, churches and other public buildings.	1510	1st June 1865	Frederick Knight.
Furnaces used in the manufacture of welded iron tubes.	1517	2nd June 1865	Thomas Pritchard.
Caloric or heated air engines - - - (*Communicated by Cyrus W. Baldwin and Walter Davis Richards.*)	1543	7th June 1865	Samuel Blackford Tucker.
Furnaces - - - - - (*Communicated by François Durand.*)	1560	12th June 1865	Richard Archibald Brooman.
Furnaces - - - - - (*Communicated by Felix Alexandre Tristal de Beauregard.*)	1570	15th June 1865	Richard Archibald Brooman.
Improvements applicable to furnace bars and fire-grates.	1572	21st June 1865	Samuel Godfrey.
Means and apparatus for consuming smoke - (*Communicated by François Augustus Fouché and Claude Morel.*)	1697	21th June 1865	William Clark.
A new or improved self-acting apparatus for distributing the feeding materials in high furnaces. (*Communicated by Emile Langen.*)	1738	29th June 1865	Alexander Prince.
Improvements in the manufacture of gas retorts and other articles made of fire clay, and in furnaces for burning the same and for other purposes.	1737	30th June 1865	William Schofield.
Improvements in steam-boilers, furnaces, and engines, and in parts connected therewith.	1745	30th June 1865	Edwin Elliott.
Improvements in locomotive engines and in springs of railway carriages. (*roofs of fire-boxes.*)	1769	4th July 1865	James Edwards Wilson.
Means and apparatus for increasing the mechanical power of steam.	1820	10th July 1865	William Alexander Lytle.

Subject-matter of Patent.	Number of Patent.	Date.	Name of Patentee.
FURNACES, &c.—*continued.*			
Treatment of copper and nickel ores - - (*Communicated by Viscount Charles de Bacqueville.*)	1831	11th July 1865	Hector Auguste Dufresi.
Construction and working of furnaces for puddling, balling, heating and melting metals.	1882	19th July 1865	David Caddick.
Locomotive boiler furnaces - - - -	1929	25th July 1865	{John Juckes, jun'. / John Swinburne.
Apparatus for burning combustible and volatile liquids for generating steam and similar purposes. (*Communicated by Patrick Hayes.*)	1935	26th July 1865	George Tomlinson Bousfield.
Means of and apparatus for treating animal and vegetable fibrous materials, which apparatus is also applicable to various useful purposes. (*gears for steam-boiler furnaces.*)	1962	27th July 1865	Henry Sherwood.
Fire-engines and hydraulic machines - - (*blow pipes of forges.*)	1963	28th July 1865	Leon Paul Laroche.
Means or apparatus for promoting the combustion of fuel in furnaces of steam-boilers, dyers' or brewers' pans and other furnaces whereby smoke is prevented and fuel economized - -	1978	31st July 1865	{Benjamin Robinson. / Joseph Varley.
Locomotive and other tubular boilers - -	1990	1st Aug. 1865	Louis Emile Constant Martin.
Machinery to be used in the manufacture of plate or sheet iron and steel. (*Communicated by Martin Diroulmand Heuvers.*)	2012	3rd Aug. 1865	Ephraim Babel.
A combination of improved method, apparatus and receptacles for storing, preserving, transferring and discharging certain fluids, for sanitary and protective purposes. (*supplying oil as fuel to furnaces.*) (*Communicated by Henry Pinkus.*)	2096	14th Aug. 1865	Robert Alexander Willis Westley.
Improvements in and connected with the manufacture of copper.	2100	14th Aug. 1865	James Thomas Loxley.
Furnaces to be used in the manufacture of glass and iron and steel, and for other like purposes. (*Communicated by Henning Bowtius.*)	2105	15th Aug. 1865	John Frederick Bannia.
Blacksmiths' bellows, more especially those used in portable forges.	2152	21st Aug. 1865	John Bowden.
Steam-boiler and other furnaces - - -	2158	22nd Aug. 1865	John Lockwood.
An improved furnace for annealing iron and steel wire or rods.	2166	23rd Aug. 1865	John Howard Scott.
Improvements in the manufacture of steel iron and metal suitable for bearings, and in apparatus for the same. (*air furnace.*)	2175	24th Aug. 1865	William Colborne Cambridge.
A new and useful steam blower or blast apparatus for furnaces. (*Communicated by John Allen Bassett.*)	2245	31st Aug. 1865	Oliver Bennett.
Improvements in boilers and furnaces, and in cleansing the flues thereof - - -	2291	6th Sept. 1865	{Edward Green. / Edward Green the younger.
Means of and apparatus for consuming smoke in furnaces.	2382	19th Sept. 1865	Charles Worsam.

Subject-matter of Patent.	Number of Patent.	Date.	Name of Patentee.
FURNACES, &c.—continued.			
Apparatus for separating dust from the gases evolved from blast furnaces for smelting iron (for heating hot-blast stoves.)	2361	19th Sept. 1865	Edward Alfred Cowper. Charles William Siemens.
Improvements in and applicable to furnaces for the consumption of smoke.	2406	21st Sept. 1865	William Watkin.
Improvements in blast furnaces and in charging the same. (Communicated by Alexandre Lebrun-Virloy.)	2413	21st Sept. 1865	Richard Archibald Brooman.
Manufacture of iron and steel, and of furnaces and machinery for purifying, puddling or heating the same	2461	26th Sept. 1865	Thomas Frederick Cashin. Joseph Felix Allender.
Collecting or drawing off the gases from blast furnaces	2507	29th Sept. 1865	John Addenbrooke. George Addenbrooke. Philip Anthony Millward.
Improvements in producing and combining gases to be used for heating purposes, and in the construction of retorts for producing and combining such gases.	2587	2nd Oct. 1865	Silas Covell Salisbury.
Blast furnaces	2588	2nd Oct. 1865	Silas Covell Salisbury.
Improvements in steam-boilers and other apparatus applicable to the heating and evaporation of liquids, parts of which improvements are applicable also to other purposes	2661	16th Oct. 1865	Francis Wise. Edward Field. Edmund Harrison Aydon.
Calorie or hot air engines (Communicated by Guillaume Reiairix.)	2673	17th Oct. 1865	Richard Archibald Brooman.
A new or improved steam consuming apparatus, or an apparatus intended to make available as fuel all or part of the steam actually evolving from engines into the atmosphere, and also to absorb the smoke resulting from the combustion.	2679	17th Oct. 1865	François Georges Ricardo.
Furnaces	2683	17th Oct. 1865	William Reardman.
Furnaces of and means of heating the feed water for steam-boilers	2713	20th Oct. 1865	John White.
An improved apparatus for calcining copper ore, and for treating the products of copper ore when being calcined.	2730	21st Oct. 1865	Arthur Bankart.
Steam-boilers	2758	23rd Oct. 1865	Alexander Chaplin.
Construction of furnaces and boilers for the consumption of smoke	2748	24th Oct. 1865	Charles Matthews. Henry Booth Southwick. John Fereday.
Furnaces	2808	31st Oct. 1865	Robert Cassels. Thomas Morton.
Improvements in the manufacture of iron and steel, and in apparatus employed in such manufacture.	2835	3rd Nov. 1865	Henry Bessemer.
Apparatus for separating dust from the gases evolved from blast furnaces.	2885	6th Nov. 1865	Charles Cochrane.
Furnaces for heating the blast for blast furnaces	2867	10th Nov. 1865	Thomas Whitwell.
Stoves for drying moulds	2943	15th Nov. 1865	Henry Cochrane.
Furnaces	2963	17th Nov. 1865	Thomas Maxwell Tennant.
Apparatus for condensing exhaust steam, and heating air by the heat abstracted in effecting the condensation of such steam. (for supplying oxygen to boiler furnaces.) (Communicated by Addison Calvin Fletcher.)	2996	21st Nov. 1865	Alfred Vincent Newton.

Subject-matter of Patent.	Number of Patent.	Date.	Name of Patentee.
FURNACES, &c.—continued.			
Furnaces -	8025	25th Nov. 1865	William Alexander Lyttle.
Means and apparatus for raising heat by the combustion of fuels of various kinds.	8029	25th Nov. 1865	John Francis Bennett.
Means or apparatus for economising and inducing more perfect combustion of fuel in furnaces.	8082	29th Nov. 1865	Thomas Lancaster.
Improvements in the manufacture and treatment of railway bars, tyres and axles, also in the construction of furnaces, machinery and apparatus connected therewith.	3084	1st Dec. 1865	Thomas Weatherburn Dodds.
Improvements in the manufacture of salt, and in machinery or apparatus for that purpose. (feeding the fire with small coal.)	3106	4th Dec. 1865	Dennis Hall.
Certain improvements in the construction of forge furnaces.	3109	4th Dec. 1865	William Beardmore.
Improvements in puddling, heating and other reverberatory furnaces used in the manufacture of iron and steel, and for other purposes.	3136	6th Dec. 1865	Thomas Lewis Nicklin.
A new and improved fire pot and retort for stoves, ranges and furnaces in which steam is generated and superheated.	3140	6th Dec. 1865	William Ennis.
Improvements in steam-boilers and in the furnaces and grates thereof, the same improvements in furnaces and grates being also applicable to other furnaces and to stoves. (Communicated by Robert Winslow Davis, Daniel Davis and Henry Sheldon Anable.)	3141	6th Dec. 1865	William Edward Newton.
Improvements in steam-boilers and in apparatus adapted for cleaning the flues of boilers. (annular or segmental grate.)	3181	9th Dec. 1865	Norman Willis Wheeler.
Improvements in locomotive engines and in the means employed for generating steam therein. (fire-box.)	8185	9th Dec. 1865	Robert Francis Fairlie.
Construction of fire-places and furnaces - .	3247	15th Dec. 1865	George Warriner.
Certain improvements in the means of collecting waste gases arising from blast furnaces - .	3251	14th Dec. 1865	Samuel Whitehouse the elder. Samuel Whitehouse the younger. Jeremiah Whitehouse. William Whitehouse.
Improvements in the manufacture of steel and purified iron, and in the apparatus employed therein. (Communicated by Antoine Goly-Cazalat.)	3300	21st Dec. 1865	Henri Adrien Bonneville.
Fire-places, furnaces and stoves - . .	3337	23rd Dec. 1865	Julius Jeffreys.
Improvements applicable to steam-boilers, iron, steel, retort and other furnaces.	3338	26th Dec. 1865	Joshua Fisher.
Improvements in the manufacture of soda and in the apparatus employed in the said manufacture. (Communicated by Alphonse Lautrat.)	3340	26th Dec. 1865	Michael Henry.

Subject-matter of Patent.	Number of Patent.	Date.	Name of Patentee.
FURNITURE;—BEDSTEADS, TABLES, CHAIRS, CRADLES AND NURSING-APPARATUS ; CASTORS, BEDSTEAD-BOTTOMS.			
Improvements in the manufacture of metallic bedsteads, which improvements are also applicable to the manufacture of other metallic articles.	59	7th Jan. 1865	James Atkins.
An improved elastic mattress or bedstead - (Communicated by François Carré.)	87	11th Jan. 1865	William Edward Gedge.
An improved kind of bedstead suitable for camp and domestic purposes.	149	18th Jan. 1865	Edward Deane.
Certain improvements in rendering soundless furniture and other articles for domestic purposes.	190	23rd Jan. 1865	Adolphe Drevelle.
Folding chairs and other seats - - -	198	23rd Jan. 1865	Thomas Brown.
An improved portable folding arm chair or seat - (Communicated by Louis Leperre, junior.)	220	1st Feb. 1865	William Edward Gedge.
Fastenings for doors, windows, drawers and other like purposes - - - - -	369	9th Feb. 1865	George Edward Mark. William Howes Howes.
Construction of cabinet-work and chair bedsteads	476	20th Feb. 1865	Andrew Sharp.
Portable invalid or bed tables - - -	535	24th Feb. 1865	Charles James Rowe.
Improved portable frames and joints for tables and other articles, applicable also for building purposes and the like.	549	27th Feb. 1865	Charles Whiting.
Improvements in the manufacture of metallic bedsteads, which improvements are also applicable to the manufacture of other metallic articles.	699	13th March 1865	James Atkins.
Cabin furniture for ships and other vessels -	929	24th March 1865	Charles Revas.
A portable covered hammock - - - (Communicated by Sigge Flach.)	894	30th March 1865	Thorsten Wilhelm Nordenfelt.
A new or improved table and support for invalids -	1069	15th April 1865	Thomas Edward Harding.
Folding beds and bedsteads - - - (Communicated by Frederick Menhrow Payne and John Spencer Giles.)	1290	2nd May 1865	William Edward Newton.
A new or improved chair-ladder - - -	1273	3rd May 1865	Jean Baptiste Lavanchy.
Construction of bedsteads - - -	1370	10th May 1865	Cyrus Copus.
Mechanism for locking or fastening tiers or sets of drawers arranged in writing tables, cabinets, chests or other articles of furniture.	1462	27th May 1865	Ludwig Dicle.
An improved exercising chair for infants -	1506	1st June 1865	Thomas Brinsmead.
An improved elastic mattress or spring bed - (Communicated by Henry Merle Hingand de Saint Mour.)	1652	20th June 1865	William Edward Gedge.
Machinery for cutting dovetails for joiners' work - (for articles of furniture.)	1671	21st June 1865	William Roberts.
Castors - - - - - -	1689	24th June 1865	Robert Eastman.
An improved portable table or seat - - (Communicated by Charles Joseph Berricks.)	1691	24th June 1865	Richard Archibald Beauman.
A new or improved table or support to be employed in the dressing and finishing of churns.	1783	28th June 1865	William Percival.
The use and application of paper, printed or otherwise ornamented with water colors, for covering floors and other analogous purposes, as a substitute for carpets and oil cloths, and of an improved coating or varnish to be applied to the same, to protect its surface from injury and wear. (and for covering counters, desks, &c.)	1873	19th July 1865	Anson Henry Platt.

Subject-matter of Patent.	Number of Patent.	Date.	Name of Patentee.
FURNITURE, &c.—continued.			
Bedsteads, sofas and chairs . . .	1912	22nd July 1866	{ George Wilson. / James Goodfellow.
Ornamental tables and table stands, such as cruet frames, liquour frames, flower, egg and other stands	1925	25th July 1865	{ Louis Pître. / Edward Samuel Tasks.
Improvements in the making of metallic and other bedsteads, sofas, couches and other like articles, which said improvements may also be applied to the seats of chairs, railway carriages and other articles. (Communicated by Thomas Tunnington.)	2039	6th Aug. 1865	Henry Gerring.
Manufacture and ornamenting of carpets, rugs and other fabrics. (chair covers.)	2151	25th Aug. 1865	Lemuel Clayton.
Folding chairs . . . . . . (Communicated by James Gourley English and Edward Francis Merock.)	2200	26th Aug. 1865	George Tomlinson Bousfield.
An improved reclining chair . . . (Communicated by William Henry Fox Northwick.)	2504	29th Sept. 1865	George Davies.
Improvements in rules for measuring, and in other instruments or articles requiring to be adjusted or disposed at various angles. (desks.)	2618	10th Oct. 1865	Arthur Nicholls.
Rendering wood for building and other purposes non-combustible or non-inflammable. (fireproofing wood for furniture.)	2625	11th Oct. 1865	William Ball.
Bedsteads, seats, couches and other articles for sitting and reclining on.	2656	14th Oct. 1865	James Lamb Hancock.
Folding chairs . . . . . . (Communicated by Auguste Emmanuel Elmers.)	2676	17th Oct. 1865	George Davies.
An improved process for bending or arching wood. (Communicated by Louis Parrubhtr.)	2722	21st Oct. 1865	William Edward Gedge.
Improvements in roller skates, and in the rollers to be used therewith and for other purposes. (applicable to furniture.)	2770	27th Oct. 1865	Robert Bell Sames.
Cabinet furniture	2901	11th Nov. 1865	Daniel Slater.
An improved piece of furniture convertible into a seat with back on either side, a seat with desk on either side or a seat with table on either side.	3057	29th Nov. 1865	Thomas Lourie.
Improvements in machinery employed when weaving hair, and in preparing and treating hair for weaving. (making furniture seating.) (Communicated by Charles Bradley.)	3058	29th Nov. 1866	George Tomlinson Bousfield.
Certain improvements in the manufacture of knobs for doors, cupboards, ashpans, and for other like purposes.	3061	1st Dec. 1865	John Wilson.
A new or improved cement or composition, applicable to the agglomeration or moulding of various materials, and to other useful and decorative purposes. (for tables or panels.) (Communicated by Stanislas Sorel and Emile Justin Mesnir.)	3119	5th Dec. 1865	Richard Archibald Brooman.
Construction or manufacture of metal bedsteads .	3135	6th Dec. 1865	Henry Berkeley Hamilton.

Subject-matter of Patent.	Number of Patent.	Date.	Name of Patentee.
FURNITURE, &c.—continued.			
Furnishing and adapting ordinary tables for playing billiards.	3166	9th Dec. 1865	Henry Stuart Marshall.
Construction of castors - - - -	3294	20th Dec. 1865	Robert MacLeod Claypole.
Preparation of glue or gelatine so as to render it insoluble in water, and applicable by the admixture of other substances to various purposes for which common glue or gelatine cannot now be used. (for renewing furniture, for chair bottoms, &c.) (Communicated by Henry Wurtz.)	3325	23rd Dec. 1865	William Edward Newton.
Obtaining and employing continuous lengths of tanned leather for various useful purposes - (lacing hose for bedsteads, for making bed sacking, &c.)	6334	23rd Dec. 1865	{ George Horn. Daniel Horn.
Construction of show-cases, picture-frames, house and shop furniture and fittings, and other similar articles.	3364	29th Dec. 1865	David Vogl.
GAMES AND EXERCISES; BILLIARDS AND BAGATELLE.			
Cushions for billiard and other like tables - -	819	4th Feb. 1865	James Lyne Hancock.
Improvements in boxing, fencing and cricket gloves, and in cricket pads or guards.	862	10th Feb. 1865	Henry Esmond.
Cricket, racket and tennis balls - - -	890	11th March 1865	Charles Huntley.
Rests or supports for cues or other similar instruments used for billiards or other similar games.	1048	12th April 1865	George Jackson.
An improvement in mallets used in the game of croquet and other similar games.	1191	27th April 1865	Joseph Frederick Feltham.
An improved croquet stand - - -	1214	1st May 1865	Walter Thomas Whitmore Jones.
Wickets for the game of cricket - - -	1478	30th May 1865	William Hubert Stanley.
An improved exercising chair for infants - -	1508	1st June 1866	Thomas Heimvand.
Croquet mallets - - - - -	1704	26th June 1865	Samuel Stephen Halemon.
An improved circular endless railway - - (used as a pastime.) (Communicated by Ernest Michaux.)	1771	5th July 1865	William Edward Gedge.
An improved combination of materials for the manufacture of carpets, floor cloth, felt, wall paper, fireproof flexible roofing, ship and boat building, and for other similar purposes - - (billiard table mats.)	1778	5th July 1865	{ John Longbottom. Abram Longbottom.
Improved means for marking progress in the game of croquet and other games - - -	1829	11th July 1865	{ James Nasmyth, sen'. Thomas Christie.
A toy or game called flying fish - - -	3148	19th Aug. 1865	George Whitford.
Improvements in ice houses and in glaciaria or skating places, and in baths.	2292	6th Sept. 1865	Augustus William Parker.
Cricket, racket, tennis and foot balls - -	2326	11th Sept. 1865	Charles Huntley.
An improved billiard marker - - - -	2402	21st Sept. 1865	Newman Burdon Thoyts.

Subject-matter of Patent.	Number of Patent.	Date.	Name of Patentee.
GAMES, &c.—continued.			
Improvements in the construction of billiard tables, and improved apparatus for ascertaining the degree of elasticity of the cushions and the strength of the cloth. (Communicated by Eugene Pomara, junior.)	2608	10th Oct. 1865	William Edward Gedge.
An improved apparatus for gymnastic exercises (Partly communicated by Edwin Faxon Bacon.)	2707	26th Oct. 1865	George Washington Bacon.
Implements or articles employed in the game of indoor croquet.	2831	2nd Nov. 1865	Henry Jones.
Manufacture of cushions for billiard tables	2874	7th Nov. 1865	George Alexander Smith.
Furnishing and adapting ordinary tables for playing billiards.	3166	9th Dec. 1865	Henry Stuart Marshall.
An improvement in swings (Communicated by Julius Walter Sperry.)	3229	14th Dec. 1865	Charles Pomeroy Barton.
Machines called roundabouts	3271	19th Dec. 1865	George Stephen Harrison. Stephen Everafield Featherstone.
Preparation of glue or gelatine so as to render it insoluble in water, and applicable by the admixture of other substances to various purposes for which common glue or gelatine cannot now be used. (for billiard balls.) (Communicated by Henry Werts.)	3325	22nd Dec. 1865	William Edward Newton.
Obtaining and employing continuous lengths of tanned leather for various useful purposes (for swings, shipping ropes, &c.)	3334	23rd Dec. 1865	George Hunt. Daniel Hunt.
GAS, GASOMETERS, HOLDERS AND RETORTS ; OXYGEN.			
Improvements in the manufacture of oxygen gas and in treating and economising the residual products of the said manufacture	6	2nd Jan. 1866	John Frederick Parker. Joseph Tanner.
Producing gases and vapour in a heated state	127	14th Jan. 1866	James Young.
Apparatus for charging and drawing gas retorts and for other purposes	142	17th Jan. 1866	Sealy James Best. James John Holden.
Improvements in lining the sides and bottoms of puddling furnaces and other furnaces employed in the manufacture of iron or steel, and in mending, repairing and fettling the sides and bottoms of the said puddling and other said furnaces. (gas furnaces.)	294	26th Jan. 1866	Robert Mushet.
Purification of coal gas	298	26th Jan. 1866	Alexander Angus Croll.
An improved method of and improvements in apparatus for extracting gases from mineral oils, and employing the same for illuminating purposes.	344	7th Feb. 1866	William Sen.
Apparatus for distilling petroleum and other volatile liquids and for making gas. (Communicated by George Hughes Sinclair Duffus.)	447	16th Feb. 1866	William Edward Newton.

Subject-matter of Patent.	Number of Patent.	Date.	Name of Patentee.
GAS, &c.—continued.			
Converting coal oil into gas suitable for use as an illuminator.	528	24th Feb. 1865	James Nicholas.
An improved method of extracting gases from mineral oils, and in employing the same for illuminating and heat producing purposes, and in the machinery or apparatus connected therewith.	549	27th Feb. 1865	William Sim.
An improvement in carburetting gas, also in the preparation of hydrocarbons for carburetting gas, and improved methods of treating alkali which has been used to purify coal oils, shale oils, petroleum and other mineral oils.	696	3rd March 1865	William Renwick Bowditch.
Apparatus for vaporising hydrocarbon liquids for illuminating and heating. (Communicated by Jonathan Griffen.)	717	14th March 1865	George Tomlinson Bousfield.
Constructing gasometers, tanks, casks and similar vessels.	761	21st March 1865	Charles Hill Pennycook.
Apparatus for the distillation of coal and peat, and such other substances as are or may be used for the manufacture of solid and liquid volatile hydrocarbons, or for the manufacture of the said hydrocarbons and coke. (See "DISTILLING.")	799	22nd March 1865	William Mattieu Williams.
Improvements in the manufacture or preparation of materials for and in their application to lighting and heating purposes, also in apparatus used for the same. (Communicated by Auguste de Peyronnet.)	856	25th March 1865	William Clark.
Means of and apparatus for increasing the illuminating power of hydrocarbons, oils and gases. (Communicated by Thomas Say Speakman.)	960	6th April 1865	George Davies.
Improvements in the mode of and apparatus for purifying smoke, which improvements are also applicable to other purposes in which gas or vapour is to be separated from substances combined therewith or held in suspension therein. (Communicated by Joseph Bourgeois and Jules Malkin.)	1001	7th April 1865	Michael Henry.
Manufacture of coal gas - - - -	1266	6th May 1865	Israel Swindells.
An improved method of mixing gases and vapour, and in the machinery or apparatus connected therewith.	1287	9th May 1865	William Jackson.
Obtaining certain compounds of nitrogen and of sulphur - - - - - - - (See "ALKALIES.")	1384	19th May 1865	Thomas Richardson. Martin Diederich Rücker.
Apparatus for washing or purifying coal gas, and for producing ammoniacal water therefrom.	1386	19th May 1865	William Davey.
Improvements in the retorts used in the manufacture of gas and in other distillations, which improvements are adaptable to evaporating vessels.	1424	25th May 1865	John Ambrose Coffey.
Improvements in the means of carburetting or treating aëriform fluids for lighting and heating purposes, and in apparatus for the same. (Communicated by Henri Auguste Georges du Verger Marquis de la Roche Jaquelein.)	1507	1st June 1865	William Clark.
An improved method and apparatus for distilling coal shale and other carbonaceous substances. (Communicated by John Howarth.)	1683	7th June 1865	James Howarth, M.D.

Subject-matter of Patent.	Number of Patent.	Date.	Name of Patentee.
GAS, &c.— continued.			
A new material to be used in the purification of heating and lighting gases.	1591	12th June 1865	John Thomas.
Furnaces - - - - - (producing gas.) (Communicated by Félix Alexandre Trotet de Beaurygard.)	1630	15th June 1865	Richard Archibald Brooman.
Means and apparatus for generating motive-power (generating gases.) (Communicated by Jules Gros.)	1656	20th June 1865	William Clark.
An improved pulping and compressing machine, for the treatment of peat as a fuel, and gas for illuminating purposes - - -	1703	26th June 1865	{ Charles Wormam. { George Evans.
Improvements in the manufacture of gas retorts and other articles made of fire clay, and in furnaces for burning the same and for other purposes.	1757	30th June 1865	William Schofield.
Means of obtaining or producing oxygen applicable to various useful purposes.	1780	6th July 1865	Hermann Brigel.
An improved portable pocket gas generator or gasogene. (See "AERATING.")	1798	7th July 1865	Augustin François Murelle.
Improvements in the production of artificial light and in the apparatus connected therewith.	1809	8th July 1865	Isham Baggs.
Treating ammoniacal liquors for purifying gas and other purposes.	1818	10th July 1865	George Thomas Livesey.
An improved process for obtaining oxygen - (Communicated by Monsieur Charles Tellier.)	1833	11th July 1865	Hector Auguste Dufrené.
Improvements in the production of gases from aqueous vapour, and in the application thereof to heating purposes.	1841	12th July 1865	Harrison Blair.
Means of and apparatus for treating animal and vegetable fibrous materials, which apparatus is also applicable to various useful purposes. (producing gases.)	1962	27th July 1865	Henry Sherwood.
Improvements in carburetting coal gas and manufacturing artificial gas, and in the machinery or apparatus employed therein.	2095	12th Aug. 1865	Henry Woodward.
Improvements in apparatus by means of which certain liquids, common air, and certain elastic fluids are made available in the production of light, and their quantity regulated and measured, parts of which improvements are applicable for other purposes. (applied to gas-holders.)	2184	25th Aug. 1865	Edwin Augustus Curley.
Method of and apparatus for treating peat and other plastic materials - - - (obtaining gas.)	2219	29th Aug. 1865	{ Hull Terrell. { Thomas Don.
Obtaining spirits of turpentine, rosin, pitch, tar, pyroligneous acid and other products, from wood. (obtaining gas.) (Communicated by Albert Hamilton Emery.)	2247	31st Aug. 1865	William Edward Newton.
Apparatus for separating dust from the gases evolved from blast furnaces for smelting iron -	2391	19th Sept. 1865	{ Edward Alfred Cowper. { Charles William Siemens.
Improvements in generating illuminating gas, and in the machinery or apparatus employed therein. (Communicated by Erasmus Allington Pond, Mark Staples Richardson and Edmund Almes Morss.)	2455	23rd Sept. 1865	John Henry Johnson.

Subject-matter of Patent.	Number of Patent.	Date.	Name of Patentee.
GAS, &c.—continued.			
Improved apparatus for generating illuminating gas (Communicated by John Irwin.)	2429	23rd Sept. 1865	Alfred Vincent Newton.
An improved mode of decarbonizing retorts (used for making gas.) (Communicated by George Washington Edge.)	2468	26th Sept. 1865	Alfred Vincent Newton.
Improvements in obtaining and applying sulphurous acid and in apparatus used therein.	2463	24th Sept. 1865	Rees Reece.
Improvements in producing and combining gases to be used for heating purposes, and in the construction of retorts for producing and combining such gases.	2627	2nd Oct. 1865	Silas Covell Salisbury.
Apparatus for decomposing and superheating liquids, vapours and gases. (producing oxygen.) (Communicated by Gustave Renard and Amédée Lipman.)	2535	3rd Oct. 1865	Richard Archibald Brooman.
Manufacture of gas	2620	11th Oct. 1865	James Croteland.
Improvements in the manufacture of inflammable gases and in their application to useful purposes.	2719	21st Oct. 1865	Johann Boggs.
An improved mode of purifying gas	2818	1st Nov. 1865	{ Charles Henry Wood, Edward Louis Barrel.
Improvements in generating and applying certain gases, and in apparatus to be employed therein.	2839	2nd Nov. 1865	James Webster.
A new or improved process for the manufacture of oxygen	2984	14th Nov. 1865	{ Jules Théodore Anatole Mallet.
Improvements in the production or manufacture of gas for heating or illuminating, and in the retorts and apparatus employed in such manufacture.	2966	17th Nov. 1865	James Harbert.
Apparatus for the production of hydrocarbon or other vapours, parts of which apparatus are also applicable to measuring gaseous or fluid matter.	2978	19th Nov. 1865	Frederick Wilkins.
Treating the oxide of iron residues of gas purifying, in order principally to extract sulphur therefrom.	3099	2nd Dec. 1865	Thomas Bell.
Compounds for deodorising and disinfecting (purifying gas.)	3255	24th Dec. 1865	{ Edward Vincent Gardner, Louis Ash Israel. Henry Ash Israel, jun'.
For carbonic acid gas, see "ABATING." For nitrous acid gas, see "ACIDS."			
GAS AND OTHER BURNERS AND REGULATORS; GAS FITTINGS; LIGHTING GAS; PREVENTING ESCAPE OF GAS.			
Taps	67	9th Jan. 1865	Joseph Calkin.
Improved pincers for gas and other pipes (Communicated by Jules Chartier.)	86	11th Jan. 1865	William Edward Gedge.
Street and other lamps and lanterns	151	19th Jan. 1865	John William Gregg.

Subject-matter of Patent.	Number of Patent.	Date.	Name of Patentee.
GAS BURNERS, &c.—*continued.*			
Improvements in shaping and forging metals and in the machinery and apparatus employed therein. ("*iron*," "*others*," &c.)	185	19th Jan. 1865	James Alfred Shipton. Robert Mitchell.
Petroleum and coal oil burners and glasses	201	23rd Jan. 1865	Michael Alexander Dixey.
Improvements in effecting the combustion of fuel in the furnaces of steam-boilers and the fire-places of stoves, and of gas in gas-burners, and in apparatus connected therewith.	511	4th Feb. 1865	Frank Clarke Hills.
An improved fluid valve	547	27th Feb. 1865	Comyn Ching.
Gas-burners	556	24th Feb. 1865	Thomas Slocombe Hall.
An improved mode of and apparatus for ascertaining and indicating the presence of explosive gases.	662	9th March 1865	George Frederick Atwell.
Apparatus for vaporising hydrocarbon liquids for illuminating and heating. (*Communicated by Jonathan Griffen.*)	717	14th March 1865	George Tomlinson Bousfield.
Argand gas-burners	809	22nd March 1865	William Morvant Baker.
Improvements in the manufacture or preparation of materials for and in their application to lighting and heating purposes, also in apparatus used for the same. (*Communicated by Auguste de Peyronny.*)	855	25th March 1865	William Clark.
Certain improvements in gas-burners	876	24th March 1865	François Adolphe Marquard.
Means and apparatus employed for illuminating lighthouses.	945	4th April 1865	John Richardson Wigham.
Apparatus for regulating the supply of gas	972	5th April 1865	Charles Esplin.
Means of and apparatus for increasing the illuminating power of hydrocarbons, oils and gases. (*Communicated by Thomas Say Speakman.*)	980	6th April 1865	George Davies.
Gas regulators and valves for the same (*Communicated by Charles Manory Crennan.*)	1109	20th April 1865	Francis Wise.
Certain improvements in apparatus for illuminating (*Communicated by Monsieur Louis Joseph Aurèle de Mannerville.*)	1269	8th May 1865	Peter Armand Le Comte de Fontaine Moreau.
Gas-burners and chimneys (*Communicated by William Reaux.*)	1384	13th May 1865	William Clark.
An improved gas-burner	1457	25th May 1865	George Bray.
An improved burner for gas and other lighting apparatus.	1494	31st May 1865	Hypolite Monier.
Lamp burners and parts connected therewith (*Communicated by Rufus Spaulding Merrill and William Lincoln.*)	1631	16th June 1865	John Henry Johnson.
Construction of taps or valves (*for gas.*) (*Communicated by Ernest Alexandre Ribert.*)	1655	20th June 1865	Edward Griffith Brewer.
Gas-burners	1656	20th June 1865	John Scholl.
Apparatus used in supplying gas to burners	1697	23rd June 1865	Henry Saxon Snell. Frederick Edward Thomas.
An improved method of and apparatus for burning liquid hydrocarbons, and the employment thereof for heating purposes. (*Communicated by Alexandre Schpakofsky and Nicolas Stange.*)	1711	27th June 1865	Richard Archibald Brooman.

Subject-matter of Patent.	Number of Patent.	Date.	Name of Patentee.
GAS BURNERS, &c.—*continued.*			
Lamps - - - - - -	1891	15th July 1865	Aaron Henry Platt.
Means of and apparatus for treating animal and vegetable fibrous materials, which apparatus is also applicable to various useful purposes. (*patent for Baker's burners.*)	1892	27th July 1865	Henry Sherwood.
Gas-burners - - - - -	1968	29th July 1865	Ferdinand Küp.
Signals for railways - - - - -	2009	3rd Aug. 1865	Edward Samuel Horridge.
With holders or burners for lamps - - -	2024	4th Aug. 1865	{ Emil Wild. Wilhelm Wessel.
Gas-burners - - - - - -	2094	12th Aug. 1865	Henry Woodward.
An improvement in gas-burners - - -	2170	24th Aug. 1865	Giacomo Bagnagatti.
Improvements in apparatus by means of which certain liquids, common air and certain elastic fluids are made available in the production of light, and their quantity regulated and measured, parts of which improvements are applicable for other purposes.	2184	25th Aug. 1865	Edwin Augustus Curley.
Certain improvements in the method of lighting gas and in apparatus connected therewith - }	2206	9th Sept. 1865	{ Alexander Mackie. James Paterson.
Means and apparatus applicable to the lighting and reviving of fires.	2229	11th Sept. 1865	Charles James Webb.
Manufacture of submarine lamps - - -	2456	26th Sept. 1865	John Rampano Starter.
Improvements in connections for and in stopping pipes used for conveying water and gas, and for other like purposes, and in preventing leakages in the said pipes, and in apparatus employed therein.	2503	29th Sept. 1865	Charles Forster Cotterill.
Paraffine lamps - - - - -	2619	10th Oct. 1866	Daniel Gallafent.
A new composition of indian-rubber mastic or cement, made in a more or less fluid state according to the use to be made of it, and the process or contrivance for applying the same. (*making gas-joints.*)	2630	12th Oct. 1865	Augusta Aimé Leremard.
An improved apparatus for burning petroleum and other volatile oils.	2689	2nd Nov. 1865	Louis Pelzeyn.
Improvements in generating and applying certain gases, and in apparatus to be employed therein.	2833	2nd Nov. 1865	James Webster.
Improvements in cocks for steam, water, air and gases at high pressures, and also in gauge cocks and water gauges for boilers, and sediment tubes for cocks and pipes.	2890	21st Nov. 1865	Samuel Bennett.
Lamps, lanterns and gas fittings - - -	3069	2nd Dec. 1865	William Johnston.
An improved mode of applying the compression of air for ventilating purpose, and the compression of any gas for hurrying along elastic fluids in conveying pipes - - - - (*propelling gas.*)	3153	8th Dec. 1865	{ Pierron de Mondésir. Paul Lebaitre. Augustin Jullienne.
A new process of lacquering and finishing metal goods, such as gas fittings, and other like articles usually finished by bronzing and lacquering.	3294	16th Dec. 1865	Joseph Harcourt.
An improved gas-burner - - - - (*Communicated by James Stratton.*)	3303	21st Dec. 1865	George Davies.
Improved apparatus for burning combustible vapor (such as that from naphtha or coal oil) for heating, cooking and lighting purposes. (*Communicated by James Stratton.*)	3317	22nd Dec. 1865	George Davies.

n 2

Subject-matter of Patent.	Number of Patent.	Date.	Name of Patentee.
GAS BURNERS &c.,—continued.			
Improvements in friction matches, in apparatus for using them, and in adapting them for lighting lamps. *(Communicated by Philos Blake Tyler.)* For gas pipes, see " PIPES."	3259	30th Dec. 1865	William Edward Newton.
GAUGES, SAFETY PLUGS, WATER LEVEL INDICATORS.			
Improved apparatus for preventing the explosion of steam-boilers.	305	3rd Feb. 1865	John Westerby.
Improvements in washing-machines and in apparatus connected therewith. *(working under pointers.)*	481	21st Feb. 1865	Robert Willison.
An improved safety apparatus for steam-boilers	1066	15th April 1865	John Minton Courtauld.
A combined safety valve regulator, pressure gauge, water indicator, alarm and " blow off " for steam generators. *(Communicated by Peter Riordan.)*	1306	11th May 1865	John Henry Johnson.
Water gauges and cocks	1330	13th May 1865	Alexander Weir.
Apparatus for indicating the pressure of steam or liquids in gauges, and for signalling.	1497	31st May 1865	Frederic Newton Gisborne.
Certain improvements on " Bourdon's " steam pressure gauge.	1509	1st June 1865	Thomas Edwin Wright.
A new or improved apparatus for supplying disinfecting liquids to water-closets, urinals and other places requiring the same.	1879	19th July 1865	Charles Nicholas.
Improvements in rules for measuring, and in other instruments or articles requiring to be adjusted or disposed at various angles. *(gauges.)*	2618	10th Oct. 1865	Arthur Nicholls.
Improvements in cocks for steam, water, air and gases at high pressures, and also in gauge cocks and water gauges for boilers, and sediment tubes for cocks and pipes.	2990	21st Nov. 1865	Samuel Bennett.
Certain improvements in water gauges to be employed in connection with steam-boilers	3026	25th Nov. 1865	{ James Draper. William Leech.
Apparatus for registering the speed of machinery, and apparatus for registering the pressure of steam and other fluids	3077	30th Nov. 1865	{ James Lee Norton. James Langfhan.
GLASS; APPLICATIONS OF GLASS.			
Improvements in the manufacture of oxygen gas and in treating and economizing the residual products of the said manufacture *(revisions for glass makers.)*	5	2nd Jan. 1865	{ John Frederick Parker. Joseph Tanner.

Subject-matter of Patent.	Number of Patent.	Date.	Name of Patentee.
GLASS—continued.			
Manufacture of enamelled glass to render it more useful in photographic art.	12	3rd Jan. 1865	William George Helsby.
Engraving upon crystal and silicious substances. (Communicated by Charles Raphael Maréchal and Cyprien Marie Tessie du Motay.)	69	11th Jan. 1865	Richard Archibald Brooman.
Certain improvements in rendering sundries furniture and other articles for domestic purposes. (glass articles.)	196	23rd Jan. 1865	Adolphe Drevelle.
Manufacture of ornamented articles of glass	497	22nd Feb. 1865	Thomas George Webb.
Manufacture of buttons. (Communicated by Joseph Edouard Mittler, &c'.)	594	2nd March 1865	William Clark.
Cotton gins	673	10th March 1865	Evan Legh.
Improvements in wine glasses and in stands or holders for the same.	699	11th March 1865	James Murdoch Napier.
Improvements in the manufacture of looking glasses or mirrors, and in apparatus employed therein. (Communicated by The Society Randal Cromwell, Alfred Tavernier and Edouard Dodé.)	756	21st March 1865	John Henry Johnson.
An improvement or improvements in ornamenting articles made of glass.	889	29th March 1865	Joseph Williams.
An improved mode of preventing corrosion or staining of the surface of glass.	994	6th April 1865	William Barrum Richards.
Protecting letters, numerals and ornamental designs on glass.	1111	21st April 1865	David Simson Buchanan.
An improved lamp or signal for calling cabs or other vehicles, by day and night. (partly composed of coloured glass.)	1115	21st April 1865	Edward Wilson.
Improvements in photographing upon wood, and in the preparation of wood, canvas, silk, glass and other substances, for the purpose of receiving and retaining impressions.	1174	26th April 1865	William Henry Smith.
Improved contrivances to facilitate the arrangement of flowers and leaves.	1167	29th April 1865	Thomas Charles March.
Manufacture and application of glass and other vitreous compositions	1220	1st May 1865	Arthur Howard Emerson. Robert Fowler.
Superseding the unsightly chimney pots now in use	1400	22nd May 1865	Robert Howell.
A new or improved compound spherical rest for ornamental turning lathes. (or for engraving glass.)	1441	25th May 1865	Thomas Hallam Hoblyn.
Improvements in securing roof lamp glasses of railway and other carriages, which improvements are also applicable to lighting the decks of ships, and other situations.	2029	4th Aug. 1865	Thomas Manley Rancy.
Improvements in the ornamentation of glass and in the application of glass so ornamented. (Communicated by The Society Randal Cromwell, Alfred Tavernier and Edouard Dodé.)	2039	5th Aug. 1865	John Henry Johnson.
Improvements in preparing and treating gunpowder in order to render the same unexplosive and to protect it from damp. (mixing glass with gunpowder.)	2057	8th Aug. 1865	James Gale, jun'.
Looms for weaving (applying glass or coating to picker spindles.)	2073	10th Aug. 1865	John Ingham. Henry Ingham. James Bradley.

Subject-matter of Patent.	Number of Patent.	Date.	Name of Patentee.
GLASS—continued.			
Gas-burners (applying a level of glass to steady flame.)	2094	12th Aug. 1866	Henry Woodward.
Furnaces to be used in the manufacture of glass and iron and steel, and for other like purposes. (Communicated by Henning Bovies.)	2106	15th Aug. 1865	John Frederick Bovien.
An improved liquid composition for cleansing, scouring and bleaching textile animal, mineral and vegetable substances (cleansing glass.)	2440	23rd Sept. 1865	Gustave Emile Rolland. Emile Léon Rolland.
Tiles for roofing (with ridges of glass.)	2663	18th Oct. 1865	John Taylor, jun'.
Preparing the surfaces of paper, leather, woven and other fabrics and substances, for receiving photographic pictures, engravings, lithographs and prints, and for rendering such substances fire and water-proof, (surfacing glass.) (Communicated by William Gibson.)	2891	9th Nov. 1865	William Edward Newton.
An improved mode of applying photographic paper pictures to glass.	3092	2nd Dec. 1865	Anne Josphine Wright.
Improvements in apparatus for mixing materials, which is also applicable for smoothing, finishing, rounding or polishing articles of metal or other material. (manufacture of glass.)	3243	14th Dec. 1865	William Robinson.
See also " BOTTLES."			
GLOVES.			
Sewing-machines (for making gloves.) (Communicated by Edmond Philippe and Dominique Gonce.)	304	3rd Feb. 1865	William Clark.
Improvements in boxing, fencing and cricket gloves, and in cricket pads or guards.	378	10th Feb. 1865	Henry Emanuel.
Sewing-machines (sewing gloves.)	2640	13th Oct. 1865	George Baldwin Woodruff.
GOVERNORS AND INDICATORS OF SPEED AND POWER FOR STATIONARY ENGINES AND MACHINERY; STARTING, STOPPING AND REVERSING APPARATUS; MACHINERY-BRAKES.			
Machinery for opening and carding cotton and other fibrous materials. (reversing gear.)	90	11th Jan. 1865	Robert Tempest.

Subject-matter of Patent.	Number of Patent.	Date.	Name of Patentee.
GOVERNORS, &c.—continued.			
Improvements in furnaces and boilers and parts connected with them, for generating steam and heating fluids, and also for improved apparatus for reducing and shutting off steam and regulating the speed of steam-engines.	626	11th Feb. 1865	John Cass.
Apparatus for rinsing and drying by centrifugal force. (Communicated by Félix Mennons and Auguste Racine.)	606	4th March 1865	Henri Adrien Bonneville.
Certain improvements in lap machines employed in preparing cotton and other fibrous substances. (stopping the machines.)	759	14th March 1865	Thomas Ogden.
Weft stop motions for looms - - -	789	18th March 1865	{ Edwin Pilling. / John Harper.
Certain improvements in governors or regulators for steam or other motive-power engines -	861	7th April 1865	{ Samuel Smith. / John William Jackson.
Machinery for cutting files - - - -	1019	8th April 1865	Thomas Turton.
Certain improvements in looms for weaving -	1070	17th April 1866	Mark Smith.
Certain improvements in looms for weaving	1069	19th April 1865	James Edward Hyde Andrew.
Machinery for carding cotton and other fibrous substances and for doubling yarns - -	1094	20th April 1865	{ James Hall. / William Dankerley. / Samuel Schofield.
Engines, machinery and implements employed in ploughing and tilling land.	1169	21st April 1865	Collinson Hall.
Improved means or apparatus for gaining or acquiring motive power.	1156	25th April 1865	Claude Jacquelin, Jun'.
File cutting machines - - - - -	1173	26th April 1865	James Dodge.
Certain improvements in machinery or apparatus for rolling or shaping metallic articles of irregular form, such as "file-blanks" and similar articles. (stopping the rollers.)	1190	27th April 1865	Edward M'Nally.
Improvements in steam-engines, relating to valve motions, governor and drain pipes - -	1198	29th April 1865	{ Andrew Wylde. / John M'Farlane Gray.
Means and apparatus for regulating the power and velocity of machinery or apparatus in motion.	1230	2nd May 1865	Charles William Simmons.
Improvements in steam generators and engines and in apparatus for feeding steam generators. (Communicated by George Bailey Brayton.)	1240	3rd May 1865	John Henry Johnson.
Printing machines - - - - -} (throwing out of gear.)	1344	15th May 1865	{ Robert Harrild. / Horton Harrild.
Screw gills or hackle frames - - - (throwing off the belts.)	1419	24th May 1865	Thompson Beanland.
Certain improvements applicable to spinning, weaving and knitting machines. (throwing out of gear.) (Communicated by Charles Arthur Radiguet and Jean Adolphe Levitor.)	1440	25th May 1865	William Edward Newton.
An improved break applicable to various descriptions of steam-engines and also to railway purposes. (Communicated by Euphe Dethril.)	1543	5th June 1865	Frederick Tolhausen.
An improvement in steam-engine governors (Communicated by Estur Lamb and Henry Stephen Maxfield and Lyman Arnold Cook.)	1561	7th June 1865	William Edward Newton.

Subject-matter of Patent.	Number of Patent.	Date.	Name of Patentee.
GOVERNORS, &c.—continued.			
Improvements in and applicable to machinery for doubling and drawing cotton and other fibrous substances. (stopping the carriage.)	1739	30th June 1865	François Dehaisne-Debauterville.
Improvements in apparatus for giving signals on board ships, and which are also applicable for other purposes.	1778	5th July 1865	Frederic Newton Gisborne.
Regulating or controlling the power employed in actuating sewing and other machines of a light nature.	1685	11th July 1865	Benjamin Fothergill.
Machinery for winding yarn cops - - - (stop lever.)	2297	7th Sept. 1865	William Oldham.
Machinery for excavating earth - - - (disconnecting the gearing.)	2405	21st Sept. 1865	John Bostock Hahne.
Construction of presses for hay, cotton, hemp and other substances. (throwing in and out of action.) (Communicated by Thomas Gamm and Thomas Bolton Webster.)	2464	25th Sept. 1865	Alfred Vincent Newton.
Machinery or apparatus for preparing and spinning cotton and other fibrous materials. (buffers or stops.)	2476	27th Sept. 1865	William Tatham.
Steam-engines - - - - - (reversing gear.)	2479	27th Sept. 1865	John Rodger Arnoldi.
Weft winding machines both for winding on bobbins and cops, also for a shuttle to hold the cop when weaving. (stopping the spindles.)	2519	30th Sept. 1865	William Longbottom.
File cutting machines - - - - (arresting the motion.)	2546	4th Oct. 1865	John Dudge.
Improvements in the propelling and steering of steam ships or other vessels, and in the machinery or apparatus employed therefor. (reversing action of propellers.)	2565	5th Oct. 1865	Robert William Fraser.
Centrifugal governors - - - - (Communicated by Thomas Richard Pickering.)	2659	12th Oct. 1865	William Edward Newton.
Transmitting motion to propelling shafts - - (reversing action.) (Communicated by James Buchanan Eads.)	2807	31st Oct. 1865	William Edward Newton.
Machinery or apparatus for reeling silk, cotton or other fibrous threads, in the form of skeins. (stop motion.)	2826	2nd Nov. 1865	Enoch Rushton.
Means of connecting drums or pulleys with their shafts or drivers. (for starting machinery.) (Communicated by Leverett Hamer Olmsted.)	2953	14th Nov. 1865	William Clark.
Apparatus for raising, lowering and moving heavy bodies, and for transmitting and arresting motion for various purposes.	3093	2nd Dec. 1865	Thomas Aldridge Weston.
Improvements in reaping and mowing machines, part of which is applicable to machinery in general. (reversing gear.)	3142	6th Dec. 1865	Adam Carlisle Bamlett.

Subject-matter of Patent.	Number of Patent.	Date.	Name of Patentee.
GRINDING AND CRUSHING CORN, GRAIN, SEEDS, &c.; DRESSING FLOUR; MILLSTONES; DECORTICATING GRAIN, GRINDING DRIED MEAT.			
Apparatus for balling grain and for reducing granular substances. (operating machine.)	36	5th Jan. 1865	Gustav Adolph Buchholz.
Improvements in the grinding and feeding apparatus of mills for grinding corn and other substances, and in the combination of such mills with flour dressing machines - - -	806	24th Jan. 1865	{ Richard Robert Ritchen. Charles James Watts.
An improvement in the construction of mills for grinding and pulverising grain and other substances.	811	25th Jan. 1865	Anthony Stevenson.
A new method for removing or destroying the momentum of heavy bodies by means of an elastic machine or machines, so as to prevent injury and damage from concussion, applicable to ship cables, ship and fort armour, railway trains, tenders to pierheads, and floating piers, gang ways, break-waters and other similar structures, also as a motive-power. (driving grinding machinery.) (Communicated by William Graham M'Ivor.)	821	6th Feb. 1865	Clements Robert Markham.
Mills for grinding wheat and other grain - -	839	6th Feb. 1865	William Pickford Wilkins.
Improvements in the means of decorticating grain and other seeds, and in apparatus for the same. (Communicated by Gustave Latour, Christophe Oura Rollet and Clément Montville.)	841	24th Feb. 1865	William Clark.
Improvements in machinery for grinding corn and other substances, and in horse gear or apparatus for driving the same, which horse gear is also applicable for driving other machinery.	652	8th March 1865	Frederick William Turner.
Combined apparatus for threshing, dressing and grinding grain and other agricultural produce.	742	16th March 1865	James Marshall.
Improvements in the treatment of meal and the dressing of flour, and the machinery and apparatus employed therein.	896	30th March 1865	William Savory.
Apparatus for grinding corn, seeds, minerals or any other substance ground on the flat surface of a stone - - - - - -	1267	6th May 1865	{ John Hart. Henry Tonge.
Treating rice and other grain for the manufacture of starch, also to prepare them for use as food and for other purposes.	1319	12th May 1865	Henry Bamford.
Flour mills - - - - - - (Communicated by Charles Simon Olivier Martineau, Norrine Justine and Nicolas François Danel-Prévost.)	1348	15th May 1865	Henri Adrien Bonneville.
Machinery for cleaning and decorticating rice and other grains and seeds.	1777	5th July 1865	Joseph Wace Gray.
Mills for grinding, of the description known as Felton's American Mill - - - -	2204	2nd Sept. 1865	{ William Barford. Thomas Perkins.
Mills for crushing and grinding wheat and other grain.	2299	20th Sept. 1865	John Tye.

Subject-matter of Patent.	Number of Patent.	Date.	Name of Patentee.
GRINDING CORN, &c.—*continued.*			
Improvements in grinding wheat and other grain, and in apparatus for drying and improving the condition of damp wheat or other grain.	2485	29th Sept. 1865	Benjamin Wren.
Machinery or apparatus for preparing and supplying food for cattle. (*corn crushers.*)	2514	30th Sept. 1865	Robert Willacy.
Apparatus for grinding corn, seeds and minerals	2562	7th Oct. 1865	{ James Priestley. William Whitworth. John Sutcliffe.
Preparation of meat for food (*grinding meat.*)	2577	17th Oct. 1865	Arthur Hill Hassall, M.D.
Constructing and mounting or hanging millstones	2592	18th Oct. 1865	William Henry Parker.
Machinery for dressing millstones (*Communicated by Kleazer A. Paine.*)	2517	1st Nov. 1865	Alfred Vincent Newton.
Mounting and driving millstones	2839	3rd Nov. 1865	Richard Smith, jun'.
An improved mode of ventilating millstones (*Communicated by Alexandre Désiré Lavoyrury.*)	2924	13th Nov. 1865	Henry Edward Newton.
An improved machine for taking off the fibre from cotton seed and cleaning it. (*using grinders.*)	2950	17th Nov. 1865	William Henry Cope.
A new or improved cement or composition, applicable to the agglomeration or moulding of various materials, and to other useful and decorative purposes. (*forming millstones.*) (*Communicated by Stanislas Sorel and Emile Justin Meunier.*)	3119	5th Dec. 1865	Richard Archibald Brooman.
Apparatus employed in grinding corn and other substances capable of being ground by millstones.	3120	6th Dec. 1865	Edward Alfred Cowper.
Means of feeding meal to the bolting reel in flouring mills.	3286	30th Dec. 1865	William Fraser Cochrane.
GRINDING AND CRUSHING MINERALS, CLAY, FIBROUS PLANTS, &C.; BREAKING STONE.			
An improvement in the construction of mills for grinding and pulverising grain and other substances. (*cereal and charcoal.*)	211	25th Jan. 1865	Anthony Stevenson.
Improvements in mortar mills, applicable also to grinding other substances.	262	28th Jan. 1865	John Raines.
Improvements in machinery for grinding corn and other substances, and in horse gear or apparatus for driving the same, which horse gear is also applicable for driving other machinery.	662	8th March 1865	Frederick William Turner.
Improvements in the manufacture of looking glasses or mirrors, and in apparatus employed thereon. (*grinding platinum.*) (*Communicated by The Society Rendel Cromwell, Alfred Turrour and Edouard Dodd.*)	766	21st March 1865	John Henry Johnson.

Subject-matter of Patent.	Number of Patent.	Date.	Name of Patentee.
GRINDING MINERALS, &c.—continued.			
Improved apparatus for collecting or receiving pulverised flint or dust. (See "VENTILATION.")	909	31st March 1865	Elias Leah.
Treating wood in order to cleanse it from burrs, seeds and other foreign matters -	1042	12th April 1865	Henry Sikes. George Jarman.
Paints or compositions for coating and preserving metallic and other substances from oxidation and decay - - - -	1154	25th April 1865	John Northall Brown. Thomas Daykin Clare.
Apparatus for disintegrating vegetable and animal substances.	1166	26th April 1865	François Dominique Pierre Jacques Calmason.
Machinery for reducing friable substances to powder	1176	27th April 1865	Henry Walker Wood.
Apparatus for grinding corn, seeds, minerals or any other substance ground on the flat surface of a stone - - - -	1867	6th May 1865	John Hart. Henry Tonge.
Improvements in the preparation of amalgams of quicksilver or mercury, and in the application of such amalgams to various purposes in the arts. (enclosing crushing rollers.) (Communicated by Henry Wurtz.)	1719	26th June 1865	William Edward Newton.
Improvements in reducing vegetable fibre to pulp and in machinery employed therein.	2002	2nd Aug. 1865	William Wharton Burdon.
Improvements in preparing and treating gunpowder in order to render the same unexplosive and to protect it from damp. (crushing plant to mix with gunpowder.)	2057	8th Aug. 1865	James Gale, jun'.
Improved machinery for mixing or grinding ointment, paints, drugs and other substances.	2290	6th Sept. 1865	Thomas Charles Gibson.
Apparatus for grinding corn, seeds and minerals -	2553	7th Oct. 1865	James Priestley. William Whitworth. John Nutcliffe.
Machinery employed for crushing, amalgamating and washing gold quartz and other minerals or matters containing gold or other metal. (Communicated by James Hart.)	2643	13th Oct. 1865	William Halse Gatty Jones.
Machinery for crushing or reducing stone, quartz, emery and other mineral substances -	2918	13th Nov. 1865	George Henry Goodman. Edward Bow.
Improved machinery to be used in the manufacture of paper. (grinding wood.) (Communicated by Heinrich Voelter.)	3041	27th Nov. 1865	William Edward Newton.
Apparatus employed in grinding corn and other substances capable of being ground by millstones. (drugs, paints, cupralions, arsenic, &c.)	3126	5th Dec. 1865	Edward Alfred Cowper.
An improved method of and apparatus for making mortars, bowls, spill pots, jelly cans, galvanic troughs and other similar articles -	3159	8th Dec. 1865	William Boulton. Joseph Worthington.
Improvements in floor cloths and similar composition fabrics, in the manufacture of such fabrics, and in machinery employed therein - (breaking up or reducing composition materials.)	3370	29th Dec. 1865	John Howard Kidd. James Chadwick Mather.

Subject-matter of Patent.	Number of Patent.	Date.	Name of Patentee.
GRINDING AND SHARPENING; FLAT GRINDING AND POLISHING; GRINDING SURFACES; EMERY, SAND AND GLASS PAPERS AND CLOTHS.			
Apparatus for cleaning and polishing knives	26	4th Jan. 1865	George Kent.
Improved means or apparatus for facing flags or smoothing the surface of stones	154	14th Jan. 1865	{ James Coulter. Herbert Harpin. }
Improvements in shaping and forging metals and in the machinery and apparatus employed therein (planishing and finishing.)	165	19th Jan. 1865	{ James Alfred Shipton. Robert Mitchell. }
Certain improvements in machinery and appliances for the manufacture of nails, pins and rivets (pointing.)	785	21st March 1865	{ Charles Farmer. Thomas Turner. }
Certain improvements in machinery or apparatus used in carding cotton or other fibrous substances (sharpening the wires.)	867	29th March 1865	{ Evan Leigh. Frederick Allen Leigh. }
Means or apparatus for effecting the cleansing and polishing of forks	950	4th April 1865	Charles Martin.
An improved machine for rounding and polishing shot, shell and other balls or spheres. (Communicated by William Davis Winsor.)	952	4th April 1865	William Clark.
New or improved apparatus for separating or sorting and washing ores, minerals, coal, emery and other substances in a granular or pulverulent state. (Communicated by Charles Prieger and Theodor Herold.)	983	5th April 1865	Henry Simm.
An improved mode of pointing or tapering the ends of metallic rods or wires, applicable to the manufacture of pins, needles, and other articles where points or tapered ends are required. (Communicated by Henri Cauderay.)	976	6th April 1865	Edwin Henry Newby.
An improved metallic preparation or composition for cleaning, sharpening, burnishing and grinding articles of cutlery, edge tools or cutting instruments, and for grinding the cards or rollers of carding-engines and the surfaces of cylinders, and covering rollers for various kinds of woollen and cotton machinery.	1054	13th April 1865	George Mountford.
Improvements in finishing and polishing metal tubes and rods, and in apparatus or machinery to be employed therein.	1229	2nd May 1865	Thomas Allcock.
Improved apparatus for cutting, turning and smoothing metal pipes, and the surfaces of bolts, rods or spindles	1611	11th May 1865	{ George Mountford. Edward Worrall. }
Improvements in vessels for containing blacking, polishing oils and other similar materials, and in apparatus connected therewith.	1327	12th May 1865	Thomas Davis.
Machinery for the manufacture of hinges (polishing the metal strips.) (Communicated by Jean Baptiste Evrard and Jean Pierre Bayer.)	1338	13th May 1865	William Clark.
Apparatus for polishing, smoothing or facing, especially applicable to lithographic stones.	1669	21st June 1865	Charles Henry Gardner.

Subject-matter of Patent.	Number of Patent.	Date.	Name of Patentee.
GRINDING, SHARPENING, &c.—*continued.*			
Regulating or controlling the power employed in actuating sewing and other machines of a light nature.	1838	11th July 1865	Benjamin Fothergill.
Improvements in the manufacture of velvets, plushes and other pile fabrics, and in the machinery or apparatus connected therewith. (*keeping the knife sharpened.*)	1937	26th July 1865	John Bellhouse the younger.
Machinery or apparatus for the manufacture of needles.	2074	10th Aug. 1865	Chauncey Orris Crosby.
Machinery for grinding, dressing, smoothing or polishing flags and stones, without the use of the ordinary cutting tools.	2413	21st Sept. 1865	Benjamin Chaffer. James Thompson. Charles Thompson.
Apparatus for grinding cards of carding engines	2516	30th Sept. 1865	Samuel Faulkner.
A new composition of Indian-rubber mastic or cement, made in a more or less solid state according to the use to be made of it, and the process or contrivance for applying the same. (*making glass and emery cloth.*)	2630	12th Oct. 1865	Auguste Aimé Letenard.
Apparatus for polishing and brushing	2655	14th Oct. 1865	James Lamb Hancock.
Machinery for the manufacture of fish hooks (*pointing lengths of wire.*)	2673	17th Oct. 1865	Albert Fenton.
Certain new or improved machinery for the manufacture of anils. (*pointing.*)	2769	30th Oct. 1865	William Whittle.
Means and apparatus for finishing the soles of boots and shoes.	2857	6th Nov. 1865	Robert Flude.
Apparatus for grinding and pointing the cards on carding-engines.	2876	8th Nov. 1865	Robert Swires.
Machinery for crushing or reducing stone, quartz, emery and other mineral substances	2918	13th Nov. 1865	George Henry Goodman. Edward Bow.
Certain improvements in the manufacture of brushes. (*for polishing.*)	6060	29th Nov. 1865	James Stokes. Thomas Gray.
A new or improved cement or composition, applicable to the agglomeration or moulding of various materials, and to other useful and decorative purposes. (*forming grindstones.*) (*Communicated by Stanislas Sorel and Emile Justin Mouler.*)	3119	5th Dec. 1865	Richard Archibald Brooman.
Improved machinery for manufacturing sewing-machine needles. (*pointing the wire.*) (*Partly communicated by Joseph Thorne.*)	3143	6th Dec. 1865	Nahum Salamon. William John Lawrence Davids.
Machinery for grinding pit frame, crosscut, mill, carpenters' hand back and other saws, and other like metal surfaces where great truth and accuracy is required	3223	13th Dec. 1865	George Atkin. Edwin Atkin. Alfred Amos Atkin.
Improvements in apparatus for mixing materials, which is also applicable for smoothing, finishing, rounding or polishing articles of metal or other material.	3243	14th Dec. 1865	William Robinson.
Improvements in the manufacture of floor cloth and in apparatus employed therein. (*grinding the surface.*)	3252	15th Dec. 1865	Frederick Walton.

Subject-matter of Patent.	Number of Patent.	Date.	Name of Patentee.
GRINDING, SHARPENING, &c.—*continued.*			
Preparation of glue or gelatine so as to render it insoluble in water, and applicable by the admixture of other substances, to various purposes for which common glue or gelatine cannot now be used. (*for making emery, sand and glass papers.*) (*Communicated by Henry Waris.*)	3325	23rd Dec. 1865	William Edward Newton.
GUNPOWDER AND EXPLOSIVE COMPOUNDS; POWDER FLASKS.			
Improvements in the construction of shells, and in the explosive powder and fuse to be used therewith and for other purposes.	188	16th Jan. 1865	John Berkeley Cotler.
A self adjusting lever powder and shot charger for fire-arms.	509	3rd Feb. 1865	William Bartram.
An improved gunpowder - - - -	403	13th Feb. 1865	Louis Henry Gustavus Ehrhardt.
Preparing explosive compounds - - } (*Communicated by Wilhelm Gerhardt.*) }	515	23rd Feb. 1865	{ Adolph Meyer. { Moritz Meyer.
Preparation and treatment of gun cotton -	1109	20th April 1865	Frederick Augustus Abel.
Certain improvements in the means employed for the prevention of the ignition of matter capable of ignition or combustion.	1515	2nd June 1865	Herbert Allman.
Gunpowder for mining and war purposes - (*Communicated by Gustav Adolph Neumeyer.*)	1636	17th June 1865	August Klein.
Preparing and treating gunpowder - -	1679	21st June 1865	James Gale, jun'.
Improvements in breech-loading fire-arms and in the charges and projectiles to be used therewith.	1894	20th July 1865	William Le Posollire.
Compositions similar to gunpowder, for blasting, for use in ordnance and fire-arms, and for other purposes. (*Communicated by Petro Nisser.*)	1929	26th July 1865	Edward Spicer.
Improvements in preparing and treating gunpowder in order to render the same unexplosive and to protect it from damp.	2057	8th Aug. 1865	James Gale, jun'.
Preparing charges for fire-arms and for blasting	2266	2nd Sept. 1865	Constant Reichen.
Improvements in rifling fire-arms, and in missiles or projectiles used in such, and in the machinery for the production of these improvements. (*on explosive composition.*)	2466	24th Sept. 1865	William Ellis Metford.
Improvements in preparing compounds of xyloidine or gun cotton, and in the apparatus employed.	3162	9th Dec. 1865	Alexander Parkes.
An improved blasting powder - - - (*Communicated by Bernhard August Schäffer and Christian Friedrich Budenberg.*)	3206	12th Dec. 1865	Arnold Budenberg.
Improvements in apparatus for mixing materials, which is also applicable for smoothing, finishing, rounding or polishing articles of metal or other material. (*forming gunpowder.*)	3243	14th Dec. 1865	William Robinson.

Subject-matter of Patent.	Number of Patent.	Date.	Name of Patentee.

GUNPOWDER, &c.—continued.

Preparation of glue or gelatine so as to render it insoluble in water, and applicable by the admixture of other substances to various purposes for which common glue or gelatine cannot now be used. (*for powder horns.*) (*Communicated by Henry Wurtz.*) — 3226 — 23rd Dec. 1865 — William Edward Newton.

GUTTA-PERCHA AND INDIA-RUBBER.
(*Preparing, Treating, Vulcanising.*)

Vulcanising compounds and vulcanised fabrics. (*Communicated by Simon Stevens.*) — 170 — 20th Jan. 1865 — Benjamin Franklin Stevens.

Certain improvements in the manufacture of caoutchouc. (*Communicated by Messieurs Léon Désiré Innocent and François Perroncel.*) — 396 — 11th Feb. 1865 — Peter Armand Le Comte de Fontaine Moreau.

Improvements in cutting sheets of india-rubber and like materials into strips or threads, and in machinery or apparatus for the purpose. — 666 — 9th March 1865 — Benoni Collins.

Manufacture of a compound or material to be used as a substitute for india-rubber. (*Communicated by Henry Larrowberry and Emile Grenier.*) — 1068 — 15th April 1865 — William Clark.

Manufacture or treatment of india-rubber or gutta-percha, or compounds thereof, applicable to the production of stereotype plates and other forms. — 1257 — 5th May 1865 — Thomas Jefferson Mayall.

Preparing the surfaces of paper, leather, woven and other fabrics and substances, for receiving photographic pictures, engravings, lithographs and prints, and for rendering such substances fire and water proof. (*enamelling gutta-percha.*) (*Communicated by William Gibson.*) — 2861 — 9th Nov. 1865 — William Edward Newton.

Preparation of glue or gelatine so as to render it insoluble in water, and applicable by the admixture or other substances to various purposes for which common glue or gelatine cannot now be used. (*as vulcanised rubber compounds.*) (*Communicated by Henry Wurtz.*) — 3225 — 23rd Dec. 1865 — William Edward Newton.

GUTTA-PERCHA AND INDIA-RUBBER as APPLIED IN VARIOUS MANUFACTURES.

Coverings of telegraphic conductors and cables. — 96 — 12th Jan. 1865 — John Fuller.

Improvements in the packing of pistons and piston rods of pumps and steam and other engines, which improvements are also applicable to hydraulic presses. — 155 — 18th Jan. 1865 — William Robert Foster.

Subject-matter of Patent.	Number of Patent.	Date.	Name of Patentee.
GUTTA-PERCHA, &c.—*continued.*			
Manufacture of boots, shoes, saddlery, harness and other articles. (*Communicated by Toussaint Loudric.*)	159	19th Jan. 1865	William Clark.
Certain improvements in rendering soundless furniture and other articles for domestic purposes.	196	23rd Jan. 1865	Adolphe Dreveile.
An improved elastic valve and high pressure and general tap	283	26th Jan. 1866	{ Stephen Sharp. Daniel Smith.
Permanent way of railways	275	31st Jan. 1865	{ Ewing Pye Colquhoun. John Pardoe Ferris.
Cushions for billiard and other like tables	316	4th Feb. 1865	James Lyne Hancock.
Improvements applicable to air cushions, mattresses, portable baths, and other like air inflated articles.	317	4th Feb. 1865	Arthur Henry Robinson.
Manufacture of boots, shoes and other coverings for the feet	381	10th Feb. 1865	{ George Coles. James Archibald Jaques. John American Fanshawe.
Certain improvements in the manufacture of caoutchouc. (*Communicated by Messieurs Jean, Désiré Issoard and François Perrenot.*)	398	11th Feb. 1865	Peter Armand Le Comte de Fontaine Moreau.
Waterproofing skins, hides and leather	418	14th Feb. 1865	George Harton.
Manufacture of boots, shoes and other like coverings for the feet. (*Communicated by Alexandre Leverd.*)	442	16th Feb. 1865	Richard Archibald Brougman.
An improved method of stopping bottles	464	18th Feb. 1865	John James Chidley.
An improvement in air tight jars for preserving eggs and fruits and such like articles of food.	546	27th Feb. 1865	George Kennedy Geyelin.
An improved means of securing and protecting the india-rubber rings of buffer springs of railway carriages, which invention is also applicable to air pump and valve seatings, and lids faced with india-rubber.	636	6th March 1865	William John Oliver.
Manufacture of shoes and other coverings for the feet	687	7th March 1865	{ Alexandre Eugène Adolphe Aubert. Gustave Eugène Michel Gerard.
Water-closet apparatus	648	8th March 1865	John Shanks.
Cricket, racket and tennis balls	696	11th March 1865	Charles Huntley.
Mail and despatch bags and bags for other similar uses. (*Communicated by Thomas James Claxton.*)	788	15th March 1865	George Tomlinson Bousfield.
Improvements in the means and apparatus employed for treating timber with antiseptic or preservative fluids, also applicable to other purposes. (*india-rubber tanks.*)	734	16th March 1865	Samuel Bagster Boulton.
An improved apparatus combining a pencil shield and india-rubber.	746	17th March 1865	Charles Anthony Wheeler.
A new or improved machine for peeling or skinning almonds.	760	18th March 1865	James Henry Walkew.
Double acting lift and force pumps	942	4th April 1865	Charles Demoon Young.
Manufacture of a compound or material to be used as a substitute for india-rubber. (*Communicated by Henry Larowsbery and Emile Orosier.*)	1066	15th April 1865	William Clark.
Inkstands (*Communicated by Frank Oliver.*)	1089	19th April 1865	John Merrill.

Subject-matter of Patent.	Number of Patent.	Date.	Name of Patentee.
GUTTA-PERCHA, &c.—*continued.*			
Invalid carriages - - - - - (*Communicated by Auguste Quitrue.*)	1120	21st April 1865	Henry Edward Newton.
Improvements in the fitting of surface condenser tubes, and in the tools to be used therein, and in the means of retarding corrosion in steam-boilers. (*Communicated by William Judson.*)	1129	22nd April 1865	Alfred Vincent Newton.
A new or improved shoe or sandal for facilitating the art of swimming.	1145	24th April 1865	Aaron Atkins.
Machinery for sewing and embroidering - -	1167	25th April 1865	George Mumby.
Improvements in boring or excavating and blasting rocks and minerals, and in the treatment of the tools employed therein. (*a mixture of india-rubber for waterproofing cartridges.*)	1193	29th April 1865	Julius Bernard.
Pickers for looms. (*of india-rubber.*)	1200	29th April 1865	George Pomeroy Dodge.
An improved manufacture of waterproof fabric - (*Communicated by The American Waterproof Cloth Company.*)	1319	1st May 1865	William Edward Newton.
Means and apparatus used for stretching woven fabrics and other materials. (*Communicated by Jules Ducommun.*)	1329	3rd May 1865	William Clark.
Manufacture or treatment of india-rubber or gutta-percha, or compounds thereof, applicable to the production of stereotype plates and other forms.	1357	5th May 1865	Thomas Jefferson Mayall.
Manufacture of elastic knitted or looped fabrics -	1378	9th May 1865	Robert Barlow Cowley.
Improvements in door and other mats, part of which improvements is also applicable to brushes and brooms, and to producing card or tooth surfaces employed in operating on various fibrous substances.	1379	9th May 1865	Thomas Jefferson Mayall.
Improvements in the manufacture of hose and other flexible tubing, which improvements are also applicable in uniting surfaces of india-rubber, gutta-percha or of compounds thereof, to each other, or to woven or other fabric or material for other purposes.	1303	11th May 1865	Thomas Jefferson Mayall.
An improvement in the drawing and other rollers used in preparing and spinning cotton and other fibrous materials and textile manufactures. (*Communicated by Amos Ashom Taylor.*)	1420	25th May 1865	William Edward Newton.
Manufacture of carpets and other terry and cut pile fabrics. (*Communicated by The American Waterproof Cloth Company.*)	1400	31st May 1865	William Edward Newton.
A new or improved method of obtaining motive-power, together with certain machinery or apparatus for applying the same - - -	1504	1st June 1865	{ David Hancock. { Frederick Barnes.
Safety apparatus for steam-boilers - - -	1538	2nd June 1865	James Shepherd.
Umbrellas, parasols and sunshades - - -	1539	5th June 1865	John Stephenson.
An improved metallic stuffing box - - -	1855	7th June 1865	Victor Duterne.
An improved material for stuffing seats, cushions, mattrasses and other articles. (*Communicated by Emile Renterre.*)	1800	7th July 1865	Thomas Frederick Henley.

Subject-matter of Patent.	Number of Patent.	Date.	Name of Patentee.
GUTTA-PERCHA, &c.—continued.			
Double or single action pumps (caoutchouc spring.) (Communicated by Claude Gouin.)	8523	11th Oct. 1865	William Edward Gedge.
A new composition of india-rubber mastic or cement, made in a more or less fluid state according to the use to be made of it, and the process or contrivance for applying the same.	2530	12th Oct. 1865	Auguste Aimé Lerenard.
Apparatus for raising liquids (india-rubber washers.)	2532	12th Oct. 1865	Jean Urin Bastier.
Elastic fronts, sides and backs for boots and shoes -	2540	13th Oct. 1865	Matthew Cartwright.
A certain composition having anti-corrosive and anti-fouling properties, for the preservation of and keeping clean the bottoms of iron vessels, and also for the preservation of iron submerged and iron structures exposed to the action of the atmosphere or water (composed partly of gutta-percha.)	2585	14th Oct. 1865	William Jardine Combe Mac Millan. James Mason. John Vickers Scarborough.
Manufacture of covers applicable to drawing or printing rollers and as endless blankets -	2716	20th Oct. 1865	Manuel Leopold Jonas Larmier. John Kershaw.
An improved mode of transmitting motion to the styles or hands of the dials of counters used for indicating and registering the distances public vehicles or private carriages travel.	2736	23rd Oct. 1865	Mathieu Julien, aîné.
Improvements in the manufacture of keys for pianofortes and other musical instruments requiring such keys, and in parts connected with such keys -	2747	24th Oct. 1865	Daniel George Staight. Stephen Staight. James Cheverton.
Improvements in roller skates, and in the rollers to be used therewith and for other purposes.	2770	27th Oct. 1865	Robert Bell Sansom.
Packing and labelling bottles, jars and other fragile articles.	2775	24th Oct. 1865	George Clark.
Manufacture of cushions for billiard tables -	2874	7th Nov. 1865	George Alexander Smith.
Improvements in brushes for hair dressing and other uses, also in brooms and apparatus for cleaning, preparing, painting, coating and smoothing surfaces	2985	20th Nov. 1865	George Smith. Charles Ritchie.
Shields for trunks or packages (Communicated by Alford House and Henry Alonzo Howe.)	3022	24th Nov. 1865	William Edward Newton.
Apparatus for signalling on railways (india-rubber packings for bearings.)	3029	25th Nov. 1865	Charles Frederick Whitworth.
Improved machinery to be used in the manufacture of paper. (Communicated by Heinrich Voelter.)	3041	27th Nov. 1865	William Edward Newton.
An improved nautical safety apparatus -	3045	29th Nov. 1865	François Mole.
" Top rollers " employed in the manufacture of fibrous substances.	3078	30th Nov. 1865	John Kerfoot.
Apparatus for raising, lowering and moving heavy bodies, and for transmitting and arresting motion for various purposes.	3096	2nd Dec. 1865	Thomas Aldridge Weston.
An improved ruler (Communicated by George Schramm.)	3188	11th Dec. 1865	James Theodore Griffin.
Construction of door mats, flesh and bath brushes made principally of india-rubber.	3216	13th Dec. 1865	George Barber.

Subject-matter of Patent.	Number of Patent.	Date.	Name of Patentee.
GUTTA-PERCHA, &c.—continued.			
Apparatus for regulating heat obtained by the combustion of gas. (for vulcanising india-rubber.)	3266	18th Dec. 1866	Henry Ptasch.
Manufacture of electric conductors Insulated with india-rubber.	3347	27th Dec. 1865	Hugh Adams Silver.
HAIR-DRESSING AND PERFUMERY.			
Improvements in brushes for brushing the hair, which improvements are also applicable to brushes for other purposes.	61	7th Jan. 1865	Theophilus Harvey.
Improvements in the construction of brushes used for brushing the human or other hair, and in the apparatus or means connected therewith.	214	25th Jan. 1865	Casimir Roques.
Hair pins . . . . . (Communicated by Joseph Charles Howells.)	325	6th Feb. 1865	Richard Archibald Brooman.
Machinery or apparatus for brushing the hair	348	7th Feb. 1865	John Butler Watters.
Improvements in the strengthening and ornamenting of collapsible or soft metal tubes. (for cosmetics.)	667	9th March 1865	Edmund Leahy.
Machinery for cutting the human hair, the same being applicable for shearing horses.	973	6th April 1865	Robert Maynard.
The application of a certain kind of goat's hair in imitation of human hair, to the manufacture of head dresses, moustaches, and all kinds of false hair, and the process of preparing the same.	1367	18th May 1865	Henry Rushton.
Driving apparatus for hair brushing and shampooing by machinery - - - -	1490	31st May 1865	Thomas Appleton Browne. John Knight.
Improved preparations for the treatment and preservation of the hair. (Communicated by Max Oldradorff and Pierre Léry.)	1647	19th June 1865	John Henry Johnson.
An improved arrangement of machinery for brushing hair.	2068	8th Aug. 1865	Samuel Middleton.
Improvements in apparatus by means of which certain liquids, common air, and certain elastic fluids are made available in the production of light, and their quantity regulated and measured, parts of which improvements are applicable for other purposes. (impregnating the air with perfumes.)	2184	25th Aug. 1865	Edwin Augustus Curley.
Brushes - - - - - (for the hair.)	2226	30th Aug. 1865	George Smith. Charles Ritchie.
Hair brushing machinery or apparatus .	2278	5th Sept. 1865	Joseph Neat. Francis Ford.
A new or improved method of and apparatus for heating instruments or irons for curling, waving and frissling hair, and for other purposes to which heated instruments or irons are applicable. (Communicated by Hyppolyte Gillot.)	2283	6th Sept. 1865	Louis Gachin.

Subject-matter of Patent.	Number of Patent.	Date.	Name of Patentee.
HAIR-DRESSING, &c.—*continued.*			
Machinery for brushing hair - • • •	2417	22nd Sept. 1865	Frederick Thomas Broadreth. John Henry Brandreth.
Manufacture of scent and emulsifying bottles - •	2549	9th Oct. 1865	Thomas Miles.
A new or improved bottle fountain for pocket and other purposes.	2847	4th Nov. 1865	Jean Nadal.
Improvements in brushes for hair dressing and other uses, also in brooms and apparatus for cleaning, preparing, painting, coating and smoothing surfaces - • • • • • •	2966	20th Nov. 1865	George Smith. Charles Ritchie.
Hair brushing apparatus • • • •	2994	21st Nov. 1865	George Smith. George Smith, Junr. Charles William Smith.

HAMMERS, ANDS, PICKS, SCREW-DRIVERS.

Subject-matter of Patent.	Number of Patent.	Date.	Name of Patentee.
Improvements in steam hammers and in apparatus employed in combination with steam hammers.	89	11th Jan. 1865	John Ramsbottom.
Hammers and pile-drivers to be worked by steam or other power. (Communicated by Charles Michel Nillus, Ernest Ferdinand Nillus, Albert Emmanuel Nillus and Jean Joseph Mondrat Crouen.)	151	20th Jan. 1865	William Edward Newton.
Machinery for rolling and hammering iron and other metals.	375	10th Feb. 1865	John Ramsbottom.
Improvements in steam hammers applicable to the manufacture of files, to welding types of cotton machinery and to other purposes.	641	7th March 1865	James Dodge.
Forging machines • • • • •	822	24th March 1865	Joseph Wright.
Improvements in steam and atmospheric hammers and presses, which improvements are also applicable to steam-engines.	962	4th April 1865	Joseph Vaughan.
Mode of making or forming the links of iron or steel chains and chain cables, and for machinery to be used therein.	1006	8th April 1865	Alfred Homfray.
Machinery for cutting files • • • •	1018	8th April 1865	Thomas Torton.
Manufacture of iron and steel • • •	1082	11th April 1865	Charles Vaughan.
Cushions for steam cylinders • • • (Communicated by Henry Johnson.)	1079	18th April 1865	Frederick Collier Bakewell.
Machinery for cutting and dressing stones and other hard substances. (Communicated by Gustavus Cappers.)	1093	19th April 1865	Maurice Vogt.
Machinery or apparatus for working or cutting coal or minerals, and for compressing or exhausting air to be employed therein or for other purposes. same parts of which apparatus are also applicable to upright shafts, and other parts for regulating the flow or discharge of steam or other elastic fluids. (construction of picks.)	1209	29th April 1865	William Leatham.
An improvement in atmospheric forging hammers -	1320	19th May 1865	Edward Augustus Raymond.

Subject-matter of Patent.	Number of Patent.	Date.	Name of Patentee.
HAMMERS, &c.—continued.			
Construction of screws and screw drivers - - (Communicated by Jared Augustus Ayres.)	1367	19th May 1865	Alfred Vincent Newton.
Certain improvements in steam hammers, partly applicable to steam-engines.	1491	31st May 1865	Peter Pilkington.
Certain improvements in the manufacture of axes, adzes, picks, and other like tools having a hole or eye formed in them for receiving a handle.	1558	7th June 1865	Thomas Smith.
Hammers and other machines actuated by steam or other fluid or vapour - - - - }	1607	14th June 1865	{ Benjamin Massey. Stephen Massey.
Steam hammers - - - - -	2174	24th Aug. 1865	David Davies.
Chucks for turning lathes - - - - (and turning handles for picks.)	2690	17th Oct. 1865	Robert Barley.
Improvements in forging and swaging steel and iron wheel tyres, and in the apparatus or tools employed for that purpose.	2695	19th Oct. 1865	Josiah Paxton.
Construction of mining picks - - - (Communicated by The Incorporated Washer Tool Company.)	2798	30th Oct. 1865	William Edward Newton.
Improvements in steam hammers and in means of applying them to the manufacture of boilers and tubes.	2805	31st Oct. 1865	Charles Emmet.
Improvements in the construction and manufacture of steel castings for railways, and in the moulds for casting the same, all or part of which said improvements in moulds are applicable for casting other articles. (casting hammer blocks.)	3323	23rd Dec. 1865	Francis William Webb.
HARNESS, SADDLES, BITS, BLINKERS, STIRRUPS AND WHIPS; HARNESSING, RELEASING FROM HARNESS; SHEARING, GROOMING AND SHAMPOOING HORSES.			
Bits for horses and other animals - - -	66	9th Jan. 1865	Lionel Weber.
Manufacture of boots, shoes, saddlery, harness and other articles. (Communicated by Toussaint Landrin.)	139	19th Jan. 1865	William Clark.
Improvements in the manufacture of saddle trees and in the spring bars of saddle trees - }	230	27th Jan. 1865	{ John Southall the younger. Henry Southall.
Waterproofing skins, hides and leather - - (for harness.)	418	14th Feb. 1865	George Harton.
A chemical combustible substance and apparatus to which it is applicable. (for harness's stirrup.) (Communicated by François Stahr.)	477	20th Feb. 1865	William Edward Gedge.
Arrangements or apparatus to be applied to vehicles drawn by horses to restrain and prevent them from running away.	559	2nd March 1865	Peter Rothwell.
Improved apparatus for promptly disconnecting horses from carriages and other vehicles.	682	11th March 1865	Pierre Marraud.

Subject-matter of Patent.	Number of Patent.	Date.	Name of Patentee.
HARNESS, &c.—*continued.*			
A new or improved apparatus for grooming horses.	869	29th March 1865	John Norris, jun'.
An improved application of rotating brushes, and in the mechanism and apparatus connected therewith. (*for grooming horses.*)	890	1st April 1865	John Drinkwater.
Machinery for cutting the human hair, the same being applicable for shearing horses.	978	6th April 1865	Robert Maynard.
An improved application of rotating brushes to the grooming or cleaning of horses and other quadrupeds.	1039	12th April 1865	John Haworth.
Manufacture of flock fabrics (*for saddle cloths.*) (*Communicated by The American Waterproof Cloth Company.*)	1219	1st May 1865	William Edward Newton.
Fasteners for driving-bands, straps, belts, harness or other such like purposes	1283	1st May 1865	{ Joseph Felix Allender. Thomas Frederick Cashin.
An improved safety stirrup for ladies' and gentlemen's riding saddles.	1285	9th May 1865	Samuel Hudson.
An improved dog leash or slip	1476	30th May 1865	Samuel Davis.
Driving apparatus for hair brushing and shampooing by machinery (*horses and cattle.*)	1490	31st May 1865	{ Thomas Appleton Browne. John Knight.
An improved bit for subduing or stopping runaway or restive horses.	1617	14th June 1865	Jules François Dubois.
Apparatus for shearing or "clipping" horses or other animals. (*Communicated by François Romain Corron, jun'.*)	2172	23rd Aug. 1865	John Gerrit Tongue.
Machinery or apparatus for disengaging runaway horses from carriages and stopping them so as to prevent accidents.	2214	29th Aug. 1865	Robert Thomas Holmes.
Improved apparatus for promptly disconnecting horses from carriages and other vehicles.	2271	4th Sept. 1865	Pierre Marraud.
An improved stirrup latch bar	2390	11th Sept. 1865	Samuel Davis.
Saddles and harness (*Communicated by Chevalier Achille Angelini.*)	2389	13th Sept. 1865	William Clark.
Tanning or treating hides applicable for machine bands and other purposes. (*for harness.*)	2591	7th Oct. 1865	William Harris.
Coating iron and steel with gold, silver, platinum or copper. (*carriage harness.*)	2592	7th Oct. 1865	Jacob Baynes Thompson.
Manufacture of bands, belts or straps for harness, for driving machinery or for other purposes.	2619	11th Oct. 1865	James Crutchett.
A new composition of india-rubber mastic or cement, made in a more or less fluid state according to the use to be made of it, and the process or contrivance for applying the same. (*coating saddlery.*)	2620	12th Oct. 1865	Auguste Aimé Lewuaud.
An improvement in blinkers for horses and other animals.	2654	14th Oct. 1865	Charles Alfred Elliott.
Saddles	2686	18th Oct. 1865	{ Thomas Jones. Edward King Mason.
A new or improved double acting safety stirrup bar.	2704	20th Oct. 1865	William Johns.

Subject-matter of Patent.	Number of Patent.	Date.	Name of Patentee.
HARNESS, &c.—*continued.*			
Fasteners for driving bands, straps, belts, harness or other such like purposes - - - }	2808	31st Oct. 1865	{ Thomas Frederick Cabin Joseph Felix Allender.
A new or improved swivel snap - - } (*for harness chains.*)	3096	2nd Dec. 1865	{ Emile Morin. Roman Schweizer.
Preparation of glue or gelatine so as to render it insoluble in water, and applicable by the admixture of other substances to various purposes for which common glue or gelatine cannot now be used.) (*for whip stocks.*) (*Communicated by Henry Wertz.*)	3338	23rd Dec. 1865	William Edward Newton.
Obtaining and employing continuous lengths of tanned leather for various useful purposes - } (*for traces, bridles and reins, collars, &c.*)	3354	23rd Dec. 1865	{ George Haro. Daniel Haro.

HATS, CAPS, BONNETS, LADIES' CAPS, CAP-FRONTS; COVERINGS FOR THE HEAD, HEAD DRESSES, HEAD ORNAMENTS.

Subject-matter of Patent.	Number of Patent.	Date.	Name of Patentee.
Apparatus for ironing and dressing woollen and other tissues. (*felt hats or bonnets.*) (*Communicated by André Lyon.*)	148	18th Jan. 1865	François Paul Henri Cabanac.
Improved machinery for shaping hat and bonnet blocks.	250	28th Jan. 1865	William Hiram Higgins.
Sewing-machines - - - - - - (*for sewing hat leathers.*) (*Communicated by Edmund Philippe and Dominique Gester.*)	304	3rd Feb. 1865	William Clark.
Dying the herbs and straw used in the manufacture of straw hats and artificial flowers, or other fancy articles.	463	18th Feb. 1865	Emile Carchon.
A chemical combustible substance and apparatus to which it is applicable. (*to apparatus for hatters.*) (*Communicated by François Sicher.*)	477	20th Feb. 1865	William Edward Gedge.
Apparatus for ventilating hats - - -	489	22nd Feb. 1865	John Carter.
Manufacture of felt hats - - - -	941	3rd April 1865	Charles Vero.
An improved hat ventilator - - -	961	5th April 1865	Robert Stanley.
Manufacture of flock fabrics - - - (*for hats and caps.*) (*Communicated by The American Waterproof Cloth Company.*)	1216	1st May 1865	William Edward Newton.
Improved machinery for filling fur hats or felt hats (*Communicated by Ouzeppe Silvio.*)	1314	12th May 1865	Etienne Lucien Girard.
An improved chaplet or head dress - -	1539	13th May 1865	Henry James Bart.
The application of a certain kind of goat's hair in imitation of human hair, to the manufacture of head dresses, moustaches, and all kinds of false hair, and the process of preparing the same.	1297	18th May 1865	Henry Bashton.

Subject-matter of Patent.	Number of Patent.	Date.	Name of Patentee.
HATS, &c.—continued.			
An improved composition to be employed in the manufacture of bonnets and hats.	1642	25th May 1865	Jeffery Eustace.
Manufacture of hats and other felted goods and fabrics. (Communicated by Edwin Dodd M'Cracken, James M'Cracken, Charles Edward M'Cracken, John Adams Southwoyd and Robert Warner Southwoyd.)	1707	26th June 1865	William Edward Newton.
Certain new and useful improvements in the construction of hats. (Communicated by Elias Rawaguig.)	1871	31st July 1865	Thomas Drew Stetson.
Adaptation of elastic material to articles requiring a bellows arrangement, or a partially rigid and partially expandible arrangement. (for hat cases.)	2423	22nd Sept. 1865	Matthew Cartwright.
Coverings for the head. (Communicated by Alfred Apord.)	3069	29th Nov. 1865	Henri Adrien Bonturville.
Manufacture of navy, yachting and other seaman's hats.	3241	14th Dec. 1865	James Lancaster.
Machinery for the manufacture of felt hats. (Communicated by The Eichveuryer Hat Blocking Machine Company.)	3361	19th Dec. 1865	William Edward Newton.
Preparation of glue or gelatine so as to render it insoluble in water, and applicable by the admixture of other substances to various purposes for which common glue or gelatine cannot now be used. (for stiffening rims of hats.) (Communicated by Henry Warts.)	3726	23rd Dec. 1865	William Edward Newton.
Obtaining and employing continuous lengths of tanned leather for various useful purposes (for hat bands, trimmings and flowers.)	3254	23rd Dec. 1865	{ George Hurn. Daniel Hurn.

HEATING AND EVAPORATING; REGULATING HEAT.

Subject-matter of Patent.	Number of Patent.	Date.	Name of Patentee.
An improved jacket or protector for metallic and other vessels and structures containing solid substances, liquids or gases, to prevent radiation of heat from or communication of heat to such vessels and structures.	4	2nd Jan. 1865	{ Edward Beven. Abel Fleming.
Means of and apparatus for generating steam and heat.	33	5th Jan. 1865	John Malsbury Kirby.
Construction of vacuum pans.	57	7th Jan. 1865	{ Edward Reanes. Conrad William Finzel.
Construction of railway carriages (and warming.)	96	11th Jan. 1865	Roch Chidley.
Producing gases and vapour in a heated state.	127	14th Jan. 1865	James Young.
Manufacture of boots, shoes, saddlery, harness and other articles. (Communicated by Townsend Lawbrin.)	169	19th Jan. 1865	William Clark.

Subject-matter of Patent.	Number of Patent.	Date.	Name of Patentee.
HEATING, &c.—*continued.*			
Improvements in steam generators or steam-boilers and furnaces, part of which is also applicable to other heat generating apparatus.	243	27th Jan. 1865	Joseph Twibill.
Improvements in effecting the combustion of fuel in the furnaces of steam-boilers and the fire-places of stoves, and of gas in gas-burners, and in apparatus connected therewith.	311	4th Feb. 1865	Frank Clarke Hills.
Improvements in the ventilation of pressing irons heated by gas, and for preventing the condensation of the vapour in the tubes or flues leading therefrom.	350	7th Feb. 1865	Samuel Egan Romer.
Improvements in apparatus for heating water and in connecting hot water and other metal pipes.	690	11th Feb. 1865	Andrew M'Laren.
Improvements in furnaces and boilers and parts connected with them, for generating steam and heating fluids, and also for improved apparatus for reducing and shutting off steam and regulating the speed of steam-engines.	395	11th Feb. 1865	John Cam.
Improvements in the mode of treating for evaporating and concentrating purposes, cane juice and saccharine and other solutions and liquids, and also in machinery or apparatus for the concentration of cane juice and saccharine and other solutions, and for the evaporation of liquids.	418	14th Feb. 1865	Alfred Fryer.
Improvements in puddling furnaces and in apparatus connected therewith. (*utilising waste heat.*)	473	18th Feb. 1865	John Guy Newton Alleyne.
A chemical combustible substance and apparatus to which it is applicable. (*for foot warmers, heating carriages, &c.*) (*Communicated by François Stoher.*)	477	20th Feb. 1865	William Edward Gedge.
Obtaining motive-power from aëriform fluids and from liquids.	501	22nd Feb. 1865	Matthew Piers Watt Boulton.
Method of and apparatus for generating heat	516	24th Feb. 1865	{ Joseph Jacob. Rudolph Pilzinger.
An improved method of extracting gases from mineral oils, and in employing the same for illuminating and heat producing purposes, and in the machinery or apparatus connected therewith.	549	27th Feb. 1865	William Sim.
An improved atmospheric pressure lamp for the burning of creosote, paraffin, naphtha or other volatile oils, which lamp may be used for all the purposes for which lamps are usually required, either for lighting, cooking, heating or other purposes. (*Partly communicated by John Joseph Riddle.*)	562	28th Feb. 1865	William Bell Dalston.
Drying apparatus (*Communicated by Félix Mommen and Auguste Racinet.*)	605	4th March 1865	Henri Adrien Bonneville.
Apparatus for heating and cooling atmospheric air and other aëriform bodies, and for heating ovens, and for heating and ventilating buildings.	636	7th March 1865	Loftus Perkins.
Stoves for heating air supplied to blast furnaces	650	8th March 1865	Richard Howson.
Apparatus used for handling the ends of walking sticks, and the sticks or handles of umbrellas and parasols	682	10th March 1865	{ Joshua James. Richard Daniel Jowra.

Subject-matter of Patent.	Number of Patent.	Date.	Name of Patentee.
HEATING, &c.—continued.			
Construction of steam generators and evaporators - (Communicated by Eli Thayer and Sabin Peter Pond.)	742	16th March 1865	Alfred Vincent Newton.
Heating preparatory to and for the purpose of hardening or tempering of knives, files, tools, and all other descriptions of cutlery or hardware usually subject to the process of hardening or tempering.	747	17th March 1865	Henry Wetherred.
Means and apparatus for utilising the heat of steam.	854	25th March 1865	David Esther Blachie.
Improvements in the manufacture or preparation of materials for and in their application to lighting and heating purposes, also in apparatus used for the same. (Communicated by Auguste de Peyrousy.)	855	25th March 1865	William Clark.
Certain improvements in non-conducting composition for preventing the radiation or transmission of heat or cold.	864	27th March 1865	Ferdinand Le Boy.
Apparatus employed in the concentration of all solutions where quick or speedy concentration or evaporation is required.	872	28th March 1865	William Walsh.
Furnaces or apparatus for heating the blast for furnaces used in smelting iron, and for other furnaces.	891	29th March 1865	John Player.
Kitchen ranges - - - - -	940	3rd April 1865	Frederick Brown.
Improvements in or applicable to boilers furnished with pipes for the circulation of water for domestic purposes.	974	6th April 1865	John Brown.
Fire-places and flues and apparatus connected therewith.	989	7th April 1865	Edward Welch.
Improvements in the method of mixing gases and vapours, and in the machinery or apparatus connected therewith.	997	7th April 1865	William Jackson.
Heating flies and file blanks - - -	1070	10th April 1865	William Brooks.
Manufacture of a compound or material to be used as a substitute for india-rubber. (Communicated by Henry Lowrandry and Emile Grasier.)	1068	15th April 1865	William Clark.
Certain improvements in gas-ammoniacal engines -	1074	17th April 1865	Louis De St. Céran.
Constructing portable hot rooms or chambers for drying cloths and other articles.	1136	24th April 1865	Welburn Williamson.
Machinery or apparatus employed in breweries and distilleries.	1204	29th April 1865	Francis Gregory.
Improvements in steam generators and engines, and in apparatus for feeding steam generators. (and treating feed water.) (Communicated by George Bailey Brayton.)	1240	3rd May 1865	John Henry Johnson.
An improved method of mixing gases and vapour, and in the machinery or apparatus connected therewith.	1297	9th May 1865	William Jackson.
Production and application of electricity - - (for heating metals.)	1412	23rd May 1865	Henry Wilde.
Improvements in the retorts used in the manufacture of gas and in other distillations, which improvements are adaptable to evaporating vessels.	1434	25th May 1865	John Ambrose Coffey.

Subject-matter of Patent.	Number of Patent.	Date.	Name of Patentee.
HEATING, &c.—*continued.*			
Foundry cupolas - - - - - (heating the blast.)	1488	31st May 1865	Thomas Summerson.
Improvements in the means of carburetting or treating aeriform fluids for lighting and heating purposes, and in apparatus for the same. (Communicated by Henri Auguste Georges du Vergier Marquis de la Roche Jaqueleis.)	1507	1st June 1865	William Clark.
An improved economic boiler for hot water apparatus, applicable for the heating of hothouses, churches and other public buildings.	1510	1st June 1865	Frederick Knight.
An improved method of generating heat, and apparatus or means for riveting the same - - }	1559	7th June 1865	{ William Sim. Arthur Barff.
An improved process for penetrating or impregnating woods with various substances. (Communicated by Jules Louis Hessard.)	1575	9th June 1865	William Edward Gedge.
Multitubular hot water boilers - - -	1614	14th June 1865	Henry Ormson.
Generating steam - - - -	1622	15th June 1865	Matthew Piers Watt Boulton.
An improved method of and apparatus for burning liquid hydrocarbons, and the employment thereof for heating purposes. (Communicated by Alexandre Schpakofsky and Nicolas Stange.)	1711	27th June 1865	Richard Archibald Brooman.
Heating chisels, knives, plane irons, gouges, augers, steels, shears, scythes and saws.	1715	27th June 1865	William Brooks.
Improvements in the production of artificial light, and in the apparatus connected therewith.	1808	8th July 1865	Johann Baggs.
An improved self-acting apparatus for obtaining a circulation of volatile liquids. (Communicated by Messieurs Francisque Massal and Auguste Jaquin.)	1819	8th July 1865	Hector Auguste Dubreuil.
Means and apparatus for increasing the mechanical power of steam.	1830	10th July 1865	William Alexander Lyttle.
An improved process for obtaining oxygen - (Communicated by Monsieur Charles Tellier.)	1833	11th July 1865	Hector Auguste Dubreuil.
Improvements in the production of gases from aqueous vapour, and in the application thereof to heating purposes.	1841	12th July 1865	Harrison Blair.
Motive-power by capillary attraction - - - (adapted to heating.)	1874	19th July 1865	Johann Ernst Friedrich Lüdeke.
Construction and working of furnaces for puddling, balling, heating and melting metals.	1882	19th July 1865	David Caddick.
Manufacture of pots and crucibles wherein metals and other materials may be heated or melted.	1884	19th July 1865	George Nimmo.
Obtaining motive-power when heated air or aeriform fluid is employed. (heating aeriform liquid.)	1915	22nd July 1865	Matthew Piers Watt Boulton.
Means or method of applying mineral oils for generating steam and heat. (Partly communicated by Alexandre Sepis.)	1926	25th July 1865	Wladislaus Zbyszewski.
Construction of cooking stoves and ranges - -	1944	26th July 1865	William Barton.
An improved process for applying airproof solutions to the interior of casks and barrels. (heating the interior.) (Communicated by Edward Delevan Woodruff.)	1967	24th July 1865	William Edward Newton.

Subject matter of Patent.	Number of Patent.	Date.	Name of Patentee.
HEATING, &c.—continued.			
Obtaining motive-power by heat - - - (heating airyform fluids.)	1947	1st Aug. 1865	Matthew Piers Watt Boulton.
Improvements in generating steam and in heating steam and airiform fluids.	2051	7th Aug. 1865	Matthew Piers Watt Boulton.
Heating and evaporating - - - - (Partly communicated by Hippolite Girard.)	2073	10th Aug. 1865	Thomas Frederick Henley.
A combination of improved method, apparatus and receptacles for storing, preserving, transferring and discharging certain fluids, for sanitary and productive purposes. (and more safely supplying oil for heating purposes.) (Communicated by Henry Pinkus.)	2094	14th Aug. 1865	Robert Alexander William Westley.
Furnaces to be used in the manufacture of glass and iron and steel, and for other like purposes. (heating the air.) (Communicated by Henning Bostius.)	2108	15th Aug. 1865	John Frederick Bostius.
Method of heating the ovens and boilers of kitchen ranges or cooking stoves.	2170	24th Aug. 1865	Frederick Thomas.
Improvements in apparatus by means of which certain liquids, common air, and certain elastic fluids are made available in the production of light, and their quantity regulated and measured, parts of which improvements are applicable for other purposes. (preserving uniform temperature in ovens, &c.)	2184	25th Aug. 1865	Edwin Augustus Carley.
Construction of apparatus for distilling and rectifying alcohols. (wash heaters.) (Communicated by François Désiré Savalle.)	2203	28th Aug. 1865	Henri Adrien Bonneville.
Improved steam heating apparatus - - (Communicated by Henry Bailley.)	2255	1st Sept. 1865	Alfred Vincent Newton.
Apparatus for preventing incrustation in steam-boilers, and for preventing explosion of such boilers, heating the feed water, and consuming smoke - - - - - -	2273	4th Sept. 1865	James Howard. William Stafford. William Parker M'Callum.
A new or improved method of and apparatus for heating instruments or irons for curling, waving and frizzling hair, and for other purposes to which heated instruments or irons are applicable. (Communicated by Hippolyte Gillet.)	2283	6th Sept. 1865	Louis Guchin.
Improvements in cooling, heating and evaporating, and in apparatus employed therein.	2361	15th Sept. 1865	Walter Blundell.
Improvements in the machinery or apparatus and in the processes for the treatment and manufacture of sugar.	2385	19th Sept. 1865	John Fletcher.
Apparatus for separating dust from the gases evolved from blast furnaces for smelting iron - (for heating boilers, &c.)	2391	19th Sept. 1865	Edward Alfred Cowper. Charles William Siemens.
Construction of vessels for preserving food and liquids.	2473	27th Sept. 1865	Louis Henri Gillet.
Apparatus for heating, evaporating and cooling liquids - - - - - -	2494	28th Sept. 1865	Isaac Smith. William Fothergill Batho.
Apparatus for lighting and heating, suitable for sick rooms and nurseries, and applicable also as holders for matches, watches, and other necessary articles. (Communicated by François René Mennad and Charles Louis Marie Mennad.)	2515	30th Sept. 1865	John Henry Johnson.

Subject-matter of Patent.	Number of Patent.	Date.	Name of Patentee.
HEATING, &c.—continued.			
Improvements in producing and combining gases to be used for heating purposes, and in the construction of retorts for producing and combining such gases.	2527	2nd Oct. 1865	Silas Covell Salisbury.
Blast furnaces	2529	2nd Oct. 1865	Silas Covell Salisbury.
Apparatus for decomposing and superheating liquids, vapours and gases. (Communicated by Gustave Renard and Amédée Lipman.)	2535	3rd Oct. 1865	Richard Archibald Brooman.
Improvements in evaporating and distilling liquids, and in the apparatus employed therein.	2590	7th Oct. 1865	Tomlin Camphell.
Apparatus for mangling and calendering (heating the rollers.)	2597	9th Oct. 1865	Robert Walmsley.
An improved mode of generating steam	2604	10th Oct. 1865	John Sturgeon.
Improvements in the construction of steam generators, applicable also to the construction of condensers, the heating of water generally, and to the warming of buildings. (Communicated by Joseph Harrison, jun'. and Thomas Landers.)	2610	10th Oct. 1865	John Henry Johnson.
Manufacture of gas (for heating.)	2620	11th Oct. 1865	James Crutchett.
Heating calender bowls and other cylinders or rollers.	2626	12th Oct. 1865	William Mather.
Improvements in steam-boilers and other apparatus applicable to the heating and evaporation of liquids, parts of which improvements are applicable also to other purposes	2661	16th Oct. 1865	Francis Wise, Edward Field. Enoch Harrison Aydon.
Means of securing the handles of table knives and forks and other similar articles.	2671	16th Oct. 1865	Thomas M'Grah.
Cabriole or hot air engines (Communicated by Guillaume Reinleto.)	2676	17th Oct. 1865	Richard Archibald Brooman.
Improvements in desiccating the leaves and flowers of plants and other vegetable substances, and in the apparatus to be employed therein. (Communicated by Benjamin Dickinson.)	2708	20th Oct. 1865	Allan Lawrie M'Clavie.
Furnaces of and means of heating the feed water for steam-boilers.	2712	20th Oct. 1865	John White.
Improvements in the manufacture of inflammable gases and in their application to useful purposes. (for heating.)	2719	21st Oct. 1865	Isham Baggs.
Improvements in the method of and apparatus for utilising the liquors used in the treatment of straw or other fibrous materials for the manufacture of paper, which improvements are also applicable to the evaporation of liquids generally. (Communicated by Kaytene Perron.)	2726	21st Oct. 1865	James Wright.
Improvements in sewing machinery for using waxed thread. (Communicated by Thomas John Hallipers.)	2748	24th Oct. 1865	Alfred Vincent Newton.
Skates (with heater attached.) (Communicated by Oscar Wilson Toft.)	2780	30th Oct. 1865	Frederick Tolhausen.
An improved apparatus for increasing draught in and preventing or curing smoky chimneys, and economising heat. (Communicated by François Perrochon.)	2822	2nd Nov. 1865	William Edward Gedge.

Subject-matter of Patent.	Number of Patent.	Date.	Name of Patentee.
HEATING, &c.—continued.			
Manufacture of coloring matter for dyeing and printing. (*heating mixtures.*)	2825	2nd Nov. 1865	Ludwig Schad.
Improvements in generating and applying certain gases, and in apparatus to be employed therein.	2823	2nd Nov. 1865	James Webster.
An improved non-conducting composition for preventing the radiation or transmission of heat or cold.	2853	4th Nov. 1865	James Thye.
Machinery or apparatus employed for sizing yarns -	2865	8th Nov. 1865	James Eastwood.
Furnaces for heating the blast for blast furnaces -	2897	10th Nov. 1865	Thomas Whitwell.
Treating brewers' grains in order to render them more suitable for the food of animals. (*subjecting to heat.*)	2908	10th Nov. 1865	Edward John Davis.
Apparatus for heating the feed water for steam-boilers.	2920	13th Nov. 1865	James Heywood Whitehead.
Improvements in the production or manufacture of gas for heating or illuminating, and in the retorts and apparatus employed in such manufacture.	2965	17th Nov. 1865	James Harkart.
An improved trap or liquid sealing to the covers of cisterns, pans, jars, tubs and other vessels or chambers - - - - - (*for retaining heat.*)	2986	20th Nov. 1865	George Putland Henning. Henry Coyle.
Apparatus for condensing exhaust steam, and heating air by the heat abstracted in effecting the condensation of such steam. (*Communicated by Addison Calvin Fletcher.*)	2996	21st Nov. 1865	Alfred Vincent Newton.
Means and apparatus for raising heat by the combustion of fuels of various kinds. (see " FURNACES.")	3029	25th Nov. 1865	John Francis Brunett.
An improved composition for enamel, paint, varnish, cement or plaster. (*Communicated by William Harvey Watkins.*)	3042	27th Nov. 1865	William Robert Lake.
An improved method of utilising the waste heat of coke ovens. (*for heating boilers.*) (*Communicated by Antoine Barbier-Perrotin.*)	3048	24th Nov. 1865	William Edward Gedge.
A new or improved method of (preventing the) escape of heat from steam cylinders - -	3081	24th Nov. 1865	William Symons. Andrew Brown.
Apparatus for increasing the safety of railway passengers and trains, signalling and forming a communication externally and internally between all parts of such trains, lighting, warming and securing the doors of the carriages, and indicating therein and at the stations the names of the places at which the train stops.	3068	25th Nov. 1865	Richard Howarth.
Improvements in the manufacture and treatment of railway bars, tyres and axles, also in the construction of furnaces, machinery and apparatus connected therewith. (*heating the furnaces.*)	3084	1st Dec. 1865	Thomas Westburburn Dodds.
Apparatus for cooking by steam - - - (*or heating dishes.*) (*Communicated by Francis Millière.*)	3169	6th Dec. 1865	George Tomlinson Bousfield.
Apparatus for regulating heat obtained by the combustion of gas.	3269	19th Dec. 1865	Henry Planch.

Subject-matter of Patent.	Number of Patent.	Date.	Name of Patentee.
HEATING, &c. — continued.			
Boilers or apparatus for generating steam (for heating.) (Communicated by Julien Belleville.)	3269	18th Dec. 1865	Richard Archibald Brooman.
Foot protectors	3278	19th Dec. 1865	Augustus Henry Thorpe.
Improved apparatus for burning combustible vapor (such as that from naphtha or coal oil) for heating, cooking and lighting purposes. (Communicated by James Stratton.)	3317	22nd Dec. 1865	George Davies.
An improved method of and apparatus for preserving, purifying, mixing, separating, cooling, aërating, roasting and otherwise treating grain, ores and various other matters.	3344	27th Dec. 1865	Gaston Charles Auguste Marquis D'Azey.
Treating hydrocarbon oils	3345	27th Dec. 1865	James Young, jun'.
Steam-boilers or generators	3369	29th Dec. 1865	Andrew Barclay.
See also "FIRE-PLACES." *See also* "FURNACES."			

HOISTS, CRANES, CAPSTANS, WINDLASSES; RAISING AND LOWERING HEAVY BODIES; RAISING FROM MINES; RAISING SUNKEN SHIPS; MOVING HEAVY BODIES.

Subject-matter of Patent.	Number of Patent.	Date.	Name of Patentee.
Drilling apparatus for hand or steam power, adaptable also as a vice and for lifting purposes (screw jack.)	18	3rd Jan. 1865	George Hodgson. James Fea.
Mode of working hydraulic lifts	180	24th Jan. 1865	William Clay.
Applying power to the working of ships' windlasses, winches, capstans, pumps and other ships' gear.	248	27th Jan. 1865	Handel Moore.
Apparatus for relieving wire ropes from strain when used in lifting and lowering weights.	302	30th Jan. 1865	John Gibson.
A new method for removing or destroying the momentum of heavy bodies by means of an elastic machine or machines, so as to prevent injury and damage from concussion, applicable to ship cables, ship and fort armour, railway trains, tenders to piertheads and floating piers, gangways, breakwaters and other similar structures, also as a motive-power. (motive-power for hoisting.) (Communicated by William Graham M'Iver.)	331	6th Feb. 1865	Clements Robert Markham.
Hydraulic lifting or hoisting apparatus	338	6th Feb. 1865	Alexander Stern.
Improvements in apparatus for discharging coals and other cargo from ships' holds, applicable also to the raising and transferring of weights from one point to another	350	6th Feb. 1865	George Elliot. Henry Coxon.
Apparatus for lifting and tilting casks containing liquids.	446	16th Feb. 1865	Charles Octavius Stanton.
A new or improved instrument or apparatus for raising weights, for moving heavy bodies, and for other like purposes.	526	24th Feb. 1865	James Handy.

Subject-matter of Patent.	Number of Patent.	Date.	Name of Patentee.
Hoists, &c.—*continued.*			
Differential wheel gearing - - - (*for cranks, hoists, cranes, &c.*)	744	17th March 1865	John Standfield.
Cranes - - - - - -	834	29th March 1865	William Irlam.
A new or improved arrangement of mechanism for propelling waggons in connection with railway hoists.	895	30th March 1865	George Gremish.
An improved safety tackle for raising and lowering heavy weights.	937	3rd April 1866	Pierre Joseph Jamet.
"Pulleys" used by brewers and others for lifting and lowering weights into and out of carts, waggons or trucks.	1091	19th April 1865	Fredric William Gilbert.
Hydraulic pulling jacks - - - -	1176	27th April 1865	Joseph Thagyr.
Steam cranes - - - - -	1348	15th May 1865	Charles James Appleby.
Hydraulic cranes - - - - - (*Communicated by Alfred Corenwile.*)	1491	24th May 1865	Henri Adrien Bocoeville.
Manufacture of iron piers or erections, applicable more especially for carrying bridges at high elevations, or available for shear legs and lighthouses.	1583	5th June 1865	Charles De Bergue.
An improved fire-escape, applicable also to raising loads from mines and other purposes. (*Communicated by Xavier Philippart.*)	1666	21st June 1865	William Edward Gedge.
Improvements in tubular structures rendering them specially applicable for ships' masts and building purposes. (*hoists and hoist shafts.*)	1755	3rd July 1865	Edward Dunn.
Lifts for transferring passengers, goods and heavy weights, from the lower to the upper floors of hotels, club houses and other buildings, with greater safety than heretofore.	1812	10th July 1865	David Cowan.
A new and improved mode of elevating ships or boats in the water, to enable them to pass over mud bars, shallows and the like, and for raising sunken vessels and docks.	1838	12th July 1865	Thomas Cato M'Kean.
Applying and utilising water power - (*driving cranes.*)	1967	25th July 1865	Valentine Baker.
Apparatus for sustaining and lowering ships' boats	2041	5th Aug. 1865	Cortland Herbert Simpson.
Machinery or apparatus for raising and lowering } heavy bodies - - - - }	2276	5th Sept. 1865	{ John Campbell Evans. William Fairlie.
Pulleys for raising and lowering heavy bodies	2333	13th Sept. 1865	{ George Tangye. Joseph Jewsbury.
Safety apparatus for cages and hoists - -	2363	19th Sept. 1865	Jubal Charlton Broadbent.
Hoisting machines - - - - (*Communicated by William Miller.*)	2416	21st Sept. 1865	William Robert Lake.
Travelling cranes - - - -	2524	2nd Oct. 1865	{ David Greig. Robert Burton.
A new apparatus for raising weights by means of the feet or hands. (*Communicated by Messieurs Jean Baptiste Veyre and Julien Nicolas Hubert Gauthier.*)	2560	5th Oct. 1865	Hector Auguste Dufrené.
Capstans - - - - - -	2676	6th Oct. 1865	William Dakin Grimshaw.
An improved method of working windlasses -	2855	12th Oct. 1865	{ George Deslandes. Albert Deslandes.

Subject-matter of Patent.	Number of Patent.	Date.	Name of Patentee.
HOISTS, &c.—continued.			
Construction of ships for raising ballast, corn, coal, minerals and other matters in bulk.	2669	16th Oct. 1865	Charles Henry Murray.
Raising sunken vessels	2764	26th Oct. 1865	Thomas Page.
Means of preventing vessels from sinking, which means are also applicable for raising sunken vessels.	2851	4th Nov. 1865	Thomas Page.
Hydraulic steam and other "lifts" for raising passengers or goods.	2900	11th Nov. 1865	James Norris.
Apparatus for raising, lowering, moving or transporting heavy bodies	2931	14th Nov. 1865	Thomas Aldridge Weston. James Tangye. Richard Chapman.
Improvements in the hulls and tackle of navigable vessels, and in the gear for propelling the same by wind and steam or other motive-power engine, and clearing the same from water, and in apparatus connected therewith to enable the said vessels to be converted in floating graving docks, or lifts for raising vessels and other submerged or partially submerged heavy bodies to or above the surface of the water	3021	25th Nov. 1865	John Ferrier.
Apparatus for raising, lowering and moving heavy bodies, and for transmitting and arresting motion for various purposes.	3095	2nd Dec. 1865	Thomas Aldridge Weston.
Steam cranes and hoists	3180	6th Dec. 1865	Andrew Betts Brown.
An improvement in apparatus for elevating hay, grain or similar materials, and discharging the same from the said apparatus.	3196	11th Dec. 1865	Edward Livingston Walker.
Boilers or apparatus for generating steam. (for cranes.) (Communicated by Julien Belleville.)	3269	16th Dec. 1865	Richard Archibald Brooman.
Pipes, tubular columns and hollow structures, for masts, oars, chear legs, lift boats and ordinary boats, for water, gas and waste water pipes, and for other similar constructions where great strength is required. (shear legs for hoists.)	3314	22nd Dec. 1865	Edward Deane.
Machinery for paying out and hauling in or picking up, particularly applicable to paying out and hauling in telegraph cables.	3345	27th Dec. 1865	Samuel Griffith.
HORSE-SHOES, SHOEING HORSES.			
Shoes for horses and other animals. (Communicated by Pierre Charlier.)	639	7th March 1865	William Clark.
Horse-shoes. (Communicated by Jesse Fraser Mallett.)	1028	11th April 1865	William Clark.
Improvements in the manufacture of shaping of iron intended for the shoes of horses and other animals, and in machinery employed therein. (Communicated by Hector Edward Bastien.)	1629	16th June 1865	Richard Archibald Brooman.

Subject-matter of Patent.	Number of Patent.	Date.	Name of Patentee.
Horse-shoes, &c.—*continued.*			
Certain improvements in machinery for the manufacture of horse-shoes and other nails. (Communicated by Messieurs Bernard Clairvoisier, Maxime Antoine Durio and François Bigny.)	1693	24th June 1865	Peter Armand Le Comte de Fontaine Moreau.
Shoeing horses	1697	19th July 1865	Thomas Henry Ince.
Machinery to be used in the manufacture of horse-shoes, shoe heel and toe-tips, and other similar articles.	2017	3rd Aug. 1865	Luke Anderson.
Improvements in the manufacture of horse-shoes and in machinery used in the said manufacture.	2197	25th Aug. 1865	John Symmons.
Improvements in the manufacture of horse-shoes, and in the machinery used for such manufacture. (Communicated by Léon Chrysostôme Viel and Pierre Michel Sibut.)	2453	23rd Sept. 1865	George Davies.
Shoeing horses . . . . . (Communicated by Alphonse Auguste Watrin.)	2498	28th Sept. 1865	William Edward Newton.
Shoeing horses, ponies and mules, by using shoes without nails.	3134	6th Dec. 1865	John Nainty.

Horticulture, Conservatories, Vineries, Flower Stands, Lawn Mowing, Training Plants.

Subject-matter of Patent.	Number of Patent.	Date.	Name of Patentee.
Means of and apparatus for generating steam and heat. (For warming greenhouses.)	55	5th Jan. 1865	John Malsbury Kirby.
An improved ornamental flower box . . .	126	14th Jan. 1865	George Colsen.
Ground vineries or glass ridges for the cultivation of grapes or other fruit.	204	24th Jan. 1865	Charles Tennant Wells.
Improvements in fixing frost screen awnings and nettings, for protecting wall fruit trees, in fixing trellis for training fruit and other trees to walls, and in bricks therefor.	297	1st Feb. 1865	Charles Anthony Wheeler.
Apparatus for ventilating horticultural and other buildings.	532	6th Feb. 1865	Charles Hearl.
Improvements in apparatus for heating water and in connecting hot water and other metal pipes. (For warming conservatories.)	590	11th Feb. 1865	Andrew M'Laren.
An improved machine for clearing, sweeping and removing the refuse from highways, streets and roads or ways, applicable also for removing the leaves of cut grass and other refuse from lawns and other grass lands and walks.	646	16th Feb. 1865	Henry John Pickard.
Lawn-mowing machines	656	17th Feb. 1865	James Bryce Brown.
Boilers for heating water and delivering it at an equal temperature to any number of flow pipes, and also for the generation of steam. (heating horticultural buildings.)	683	21st Feb. 1865	Jasper Hulley.
Construction of walls, houses and other buildings . (garden walls.)	822	23rd March 1865	Joseph Tall.

o 2

Subject-matter of Patent.	Number of Patent.	Date.	Name of Patentee.
HORTICULTURE, &c.—*continued.*			
An improvement or improvements in ornamenting articles made of glass. (*flower stands.*)	888	28th March 1865	Joseph Williams.
Improved contrivances to facilitate the arrangement of flowers and leaves.	1187	29th April 1865	Thomas Charles March.
An improved economic boiler for hot water apparatus, applicable for the heating of hothouses, churches and other public buildings.	1510	1st June 1865	Frederick Knight.
Multitubular hot water boilers . . . (*for conservatories.*)	1614	14th June 1865	Henry Ormson.
Ornamental fences and baskets to contain flowers and other articles.	1806	7th July 1865	William Goulding.
Utilising the stalks, smalls and waste of tobacco for certain purposes . . . (*fumigating greenhouses.*)	1844	13th July 1865	{ George Clayton Collyer. Charles Lewis Roberts.
Ornamental tables and table stands, such as cruet frames, liqueur frames, flower, egg and other stands . . .	1926	25th July 1865	{ Louis Peire. Edward Samuel Tucker.
Improvements in apparatus by means of which certain liquids, common air, and certain elastic fluids are made available in the production of light, and their quantity regulated and measured, parts of which improvements are applicable for other purposes. (*preserving uniform temperature in hothouses.*)	2184	25th Aug. 1865	Edwin Augustus Curby.
Brushes . . . . . . (*for sweeping gardens.*)	2238	29th Aug. 1865	{ George Smith. Charles Ritchie.
Improved steam heating apparatus . . . (*Communicated by Henry Bolliey.*)	2235	1st Sept. 1865	Alfred Vincent Newton.
Improvements in apparatus and means for extinguishing fires, part of such improvements being applicable for other purposes. (*for watering gardens.*)	2559	5th Oct. 1865	William Henry Phillips.
A new composition of indian-rubber mastic or cement, made in a more or less fluid state according to the use to be made of it, and the process or contrivance for applying the same. (*coating graftings of fruit trees, &c.*)	2630	12th Oct. 1865	Auguste Aimé Lermard.
Greenhouses	2684	16th Oct. 1865	Thomas Harcgate Preston Dennis.
Improvements in brushes for hair dressing and other uses, also in brooms and apparatus for cleaning, preparing, painting, coating and smoothing surfaces . . . (*for gardens.*)	2985	20th Nov. 1865	{ George Smith. Charles Ritchie.
Apparatus for regulating heat obtained by the combustion of gas. (*for greenhouses.*)	3268	16th Dec. 1865	Henry Plarck.
Obtaining and employing continuous lengths of tanned leather for various useful purposes (*for tackle for garden rollers, hose for greenhouses, &c.*)	3354	23rd Dec. 1865	{ George Hara. Daniel Hara.

Subject-matter of Patent.	Number of Patent.	Date.	Name of Patentee.
INKS AND INKSTANDS.			
A new typographic ink	390	6th Feb. 1865	Anatole Auguste Halot.
Manufacture of ink (Communicated by Josiah Vincent Lezorn.)	836	24th March 1865	William Edward Newton.
Inkstands (Communicated by Frank Oliver.)	1089	19th April 1865	John Merritt.
Inkstands (and pen racks.) (Communicated by Thomas Lawrence.)	1484	31th May 1865	Benjamin Lawrence.
Improvements in copying letters, plans and other manuscripts, and in the apparatus and substances employed therein. (Communicated by Edward Cusper.)	1846	14th July 1865	Henri Adrian Bonneville.
Improvements in the manufacture of compounds of silica and in the production of silicated alkaline inks, colours and dyes.	2267	2nd Sept. 1865	Henry Ellis.
Preparation of glue or gelatine so as to render it insoluble in water, and applicable by the admixture of other substances to various purposes for which common glue or gelatine cannot now be used. (substitute for oil in printers' ink.) (Communicated by Henry Wurtz.)	3325	23rd Dec. 1865	William Edward Newton.

INLAYING; INLAID-WORK.

Improvements in taking impressions from the grain of wood, and in transferring the same on to various surfaces (and for inlaying.)	1117	21st April 1865	William Scarratt. William Dean.
Staining and graining woods (in imitation of inlaid-work.)	1851	14th July 1865	John Morrough Murphy. James Morrough Murphy.
A new or improved cement or composition, applicable to the agglomeration or moulding of various materials, and to other useful and decorative purposes. (for inlaid flooring, mosaics, parquet tiles, &c.) (Communicated by Stanislas Sorel and Emile Justin Mercier.)	3119	5th Dec. 1865	Richard Archibald Brennan.

JEWELLERY, LOCKETS, BROOCHES, BRACE-LETS, WATCH CHAINS, SWIVELS AND KEYS.

Certain improvements in brooch or other like fastenings.	60	7th Jan. 1865	Joseph Josiah Blackham.
Clasps and snaps or other similar fastenings	185	21st Jan. 1865	Alice Isabel Larna Gordon.

Subject-matter of Patent.	Number of Patent.	Date.	Name of Patentee.
JEWELLERY, &c.—continued.			
Certain improvements in the manufacture of pencil cases. (combined with watch keys.)	296	3rd Feb. 1865	William Vale.
Certain improvements in the manufacture of brooches, part of which said improvements are applicable to the manufacture of lockets - .	365	11th Feb. 1865	{ George Carter Hamler. / John Bush Hamler. }
Manufacture of jewelry cases and other similar such.	503	22nd March 1865	John James Carter.
Manufacture of ornamental metallic chains - -	643	25th March 1865	Edwin Wolverson.
Fastenings for pins, buttons and other articles with metallic backs.	681	30th March 1865	Isaac Louis Pulvermacher.
Fastenings for sleeve-links, solitaires and other like purposes.	947	4th April 1865	Henry Jenkins.
A new manufacture of or improvement in ornaments for personal wear.	1770	5th July 1865	Harry Emanuel.
Manufacture of chains, bracelets, necklaces and other articles of jewelry.	1794	7th July 1865	Pierre Mathurin Charles Béraud.
Regulating or controlling the power employed in winding sewing and other machines of a light nature. (jewellers' polishing machines.)	1885	11th July 1865	Benjamin Fothergill.
An improved shank for buttons, studs and solitaires.	1930	25th July 1865	Henry Wright.
Fastenings for sleeve-links, solitaires, brooches and other articles of jewellery	2103	15th Aug. 1865	{ Reuben Cornelius Lilly. / James Sunderland. }
Manufacture of swivels - - - -	2334	12th Sept. 1865	Joseph Welch.
Manufacture of chains, bracelets, necklaces and other analogous articles.	2497	29th Sept. 1865	Carlo Guiliaum.
Manufacture of scent and smelling bottles - - (containing lockets.)	2599	9th Oct. 1865	Thomas Miles.
Certain improved methods of manufacturing or arranging the spring bolts and attendant parts of sleeve-links, and other like articles where the means of a portable connection are required	2665	16th Oct. 1865	{ John Reading. / Samuel Alfred Reading. / George Edward Reading. / Frederick Francis Reading. }
Manufacture of gold and other ornamental chains -	3078	30th Nov. 1865	{ John Hollands. / Edward Richard Hollands. / Thomas Hollands. }
A new or improved swivel snap - - - } (see " CHAINS.")	3098	2nd Dec. 1865	{ Emile Mevin. / Roman Schweizer. }
Improved mechanism for winding keyless watches -	3230	14th Dec. 1865	August Guye.
An improved kind of clasp or dress preserver, to prevent ladies' dresses from trailing along the ground. (application of brooches.) (Communicated by Marie Louise Changeur.)	3298	20th Dec. 1865	Henry Edward Newton.
Preparation of glue or gelatine so as to render it insoluble in water, and applicable by the admixture of other substances to various purposes for which common glue or gelatine cannot now be used. (for jewellery.) (Communicated by Henry Wurtz.)	3325	23rd Dec. 1865	William Edward Newton.

Subject-matter of Patent.	Number of Patent.	Date.	Name of Patentee.
JOINING, JOINTING, COUPLING ; PIPE JOINTS, RAILWAY JOINTS, FURNITURE JOINTS AND HINGES; PACKING FOR JOINTS.			
Improvements in the manufacture of metallic bedsteads, which improvements are also applicable to the manufacture of other metallic articles.	52	7th Jan. 1865	James Atkins.
Certain improvements in brooch or other like fastenings.	60	7th Jan. 1865	Joseph Josiah Blackham.
Improved arrangements for coupling steam-engines, turbines or other apparatus employed as motive-power. (Communicated by Ludwig August Riedinger.)	159	19th Jan. 1865	Adolf Wilhelm Preyer.
Improvements in shaping and forging metals and in the machinery and apparatus employed therein - - - - - ("couplings" for gas fittings.)	165	19th Jan. 1865	James Alfred Shipton. Robert Mitchell.
Manufacture of boots, shoes, saddlery, harness and other articles. (Communicated by Toussaint Loudrin.)	169	19th Jan. 1865	William Clark.
Packing for steam joints, stuffing boxes, pistons and the like.	217	26th Jan. 1865	William Paton.
Improvements in steam generators or steam-boilers and furnaces, part of which is also applicable to other heat generating apparatus. (jointing ends of tubes.)	243	27th Jan. 1865	Joseph Twibill.
An improved socket for pipes and method of joining the same.	295	1st Feb. 1865	George Henry Pierce.
Improvements in apparatus for heating water and in connecting hot water and other metal pipes.	390	11th Feb. 1865	Andrew M'Laren.
Improvements in breech-loading fire-arms and in cartridges for breech-loading fire-arms.	421	14th Feb. 1865	Johann Von der Poppenbuy.
Mode of making or forming the links of iron or steel chains, chain cables, shackles, couplings or parts of the same, and for machinery to be used therein.	422	14th Feb. 1865	George Humfrey.
Sewing-machines - - - - - (Communicated by Elias Howe, jun'.)	430	15th Feb. 1865	Alfred Vincent Newton.
Construction of cabinet sofa and chair bedsteads -	476	20th Feb. 1865	Andrew Sharp.
Certain improvements in hydraulic pumps in connexion with engines of motive-power.	521	21th Feb. 1865	William Oram.
Improved portable frames and joints for tables and other articles, applicable also for building purposes and the like.	542	27th Feb. 1865	Charles Whiting.
Making the joints of steam generators and parts connected therewith.	562	2nd March 1865	John Muir Hetherington.
Apparatus for coupling and uncoupling railway waggons or carriages - - - -	609	4th March 1865	Daniel Morris. Joseph Morris. James Morris.
Construction of bridges - - - -	633	7th March 1865	Edward William Young.
Improvements in the construction of joints for boxes, drawers and other like articles, and for planks and timbers, and in machinery to be used in the preparation of such joints.	640	7th March 1865	Henry William Wimshurst.

Subject-matter of Patent.	Number of Patent.	Date.	Name of Patentee.
JOINING, &c.—continued.			
Rolls for connecting sheets of zinc and other metals employed for covering roofs and other enclosures.	662	9th March 1865	Rowland George Fisher.
An improved method of connecting together tubes or pipes used for conveying gas and water, and for other purposes.	669	9th March 1865	Victor Delperdange.
An improved combined tee-piece and valve - -	884	11th March 1865	Charles Johnson.
Improvements in the manufacture of metallic bedsteads, which improvements are also applicable to the manufacture of other metallic articles.	698	13th March 1865	James Atkins.
An improved application of steam power to locomotion on ordinary roads. (Communicated by Alfred Taillradeau.)	1002	6th April 1865	William Edward Gedge.
Couplings for railway carriages, waggons, trucks and other vehicles.	1035	11th April 1865	Josiah Dudley.
An improved chain or iron-cable shackle - -	1036	11th April 1865	Robert Turner.
Improvements in fire-arms, and in cartridges to be used therewith and with other fire-arms.	1040	12th April 1865	Thomas Jefferson Mayall.
An improved guide applicable to sewing-machines -	1047	12th April 1865	Frederic Bapty. Edward Brydges Bayers.
Pipes for conveying water and gas and for other like purposes, and a new or improved composition for joining the said pipes and other similar pipes.	1058	13th April 1865	Charles Fenner Cotterill.
A new or improved table or support for invalids -	1089	15th April 1865	Thomas Edward Harding.
Improvements in the fitting of surface condenser tubes, and in the tools to be used therein, and in the means of retarding corrosion in steam-boilers. (Communicated by William Judson.)	1138	22nd April 1865	Alfred Vincent Newton.
Improvements in motive-power machinery for cultivating land, part of which improvements is applicable to driving machinery generally - .	1184	22nd April 1865	James Howard. Edward Tenney Bousfield.
Improved contrivances to facilitate the arrangement of flowers and leaves. (connecting tubes for the reception of flowers.)	1187	24th April 1865	Thomas Charles March.
Improvements in apparatus for raising water and other fluids, and in raising and lowering such apparatus.	1191	26th April 1865	Julius Bernard.
Improvements in iron fortifications, such improvements being applicable to the construction and protection of ships and floating batteries. (joining armour plates.)	1209	1st May 1865	George Johnson.
Shackles or links for connecting chain cables and other chains.	1250	4th May 1865	William Roberts.
Certain improvements in the manufacture of "moulds" for metallic castings having a cylindrical form. (" elbows.")	1286	10th May 1865	David Hartley.
Improvements in the manufacture of hose and other flexible tubing, which improvements are also applicable to uniting surfaces of india-rubber, gutta-percha or of compounds thereof, to each other, or to woven or other fabric or material for other purposes.	1309	11th May 1865	Thomas Jefferson Mayall.

Subject-matter of Patent.	Number of Patent.	Date.	Name of Patentee.

JOINING, &c.—continued.

Subject-matter of Patent.	Number of Patent.	Date.	Name of Patentee.
Machinery for the manufacture of hinges - (Communicated by Jean Baptiste Errard and Jean Pierre Boyer.)	1635	12th May 1865	William Clark.
Printing machines - - - - -	1344	15th May 1865	Robert Harrild, Horton Harrild.
Reaping and mowing machines - - -	1871	19th May 1865	William Magwaring.
An improvement in atmospheric forging hammers -	1380	19th May 1865	Edward Augustus Raymond.
Knitting machines - - - - - (Communicated by Isaac Wixom Lamb.)	1445	26th May 1865	William Clark.
Improved means of conducting electric currents through railway trains, and of actuating signals or alarums therein. (forming mercurial joints.)	1609	14th June 1865	Andrew Edmund Bear.
Lamp burners and parts connected therewith - (Communicated by Rufus Spaulding Merrill and William Lincoln.)	1631	16th June 1865	John Henry Johnson.
Improvements in lamps for railway and other carriages, and in connecting lamps to carriages, a part of which improvements may also be applied to handles for carriages - - -	1687	17th June 1865	Walter Howra, William Borley.
Forming the permanent ways of railways - -	1706	26th June 1865	John Whittle.
Improvements in steam-boilers, furnaces and engines, and in parts connected therewith.	1746	29th June 1865	Edwin Elliott.
Mode of connecting rails for railways and tramways.	1876	19th July 1865	Constantine Henderson.
An improvement in the mode of uniting different metals, such as iron and copper or alloys, to form compound metallic castings.	1885	19th July 1865	George Nimmo.
Apparatus applicable as a motive-power engine, a pump or fluid meter. (Communicated by Francis Bernard de Kerreveun.)	2021	4th Aug. 1865	William Clark.
A self-acting coupling for railway carriages and wagons - - - - - - -	2037	5th Aug. 1865	Thomas Smith, John Hawk.
Couplings or fastenings of railway carriages or trucks.	2092	11th Aug. 1865	Richard Douglas Morgan.
Improved safety couplings for railway carriages -	2159	22nd Aug. 1865	Frederick Charles Hynn Robinson.
Permanent way of railways - - - - (Communicated by John Vauthrin.)	2259	1st Sept. 1865	William Clark.
A new shackle or coupling for connecting railway carriages, wagons and other vehicles used on railroads, whereby going between the carriages, wagons or other vehicles, to couple or uncouple, is rendered totally unnecessary - - -	2263	4th Sept. 1865	Samuel Richards Freeman, Abraham Grundy.
Construction of iron safes, strong boxes and other receptacles.	2284	7th Sept. 1865	John Matthias Hart.
Improvements in locomotive engines, parts of which improvements are also applicable to railway carriages. (friction coupling.)	2370	1?th Sept. 1865	Russel Aithen.
Railway carriages and other vehicles - - (Communicated by Henry Hudson Trevor.)	2394	20th Sept. 1865	John Henry Johnson.
Machinery for making casks, barrels and other wooden vessels of capacity. (jointing screw.)	2426	22nd Sept. 1865	James Davidson.

Subject-matter of Patent.	Number of Patent.	Date.	Name of Patentee.
JOINING, &c.—continued.			
Construction of presses for hay, cotton, hemp and other substances. (Communicated by Thomas Clemson and Thomas Bolton Webster.)	2454	25th Sept. 1865	Alfred Vincent Newton.
Manufacture of submarine lamps - - .	2458	26th Sept. 1865	John Sampson Starnes.
Certain sanitary improvements in coffins - .	2459	26th Sept. 1865	John Hargreaves.
Improvements in coke and charcoal ovens and in the manufacture of coke, parts of which are applicable to bread, biscuit and pastry ovens. (liquid joint.)	2477	27th Sept. 1865	William Morgan.
Improvements in connections for and in stopping pipes used for conveying water and gas, and for other like purposes, and in preventing leakages in the said pipes, and in apparatus employed therein.	2503	29th Sept. 1865	Charles Forster Cotterill.
An improved reclining chair - - . (Communicated by William Henry Von Nostrick.)	2504	29th Sept. 1865	George Davies.
Means employed for fixing sheet metal for roofing and other purposes.	2522	2nd Oct. 1865	James William Tyler.
Improvements in rules for measuring, and in other instruments or articles requiring to be adjusted or disposed at various angles.	2613	10th Oct. 1865	Arthur Nicholls.
Double or single action pumps - - . (Communicated by Claude Genie.)	2623	11th Oct. 1865	William Edward Gedge.
A new composition of Indian-rubber mastic or cement, made in a more or less fluid state according to the use to be made of it, and the process or contrivance for applying the same. (making steam-joints.)	2630	12th Oct. 1865	Auguste Aimé Leronard.
Clod crushers and chain harrows - - . (coupling.)	2634	12th Oct. 1865	William Colhorne Cambridge.
Certain improved methods of manufacturing or arranging the spring bolts and attendant parts of sleeve-links, and other like articles where the means of a portable connection are required .	2666	16th Oct. 1865	John Reading. Samuel Alfred Reading. George Edward Reading. Frederick Francis Reading.
Folding chairs - - - . (Communicated by Auguste Emanuel Eliaers.)	2676	17th Oct. 1865	George Davies.
Improvements in common road carriages and in breaks for the same.	2697	18th Oct. 1865	James Rock the younger.
Wheels for carriages and other vehicles - .	2708	20th Oct. 1865	Samuel Richard Rowe.
An improved mode of uniting pieces of leather, more especially adapted to the manufacture of boots and shoes. (Communicated by John Chipman Handley.)	2750	25th Oct. 1865	George Haseltine.
A combined adjustable spanner, tube cutter and pipe wrench. (wrench to screw and unscrew couplings.) (Communicated by Henry Hitchings Baragwanath and Martin Van Winkler.)	3035	27th Nov. 1865	John Phillips Baragwanath.
Coverings for the head - - - . (lamped brim.) (Communicated by Alfred Apard.)	3056	29th Nov. 1865	Henri Adrien Bonneville.

Subject-matter of Patent.	Number of Patent.	Date.	Name of Patentee.
JOINING, &c.,— continued.			
Apparatus for increasing the safety of railway passengers and trains, signalling and forming a communication externally and internally between all parts of such trains, lighting, warming and securing the doors of the carriages, and indicating therein and at the stations the names of the places at which the train stops. (coupling shafts and gas pipes.)	3088	29th Nov. 1865	Richard Howarth.
Apparatus for raising, lowering and moving heavy bodies, and for transmitting and arresting motion for various purposes. (adapting the coupling to shafts.)	3093	2nd Dec. 1865	Thomas Aldridge Weston.
A new or improved cement or composition, applicable to the agglomeration or moulding of various materials, and to other useful and decorative purposes. (walling stone, &c.) (Communicated by Stanislas Sorel and Emile Justin Mesler.)	3119	5th Dec. 1865	Richard Archibald Brooman.
Certain improvements in the manufacture of railway chairs and in the manner of securing rails thereto.	3131	6th Dec. 1865	Joseph Taylor.
Boilers or apparatus for generating steam. (pipe joints.) (Communicated by Julien Belleville.)	3269	13th Dec. 1865	Richard Archibald Brooman.
Certain improvements in the method of attaching and securing together the ends of strapping employed in machinery.	3302	21st Dec. 1865	William Barnsley.
Improvements in the manufacture of axles for carriages and spindles for various purposes, and in machinery to be employed in the said manufacture, part of which improvements in machinery may also be applied to other purposes (coupling for machinery.)	3330	26th Dec. 1865	Eliza Lonax. Joseph Constant Lonax. John Lonax. John Revitell. Thomas Revitell. Charles Vernon.
Brakes or apparatus for stopping or retarding railway trains. (coupling.)	3300	30th Dec. 1865	David William Thomas.
KNIVES, FORKS, SPOONS, SCISSORS, SHEARS; CLEANING KNIVES, FORKS AND SPOONS; NUT AND LOBSTER CRACKERS.			
Apparatus for cleaning and polishing knives	36	4th Jan. 1865	George Kent.
Manufacture of sheep shears	306	2nd Feb. 1865	James Ball.
A new or improved machine for trimming or cutting the edges of books, magazines and such like articles	334	6th Feb. 1865	William Henry Latham. Frederic Cartwright Ward Latham.
Manufacture of trimmers, shears and edge tools (Partly communicated by Charles Lingard, jun'.)	379	10th Feb. 1865	Charles Lingard.

Subject-matter of Patent.	Number of Patent.	Date.	Name of Patentee.
KNIVES, &c.—_continued._			
Case hardening or converting partially into steel, articles of wrought or malleable iron. _(edges of cutlery.)_ _(Partly communicated by Anthony Leonard Fleury.)_	693	11th Feb. 1865	Edwin Henry Newby.
An improved apparatus for shearing and burling all sorts of woven fabrics. _(toothed blades.)_ _(Communicated by Caliste Hippolyte Jean Pierre Damoye and Jean Compagnon.)_	817	24th Feb. 1865	William Edward Gedge.
Making solid iron scales with bolsters, for all kinds of spring knives.	860	28th Feb. 1865	Arthur Davy.
Manufacture of sheep shears	912	4th March 1865	William Clulow.
Machinery or apparatus for rolling, shaping or forging metals. _(knife blades, &c.)_	701	13th March 1865	Robert Marsden.
Treating preparatory to and for the purpose of hardening or tempering of knives, files, tools, and all other descriptions of cutlery or hardware usually subject to the process of hardening or tempering.	747	17th March 1865	Henry Wetherad.
An improved method of treating, cleaning or preparing painted or other canvas, tarpaulins and dirty cotton waste, so as to render the same suitable to be used for household and other purposes for which they may be applicable. _(for knife cloths, &c.)_	758	17th March 1865	William Maurice Williams.
Manufacture of letter clips, bookmarkers, paper knives, and clips for suspending stationery, drapery and pictures, and for other such like purposes	838	3rd April 1865	{ Thomas Corbett. Robert Harrington.
Means or apparatus for effecting the cleansing and polishing of forks.	860	4th April 1865	Charles Martin.
Machinery for cutting the human hair, the same being applicable for shearing horses.	973	6th April 1865	Robert Maynard.
Improvements in the manufacture of the handles of nut crackers, lobster crackers and grape scissors, which said improvements are also applicable to the manufacture of the handles of knives, spoons and other articles.	993	7th April 1865	Thomas White.
An improved metallic preparation or composition for cleaning, sharpening, burnishing and grinding articles of cutlery, edge tools or cutting instruments, and for grinding the cards or rollers of carding-engines and the surfaces of cylinders, and covering rollers for various kinds of woollen and cotton machinery.	1084	13th April 1865	George Mountford.
Knife cleaning machines	1212	1st May 1865	John Charles Davis.
Machinery or apparatus for cutting cylindrical or conical articles.	1247	4th May 1865	George Enthrup.
Heating chisels, knives, plane irons, gougers, augers, steels, shears, scythes and saws.	1718	27th June 1865	William Brooks.
Apparatus for cutting scales for knives, and forming metal arbs for knives.	1989	1st Aug. 1865	William Singleton.
Sheet metal handles for spoons, saucepans, and other utensils for culinary purposes. _(forks, ladles, &c.)_	2255	30th Aug. 1865	James Fellows.

Subject-matter of Patent.	Number of Patent.	Date.	Name of Patentee.
KNIVES, &c.—continued.			
Improvements in the manufacture of spoons, forks and other similar articles, and in apparatus or machinery to be employed therein.	2597	20th Sept. 1865	Daniel Joseph Fleetwood.
Coating iron and steel with gold, silver, platinum or copper. (knife and fork blades.)	2562	7th Oct. 1865	Jacob Baynes Thompson.
Means of securing the handles of table knives and forks and other similar articles.	2671	16th Oct. 1865	Thomas M'Grah.
A spoon rest - - - - - -	3060	1st Dec. 1865	Joseph Roberts.
Machinery or apparatus for cutting bread - -	3281	15th Dec. 1865	Henry Charles Litchfield.
Shears and scissors - - - - -	3254	16th Dec. 1865	Rollo Radger.
Preparation of glue or gelatine so as to render it insoluble in water, and applicable by the aid of mixture of other substances to various purposes for which common glue or gelatine cannot now be used. (for paper knives, handles, &c.) (Communicated by Henry Wurtz.)	3385	23rd Dec. 1865	William Edward Newton.

LAMPS, LANTERNS, CHANDELIERS, CANDLE- STICKS; LAMP FURNITURE, GLASSES AND SHADES; LIGHTING; PRODUCING LIGHT.

Subject-matter of Patent.	Number of Patent.	Date.	Name of Patentee.
Lamps for burning the vapour of volatile fluids -	41	6th Jan. 1865	John Clowes Barley. Daniel Campbell.
Motive-power and means of communication between passengers while travelling, and appliances connected therewith.	55	7th Jan. 1865	George Bell Galloway.
Improvements in producing and finishing photographs and photographic transparencies on paper and other suitable substances, and in the machinery employed therein - - - - (for lamp shades.)	56	7th Jan. 1865	Barrowclough Wright Bentley. William Henry Bailey.
An improved method of lighting street and other lamps, and in the apparatus or means connected therewith.	65	9th Jan. 1865	John Welsh.
Street and other lamps and lanterns - -	151	18th Jan. 1865	John William Gregg.
Petroleum and coal oil burners and glasses -	202	23rd Jan. 1865	Michael Alexander Dietz.
Lanterns for burning hydrocarbon fluids -	250	24th Jan. 1865	Alexander Septimus Macrae.
An improvement in shades or globes for lamps and other lights. (Communicated by Henri Berial.)	299	30th Jan. 1865	Richard Archibald Brooman.
Candlesticks and candle holders - - -	539	7th Feb. 1865	Alice Isabel Lucas Gordon.
An improved reflecting apparatus for street and other lamps.	542	7th Feb. 1865	Romain De Bray.
Improvements in the miner's safety lamp - -	553	8th Feb. 1865	Richard Clarke Thorp. Philip Young.
A new or improved signal applicable to railways, ships, telegraphs and other such like purposes.	557	8th Feb. 1865	Alfred Ware Banks.

Subject-matter of Patent.	Number of Patent.	Date.	Name of Patentee.

LAMPS, &c.—*continued.*

Subject-matter of Patent.	Number of Patent.	Date.	Name of Patentee.
Improved apparatus for supplying with a constant and regular pressure air to burners for consuming or burning hydrocarbons for illuminating purposes.	408	13th Feb. 1865	Edward John Cowling Welch.
An improved atmospheric pressure lamp for the burning of benzole, paraffin, naphtha, or other volatile oils, which lamp may be used for all the purposes for which lamps are usually required, either for lighting, cooking, heating or other purposes. (*Partly communicated by John Joseph Riddle.*)	602	20th Feb. 1865	William Ball Dalston.
An improved instrument for concentrating light, applicable to dental, surgical and other operations.	691	2nd March 1865	Charles Rahn.
Improvements in the manufacture of metallic tramrails, which improvements are also applicable to the manufacture of other metallic articles. (*uprights for chandeliers.*)	699	13th March 1865	James Atkins.
Apparatus for holding and regulating the position of lamp shades or reflectors. (*Communicated by Guillaume Pascal.*)	704	13th March 1865	William Clark.
Construction of bracket, pillar and suspended lamps and lanterns. (*Communicated by James Ives.*)	753	17th March 1865	Alfred Vincent Newton.
Apparatus for obtaining light - - -	841	24th March 1865	Giacomo Felice Marchisio.
Improvements in the manufacture or preparation of materials for and in their application to lighting and heating purposes, also in apparatus used for the same. (*Communicated by Auguste de Peyrousay.*)	865	25th March 1865	William Clark.
Manufacture of reflectors for lamps and of surfaces for reflecting light generally.	897	30th March 1865	Benjamin Baugh.
Means and apparatus employed for illuminating lighthouses.	945	4th April 1865	John Richardson Wigham.
Means of and apparatus for increasing the illuminating power of hydrocarbons, oils and gases. (*Communicated by Thomas Sey Spearman.*)	980	6th April 1865	George Davies.
Improvements in apparatus for lighting and ventilating ships, part of which is also applicable for producing fresh water at sea.	998	7th April 1865	Henry Edmonds.
Lamps for burning petroleum, naphtha, or other mineral oils - - - -	1040	12th April 1865	Charles Rourban. Josef Bindthwr. William Callon.
Means of communicating and signalling between the passengers, guards and drivers of railway trains.	1078	17th April 1865	George William Garrood.
An improved lamp or signal for calling cabs or other vehicles, by day and night.	1115	21st April 1865	Edward Wilson.
Oiling cans - - - - -	1119	21st April 1865	George Whitlock.
Improved apparatus for administering nourishment to the sick or infirm. (*night lamp for heating drinks.*) (*Communicated by Bernard Maillet.*)	1140	24th April 1865	William Edward Gedge.
Philosophical examination into the alleged spirit manifestations, consisting of a lamp and a close tunnel. (*see "DRAMATIC EFFECTS."*)	1148	24th April 1865	Owen Grenville Warren.

Subject-matter of Patent.	Number of Patent.	Date.	Name of Patentee.
LAMPS, &c.—continued.			
Improved apparatus for pouring and decanting liquids. *(supplying lamps.)*	1149	25th April 1865	Nicholas Sibly.
A new illuminating apparatus for burning petroleum *(Communicated by Messieurs Jules Bontems and Louis Pelegry.)*	1237	3rd May 1865	Peter Armand Le Comte de Fontaine Moreau.
Reflecting lamps - - - - -	1268	4th May 1865	William Charles Cropp.
Certain improvements in apparatus for illuminating *(Communicated by Monsieur Louis Joseph Aurelin de Monnerville.)*	1269	4th May 1865	Peter Armand Le Comte de Fontaine Moreau.
Safety lamps - - - - - *(Communicated by Ferdinand Sart.)*	1274	4th May 1865	John Henry Johnson.
Gas-burners and chimneys - - - *(Communicated by William Rreu.)*	1334	13th May 1865	William Clark.
Sliding gas pendents or chandeliers - -	1381	19th May 1865	George Henry Brookes.
Certain Improvements in lamps for burning mineral oils. *(Communicated by Monsieur Louis Theodore Letourneau.)*	1410	22nd May 1865	Peter Armand Le Comte de Fontaine Moreau.
Lamps - - - - - - *(Communicated by Adolf Forstlin.)*	1423	24th May 1865	Carl Theodor Müller.
Apparatus for increasing the safety of railway passengers and trains, signalling, lighting, and forming a communication between all parts of such trains, also for securing the carriage doors.	1498	31st May 1865	Richard Howarth.
Improvements in the means of carburetting or treating aeriform fluids for lighting and heating purposes, and in apparatus for the same. *(Communicated by Henri Auguste Georges de l'evytir Marquis de la Roche Jacquelein.)*	1507	1st June 1865	William Clark.
An improved pocket lantern - - - *(Communicated by John Augustus Miller.)*	1518	1st June 1865	William Edward Newton.
Improvements in lamps for railway and other carriages, and in connecting lamps to carriages, a part of which improvements may also be applied to handles for carriages - - -	1597	17th June 1865	{ Walter Howes. William Hurley.
Producing a light applicable to photographic purposes, to lighthouses, and to other illuminations.	1583	20th June 1865	Prospero Carlevaris.
Preparation of magnesium for illuminating purposes. *(Communicated by François Pierre Le Roux.)*	1696	24th June 1865	Joseph Solomon.
A new or improved apparatus for producing the magnesium light.	1696	24th June 1865	Charles Ross Bamber.
Means of obtaining or producing oxygen applicable to various useful purposes. *(for generating light.)*	1780	6th July 1865	Hermann Beigel.
Improvements in the production of artificial light and in the apparatus connected therewith.	1809	8th July 1865	Isham Baggs.
An improved process for obtaining oxygen - *(Communicated by Monsieur Charles Trihir.)*	1853	11th July 1865	Hector Auguste Dufresné.
Lamps - - - - - -	1863	15th July 1865	Arson Henry Platt.
Motive-power by capillary attraction - *(adapted to lighting.)*	1874	19th July 1865	Johann Ernst Friedrich Lüdeke.
Signals for railways - - - -	2000	3rd Aug. 1865	Edward Samuel Horridge.

Subject-matter of Patent.	Number of Patent.	Date.	Name of Patentee.
LAMPS, &c.—*continued.*			
Improvements in securing roof lamp glasses of railway and other carriages, which improvements are also applicable to lighting the decks of ships, and other situations.	2035	4th Aug. 1865	Thomas Stanley Raney.
Lamps for burning paraffin oil and other volatile oils.	2043	7th Aug. 1865	Abraham Follet Osler.
A combination of improved method, apparatus and receptacles for storing, preserving, transferring and discharging certain fluids, for sanitary and protective purposes. (*and more safely supplying oil for lighting.*) (*Communicated by Henry Pinkus.*)	2098	14th Aug. 1865	Robert Alexander William Wenley.
Floating lights, beacons, floating batteries and other vessels.	2172	24th Aug. 1865	John Moody.
Improvements in apparatus by means of which certain liquids, common air, and certain elastic fluids are made available in the production of light, and their quantity regulated and measured, parts of which improvements are applicable for other purposes.	2184	25th Aug. 1865	Edwin Augustus Curley.
Improvements in the manufacture of night lights and in apparatus employed therein · · · }	2367	15th Sept. 1865	{ Frederick Meyer. Joseph William Freestone. }
Save-alls · · · · · · · (*Communicated by Jacques Jean Frisouil.*)	2369	16th Sept. 1865	Henri Adrien Bonneville.
Safety lamps for use in mines and other localities · (*Communicated by André Jean Olanier.*)	2370	16th Sept. 1865	Henri Adrien Bonneville.
An improved apparatus for and method of ascertaining the state of sewers, tunnels, drifts or other subterranean works, without descending therein, by means of the natural, artificial or magnesium light, part of which apparatus is applicable to levelling purposes.	2440	25th Sept. 1865	Richard William Barrow.
An improved arrangement of apparatus and materials to be employed for effecting the deodorising of the noxious gases arising from sewers and drains, and for the more effectual ventilation and inspection of such sewers and drains.	2451	25th Sept. 1865	Edward Brooke the younger.
Manufacture of submarine lamps · · · ·	2465	25th Sept. 1865	John Sampson Starnes.
Improvements in lamps for burning schist, petroleum and other similar oils, and in the means to be employed in lighting the same.	2487	29th Sept. 1865	Jean Mauhlane.
Candlesticks · · · · · ·	2513	30th Sept. 1865	Arthur Hill.
Apparatus for lighting and heating, suitable for sick rooms and nurseries, and applicable also as holders for matches, watches, and other necessary articles. (*Communicated by François René Ménard and Charles Louis Marie Ménard.*)	2515	30th Sept. 1865	John Henry Johnson.
Improvements in lamps for burning paraffin, and in feeding apparatus for supplying the same.	2545	4th Oct. 1865	Levi Hewitt.
Manufacture of railway station and other gas lamps	2615	10th Oct. 1865	John Joseph Parkes.
Paraffine lamps · · · · ·	2616	10th Oct. 1865	Daniel Gallafent.
Manufacture of gas · · · · · (*for lighting.*)	2630	11th Oct. 1865	James Cratchett.
Improvements in the manufacture of inflammable gases and in their application to useful purposes. (*for lighting.*)	2719	21st Oct. 1865	Isham Baggs.

Subject-matter of Patent.	Number of Patent.	Date.	Name of Patentee.

LAMPS, &c.—continued.

Hydrocarbon lamps (Communicated by Dr. Moritz Herzog and David Leopold Cohn.)	2742	24th Oct. 1865	William Snell.
Improvements in lamps for the combustion of magnesium and in preparing magnesium for burning.	2786	26th Oct. 1865	Henry Larkin.
Lamps for burning paraffin oil and other volatile liquid hydrocarbons - - - -	2767	26th Oct. 1865	{ James Hinks. Joseph Hinks.
Lanterns for burning coal oil, petroleum and other hydrocarbon fluids. (Communicated by William Westlake.)	2809	1st Nov. 1865	Edwin Addison Phillips.
An improved apparatus for burning petroleum and other volatile oils.	2820	2nd Nov. 1865	Louis Pribyre.
Apparatus for obtaining artificial light from volatile liquids or fluids - - - - -	2995	22nd Nov. 1865	{ William Wells. National Marland.
Apparatus for increasing the safety of railway passengers and trains, signalling and forming a communication externally and internally between all parts of such trains, lighting, warming and securing the doors of the carriages, and indicating therein and at the stations the names of the places at which the train stops.	3068	29th Nov. 1865	Richard Howarth.
Lamps for burning petroleum, paraffin and other hydrocarbon liquids, without a glass chimney, in the roofs of railway carriages and other like places and positions.	6070	30th Nov. 1865	James Turner Hall.
Lamps, lanterns and gas fittings - - -	3069	2nd Dec. 1865	William Johnston.
Cups or sockets applied to candles and other lights. (Communicated by Clémathe St. Cembury.)	3127	9th Dec. 1865	William Clark.
Producing an oxy-hydro-magnesian light, applicable to photographic purposes, to lighthouses, and to other illuminations. (Communicated by Prospero Carleveris.)	3246	16th Dec. 1865	Thomas Parkes.
Improved apparatus for burning combustible vapor (such as that from naphtha or coal oil) for heating, smoking and lighting purposes. (Communicated by James Stratton.)	3317	22nd Dec. 1865	George Davies.
Preparation of glue or gelatine so as to render it insoluble in water, and applicable by the admixture of other substances to various purposes for which common glue or gelatine cannot now be used. (transparencies for lanterns, &c.) (Communicated by Henry Watt.)	3334	23rd Dec. 1865	William Edward Newton.
Improvements in friction matches, in apparatus for using them, and in adapting them for lighting lamps. (Communicated by Philos Blake Tyler.)	3385	30th Dec. 1865	William Edward Newton.

For lamp burners, see " Gas Burners."

Subject-matter of Patent.	Number of Patent.	Date.	Name of Patentee.
LEATHER, SKINS AND HIDES; ARTIFICIAL LEATHER AND PARCHMENT; CURRYING, TANNING, CUTTING AND ORNAMENTING LEATHER.			
Dyeing leather - - - - -	166	19th Jan. 1865	{ Tasso Lahrouuer. John Kelly.
Machinery or apparatus employed for fluting, dicing, cross graining, glazing and all kinds of jiggered work on skins or hides, and having a self acting table and revolving friction wheel or roller - - - - -	178	20th Jan. 1865	{ John Torney the younger. George Wood.
Improvements in tanning hides and skins, and in apparatus employed therein.	270	31st Jan. 1865	William Hinkes Cox.
Certain improvements in the manufacture of caoutchouc. (for replacing leather.) (Communicated by Messieurs Léon Désiré Innocent and François Perrucel.)	396	11th Feb. 1865	Peter Armand Le Comte de Fontaine Moreau.
Waterproofing skins, hides and leather - -	412	14th Feb. 1865	George Harton.
An improved composition as a substitute for leather or other similar materials -	465	18th Feb. 1865	{ Christopher Brakell. William Horkl. William Günther.
Machinery for sewing or uniting leather and other hard substances, particularly applicable to the manufacture of boots and shoes.	484	21st Feb. 1865	Charles Baulch.
Preparing or treating hides for tanning - - (Communicated by Wilhelm Maris.)	531	6th March 1865	William Clark.
Engraving on metal - - - - (for printing on leather.) (Communicated by Narcisse Guilbat and Pierre Horiter.)	607	22nd March 1865	Richard Archibald Brooman.
A new process of tanning leather and other skins -	1126	23rd April 1865	{ Emile Stanislas Beaux. Edward Pannifer.
Means and apparatus used for stretching woven fabrics and other materials. (leather, skins, &c.) (Communicated by Jules Durommun.)	1239	3rd May 1865	William Clark.
Ornamentation of fabrics and leather - - (Communicated by Miss Nathalie Kolb.)	1389	19th May 1865	William Clark.
Improvements in tanning hides and in apparatus connected therewith. (Communicated by Emile Stanislas Beaux and Edward Pannifer.)	1554	7th June 1865	Arthur Charles Henderson.
Apparatus for "lap" and "surface shaving," the splitting and bevilling of leather and other like substances, in sheets and strips.	1635	17th June 1865	Henry Everard Clifton.
Compounds for waterproofing and insulating purposes.	1982	29th July 1865	Frederick Augustus Abel.
Apparatus used in rolling leather - - -	2007	2nd Aug. 1865	John Henry Tyler.
Improved machinery or apparatus for reducing the thickness of parts of calf skins or of other skins or hides. (Communicated by Adolphe Brl.)	2138	18th Aug. 1865	William Edward Gedge.
Improvements in tanning and in the preparation of extracts to be used therein. (Communicated by Emanuel Desiré Colt.)	2231	30th Aug. 1865	John Henry Johnson.

Subject-matter of Patent.	Number of Patent.	Date.	Name of Patentee.
LEATHER, &c.—continued.			
Machines for splitting, shaving and paring hides, skins and leather.	2258	6th Sept. 1865	Henry Harrison Doty.
Improved means for rendering leather more durable and flexible - - - - -	2367	15th Sept. 1865	{ Louis Gustave Rouxnac. { Louis Hombail.
An improved process for preparing skins and hides or leather, so as to render such substances water-proof and more durable than heretofore.	2516	30th Sept. 1865	John William Moore Miller.
Instruments for punching or perforating leather and other materials - - - -	2556	6th Oct. 1865	{ Edward Marsland. { Peter Williams.
Apparatus for preparing skins for tanning and for currying or dressing the same. (Communicated by Prosper Dumas.)	2585	7th Oct. 1865	Henri Adrien Bonneville.
Tanning or treating hides applicable for machine bands and other purposes.	2601	7th Oct. 1865	William Harris.
Improvements in satchels and in the manufacture of the gussets of leather satchels, bags and purses, and of the gussets of other articles made of leather.	2707	20th Oct. 1865	Frederick Thompson.
An improved mode of making pieces of leather, more especially adapted to the manufacture of boots and shoes. (Communicated by John Chipman Handley.)	2750	25th Oct. 1865	George Hawkins.
Preparing the surfaces of paper, leather, woven and other fabrics and substances, for receiving photographic pictures, engravings, lithographs and prints, and for rendering such substances fire and water proof. (Communicated by William Gibson.)	2891	9th Nov. 1865	William Edward Newton.
Utilization of waste leather to be employed as a fertilizer. (Communicated by Orazio Lays.)	3054	24th Nov. 1865	Alfred Vincent Newton.
Improvements in sewing-machines and in sewing or embroidering. (sewing leather.)	3079	1st Dec. 1865	Isaac Merritt Singer.
An improved leather shaving machine - -	3138	5th Dec. 1865	William Samuel Clodevay.
Manufacture of leather driving belts - -	3146	7th Dec. 1865	{ Clarke Duchesne Hitchcock. { John Shimmon.
Utilizing scraps or small pieces of leather - -	3263	18th Dec. 1865	{ John Farmerley Dickson. { John Barrs.
Machinery for splitting leather, skins and other similar articles. (Communicated by Sewell Brown Noyes.)	3277	19th Dec. 1865	George Tomlinson Bousfield.
Preparation of glue or gelatine so as to render it insoluble in water, and applicable by the admixture of other substances to various purposes for which common glue or gelatine cannot now be used. (for stiffening leather.) (Communicated by Henry Warts.)	3325	23rd Dec. 1865	William Edward Newton.
Obtaining and employing continuous lengths of tanned leather for various useful purposes -	3354	23rd Dec. 1865	{ George Hurn. { Daniel Hurn.

Subject-matter of Patent.	Number of Patent.	Date.	Name of Patentee.

Locks, Latches, Bolts, Lock Furniture; Keys, Safes, Strong Boxes, Money Tills.

Subject-matter of Patent.	Number of Patent.	Date.	Name of Patentee.
An improved method of preserving from fire books and other articles in safes.	71	9th Jan. 1865	Friedrich Wiese.
Construction of keys and locks - - -	92	11th Jan. 1865	John Fry Heather.
Improvements in tills and the means of securing and checking money taken by servants.	104	12th Jan. 1865	George Gass.
A new or improved instrument for removing dirt from the inside of the barrels of keys, and an improvement in the manufacture of keys.	229	27th Jan. 1865	Robert Habham.
Window safes for the protection of property (see "Show Cases.")	526	6th Feb. 1865	Robert Shaw.
Iron safes and strong rooms - - -	364	9th Feb. 1865	John Chubb.
Fastenings for doors, windows, drawers and other like purposes - - - - -	369	9th Feb. 1865	{ George Edward Mash. William Howes Howes.
Burglar-proof and fireproof safes - - -	430	15th Feb. 1865	Alexander Clark.
Safes - - - - - -	450	16th Feb. 1865	Joseph Thompson.
An improved means of securing the safety of railway passengers.	454	17th Feb. 1865	Coleman Defries.
Iron safes and strong rooms - - -	459	17th Feb. 1865	James Ferguson.
New or improved indicating apparatus for the protection of railway passengers, buildings, rooms, safes and other objects (see "Signals.")	472	18th Feb. 1865	{ Leicester William Glen Boure. Adolphe Boah.
Iron safes and strong rooms - - -	499	22nd Feb. 1865	George Nathaniel Shore.
Locks or fastenings for safes or strong boxes	507	23rd Feb. 1865	Samuel Whitfield.
Manufacture of safes or strong boxes	508	23rd Feb. 1865	Walter Randall Mappin.
Means and apparatus employed for protecting bullion, jewelry or other valuable property contained in safes, from being stolen or damaged by fire.	514	23rd Feb. 1865	Henry Kindon Taylor.
Fire and thief proof safes, chests and strong room doors.	543	27th Feb. 1865	Walter Henry Tucker.
A combined key and weapon of defence - (Communicated by Theodore de Bouvrier de Laffer.)	552	27th Feb. 1865	Richard Archibald Brosman.
Improvements in the construction of doors or other covers of safes or depositories, and in parts connected therewith, for the purpose of obtaining increased security.	559	28th Feb. 1865	John Matthias Hart.
Locks and bolts for fastening doors, door bars and drawers.	570	1st March 1865	Samuel Whitfield.
Improvements in the manufacture of safes and in apparatus connected therewith.	585	2nd March 1865	Samuel Chatwood.
Improved apparatus for the protection of houses and property from burglars, parts of the invention being applicable for other purposes.	619	6th March 1865	Cromwell Fleetwood Varley.
Safes - - - - - -	621	6th March 1865	{ Samuel Phillips. Joseph Groves.
Iron safes - - - - -	653	8th March 1865	Arthur Edwin Taylor.
An improved burglary alarum - - -	664	9th March 1865	William Henry Hudson.
Construction of fastenings or bolts for window sashes and other purposes.	678	10th March 1865	William Smith.

Subject-matter of Patent.	Number of Patent.	Date.	Name of Patentee.
LOCKS, &c. —continued.			
Fire and burglar proof safes, chests, doors and iron rooms.	696	11th March 1865	John Tann.
An improvement in securing safes and strong rooms.	702	13th March 1865	Henry Hill.
Construction of safes for securing valuable articles from thieves and fire.	714	14th March 1865	Edmund Dorman Hodgson.
Construction of safes or receptacles for securing and protecting valuable property.	783	15th March 1865	Edward Loyal.
Locks for safes, strong rooms and other purposes	779	20th March 1865	Samuel Chatwood.
Certain improvements in the fastenings to be employed in metallic "safes" or other similar depositories	903	31st March 1865	William Milner. Daniel Rowlinson Ratcliff.
Construction of safes or depositories intended to contain valuable property.	904	31st March 1865	Thomas Cook.
Improvements in locks, and in fixing knobs and spindles to doors and latches.	944	4th April 1865	Richard Nabbs.
Securing the doors of safes and other doors	946	4th April 1865	George Carr Thompson.
Locks (for safes.)	999	7th April 1865	Nathan Gold Kimberley.
Construction of safes or receptacles for securing and protecting valuable property.	1000	7th April 1865	Thomas Skidmore.
Door locks and latches	1043	12th April 1865	John Walker.
Bolting and locking arrangements for safe and other doors.	1045	12th April 1865	John Matthias Hart.
Iron safes and strong rooms	1056	13th April 1865	John Chubb. Robert Goater.
Indicators and fastenings for watercloset and other purposes.	1096	20th April 1865	Henry Kinder Taylor.
Locks and lock furniture	1194	29th April 1865	Walter Henry Tucker.
Locks and other fastenings (Communicated by Paul Bendet.)	1201	29th April 1865	William Clark.
An improved safety lock (Communicated by Matthieu Prosper Mareite.)	1402	22nd May 1865	William Edward Gedge.
Locks (Communicated by James Hutson.)	1408	22nd May 1865	William Hodson.
Mechanism for locking or fastening tiers or sets of drawers arranged in writing tables, cabinets, chests or other articles of furniture.	1462	27th May 1865	Ludwig Diehl.
Keys of locks having through holes	1485	30th May 1865	Sidney Grafton.
Construction of locks	1487	30th May 1865	John Calvert.
An improved system of telegraphic communication on railways, parts of which invention are also applicable to other telegraphic purposes.	1545	6th June 1865	Alice Isabel Lucas Gordon.
Fastenings for doors, windows, drawers and other like purposes	1578	9th June 1865	George Edward Mark. William Howes Howes.
Improved means or apparatus to be applied to doors and windows for the purpose of supporting or maintaining them in any required position when open, and in securing them when shut.	1583	10th June 1865	Arthur Hamilton Gilmore.
Preventing the forcing or wedging open iron safes, iron doors and strong rooms	1657	20th June 1865	James Parrish. Charles Thatcher. Thomas Glasscock.

Subject-matter of Patent.	Number of Patent.	Date.	Name of Patentee.
LOCKS, &c.—continued.			
Locks (Communicated by Frank Grant Johnson, Edwin Drew and Joy Jervis Jones.)	1786	29th June 1865	William Edward Newton.
Improvements in locks and latches, and in staples and spindles for the same.	1782	6th July 1865	George Carter.
Construction of locks and keys	1812	8th July 1865	John Fry Heather.
Improvements in locks and in latch bolts for locks and latches	1908	21st July 1865	James Walton.
Construction of safes or strong receptacles for the protection of property.	1911	22nd July 1865	William Diaper.
Improved mechanical arrangements or fastenings applicable to the doors and cases of safes and strong rooms, for the purpose of preventing the opening thereof by wedges or levers	1995	2nd Aug. 1865	{ Thomas Andrew. James Whiley Taylor. }
An improved fastening or lock	2003	2nd Aug. 1865	{ Richard Bailey. Joseph England. }
Burglar proof safes	2006	2nd Aug. 1865	Herbert Allman.
Certain improvements in the mode of fixing safes, boxes or other depositories for the protection of papers or other materials from fire.	2081	11th Aug. 1865	Peter Carlsson Kjellberg.
An improved burglar proof lock (Communicated by Charles Cushing Dickerman and Gilbert Smith.)	2092	12th Aug. 1865	William Edward Newton.
Certain improvements in the manufacture of safes	2121	17th Aug. 1865	{ Samuel Phillips. Joseph Groves. }
Manufacture of locks	2196	26th Aug. 1865	Edmund Durman Hodgson.
Iron safes	2244	31st Aug. 1865	Henry Clarke Ash.
Improvements in the manufacture of metallic safes and strong rooms, and in apparatus connected therewith.	2256	2nd Sept. 1865	Samuel Chatwood.
Construction of iron safes, strong boxes and other receptacles.	2294	7th Sept. 1865	John Matthias Hart.
Apparatus connected with safes for protecting valuables from fire	2318	9th Sept. 1865	{ Adolf Erik Nordenskjöld. John William Smith. }
Locks for trunks, bags, dressing-cases and other like articles. (Communicated by Nicolas Chrétien Goynand.)	2360	15th Sept. 1865	Richard Archibald Brooman.
An improved apparatus or mechanism for locking and unlocking railway carriage doors, and for making signals with reference thereto.	2442	23rd Sept. 1865	John Hawkins Simpson.
Improvements in the construction of safes, strong rooms and other similar depositories, and in the locks thereof	2457	26th Sept. 1865	{ Claude Parigot. Antoine Crival the younger. }
Locks and latches	2454	26th Sept. 1865	Cyrus Price.
Fasteners for doors	2566	6th Oct. 1865	Charles Fitz Gerald.
Locks	2852	4th Nov. 1865	William Gardner.
Locks and such like fastenings	2878	6th Nov. 1865	Jules Adolphe Raiset.
Improvements in the construction of door locks, latches and such like fastenings, and in knob and handle spindles and furniture used therewith.	2880	9th Nov. 1865	Benjamin Piat.
Locks or catches for portmonnaies, portfolios or other articles	2939	15th Nov. 1865	{ George Chambers. George Gregory. }

Subject-matter of Patent.	Number of Patent.	Date.	Name of Patentee.

Locks, &c.—continued.

Fastenings for safe doors and other doors and lids, and for other like purposes.	2979	20th Nov. 1865	Joseph Beverley Fenby.
Locks . . . . (Communicated by William Hudson and James Hutson.)	2991	21st Nov. 1865	Frederic Pope.
Manufacture of safes	3065	1st Dec. 1865	William Fothergill Batho.
Improvements in the construction of safes, strong rooms and other similar depositories, and in the locks thereof.	3169	9th Dec. 1865	Antoine Grivel the younger.
Improvements in locks and latches, and in attaching the knobs of locks and latches and other knobs to their spindles	3274	19th Dec. 1865	{ John Thomas Dawes. John Robbins. }
Improvements in the furniture of door locks and latches and in the means used in applying the same.	3290	20th Dec. 1865	John Martin.
Fireproof safes	3306	21st Dec. 1865	John William Blackman.
Improvements in the manufacture of safes and in apparatus connected therewith.	3321	23rd Dec. 1865	Samuel Chatwood.
Improvements in safes and in protecting the locks and bolts of safes, and other locks and bolts .	3334	23rd Dec. 1865	{ Joseph Grover. George Robinson the younger. }
Locks and keys for the same . . . (Communicated by Edrick Francis Young and Joshua Grenville Nickerson.)	3362	30th Dec. 1865	William Edward Newton.

Looking Glasses and Frames.

Improvements appertaining to reflectors .	288	2nd Feb. 1865	Alexander Southwood Stocker.
Manufacture of mirrors . . . . (Communicated by Lewis Paul Angenard.)	554	27th Feb. 1865	George Haseltine.
Improvements in the manufacture of looking glasses or mirrors, and in apparatus employed therein. (Communicated by The Society Rendal Cromwell, Alfred Tevernier and Edouard Dodd.)	786	21st March 1865	John Henry Johnson.
Manufacture of frames for looking glasses -	1564	6th June 1865	{ Henry Hunt. Richard Hunter. }
Improvements in the preparation of amalgams of quicksilver or mercury, and in the application of such amalgams to various purposes in the arts. (for coating mirrors.) (Communicated by Henry Warts.)	1719	29th June 1865	William Edward Newton.
Improvements in the ornamentation of glass and in the applications of glass so ornamented. (Communicated by The Society Rendal Cromwell, Alfred Tevernier and Edouard Dodd.)	2029	5th Aug. 1865	John Henry Johnson.
Apparatus for raising, lowering and moving heavy bodies, and for transmitting and arresting motion for various purposes. (applicable to looking-glasses.)	3098	2nd Dec. 1865	Thomas Aldridge Weston.

Subject-matter of Patent.	Number of Patent.	Date.	Name of Patentee.
LOOKING GLASSES, &c.—*continued.*			
Preparation of glass or gelatine so as to render it insoluble in water, and applicable by the admixture of other substances to various purposes for which common glue or gelatine cannot now be used. *(for mirror frames.)* *(Communicated by Henry Harris.)*	3325	23rd Dec. 1865	William Edward Newton.
MANGLING, IRONING, GOFFERING, ROUCHING.			
Washing, squeezing and mangling machinery	22	5th Jan. 1865	John William Brasford
Apparatus for ironing and dressing woollen and other tissues. *(Communicated by André Lyon.)*	146	19th Jan. 1865	François Paul Henri Cahuzac.
A chemical combustible substance and apparatus to which it is applicable. *(heating smoothing irons, goffering cylinders, &c.)* *(Communicated by François Stoher.)*	477	20th Feb. 1865	William Edward Gedge.
An improved machine for washing, wringing and mangling.	837	24th March 1865	James Andrew Swasey.
Mangles	1217	1st May 1865	{ William Watts. John Joseph Coope.
Machinery for stretching cotton and other fabrics or materials. *(applied to mangles.)*	1317	12th May 1865	James Heaford.
An improved mangle	1418	24th May 1865	Henry Nunn.
An improved plain or graduated gophering or puffing and pressing machine	1464	26th May 1865	{ Charles Cotton. Francis Anderson. Daniel Booker.
An improvement or improvements in the manufacture of the handles of smoothing irons or said irons, which said improvement or improvements may also be applied to the manufacture of the handles of various other articles.	1798	7th July 1865	Thomas Sheldon.
Machinery for washing, wringing, mangling and drying domestic clothes or other fabrics and fibrous substances	1827	10th July 1865	{ Henry Fearnley. Christopher Smith.
An improved apparatus for cooking, a portion of the same being applicable for washing and ironing.	1917	22nd July 1865	William Wapshare.
Manufacture of box-irons	2368	15th Sept. 1865	John Whitehouse.
An improved arrangement and combination of the working parts of machinery or apparatus employed for washing, wringing and mangling clothes and fabrics.	2450	25th Sept. 1865	George Frederic Seaward.
Apparatus for mangling and callendering	2597	9th Oct. 1865	Robert Walmsley.
Apparatus for finishing textile fabrics	2647	13th Oct. 1865	{ William Robertson. James Guthrie Orchar.
Goffering and plaiting machines	2823	2nd Nov. 1865	William Born West.

Subject-matter of Patent.	Number of Patent.	Date.	Name of Patentee.
MANTEL-PIECES.			
Manufacture and application of glass and other vitreous compositions - - - - (*for chimney-pieces.*)	1280	1st May 1865	Arthur Howard Emerson. Robert Fowler.
A new or improved cement or composition, applicable to the agglomeration or moulding of various materials, and to other useful and decorative purposes. (*for chimney-pieces.*) (Communicated by *Stanislas Sorel and Emile Justin Menier.*)	3119	5th Dec. 1865	Richard Archibald Brootman.
MANURE; TREATING SEWAGE.			
An improved method of treating apatite and other mineral phosphates. (Communicated by *Mr. John Oliver.*)	3	2nd Jan. 1865	Montagne Richard Leverson.
Improvements in the manufacture of oxygen gas and in treating and economising the residual products of the said manufacture - - (obtaining a compost or fertiliser for cereals.)	6	2nd Jan. 1865	John Frederick Parker. Joseph Tanner.
Treating guano - - - - -	50	6th Jan. 1865	Thomas Richardson. Martin Diederich Rücker.
Treating phosphates of lime and salts of potass and soda in order to fit them for agricultural uses. (Communicated by *Georges Ville.*)	140	17th Jan. 1865	Richard Archibald Brootman.
Manufacture of manure - - - -	202	23rd Jan. 1865	Benjamin King.
Preparation of superphosphate of lime - - (Communicated by *Robert Barnhill Potts.*)	330	4th Feb. 1865	William Edward Newton.
Improvements in treating sewage and in arranging apparatus in sewers and culverts to facilitate the ventilation of such structures.	451	16th Feb. 1865	Richard Smith.
An improved mode of preparing fertilising compounds or artificial manures. (Communicated by *Gustave Adolph Liebig.*)	518	23rd Feb. 1865	William Edward Newton.
An improved process for reducing or preparing waste animal matters, for the purpose of employing the same in the preparation of manures or fertilising compounds.	888	29th March 1865	William Moxon Fuller.
Manufacture of soluble and assimilable superphosphate of lime, by the application of phosphoric acid and acid phosphates. (Communicated by *Lucien Henri Blanchard and Théodore Chateau.*)	1161	25th April 1865	William Clark.
Obtaining certain compounds of nitrogen and of sulphur - - - -	1388	19th May 1865	Thomas Richardson. Martin Diederich Rücker.
Certain improvements in the manufacture of lime - (*for agricultural purposes.*) (Communicated by *Monsieur Louis Poulet.*)	1407	20th May 1865	Peter Armand Le Comte De Fontaine Moreau.
Certain improvements in the manufacture of superphosphate of lime from guano. (Communicated by *Gustave Adolph Liebig.*)	1790	6th July 1865	Alfred Vincent Newton.

Subject-matter of Patent.	Number of Patent.	Date.	Name of Patentee.
MANURE, &c.—continued.			
An improved process of preparing sea weeds and other vegetable substances for the production of artificial guano, felt, alkaline salts and iodine.	1877	19th July 1865	Donald McCrummen.
Preparation of soils to promote general vegetation. (applying metallic oxides.)	1935	26th July 1865	Thomas Spencer.
Manufacture of the straw of rye and other straws and grasses into fibre, and utilising the refuse. (for artificial manure.)	2171	23rd Aug. 1866	Edward Henry Cradock Monckton.
Means and apparatus to be employed in the manufacture of sugar. (applying refuse of sugar refining as manure.) (Partly communicated by Absalom Hippolyte Lepley.)	2606	10th Oct. 1865	Jean Adolphe Léon.
The utilization of town sewage for agricultural purposes, and also to prevent the pollution of rivers and streams, and the machinery and apparatus for effecting the same.	2639	12th Oct. 1865	John Linton.
Manufacture of paper from marine vegetable matters (refuse used as manure.) (Communicated by Pierre Erard Gérymon and Charles Marie Gagnage.)	2741	23rd Oct. 1865	William Clark.
Treatment and deodorization of sewage water	2808	31st Oct. 1865	Henry Young Darracott Scott.
Artificial manure	2830	2nd Nov. 1865	George Bartlett.
Utilization of waste leather to be employed as a fertiliser. (Communicated by Orazio Lopa.)	3064	24th Nov. 1865	Alfred Vincent Newton.
Manufacture of disinfectants (for manure.)	3115	4th Dec. 1865	John Thomlinson.
Apparatus employed in grinding corn and other substances capable of being ground by millstones. (corpulites, bones, &c.)	3126	5th Dec. 1865	Edward Alfred Cowper.
MAPS AND GLOBES.			
Dissected maps and charts (Communicated by François Auguste Laurvinyac.)	1137	24th April 1865	Henri Adrien Bonneville.
A covering or cap for protecting the ends of maps, drawings, rolls of paper and other materials that are capable of being rolled up.	3175	9th Dec. 1865	Saint George Howard Darien-Gwyn.
MATCHES, FUSEE, PIPE AND CIGAR LIGHTS.			
An improvement in machines for cutting match splints, toothpicks and similar articles.	74	10th Jan. 1865	Jonathan Clark Brown.
Improvements in the construction of shells, and in the explosive powder and fuse to be used therewith and for other purposes.	130	16th Jan. 1865	John Berkeley Cotter.

Subject-matter of Patent.	Number of Patent.	Date.	Name of Patentee.
MATCHES, &c.—continued.			
Mechanism applicable to frame-filling machines for wooden matches, vestas and vesuvians	1003	6th April 1865	Henry Joseph Simkirk.
The manufacture of an improved safety fuse	1049	13th April 1865	John Soloman Bickford.
Cases or receptacles for matches, stamps, cards and other articles	1121	21st April 1865	George Betjemann. George William Betjemann. John Betjemann.
An improved pocket lantern (Communicated by John Augustus Miner.)	1513	1st June 1865	William Edward Newton.
Fuzes and projectiles for rifled ordnance (Communicated by Benjamin Berkley Hotchkiss.)	1588	6th June 1865	George Haseltine.
Fuzes for shells for ordnance (Communicated by Frederick Schenkl.)	1585	13th June 1865	George Haseltine.
Fuzes for shells	1989	1st Aug. 1865	Andrew Noble.
Friction matches, lucifer matches, and matches for relighting, called tapex matches.	2153	21st Aug. 1865	Gideon G. Dennis.
Apparatus for lighting and heating, suitable for sick rooms and nurseries, and applicable also as holders for matches, watches and other necessary articles. (Communicated by François René Menaud and Charles Louis Marie Menaud.)	2315	30th Sept. 1865	John Henry Johnson.
Machinery or apparatus for the manufacture of wooden spills.	2577	6th Oct. 1865	Thomas Machin.
Improvements in block matches and in machinery for making the same	2690	18th Oct. 1865	James Whitford Truman. Henry Lovi.
An improved apparatus for igniting cigars or tobacco.	2868	7th Nov. 1865	Hyde Bateman.
Certain improvements in cutting or dividing timber, and in the machinery or apparatus connected therewith. (for lucifer matches.)	2923	13th Nov. 1865	John Jex Long.
An improvement in the manufacture of friction matches and tapers.	3002	22nd Nov. 1865	Samuel Alexander Bell.
An improved method of and apparatus for making mortars, bowls, spill pots, jelly cans, galvanic troughs and other similar articles	3189	8th Dec. 1865	William Boulton. Joseph Worthington.
An improved mode of igniting cigars, cigarettes, and other similar articles.	3380	24th Dec. 1865	Charles Leamington Williams Kneller.
Improvements in friction matches, in apparatus for using them, and in adapting them for lighting lamps. (Communicated by Philos Blake Tyler.)	3363	30th Dec. 1865	William Edward Newton.

Subject-matter of Patent.	Number of Patent.	Date.	Name of Patentee.
MEASURING AND GAUGING LENGTH, SIZE AND QUANTITY; LOOM AND OTHER MACHINE REGISTERS; APPOINTMENT AND DATE INDICATORS; CHECKS FOR CASH TAKING.			
Improved means of checking the receipts of railway clerks.	29	4th Jan. 1865	William Henry Roy.
An improved apparatus for registering the distance travelled by vehicles or the speed of machinery.	61	11th Jan. 1865	Claude Marie Bathias.
Improvements in tills and the means of securing and checking money taken by servants.	104	12th Jan. 1865	George Gaze.
Apparatus for counting coins of money, tickets and other similar articles, and indicating the number thereof.	363	11th Feb. 1865	Jacob Schoeruhr.
An improved winder and arrangement for winding and putting up velvet and other ribands ·	389	11th Feb. 1865	Theodor Anton Verkruzen. Martin Anton Verkruzen.
Stoppering bottles or other similar vessels, and measuring quantities therefrom.	414	14th Feb. 1865	William Conway Hine.
Certain improvements in mechanism or apparatus for "blocking," rolling and measuring calico, linen, flannel or other woven fabrics ·	536	25th Feb. 1865	Thomas Dronsfield. Thomas Edwin Jones. John Ashton.
An improved method of and means or apparatus for measuring the human body.	638	7th March 1865	John Howigrave Wilson.
Tablets, tickets or instruments to be used when drawing lots and prizes, and for such like purposes.	1106	29th April 1865	Charles Gassman.
Jacquard and indexing machines · · ·	1261	5th May 1865	Joseph Wadsworth. Henry Dansse. James M'Murdo.
Apparatus for measuring the human figure for garments.	1528	3rd June 1865	Edward Eastman.
Apparatus for the reception of coin · · (fares and entrance money.)	1676	22nd June 1865	Julian Mann Abrams.
Improved apparatus for gauging and marking the width of tucks and pleats on fabrics under operation in sewing-machines.	1811	8th July 1865	George Baldwin Woodruff.
Checking or controlling the payment of fares in cabs and other public vehicles. (Communicated by John Becker and Joseph Leib.)	2029	4th Aug. 1865	Henri Adrien Bonneville.
An improved numerical registering machine ·	2035	5th Aug. 1865	Samuel Burton.
Apparatus for taking measurements · · (Communicated by George Reord.)	2112	16th Aug. 1865	William Clark.
A new or improved date and other indicator, together with an improved method of arranging the date papers thereon.	2565	5th Oct. 1865	Louis Rollier Whitehead.
Improvements in rules for measuring, and in other instruments or articles requiring to be adjusted or disposed at various angles.	2613	10th Oct. 1865	Arthur Nicholls.
Apparatus for finishing textile fabrics · ·	2647	13th Oct. 1865	William Robertson. James Guthrie Orchar.
Machinery or apparatus for reeling silk, cotton or other fibrous threads, in the form of skeins. (reel and slap motions.)	2896	2nd Nov. 1865	Enoch Humason.

Subject-matter of Patent.	Number of Patent.	Date.	Name of Patentee.
MEASURING LENGTH, &c.—continued.			
Machinery for measuring woollen and other cloths	2942	6th Nov. 1865	William Herbdon.
Steering indicators and tell-tales - - -	2904	7th Nov. 1865	Charles Jullien Vishoff. James Adolphe Matthissen.
Apparatus for separating dust from the grain evolved from blast furnaces.	2825	8th Nov. 1865	Charles Cochrane.
An improved method of draughting patterns for coats, waistcoats and other close fitting garments, and apparatus to be used in obtaining the measurements for the same - -	2966	17th Nov. 1865	John Henry Smith. George Robert Smith.
Improvements in and adaptation of cylinder printing machines to the double purpose of letter press and lithography, also a new mode of damping litho stones, and a new mode of registering and printing in such machines.	2999	22nd Nov. 1865	Thomas William Nicholson.
Apparatus for registering the speed of machinery, and apparatus for registering the pressure of steam and other fluids - - -	3077	30th Nov. 1865	James Lee Norton. James Landless.
An improved apparatus for apportioning the fodder of horses, cattle and other domestic animals.	3237	14th Dec. 1865	Jacques Masson.
Obtaining and employing continuous lengths of tanned leather for various useful purposes - (for measuring lines.)	3354	23rd Dec. 1865	George Harn. Daniel Harn.

For measuring angles, see "COMPASSES."

MEASURING AND REGISTERING PROGRESS OF LOCOMOTIVES, CARRIAGES AND SHIPS; COUNTING AND MILEAGE APPARATUS OR TURNSTILES FOR CABS, &c.; LOGS AND SOUNDERS.

Subject-matter of Patent.	Number of Patent.	Date.	Name of Patentee.
An improved apparatus for registering the distance travelled by vehicles or the speed of machinery.	91	11th Jan. 1865	Claude Marie Rathins.
Improvements applicable to ships' logs and sounding machines.	233	26th Jan. 1865	John Edward Massey.
An improved arrangement of and addition to certain parts of omnibuses and other vehicles to indicate the number of passengers carried.	586	2nd March 1865	John Kirkland.
An improved system of telegraphic communication on railways, parts of which invention are also applicable to other telegraphic purposes.	1543	5th June 1865	Alice Isabel Lucas Gordon.
Ships' logs - - - -	1820	11th July 1865	Frederick Massey.
An improved mode of transmitting motion to the styles or hands of the dials of counters used for indicating and registering the distances public vehicles or private carriages travel.	2736	23rd Oct. 1865	Mathian Jakira, sen'.
An improved self-acting regulator or dial applicable to all descriptions of public conveyances.	2890	9th Nov. 1865	Joseph Ernest Avy.

Subject-matter of Patent.	Number of Patent.	Date.	Name of Patentee.
MEDICAL TREATMENT OF ANIMALS, CLEANSING HORSES.			
An improved application of rotating brushes to the grooming or cleaning of horses and other quadrupeds.	1036	12th April 1865	John Haworth.
Preparation of sheep ointment . . .	3208	12th Dec. 1865	Charles Knowles Tomlinson. Charles John Hayward.
Improvements in the treatment of animals intended for human food, and in the preservation of meat.	3293	20th Dec. 1865	John Gamgee.
MEDICINES AND CURATIVE APPARATUS; MEDICAL BATHS; INHALING AND RESPIRATORY APPARATUS.			
An improved portable pneumatic apparatus applicable in surgery and medicine for all purposes as a douche, for affusion, irrigation, injection, and for enemas.	16	3rd Jan. 1865	Thomas John Ashton.
Impregnating air for hygienic or therapeutic purposes with the vapours or emanations arising from tar, creosote or other suitable liquid antiseptic or antiputrid substances, or disseminating in the air for the said purpose suitable pulverized substances.	112	13th Jan. 1865	Antoine Joseph Sax.
Stoppering bottles or other similar vessels, and measuring quantities therefrom. (for medicines.)	414	14th Feb. 1865	William Conway Hine.
A new or improved invalid or siphon drinking cup	437	15th Feb. 1865	Robert Henry Emerson.
Certain improvements in the manufacture of magnesium and its compounds (sulphate of magnesia.)	456	17th Feb. 1865	John Osborne Christian, F.C.S. John Charlton. Henry Charlton.
Obtaining sulphates and carbonates of potash and soda.	460	17th Feb. 1865	Charles Frederick Claus.
A new febrifuge and digestive elixir - (Communicated by Monsieur Alexandre Gearon.)	674	28th March 1865	Alexandre Denis Gearon.
Improved apparatus for administering nourishment to the sick or infirm. (Communicated by Bernard Maillet.)	1140	21th April 1865	William Edward Gedge.
A new and improved food or fluid regulator for feeding bottle and other tubes.	1727	29th June 1865	William Botham.
Means of obtaining or producing oxygen applicable to various useful purposes. (for inhalers.)	1780	6th July 1865	Hermann Beigel.
An improved self-acting apparatus for obtaining a circulation of volatile liquids. (infusing drops.) (Communicated by Messieurs Françisque Masson and Auguste Jacquin.)	1818	8th July 1865	Hector Auguste Dufresné.

Subject-matter of Patent.	Number of Patent.	Date.	Name of Patentee.
MEDICINES, &c.—continued.			
A combination of improved method, apparatus and receptacles for storing, preserving, transferring and discharging certain fluids, for sanitary and protective purposes. (Communicated by Henry Pinkus.)	2096	14th Aug. 1865	Robert Alexander William Westley.
A new medicine for the cure of the disease of the stomach (dyspepsy, cardialgy, indigestion) and the hemorrhoids.	2127	17th Aug. 1865	Oscar Laurence.
Improved machinery for mixing or grinding ointment, paints, drugs and other substances.	2290	6th Sept. 1865	Thomas Charles Gibson.
Apparatus for administering injections and douches to the human body.	2555	5th Oct. 1865	William Robert Barker.
A new or improved apparatus for producing artificial respiration.	2721	21st Oct. 1865	William Hills Kitchen.
Bath apparatus (Communicated by Aloys Bongros.)	2749	25th Oct. 1865	William Clark.
Apparatus employed in grinding corn and other substances capable of being ground by millstones. (drugs.)	3126	5th Dec. 1865	Edward Alfred Cowper.
An improved method of and apparatus for making mortars, bowls, spill pots, jelly cans, galvanic troughs and other similar articles	3169	8th Dec. 1865	{ William Boulton. Joseph Worthington. }
Manufacture of bichloride of carbon, and chloride of sulphur. (as anæsthetic.)	3283	15th Dec. 1865	Richard Ransford.

METALLIC SALTS AND OXIDES.

Purification of lead to be employed for the manufacture of white lead, red lead and litharge.	310	4th Feb. 1865	John Arthur Phillips.
Production of substances to be used in place of the pigment usually termed satin white.	571	9th Feb. 1865	John Dale.
Certain improvements in the manufacture of magnesium and its compounds	456	17th Feb. 1865	{ John Osborne Christian, F.C.S. John Charlton. Henry Charlton. }
Preparation of hydrated oxide of chromium (Communicated by Charles Kratcrr.)	788	21st March 1865	Richard Archibald Brooman.
Apparatus employed in the concentration of all solutions where quick or speedy concentration or evaporation is required. (manufacture of chloride of sodium.)	872	24th March 1865	William Walsh.
An improved system of manufacturing salts, sulphates and acetates of chrome, and of applying them as mordants, in dyeing and printing textile substances both animal and vegetable.	1905	21st July 1865	Jean Henri Chandet.
Preparation of soils to promote general vegetation (applying metallic oxides.)	1868	26th July 1865	Thomas Spencer.
Manufacture of white lead	2427	22nd Sept. 1865	Peter Spence.
Treating the oxide of iron residues of gas purifying, in order principally to extract sulphur therefrom.	3099	2nd Dec. 1865	Thomas Ball.

Subject-matter of Patent.	Number of Patent.	Date.	Name of Patentee.

METALLIC SALTS, &c.—*continued.*

Improvements in smelting copper and in obtaining products from the gases and vapours given off during the said smelting. (collecting arsenic compounds.)	3287	16th Dec. 1865	Henry Caesar Emmill.
Preparation of glue or gelatine so as to render it insoluble in water, and applicable by the admixture of other substances to various purposes for which common glue or gelatine cannot now be used. (for imitating malachite.) (Communicated by Henry Wurtz.)	3325	23rd Dec. 1865	William Edward Newton.
Manufacture of acetate of lead - . - (Communicated by Jules Fournier Laigny.)	3368	29th Dec. 1865	Richard Archibald Brooman.

METALS.

I.—Smelting, Extracting and Reducing Metals; Treating Ores; Refining, Tempering and Annealing Metals; Manufacture of Iron and Steel; Metallic Alloys.

An improved jacket or protector for metallic and other vessels and structures containing solid substances, liquids or gases, to prevent radiation of heat from or communication of heat to such vessels and structures - - - (for blast furnaces.)	4	2nd Jan. 1865	{ Edward Bevan. { Abel Fleming.
Improvements in smelting zinc ores and in apparatus employed therein.	44	6th Jan. 1865	Arthur Reynolds.
Manufacture and refining of iron and steel - -	55	7th Jan. 1865	William Baker.
Furnaces - - - - - - - (Communicated by Dominique Chiode.)	103	12th Jan. 1865	Michael Henry.
Furnaces - - - - - - -	110	13th Jan. 1865	{ William Smith Longridge. { James Mash.
An improved method of purifying and oxidising metallic ores.	160	19th Jan. 1865	Melchior Belshazzar Mason.
Improvements in puddling, heating and other reverberatory furnaces used in the manufacture of iron and steel and for other purposes, which improvements may also be applied to steam-boiler furnaces.	179	20th Jan. 1865	John Hewes.
A new or improved process or method of treating articles of cast iron and of cast iron mixed with other metals. (hardening.)	182	23rd Jan. 1865	Percival Moses Parsons.
Furnaces for melting metals and smelting ores -	208	24th Jan. 1865	{ William Woodward. { Robert Woodward. { John Woodward. { Adam Woodward, jun'.
Improvements in lining the sides and bottoms of puddling furnaces and other furnaces employed in the manufacture of iron or steel, and in mending, repairing and fettling the sides and bottoms of the said puddling and other said furnaces.	224	26th Jan. 1865	Robert Mushet.

Subject-matter of Patent.	Number of Patent.	Date.	Name of Patentee.
METALS (Smelting)—continued.			
Manufacture of iron and steel - - -	229	26th Jan. 1865	Jacob Geoghegan Williams.
Furnaces - - - - - - -	240	27th Jan. 1865	Charles de Bergue.
Coating the bottoms and sides of ships and other submerged structures, to prevent fouling and decay. (euselgem.)	284	1st Feb. 1865	John Moyney.
Purification of lead to be employed for the manufacture of white lead, red lead and litharge.	310	4th Feb. 1865	John Arthur Phillips.
Improvements in furnaces for smelting iron ores, commonly called blast furnaces, also in cupolas used in founderies, for rendering down or melting iron or other metals.	574	11th Feb. 1866	Evan Leigh.
Extracting and separating gold and silver from their ores or matrices.	591	11th Feb. 1865	William Crookes, F.R.S.
Case hardening or converting partially into steel, articles of wrought or malleable iron. (Partly communicated by Anthony Leonard Fleury.)	593	11th Feb. 1865	Edwin Henry Newby.
Cupolas and blast furnaces - - - -	597	11th Feb. 1865	Henry Houldsworth Greenan. John Merviam Bigby.
Manufacture of sheet iron - - - (Communicated by Daniel Pratt.)	609	13th Feb. 1865	William Edward Newton.
Furnaces for smelting or reducing ores and for melting metals - - - - -	411	14th Feb. 1865	Herbert John Waldurk. Edward Barton.
Manufacture of cast and wrought iron - - (Communicated by Anthony Leonard Fleury.)	419	14th Feb. 1865	Edwin Henry Newby.
Furnaces - - - - -	443	15th Feb. 1865	Edward Brown Wilson.
Certain improvements in the manufacture of magnesium and its compounds - - -	455	17th Feb. 1865	John Osborne Christian, F.C.S. John Charlton. Henry Charlton.
Treating products obtained when roasting iron with zinc.	468	18th Feb. 1865	James Graham.
Improvements in the manufacture of iron and in articles made thereof.	470	18th Feb. 1865	William Robinson.
Improvements in puddling furnaces and in apparatus connected therewith.	472	18th Feb. 1865	John Gay Newton Alleyne.
An improvement in the utilization of the waste gases of blast furnaces.	476	20th Feb. 1865	Joseph Cliff.
Preparation of certain iron ores or residues for use in the blast furnace.	534	25th Feb. 1865	Frederic Claudet.
Treatment of certain products obtained in the smelting of iron - - - - -	560	2nd March 1865	Thomas Horton. David Simpson Price.
Improvements in converting cast iron or pig iron into wrought iron or steel, and in machinery employed therein.	649	8th March 1865	Morgan Morgans.
Stoves for heating air supplied to blast furnaces -	650	8th March 1865	Richard Hownon.
An improved manufacture of iron forgings -	654	8th March 1865	William Clay.
Manufacture of steel and homogeneous iron -	657	9th March 1865	Robert Mushet.
An improvement in the construction of hot air stoves for blast furnaces.	666	9th March 1865	Joseph Cliff.
Manufacture of iron and steel - - -	689	11th March 1865	James Henderson.
Furnaces and fire-places - - - -	692	11th March 1865	Edward Brown Wilson.

Subject-matter of Patent.	Number of Patent.	Date.	Name of Patentee.
METALS (*Smelting*)— *continued.*			
Apparatus for treating metals and metallic ores	697	13th March 1865	Robert Martin Roberts.
Puddling, heating and other furnaces	700	13th March 1865	Joseph Wright.
Improvements in drying and sorting coals, peat and mineral ores, in separating extraneous matters therefrom, and in apparatus used in those processes.	715	14th March 1865	Ferdinand Henry Wurlich.
Water tuyers for blast furnaces (*Partly communicated by Mr. Norris Best.*)	722	15th March 1865	Nathaniel Neal Solly.
Apparatus for smoke vents or chimneys	734	16th March 1865	Thomas Kennedy.
Heating preparatory to and for the purpose of hardening or tempering of knives, files, tools, and all other descriptions of cutlery or hardware usually subject to the process of hardening or tempering.	747	17th March 1865	Henry Wetherel.
Manufacture of puddled iron bars and every description of malleable iron	777	20th March 1865	{ Robert Thompson Crawshay. Isaac Arriston Lewis.
Machinery for working puddled balls or blooms of iron and steel.	779	20th March 1865	William Menelaus.
Manufacture and refining of iron and steel	806	22nd March 1865	Morgan Marquats.
Hardening and tempering steel	820	24th March 1865	Elliot Savage.
Furnaces or apparatus for heating the blast for furnaces used in smelting iron and for other furnaces.	821	25th March 1865	John Player.
A new or improved mode of rapidly reducing, reconverting and melting and other ores, also iron slag or cinders, dross and scales or crust, to produce directly therefrom steel or malleable or cast iron. (*Communicated by Jean Baptiste Helom.*)	839	30th March 1865	William Bronkes.
Apparatus applicable to furnaces for smelting ores and melting metals	842	3rd April 1865	{ Henry Brook. John Eastwood. George Brook, jun'.
Manufacture of balls, blooms or slabs of malleable iron or steel.	857	4th April 1865	John Player.
New or improved apparatus for separating or sorting and washing ores, minerals, coal, emery and other substances in a granular or pulverulent state. (*Communicated by Charles Prieger and Theodor Handt.*)	863	5th April 1865	Henry Simon.
An improved rabble or bar used in puddling iron	868	5th April 1865	George Walter Dyson.
Manufacture of iron and steel	1022	11th April 1865	Charles Vaughan.
Arrangement of furnaces used for puddling and reheating iron, the generation of steam and other similar purposes.	1004	13th April 1865	William Beardmore.
Improvements in the manufacture of iron, and in preparing fuel to be used in the manufacture and melting of iron.	1152	25th April 1865	{ John Northall Brown. Thomas Deykin Clare.
Furnaces used for smelting and melting iron and other metals.	1162	27th April 1865	William Balk.
Furnaces	1160	27th April 1865	Dundas Simpson.
Improvements in the manufacture of pig iron or foundry metal, and in making and treating castings of such metal.	1306	1st May 1865	Henry Bessemer.

Subject-matter of Patent.	Number of Patent.	Date	Name of Patentee.
METALS (*Smelting*)—*continued.*			
Means and apparatus for puddling iron -	1391	1st May 1865	{ Thomas Frederick Cushin. Joseph Felix Allender.
Extracting copper and several other metals from certain ores of them metals.	1355	5th May 1865	William Henderson,
Manufacture of iron and steel - - -	1310	11th May 1865	Joseph Bearott,
Improvements in the treatment of the waste liquors obtained after treating burnt ores of copper, such improvements having for their object the production or extraction of cobalt and nickel.	1352	16th May 1865	William Wright.
Cupola and other blast furnaces - - -	1445	26th May 1865	Richard Canham.
Improvements in the manufacture of steel, and in furnaces used in such manufacture. (*Communicated by Jules Paulis.*)	1490	27th May 1865	Louis Mouer.
Annealing pots and mueere for annealing iron and steel wire, short metal and other articles.	1460	30th May 1865	John Hibell.
Certain improvements in the manufacture of iron and steel, and in apparatus connected therewith.	1505	1st June 1865	Herbert Allman.
Manufacture of steel - - - -	1580	7th June 1865	{ John Ferguson. Robert Miller.
Preparation of magnesium for illuminating purposes (*Communicated by François Pierre Le Roux.*)	1695	24th June 1865	Joseph Solomon.
Improvements in the preparation of amalgams of quicksilver or mercury, and in the application of such amalgams to various purposes in the arts. (*Communicated by Henry Wurtz.*)	1710	26th June 1865	William Edward Newton.
A new or improved self-acting apparatus for distributing the feeding materials in high furnaces. (*such as ores.*) (*Communicated by Emile Langen.*)	1783	29th June 1865	Alexander Prince.
Improvements in the conversion of wrought or malleable iron into steel, and in the means or apparatus employed therein.	1778	5th July 1865	{ John Johnson. John Farmerley Dickson.
Manufacture of iron - - - - (*Communicated by John Williams and Josiah Copley.*)	1793	7th July 1865	James Marius Macrum.
Manufacture of cast steel - - - (*Communicated by Charles Puxtort.*)	1618	8th July 1865	Richard Archibald Brooman.
Treatment of copper and nickel ores - - (*Communicated by Vincent Charles de Serquerville.*)	1631	11th July 1865	Hector Auguste Dufrené.
An improved process for obtaining oxygen - (*to melt metals.*) (*Communicated by Monsieur Charles Tellier.*)	1833	11th July 1865	Hector Auguste Dufrené.
Separating gold from ores containing copper and and gold.	1855	14th July 1865	Andrew Edward Molin.
Construction and working of furnaces for puddling, balling, heating and melting metals.	1868	19th July 1865	David Caddick.
Manufacture of pots and crucibles wherein metals and other materials may be heated or melted.	1864	19th July 1865	George Nimmo.
An improvement in the mode of uniting different metals, such as iron and copper or alloys, to form compound metallic castings.	1866	19th July 1865	George Nimmo.
Means or method of applying mineral oils for generating steam and heat. (*for smelting.*) (*Partly communicated by Alexandre Sepis.*)	1926	25th July 1865	Wladislaus Zbyszewski.

Subject-matter of Patent.	Number of Patent.	Date.	Name of Patentee.
METALS (Smelting)—continued.			
Means of and apparatus for treating animal and vegetable fibrous materials, which apparatus is also applicable to various useful purposes. (gums used in smelting.)	1868	27th July 1865	Henry Sherwood.
Manufacture of iron and steel (see "METALS—Forging.") (Communicated by Martin Dieudonné Heur, etc.)	1864	29th July 1865	Ephraim Sabel.
Manufacture of iron	1970	29th July 1865	William Worthington Biggs.
Improved means of testing alloys of gold	1994	2nd Aug. 1865	Henry Levy.
Machinery to be used in the manufacture of plate or sheet iron and steel. (Communicated by Martin Dieudonné Heurtaux.)	2012	3rd Aug. 1865	Ephraim Sabel.
Machinery to be used in the manufacture of iron. (Communicated by Martin Dieudonné Heurtaux.)	2018	4th Aug. 1865	Ephraim Babel.
Improvements in and connected with the manufacture of copper.	8100	14th Aug. 1865	James Thomas Lockey.
Furnaces to be used in the manufacture of glass and iron and steel, and for other like purposes. (Communicated by Henley Bordiss.)	2105	15th Aug. 1865	John Frederick Boctins.
Improvements in the preparation or production of spongy metals, and in their applications. (Communicated by François Briser.)	2106	15th Aug. 1865	John Henry Johnson.
Manufacture of cast steel and cast iron, and the manufacture of a unged metal. (Communicated by Emile Martin and Pierre Emile Martin.)	2187	19th Aug. 1865	Richard Archibald Brooman.
An improved furnace for annealing iron and steel wire or rods.	8165	23rd Aug. 1865	John Howard Scott.
Improvements in the manufacture of steel iron and metal suitable for bearings, and in apparatus for the same.	2175	24th Aug. 1865	William Colburne Cambridge.
Improvements in condensing and utilising sulphurous smokes and vapours, and in apparatus to be used for that purpose. (From smelting works.)	2216	29th Aug. 1865	Adolf Gurlt.
Improvements in extracting and separating gold and silver from their ores or matrices, and in the treatment of mercury employed for such purposes.	2249	5th Aug. 1865	William Crookes, F.R.S.
Manufacture of iron	2307	9th Sept. 1865	William Unwin.
Apparatus used for calcining and roasting copper and other ores and substances containing sulphur.	2350	14th Sept. 1865	Thomas Bell. Thomas Lonnie Gregson Bell.
Apparatus for separating dust from the gases evolved from blast furnaces for smelting iron.	8391	15th Sept. 1865	Edward Alfred Cowper. Charles William Siemens.
Improvements in and applicable to furnaces for the consumption of smoke. (smelting furnaces.)	2405	21st Sept. 1865	William Watkin.
Improvements in blast furnaces and in charging the same. (Communicated by Alexandre Leleux-Faing.)	8412	21st Sept. 1865	Richard Archibald Brooman.
Manufacture of balls, blooms or slabs of malleable iron or steel.	2444	23rd Sept. 1865	John Player.

Subject-matter of Patent.	Number of Patent.	Date.	Name of Patentee.
METALS (*Smelting*)—*continued*.			
Manufacture of iron	2448	25th Sept. 1865	William Unwin.
Manufacture of cast iron, malleable iron and steel	2456	26th Sept. 1865	Nicholas Korshunoff.
Manufacture of iron and steel, and of furnaces and machinery for purifying, puddling or heating the same	2461	26th Sept. 1865	Thomas Frederick Cabbin. Joseph Felix ABender.
Separating phosphorus from iron and other metals, in metallurgical processes.	2462	27th Sept. 1865	Carl Heinrich Ludwig Wintzer.
Collecting or drawing off the gases from blast furnaces	2507	29th Sept. 1865	John Addenbrooke. George Addenbrooke. Philip Anthony Millward.
Blast furnaces	2528	2nd Oct. 1865	Silas Covell Salisbury.
Machinery employed for crushing, amalgamating and washing gold quartz and and other minerals or matters containing gold or other metal. (*Communicated by James Hatt.*)	2543	13th Oct. 1865	William Halse Gatty Jones.
Apparatus for applying carbonic and other gases to iron and other metals in a molten state.	2557	14th Oct. 1865	James Cartmell Ridley.
Improvements in steam-boilers and other apparatus applicable to the heating and evaporation of liquids, parts of which improvements are applicable also to other purposes (*puddling furnaces*.)	2601	16th Oct. 1865	Francis Wise. Edward Field. Enoch Harrison Aydon.
Treatment of copper ores in the manufacture of copper. (*Communicated by Frédéric Le Clerc.*)	2605	16th Oct. 1865	William Clark.
Furnaces	2628	17th Oct. 1865	William Beardmore.
Improvements in the manufacture of inflammable gases and in their application to useful purposes. (*for smelting.*)	2710	21st Oct. 1865	Isham Baggs.
An improved apparatus for calcining copper ore, and for treating the products of copper ore when being calcined.	2730	31st Oct. 1865	Arthur Bankart.
Improvements in lamps for the combustion of magnesium and in preparing magnesium for burning.	2769	24th Oct. 1865	Henry Larkin.
Furnaces	2808	31st Oct. 1865	Robert Cassels. Thomas Morton.
Improvements in the manufacture of iron and steel, and in apparatus employed in such manufactures.	2835	3rd Nov. 1865	Henry Bessemer.
Manufacture of copper from copper ore	2838	3rd Nov. 1865	James Balkay Filkington.
Plating or combining gold, platinum and other metals or their alloys. (*making alloys.*)	2842	3rd Nov. 1865	Edward John Northwood.
Manufacture of steel (*Communicated by Isidore Rosenthal and Ferdinand Gierou.*)	2870	7th Nov. 1865	Francis Prange.
Furnaces for heating the blast for blast furnaces	2897	11th Nov. 1865	Thomas Whitwell.
Making amalgams or alloys of metals (*Communicated by Henry Wertz.*)	2903	11th Nov. 1865	William Edward Newton.
Purifying or refining iron	2929	14th Nov. 1865	John Dixon.
An improved process for hardening malleable and non-malleable cast iron. (*Communicated by Thomas Henry Jenkins.*)	2964	17th Nov. 1865	William Edward Newton.

Subject-matter of Patent.	Number of Patent.	Date.	Name of Patentee.
METALS (Smelting)—continued.			
Improvements in the manufacture of sulphur by the reduction of the sulphurous acid accruing from the roasting of sulphuretted ores, and in apparatus for the same.	2968	21st Nov. 1865	Alexandre Colley Sa. Paul de Sincay.
Furnaces - - - - -	3025	24th Nov. 1865	William Alexander Lyttle.
Means and apparatus for raising heat by the combustion of fuels of various kinds.	3029	25th Nov. 1865	John Francis Bennett.
Making wrought iron - - -	3034	25th Nov. 1865	George Tomlinson Bonsfield.
(Communicated by Charles Meredith Dupuy.)			
Improvements in the manufacture and treatment of railway bars, tyres and axles, also in the construction of furnaces, machinery and apparatus connected therewith.	3064	1st Dec. 1865	Thomas Weatherburn Dodds.
(crossuting or converting furnaces.)			
Furnaces - - - - -	3095	2nd Dec. 1865	Edward Brown Wilson.
Improvements in puddling, heating and other reverberatory furnaces used in the manufacture of iron and steel, and for other purposes.	3136	5th Dec. 1865	Thomas Lewis Nicklin.
Treatment of sulphurous and arsenical pyrites containing copper and tin.	3256	16th Dec. 1865	Charles Pengilly.
Certain improvements in the means of collecting waste gases arising from blast furnaces -	3261	16th Dec. 1865	Samuel Whitehouse the elder. Samuel Whitehouse the younger. Jeremiah Whitehouse. William Whitehouse.
Improvements in smelting copper and in obtaining products from the gases and vapours given off during the said smelting.	3267	18th Dec. 1865	Henry Cusers Ensell.
Certain improvements in the manufacture of steel -	3288	20th Dec. 1865	John Birch.
Improvements in the manufacture of steel and purified iron, and in the apparatus employed therein.	3300	21st Dec. 1865	Henri Adrien Bonneville.
(Communicated by Antoine Galy-Cazalat.)			
Improvements applicable to steam boilers, iron, steel, retort and other furnaces.	3329	26th Dec. 1865	Joshua Fisher.
An improved method of and apparatus for preserving, purifying, mixing, separating, cooling, aerating, roasting and otherwise treating grain, ores and various other matters.	3344	27th Dec. 1865	Gaston Charles Ange Marquis D'Aury.
III.—Casting and Moulding Metals; Moulds and Core Boxes.			
Improvements in the manufacture of metallic bedsteads, which improvements are also applicable to the manufacture of other metallic articles.	55	7th Jan. 1865	James Atkins.
A new or improved process or method of treating articles of cast iron, and of cast iron mixed with other metals.	173	23rd Jan. 1865	Percival Moses Parsons.
Improvements in the manufacture of ordnance and other like castings and in the apparatus employed therein, also in carriages or moulds for the same.	225	2nd Feb. 1865	John Henry Johnson.
(Communicated by William Jones.)			
An improved mode of making metal pipes -	366	9th Feb. 1865	William Anderson.

Subject-matter of Patent.	Number of Patent.	Date.	Name of Patentee.
METALS (Casting)—continued.			
An improved " core " to be employed in the casting of metallic pipes or tubes.	587	2nd March 1865	David Hartley.
Casting steel railway wheel tyres - - -	614	4th March 1865	Joseph Whitley.
Manufacture of crucibles and pots in which metals or other substances may be melted.	620	6th March 1865	George Nimmo.
Improvements in the manufacture of railway wheel tyres, and in the implements or tools employed in such manufacture.	666	9th March 1865	William Daniel Allen.
Improvements in the manufacture of metallic bedsteads, which improvements are also applicable to the manufacture of other metallic articles.	699	13th March 1865	James Atkins.
Casting ingots of steel and malleable iron - -	662	27th March 1865	Carl Johan Laurentz Leffer.
Manufacture of steel tires for railway wheels -	678	24th March 1865	Francis William Webb.
Certain improvements in machinery or apparatus used in carding cotton or other fibrous substances - -	687	29th March 1865	Eran Leigh. Frederick Allen Leigh.
Manufacture of plough-shares, socks or points for ploughs, cultivators or scurrifurrows, and other implements used in the cultivation of the land where these points are used or required - -	906	7th April 1865	William Gray. Edward Gray. John Gray.
Manufacture of malleable iron sheaves and bushes for pulley blocks - - -	1085	19th April 1865	Joseph Gardner. Richard Lee. George Henry Wain. Samuel Hargrove. Charles Hargrove. Samuel Hargrove, jun'.
Casting and working so-called " Bessemer steel " ingots " - - -	1100	20th April 1865	Thomas Hampton. James Abbott.
Machinery for moulding and making cores for moulding or casting metals.	1128	21st April 1865	Richard Canham.
Making moulds for casting pipes and other articles of various sizes.	1209	1st May 1865	David Yoolow Stewart.
Improvements in the manufacture of pig iron or foundry metal, and in making and treating castings of such metals.	1208	1st May 1865	Henry Bessemer.
Certain improvements in the manufacture of " moulds " for metallic castings having a cylindrical form.	1288	10th May 1865	David Hartley.
Improvements in casting iron girders and in apparatus therefor.	1304	11th May 1865	James Goodwin.
Improvements in the manufacture of crossings for the permanent way of railways, and also in tyres for wheels.	1396	20th May 1865	Joseph Armstrong.
Apparatus for making cores and moulds for casting	1489	25th May 1865	David Law. James Bennett.
A new and improved mode of making and working cores and parts of moulds, to be used in the casting of iron or other metal. (Communicated by Joseph Harrison, jun'.)	1494	25th May 1865	John Henry Johnson.
An improved method of and apparatus for moulding wheels.	1489	30th May 1865	Luke Martin.
Foundry cupolas - - - -	1498	31st May 1865	Thomas Santeman.
An improved system of wheels for railway carriages	1665	7th June 1865	Emile Dupont.

Subject-matter of Patent.	Number of Patent.	Date.	Name of Patentee.
METALS (*Casting*)—*continued.*			
Manufacturing gun barrels and tubes of cast steel and homogeneous iron.	1739	30th June 1865	Henry Powell Tippet.
An improvement or improvements in the manufacture of the handles of smoothing irons or and irons, which said improvement or improvements may also be applied to the manufacture of the handles of various other articles. (*moulding.*)	1796	7th July 1865	Thomas Sheldon.
Manufacture of cast steel - - - (*Communicated by Charles Powers.*)	1813	8th July 1865	Richard Archibald Brooman.
An improved process for obtaining oxygen - (*and in preparing moulds for casting.*) (*Communicated by Monsieur Charles Tellier.*)	1832	11th July 1865	Hector Auguste Dufresi.
Apparatus employed in the manufacture of tin and terne plates - - - - -	1843	12th July 1865	{ John Saunders. Joseph Piper.
Improvements in ingot moulds and in casting metals.	1849	14th July 1865	John Clayton.
An improvement in the mode of uniting different metals, such as iron and copper or alloys, to form compound metallic castings.	1865	19th July 1865	George Nicann.
Improvements in the manufacture of hoops and tyres, and in the machinery employed therein.	1975	31st July 1865	John Ramsbottom.
Burglarproof safes - - - - -	2008	2nd Aug. 1865	Herbert Allman.
Railway chairs - - - - -	2099	14th Aug. 1865	William Frederick Hamer.
Moulds for casting metallic pipes, retorts and other articles.	2215	29th Aug. 1865	George Robinson.
Manufacture of cast steel or other metallic tubes -	2241	31st Aug. 1865	William Henry Boven.
Improvements in the manufacture of metallic safes and strong rooms, and in apparatus connected therewith.	2268	2nd Sept. 1865	Samuel Chatwood.
Improvements in founding or casting metals, and in moulds used for the same.	2401	20th Sept. 1865	Daniel Spink.
Improvements in the construction of steam generators, applicable also to the construction of condensers, the heating of water generally, and to the warming of buildings. (*Communicated by Joseph Harrison, jun'. and Thomas Lasbrs.*)	2610	10th Oct. 1865	John Henry Johnson.
Apparatus for raising liquids - - -	2632	12th Oct. 1865	Jean Urain Fastier.
Apparatus for moulding toothed or other wheels or pullies or portions of circles, for casting.	2751	25th Oct. 1865	George Lamb Scott.
Certain improvements in apparatus employed in the manufacture and production of metallic pipes, tubes or other similar hollow castings. (*moulds and cores.*) (*Communicated by Alfred Bertard.*)	2804	31st Oct. 1865	Arthur Denlasdes.
Casting hoops of steel suitable for making tyres -	2898	9th Nov. 1865	William Daniel Allm.
Stoves for drying moulds - - -	2943	15th Nov. 1865	Henry Cochrane.
Machinery for the manufacture of moulds for casting metallic wheels.	2969	17th Nov. 1865	Thomas Joseph Perry.
An improvement in the manufacture of steel castings - - - - - }	2970	16th Nov. 1865	{ George Taylor. John Fernie.
Cotton gins - - - - -	2984	20th Nov. 1865	William James Buqun.

Subject-matter of Patent.	Number of Patent.	Date.	Name of Patentee.

METALS (*Casting*)—*continued.*

Improvements in casting iron and steel and in apparatus employed for this purpose.	3018	24th Nov. 1865	Joseph Whitworth.
Moulding for casting steel, iron and other metals -	8030	25th Nov. 1865	{ Frederick Trueheart. William Hall.
Improvements in the manufacture of axles and in apparatus connected therewith.	3221	23rd Dec. 1865	Samuel Chatwood.
Improvements in the construction and manufacture of steel crossings for railways, and in the moulds for casting the same, all or part of which said improvements in moulds are applicable for casting other articles,	3353	23rd Dec. 1865	Francis William Webb.

III.—Forging, Rolling, Hammering, Rivetting, Bending, Welding and Shaping Metals; Steam Hammers, Anvils.

Improvements in steam hammers and in apparatus employed in combination with steam hammers.	69	11th Jan. 1865	John Ramsbottom.
Improvements in driving rolls for rolling metals, and in apparatus employed therein. (Communicated by Antoine François Morvel.)	125	16th Jan. 1865	Richard Archibald Brooman.
Improvements in the permanent way of railways and in buckled plates to be used therein, the same being applicable to the construction of fire-proof buildings, bridges and other like structures, also in the machinery or apparatus for producing such improved plates.	164	19th Jan. 1865	Robert Mallet.
Improvements in shaping and forging metals and in the machinery and apparatus employed therein - - - - -	166	19th Jan. 1865	{ James Alfred Shipton. Robert Mitchell.
Manufacturing ordnance and gun barrels of cast steel or of homogeneous iron -	218	25th Jan. 1865	{ John Marshall. Henry Mills.
Improvements in armour plated ships, forts, gun carriages and works of defence, and in fastenings to be employed thereto.	292	2nd Feb. 1865	Charles Langley.
Improvements in the manufacture of ordnance and other like castings and in the apparatus employed therein, also in carriages or moulds for the same. (Communicated by William Jones.)	295	2nd Feb. 1865	John Henry Johnson.
Machinery or apparatus for forming certain parts of metallic casks and drums.	327	6th Feb. 1865	George Duncan.
Manufacture of scissors, shears and edge tools - (Partly communicated by Charles Lingard, junior.)	373	10th Feb. 1865	Charles Lingard.
Machinery for rolling and hammering iron and other metals.	375	10th Feb. 1865	John Ramsbottom.
Machinery for rivetting and for making rivets -	400	13th Feb. 1865	Henry Martyn Kennard.
Mode of making or forming the links of iron or steel chains, chain cables, shackles, couplings or parts of the same, and for machinery to be used therein.	432	14th Feb. 1865	George Bombay.
An improved blowing apparatus - - - (for smiths' hearths.)	457	15th Feb. 1865	{ Samuel Richards Freeman. Abraham Grundy.

Subject-matter of Patent.	Number of Patent.	Date.	Name of Patentee.
METALS (*Forging*)—*continued.*			
Improvements in cast steel or other metal chains for cables and for other purposes, and in machinery or apparatus for manufacturing the same.	481	15th Feb. 1865	William Henry Brown.
Permanent way and rolling stock of railways (*rolling rails in halves.*)	520	24th Feb. 1865	John Kennedy Donald.
Making solid iron scales with bolsters, for all kinds of spring knives.	560	28th Feb. 1865	Arthur Dary.
Improvements in steam hammers applicable to the manufacture of files, to welding flyers of cotton machinery and to other purposes.	641	7th March 1865	James Dodge.
An improved manufacture of iron forgings	654	8th March 1865	William Clay.
Improvements in the manufacture of railway wheel tyres, and in the implements or tools employed in such manufacture.	665	9th March 1865	William Daniel Allen.
Machinery or apparatus for rolling, shaping or forging metals.	701	13th March 1865	Robert Marsden.
Machinery for rolling and shaping metals	758	16th March 1865	John Ramsbottom.
Apparatus for blowing smiths' and other fires	755	18th March 1865	{ James Cookson. Philip Billington.
Machinery for cutting, punching, raising, shaping or drawing through sheet metal, by means of tools and dies.	798	22nd March 1865	George Farmer.
Manufacture of steel tires for railway wheels	876	24th March 1865	Francis William Webb.
Forging machines	862	24th March 1865	Joseph Wright.
Shaping machines	896	30th March 1865	Walter Montgomerie Neilson.
Improvements in the manufacture of iron rods and bars of different forms, and in the apparatus relating thereto. (*Communicated by Adolphe Paul Empleirane, Philippe Cabert and Constant Fourbois.*)	918	31st March 1865	Henri Adrien Bonneville.
Rolling or forging steel or wrought iron in bars, to be used as beaters or beating bars upon the drum concaves or beater plates of concaves in thrashing machines.	925	1st April 1865	William Gray.
Improvements in steam and atmospheric hammers and presses, which improvements are also applicable to steam-engines.	958	4th April 1865	Joseph Vaughan.
Mode of making or forming the links of iron or steel chains and chain cables, and for machinery to be used therein.	1004	8th April 1865	Alfred Homfray.
An improved method of forming tapered rods and bits. (*Communicated by Cæsar Auguste Deverie.*)	1018	10th April 1865	Richard Archibald Brogman.
Manufacture of iron and steel	1022	11th April 1865	Charles Vaughan.
Certain improvements in the manufacture of hoop or narrow strip iron.	1063	13th April 1865	Thomas Bennett.
Cushions for steam cylinders (*Communicated by Henry Johnson.*)	1079	18th April 1865	Frederick Collier Bakewell.
An improved machine for straightening, bending, curving and circling beams, bars and plates of iron or other metals.	1083	18th April 1865	John Todd.
Construction of the permanent way of railways (*Communicated by Moritz Hilf.*)	1151	22nd April 1865	William Slinger.

Subject-matter of Patent.	Number of Patent.	Date.	Name of Patentee.
METALS (*Forging*)—*continued.*			
Certain improvements in machinery or apparatus for rolling or shaping metallic articles of irregular form, such as "file blanks" and similar articles.	1180	28th April 1865	Edward McNally.
Machinery for drilling boiler and other plates of metal, and for rivetting them together.	1291	10th May 1865	Daniel Adamson.
Machinery or apparatus for tapering, pointing or reducing wires or rods for spindles, hatchel teeth, pins for drawers, and similar articles.	1348	16th May 1865	Chauncey Orris Crosby.
An improvement in atmospheric forging hammers.	1380	19th May 1865	Edward Augustus Raymond.
Production and application of electricity (*for rolling and welding metals.*)	1412	23rd May 1865	Henry Wilde.
Machinery employed in the manufacture of hoops and tyres. (*rolls.*)	1425	25th May 1865	John Ramsbottom.
Manufacture of cast steel railway tires.	1428	25th May 1865	John Firth.
Improvements in making cast-steel railway tires, and in apparatus therefor.	1455	27th May 1865	John Martin Bowns.
Certain improvements in steam hammers, partly applicable to steam-engines.	1491	31st May 1865	Peter Pilkington.
Certain improvements in the manufacture of iron and steel, and in apparatus connected therewith.	1504	1st June 1865	Herbert Allman.
Furnaces used in the manufacture of welded iron tubes.	1517	2nd June 1865	Thomas Pritchard.
Machinery or apparatus for bending and straightening angle iron, T iron and other iron bars.	1532	6th June 1865	Charles De Bergue.
Hammers and other machines actuated by steam or other fluid or vapour.	1607	14th June 1865	{ Benjamin Massey. { Stephen Massey.
Improvements in the manufacture or shaping of iron intended for the shoes of horses and other animals, and in machinery employed therein. (*Communicated by Hector Edouard Bassin.*)	1689	16th June 1865	Richard Archibald Brooman.
Machinery for rivetting and for making rivets.	1709	27th June 1865	Henry Martyn Kennard.
Heating chisels, knives, plane irons, gouges, augers, steels, shears, scythes and saws.	1715	27th June 1865	William Brooks.
Machinery or apparatus for cutting, punching and bending sheet metal. (*Communicated by Nathan Harper.*)	1788	29th June 1865	Robert Henry Lenne.
Manufacturing gun barrels and tubes of cast steel and homogeneous iron.	1789	30th June 1865	Henry Powell Tipper.
Making shelps for iron or steel tubes direct from the rolls, and for machinery to be used in the same.	1858	15th July 1865	Samuel Hingley.
Manufacture of iron and steel (*rolling.*) (*Communicated by Martin Diraudeaud Heureux.*)	1964	29th July 1865	Ephraim Sabel.
Improvements in the manufacture of hoops and tyres, and in the machinery employed therein. (*expanding.*)	1975	31st July 1865	John Ramsbottom.
Manufacture of iron rails and girders (*Communicated by Martin Diraudeaud Heureux.*)	1979	31st July 1865	Ephraim Sabel.
Iron horns and riders for ships' fastenings, and iron frames for wood and iron ships.	2010	3rd Aug. 1865	Peter Cato.

Subject-matter of Patent.	Number of Patent.	Date.	Name of Patentee.
METALS (Forging)—*continued.*			
Machinery to be used in the manufacture of plate or sheet iron and steel. (*Communicated by Martin Diredan and Herroux.*)	2019	3rd Aug. 1865	Ephraim Sabel.
Blacksmiths' bellows, more especially those used in portable forges.	2108	21st Aug. 1865	John Bowden.
Steam hammers - - - - -	2174	24th Aug. 1865	David Davies.
Improvements in the manufacture of horse shoes and in machinery used in the said manufacture.	2197	26th Aug. 1865	John Symmons.
Sheet metal handles for spoons, saucepans and other utensils for culinary purposes.	2228	29th Aug. 1865	James Fallows.
The manufacture of boiler and tea kettle bottoms, and every other description of die-struck hollow ware.	2257	31st Aug. 1865	Michael Judge.
Treating, working or manipulating cast steel, for the manufacture of wheel tires, armour plates or other articles requiring great hardness and tensile strength.	2277	5th Sept. 1865	Julien Grand.
Improvements in the manufacture of tubes for gun barrels and other purposes, parts of which improvements are also applicable to the manufacture of rods or bars, and to the rifling of ordnance and fire-arms.	2351	11th Sept. 1865	Gustavus Palmer Harding.
Machinery or apparatus for shaping metal articles. (*see* "NAILS.") (*Communicated by Robert Heapp Butcher.*)	2371	16th Sept. 1865	John Henry Johnson.
Improvements in the manufacture of horse shoes and in the machinery used for such manufacture. (*Communicated by Jean Chrysostôme Viel and Pierre Michel Sébut.*)	2423	23rd Sept. 1865	George Davies.
Improvements in the manufacture of sheet iron or steel cylinders for boilers and similar articles, and in the apparatus relating thereto. (*rolling apparatus.*) (*Communicated by Benoit Rousierel.*)	2529	3rd Oct. 1865	Henri Adrien Bonterville.
Machinery for shaping metal and other substances.	2542	5th Oct. 1865	Hesketh Hughes.
Bolts, rivets and the like fastenings, for connecting together pieces of metal and other material.	2612	11th Oct. 1865	Frederic Felham Warren.
Manufacture of tyres for railway wheels - -	2654	14th Oct. 1865	William James Armitage. Fairfax Wooler. John Hodgson.
Improvements in wheels for common road carriages, in tyres for the same, and in machinery for bending the tyre.	2688	16th Oct. 1865	James Lamb Hancock.
Improvements in forging and swaging steel and iron wheel tyres, and in the apparatus or tools employed for that purpose.	2698	19th Oct. 1865	Josiah Penton.
Manufacture of ordnance whole or in parts - -	2795	30th Oct. 1865	William Deakin. John Bagnall Johnson.
Improvements in steam hammers and in means of applying them to the manufacture of boilers and tubes.	2805	31st Oct. 1866	Charles Emmet.
Improvements in forges and in apparatus for lubricating parts thereof, which apparatus is also applicable for lubricating other moving parts of machinery. (*Communicated by Claude Henri Turge, senior.*)	2878	6th Nov. 1865	William Edward Gedge.

Subject-matter of Patent.	Number of Patent.	Date.	Name of Patentee.
METALS (*Forging*)—*continued.*			
Machinery for rolling shafts and axles (*Communicated by Thomas Cooper.*)	2904	11th Nov. 1865	Alfred Vincent Newton.
Crank axles of locomotives for railroads (*Communicated by Dyer Williams.*)	2908	11th Nov. 1865	William Robert Lake.
Manufacture of beaters for threshing machines (*rolling the steel.*)	2993	21st Nov. 1865	William Gray. Edward Gray. John Gray.
An improved machine or apparatus for shaping and forging iron.	3027	25th Nov. 1865	John Arrowsmith.
Improvements in the manufacture and treatment of railway bars, tyres and axles, also in the construction of furnaces, machinery and apparatus connected therewith. (*hammering.*)	3084	1st Dec. 1865	Thomas Weatherburn Dodds.
Certain improvements in the construction of large furnaces.	3109	4th Dec. 1865	William Brackmore.
Manufacture of metal tubes	3117	5th Dec. 1865	Philip Albert Moats.
Machinery for rolling gun barrels and other articles.	8185	8th Dec. 1865	Thomas Claridge.
Certain improvements in the manufacture of tyres for railway wheels and in apparatus connected therewith.	3185	8th Dec. 1865	Richard Evan Price.
Improvements in the manufacture of metal tubes for gun barrels and other purposes, and in machinery or apparatus employed therein. (*rolling.*)	3269	20th Dec. 1865	Thomas Birkett.
Improvements in the manufacture of steel and purified iron, and in the apparatus employed therein. (*rolling.*) (*Communicated by Antoine Galy-Carolet.*)	3300	21st Dec. 1865	Henri Adrien Bonneville.
Machinery for raising or forming articles of sheet metal. (*Communicated by Mollen Bray.*)	3312	22nd Dec. 1865	George Tomlinson Bousfield.
Improvements in the construction and manufacture of steel crossings for railways, and in the moulds for casting the same, all or part of which said improvements in moulds are applicable for casting other articles. (*casting anvil blocks.*)	3358	23rd Dec. 1865	Francis William Webb.
Improvements in the manufacture of axles for carriages and spindles for various purposes, and in machinery to be employed in the said manufacture, part of which improvements in machinery may also be applied to other purposes. See also "NAILS."	3398	26th Dec. 1865	Elias Lones. Joseph Constant Lones. John Lones. John Bertrell. Thomas Bertrell. Charles Vernon.
IV.—Cutting, Planing, Punching, Boring and Sliting Metals.			
An improved apparatus for cutting iron gas or other pipes. (*Communicated by Jules Charies.*)	88	11th Jan. 1865	William Edward Gedge.
Improvements in certain sewing-machine shuttles, and in the mode of and tools for manufacturing the same.	169	19th Jan. 1865	George Francis Bradbury.

Subject-matter of Patent.	Number of Patent.	Date.	Name of Patentee.
METALS (*Cutting*)—*continued.*			
Improvements in fire-arms and in ammunition for the same. (*rifling barrels.*)	188	21st Jan. 1865	Jacob Snider, Jun'.
Improvements in preparing for fixing and in fixing plates or sheets of metal, such as are used for roofing and other similar purposes.	238	26th Jan. 1865	George Dibley.
Action and arrangement of drilling machines, turning lathes and other machine tools in which a variable speed is required.	241	27th Jan. 1865	John Combe.
Improvements in screw taps more especially designed for cutting threads in the fittings and connections for gas, steam and water pipes.	257	24th Jan. 1865	William Foster.
Machinery and tools for making collars, cuffs, wristbands and other articles of dress, also adapted for cutting metal blanks	399	13th Feb. 1865	David Barr. William Henry Page. James Clement Newey.
Mode of making or forming the links of iron or steel chains, chain cables, shackles, couplings or parts of the same, and for machinery to be used therein.	422	14th Feb. 1865	George Homfray.
Armour plates for vessels of war and for other similar purposes. (*grooving.*)	458	17th Feb. 1865	John Brown.
Apparatus for operating engineers' and carpenters' tools by hand or other power. (*for boring, planing, &c.*) (*Communicated by Henry Winans.*)	600	3rd March 1865	James Spruce.
Machinery or apparatus for cutting and shaping metals, making nails, rivets and similar articles	644	6th March 1865	Joseph Wadsworth. James Wadsworth.
Machinery for cutting, punching, raising, shaping or drawing through sheet metal, by means of tools and dies.	705	22nd March 1865	George Farmer.
Machinery or apparatus for cutting or chasing the threads of screws or worms.	835	24th March 1865	Joseph Green.
Machines for planing and shaping metals	856	27th March 1865	John Todd.
Machinery or apparatus for cutting scrolls, frets and filigree work.	926	1st April 1865	James Kennan.
Certain improvements in the manufacture of hoop or narrow strip iron.	1063	13th April 1865	Thomas Bennett.
Casting and working so-called "Bessemer steel ingots"	1100	20th April 1865	Thomas Hampton. James Abbott.
Improvements in the fitting of surface condenser tubes, and in the tools to be used therein, and in the means of retarding corrosion in steam-boilers. (*Communicated by William Judson.*)	1132	22nd April 1865	Alfred Vincent Newton.
An improved cigar cutter	1189	24th April 1865	Henry Charles Butcher.
Machinery for cutting or shaping masts, spars and other beams and articles of wood.	1279	27th April 1865	Samuel Harvey.
Improvements in means or apparatus for fixing or tightening the ends of boiler and other tubes, and in cutting the ends or other parts of such tubes.	1282	9th May 1865	Ralph Hart Tweddell.
Machinery for drilling boiler and other plates of metal, and for rivetting them together.	1291	10th May 1865	Daniel Adamson.

Subject matter of Patent.	Number of Patent.	Date.	Name of Patentee.
METALS (Cutting)—continued.			
Improvements in power looms for weaving and in apparatus connected therewith. (punching holes in metal cylinders.)	1607	11th May 1865	William Jamieson.
Improved apparatus for cutting, turning and smoothing metal pipes, and the surfaces of bolts, rods or spindles	1611	11th May 1865	George Mountford. Edward Worroll.
Improvements in the mode of rifling muzzle-loading cannon, and in projectiles for the same. (Communicated by John Seigel.)	1322	13th May 1865	William Spence.
Machinery for the manufacture of hinges - (punching the strips.) (Communicated by Jean Baptiste Evrard and Jean Pierre Boyer.)	1335	13th May 1865	William Clark.
Certain improvements in the manufacture of gun barrels and ordnance	1341	15th May 1865	William Drakin. John Bagnall Johnson.
Certain improvements in apparatus for cutting or forming screws, which is also applicable for cutting pipes or tubes.	1411	23rd May 1865	Edward M'Nally.
Machinery employed in the manufacture of hoops and tyres. (making grooves on roughing rolls.)	1425	24th May 1865	John Ramsbottom.
Improvements in making cast-steel railway tires, and in apparatus therefor.	1455	27th May 1865	John Martin Rowan.
Tube cutters and screw stocks	1527	3rd June 1865	Charles Taylor.
Machinery or tools for cutting metals or other materials.	1571	9th June 1865	William Wilson Hulse.
Hammers and other machines actuated by steam or other fluid or vapour - (machines for cutting and punching.)	1607	14th June 1865	Benjamin Meaury. Stephen Meaury.
Portable punching apparatus	1708	26th June 1865	John Medhurst.
Machinery or apparatus for cutting, punching and branding sheet metal. (Communicated by Nathan Harper.)	1723	29th June 1865	Robert Henry Lenox.
Improvements in portable cartridge holders for breech-loading guns, whether single or double barrelled, as also in the means of manufacturing the said holders and in exploding the charge.	1888	20th July 1865	Charles Reason.
Machinery for planing metals (Communicated by William Sellers.)	1942	26th July 1865	William Edward Newton.
Improvements in the manufacture of hoops and tyres, and in the machinery employed therein. (perforating discs.)	1975	31st July 1865	John Ramsbottom.
Apparatus for cutting scales for knives and forming metal webs for knives.	1985	1st Aug. 1865	William Singleton.
A new portable machine or apparatus for the cutting of screw threads on pipes or on solid materials, and for the cutting of pipes asunder.	2065	9th Aug. 1865	Thomas Goode Messenger.
An improvement in the manufacture of metallic capsules.	2125	17th Aug. 1865	Eugene Rimmel.
Improvements in the manufacture of tubes for gun barrels and other purposes, parts of which improvements are also applicable to the manufacture of rods or bars, and to the rifling of ordnance and fire-arms.	2351	14th Sept. 1865	Gustavus Palmer Harding.

Subject-matter of Patent.	Number of Patent.	Date.	Name of Patentee.
METALS (Cutting,—continued.			
An improved form of rifling for fire-arms and ordnance.	2254	14th Sept. 1865	William Burrows Edward Ellis.
A new or improved method of and apparatus for securing or fastening metal plates to boats, rafters and other places, for roofing and other purposes.	2394	19th Sept. 1865	Robert Fox.
Improvements in the manufacture of horse-shoes and in the machinery used for such manufacture. (Communicated by Leon Chrymardear Val and Pierre Michel Silvat.)	2423	23rd Sept. 1865	George Davies.
Tools for securing tubes in tube plates, and for other purposes where concentrated power or adjustment is necessary. (for working punches, adjusting cutters, &c.'	2455	26th Sept. 1865	Richard Taylor Ndam Howry.
Improvements in rifling fire-arms, and in missiles or projectiles used in such, and in the machinery for the production of these improvements.	2488	29th Sept. 1865	William Ellis Metford.
Improvements in connections for and in stopping pipes used for conveying water and gas, and for other like purposes, and in preventing leakages in the said pipes, and in apparatus employed therein. (and drilling.)	2503	29th Sept. 1865	Charles Forster Cottrill.
Machinery for cutting screws - - -	2562	11th Oct. 1865	Joseph Tangye.
Manufacture of tyres for railway wheels - -	2564	14th Oct. 1865	William James Armitage. Fairfax Wooler. John Hodgson.
Machinery for the manufacture of fish hooks -	2570	17th Oct. 1865	Albert Fenton.
Reeds for weaving cocoa-nut, jute and other fibres. (cut from metal.)	2591	19th Oct. 1865	Thomas Catchpole.
Improvements in the manufacture of wheels for railway carriages, and in the machinery to be employed therein. (drilling machines.)	2771	27th Oct. 1865	Thomas Greenwood.
Manufacture of spikes - - - -	2806	31st Oct. 1865	Messrs Bayliss.
Machinery for mortising, tenoning and boring hard or soft woods, and drilling iron.	2830	2nd Nov. 1865	James Curtis.
An improved bit for boring mortices in wood or other material.	2857	6th Nov. 1865	William Tighe Hamilton.
Fire-arms and projectiles - - - (rifling barrels.)	2902	11th Nov. 1865	Charles William Jones.
Machinery for cutting or shearing sheet iron and other metallic sheets or plates - - -	2989	21st Nov. 1865	Richard Walters. Thomas Edwin Mans Walters.
Manufacture of beaters for threshing machines - (fluting or grooving.)	2992	21st Nov. 1865	William Gray. Edward Gray. John Gray.
A combined adjustable spanner, tube cutter and pipe wrench. (Communicated by Henry Hitchings Barnswworth and Martin Van Wisler.)	3026	27th Nov. 1865	John Phillips Bangermath.
Improved machinery for manufacturing sewing-machine needles (cutting and grooving wire.) (Partly communicated by Joseph Throw.)	3143	6th Dec. 1865	Nahum Salamon. William John Lawrence Davids.
An improved screwing and tapping machine -	3166	9th Dec. 1865	Emile Wattern.

Subject-matter of Patent.	Number of Patent.	Date.	Name of Patentee.
METALS (*Cutting*)—*continued.*			
Improvements in the furniture of door locks and latches, and in the means used in applying the same. (*apparatus for cutting holes.*)	3290	20th Dec. 1865	John Martin.
Improvements in the construction and manufacture of steel crossings for railways, and in the moulds for casting the same, all or part of which said improvements is moulds are applicable for casting other articles. (*casting punch blocks.*)	3333	23rd Dec. 1865	Francis William Webb.
Machinery for boring, turning and shaping articles of metal	3368	29th Dec. 1865	William Harrison. Thomas Walker.
V.—Plating and Coating Metallic Surfaces with Silver; Finishing and Ornamenting Metallic Surfaces.			
Improvements in shaping and forging metals, and in the machinery and apparatus employed therein (*planishing and finishing.*)	166	19th Jan. 1866	James Alfred Shipton. Robert Mitchell.
Treating products obtained when coating iron with zinc.	469	18th Feb. 1865	James Graham.
Rolls for connecting sheets of zinc and other metals employed for covering roofs and other enclosures.	669	9th March 1865	Rowland George Fisher.
Improvements in the strengthening and ornamenting of collapsible or soft metal tubes.	607	9th March 1866	Edmund Leahy.
Locks for safes, strong rooms and other purposes -	773	20th March 1865	Samuel Chatwood.
Manufacture of tin and terne plates	1081	14th April 1865	John Jones Jenkins.
Paints or compositions for coating and preserving metallic and other substances from oxidation and decay	1154	25th April 1865	John Nuttall Brown. Thomas Baykin Clare.
Improvements in finishing and polishing metal tubes and rods, and in apparatus or machinery to be employed therein.	1229	2nd May 1865	Thomas Allcock.
Certain improvements in the formation and construction of metallic vessels, chambers or hollow cylinders used in hydraulic apparatus, ramms or heavy guns, and for like purposes.	1505	1st June 1865	Herbert Allonea.
Improvements in the preparation of amalgams of quicksilver or mercury, and in the application of such amalgams to various purposes in the arts. (*coating iron surfaces.*) (*Communicated by Henry Werts.*)	1719	24th June 1865	William Edward Newton.
Improvements in the manufacture of certain kinds of metallic tubes and rods, and in ornamenting metallic tubes and rods.	1749	1st July 1865	James Atkins.
Apparatus employed in the manufacture of tin and terne plates	1843	12th July 1865	John Saunders. Joseph Piper.
Protecting crinoline steel, stay busks, springs for leggings or gaiters, and other similar fastenings.	1863	19th July 1865	William Edwards.

x

Subject-matter of Patent.	Number of Patent.	Date.	Name of Patentee.
METALS (*Plating*)—*continued.*			
Manufacture of pots and crucibles wherein metals and other materials may be heated or melted.	1894	19th July 1865	George Nimmo.
Improvements in the mode or method of preparing materials for, and in the manufacture of submarine telegraphic cables, the same being generally applicable for other purposes.	2025	4th Aug. 1865	Frederick George Mulholland.
Construction of submarine telegraph cables	2088	11th Aug. 1865	Henry Robert Gay.
Manufacturing wire conductors for electro-telegraphic purposes.	2416	22nd Sept. 1865	William Boggett.
An improved liquid composition for cleansing, scouring and bleaching textile animal, mineral and vegetable substances. (*cleansing metal.*)	2440	23rd Sept. 1865	{ Gustave Emile Rolland. Emile Léon Rolland.
Preparation of iron, steel and alloyed metals, for electro-plating.	2521	2nd Oct. 1865	Thomas Allan.
Coating iron and steel with gold, silver, platinum or copper.	2592	7th Oct. 1865	Jacob Baynes Thompson.
Improvements in the construction of steam generators, applicable also to the construction of condensers, the heating of water generally, and to the warming of buildings. (*Communicated by Joseph Harrison, junior, and Thomas Leders.*)	2610	10th Oct. 1865	John Henry Johnson.
Improvements in the construction and working of electric telegraphs, and in apparatus connected therewith, partly applicable to other purposes. (*electro-deposition of metals.*)	2763	26th Oct. 1865	Henry Wilde.
Plating or combining gold, platinum and other metals or their alloys.	2842	3rd Nov. 1865	Edward John Northwood.
Making amalgams or alloys of metals (*coating metals with fused metals.*) (*Communicated by Henry Wurts.*)	2905	11th Nov. 1865	William Edward Newton.
Improvements in the construction of and in the method of laying submarine electric cables. (*coating copper wire with gold.*)	2948	16th Nov. 1865	John De La Haye.
Improvements in steam-boilers and in the furnaces and grates thereof, the same improvements in furnaces and grates being also applicable to other furnaces and to stoves. (*covering and lining mixing chambers.*) (*Communicated by Robert Winslow Davis, Daniel Davis and Henry Sheldon Anable.*)	3141	6th Dec. 1865	William Edward Newton.
Construction of wire conductors for electro-telegraphic purposes.	3180	9th Dec. 1865	William Boggett.
Improvements in coating metals and in apparatus to be used for this purpose. (*and finishing.*)	3183	9th Dec. 1865	Edmund Morewood.
Improvements in apparatus for mixing materials, which is also applicable for smoothing, finishing, rounding or polishing articles of metal or other material.	3242	14th Dec. 1865	William Robinson.
A new process of lacquering and finishing metal goods, such as gas fittings, and other like articles usually finished by bronzing and lacquering.	3284	16th Dec. 1865	Joseph Harcourt.

Subject-matter of Patent.	Number of Patent.	Date.	Name of Patentee.
METALS (*Plating*)—*continued.*			
Preparation of glue or gelatine so as to render it insoluble in water, and applicable by the admixture of other substances to various purposes for which common glue or gelatine cannot now be used. (*a gold lacquer for imitation gilding.*) (*Communicated by Henry Wurtz.*)	3326	23rd Dec. 1865	William Edward Newton.
Improvements in breech-loading fire-arms, and in cartridges for the same. (*coating metallic cartridge cases with tin.*)	3348	27th Dec. 1865	William Castle Dodge.
METERS FOR GAS AND FLUIDS.			
Means or apparatus for measuring water or other liquids.	20	4th Jan. 1865	Walter Payton.
Apparatus for supplying regulated or measured quantities of water and other fluids.	707	13th March 1865	Robert Gordon Rattray.
Improvements in gas-meters and in the machinery or apparatus connected therewith.	917	31st March 1865	James Bashgate.
Wet gas-meters - - - - -	1072	17th April 1865	Thomas Newbigging. Alexander Hindle.
Improvements in means or apparatus for measuring the flow or pressure of liquids, which improvements are also applicable in obtaining motive-power.	1150	25th April 1865	Thomas Walker.
Apparatus for measuring spirits (*Communicated by John Hutchings Cox, John Murphy and William Murphy.*)	1272	8th May 1865	John Henry Johnson.
Wet gas-meters - - - - -	1296	10th May 1865	Edward Myers.
Dry gas-meters - - - - -	1370	14th May 1865	William Richard Williams.
Wet gas-meters - - - - -	1296	20th May 1865	William Smith. George Brown Smith.
Apparatus for measuring gas and other fluids (*Communicated by Jean Théodore Scholtz.*)	1450	27th May 1865	Richard Archibald Brooman.
A new or improved machine for obtaining motive-power and other useful purposes. (*a water meter.*)	1468	29th May 1865	Henry Moseley.
Dry gas-meters - - - - -	1548	6th June 1865	Henry Hermann Kromschroder. John Frederick Gustav Kromschroder.
Apparatus for measuring fluids (*Communicated by Jean Behrend.*)	1607	21st June 1865	Michael Henry.
Certain improvements in apparatus for measuring and indicating the flow of liquids.	1674	22nd June 1865	Edward Kenworthy Dutton.
Dry gas-meters - - - - -	1732	29th June 1865	George Lizars.
An improved portable chamber or receptacle to contain aërated liquids, and the apparatus connected therewith, by which the flow of such liquid is regulated and measured.	1923	24th July 1865	Max Benjamin Schumann.
Fluid meters - - - - -	1940	26th July 1865	Samuel Losty.

Subject-matter of Patent.	Number of Patent.	Date.	Name of Patentee.
METERS, &c.—continued.			
An improved water meter, which may be employed as a water, steam or gas engine. (Communicated by Henry Isham.)	1956	24th July 1865	William Edward Newton.
Apparatus applicable as a motive-power engine, a pump or fluid meter. (Communicated by Francis Bernard de Kerovenen.)	2021	4th Aug. 1865	William Clark.
Apparatus for regulating the passage or flow of steam, water and other fluids.	2043	7th Aug. 1865	Adrienne Anastasie Foubert.
Improvements in apparatus by means of which certain liquids, common air, and certain elastic fluids are made available in the production of light, and their quantity regulated and measured, parts of which improvements are applicable for other purposes.	2181	25th Aug. 1865	Edwin Augustus Curley.
An improved construction of spirit meter. (Communicated by Edward Payne.)	2183	26th Aug. 1865	John Pollock Hearsey.
Apparatus for supplying regulated or measured quantities of water.	2199	26th Aug. 1865	Robert Gordan Rattray.
Meters or apparatus for measuring water or other fluids, partly applicable for exhausting air or other gases.	2259	1st Sept. 1865	Charles Horsley.
Construction of gas-meters	2372	16th Sept. 1865	William Eason.
Gas-meters	2549	4th Oct. 1865	James Webster.
Arrangement and construction of wet gas-meters	2893	10th Nov. 1865	Edward Myers.
Improvements in means or apparatus for measuring the passage or flow of liquids, for raising and forcing fluids, and for obtaining motive-power, also in means for the manufacture of parts of such apparatus.	2968	17th Nov. 1865	Walter Payton.
Apparatus for the production of hydrocarbon or other vapours, parts of which apparatus are also applicable to measuring gaseous or fluid matter.	2973	18th Nov. 1865	Frederick Wilkins.

MINING; BORING AND BLASTING ROCK; RAISING COALS, &c. FROM MINES; DRAINING, LIGHTING AND VENTILATING MINES; SINKING WELLS.

Improvements in machinery used for condensing atmospheric air, and in machinery worked by compressed air, employed in getting coal, stone and minerals.	96	11th Jan. 1865	James Grafton Jones.
Improvements in the construction of shells, and in the explosive powder and fuse to be used therewith and for other purposes. (mining and blasting powder.)	136	16th Jan. 1865	John Berkeley Cotter.
Apparatus for relieving wire ropes from strain when used in lifting and lowering weights.	262	30th Jan. 1865	John Gibson.
Improvements in the miner's safety lamp	353	8th Feb. 1865	{ Richard Clarke Thorp. Philip Young.

Subject-matter of Patent.	Number of Patent.	Date.	Name of Patentee.
MINING, &c.—continued.			
Apparatus for giving alarms - - - - (in mines.)	892	11th Feb. 1865	Charles West.
Machinery for mining coal and other substances - (Communicated by William Watson Grier and Robert H. Boyd.)	558	24th Feb. 1865	George Leader.
An improved mode of and apparatus for ascertaining and indicating the presence of explosive gases.	668	9th March 1865	George Frederick Ansell.
Machinery and apparatus for mining or working } coal and other minerals - - - - }	787	16th March 1865	{ James Farrar. { Edwin Booth.
An improved safety tackle for raising and lowering heavy weights. (in mines.)	897	3rd April 1865	Pierre Joseph James.
Improvements in machinery or apparatus for drilling or boring rocks and other hard substances, in tunnelling, mining and other like operations, parts of which improvements are also applicable to the ventilating of the workings in mines and similar places. (Communicated by Herman Hampt.)	981	6th April 1865	John Henry Johnson.
Apparatus employed to actuate the valves of engines worked by steam, air or other fluid. (for getting coal.)	982	6th April 1865	James Grafton Jones.
Improvements in apparatus for raising water and other fluids, and in raising and lowering such apparatus.	1101	25th April 1865	Julian Bernard.
Improvements in boring or excavating and blasting rocks and minerals and in the treatment of the tools employed therein.	1102	25th April 1865	Julian Bernard.
Machinery or apparatus for working or cutting coal or minerals, and for compressing or exhausting air to be employed therein or for other purposes, some parts of which apparatus are also applicable to upright shafts, and other parts for regulating the flow or discharge of steam or other elastic fluids.	1203	25th April 1865	William Lambton.
Safety lamps - - - - - - - (Communicated by Ferdinand Serk.)	1274	5th May 1865	John Henry Johnson.
A new or improved spring apparatus to be applied } to the bearings of the axles of pulleys or drums } used in collieries - - - - - }	1848	16th May 1865	{ George Elliot. { Samuel Bailey Coxon.
An improved method of and machinery for cutting and excavating rock for railway tunnels and other purposes. (Communicated by Thales Lindsley.)	1847	12th June 1865	George Hamilton.
Gunpowder for mining and war purposes - - (Communicated by Gustav Adolph Neumayer.)	1636	17th June 1865	August Klein.
An improved fire-escape, applicable also to raising loads from mines and other purposes. (Communicated by Xavier Philippart.)	1689	21st June 1865	William Edward Gedge.
Improved machinery for boring rocks and hard substances.	1778	5th July 1865	George Low.
Means of obtaining or producing oxygen applicable to various useful purposes. (for purifying air in mines.)	1780	6th July 1865	Hermann Beigel.

Subject-matter of Patent.	Number of Patent.	Date.	Name of Patentee.
MINING, &c.—continued.			
Improvements in the raising, lifting or drawing and forcing of water and other liquids, and in the apparatus and means employed therefor (from mines, quarries, &c.)	1998	2nd Aug. 1865	{ James M'Ewan. William Neilson.
Well sinking tubes - - - (Communicated by Hiram John Messenger, Stephen Brewer and Byron Mudge.)	2178	24th Aug. 1865	William Edward Newton.
Preparing charges for fire-arms and for blasting -	2289	2nd Sept. 1863	Constant Reichen.
Improved machinery for cutting stone - (Communicated by George Jeffords Wardwell.)	2362	15th Sept. 1865	Alfred Vincent Newton.
Safety lamps for use in mines and other localities - (Communicated by André Jean Olivier.)	2370	16th Sept. 1865	Henri Adrien Bonneville.
Safety apparatus for cages and hoists - -	2363	19th Sept. 1865	John Charlton Broadbent.
Construction of skips for raising ballast, ores, coal, minerals and other matters in bulk.	2663	16th Oct. 1865	Charles Henry Murray.
Improvements in tools and apparatus employed in blasting, boring and cutting rock, stone and other hard substances, and in the means employed for making such tools.	2774	27th Oct. 1865	Julian Bernard.
Construction of mining picks - - (Communicated by The Incorporated Washer Tool Company.)	2798	30th Oct. 1865	William Edward Newton.
Improved machinery for cutting tunnels and sinking shafts - - - - }	2940	15th Nov. 1865	{ Alexander Allison. Henry Hoskings.
Construction of pumps for raising water and other liquids. (for collieries.)	2946	15th Nov. 1865	William Easton.
Lamps for burning petroleum, paraffin and other hydrocarbon liquids, without a glass chimney, in the roofs of railway carriages and other like places and positions.	3070	30th Nov. 1865	James Turner Hall.
Improvements in sinking and operating wells, and in the apparatus employed therein. (Communicated by James Suggett.)	3074	30th Nov. 1865	John Henry Johnson.
Machinery employed when getting coal and other minerals.	3127	4th Dec. 1865	George Edmund Donisthorpe.
An improved mode of applying the compression of air for ventilating purpose, and the compression of any gas for hurrying along elastic fluids in conveying pipes - - (ventilating mining galleries.)	3153	6th Dec. 1865	{ Flavron de Mondésir. Paul Lebaitre. Augustin Jullienne.
An improved apparatus for signalling between passengers, guards and engine drivers of railway trains, which said apparatus is applicable also for other purposes - - (for collieries.)	3176	9th Dec. 1865	{ Robert Fishup. John Hauld.
An improved blasting powder - (Communicated by Bernhard August Schäffer and Christian Friedrich Budenberg.)	3206	12th Dec. 1865	Arnold Badenberg.
Machinery for boring rock and other mineral (Communicated by Carl Sachs.)	3212	13th Dec. 1865	Frederick Bernard Dering.
Construction of fire-places and furnaces - (for mines.)	3247	15th Dec. 1865	George Warriner.

Subject-matter of Patent.	Number of Patent.	Date.	Name of Patentee.
MINING, &c.—continued.			
An improved mode of and apparatus for purifying and deodorising impure air, whether in buildings, ships, mines or sewers, which improvement is also applicable for ventilating purposes	3287	20th Dec. 1865	{ Joseph John Harrison. Edward Harrison.
Machinery for cutting or getting slate, stone, coal and other substances	3297	20th Dec. 1865	{ William Fothergill Cooke. George Hunter.
Pumps (for mining purposes.)	6230	23rd Dec. 1865	{ Henry Davis Honhold. William Blazeb Brelo.
MIXING, MASHING, STIRRING, AGITATING.			
Improvements in washing machines and in apparatus connected therewith.	421	21st Feb. 1865	Robert Williman.
Improvements in refining sugar and in apparatus employed therein. (Communicated by Alfred Guillou.)	598	3rd March 1865	Richard Archibald Brooman.
Preparation of turpentine and varnishes	670	10th March 1865	{ Joseph Freeman. Edward Grace Freeman. Charles Henry Freeman.
Manufacture of yarn so as to render same applicable as a substitute for woollen yarn, for manufacturing into shawls and other textile fabrics.	774	20th March 1865	Isidor Philippothal.
Manufacture of puddled iron bars and every description of malleable iron	777	27th March 1865	{ Robert Thompson Crawshay. Isaac Arintzen Lewis.
Apparatus for obtaining light	841	24th March 1865	Giacomo Felice Macchisio.
Improvements in the method of mixing gases and vapour, and in the machinery or apparatus connected therewith.	997	7th April 1865	William Jackson.
An improved metallic preparation or composition for cleaning, sharpening, burnishing and grinding articles of cutlery, edge tools or cutting instruments, and for grinding the cards or rollers of carding-engines and the surfaces of cylinders, and covering rollers for various kinds of woollen and cotton machinery.	1054	13th April 1865	George Mountford.
Machinery or apparatus employed in breweries and distilleries.	1204	29th April 1865	Francis Gregory.
Improvements in brewing, distillation, the production of vinegar, and the extract of malt and other grain.	1283	5th May 1865	Solomon Banturti.
An improved method of mixing gases and vapour, and in the machinery or apparatus connected therewith.	1287	5th May 1865	William Jackson.
Improvements in the manufacture of soap and in apparatus employed therein. (agitating ingredients for making soap.) (Communicated by Jacob Beers Bennett and James Sidney Gibbs.)	1540	5th June 1865	Richard Archibald Brooman.
Preparing and treating gunpowder	1679	22nd June 1865	James Gale, jun'.

Subject-matter of Patent.	Number of Patent.	Date.	Name of Patentee.
MINING, &c. — *continued.*			
An improved machine for the manufacture of aerated waters.	1774	5th July 1865	William Saunders Perfitt.
Manufacture of iron - - - - (*Communicated by John Williams and Josiah Copley.*)	1798	7th July 1865	James Marius Marcus.
Compositions similar to gunpowder, for blasting, for use in ordnance and fire-arms, and for other purposes. (*Communicated by Pedro Nixon.*)	1939	25th July 1865	Edward Spicer.
Improvements in drying grass, hay and other substances, and in the machinery for effecting the same - - - - - (*and shaking or stirring up.*)	1962	29th July 1865	{ Baldwin Latham. Robert Campbell.
Treatment of hydrocarbons or paraffin oils - -	2006	3rd Aug. 1865	John William Perkins.
Improvements in the manufacture of steel iron and metal suitable for bearings, and in apparatus for the same.	2175	24th Aug. 1865	William Colburne Cambridge.
Improved machinery for mixing or grinding ointment, paints, drugs and other substances.	2290	6th Sept. 1865	Thomas Charles Gibson.
Improvements in the machinery or apparatus and in the processes for the treatment and manufacture of sugar.	2388	19th Sept. 1865	John Fletcher.
Process of and machinery for preparing flax, hemp, jute, china grass and other analogous vegetable fibres for spinning. (*cutting and mixing.*)	2728	21st Oct. 1865	James Hill Dickson.
Improved machinery to be used in the manufacture of paper. (*Communicated by Heinrich Voelter.*)	3041	27th Nov. 1865	William Edward Newton.
Improvements in the treatment of grain and in the process of malting, and in the apparatus employed therein. (*agitating or stirring.*)	3057	1st Dec. 1865	William Rowland Taylor.
Dyeing, printing and other operations based on chemical reactions. (*mixing colours.*) (*Communicated by Mathias Paraf-Javal.*)	3110	4th Dec. 1865	Richard Archibald Brooman.
Improvements in steam-boilers and in the furnaces and grates thereof, the same improvements in furnaces and grates being also applicable to other furnaces and to stoves. (*gas mixing chambers.*) (*Communicated by Robert Winslow Davis, Daniel Harris and Henry Sheldon Ausdio.*)	3141	9th Dec. 1865	William Edward Newton.
Improvements in preparing compounds of xyloidine or gun cotton, and in the apparatus employed.	3162	8th Dec. 1865	Alexander Parkes.
Improvements in apparatus for mixing materials, which is also applicable for smoothing, finishing, rounding or polishing articles of metal or other materials.	3243	14th Dec. 1865	William Robinson.
An improved method of and apparatus for preserving, purifying, mixing, separating, cooling, aërating, roasting and otherwise treating grain, ores and various other matters.	3244	27th Dec. 1865	Gaston Charles Ange Marquis D'Ausy.

Subject-matter of Patent.	Number of Patent.	Date.	Name of Patentee.
MOTIVE-POWER MACHINES ; OBTAINING MOTIVE-POWER.			
1.—Air, Gas and Wind Engines and Elastic Pneumatic Motive power.			
Motive-power and means of communication between passengers while travelling, and appliances connected therewith.	55	7th Jan. 1865	George Bell Galloway.
Regulating and working the valves of steam and other engines.	52	11th Jan. 1865	John Frederick Spencer.
Steam-engines ... (or gas-engines.)	166	19th Jan. 1865	William Cleveland Hinks.
Obtaining motive-power ...	331	6th Feb. 1865	John Isaac Watts.
Beam engines ...	442	14th Feb. 1865	James Grafton Jones.
Obtaining motive-power from uniform fluids and from liquids.	501	22nd Feb. 1865	Matthew Piers Watt Boulton.
Machinery for obtaining motive-power from ammoniacal gas. (*Communicated by Joseph Flandrin.*)	611	4th March 1865	Richard Archibald Brooman.
Motive-power engines ... (*Communicated by Auguste Gerin.*)	651	8th March 1865	William Clark.
Gas engines ...	731	15th March 1865	Hugh Smith.
An elementary power engine or a new or improved compressed air engine, for imparting power and motion to all kinds of machinery.	628	23rd March 1865	Anthony Bernhard Baron Von Rathen.
Obtaining motive-power from uniform fluids and from liquids.	827	23rd March 1865	Matthew Piers Watt Boulton.
Improvements in obtaining motive-power, parts of which improvements are applicable to the compressing of air and gases.	840	24th March 1865	Valentine Baker.
An improvement in engines worked by heated air or gases.	805	31st March 1865	John Pinchbeck.
Navigable balloons ...	830	1st April 1865	Paul Haenlein.
Means or apparatus for obtaining motive-power by the aid of steam, gas or other fluids. (*Communicated by Joseph Perrigault, Marie Joseph Denis Forest, Jean Joseph Leon Forest, Michel Basile Abel Forest, Joseph Etienne Eloi Chilters and Emmanuel Denis Forest.*)	940	4th April 1865	William Brookes.
Apparatus employed to actuate the valves of engines worked by steam, air or other fluid.	992	6th April 1865	James Grafton Jones.
Certain improvements in gas engines ...	996	6th April 1865	Pierre Hugon.
Certain improvements in gas-ammoniacal engines	1074	17th April 1865	Louis De St. Céran.
Machinery for obtaining motive-power ...	1301	10th May 1865	William Joseph Rice.
An improved metallic stuffing box ...	1555	7th June 1865	Victor Dotresse.
Caloric or heated air engines ... (*Communicated by Cyrus W. Baldwin and Walter Davis Richards.*)	1583	9th June 1865	Samuel Blatchford Tucker.
Means and apparatus for generating motive-power - (*Communicated by Jules Gros.*)	1664	20th June 1865	William Clark.
Obtaining motive-power ... (*Communicated by Monsieur Charles Tellier.*)	1822	11th July 1865	Hector Auguste Dufrend.
Certain improvements in the method of obtaining motive-power and in apparatus connected therewith.	1910	22nd July 1865	Edmund Perré.

Subject-matter of Patent.	Number of Patent.	Date.	Name of Patentee.
MOTIVE-POWER, &c.—continued.			
Obtaining motive-power when heated air or æriform fluid is employed.	1815	22nd July 1865	Matthew Piers Watt Boulton.
Means of and apparatus for treating animal and vegetable fibrous materials, which apparatus is also applicable to various useful purposes. (years for gas-engines.)	1952	27th July 1866	Henry Sherwood.
An improved water meter, which may be employed as a water, steam or gas engine. (Communicated by Henry Liston.)	1958	28th July 1865	William Edward Newton.
Applying and utilising water power (for working air-engines.)	1987	29th July 1865	Valentine Baker.
Obtaining motive-power by heat	1972	1st Aug. 1865	Matthew Piers Watt Boulton.
Improvements in generating steam and in heating steam and æriform fluids.	2061	7th Aug. 1865	Matthew Piers Watt Boulton.
Apparatus for obtaining and applying motive-power to various useful purposes	2080	11th Aug. 1865	William Thomas Cole. Henry Spick Swift. Auguste Soares.
Improved machinery or apparatus for obtaining motive-power by expansion of air. (Communicated by Abraham Désiré Chergis.)	2800	9th Oct. 1865	William Edward Gedge.
Caloric or hot air engines (Communicated by Guillaume Revелин.)	2675	17th Oct. 1865	Richard Archibald Brooman.
New or improved means and apparatus for destroying ships and such like floating bodies, parts of which said apparatus are also applicable to saving life and property at sea. (gas-engine.) (Communicated by Monsieur Stanislas Sorel.)	2758	26th Oct. 1865	Hector Auguste Dufresni.
Improvements in obtaining motive-power and in apparatus employed therein.	3016	24th Nov, 1865	Jules Wanthier.
Producing and applying rotating motion by means of an apparatus to be worked by fluids, steam, compressed air, or by water or by gas.	3278	19th Dec. 1865	John Wright Carr.
Improvements in propellers for ships and vessels, parts of which are applicable to windmill sails and fan blowers	3295	20th Dec. 1865	Frederick Lamb Hancock. Charles Lamb Hancock.
Obtaining and employing continuous lengths of tanned leather for various useful purposes (for making mill sails.)	3334	23rd Dec. 1865	George Harn. Daniel Horn.
Improvements in obtaining motive-power, and in apparatus employed therein. (from ammonia.) (Communicated by Jean Frat.)	3359	24th Dec. 1865	Richard Archibald Brooman.

See also "GOVERNORS."

IX.—Steam-Engines.

(Stationary, Locomotive and Marine.)

Improvements in the manufacture of elastic packings for pistons, and in lubricating compositions therefor.	19	4th Jan. 1865	Edward Kirby.
Improvements in locomotive engines and in the springs of railway carriages.	86	5th Jan. 1865	James Edward Wilson.

Subject-matter of Patent.	Number of Patent.	Date.	Name of Patentee.
MOTIVE-POWER, &c.—continued.			
Locomotive engines (Communicated by Auguste De Bergue.)	45	6th Jan. 1865	Charles De Bergue.
Regulating and working the valves of steam and other engines.	62	11th Jan. 1865	John Frederick Spencer.
Steam-engines (Communicated by Philibert Vair.)	111	13th Jan. 1865	William Bowles.
Apparatus for transmitting and converting reciprocating motion into rotary motion, applicable to various useful purposes. (locomotive engines.)	145	17th Jan. 1865	William John Cunningham.
Improvements in the packings of pistons and piston rods of pumps and steam and other engines, which improvements are also applicable to hydraulic presses.	155	18th Jan. 1865	William Robert Fowler.
Improved arrangements for coupling steam-engines, turbines or other apparatus employed as motive-power. (Communicated by Ludwig August Riedinger.)	159	19th Jan. 1865	Adolf Wilhelm Prager.
Steam-engines	166	19th Jan. 1865	William Cleveland Hicks.
Locomotive and other steam-engines	167	19th Jan. 1865	Thomas Charles Durham.
Steam-engines	163	21st Jan. 1865	Thomas Lester.
Improved apparatus for adjusting the weight of railway carriages and engines. (Communicated by Johann Heinrich Ehrhardt.)	216	25th Jan. 1865	Otto Gossell.
Construction of steam-engines (Communicated by Pierre Jean Lacoste.)	260	30th Jan. 1865	George Davies.
The application of hydro-electricity to steam for the purpose of increasing its expansion and power, and the machinery or apparatus connected therewith, and also the application of galvanic or frictional electricity for the same purposes	273	31st Jan. 1865	{ Joseph Fletcher. { Daniel Hamer.
An improved construction of lubricating apparatus for steam-engine purposes	274	31st Jan. 1865	{ Ewing Pye Colquhoun. { John Pardoe Perris.
Steam-engines	336	7th Feb. 1865	Charles Langley.
Expansion gear for steam-engines	415	14th Feb. 1865	William Fothergill Batho.
Beam engines	469	18th Feb. 1865	James Grafton Jones.
Steam-engines	485	21st Feb. 1865	John Russell Swann.
A new and improved balanced slide valve (Communicated by James Renkin.)	496	22nd Feb. 1865	William Edward Newton.
Steam-engines applicable to ploughing and other agricultural purposes.	522	24th Feb. 1865	James Howard.
Marine steam-engines	643	8th March 1865	John Dean.
Motive-power engines (Communicated by Auguste Givric.)	681	8th March 1865	William Clark.
Increasing the mechanical value of steam as a motive agent. (Communicated by Thomas Embrel.)	748	17th March 1865	Benjamin Lawrence.
Improved combinations of direct acting steam-engines with single or double acting pumps, for pumping water, air or gases.	751	17th March 1865	Jacob Goodfellow.
Locomotive engines and carriages for common roads and tramways, and also for agricultural and other purposes.	780	20th March 1865	Alexander Richard Mackenzie.

Subject-matter of Patent.	Number of Patent.	Date.	Name of Patentee.
MOTIVE-POWER, &c.—*continued.*			
Double cylinder steam-engines - - -	880	27th March 1865	Joshua Rooks.
Traction engines - - - - -	882	27th March 1865	{ John Bruckshaw. { William Scott Underhill.
Improvements in the construction of locomotive engines and railway carriages, for facilitating their passage round curves - - (*Communicated by George John Horner.*)	916	31st March 1865	{ George Robert Stephenson. { George Henry Phipps.
Improvements in paddle wheels, parts of which are applicable to other purposes. (*to steam-engines.*)	935	3rd April 1865	William Cantrill Gollings.
Means or apparatus for obtaining motive-power by the aid of steam, gas or other fluids. (*Communicated by Joseph Perrigault, Marie Joseph Denis Ferrot, Jean Joseph Leon Ferrot, Michel Basile Abel Ferrot, Joseph Etienne Elei Cildren and Emmanuel Denis Ferrot.*)	949	4th April 1865	William Brookes.
Improvements in steam and atmospheric hammers and presses, which improvements are also applicable to steam-engines.	953	4th April 1865	Joseph Vaughan.
Traction engines - - - - -	982	5th April 1865	John Guy Newton Alleyne.
Apparatus employed to actuate the valves of engines worked by steam, air or other fluid.	982	6th April 1865	James Grafton Jones.
An improved application of steam power to locomotion on ordinary roads. (*Communicated by Alfred Taillendron.*)	1002	8th April 1865	William Edward Gedge.
Improvements in steam-engines, relating to valve motions, governor and drain pipes - -	1195	29th April 1865	{ Andrew Wyllie. { John M'Farlane Gray.
Marine steam-engines - - - - -	1212	1st May 1865	Daniel Rankin.
Improvements in steam generators and engines, and in apparatus for feeding steam generators. (*Communicated by George Briley Brayton.*)	1240	3rd May 1865	John Henry Johnson.
Improvements in or applicable to marine condensing steam-engines.	1255	4th May 1865	Thomas Ward.
Steam-engines - - - - - (*Communicated by Ebenezer Dayford.*)	1284	6th May 1865	William Edward Newton.
Mode of and apparatus for obtaining and applying motive-power - - - - -	1303	10th May 1865	{ Stanislas Polutynski. { Michel Mycielski.
Means and apparatus for effecting traction on railways and roads where traction is used - -	1328	12th May 1865	{ Richard Edward Donovan. { Daniel O'Brien.
Locomotive engines - - - - -	1359	16th May 1865	Walter Montgomerie.
A new system of rotative machines to be used as steam-engines and water pumps.	1447	20th May 1865	Jean Alphonse Heinrich.
A new or improved machine for obtaining motive-power and other useful purposes.	1468	29th May 1865	Henry Mowbry.
Certain improvements in steam hammers, partly applicable to steam-engines.	1491	31st May 1865	Peter Pilkington.
Improvements in machinery or apparatus for actuating the slide-valves of marine engines, and in the slide-valves thereof.	1555	5th June 1865	John Robertson.
An improved break applicable to various descriptions of steam-engines and also to railway purposes. (*Communicated by Eugene Dutheil.*)	1559	5th June 1865	Frederick Tolhausen.

Subject-matter of Patent.	Number of Patent.	Date.	Name of Patentee.
MOTIVE-POWER, &c.—continued.			
An improved metallic stuffing box . . .	1566	7th June 1865	Victor Duterne.
Improvements in safety valves, which improvements are also applicable to steam-engine and other valves	1578	9th June 1865	Charles Vernon. William Hodgkins.
Improvements in the permanent way of railways and in locomotives applicable thereto.	1583	13th June 1865	William James Hixon.
Locomotive engines and railway carriages . .	1646	19th June 1865	George Ruith the younger.
Improvements in surface condensers for steam-engines, and in feeding boilers therefrom.	1669	21st June 1865	Charles Talbot Porter.
Surface condensers . . . . . (Communicated by Alban Crawler Stimers.)	1677	22nd June 1865	William Edward Newton.
Improvements in steam-boilers, furnaces, and engines, and in parts connected therewith.	1746	30th June 1865	Edwin Elliott.
Locomotive engines . . . . . (Communicated by Auguste De Bergue.)	1764	3rd July 1865	Charles De Bergue.
Steam pumping machines or engines . .	1780	3rd July 1865	Martin Benson.
Improvements in locomotive engines and in springs of railway carriages.	1789	4th July 1865	James Edwards Wilson.
Means and apparatus for increasing the mechanical power of steam.	1830	10th July 1865	William Alexander Lyttle.
Improvements in steam carriages and in adapting wheels for common roads to railways. (Communicated by Joseph Alphonse Loubat.)	1831	10th July 1865	Richard Archibald Brooman.
Obtaining motive-power . . . . (Communicated by Monsieur Charles Triller.)	1838	11th July 1865	Hector Auguste Duftené.
Steam and water valves	1834	11th July 1865	Nathaniel Jenkins.
Traction engines . . . . . (Communicated by Alexander Kwat Richards.)	1838	11th July 1865	Morris Horsey Keene.
Slide valves	1883	20th July 1865	Richard Clark Bristol.
Condensing apparatus for steam-engines .	1897	20th July 1865	Morgan Lawrence Parry.
Construction of valves for steam and other engines (Communicated by Thomas Shrimton Davis.)	1913	22nd July 1865	William Edward Newton.
Conical plug steam-valves . . . . (Communicated by John Wesley Carhart.)	1956	28th July 1865	William Edward Newton.
An improved water motor, which may be employed as a water, steam or gas engine. (Communicated by Henry Isham.)	1958	28th July 1865	William Edward Newton.
Obtaining motive-power by heat . . .	1993	1st Aug. 1865	Matthew Piers Watt Boulton.
Improvements in and apparatus for treating peat in bogs and obtaining it therefrom, also applicable to tilling and cultivating land.	2004	2nd Aug. 1865	Charles Hodgson.
Apparatus applicable as a motive-power engine, a pump or fluid meter. (Communicated by Francis Bernard de Kerarenn.)	2021	4th Aug. 1865	William Clark.
Construction of steam-engines . . .	2062	9th Aug. 1865	Henry Cartwright.
An improved mode of relieving slide-valves of back pressure.	2068	9th Aug. 1865	James William Longs-off.
Apparatus for obtaining and applying motive-power to various useful purposes . .	2080	11th Aug. 1865	William Thomas Cole. Henry Spink Swift. Augusto Soares.

Subject-matter of Patent.	Number of Patent.	Date.	Name of Patentee.
MOTIVE-POWER, &c.—*continued.*			
Steam-engines - - - - - (Communicated by Giovanni Batista Venturi.)	2130	16th Aug. 1865	James Stevenson.
Certain improvements in rotatory engines - -	2202	28th Aug. 1865	William Graham. John Broughton. Thomas Corkhill.
Traction engines and other vehicles - - -	2234	3rd Aug. 1865	Samuel Lawrence James.
Certain improvements in steam-engines and valves (Communicated by George Ichabod Washburn.)	2306	6th Sept. 1865	William Clark.
A new method of and apparatus for condensing the steam of steam-engines - - -	2376	13th Sept. 1865	Francesco Daina.
Improvements in locomotive engines, parts of which improvements are also applicable to railway carriages.	2379	14th Sept. 1865	Russel Aitken.
Apparatus for lubricating machinery - - (steam-engines.) (Communicated by Joseph Bonillon.)	2429	23rd Sept. 1865	Henri Adrien Bonneville.
An improved construction of engine which can be used either as a motor or for pumping. (Communicated by John Benjamin Root and William Benjamin.)	2453	25th Sept. 1865	William Edward Newton.
Tools for securing tubes in tube plates, and for other purposes where concentrated power or adjustment is necessary. (for tightening piston packing rings.)	2455	26th Sept. 1865	Richard Taylor Nelson Howey.
Steam-engines - - - - -	2470	27th Sept. 1865	John Roger Arnoldi.
Compositions used for coating metallic surfaces - (steam cylinders.)	2480	27th Sept. 1865	John Boffey. Charles William Smith.
Steam-engines - - - - - (Communicated by Nicolas Chenot and Pierre Jean Lacaze.)	2502	29th Sept. 1865	William Edward Gedge.
Improvements in the propelling and steering of steam ships or other vessels, and in the machinery or apparatus employed therefor. - -	2543	5th Oct. 1865	Robert William Fraser.
Rotary engines and pumps - - - (Communicated by Noble Chatelain.)	2547	6th Oct. 1865	Richard Archibald Brooman.
Construction of compound cylinder engines - (Communicated by Matthew Murray Jackson.)	2557	7th Oct. 1865	John Howard.
Railway carriages and locomotives - - (Communicated by Henry Gifford.)	2621	11th Oct. 1865	Michael Henry.
Improvements in and applicable to slide-valves, pistons and glands - - - -	2700	19th Oct. 1865	Thomas Adams. George John Parson.
Steam-engines - - - - -	2759	26th Oct. 1865	Edmund Hunt.
Certain improvements in mechanism or apparatus to be employed for lubricating the cylinders of steam-engines, or other similar frictional surfaces - - - - - -	2891	8th Nov. 1865	Neville Beard. John Maiden.
Railway steam-engines and carriages - -	2926	14th Nov. 1865	Joseph Alphonse Loubat.
A new or improved steam wheel and apparatus connected therewith. (Communicated by Jean Gabriel Alphonse Appel.)	3057	27th Nov. 1865	William Edward Gedge.
A new or improved method of preventing the escape of heat from steam cylinders - -	3051	24th Nov. 1865	William Simons. Andrew Brown.
Improvements in locomotive engines and in the means employed for generating steam therein	3128	9th Dec. 1865	Robert Francis Fairlie.
Steam-engines - - - - -	3213	13th Dec. 1865	Joseph Stocker.

Subject-matter of Patent.	Number of Patent.	Date.	Name of Patentee.
MOTIVE-POWER, &c.—continued.			
An improved construction of rotary engine	3225	13th Dec. 1865	Peter Gardner.
Machinery or apparatus for cultivating land by steam power.	3228	13th Dec. 1865	Pryce William Bowen.
Locomotive engines	3269	16th Dec. 1865	James Atkinson Longridge.
Producing and applying rotating motion by means of an apparatus to be worked by fluids, steam, compressed air, or by water or by gas.	3373	19th Dec. 1865	John Wright Carr.
Pistons (Communicated by David Lister.)	3379	19th Dec. 1865	John Henry Johnson.
Steam engines (Communicated by George Brader Whiting and Thomas Fitch Rowland.)	3308	22nd Dec. 1865	William Clark.
Duplex steam-engines	3350	27th Dec. 1865	Norman Willis Wheeler.
Steam-engines	3380	30th Dec. 1865	Richard Reck.

See also "GAUGES."
See also "GOVERNORS."

XXI.—Waterwheels and Engines; Hydraulic Motive-power.

Motive-power and means of communication between passengers while travelling, and appliances connected therewith.	65	7th Jan. 1865	George Bell Galloway.
Improved arrangements for coupling steam-engines, turbines or other apparatus employed as motive-power. (Communicated by Ludwig August Birkinger.)	150	19th Jan. 1865	Adolf Wilhelm Proger.
Steam-engines (or water-engines.)	168	19th Jan. 1865	William Cleveland Hicks.
Beam engines	449	16th Feb. 1865	James Grafton Jones.
An improved mercury-hydraulic motor (Communicated by Pierre Eugene Lourier.)	472	22nd Feb. 1865	Richard Archibald Brouman.
Obtaining motive-power from uniform fluids and from liquids.	501	22nd Feb. 1865	Matthew Piers Watt Boulton.
An improved arrangement of valves and other appliances for a new description of hydraulic engine for raising water and other fluids above their common level, the fluids so raised to be used as a motive-power	791	21st March 1865	{James Smith. Sydney Arthur Cheese.}
Obtaining motive-power	609	22nd March 1865	Valentine Baker.
Improvements in obtaining motive-power, parts of which improvements are applicable to the compressing of air and gases.	640	24th March 1865	Valentine Baker.
Improvements in paddle wheels, parts of which are applicable to other purposes. (to water-engines.)	835	3rd April 1865	William Cantrill Golling.
Means or apparatus for obtaining motive-power by the aid of steam, gas or other fluids. (Communicated by Joseph Perrigault, Marie Joseph Denis Forcet, Jean Joseph Leon Forcet, Michel Basile Abel Forcet, Joseph Etienne Eloi Chateau and Emmanuel Denis Forcet.)	849	4th April 1865	William Brookes.
A new motive-power engine	1059	19th April 1865	Herman Lamhardt.

Subject-matter of Patent.	Number of Patent.	Date.	Names of Patentees.
MOTIVE-POWER, &c.—*continued.*			
A new method of obtaining and applying water as a motive-power for propelling ships, boats and other vessels.	1058	13th April 1865	George Rommel.
Improvements in means or apparatus for measuring the flow or passage of liquids, which improvements are also applicable in obtaining motive-power.	1150	25th April 1865	Thomas Walker.
Improved means or apparatus for gaining or acquiring motive-power.	1156	25th April 1865	Claude Jacquelin, jun'.
Certain improvements in waterwheels (Communicated by Eugène Romerstin.)	1189	29th April 1865	Arthur Charles Henderson.
A new or improved method of obtaining motive-power, together with certain machinery or apparatus for applying the same	1504	1st June 1865	David Hancock. Frederick Barton.
Machinery for obtaining power when fluid pressure is employed.	1576	9th June 1865	Lieutenant Colonel James Baker.
Hydraulic motive-power machinery	1642	17th June 1865	Valentine Baker.
An improved hydraulic apparatus for producing motive-power.	1701	26th June 1865	Jome Egide Spanoghe.
Construction or arrangement of sluices or dams	1870	19th July 1865	Timothy Ward Wood.
Certain improvements in the method of obtaining motive-power and in apparatus connected therewith.	1910	22nd July 1865	Edmund Ferré.
Means of and apparatus for raising water for agricultural and other useful and ornamental purposes. (Communicated by Jean Louis Célestin Achard.)	1919	22nd July 1865	William Edward Gedge.
An improved water meter, which may be employed as a water, steam or gas engine. (Communicated by Henry Isham.)	1959	24th July 1865	William Edward Newton.
Applying and utilising water power	1987	29th July 1865	Valentine Baker.
Means of and mechanism for obtaining motive-power.	2030	4th Aug. 1865	Adderley Sleigh.
Apparatus for obtaining motive-power	2425	22nd Sept. 1865	George Binnie McNicol.
Hydraulic pressure engines	2445	23rd Sept. 1865	Jacob Dreissorner.
A new method of obtaining and applying water as a motive-power, for propelling ships by means of paddle wheels, inside and outside.	2641	13th Oct. 1865	George Rommes.
Improvements in means or apparatus for measuring the passage or flow of liquids, for raising and forcing fluids, and for obtaining motive-power, also in means for the manufacture of parts of such apparatus.	2949	17th Nov. 1865	Walter Payton.
Turbines for obtaining motive-power, applicable also to raising and forcing fluids, and to propelling ships or vessels. (Communicated by Joseph Denis Ferrot, Jean Joseph Léon Ferrot, Michel Basile Abel Ferrot, Joseph Etienne Eloi Chatron and Emmanuel Denis Ferrot.)	3222	13th Dec. 1865	William Brookes.
Producing and applying rotating motion by means of an apparatus to be worked by fluids, steam, compressed air, or by water or by gas.	3272	19th Dec. 1865	John Wright Carr.

Subject-matter of Patent.	Number of Patent.	Date.	Name of Patentee.
MOTIVE-POWER, &c.—continued.			
A new or improved method of and apparatus or machinery for applying water or other fluid as a motive-power - - - - - -	3323	23rd Dec. 1865	{ Edmund Dwyer. Henry Nooe.
See also "GOVERNORS."			
IV.—Electro-Magnetic Engines ; Electro Motive-power.			
Motive-power and means of communication between passengers while travelling, and appliances connected therewith.	55	7th Jan. 1865	George Bell Galloway.
The application of hydro-electricity to steam for the purpose of increasing its expansion and power, and the machinery or apparatus connected therewith, and also the application of galvano or frictional electricity for the same purpose - - - - -	273	31st Jan. 1865	{ Joseph Fletcher. Daniel Harmer.
The improved use of magnets in overbalancing weights.	461	18th Feb. 1865	Thomas Philip Tregaskis.
Electro-magnetic engines - - - -	1012	8th April 1865	Sigmund Moore.
Rotary magneto-electric machines - - (Communicated by Mr. Henry Brandon.)	1868	19th May 1865	Thomas Fanshaw.
Obtaining motive-power by heat - - (producing electro motive-power.)	1992	1st Aug. 1865	Matthew Piers Watt Boulton.
Obtaining motive-power applicable to various useful purposes. (by magnetism.)	3250	16th Dec. 1865	Cecil Loftus Wellesley Reade.
Electro-magnetic engines - - - - (Communicated by Laban Clarke Stuart.)	3262	19th Dec. 1865	Alfred Vincent Newton.
V.—Mechanical Motive-power, Horse-power.			
A new method for removing or destroying the momentum of heavy bodies by means of an elastic machine or machinery, so as to prevent injury and damage from concussion, applicable to ship cabins, ship and fort armour, railway trains, tenders to perihends, and floating piers, gangways, breakwaters and other similar structures, also as a motive-power. (Communicated by William Graham M'Iver.)	331	6th Feb. 1865	Clemerus Roberts Markham.
An improved mercuro-hydraulic motor - (Communicated by Pierre Eugene Lourier.)	499	22nd Feb. 1865	Richard Archibald Brooman.
Improvements in motive-power machinery for cultivating land, part of which improvements is applicable to driving machinery generally -	1154	22nd April 1865	{ James Howard. Edward Tenney Bousfield.
Motive-power by capillary attraction -	1874	19th July 1865	Johann Ernst Friedrich Lüdeke.
A new self-generating continuous motive-power -	1973	31st July 1865	John James Stoll.
Machinery for deriving motive-power from the application of the force of gravitation alone, without the aid of steam, water, wind, compressed air, or any other similar means.	3048	24th Nov. 1865	Robert Martin Roberts.

Subject-matter of Patent.	Number of Patent.	Date.	Name of Patentee.
MOTIVE-POWER, &c.—continued.			
Obtaining motive-power applicable to various useful purposes. (by percussion.)	3280	16th Dec. 1865	Cecil Loftus Wellesley Reade.
MOULDINGS AND ARCHITECTURAL ORNAMENTS.			
Machinery or apparatus for planing and moulding or otherwise shaping wood - - -	143	17th Jan. 1865	John Robinson. John Smith.
Machinery or apparatus for cutting scrolls, frets and figure work.	926	1st April 1865	James Keenan.
Staining and graining woods - - - (transferring designs for ornamental scrolls.)	1851	14th July 1865	John Marrough Murphy. James Marrough Murphy.
Certain improvements in window fittings -	2603	10th Oct. 1865	William Cooke.
An improved preparation or composition for coating, covering or colouring walls and other surfaces or parts of buildings, and for forming mouldings, cornices and other decorative parts of houses.	2636	12th Oct. 1865	William Berwick.
Machinery or apparatus for moulding or cutting moulds, and planing wood and other similar materials - - - - -	2711	20th Oct. 1865	William Blackett Haigh. William Bissell.
Manufacture of embossed wood - - - (for mouldings.) (Communicated by Henry May and Henry Taylor Blake.)	2896	10th Nov. 1865	Alfred Vincent Newton.
Machinery for cutting mouldings in wood - (Communicated by John Bartlett Winslow.)	3040	27th Nov. 1865	William Edward Newton.
Machinery or tools for cutting wood or other substances. (moulding-machines.)	3166	9th Dec. 1865	William Wilson Hulse.
MUSICAL INSTRUMENTS AND NOTATION; TURNING OVER LEAVES OF MUSIC, METRONOMES; TUNING INSTRUMENTS; TRANSPOSING MUSIC.			
Instruments or apparatus for teaching and transposing music. (Communicated by Ferdinand Bellows.)	102	12th Jan. 1865	Richard Archibald Brooman.
Certain improvements in the manufacture and construction of pianofortes or similar stringed instruments.	141	17th Jan. 1865	Francis Henry Lakin.
An improvement in clarinets - - - -	502	4th Feb. 1865	James Park.
Organs and harmoniums - - - -	641	25th Feb. 1865	Ralph Smyth.

Subject-matter of Patent.	Number of Patent.	Date.	Name of Patentee.
MUSICAL INSTRUMENTS, &c.—continued.			
Musical instruments in the nature of organs in which reeds are employed.	579	1st March 1865	Augustine Thomas Godfrey.
An improved method of and apparatus for facilitating the proper action of the hands of players upon the piano, organ, harmonium or other like keyed instruments.	655	9th March 1865	William Tighe Hamilton.
Musical instruments - (Communicated by Pierre Louis Gautrot, aind.)	741	16th March 1865	William Brookes.
Bringing and tuning pianofortes and other stringed musical instruments - - - }	964	4th April 1865	{ William Moody. William James Huband. }
Pianofortes - - - - -	985	5th April 1865	Benjamin Johnson.
Improvements in reproducing or producing copies of writings, drawings, music and other characters, and in preparing originals to be transmitted by electric telegraph. (Communicated by Jacques Paul Landrigot.)	1457	27th May 1865	Richard Archibald Brooman.
Manufacture of pianofortes. (Communicated by Maurice Vreyart.)	1623	15th June 1865	George Edgar Way.
Castors - - - - - (for pianofortes.)	1660	24th June 1865	Robert Eastman.
Pianofortes - - - - - (Communicated by Herman Lindman and Henry Lindman.)	1706	26th June 1865	William Edward Newton.
Apparatus for tuning pianos - - - (Communicated by François Debarrie.)	1742	30th June 1865	Richard Archibald Brooman.
Improvements in harmoniums, organs or other musical instruments, a part of which invention is applicable to turning over the leaves of music.	1763	6th July 1865	James Henry Smith.
Organs, harmoniums and other similar keyed wind musical instruments - - - }	1802	7th July 1865	{ John Hophinson. John Whitelock. }
Organs and harmoniums and similar keyed instruments - - - - - }	1896	20th July 1865	{ Ralph Smyth. Wardle Eastland Evans. }
A new or improved keyed musical instrument -	2034	5th Aug. 1865	Hubert Cyrille Baudet.
Manufacture of keys for pianofortes and other musical instruments requiring such keys - }	2158	22nd Aug. 1865	{ Daniel George Maight. Stephen Maight. }
Improvements in apparatus by means of which certain liquids, common air and certain elastic fluids are made available in the production of light, and their quantity regulated and measured, parts of which improvements are applicable for other purposes. (supplying air for organs.)	2194	25th Aug. 1865	Edwin Augustus Curley.
Adaptation of elastic material to articles requiring a bellows arrangement, or a partially rigid and partially expansible arrangement. (for concertinas.)	2423	22nd Sept. 1865	Matthew Cartwright.
Pianofortes - - - - -	2540	3rd Oct. 1865	{ Enoch Farr. William Tarr. Isaac Gregory, F.R.G.S. }
Improvements in musical reed instruments of the harmonium class, and improvements also forming in combination a small instrument of a novel construction. (Communicated by Alexandre François Debain.)	2541	4th Oct. 1865	Frederick Tolhausen.
Pianofortes - - - - -	2562	5th Oct. 1865	Benjamin Johnson.

Subject-matter of Patent.	Number of Patent.	Date.	Name of Patentee.

MUSICAL INSTRUMENTS, &c.—continued.

Subject-matter of Patent.	Number of Patent.	Date.	Name of Patentee.
Action of upright pianofortes - - -	2607	10th Oct. 1865	George Glover Rich.
Pianofortes, harmoniums and organs - -	2663	14th Oct. 1865	Isaac Gregory, F.R.G.S. Enoch Farr. William Farr.
Improvements in the manufacture of keys for pianofortes and other musical instruments requiring such keys, and in parts connected with such keys - - - - - -	2747	24th Oct. 1865	Daniel George Staight. Stephen Staight. James Cherrrton.
An improved metronome or apparatus for measuring intervals of time.	2999	11th Nov. 1865	Henry Carnegie Carden.
Construction of pianofortes - - -	3064	29th Nov. 1865	Enoch Farr. Isaac Gregory, F.R.G.S.
Harmoniums, pianofortes, organs, and other similar keyed instruments.	3149	7th Dec. 1865	Wardle Eastland Evans.
Improved means of assisting the teaching and study of musical notation.	3196	11th Dec. 1865	Alexander Victor Martinus Marie.
Preparation of glue or gelatine so as to render it insoluble in water, and applicable by the admixture of other substances to various purposes for which common glue or gelatine cannot now be used. (for piano keys, &c.) (Communicated by Henry Harris.)	3285	23rd Dec. 1865	William Edward Newton.
Obtaining and employing continuous lengths of tanned leather for various useful purposes . (for drum cords.)	3334	23rd Dec. 1865	George Hum. Daniel Hum.

NAILS, SPIKES, BOLTS, RIVETS, SCREWS, NUTS, WASHERS AND DIES; ANGLE IRON, T IRON, IRON KEYES.

Subject-matter of Patent.	Number of Patent.	Date.	Name of Patentee.
Improvements in screw taps more especially designed for cutting threads in the fittings and connections for gas, steam and water pipes.	257	24th Jan. 1865	William Foster.
Improvements in armour plated ships, forts, gun carriages and works of defence, and in fastenings to be employed therein. (forming bolts hollow.)	392	2nd Feb. 1865	Charles Langley.
Railway chairs, fastenings and sleepers - -	416	4th Feb. 1865	Robert Richardson.
Machinery for preparing cotton and other fibrous substances. (constructing screw nuts.)	476	10th Feb. 1865	Edward Lord.
Machinery for rivetting and for making rivets -	400	13th Feb. 1865	Henry Martyn Kennard.
Dies for cutting screws - - - - - (Communicated by Robert Kennedmann.)	565	24th Feb. 1865	George Weigmann.
An improved machine for pointing or drawing down railway spikes, and which said improved machine is also applicable for forming or drawing down the shanks of ordinary spikes and other articles of irregular shape.	576	1st March 1865	Moses Bayliss.

Subject matter of Patent.	Number of Patent.	Date.	Name of Patentee.
Nails, &c.—continued.			
Machinery or apparatus for cutting and shaping metals, making nails, rivets and similar articles -	644	14th March 1865	{ Joseph Wadsworth. James Wadsworth.
Certain improvements in machinery and appliances for the manufacture of nails, pins and rivets -	765	21st March 1865	{ Charles Farmer. Thomas Turner.
Machinery or apparatus for cutting or chasing the threads of screws or worms.	835	24th March 1865	Joseph Green.
Improvements in machinery for the cutting of nails, brads or spikes, and in the conformation of some of such nails and spikes.	886	29th March 1865	Richard Cardwell Robinson.
Machinery for the manufacture of railway bolts and spikes and other like articles.	962	7th April 1865	Thomas Wilkes.
An improved nail - - - - -	964	7th April 1865	James Brown.
Construction of fireproof buildings - - -	1170	26th April 1865	John Cunningham.
Straight line dividing engines and tools for regulating distances. (cutting threads of screws.)	1245	4th May 1865	William Ford Stanley.
Improved apparatus for cutting, turning and smoothing metal pipes, and the surfaces of bolts, rods or spindles - - - - -	1311	11th May 1865	{ George Mountford. Edward Worrall.
Machinery for making rivets, bolts, spikes and other similar articles.	1357	16th May 1865	Richard Leddicoat.
Construction of screws and screw drivers - - (Communicated by Jared Augustus Ayres.)	1387	19th May 1865	Alfred Vincent Newton.
Certain improvements in apparatus for cutting or forming screws, which is also applicable for cutting pipes or tubes.	1411	23rd May 1865	Edward McNally.
Improvements in locking screws and the nuts of bolts, as also in preventing an unequal straining of their threads.	1476	29th May 1865	Frederick Arthur Paget.
Tube cutters and screw stocks - - -	1527	3rd June 1865	Charles Taylor.
Apparatus for the manufacture of rivets - -	1531	5th June 1865	Charles De Bergue.
Machinery or apparatus for bending and straightening angle iron, T iron and other iron bars.	1532	5th June 1865	Charles De Bergue.
Machinery and apparatus for the manufacture of rivets, bolts, spikes and similar articles.	1688	23rd June 1865	Edward Finch.
Certain improvements in machinery for the manufacture of horse shoes and other nails. (Communicated by Messieurs Bernard Courreisier, Maxime Antoine Davis and François Bigoy.)	1693	24th June 1865	Peter Armand Le Comte de Fontaine Moreau.
Machinery for rivetting and for making rivets -	1709	27th June 1865	Henry Martyn Kennard.
Certain improvements in machinery or apparatus to be employed in the manufacture of metallic bolts, rivets and spikes.	1788	7th July 1865	Eric Hugo Waldenström.
Shearing horse - - - - - -	1887	19th July 1865	Thomas Henry Ince.
Bolt screwing machines - - - - - (Communicated by William Sellers and Coleman Sellers.)	1949	27th July 1865	William Edward Newton.
Manufacture of iron and steel - - - - (forming angle iron.) (Communicated by Martin Diridoned Hermann.)	1994	29th July 1865	Ephraim Fahel.
Iron keers and rulers for ships' fastenings, and iron frames for wood and iron ships.	2010	3rd Aug. 1865	Peter Cato.
Means of fastening or securing the toogram or roods of log horns.	2011	3rd Aug. 1865	William Henry Brookes.

Subject-matter of Patent.	Number of Patent.	Date.	Name of Patentee.
NAILS, &c.—continued.			
Machinery for screwing bolts and nuts - -	2080	9th Aug. 1865	George Harvey. Alexander Harvey, jun'.
Bolt heading machines - - - -	2104	15th Aug. 1865	John William M'Dermott.
Improvements in boots and other coverings for the feet, which improvements are applicable also to trunks and other articles, for the purpose of strengthening, preserving or protecting them. (substitutes for nails.) (Communicated by Jacob Nichols and Moses Pettee.)	2133	16th Aug. 1865	Phineas Lawrence.
Manufacture of screws - - - -	2240	31st Aug. 1865	William Carron.
Machinery for making rivets, spikes, screw blanks, bolts, nuts and other such like articles.	2352	14th Sept. 1865	John Lewin.
Machinery for the manufacture of rivets - -	2355	14th Sept. 1865	John Wakefield.
Machinery or apparatus for shaping metal articles - (heading bolts.) (Communicated by Robert Heppy Butcher.)	2371	16th Sept. 1865	John Henry Johnson.
Bolts, rivets and the like fastenings, for connecting together pieces of metal and other material.	2618	11th Oct. 1865	Frederic Pelham Warren.
Machinery for cutting screws - - - -	2652	14th Oct. 1865	Joseph Taggye.
Certain new or improved machinery for the manufacture of nails.	2769	30th Oct. 1865	William Whittle.
Manufacture of spikes - - - -	2808	31st Oct. 1865	Moses Bayliss.
A new and useful improvement in nail machines or the feeding mechanism therefor. (Communicated by Cyrus Chester Hunt.)	2931	13th Nov. 1865	Henry Cogswell Davis.
Improvements in the manufacture of bevilled or convex iron washers, and in machinery to be employed in the said manufacture.	2957	17th Nov. 1865	George Carter.
Improvements in the construction of railways and in spikes for securing the rails in position. (chamfering spikes.) (Communicated by John M'Murtry.)	3024	24th Nov. 1865	Alfred Vincent Newton.
A combined adjustable spanner, tube cutter and pipe wrench. (spanner for unscrewing nuts and bolts.) (Communicated by Henry Hitchings Barogarauth and Martin Van Wisher.)	3038	27th Nov. 1865	John Phillips Barrogarauth.
An improved screwing and tapping machine -	3166	9th Dec. 1865	Emile Watteau.
Machinery for finishing rivets - - -	3200	11th Dec. 1865	Henry Kinnaird York.
Machinery for manufacturing bolts and rivets - (Communicated by Alexander M'Connell White and Benjamin Ratterworth.)	3215	12th Dec. 1865	Alfred Vincent Newton.
Improvements in machines for making metal nuts and in dies for the same.	3306	18th Dec. 1865	Orrin Clarke Burdict.
Preparation of glue or gelatine so as to render it insoluble in water, and applicable by the admixture of other substances to various purposes for which common glue or gelatine cannot now be used. (for elastic washers in oil boxes.) (Communicated by Henry Wurtz.)	3325	23rd Dec. 1865	William Edward Newton.

Subject-matter of Patent.	Number of Patent.	Date.	Name of Patentee.

OIL-CLOTHS, FLOOR-CLOTHS, TABLE-COVERS AND FURNITURE-COVERS; TARPAULINS, RICK-CLOTHS, TENT-COVERS, AWNING.

Subject-matter of Patent.	Number of Patent.	Date.	Name of Patentee.
Manufacture of floor-cloths - - -	197	23rd Jan. 1865	John Bland Wood.
Improvements in the treatment of oils obtained from the distillation of tar, and in the application of the same to the purposes for which ordinary drying oils are applicable. (*for oil-cloths.*) (*Communicated by Claudius Cordier and Vincent Cordier.*)	344	27th Jan. 1865	John Henry Johnson.
Sewing-machines - - - - - (*for making awnings.*) (*Communicated by Edmond Philippe and Dominique Genre.*)	304	3rd Feb. 1865	William Clark.
Certain improvements in the manufacture of caoutchouc. (*for replacing oil-cloth.*) (*Communicated by Messieurs Léon Désiré Imnervos and François Perruecel.*)	595	11th Feb. 1865	Prize Armand Le Comte de Fontaine Moreau.
Manufacture or treatment of floor-cloths - -	648	27th Feb. 1865	Michael Barker Nairn.
Improvements in the manufacture of textile fabrics and in the machinery or apparatus employed therefor. (*cloths for tarpaulings.*)	663	28th Feb. 1865	David Chalmers.
An improved method of treating, cleaning or preparing painted or other canvas, tarpauline and dirty cotton waste, so as to render the same suitable to be used for household and other purposes for which they may be applicable.	762	17th March 1865	William Maurice Williams.
Improvements in floor-cloth and in machinery for the manufacture of floor-cloth - - -	785	18th March 1865	{ John Howard Kidd. James Chadwick Mather.
Certain improvements in dyeing or printing upon the fabric known as "sail cloth."	1006	8th April 1865	James Isherwood.
Apparatus for covering railway trucks or vans and other carriages - - - - -	1078	17th April 1865	{ Edward Morgan. George Henry Morgan.
Means of covering railway trucks, vans and other carriages.	1090	19th April 1865	William Riddell.
Improvements in taking impressions from the grain of wood, and in transferring the same on to various surfaces - - - (*such as oil-cloths.*)	1117	21st April 1865	{ William Scarratt. William Dean.
Improved means or apparatus for printing felts, floor-cloths, carpets and woven fabrics.	1156	25th April 1865	John Wilkinson the younger.
Improvements in photographing upon wood, and in the preparation of wood, canvas, silk, glass and other substances, for the purpose of receiving and retaining impressions.	1174	26th April 1865	William Henry Smith.
Manufacture of flock fabrics - - - (*for furniture covers.*) (*Communicated by The American Waterproof Cloth Company.*)	1215	1st May 1865	William Edward Newton.
Ornamenting table cloths and other articles with embroidery.	1433	25th May 1865	William Maddere.

Subject-matter of Patent.	Number of Patent.	Date.	Name of Patentee.
OIL-CLOTH, &c.—continued.			
Manufacture of carpets and other terry and cut pile fabrics. (When worn will serve as tent covers.) (Communicated by The American Waterproof Cloth Company.)	1498	31st May 1865	William Edward Newton.
Manufacture of mats, matting and brushes (floor-cloths.)	1758	3rd July 1865	{ George Hurn. Daniel Hurn.
An improved combination of materials for the manufacture of carpets, floor-cloth, felt, wall paper, fire proof flexible roofing, ship and boat building, and for other similar purposes	1775	5th July 1865	{ John Longbottom. Abram Longbottom.
The use and application of paper, printed or otherwise ornamented with water colors, for covering floors and other analogous purposes, as a substitute for carpets and oil-cloths, and of an improved coating or varnish to be applied to the same, to protect its surface from injury and wear.	1878	19th July 1865	Anson Henry Platt.
Construction of sewing-machines particularly adapted for sewing sacks and bags (used for sewing tarpaulings.)	2057	9th Aug. 1865	{ Barnabas Bass. Edward Gandell the younger.
Manufacture and ornamenting of carpets, rugs and other fabrics. (table covers.)	2181	25th Aug. 1865	Lemuel Clayton.
Ornamenting and protecting the edges of bed quilts, counterpanes, toilet covers, carriage rugs and other similar coverings, by edging, binding or fringing by machinery	2255	1st Sept. 1865	{ Robert Knowles. Joseph Lindley.
An improved composition or material to be employed in waterproofing or rendering woven fabrics impervious to moisture. (cover for carriages, stacks, &c.)	2549	6th Oct. 1865	Henry Francis Smith.
A new composition of india-rubber mastic or cement, made in a more or less fluid state according to the use to be made of it, and the process or contrivance for applying the same. (coating wagon tilts, tents, &c.)	2630	12th Oct. 1865	Auguste Aimé Levoord.
Improvements in the manufacture of floor-cloth and in apparatus employed therein.	3242	15th Dec. 1865	Frederick Walton.
Manufacture of bed quilts, table and toilet covers	3265	16th Dec. 1865	{ Thomas Jones. Joseph Buckley.
Obtaining and employing continuous lengths of tanned leather for various useful purposes (for railway sheets, rick-cloths, floor-cloths, toilet covers, &c.)	3354	23rd Dec. 1865	{ George Hurn. Daniel Hurn.
Improvements in floor-cloths and similar compositions fabrics, in the manufacture of such fabrics, and in machinery employed therein	3570	29th Dec. 1865	{ John Howard Kidd. James Chadwick Mather.
Coverings for floors (Communicated by Antoine Perrin and Achille Baudouin.)	3594	30th Dec. 1865	John Henry Johnson.

Subject-matter of Patent.	Number of Patent.	Date.	Name of Patentee.
OILING OR LUBRICATING ; MATERIALS FOR OILING ; OIL CANS AND LUBRICATORS.			
An improved method of and apparatus for lubricating the axles or journals of coal or iron tram waggons or tubs, or of other carriages or rolleys used upon tramways or railways, for carrying mineral or other material	6	2nd Jan. 1865	Joseph Smith, jun'. John Williamson.
Improvements in the manufacture of elastic packings for pistons, and in lubricating compositions therefor.	19	4th Jan. 1865	Edward Kirby.
Bearings for general mechanical purposes, and the application of fluid metallic in lieu of oleaginous or other lubricants to prevent friction	109	13th Jan. 1865	Frederick George Mulholland. Thomas Dugard.
An improved construction of lubricating apparatus for steam-engine purposes	274	31st Jan. 1865	Ewing Pye Colquhoun. John Purdue Ferris.
Manufacture of grease for lubricating purposes	354	8th Feb. 1865	John Drummond.
Certain improvements in mechanism or apparatus for lubricating the cylinders of " slashing " and " taping " machines, such machinery being employed in the sizing of cotton and other yarns.	488	18th Feb. 1865	Thomas Ogden.
Apparatus for sizing and drying by centrifugal force. (Communicated by Félix Monneau and Auguste Racinet.)	604	4th March 1865	Henri Adrien Bonneville.
Improved screws or apparatus for lubricating vertical or diagonal spindles and shafts.	732	21st March 1865	James Waterhouse Midgley.
Oil feeders or cans (Communicated by Charles Churchill.)	859	27th March 1865	James Buckingham.
Preparing lubricating compounds	897	27th March 1865	William West.
Manufacture of lubricating oil and grease (Communicated by Émile Lepeudie.)	968	5th April 1865	William Trall. Louis Lepaige. Edward Thornhill Simpson.
A new or improved compensating wheel to be used with locomotives, carriages and other vehicles on railway and tram roads, in conjunction with or without the wheels now used, in order to obtain at curves and other parts of the road a rolling instead of a dredging motion now effected by wheels in general use on railway and other tram roads.	1022	11th April 1865	James John Myers.
Lamps for burning petroleum, naphtha or other mineral oils	1040	12th April 1865	Charles Rouchan. Josef Bindtner. William Caffou.
Apparatus for lubricating spindles, shafts or other frictional surfaces. (Communicated by William Francis Rippon.)	1060	13th April 1865	James Rippon.
Oiling cans	1119	21st April 1865	George Whillock.
Certain improvements in apparatus for lubricating frictional surfaces, and in the lubricant to be employed therewith.	1178	27th April 1865	Joseph Wilson Lowther.
Purifying animal and vegetable oils or fatty matters to be used for lubricating and other purposes.	1465	27th May 1865	Scipion Sequelin.
Oil and other liquid feeders	1556	7th June 1865	Frederick Foster.
Construction of taps or valves (facilitating lubrication.) (Communicated by Ernest Alexandre Ribert.)	1655	30th June 1865	Edward Griffith Brewer.

Subject-matter of Patent.	Number of Patent.	Date.	Name of Patentee.
OILING, &c.—*continued.*			
Improvements in the preparation of amalgams of quicksilver or mercury, and in the application of such amalgams to various purposes in the arts. (*for lubricating bearings.*) (*Communicated by Henry Wurtz.*)	1719	24th June 1865	William Edward Newton.
Locomotive engines . . . (*lubricating the valves.*) (*Communicated by Auguste De Bergue.*)	1784	3rd July 1865	Charles De Bergue.
Apparatus applicable as a motive-power engine, a pump or fluid meter. (*Communicated by François Bernard de Kéravenan.*)	2021	4th Aug. 1865	William Clark.
Improvements in the lubricating of spindles, the necks or bolsters in which the said spindles revolve having a traversing motion in the said neck or bolster.	2059	9th Aug. 1865	Jacob Henry Radcliffe.
Machinery for preparing cotton, wool and other fibrous materials . . .	2069	12th Aug. 1865	{ Jonas Tatham. John Smith.
Machinery for lubricating the axles of colliery and other similar waggons or trucks.	2090	12th Aug. 1865	James Knowles.
Improvements in revolving fire-arms, in projectiles and cartridges. (*lubricating fire-arms.*)	2108	15th Aug. 1865	James Brown.
Preparing lubricating compounds - - -	2118	16th Aug. 1865	William West.
Apparatus for lubricating shafts and other running surfaces.	2286	6th Sept. 1865	William Mycock.
Lubricating apparatus . . .	2352	14th Sept. 1865	Isaac Rennish.
Apparatus for lubricating machinery - (*Communicated by Joseph Bonillon.*)	2469	23rd Sept. 1865	Henri Adrien Bonneville.
Improved machinery for feeding fibrous substances to preparing, carding and other machinery for working wool and other filamentous substances. (*Communicated by Alexandre Dura.*)	2517	30th Sept. 1865	William Edward Newton.
An improved axle-box for supplying oil to the journals of railway vehicles. (*Communicated by Prosper Piot and Edmond Piot.*)	2757	23rd Oct. 1865	William Edward Gedge.
Improvements in the construction and working of electric telegraphs, and in apparatus connected therewith, partly applicable to other purposes. (*lubricating commutators.*)	2782	26th Oct. 1865	Henry Wilde.
Improvements in forges and in apparatus for lubricating parts thereof, which apparatus is also applicable for lubricating other moving parts of machinery. (*Communicated by Claude Henri Turpe, and.*)	2878	6th Nov. 1865	William Edward Gedge.
Certain improvements in mechanism or apparatus to be employed for lubricating the cylinders of steam-engines, or other similar frictional surfaces.	2861	9th Nov. 1865	{ Neville Beard. John Maiden.
Improvements in the mode of applying mineral soaps to the scouring and lubrication of textile matters and machinery, and in the manufacture of soap.	3107	4th Dec. 1865	Leopold Joseph Bouchart.
Means or apparatus for preparing and combing wool and other fibrous substances. (*oiling gill combs.*)	3123	5th Dec. 1865	Isaac Holden, M.P.

Subject-matter of Patent.	Number of Patent.	Date.	Name of Patentee.
OILING, &c.— *continued.*			
Improvements in reaping and mowing machines, part of which is applicable to machinery in general. (*lubricating crank pins.*)	3148	6th Dec. 1865	Adam Carlisle Ramlett.
Preparation of glue or gelatine so as to render it insoluble in water, and applicable by the admixture of other substances to various purposes for which common glue or gelatine cannot now be used. (*for matters in oil base.*) (*Communicated by Henry Werts.*)	3325	23rd Dec. 1865	William Edward Newton.
Improvements applicable to the lubrication of machinery.	3342	27th Dec. 1865	Joshua Rea.
An improved mechanical oil for lubricating machinery and other purposes.	3349	27th Dec. 1865	John Henry Lester.
An improved piston and tallow or grease cup	3353	24th Dec. 1865	John Bates. Edward Brookes. Edmond William Brookes.

OILS FROM SEEDS ; ANIMAL AND VEGETABLE OILS ; TREATING FATTY AND OILY MATTERS.

Treating the pitch obtained in or resulting from the distillation of palm oil and other fats, in candle making.	9	2nd Jan. 1865	Robert Irvine.
Improvements in extracting and purifying fats and other products from bones and other animal substances, and in apparatus for the same.	93	11th Jan. 1865	Alfred George Lock.
Presses for the expression of fluids from substances containing the same.	134	16th Jan. 1865	John Marshall.
Filtering apparatus (*oils, &c.*)	249	28th Jan. 1865	Victor Burq.
Means or apparatus for extracting or expressing oil or grease from the greasy waste of fibrous substances or other substances containing oil or grease	261	30th Jan. 1865	William Teall. Abraham Naylor.
Manufacture of grease for lubricating purposes	354	8th Feb. 1865	John Dermontila.
The manufacture or production of oil for the use of machinery or for other similar purposes.	388	11th Feb. 1865	Joseph Hall.
A new or improved apparatus and means for ascertaining the quality and condition of grain and seed. (*quality of oil.*) (*Communicated by Christian Joseph Schmitz.*)	632	7th March 1865	William Rünger.
Treating and purifying oils and fats	738	15th March 1865	Campbell Morfit.
Treating fats and fatty matters for the manufacture of candles. (*Communicated by Emile Dangiville and Victor Babet.*)	817	23rd March 1865	Richard Archibald Brooman.
An improved method of treating fatty matters	879	25th March 1865	Samuel Childs, jun'.

Subject-matter of Patent.	Number of Patent.	Date.	Name of Patentee.
OILS FROM SEEDS, &c.—*continued.*			
Improvements in vessels for containing bleaching, polishing oils and other similar materials, and in apparatus connected therewith.	1287	12th May 1865	Thomas Davis.
Vessels or receptacles for containing oil and other liquids.	1359	16th May 1865	Svend Svendsen.
Purifying animal and vegetable oils or fatty matters to be used for lubricating and other purposes.	1453	27th May 1865	Scipion Nequelin.
A new method of manufacturing oil from fatty matters or the residuum arising from the distillation of fatty matters, the manufacture of stearic acid, soap, and purification of oils. *(Communicated by Pierre René Bernaout.)*	1456	27th May 1865	Richard Archibald Brooman.
Construction of reservoirs for containing and storing petroleum and other oils. *(Communicated by Paul Jacotueo.)*	1549	6th June 1865	Richard Archibald Brooman.
Purifying cotton seed oil - - -	1628	17th June 1865	George Payne.
Improved preparations for the treatment and preservation of the hair. *(oils.)* *(Communicated by Mas Oldendorff and Pierre Lévy.)*	1647	19th June 1865	John Henry Johnson.
Manufacture of lamp oils - - - -	1768	4th July 1865	William Jenkins.
Manufacturing grease from soap ends - -	1797	7th July 1865	{ Isaac Peel. / William Hargreaves.
Machinery for treating cotton seeds in order to remove the cotton therefrom, and to prepare the seeds for crushing.	2196	26th Aug. 1865	François Antoine Edmond Guironnet de Masmes.
Construction of hydrostatic presses - -	2304	8th Sept. 1865	{ John Wrenn. / William Wrenn.
Manufacture of insoluble oils and greases - -	2390	19th Sept. 1865	Isaac Salmwell M'Dougall.
Construction of casks to be used more especially for the transport of oil.	2500	29th Sept. 1865	Johann Heinrich Pinchvom.
Machinery or apparatus for preparing and supplying food for cattle. *(oil cake mills.)*	2514	30th Sept. 1865	Robert Willacy.
Cleaning cotton seeds - - - *(for the oil press.)* *(Communicated by Etienne Laporte.)*	2654	5th Oct. 1865	John Charles Stovin.
OILS OF TAR, BITUMEN AND RESIN; NAPHTHA, PARAFFINE, &c.; MINERAL OILS; HYDROCARBONS, PHOSPHORUS.			
Improvements in the treatment of oils obtained from the distillation of tar, and in the application of the same to the purposes for which ordinary drying oils are applicable. *(Communicated by Claudius Cordier and Vincent Cordier.)*	244	27th Jan. 1865	John Henry Johnson.

Subject-matter of Patent.	Number of Patent.	Date.	Name of Patentee.
OILS OF TAR, &c.—continued.			
Treatment of tar oils for the purpose of employing the same as paint. (Communicated by Vincent Cordier, Claudius Cordier and John Gatley.)	245	27th Jan. 1865	Alexander Horace Brandon.
Extracting turpentine and tar from resinous wood -	408	13th Feb. 1865	Jean Antoine Pastorelly.
Apparatus for distilling petroleum and other volatile liquids and for making gas. (Communicated by George Hughes Sinclair Duffus.)	447	16th Feb. 1865	William Edward Newton.
Apparatus for extracting liquid from solid substances. (oil from paraffine.) (Communicated by Lyman Smith.)	496	21st Feb. 1865	William Edward Newton.
Process and apparatus for producing oil and coke from coal and slack.	600	22nd Feb. 1865	James Nicholas.
Improvements in treating certain hydrocarbon oils and in vessels for containing the same.	664	24th Feb. 1865	John Fardred.
Treatment of certain products obtained in the smelting of iron. (collecting condensible hydrocarbons.)	680	2nd March 1865	{ Thomas Horton. David Simpson Price. }
An improvement in carburetting gas, also in the preparation of hydrocarbons for carburetting gas, and improved methods of treating alkali which has been used to purify coal oils, shale oils, petroleum and other mineral oils.	698	3rd March 1865	William Renwick Bowditch.
Preparation of turpentines and varnishes - -	670	10th March 1865	{ Joseph Freeman. Edward Grace Freeman. Charles Henry Freeman. }
Apparatus for vapourising hydrocarbon liquids for illuminating and heating. (Communicated by Jonathan Griffen.)	727	14th March 1865	George Tomlinson Bousfield.
Apparatus for distilling oils and other liquids from coal and other substances. (Communicated by William George Washington Jaeger.)	787	15th March 1865	William Edward Newton.
Apparatus for the distillation of coal and peat, and such other substances as are or may be used for the manufacture of solid and liquid volatile hydrocarbons, or for the manufacture of the said hydrocarbons and coke.	796	22nd March 1865	William Mattieu Williams.
Casks or vessels for storing petroleum and hydrocarbons.	834	24th March 1865	John Bailey Brown.
Means of and apparatus for increasing the illuminating power of hydrocarbons, oils and gases. (Communicated by Thomas Say Speakman.)	980	6th April 1865	George Davies.
Apparatus for storing petroleum and other inflammable liquids of less specific gravity than water. (Communicated by Félix Bizard and Pierre Lelarre.)	1027	11th April 1865	Richard Archibald Brooman.
Apparatus for distilling hydrocarbons from coals, schists and other materials.	1078	17th April 1865	Joseph Dougan.
Manufacture of parkesine or compounds of pyroxyline, and also solutions of pyroxyline known as collodion.	1313	11th May 1865	Alexander Parkes.
Apparatus used in distilling hydrocarbons - -	1391	16th May 1865	George Walton.

Subject-matter of Patent.	Number of Patent.	Date.	Name of Patentee.
OILS OF TAR, &c.—continued.			
Apparatus for raising oil and other liquids from deep wells. (see "PUMPS.") (Communicated by Francis Stebbins Pease.)	1092	20th May 1865	William Edward Newton.
Construction of reservoirs for containing and storing petroleum and other oils. (Communicated by Paul Jacovaco.)	1549	6th June 1865	Richard Archibald Brooman.
An improved method and apparatus for distilling coal shale and other carbonaceous substances. (Communicated by John Howarth.)	1553	7th June 1865	James Howarth, M.D.
Purifying paraffine	1586	12th June 1865	John Edgar Poynter.
An improved method of and apparatus for burning liquid hydrocarbons, and the employment thereof for heating purposes. (see "HEATING.") (Communicated by Alexandre Schpakofsky and Nicolas Stange.)	1711	27th June 1866	Richard Archibald Brooman.
Apparatus for the decantation and raising of petroleum and other oils.	1724	24th June 1865	Paul Jacovaco.
Manufacture of lamp oils	1768	4th July 1865	William Jenkins.
Apparatus for burning combustible and volatile liquids for generating steam and similar purposes. (Communicated by Patrick Hayes.)	1838	25th July 1865	George Tomlinson Bousfield.
An improvement in refining petroleum and other hydrocarbon oils. (Communicated by Robert Augustus Chesebrough.)	1980	31st July 1865	Alfred Vincent Newton.
Treatment of hydrocarbon or paraffin oils	2009	3rd Aug. 1865	John William Perkins.
Stills for the distillation of petroleum and other oily substances.	2040	5th Aug. 1865	Adolphe Millochau.
Improvements in carburetting coal gas and manufacturing artificial gas, and in the machinery or apparatus employed therein.	2096	12th Aug. 1865	Henry Woodward.
Tanks and other receptacles for obtaining and transporting petroleum, naphtha and other oils and liquids, to prevent wastage by fire or filtration or evaporation, or hazard of life.	2185	25th Aug. 1865	George Washington Howard.
Treatment of certain products obtained in the refining of petroleum and of other hydrocarbon oils.	2196	26th Aug. 1865	John Fordred.
Obtaining spirits of turpentine, rosin, pitch, tar, pyroligneous acid and other products from wood. (Communicated by Albert Hamilton Emery.)	2247	31st Aug. 1865	William Edward Newton.
Separating phosphorus from iron and other metals, in metallurgical processes.	2422	27th Sept. 1865	Carl Heinrich Ludwig Winter.
Apparatus for extracting oil from coal shale and other minerals.	2544	4th Oct. 1865	Allan Craig.
An improved mode of treating or preparing casks and other vessels, to make them tight and suitable for containing hydrocarbon and other fluids.	2644	13th Oct. 1865	George Marshall.
Purification and preparation of animal and vegetable wax, stearine, spermaceti, paraffine and other solid, waxy or fatty substances.	2769	27th Oct. 1865	Scipion Saquelin.
Improvements in the distillation of coal and shale, and in the apparatus employed therein.	2793	30th Oct. 1865	Edward Meldrum.

Subject-matter of Patent.	Number of Patent.	Date.	Name of Patentee.
OILS OF TAR, &c.—continued.			
A combination of improved method, apparatus and receptacles for storing, preserving, transferring and discharging certain fluids, for sanitary and protective purposes. (Communicated by Henry Pinkus.)	2206	14th Aug. 1865	Robert Alexander William Westley.
Manufacture or purification of hydrocarburets, and especially of petroleum oils used for lighting purposes. (Communicated by Doctor Pierre Gédéon Barry and Chevalier Bartholomy Lupula.)	2945	15th Nov. 1865	William Clark.
Improved apparatus for facilitating the treating or preparing of casks and other vessels, to make them tight, and suitable for containing hydrocarbon and other fluids.	3081	25th Nov. 1865	George Marshall.
Apparatus for distilling oils and condensing oily vapours. (from shale.)	3101	2nd Dec. 1865	Thomas Newton Brazie.
An improved retort for distilling or extracting products from cannel, coal, shale or schist, and more especially from the small coal or dust technically known as " slack."	3285	20th Dec. 1865	John Gibbon.
Obtaining oil and other products from bituminous shale - - - - - - - - -	3296	20th Dec. 1865	{ John Watson. / John Player.
Purification, refining and treatment of the volatile and fixed oils produced from the destructive distillation of peat or turf.	3312	22nd Dec. 1865	Denis M'Grath.
Treating hydrocarbon oils - - - -	3345	27th Dec. 1865	James Young, jun'.
OPTICAL INSTRUMENTS, TELESCOPES, MICROSCOPES, STEREOSCOPES, LENSES; OPTICAL ILLUSIONS.			
A new or improved apparatus for illusory exhibitions	223	26th Jan. 1865	{ John Henry Pepper. / Thomas William Tobin.
An improved instrument for concentrating light, applicable to dental, surgical and other operations. (combination of lenses.)	591	2nd March 1865	Charles Rahn.
Philosophical examination into the alleged spirit manifestations, consisting of a lamp and a close room.	1148	24th April 1865	Owen Grenliffe Warren.
Spectacles, opera glasses, telescopes and similar apparatus. (Communicated by Etienne Boudry.)	1206	29th April 1865	Jean Gutmann.
A new or improved method of obtaining or producing optical illusions.	1569	12th June 1865	Gaetan Bonelli.
A new or improved apparatus for illusory exhibitions	1983	1st Aug. 1865	{ Thomas William Tobin. / Colonel Stodare.
Mounting telescopes and microscopes - -	2075	10th Aug. 1865	Carl Johann Reinhart Johns.
Improvements in rules for measuring, and in other instruments or articles requiring to be adjusted or disposed at various angles. (telescopes.)	2618	10th Oct. 1865	Arthur Nicholls.

Subject-matter of Patent.	Number of Patent.	Date.	Name of Patentee.

OVENS, &c.—continued.

Furnaces for heating the blast for blast furnaces (and cleansing ovens.)	2897	10th Nov. 1865	Thomas Whitwell.
Cooking apparatus - - - - -	2971	14th Nov. 1865	Samuel Hazard Huntly.
An improved method of utilising the waste heat of coke ovens. (Communicated by Antoine Barbier-Perrain.)	3046	24th Nov. 1865	William Edward Gedge.
Construction of kitchen stoves and cooking ranges -	3144	6th Dec. 1865	George Fitzjames Russell.
Construction of fire-places and furnaces - - (with oven.)	3247	15th Dec. 1865	George Warriner.
Boilers or apparatus for generating steam - - (for baking.) (Communicated by Julien Belleville.)	3369	14th Dec. 1865	Richard Archibald Brooman.

OXIDATION AND INCRUSTATION (Preventing and Removing).

A method of and apparatus for preventing incrustation or calcareous deposits in steam-boilers. (Communicated by Alexander Forbes Porter.)	119	14th Jan. 1865	George Davies.
A new or improved apparatus applicable to steam-boilers for preventing deposits therein. (Communicated by Louis Hippolyte Courtois-Rambert.)	219	26th Jan. 1865	Charles Denton Abel.
A metallic anti-corrosive varnish for protecting the surfaces of metals from oxidation.	259	30th Jan. 1865	John M'Innes.
Coating the bottoms and sides of ships and other submerged structures to prevent fouling and decay.	384	1st Feb. 1865	John Moyery.
An improved varnish for preserving wood, and for protecting iron ships and other metal work from oxydation and from fouling. (Communicated by Adolphe Guibert.)	315	4th Feb. 1865	Richard Archibald Brooman.
Protecting wooden surfaces from the fouling and injury to which they are ordinarily liable in sea water.	369	9th Feb. 1865	John Cornelius Craigie Halkett.
Improvements in coatings for the prevention of the fouling to which iron and other ships and structures are ordinarily liable to sea water.	424	6th March 1865	Francis Cruickshank.
Improvements in coating the bottoms of iron ships and other surfaces, to prevent oxidation, the adhesion of marine animals and plants, and in compositions to be therein employed.	661	10th March 1865	Richard Perry Roberts.
Protecting iron ships and other submerged structures from oxidation and corrosion.	970	5th April 1865	Edward Ritherdon.
An improved composition for preventing the fouling of ships and other vessels. (Communicated by William Baliver Davis.)	1009	14th April 1865	George Davies.
Improvements in the fitting of surface condenser tubes, and in the tools to be used therein, and in the means of retarding corrosion in steam-boilers. (Communicated by William Judson.)	1183	22nd April 1865	Alfred Vincent Newton.

Subject-matter of Patent.	Number of Patent.	Date.	Name of Patentee.
OXIDATION, &c.—*continued.*			
Paints or compositions for coating and preserving metallic and other substances from oxidation and decay - - - - -	1154	25th April 1865	{ John Nuthall Brown. Thomas Deykin Clarr.
An improved composition for coating iron or other vessels, and for other similar purposes.	1278	9th May 1865	John Cornelius Craigie Halkett.
An improved composition for preventing incrustation in steam-boilers.	1394	12th May 1865	William Hewitt.
Annealing pots and saucers for annealing iron and steel wire, sheet metal and other articles. (*avoiding production of scale.*)	1490	20th May 1865	John Hibell.
Composition and manufacture of paints applicable to iron and other ships' bottoms, and for other general purposes.	1489	31st May 1865	Thomas Spencer.
Steam-boilers - - - - - (*Communicated by Abram Samuel Mitchell.*)	1521	2nd June 1865	Henry Edward Newton.
Caloric or heated air engines - - - (*Communicated by Cyrus W. Baldwin and Walter Davis Richards.*)	1543	8th June 1865	Samuel Blatchford Tucker.
Improvements in the manufacture of paper and paper stock, and in the utilisation of certain waste products resulting therefrom (*to prevent incrustation in steam-boilers.*)	1602	13th June 1865	Thomas Routledge. William Henry Richardson.
Improvements in the preparation of amalgams of quicksilver or mercury, and in the application of such amalgams to various purposes in the arts. (*removing films from metals.*) (*Communicated by Henry Warts.*)	1719	29th June 1865	William Edward Newton.
Preventing the incrustation of steam-boilers - (*Communicated by Charles James Eames.*)	1734	29th June 1865	William Edward Newton.
An improved composition for coating ships' bottoms, and the surfaces of other vessels or structures which are exposed to the action of sea water - - - - -	1943	26th July 1865	{ Frederick Pulman. Richard Gimson.
An improved composition for coating the bottoms of iron and wooden ships, by which the same are preserved from fouling and the iron from corrosion, whether internally or externally, by sea or other water or moisture, which is applicable to iron of any kind exposed to the action of moisture.	1988	1st Aug. 1865	William La Penotière.
Improvements in cleansing and coating the bottoms of ships and other submerged surfaces, to prevent oxidation and the adhesion of marine animals and plants, also in compositions to be employed for these purposes.	2316	9th Sept. 1865	Richard Perry Roberts.
An improved mode of removing and preventing the incrustation of steam-boilers - - }	2331	11th Sept. 1865	{ William Tyne. Stephen Tyne. Robert Clayton.
An improved composition for preventing incrustation in steam-boilers.	2332	11th Sept. 1865	William Hewitt.
Compositions used for coating metallic surfaces -	2490	27th Sept. 1865	{ John Boffey. Charles William Smith.
An improved liquid compound for purifying sea and other waters. (*preventing incrustation.*) (*Communicated by Léandre Danjoe.*)	2646	13th Oct. 1865	Richard Archibald Brooman.

Subject matter of Patent.	Number of Patent.	Date.	Name of Patentee.

OXIDATION, &c.—continued.

Subject matter of Patent.	Number of Patent.	Date.	Name of Patentee.
A certain composition having anti-corrosive and anti-fouling properties, for the preservation of and keeping clean the bottoms of iron vessels, and also for the preservation of iron submerged and iron structures exposed to the action of the atmosphere or water - - - -	2655	14th Oct. 1865	William Jardine Combe Mac Millan. Jasper Mason. John Vickers Scarborough.
Improvements in steam-boilers and other apparatus applicable to the heating and evaporation of liquids, parts of which improvements are applicable also to other purposes - - -	2601	16th Oct. 1865	Francis Wise. Edward Field. Enoch Harrison Ayden.
Apparatus for indicating and registering high temperatures. (*protecting fusible metals from oxidation.*)	2790	24th Oct. 1865	Frederick Herbert Gossage.
An improved coating for covering the bottoms of iron and steel ships and other navigable vessels and marine works, to prevent oxidation and the adhesion of animal and vegetable matter thereto.	2791	30th Oct. 1865	Robert Dwyne Dwyer.
Improvements in the manufacture of salt, and in machinery or apparatus for that purpose. (*preventing formation of pan scale.*)	3105	4th Dec. 1865	Dennis Hall.
Dyeing, printing and other operations based on chemical reactions. (*preventing oxidation of printing rollers.*) (*Communicated by Mathan Percy-Jorel.*)	3110	4th Dec. 1865	Richard Archibald Brooman.
Apparatus for preventing incrustation in steam-boilers.	3121	5th Dec. 1865	Josef Toth.
Boilers or apparatus for generating steam - - (*securing from incrustation.*) (*Communicated by Julien Belleville.*)	3246	18th Dec. 1865	Richard Archibald Brooman.
Improvements in caps employed in spinning, and in the manufacture thereof. (*preventing corrosion.*)	3323	23rd Dec. 1865	Edward Clifton.

PAINTING, COLOURING AND VARNISHING; PAINTS, COLOURS, VARNISHES, GLAZES AND LACQUER.

Subject matter of Patent.	Number of Patent.	Date.	Name of Patentee.
Apparatus for painting venetian blinds and similar articles - - - - -	170	20th Jan. 1865	Donald Munro. Thomas Wright.
Improvements in the treatment of oils obtained from the distillation of tar, and in the application of the same to the purposes for which ordinary drying oils are applicable. (*for painting, varnishing, &c.*) (*Communicated by Claudius Cordier and Vincent Cordier.*)	244	27th Jan. 1865	John Henry Johnson.
Treatment of tar oils for the purpose of employing the same as paint. (*Communicated by Vincent Cordier, Claudius Cordier and John Gailiff.*)	245	27th Jan. 1865	Alexander Horace Brandon.
A metallic anti-corrosive varnish for protecting the surfaces of metals from oxidation.	250	30th Jan. 1865	John M'Innes.

Subject-matter of Patent.	Number of Patent.	Date.	Name of Patentee.
PAINTING, &c.—continued.			
Improvements in the manufacture of carbonate of ammonia, and in the utilization of the product obtained in such manufacture. (obtaining pigments.) (Communicated by Dr. Hugo Kunheim.)	1933	25th July 1865	Astley Paston Price.
Paints or preparations for coating surfaces - -	2016	3rd Aug. 1865	Ernest Leslie Ransome.
Improvements in the mode or method of preparing materials for, and in the manufacture of submarine telegraphic cables, the same being generally applicable for other purposes. (making protective compositions applicable as paints, for railways, bridges, &c.)	2025	4th Aug. 1865	Frederick George Mulholland.
A new composition suitable for use as paint and protective coating. (Communicated by William Potter.)	2163	22nd Aug. 1865	John Gilbert Avery.
An improvement in the treatment of tar and other substances suitable to be used in the manufacture of paint and for other purposes.	2191	25th Aug. 1865	John Monle.
Treatment of certain products obtained in the refining of petroleum and of other hydrocarbon oils. (oils for mixing paints or varnishes.)	2196	25th Aug. 1865	John Fordred.
Improvements in cleansing and coating the bottoms of ships and other submerged surfaces, to prevent oxidation and the adhesion of marine animals and plants, also in compositions to be employed for these purposes. (compounding varnish.)	2316	9th Sept. 1865	Richard Perry Roberts.
Manufacture of white lead - - - -	2427	22nd Sept. 1865	Peter Spence.
A new or improved colour slide and case for the use of artists and painters.	2588	9th Oct. 1865	John Robertson.
Improved apparatus to be fitted to windows when cleaning, painting or otherwise.	2737	21st Oct. 1865	Joseph William Lea.
Improvements in brushes for hair dressing and other uses, also in brooms and apparatus for cleaning, preparing, painting, coating and smoothing surfaces - - - -	2985	20th Nov. 1865	{ George Smith. Charles Ritchie.
An improved composition for enamel, paint, varnish, cement or plaster. (Communicated by William Berney Watkins.)	3049	27th Nov. 1865	William Robert Lake.
Dyeing, printing and other operations based on chemical reactions. (painting.) (Communicated by Mathias Parof-Javal.)	3110	4th Dec. 1865	Richard Archibald Brooman.
Apparatus employed in grinding corn and other substances capable of being ground by millstones. (paints.)	3126	5th Dec. 1865	Edward Alfred Cowper.
A new process of lacquering and finishing metal goods, such as gas fittings, and other like articles usually flambed by brassing and lacquering.	3264	18th Dec. 1865	Joseph Harcourt.
Preparation of glue or gelatine so as to render it insoluble in water, and applicable by the admixture of other substances to various purposes for which common glue or gelatine cannot now be used. (for a varnish, vehicle for pigments, &c.) (Communicated by Henry Wurtz.)	3328	23rd Dec. 1865	William Edward Newton.

Subject-matter of Patent.	Number of Patent.	Date.	Name of Patentee.

PAPER, PASTEBOARD AND PAPIER-MÂCHÉ; PAPER-HANGINGS.

I.—Making Paper, Papier-mâché, Preparing Pulp, &c.

Machinery for smoothing or finishing paper -	8	2nd Jan. 1865	James Roger Crompton.
Manufacturing paper - (Communicated by Jules Joseph Manery.)	15	3rd Jan. 1865	Léopold D'Aubréville.
Machinery for making paper board -	25	4th Jan. 1865	John Franklin Jones.
Machinery for the manufacture of paper board	62	7th Jan. 1865	John Franklin Jones.
Preparing or treating wood and other vegetable fibrous materials for the manufacture of pulp for paper. (Communicated by Zephiria Gaspard Alexandre Nathan Pétrone Oriali, Amable Alfred Froulet and Pierre Amable Henri Matamière.)	80	10th Jan. 1865	William Clark.
Apparatus for drying paper in sheets	196	23rd Jan. 1865	Alfred Sheldon.
Filtering apparatus - (for straining paper pulp.)	249	30th Jan. 1865	Victor Butq.
Treating spent or used leys resulting from the preparation of fibrous substances used in the manufacture of paper stock.	297	2nd Feb. 1865	Thomas Routledge.
Improved machinery for cutting, sifting, separating, bruising, sucking and preparing straw and other vegetable fibrous substances to be employed in the manufacture of various kinds of paper, and also for preparing food for cattle -	340	7th Feb. 1865	{ John Corner. William Simpson. }
Treatment and utilization of certain products obtained in the manufacture of paper or of paper stock -	532	24th Feb. 1865	{ Thomas Routledge. Thomas Richardson. }
Machinery or apparatus used in the manufacture of paper -	552	25th Feb. 1865	{ James Hyndford Rawlins. Joseph Chappell. }
Improvements in machinery employed in the manufacture of paper, part of which is applicable to drying cylinders for other purposes.	581	2nd March 1865	James Park.
An improvement in putting up tobacco for smoking, and in the implements or pipes for smoking the same, and in making tobacco paper. (see "TOBACCO.") (Communicated by Luther Holman Hale.)	615	4th March 1865	William Edward Newton.
Application and utilization of certain materials suitable for the manufacture of paper. (Communicated by Joachim John Monteiro.)	708	13th March 1865	John Webb.
An improved method of treating, cleaning or preparing painted or other canvas, tarpaulins and dirty cotton waste, so as to render the same suitable to be used for household and other purposes for which they may be applicable. (for manufacture of paper.)	752	17th March 1865	William Maurice Williams.
Separating fibre from vegetable materials containing the same. (Communicated by Antonio Mrucri.)	968	4th April 1865	George Tomlinson Bousfield.
Improved apparatus for reducing wheat and other straw. (for paper making.)	985	6th April 1865	Richard Garrett, jun.
Improvements in sizing paper and in the machinery employed therein.	1006	8th April 1865	William Weatherley.

Subject-matter of Patent.	Number of Patent.	Date.	Name of Patentee.
PAPER, &c. — *continued.*			
Washing or steeping and bleaching textile or fibrous materials. (*Communicated by Messieurs Negret, Oriol and Fredel.*)	1144	24th April 1865	William Clark.
Apparatus for disintegrating vegetable and animal substances.	1168	26th April 1865	François Dominique Pierre Jacques Cabasson.
Improvements in photographing upon wood, and in the preparation of wood, canvas, silk, glass and other substances, for the purpose of receiving and retaining impressions.	1174	26th April 1865	William Henry Smith.
Certain improvements in mechanism or apparatus for making and cutting cardboard.	1366	17th May 1865	William Haigh.
Process and apparatus for the treatment of materials for the manufacture of paper and other purposes.	1488	30th May 1865	Robert Hanham Collyer.
Improvements in paper or cloth-lined paper collars, and in the machinery for manufacturing the same.	1537	5th June 1865	James Atkins Woodbury.
Certain improvements in machinery employed in and for the manufacture of paper · · ·	1566	13th June 1865	Jonathan Alonzo Millington. Alfred Allnutt.
Improvements in the manufacture of paper and paper stock, and in the utilisation of certain waste products resulting therefrom · · ·	1602	13th June 1865	Thomas Routledge. William Henry Richardson.
An improvement in the preparation of vegetable fibre for the manufacture of paper.	1684	17th June 1865	William Dellour.
Machines for making paper board · · ·	1756	3rd July 1865	John Franklin Jones.
Machinery for the manufacture of paper board and paper.	1787	6th July 1865	John Franklin Jones.
Means of and apparatus for treating animal and vegetable fibrous materials, which apparatus is also applicable to various useful purposes.	1962	27th July 1865	Henry Sherwood.
Improvements in the raising, lifting or drawing and forcing of water and other liquids, and in the apparatus and means employed therefor · (*for paper mills.*)	1996	2nd Aug. 1865	James M'Ewan. William Neilson.
Manufacture of paper · · · ·	2076	10th Aug. 1865	Alexandre Mendel.
An improved preparation for the prevention of forgery of bank cheques, bills and other documents · · ·	2101	14th Aug. 1865	John Gallemore Dale. Richard Samuel Dale.
Manufacture of paper boards and pipes · ·	2126	17th Aug. 1865	Nicholas Charles Saurel-mey.
Manufacture of the straw of rye and other straws and grasses, into fibre, and utilising the refuse. (*for papier-mâché.*)	2171	23rd Aug. 1865	Edward Henry Cradock Monckton.
An improvement in the manufacture of paper pulp. (*Communicated by James Brewer Brown.*)	2248	31st Aug. 1865	William Edward Newton.
Manufacture of paper · · · ·	2404	21st Sept. 1865	Sanders Trotman.
Improvements in the manufacture of paper by the introduction therein of a new vegetable fibrous substance.	2478	27th Sept. 1865	George Eveleigh.
Mode of treating the roots of the locust plant, for the purpose of manufacturing paper, pasteboard, fabrics and ropes therefrom. (*Communicated by John Peter Cominade.*)	2525	2nd Oct. 1865	Charles Denton Abel.

Subject-matter of Patent.	Number of Patent.	Date.	Name of Patentee.
Paper, &c.—continued.			
Apparatus for steeping or treating paper pulp and other matters subjected to the action of alkalies. (*Communicated by Messieurs. Neyret, Oriali and Fredet.*)	2574	6th Oct. 1865	William Clark.
An improvement in preparing paper and the surfaces of other materials for use in photography.	2649	13th Oct. 1865	Johannes De Witt Brinckerhoff.
Improvements in the method of and apparatus for utilising the liquors used in the treatment of straw or other fibrous materials for the manufacture of paper, which improvements are also applicable to the evaporation of Liquids generally. (*Communicated by Eugene Porion.*)	2726	21st Oct. 1865	James Wright.
Manufacture of paper from marine vegetable matters (*Communicated by Pierre Ernest Gégann and Charles Marie Gognage.*)	2741	23rd Oct. 1865	William Clark.
Treating vegetable fibres used in the manufacture of paper and other similar substances made from pulp. (*Communicated by Louis Horal.*)	2882	8th Nov. 1865	Godfrey Anthony Erzam.
An improved method or process for producing paper makers' pulp from cane, bamboo and other analogous substances. (*Communicated by Charles Heaton.*)	2923	13th Nov. 1865	William Robert Lake.
Application of photography to the obtaining of printed proofs or impressions or engravings - (*photographic paper.*)	2964	17th Nov. 1865	{ Edward Bullock. James Bullock.
Manufacture of endless cloths (*used in paper making.*)	2966	17th Nov. 1865	James Heywood Whitehead.
Improved machinery to be used in the manufacture of paper. (*Communicated by Heinrich Voelter.*)	3041	27th Nov. 1865	William Edward Newton.
Improvements in the process of treating materials for the manufacture of paper and other similar textile fabrics, and in apparatus for the same. (*Communicated by Robert Hawkes Collyer.*)	3067	29th Nov. 1865	Charles Stuart Baker.
The manufacture of pulp from " Lygeum Spartnum " (*Communicated by Antonio Escubos.*)	3219	13th Dec. 1865	Richard Archibald Brooman.
Improved apparatus for manufacturing paper pulp	3245	14th Dec. 1865	William Alfred West.
Improvements in the manufacture of yarns, string and paper, and in the preparation of dyes, and in dyeing fabrics, by the application of vegetable substances not hitherto used for such purposes.	3318	22nd Dec. 1865	John Alexander Cooper.
Preparation of glue or gelatine so as to render it insoluble in water, and applicable by the admixture of other substances, to various purposes for which common glue or gelatine cannot now be used. (*applicable as papier-mâché, for stiffening paper, &c.*) (*Communicated by Henry Wurtz.*)	3325	23rd Dec. 1865	William Edward Newton.
III.—Cutting, Folding and Ornamenting Paper and Papier-mâché; Applications of Paper.			
Machinery and tools for making collars, cuffs, wristbands and other articles of dress, also adapted for cutting metal blanks - (*from paper.*)	399	13th Feb. 1865	{ David Barr. William Henry Page. James Clement Newey.

Subject-matter of Patent.	Number of Patent.	Date.	Name of Patentee.

PAPER, &c.— continued.

Subject-matter of Patent.	Number of Patent.	Date.	Name of Patentee.
An improved composition as a substitute for leather or other similar materials . . .	465	18th Feb. 1865	Christopher Brakell. William Bonhl. William Günther.
Apparatus for folding envelopes . . .	470	20th Feb. 1865	John Davidson Nichol.
Paper and cloth-lined paper collars for ladies and gentlemen.	556	28th Feb. 1865	Solomon Nelly Gray.
Certain improvements in apparatus for cutting paper, pasteboard and similar substances.	557	28th Feb. 1865	Mark Mason.
Improvements in machinery employed in the manufacture of paper, part of which is applicable to drying cylinders for other purposes.	561	2nd March 1865	James Park.
Improved machinery for manufacturing paper and cloth-lined paper collars for gentlemen and ladies.	769	20th March 1865	Solomon Nelly Gray.
Apparatus for cutting pasteboard and other like boards. (Communicated by Elizur Ely Clarke.)	789	21st March 1865	William Clark.
Manufacture of jewelry cases and other similar cases	803	22nd March 1865	John James Carter.
Ornamenting the surfaces of japanned goods and papier maché goods, and other varnished surfaces	831	27th March 1865	Thomas Farmer. Frederick Lewis.
Improved means of preventing the leakage of barrels, and of rendering packages and fabrics impervious to air and gases. (coating paper.) (Communicated by Lewis Francis and Cyrus Loutrel.)	913	31st March 1865	Alfred Vincent Newton.
Manufacture of letter-clips, book-markers, paper-knives, and clips for suspending stationery, drapery and pictures, and for other such like purposes . . .	938	3rd April 1865	Thomas Corbett. Robert Harrington.
Improvements in embossing presses to facilitate the operation of relief coloring on envelopes, note paper and other similar articles of stationery.	1254	2nd May 1865	Best Feamr.
Certain improvements in mechanism or apparatus for making and cutting cardboard.	1368	17th May 1865	William Haigh.
An improvement in the manufacture of envelopes -	1416	23rd May 1865	Henry Gibbs.
Improvements in reproducing or producing copies of writings, drawings, music and other characters, and in preparing originals to be transmitted by electric telegraph. (preparing a metallic paper.) (Communicated by Jacques Paul Lambrigot.)	1457	27th May 1865	Richard Archibald Brooman.
Certain improvements in machinery employed in and for the manufacture of paper . . .	1596	13th June 1865	Jonathan Alonzo Millington. Alfred Allenn.
The use and application of paper, printed or otherwise ornamented with water colors, for covering floors and other analogous purposes, as a substitute for carpets and oil cloths, and of an improved coating or varnish to be applied to the same, to protect its surface from injury and wear.	1878	19th July 1865	Amson Henry Platt.
Compounds for waterproofing and insulating purposes.	1969	29th July 1865	Frederick Augustus Abel.
Improvements in reducing vegetable fibre to pulp and in machinery employed therein.	2002	2nd Aug. 1865	William Wharton Burdon.
Printing machines	2066	5th Aug. 1865	William Bork.

Subject-matter of Patent.	Number of Patent.	Date.	Name of Patentee.
PAPER, &c.—continued.			
Machinery or apparatus for the manufacture of paper bags. (Communicated by Delarue Clark.)	2116	16th Aug. 1865	John Henry Johnson.
An improved covering for rollers or cylinders -	2157	23rd Aug. 1865	James Alfred Turner.
Improved machinery for the manufacture of bags and envelopes made of paper or other fibrous materials or woven or textile fabrics, either separately or combined.	2420	22nd Sept. 1865	Henry Rankin.
An improved apparatus for bordering paper and envelopes.	2441	23rd Sept. 1865	Joseph Perkins.
Manufacture of knickerbockers and such like coverings for the legs. (cloth and paper pulp.)	2460	26th Sept. 1865	William Ambler.
Pianofortes, harmoniums and organs - -	2653	11th Oct. 1865	Isaac Gregory, F.R.G.S. Enoch Farr. William Tarr.
Preparation of photographic papers - - (Communicated by Laurent de Montgolfier.)	2754	25th Oct. 1865	William Edward Newton.
Improvements in envelopes and in the construction thereof.	2764	30th Oct. 1865	Robert Girdwood.
Preparing the surfaces of paper, leather, woven and other fabrics and substances, for receiving photographic pictures, engravings, lithographs and prints, and for rendering such substances fire and water proof. (Communicated by William Gibson.)	2891	9th Nov. 1865	William Edward Newton.
Improvements in the manufacture of air tight coffins and in the mode of ornamenting or finishing the same, as also in the application of a material or composition not hitherto used in their production (of paper boards.)	3014	21th Nov. 1865	Henry John Cox. William Leach.
Apparatus for embossing - - - (and applying gold leaf.)	3083	25th Nov. 1865	John Erskine Brown.
Certain improvements having reference to shirt collars and mechanism for manufacturing the same. (paper collars.)	3085	25th Nov. 1865	George Knowles Snow.
Machinery for cutting paper - - -	3189	11th Dec. 1865	Thomas Corfauld Usher.
Envelopes - - - - -	3207	13th Dec. 1865	Henry Yates Thompson.
Apparatus for damping and gumming labels, stamps, envelopes and sheets of paper - -	3343	27th Dec. 1865	Joseph Renn. George Oswald Lochman.
III.—Paper-hangings.			
Manufacture of paper-hangings - -	329	6th Feb. 1865	John Booth.
Improvements in taking impressions from the grain of wood, and in transferring the same on to various surfaces - - - (such as paper-hangings.)	1117	21st April 1865	William Scarratt. William Dean.
Paper-hangings - - -	1243	4th May 1865	Gustave Jusse.
Apparatus for the manufacture of "improved gold" and similar paper-hangings - -	1399	22nd May 1865	John Wylie. James Kew.

Subject-matter of Patent.	Number of Patent.	Date.	Name of Patentee.

PAPER, &c.—continued.

| An improved combination of materials for the manufacture of carpets, floor cloth, felt, wall paper, fireproof flexible roofing, ship and boat building, and for other similar purposes · · | 1775 | 5th July 1865 | John Longbottom. Abram Longbottom. |
| Machinery or apparatus for cutting the edges of paper-hangings. | 1965 | 29th July 1865 | Alfred Augustus Larmuth. |

PAVING, ROAD-MAKING AND CLEANSING; PAVEMENTS.

Construction and paving of roads and other surfaces	110	13th Jan. 1865	Tommaso Guarmacchelli Pagano.
Improved means or apparatus for facing flags or smoothing the surface of stones · · ·	154	18th Jan. 1865	James Coulter. Herbert Harpin.
Improvements in the construction of roadways, pavements, and iron girders specially applicable for the purpose of constructing roads, pavements, bridges, and all description of buildings.	338	7th Feb. 1865	Constantine Headrman.
An improved machine for clearing, sweeping, and removing the refuse from highways, streets and roads or ways, applicable also for removing the leaves of cut grass and other refuse from lawns and other grass lands and walks.	444	16th Feb. 1865	Henry John Pickard.
Improvements in carriage ways and in carriages for the same.	681	9th March 1865	William Henry James.
Brushes or brooms · · · · · · (street brooms.)	704	14th March 1865	James Vero.
Constructing roads and streets · · ·	1260	5th May 1865	Joseph Mitchell.
An improved road scraper · · · · ·	1477	30th May 1865	William Smith.
Construction of roadways, floorings or other surfaces	1688	17th June 1865	Thomas Russell Crampton.
Construction of suspended bridges, roads, aqueducts or other way.	1766	4th July 1865	Sylvain Benjamin Lahouret.
Machinery for excavating earth · · · ·	2403	21st Sept. 1865	John Dastork Hulme.
Construction of roadways, floorings and other surfaces.	2766	26th Oct. 1865	Thomas Russell Crampton.
Improved machinery for cutting tunnels and sinking shafts · · · · · · · (cutting levels.)	2940	15th Nov. 1865	Alexander Allison. Henry Hoskins.
An improved system of pavement to supersede the macadamized system used in the main streets of large cities and causeways subject to a great circulation of vehicles.	3085	25th Nov. 1865	Theophilus Berrens.

Subject-matter of Patent.	Number of Patent.	Date.	Name of Patentee.
PEAT.			
Improvements in treating or manufacturing peat for fuel and in apparatus for the same.	319	4th Feb. 1865	Robert Morellet Alloway.
Improvements in drying and sorting coals, peat and mineral ores, in separating extraneous matters therefrom, and in apparatus used in those processes.	715	14th March 1865	Ferdinand Henry Warlich.
Manufacture of artificial fuel - - -	1547	6th June 1865	David Barker.
A new or improved artificial fuel - - -	1600	13th June 1865	Charles James Collins.
An improved pulping and compressing machine, for the treatment of peat as a fuel, and gas for illuminating purposes - - - -	1708	26th June 1865	Charles Wornum, George Evans.
Improvements in and apparatus for treating peat in bogs and obtaining it therefrom, also applicable to tilling and cultivating land.	2004	2nd Aug. 1865	Charles Hodgson.
Method of and apparatus for treating peat and other plastic materials - - -	2219	29th Aug. 1865	Hall Terrell, Thomas Dos.
Preparing peat or turf for fire lights and fuel, and for machinery to be employed therein.	2436	23rd Sept. 1865	Thomas Vincent Lee.
Machinery for tempering and preparing peat for fuel. (Communicated by Nathaniel Frothingham Potter.)	2469	26th Sept. 1865	George Tomlinson Bousfield.
Manufacture of candles and other illuminating bodies from peat and petroleum.	2580	7th Oct. 1865	Thomas Vincent Lee.
Arrangements of apparatus for drying peat - -	2834	2nd Nov. 1865	Murdoch Campbell, Algernon Charles Plumptre Coote, John Charles Augustus Henry Wolfram.
Purification, refining and treatment of the volatile and fixed oils produced from the destructive distillation of peat or turf.	3312	22nd Dec. 1865	Denis M'Grath.
PENS, PENHOLDERS, PENCILS AND PENCIL-CASES.			
Pencil cases usually termed ever-pointed pencils - (Communicated by Henri Louis Riottel, jun'.)	234	26th Jan. 1865	William Clark.
Certain improvements in the manufacture of pencil cases.	296	3rd Feb. 1865	William Vale.
Improvements in pencil holders and penholders, and in holders for crayons and other marking, writing or drawing materials.	332	8th Feb. 1865	William Edward Wiley.
Pen and pencil holders - - - -	394	11th Feb. 1865	Edward Jacob Hill.
Certain improvements in the manufacture of penholders.	406	13th Feb. 1865	Francis Charles Vannet.
Improvements in ornamenting china and earthenware, and in preparing materials to be employed therefor. (crayons.)	428	15th Feb. 1865	Francis Joseph Emery.

Subject-matter of Patent.	Number of Patent.	Date	Name of Patentee.
PENS, &c.—continued.			
An improved apparatus combining a pencil shield and india-rubber.	766	17th March 1865	Charles Anthony Wheeler.
Pen holders or cases (Communicated by Auguste Mouson and Pierre Hubert Cery.)	1147	21th April 1865	William Edward Newton
Ever-pointed pencils	1216	1st May 1865	William Edward Wiley.
An improved self-supplying pen	1231	2nd May 1865	Jules Catillon.
Certain improvements in the manufacture of penholders.	1266	3rd May 1865	Magloire Honoré Beguin.
Manufacture of pocket pencils	1336	13th May 1865	John Frederic Cooke.
Pencils and pencil-cases having a moveable lead	2466	26th Sept. 1865	Maurice Nopitsch.
Pens used for writing	2673	6th Oct. 1865	Robert Macintyre Cameron. Duncan Cameron.
An improved penholder	2834	3rd Nov. 1865	Reuben Cornelius Lilly.
Certain improvements in cutting or dividing timber, and in the machinery or apparatus connected therewith. (for pencils.)	2935	13th Nov. 1865	John Jex Long.
Preparation of glue or gelatine so as to render it insoluble in water, and applicable by the admixture of other substances, to various purposes for which common glue or gelatine cannot now be used. (for penholders, pencil-cases, &c.) (Communicated by Henry Wurtz.)	3225	23rd Dec. 1865	William Edward Newton.

PETTICOATS, SKIRTS, STAYS, CRINOLINES, RUFFLES, COLLARS AND OTHER LIKE ARTICLES OF LADIES' ATTIRE; SHAWLS.

Subject-matter of Patent.	Number of Patent.	Date	Name of Patentee.
Manufacture of crinoline skirts	106	13th Jan. 1865	Joseph Knight.
Fastenings for stay busks, leggings, gaiters and other similar articles.	349	7th Feb. 1865	George Twigg.
A new method (or mechanical contrivance) for lacing and fastening ladies' stays (sometimes called corsets and bodices).	351	8th Feb. 1865	Charles Field.
Certain improvements in scarfs and in the manufacture of the same. (Communicated by Leon de Mone Pariente.)	491	22nd Feb. 1865	Isaac Pariente.
Improvements in crinoline skirts and in fastenings for the steels or hoops of the same.	529	24th Feb. 1865	James Badcock.
Paper and cloth-lined paper collars for ladies and gentlemen.	666	29th Feb. 1865	Solomon Sully Gray.
Improvements in covered steel for crinoline skirts, and in the machinery for covering and uniting the same. (Communicated by Oliver Rogers Burnham.)	589	2nd March 1865	William Sparks Thomas.
An improvement in covered springs for clothing and in means for manufacturing the same, applicable also to other purposes.	623	6th March 1865	Timothy Sheldon Sperry.

Subject-matter of Patent.	Number of Patent.	Date.	Name of Patentee.
PETTICOATS, &c.—continued.			
An improved manufacture of trimming applicable to the ornamentation of ladies' dresses.	720	11th March 1865	John Peter Booth.
Machinery for cutting, punching, raising, shaping or drawing through sheet metal, by means of tools and dies. (crinoline clips.)	795	22nd March 1865	George Farmer.
Means of ornamenting linen cuffs and collars	1010	4th April 1865	Joseph Debnam.
An improved manufacture of ladies' shirts	1080	14th April 1865	John Crombie Aitken Henderson.
Improvements applicable to capes, paletôts, over-coats and other such like garments.	1128	22nd April 1865	John Emary.
Manufacture of dress shirts and dresses made by means of the stocking frame.	1188	24th April 1865	Edward Moore.
Fasteners for stays or corsets or other articles of dress.	1294	9th May 1865	George Hartley.
Means or method of securing or fastening the stiffeners or supports of stays, corsets and other such like articles of dress.	1338	13th May 1865	Richard Langridge.
An improved stay or corset busk. (Communicated by Telesphore Genty.)	1446	26th May 1865	William Edward Gedge.
An improved machine for curling or curving collars and cuffs.	1689	12th June 1865	George Speight.
Manufacture of collars and cuffs (Communicated by Henri Lacroix Girard.)	1741	30th June 1865	Richard Archibald Brooman.
Improved linings for ladies' dresses (Communicated by Friedrich August Pieper.)	1763	4th July 1865	Philip Paanvant.
Protecting crinoline steel, stay busks, springs for leggings or gaiters, and other similar fastenings.	1857	19th July 1865	William Edwards.
Crinolines	1922	24th July 1865	James Leitch.
Certain improvements in crinolines	1974	31st July 1865	Auguste Yves Behen.
A new and improved application of imitation embroidery to be employed for the ornamentation of crinolines.	2131	14th Aug. 1865	Richard Clarke.
Apparatus for raising and holding the skirts of ladies' dresses. (Communicated by Charles Deudet.)	2207	24th Aug. 1865	Henri Adrien Bonneville.
Improvements in ruffles or frills composed of strips of fabrics, and in the machinery or apparatus employed for their manufacture.	2579	6th Oct. 1865	Chauncey Orrin Crosby.
An improvement or improvements in the manufacture of stays and bodices.	3011	23rd Nov. 1865	John Ellis the younger.
Manufacture of stays, corsets and other similar articles.	3049	24th Nov. 1865	Edward Drucker.
Improvements in machinery employed when wearing hair, and in preparing and treating hair for weaving. (making crinolines.) (Communicated by Charles Bradley.)	3066	29th Nov. 1865	George Tomlinson Bousfield.
Improvements in the manufacture or production of stays, corsets and bodices and other similar articles of dress, and in the fastenings for same.	3079	30th Nov. 1865	Stephen Dixon.
Manufacture of shawls and similar ornamental coverings.	3145	6th Dec. 1865	William Houghton Claburn.
Manufacture of stays or corsets	3239	14th Dec. 1865	William Pretty.

Subject-matter of Patent.	Number of Patent.	Date.	Name of Patentee.
**PETTICOATS, &c.—*continued.*			
An improved kind of clasp or dress preserver, to prevent ladies' dresses from trailing along the ground. (*Communicated by Marie Louise Champrur.*)	8296	20th Dec. 1865	Henry Edward Newton.
Preparation of glue or gelatine so as to render it insoluble in water, and applicable by the admixture of other substances, to various purposes for which common glue or gelatine cannot now be used. (*for coating wire for hoop skirts.*) (*Communicated by Henry Wurts.*)	8325	23rd Dec. 1865	William Edward Newton.
Obtaining and employing continuous lengths of tanned leather for various useful purposes (*for crinolines, shirts, drawers, &c.*)	3334	23rd Dec. 1865	{ George Horn. Daniel Horn.

PHOTOGRAPHY AND PHOTOGRAPHIC APPARATUS.

Subject-matter of Patent.	Number of Patent.	Date.	Name of Patentee.
Mounting photographic printed and other pictures (*Communicated by Louis Streliski.*)	10	2nd Jan. 1865	Frederick Gye.
Manufacture of enamelled glass to render it more useful in photographic art.	12	3rd Jan. 1865	William George Helsby.
Improvements in producing and finishing photographs and photographic transparencies on paper and other suitable substances, and in the machinery employed therein	56	7th Jan. 1866	{ Barrowclough Wright Hentley. William Henry Bailey.
Improvements in giving permanence to and in ornamenting glass transparent positive photographs.	78	10th Jan. 1865	Edwin Pettitt.
Photo-sculpture and apparatus to be employed therein.	216	26th Jan. 1865	David Gay.
A method of or process for producing a new kind of photographic pictures.	616	4th March 1865	Edwin Pettitt.
Improvements in ascertaining the presence of "fixing" agents in photographic productions, in removing the said fixing agents therefrom, and in apparatus connected therewith. (*Communicated by Wilhelm Reissig.*)	677	10th March 1865	Theodor Reissig.
Improved processes for the production of photographic images capable of being inked with fatty inks. (*Communicated by Cyprien Marie Tessié du Motay and Charles Raphael Marichal.*)	712	14th March 1865	Richard Archibald Brooman.
Ornamenting the surfaces of japanned goods and papier maché goods, and other varnished surfaces (*applying photographic pictures.*)	831	21th March 1865	{ Thomas Farmer. Frederick Lewis.
Improved apparatus for mounting photographs	915	31st March 1865	John Henry Smith.
Photographic cameras	1009	8th April 1865	Victor Albert Prout.

Subject-matter of Patent.	Number of Patent.	Date.	Name of Patentee.
PHOTOGRAPHY, &c.—continued.			
Producing an oxy-hydro-magnesian light, applicable to photographic purposes, to lighthouses, and to other illuminations. (Communicated by Prospero Carbraris.)	3246	15th Dec. 1866	Thomas Parker.
Construction of stereoscopes and stereoscopic apparatus.	3262	29th Dec. 1865	Isham Baggs.
PICTURES, PORTRAITS AND MINIATURES; PICTURE-FRAMES.			
Mounting photographic printed and other pictures. (Communicated by Lewis Strelisky.)	10	2nd Jan. 1865	Frederick Gye.
Improvements in producing and finishing photographs and photographic transparencies on paper and other suitable substances, and in the machinery employed therein. (producing medallion portraits is referre.)	59	7th Jan. 1865	Barrowclough Wright Beatley. William Henry Bailey.
A method of or process for producing a new kind of photographic pictures.	619	4th March 1865	Edwin Pettit.
Improved processes for the production of photographic images capable of being inked with fatty inks. (Communicated by Cyprien Marie Tremit du Matoy and Charles Raphael Maréchal.)	712	14th March 1865	Richard Archibald Brooman.
Ornamenting the surfaces of japanned goods and papier maché goods and other varnished surfaces (applying portraits, &c.)	831	24th March 1865	Thomas Farmer. Frederick Lewis.
Manufacture of letter clips, book markers, paper knives, and clips for suspending stationery, drapery and pictures, and for other such like purposes	963	3rd April 1865	Thomas Corbett. Robert Harrington.
Photographic cameras	1009	8th April 1865	Victor Albert Prout.
Improvements in the manufacture and application of devices and representations to tombstones, and in other public or exposed situations, for various purposes (for preparing portraits or likenesses.)	1130	22nd April 1865	Alfred Grainger. Charles Mitchel Girdler.
Production of portraits or likenesses on certain materials by means of photography	1184	27th April 1865	Alfred Grainger. Charles Mitchel Girdler.
An improved liquid composition for cleansing, scouring and bleaching textile animal, mineral and vegetable substances (cleansing pictures.)	2440	23rd Sept. 1865	Gustave Emile Rolland. Emile Léon Rolland.
An improvement in preparing paper and the surfaces of other materials for use in photography.	2648	13th Oct. 1865	Johnners De Witt Brinckerhoff.
Manufacture of embossed wood (for picture frames.) (Communicated by Henry May and Henry Taylor Blake.)	2885	10th Nov. 1865	Alfred Vincent Newton.
An improved mode of applying photographic paper pictures to glass.	3089	2nd Dec. 1865	Anna Josephine Wright.

U

Subject-matter of Patent.	Number of Patent.	Date.	Name of Patentee.

PICTURES, &c.—continued.

Preparation of glue or gelatine so as to render it insoluble in water, and applicable by the administure of other substances to various purposes for which common glue or gelatine cannot now be used.
(*for picture frames.*)
(*Communicated by Henry Warts.*) | 8296 | 23rd Dec. 1865 | William Edward Newton.

Obtaining and employing continuous lengths of } tanned leather for various useful purposes -} (*cord for hanging pictures.*) | 8334 | 23rd Dec. 1865 | { George Hurn. Daniel Hurn.

Construction of show cases, picture frames, house and shop furniture and fittings, and other similar articles. | 8364 | 29th Dec. 1865 | David Vogl.

PILE-DRIVING AND DRAWING.

Hammers and pile drivers to be worked by steam or other power.
(*Communicated by Charles Michel Nillus, Ernest Ferdinand Nillus, Albert Emmanuel Nillus and Jean Joseph Maulins Crousés.*) | 181 | 20th Jan. 1865 | William Edward Newton.

Protecting wooden surfaces from the fouling and injury to which they are ordinarily liable in sea water.
(*piles.*) | 363 | 9th Feb. 1865 | John Cornelius Craigie Halkett.

Improvements in driving piles and in apparatus } therefor - - - - -} | 597 | 3rd March 1865 | { David Manwell. James Manwell.

An improved composition for coating iron or other vessels, and for other similar purposes. (*piles, &c.*) | 1278 | 9th May 1865 | John Cornelius Craigie Halkett.

Machinery for driving piles - - - - | 1278 | 18th May 1865 | William Eamir.

Machinery applicable to the cutting off the upper } parts of piles - - - - -} | 1408 | 22nd May 1865 | { George Furoom. James Slater.

Improved machinery or apparatus for cutting off wooden piles below water. | 1474 | 27th May 1865 | Charles Henry Murray.

PILLARS, COLUMNS, POSTS, SLABS, VASES;
STATUARY.

Photo-sculpture and apparatus to be employed therein. | 219 | 26th Jan. 1865 | David Gay.

An improvement in the manufacture of artificial stone for building and other purposes. (*for columns.*) | 441 | 16th Feb. 1865 | William Kirrage.

Improvements in the manufacture of metallic bedsteads, which improvements are also applicable to the manufacture of other metallic articles. (*columns, busts, &c.*) | 699 | 13th March 1866 | James Atkins.

Subject-matter of Patent.	Number of Patent.	Date.	Name of Patentee.
PILLARS, &c.—continued.			
Posts or supports for telegraph wires, also applicable to posts or supports employed for other purposes	749	17th March 1865	George Dibley. Frederick Bosby.
An improved socket for fencing and telegraph posts	775	20th March 1865	Arthur Giraud Browning.
Improvements in the manufacture and application of devices and representations to tombstones, and in other public or exposed situations, for various purposes.	1130	22nd April 1865	Alfred Grainger. Charles Mitchel Girdler.
Manufacture and application of glass and other vitreous compositions. *(for monumental tablets, slabs, &c.)*	1220	1st May 1865	Arthur Howard Emerson. Robert Fowler.
Certain improvements in the manufacture of "moulds" for metallic castings having a cylindrical form. *(supporting-pillars.)*	1296	10th May 1865	David Hartley.
Manufacture of slabs, beams, and other articles of artificial stone where great strength is required.	1337	13th May 1865	Frederick Ransome.
Telegraph supports, parts of the invention being applicable to other purposes	1380	20th May 1865	Cornelius Varley. Samuel Alfred Varley.
Manufacture of iron piers or erections, applicable more especially for carrying bridges at high elevations, or available for shore legs and light-houses.	1433	5th June 1865	Charles De Bergue.
An improvement in the mode of uniting different metals, such as iron and copper or alloys, to form compound metallic castings. *(adapted to ornamental columns.)*	1885	19th July 1865	George Nimmo.
Manufacture of bricks and other analogous materials. *(for columns, balustrades, &c.)*	2571	6th Oct. 1865	Victor Jean Baptiste Germain.
A new composition of India-rubber mastic or cement, made in a more or less fluid state according to the use to be made of it, and the process or contrivance for applying the same. *(coating posts.)*	2630	12th Oct. 1865	Auguste Aimé Lermard.
Purification and preparation of animal and vegetable wax, stearine, spermaceti, paraffine and other solid, waxy or fatty substances. *(for statuettes.)*	2769	27th Oct. 1865	Scipion Nequelin.
A new or improved cement or composition applicable to the agglomeration or moulding of various materials, and to other useful and decorative purposes. *(moulding statues, vases, slabs, &c.)* *(Communicated by Stanislas Sorel and Emile Justin Mesier.)*	3119	5th Dec. 1865	Richard Archibald Brooman.
Pipes, tubular columns and hollow structures, for masts, cars, shear legs, life boats and ordinary boats, for water, gas and waste water pipes, and for other similar constructions where great strength is required.	3314	22nd Dec. 1865	Edward Deane.

Subject-matter of Patent.	Number of Patent.	Date.	Name of Patentee.
PINS AND NEEDLES.			
Hair pins . . . . (Communicated by Joseph Charles Howells.)	535	6th Feb. 1865	Richard Archibald Brooman.
Machinery or apparatus for rolling and shaping metals, making nails, rivets and similar articles	644	8th March 1865	{ Joseph Wadsworth. James Wadsworth.
Certain improvements in machinery and appliances for the manufacture of nails, pins and rivets -	765	21st March 1865	{ Charles Farmer, Thomas Turner.
Fastenings for pins, buttons and other articles with metallic backs.	861	24th March 1865	Isac Louis Pulvermacher.
An improved mode of pointing or tapering the ends of metallic rods or wire, applicable to the manufacture of pins, needles, and other articles where points or tapered ends are required. (Communicated by Henri Camberay.)	916	6th April 1865	Edwin Henry Newby.
Machinery or apparatus for tapering, pointing or reducing wires or rods for spindles, hatchel teeth, pins for dressers, and similar articles.	1363	16th May 1865	Chauncey Orvis Crosby.
Machinery for the manufacture of needles - -	1688	23rd June 1865	William Lenty.
An improvement in metal pins - - -	1920	21th July 1865	Herbert William Hart.
Machinery or apparatus for the manufacture of needles.	2074	10th Aug. 1865	Chauncey Orvis Crosby.
An improved sewing machine - - - (needle.) (Communicated by Henry Hudson.)	2535	3rd Oct. 1865	William Robert Lake.
Improvements in sewing machinery for using waxed thread. (needle.) (Communicated by Thomas John Halligan.)	2748	24th Oct. 1865	Alfred Vincent Newton.
An improved needle - - - -	2768	25th Oct. 1865	Leonard Bennett.
Knitting-machine needles - - - (Communicated by Isaac Wixom Lamb.)	2960	17th Nov. 1865	William Clark.
Sewing-machines - - - - } (needles.)	3086	1st Dec. 1865	{ Henry Hedley. George Ainsley.
Improved machinery for manufacturing sewing-machine needles - - - } (Partly communicated by Joseph Thorne.)	3143	6th Dec. 1865	{ Nahum Salamon, William John Lawrence Davids.
Boxes or cases for needles - - -	3309	22nd Dec. 1865	Richard Newball.

PIPES, TUBES AND SYPHONS; TOBACCO-PIPES; JOINING PIPES.			
Stoppers for bottles, jars, vessels and tubes, also for ordnance and fire-arms.	27	4th Jan. 1865	Nathan Thompson.
An improved apparatus for cutting iron gas or other pipes. (Communicated by Jules Chartier.)	85	11th Jan. 1865	William Edward Gedge.
Packing for steam joints, stuffing boxes, pistons and the like.	217	25th Jan. 1865	William Paton.
Machinery for compressing coal dust and other materials fit for burning, also clay into bricks, tubes, pipes and other like articles.	230	25th Jan. 1865	William Smith.

Subject-matter of Patent.	Number of Patent.	Date.	Name of Patentee.
PIPES, &c.—*continued.*			
Improvements in steam generators or steam-boilers and furnaces, part of which is also applicable to other heat-generating apparatus. (*forming the transverse tubes.*)	243	27th Jan. 1865	Joseph Twibill.
Improvements in screw taps more especially designed for cutting threads in the fittings and connections for gas, steam and water pipes.	257	28th Jan. 1865	William Foster.
An improved socket for pipes and method of joining the same.	286	1st Feb. 1865	George Henry Pierce.
Improvements in armour plated and other ships or vessels, also applicable to fortifications generally. (*transport-moulded tubes.*)	296	2nd Feb. 1865	Julius Saunders Jeffreys.
An improved mode of making metal pipes	356	8th Feb. 1865	William Anderson.
Improvements in apparatus for heating water and in connecting hot water and other metal pipes.	390	11th Feb. 1865	Andrew M'Laren.
Improvements in ships of war, partly applicable to ships designed for the merchant service. (*ventilating tubes.*) (*Communicated by Augustus Walker.*)	508	23rd Feb. 1865	George Haseltine.
Musical instruments in the nature of organs in which reeds are employed.	579	1st March 1865	Augustine Thomas Godfrey.
An improved " core " to be employed in the casting of metallic pipes or tubes.	587	2nd March 1865	David Hartley.
An improvement in putting up tobacco for smoking, and in the implements or pipes for smoking the same, and in making tobacco paper. (*Communicated by Luther Holmes Hale.*)	615	4th March 1865	William Edward Newton.
Improvements in the strengthening and ornamenting of collapsible or soft metal tubes.	687	9th March 1865	Edmund Leahy.
An improved method of connecting together tubes or pipes used for conveying gas and water, and for other purposes.	689	9th March 1865	Victor Delperdange.
An improved combined tap-piece and valve	694	11th March 1865	Charles Johnson.
Improvements in the manufacture of metallic bedsteads, which improvements are also applicable to the manufacture of other metallic articles.	699	13th March 1865	James Atkins.
An improved top or mouth-piece for cigars or cheroots	770	20th March 1865	{ Thomas Oliver, Joseph William Musto.
Certain improvements in non-conducting composition for preventing the radiation or transmission of heat or cold. (*for coating pipes.*)	864	27th March 1865	Ferdinand Le Roy.
Machinery for ornamenting metal tubes	884	1st April 1865	George Burt.
Manufacture of flexible tubing or hose. (*for gas.*) (*Communicated by David Knight Harris, and Thomas Lyons Revd.*)	960	4th April 1865	George Tomlinson Bousfield.
Steam-boilers, steam-boiler tubes, sides of steam boilers, flues and furnaces.	988	7th April 1865	George Rydill.
Pipes for conveying water and gas and for other like purposes, and a new or improved composition for joining the said pipes and other similar pipes.	1086	13th April 1865	Charles Forster Cotterill.
Machinery for moulding and making cores for moulding or casting metals.	1183	21st April 1865	Richard Cashen.

Subject-matter of Patent.	Number of Patent.	Date.	Name of Patentee.
PIPES, &c.—continued.			
Improvements in the fitting of surface condenser tubes, and in the tools to be used therein, and in the means of retarding corrosion in steam-boilers. (*Communicated by William Judson.*)	1183	22nd April 1865	Alfred Vincent Newton.
Improved contrivances to facilitate the arrangement of flowers and leaves. (*making tubes for the reception of flowers.*)	1187	24th April 1865	Thomas Charles Marsh.
Improvements in steam-engines, relating to valve motions, governor and drain pipes -	1196	29th April 1865	{ Andrew Wyllie. John M'Farlane Gray
Making moulds for casting pipes and other articles of various sizes.	1206	1st May 1865	David Yonlow Stewart.
Improvements in finishing and polishing metal tubes and rods, and in apparatus or machinery to be employed therein.	1229	2nd May 1865	Thomas Allcock.
Improvements in means or apparatus for fixing or tightening the ends of boiler and other tubes, and in cutting the ends or other parts of such tubes.	1262	9th May 1865	Ralph Hart Tweddell.
Certain improvements in the manufacture of "moulds" for metallic castings having a cylindrical form. (*metallic tubes, pipes, &c.*)	1296	10th May 1865	David Hartley.
Improvements in the manufacture of hose and other flexible tubing, which improvements are also applicable in uniting surfaces of india-rubber, gutta-percha or of compounds thereof, to each other, or to woven or other fabric or material for other purposes.	1309	11th May 1865	Thomas Jefferson Mayall.
Improved apparatus for cutting, turning and smoothing metal pipes, and the surfaces of bolts, rods or spindles -	1311	11th May 1865	{ George Mountford. Edward Worrell.
Certain improvements in apparatus for cutting or forming screws, which is also applicable for cutting pipes or tubes.	1411	23rd May 1865	Edward M'Nally.
Apparatus for making cores and moulds for casting - (*pipes of small size.*)	1429	24th May 1865	{ David Law. James Bennet.
A new and improved mode of making and venting cores and parts of moulds, to be used in the casting of iron or other metal. (*casting pipes.*) (*Communicated by Joseph Harrison, jun.*)	1434	25th May 1865	John Henry Johnson.
Instruments or apparatus for cleaning the interior of tubes or hollow cylinders, gas chimneys and other hollow articles.	1479	30th May 1865	James Hare the younger.
Furnaces used in the manufacture of welded iron tubes.	1517	2nd June 1865	Thomas Pritchard.
Tube cutters and screw stocks -	1527	3rd June 1865	Charles Taylor.
Turbines -	1534	5th June 1865	{ Thomas Gentle. Joseph Allinsark.
Multitubular hot water boilers -	1614	14th June 1865	Henry Ormson.
Clay tobacco pipes -	1683	23rd June 1865	Lesley White.
An improved brewers' and distillers' refrigerator or apparatus for cooling liquids, condensing steam or other vapours.	1700	26th June 1865	Morris Ashby.

Subject-matter of Patent.	Number of Patent.	Date.	Name of Patentee.

PIPES, &c. —continued.

Subject-matter of Patent.	Number of Patent.	Date.	Name of Patentee.
A new and improved feed or fluid regulator for feeding bottle and other tubes.	1727	29th June 1865	William Botham.
Manufacturing gas barrels and tubes of cast steel and homogeneous iron.	1738	30th June 1865	Henry Powell Tipper.
Improvements in the manufacture of certain kinds of metallic tubes and rods, and in ornamenting metallic tubes and rods.	1740	1st July 1865	James Atkins.
Improvements in tubular structures, rendering them specially applicable for ships' masts and building purposes.	1755	3rd July 1865	Edward Dunn.
An improved self-acting apparatus for obtaining a circulation of volatile liquids. (Communicated by Messieurs Francisque Massot and Auguste Jaquin.)	1810	8th July 1865	Hector Augustè Dufresd.
Making skelps for iron or steel tubes direct from the rolls, and for machinery to be used in the same.	1850	15th July 1865	Samuel Illingby.
Flexible gas tubing - - - -. (Communicated by Henry Reithen.)	1861	15th July 1865	William Robert Lake.
A new portable machine or apparatus for the cutting of screw threads on pipes or on solid materials, and for the cutting of pipes asunder.	2086	8th Aug. 1865	Thomas Goode Messenger.
Manufacture of paper boards and pipes - -	2125	17th Aug. 1865	Nicholas Charles Sarsdmey.
An improvement in syphons - - -	2168	23rd Aug. 1865	Lippmann Jacob Levinska.
Well sinking tubes - - - - - (Communicated by Hiram John Messenger, Stephen Arrow and Byron Medge.)	2178	24th Aug. 1865	William Edward Newton.
An improved combination drill brace - } (cutting off the ends of tubes.)	2212	24th Aug. 1865	{ Edward Davies. Richard Hobbs Traunton.
Moulds for casting metallic pipes, retorts and other articles.	2215	29th Aug. 1865	George Robinson.
Manufacture of cast steel or other metallic tubes -	2241	31st Aug. 1865	William Henry Brown.
Manufacture of flexible tubing or hose - - (Communicated by David Knight Harris and Thomas Lyons Reed.)	2315	9th Sept. 1865	George Tomlinson Bousfield.
Pipes used for smoking - - - - -	2325	11th Sept. 1865	Charles Ambrose M'Evoy.
Improvements in the manufacture of tubes for gun barrels and other purposes, parts of which improvements are also applicable to the manufacture of rods or bars, and to the rifling of ordnance and fire-arms.	2361	14th Sept. 1865	Gustavus Palmer Harding.
Smoking pipes and cigar holders, and an improved inhereo cartridge to be used with the same. (Communicated by Elijah Mires.)	2362	15th Sept. 1865	Neal Myers.
Saddles and harness - - - - - (using india-rubber tubes.) (Communicated by Chevalier Achille Angelini.)	2369	15th Sept. 1865	William Clark.
Compositions used for coating metallic surfaces -} (of iron pipes.)	2450	27th Sept. 1865	{ John Roffey. Charles William Smith.
Improvements in connections for and in stopping pipes used for conveying water and gas, and for other like purposes, and in preventing leakages in the said pipes, and in apparatus employed therein.	2503	29th Sept. 1865	Charles Forster Cotterill.

Subject-matter of Patent.	Number of Patent.	Date.	Name of Patentees.
Pipes, &c.—continued.			
Pneumatic ways for the transmission of letters, merchandise and passengers. (Communicated by Elias Portman Needham.)	2537	3rd Oct. 1865	William Edward Newton.
Machinery for shaping metal and other substances - (tubes.)	2542	5th Oct. 1865	Herbeth Hughes.
An improved composition or material to be employed in waterproofing or rendering woven fabrics impervious to moisture. (hose pipe.)	2548	6th Oct. 1865	Henry Francis Smith.
Tanning or treating hides applicable for machine bands and other purposes. (for hose pipes.)	2561	7th Oct. 1865	William Harris.
Improvements in apparatus for the regulation of the up and down currents of air, and for the prevention and cure of smoky chimneys.	2602	10th Oct. 1865	William Cooke.
A new composition of indian-rubber mastic or cement, made in a more or less fluid state according to the use to be made of it, and the process or contrivance for applying the same. (coating sewer pipes.)	2620	12th Oct. 1865	Auguste Aimé Lavenard.
An improved apparatus for forming or repairing the mouths of boiler and other tubes. (Communicated by Edward Clark.)	2697	19th Oct. 1865	George Reverdy Ghimelin.
Machinery for screening, tempering and moulding clays and earths into bricks, tiles and other articles. (pipes.)	2728	21st Oct. 1865	Isaac Roberts.
An improved mode of and apparatus for cleaning the tubes of steam-boilers. (Communicated by Abraham Egreton.)	2761	26th Oct. 1865	George Davies.
Certain improvements in apparatus employed in the manufacture and production of metallic pipes, tubes or other similar hollow castings. (Communicated by Alfred Bertach.)	2804	31st Oct. 1865	Arthur Denlander.
Improvements in steam hammers and in means of applying them to the manufacture of boilers and tubes.	2805	31st Oct. 1865	Charles Emmet.
An improved non-conducting composition for preventing the radiation or transmission of heat or cold. (for coating steam pipes.)	2853	4th Nov. 1865	James Toya.
An improved apparatus for braiding cigars or tobacco.	2862	7th Nov. 1865	Hyde Bateman.
Stoves for drying moulds - - - - (for making pipes.)	2943	15th Nov. 1865	Henry Cochrane.
Improvements in cocks for steam, water, air and gases at high pressures, and also in gauge cocks and water gauges for boilers, and sediment tubes for cocks and pipes.	2990	21st Nov. 1865	Samuel Bennett.
A combined adjustable spanner, tube cutter, and pipe wrench. (Communicated by Henry Hitchings Borrayn eneth and Martin Van Winder).	3036	27th Nov. 1865	John Phillips Baragwanath.
"Top rollers" employed in the manufacture of fibrous substances. (india-rubber tubes as roller covers.)	3073	30th Nov. 1865	John Kerfoot.

Subject-matter of Patent.	Number of Patent.	Date.	Name of Patentee.
PIPES, &c.—continued.			
Improved means of preventing water pipes from bursting. (Communicated by John Brown.)	8088	1st Dec. 1865	Longden McMurdo Rogers.
Manufacture of metal tubes.	8117	5th Dec. 1865	Philip Albert Muntz.
Improvements in steam-boilers and in the furnaces and grates thereof, the same improvements in furnaces and grates being also applicable to other furnaces and to stoves. (steam pipe.) (Communicated by Robert Winslow Davis, Daniel Davis and Henry Sheldon Anable.)	8141	6th Dec. 1865	William Edward Newton.
Improvements in constructing atmospheric railways and carriages, and in working the same, parts of which are applicable to exhausting and condensing air for other purposes. (atmospheric tubes.)	3173	9th Dec. 1865	Alexander Doull.
Improvements in steam-boilers and in apparatus adapted for cleaning the flues of boilers. (circulating pipe.)	8184	9th Dec. 1865	Norman Willis Wheeler.
An improved construction of tool for cutting tubes. (Communicated by David Mercer Nichols.)	8214	12th Dec. 1865	Alfred Vincent Newton.
Boilers or apparatus for generating steam. (pipe joints.) (Communicated by Julien Belleville.)	8269	14th Dec. 1865	Richard Archibald Brooman.
Improvements in the manufacture of metal tubes for gun barrels and other purposes, and in machinery or apparatus employed therein.	8289	20th Dec. 1865	Thomas Bickett.
Pipes, tubular columns and hollow structures, for masts, cars, sheer legs, lift boats and ordinary boats, for water, gas and waste water pipes, and for other similar constructions where great strength is required.	8314	22nd Dec. 1865	Edward Deane.
Preparation of glue or gelatine so as to render it insoluble in water, and applicable by the admixture of other substances, to various purposes for which common glue or gelatine cannot now be used. (for flexible gas tubes.) (Communicated by Henry Wurtz.)	8325	23rd Dec. 1865	William Edward Newton.
For Copp Tubes, see "BOBBINS."			
PISTONS AND PISTON PACKINGS.			
Improvements in the manufacture of elastic packings for pistons, and in lubricating compositions therefor.	19	4th Jan. 1865	Edward Kirby.
Regulating and working the valves of steam and other engines. (air pistons.)	82	11th Jan. 1865	John Frederick Spencer.
Improvements in the packings of pistons and piston rods of pumps and steam and other engines, which improvements are also applicable to hydraulic presses.	155	18th Jan. 1865	William Robert Foster.

Subject-matter of Patent.	Number of Patent.	Date.	Name of Patentee.
PISTONS, &c.—*continued*.			
Steam-engines - - - - -	186	19th Jan. 1865	William Cleveland Hicks.
Packing for steam joints, stuffing boxes, pistons and the like.	217	25th Jan. 1865	William Paton.
An improved packing for piston and other rods - (*Communicated by William Bolivar Davis.*)	647	14th March 1865	Francis Wise.
Certain improvements in metallic pistons - -	1059	13th April 1865	{ Seth Dawson. { John Burgess. { John Wilson.
Cushions for steam cylinders - - - (*Communicated by Henry Johnson.*)	1079	14th April 1865	Frederick Collier Bakewell.
An improved packing for steam cylinders, stuffing boxes and shared vessels containing water, air, or gases and for other similar purposes. (*Communicated by Frederic Henry Brinkmann and Ernest Frederic Wachwitz, the younger.*)	1119	21st April 1865	Edward Thomas Hughes.
Improvements in steering ships or vessels, and in the machinery or apparatus connected therewith.	1187	25th April 1865	William Elder.
Mode of and apparatus for obtaining and applying } motive-power	1305	10th May 1865	{ Stanislas Pokutynski. { Michel Mycielski.
An improvement in atmospheric forging hammers - (*packing for piston rod.*)	1380	19th May 1865	Edward Augustus Raymond.
Calorie or heated air engines - - - (*Communicated by Cyrus W. Baldwin and Walter Davis Richards.*)	1565	8th June 1865	Hommel Blatchford Tucker.
Locomotive engines - - - (*lubricating the pistons.*) (*Communicated by Auguste De Bergue.*)	1754	3rd July 1865	Charles De Bergue.
Construction of valves for steam and other engines (*Communicated by Thomas Shrimton Davis.*)	1819	2nd July 1865	William Edward Newton.
Fire-engines and hydraulic machines - -	1868	24th July 1865	Leon Paul Laroche.
Apparatus applicable as a motive-power engine, a pump or fluid meter. (*Communicated by Francis Bernard de Kerareman.*)	2021	4th Aug. 1865	William Clark.
Certain improvements in steam-engines and valves (*Communicated by George Ichabod Washburn.*)	2296	6th Sept. 1865	William Clark.
An improved construction of engine which can be used either as a motor or for pumping. (*Communicated by John Benjamin Root and William Benjamin.*)	2453	23rd Sept. 1865	William Edward Newton.
Tools for securing tubes in tube plates, and for other purposes where concentrated power or adjustment is necessary. (*for tightening packing rings of pistons.*)	2455	26th Sept. 1865	Richard Taylor Nelson Howry.
Double or single action pumps - - - (*Communicated by Claude Goula.*)	2582	11th Oct. 1865	William Edward Gedge.
Improvements in and applicable to slide valves, } pistons, and glands - - - - }	2700	19th Oct. 1865	{ Thomas Adams. { George John Porton.
A new or improved method of preventing the } escape of heat from steam cylinders - } (*covering pistons with wood.*)	3051	28th Nov. 1865	{ William Simons. { Andrew Brown.
Pistons - - - - - (*Communicated by David Lister.*)	3279	19th Dec. 1865	John Henry Johnson.

Subject-matter of Patent.	Number of Patent.	Date.	Name of Patentee.
PISTONS, &c.—continued.			
An improved piston and tallow or grease cup .	3353	29th Dec. 1865	John Bates, Edward Brookes, Edmund William Brookes.
Means of feeding meal to the bolting reel in flouring mills. *(piston and packings.)*	3395	30th Dec. 1865	William Frazer Cochrane.
PLANTS, SEA-WEEDS, &c. (Treatment of.)			
Application and utilization of certain materials suitable for the manufacture of paper. *(Communicated by Joachim John Monteiro.)*	708	13th March 1865	John Webb.
Improvements in the preparation or treatment of ura-weed and in obtaining products therefrom -	877	24th March 1865	Richard Young, Charles Finby Oliphant Glassford, F.C.S.
The manufacture of a new resinous gum or balsam *(from the Australian grass tree.)* *(Communicated by Benjamin Hawkins Dods.)*	1179	26th April 1865	George Tomlinson Bousfield.
Improvements in the manufacture of paper and paper stock, and in the utilisation of certain waste products resulting therefrom - - - *(treating asparto straw.)*	1503	13th June 1865	Thomas Routledge, William Henry Richardson.
Obtaining jellies, syrups, drinks and other products, from the tree Arbutus Unedo, known as the Arbutus.	1649	20th June 1865	Philippe Mingaud.
Manufacture of hats and other felted goods and fabrics. *(Communicated by Edwin Dodd M'Cracken, James M'Cracken, Charles Edward M'Cracken, John Adam Southanyd and Robert Warner Southanyd.)*	1707	26th June 1865	William Edward Newton.
An improved process of preparing ora seeds and other vegetable substances for the production of artificial guano, felt, alkaline salts and iodine.	1877	19th July 1865	Donald M'Crummen.
Manufacture of paper - - - -	2078	10th Aug. 1865	Alexandre Merdel.
Process of and machinery for cleaning china grass and flax, and removing therefrom the resinous and woody matters that adhere to the useful fibres of the plant.	2079	10th Aug. 1865	Joseph Farra
Treating of china grass or other vegetable fibrous substances - - - - -	2114	16th Aug. 1866	John Ingham, John Culpen.
Manufacture of the straw of rye and other straws and grasses, into fibre, and utilising the refuse.	2171	23rd Aug. 1865	Edward Henry Cradock Monckton.
Improvements in the manufacture of paper by the introduction therein of a new vegetable fibrous substance.	2472	27th Sept. 1865	George Evelngb.
Mode of treating the roots of the lucerne plant, for the purpose of manufacturing paper, pasteboard, fabrics and ropes therefrom. *(Communicated by John Peter Caminade.)*	2525	2nd Oct. 1865	Charles Denton Abel.
Process of and machinery for preparing flax, hemp, jute, china grass, and other analogous vegetable fibres for spinning.	2725	21st Oct. 1865	James Hill Dickson.

Subject-matter of Patent.	Number of Patent.	Date.	Name of Patentee.
PLANTS, &c.—*continued.*			
Manufacture of paper from marine vegetable matters. *(Communicated by Pierre Ernest Gérpiron and Charles Marie Gaymay.)*	2741	23rd Oct. 1865	William Clark.
Treating vegetable fibres used in the manufacture of paper and other similar substances made from pulp. *(Communicated by Louis Horst.)*	2882	8th Nov. 1865	Godfrey Anthony Ermen.
Improvements in the process of treating materials for the manufacture of paper and other similar textile fabrics, and in apparatus for the same. *(Communicated by Robert Hanbam Collyer.)*	3097	29th Nov. 1865	Charles Stuart Baker.
An improved method in the production of fibre from various fibrous plants and animal products.	3112	4th Dec. 1865	James Start.
A new or improved method of preparing esparto, alpha or tosgador grasses or other similar vegetable substances, for spinning, weaving, and for substitution for hair and for other fibres now in use.	3155	8th Dec. 1865	Oliver Maggs. George Hedgecombe Smith.
A new method of preparing plants of the Eucalyptus family and Myrtacean plants, and the application thereof to the purposes of tobacco and snuff. *(Communicated by Prosper Vincent Ramel.)*	3174	9th Dec. 1865	Richard Archibald Brooman.
The manufacture of pulp from "Lygeum Spartum" *(Communicated by Antonio Escobar.)*	3219	13th Dec. 1865	Richard Archibald Brooman.
Improved apparatus for manufacturing paper pulp -	3246	11th Dec. 1865	William Alfred West.
Improvements in the manufacture of yarns, string and paper, and in the preparation of dyes, and in dyeing fabrics, by the application of vegetable substances not hitherto used for such purposes. *(French willow.)*	6319	22nd Dec. 1865	John Alexander Cooper.
See also " **FIBRES.** *"*			
PLATES, DISHES, CUPS AND SAUCERS; TOAST RACKS, CRUET FRAMES.			
A new or improved invalid or stephan drinking cup -	457	15th Feb. 1865	Robert Henry Emerson.
An improved method and machinery for the manufacture of various articles in pottery, earthenware or porcelain, by mechanical process. *(plates, cups, &c.)* *(Communicated by Edme Mercier.)*	488	17th Feb. 1865	William Edward Gedge.
Improvements in wine glasses and in stands or holders for the same.	698	11th March 1865	James Murdoch Napier.
Construction of toast racks - - - -	694	11th March 1865	George Carter.
An improved method in the manufacture of toast racks - - - - - -	811	23rd March 1865	John Barley. Laurence Glover.
An improvement or improvements in ornamenting articles made of glass. *(circular dishes.)*	868	24th March 1865	Joseph Williams.

Subject-matter of Patent.	Number of Patent.	Date.	Name of Patentee.
WHEELS, &c.—continued.			
Improvements in the construction of railway plant to ensure the safety of passengers' lives in the event of accident or collision - - -	688	11th March 1865	Charles Middleton Kennett. Nathaniel Symons.
A new or improved machine for dressing and rounding the inner surfaces of felloes.	704	22nd March 1865	Hiram Smith Jacobs.
Traction engines - - - - - (travelling wheels.)	663	27th March 1865	John Brockshaw. William Scott Underhill.
Manufacture of steel tires for railway wheels - -	676	29th March 1865	Francis William Webb.
An improved application of steam power to locomotion on ordinary roads. (Communicated by Alfred Taillandres.)	1002	8th April 1865	William Edward Gedge.
A new or improved compensating wheel to be used with locomotives, carriages and other vehicles on railway and tram roads, in conjunction with or without the wheels now used, in order to obtain at curves and other parts of the road a rolling instead of a sledging motion now effected by wheels in present use on railway and other tram roads.	1022	11th April 1865	James John Myers.
Improvements in carriage and other wheels and in connecting or fixing the said wheels to their axle-boxes.	1084	11th April 1865	Stephen Wright.
Wheels and the manner of applying the same to railway carriages for passengers' and goods' traffic, as also the leading wheels for locomotives.	1116	21st April 1865	William Day.
Construction of railway rails and wheels - -	1188	24th April 1865	John Townsend Bucknill.
Improvements in the manufacture of crossings for the permanent way of railways, and also in tyres for wheels.	1396	3th May 1865	Joseph Armstrong.
Machinery employed in the manufacture of hoops and tyres.	1425	25th May 1865	John Ramsbottom.
Manufacture of cast-steel railway tires - - -	1426	25th May 1865	John Firth.
Improvements in making cast-steel railway tires, and in apparatus therefor.	1455	27th May 1865	John Martin Rowan.
Wheels for locomotive engines, railway carriages and other purposes. (Communicated by Robert Elsdon.)	1601	13th June 1865	John Henry Johnson.
Locomotive engines and railway carriages - -	1646	19th June 1865	George Smith the younger.
An improved system of wheels for railway carriages	1663	20th June 1865	Emile Dupont.
Improvements in steam carriages and in adapting wheels for common roads to railways. (Communicated by Joseph Alphonse Loubat.)	1821	10th July 1865	Richard Archibald Brooman.
Traction engines - - - - - - (Communicated by Alexander Keene Richards.)	1836	11th July 1865	Morris Horsey Keene.
Manufacture of iron and steel - - - - (rolling wheel tire.) (Communicated by Martin Diradoure Hracons.)	1964	29th July 1865	Ephraim Nobel.
Improvements in the manufacture of hoops and tyres and in the machinery employed therein.	1975	31st July 1865	John Ramsbottom.
The improvement of the permanent way of railways and carriages for the same.	2207	30th Aug. 1865	James Coin Green.
Traction engines and other vehicles - - -	2204	30th Aug. 1865	Samuel Lawrence James.
Apparatus used for removing axle-boxes from wheels.	2303	4th Sept. 1865	Joseph Drabble.

Subject-matter of Patent.	Number of Patent.	Date.	Name of Patentee.
PLOUGHING, &c.—continued.			
An improved rotary spades or digging machine for tilling land. (Communicated by Cierra Comstock.)	671	10th March 1865	Edwin Addison Phillips.
An improved agricultural implement	676	11th March 1865	George Wright.
Harrows, drags, cultivators, and other similar implements to be used in the cultivation of the soil.	739	16th March 1865	Joseph Seaman.
Locomotive engines and carriages for common roads and tramways, and also for agricultural and other purposes.	760	20th March 1865	Alexander Richard Mackenzie.
Improved apparatus applicable to steam cultivation	958	4th April 1865	William Bolstrode.
Manufacture of harrows, cultivators and other similar agricultural implements.	976	6th April 1865	John Hadger.
Manufacture of plough-shares, socks or points for ploughs, cultivators or scarifarrows, and other implements used in the cultivation of the land where three points are used or required	996	7th April 1865	William Gray. Edward Gray. John Gray.
Machinery for cultivating land (Partly communicated by Max Eyth.)	1104	20th April 1865	David Graig.
Engines, machinery and implements employed in ploughing and tilling land.	1123	21st April 1865	Collinson Hall.
Digging machinery	1126	22nd April 1865	Ormrod Coffers Evans.
Improvements in motive power machinery for cultivating land, part of which improvements is applicable to driving machinery generally	1131	22nd April 1865	James Howard. Edward Tenney Bousfield.
Ploughs	1248	4th May 1865	John Mulkarts.
An improved method of and apparatus for laying single line articulated railways, and a method of propelling thereon, particularly applicable for agricultural purposes.	1321	12th May 1865	Richard Winder.
Ploughs	1389	13th May 1865	John Eddy.
Horse hoes and drills	1649	9th June 1865	James Holmes. George Thomas Holmes. Frederick Robert Holmes.
An improved method of propelling agricultural implements.	1618	15th June 1865	Virgile Posterin.
Means of and apparatus for raising water for agricultural and other useful and ornamental purposes. (washing-troughs.) (Communicated by Jean Louis Celestin Ackard.)	1918	22nd July 1865	William Edward Gedge.
Preparation of soils to promote general vegetation	1935	26th July 1865	Thomas Spencer.
Improvements in and apparatus for treating peat in bogs and obtaining therefrom, also applicable to tilling and cultivating land.	2004	2nd Aug. 1865	Charles Hodgson.
Traction engines and other vehicles (for ploughing.)	2234	30th Aug. 1865	Samuel Lawrence James.
An improved implement for cultivating or tilling land	2235	30th Aug. 1865	Samuel Gilbert. Samuel Gilbert the younger.
Manufacture of harrows, cultivators and other similar agricultural implements	2231	12th Sept. 1865	John Badger. John Henry Neff.
A new composition of indian-rubber mastic or cement, made in a more or less fluid state according to the use to be made of it, and the process or contrivance for applying the same. (coating agricultural implements.)	2630	12th Oct. 1865	Auguste Aimé Lereuard.

Subject-matter of Patent.	Number of Patent.	Date.	Name of Patentee.
PLOUGHING, &c.— continued.			
Clod crushers and chain harrows - - -	2634	12th Oct. 1865	William Colborne Cambridge.
Machinery or apparatus for cultivating land by steam power.	3296	13th Dec. 1865	Pryce William Rowen.
Boilers or apparatus for generating steam - (for agricultural engines.) (Communicated by Julien Belleville.)	3269	18th Dec. 1865	Richard Archibald Brooman.
Obtaining and employing continuous lengths of tanned leather for various useful purposes - (ropes for harrows, ploughs, &c.)	3334	23rd Dec. 1865	{ George Hurn. { Daniel Hurn.
PRESERVING AND HARDENING WOOD, METAL, STONE, SKIN AND OTHER SUBSTANCES.			
A metallic anti-corrosive varnish for protecting the surfaces of metals from oxidation.	250	30th Jan. 1865	John M'Innes.
An improved varnish for preserving wood, and for protecting iron ships and other metal work from oxydation and from fouling. (Communicated by Adolphe Guibert.)	315	4th Feb. 1865	Richard Archibald Brooman.
An improved process and apparatus for impregnating wood with chemical solutions. (Communicated by Ernest Basin and Jules Hémery.)	590	2nd March 1865	William Edward Newton.
An improvement in carburetting gas, also in the preparation of hydrocarbons for carburetting gas, and improved methods of treating alkali which has been used to purify coal oils, shale oils, petroleum and other mineral oils. (obtaining oily compounds for steeping timber.)	596	3rd March 1865	William Renwick Bowditch.
Improvements in the means and apparatus employed for treating timber with antiseptic or preservative fluids, also applicable to other purposes.	734	16th March 1865	Samuel Hegister Boulton.
Building barges, ships and other vessels - -	864	5th April 1865	John Bethell.
An improved mode of preventing corrosion or staining of the surface of glass.	984	6th April 1865	William Bartram Richards.
Paints or compositions for coating and preserving metallic and other substances from oxidation and decay - - - - - - - -	1154	25th April 1865	{ John Northall Brown. { Thomas Deykin Clare.
Improvements in photographing upon wood, and in the preparation of wood, canvas, silk, glass and other substances, for the purpose of receiving and retaining impressions.	1174	26th April 1865	William Henry Smith.
An improved process for penetrating or impregnating woods with various substances. (Communicated by Jules Louis Hessard.)	1573	9th June 1865	William Edward Gedge.
Staining and graining woods - - -	1861	14th July 1865	{ John Morrough Murphy { James Morrough Murphy.
An improved process for rendering wood incombustible.	1900	21st July 1865	Louis Alphonse Maurice Chantin.
Burglar-proof safes - - - - -	2009	2nd Aug. 1865	Herbert Allman.

Subject-matter of Patent.	Number of Patent.	Date.	Name of Patentee.
PRESERVING WOOD, &c.—*continued.*			
Improvements in the mode or method of preparing materials for, and in the manufacture of submarine telegraphic cables, the same being generally applicable for other purposes. *(making preservative compositions for wood, metal, &c.)*	2035	4th Aug. 1865	Frederick George Mulholland.
A new composition suitable for use as paint and protective coating. *(Communicated by William Potter.)*	2163	2nd Aug. 1865	John Gilbert Avery.
Manufacture of flexible tubing or hose - - *(preserving interiors.)* *(Communicated by David Knight Harris and Thomas Lyons Reed.)*	2315	9th Sept. 1865	George Tomlinson Bousfield.
Improved means for rendering leather more durable and flexible - - - - -	2357	15th Sept. 1865	{ Louis Gustave Sourrac. Louis Bombail.
Rendering wood for building and other purposes non-combustible or non-inflammable.	2625	11th Oct. 1865	William Bull.
A certain composition having anti-corrosive and anti-fouling properties, for the preservation of and keeping clean the bottoms of iron vessels, and also for the preservation of iron submerged and iron structures exposed to the action of the atmosphere or water - - -	2653	14th Oct. 1865	{ William Jardine Combe Mac Millan. James Mason. John Vickers Scarborough.
Making amalgams or alloys of metals - - *(preserving from moisture.)* *(Communicated by Henry Wurts.)*	2908	11th Nov. 1865	William Edward Newton.

PRESERVING AND PREPARING ARTICLES OF FOOD, CUTTING SUET, PEELING POTATOES, DRESSING FRUIT, SHELLING PEAS, STONING RAISINS.

An improved jacket or protector for metallic and other vessels and structures containing solid substances, liquids or gases, to prevent radiation of heat from or communication of heat to such vessels and structures - - - *(for ice safes and wine coolers.)*	4	2nd Jan. 1865	{ Edward Berne. Abel Fleming.
A new or improved method of keeping the substance of eggs fresh and sweet.	47	6th Jan. 1865	Walter Christopher Thorgar.
Preserving meat - - - - -	79	10th Jan. 1865	Thomas Bowerman Belgrave.
Mode of and means for preserving fruit and other eatables. *(Communicated by Benjamin Markley Nyce.)*	207	24th Jan. 1865	George Haseltine.
Apparatus called ice safes - - -	230	26th Jan. 1865	Charles Falck.
Certain improvements in machinery for dressing fruit.	309	2nd Feb. 1865	David Barr.
An improvement in air-tight jars for preserving eggs and fruits and such like articles of food.	546	27th Feb. 1865	George Kennedy Geyelin.

Subject-matter of Patent.	Number of Patent.	Date.	Name of Patentee.
PRESERVING FOOD, &c.—continued.			
An improved method of preserving meat (Communicated by Hubert Felix Mévissart.)	646	9th March 1865	Arthur Charles Henderson.
Improvements in securing low and uniform temperature, applicable to public and private buildings, also to refrigerators, coolers and condensers, and to ships and other vessels, and in the apparatus employed therein. (for preserving food.) (Communicated by Daniel Somes.)	710	14th March 1865	Alfred Vincent Newton.
A new or improved machine for peeling or skinning almonds.	760	18th March 1865	James Henry Walkew.
An apparatus for cutting bread or bread and butter	792	21st March 1865	William Berry.
An improved domestic implement for paring potatoes, apples and other like vegetables and fruit.	857	27th March 1865	Charles Durfill.
An improvements in paints or compositions used for coating iron or wooden vessels, and other structures exposed to the action of sea water.	871	29th March 1865	John Cornelius Craigie Halkett.
Machines for cutting or mincing meat, suet and other substances.	1077	17th April 1865	Albert Ward Hale.
An improved apparatus for shelling peas and beans, stoning fruit and other similar purposes.	1244	4th May 1865	Edward Grainger Smith.
Treating rice and other grain for the manufacture of starch, also to prepare them for use as food and for other purposes.	1310	12th May 1865	Henry Ransford.
Manufacture of wire gauze dish covers, plate covers, window blinds, fire guards, and meat safes	1401	22nd May 1865	David Powis. Henry Brittain the younger.
Apparatus used when boiling milk	1550	2nd June 1865	George Kent. William Hayward West.
An improved mode of desiccating eggs and apparatus for effecting the same.	1632	16th June 1865	Charles Augustus Lamont.
Obtaining jellies, syrups, drinks and other products, from the tree Arbutus Unedo, known as the Arbutus. (and jams.)	1649	20th June 1865	Philippe Mingaud.
Apparatus for stoning raisins	2201	7th Sept. 1865	John Askew.
Cooling bacon-curing rooms or chambers	2336	12th Sept. 1865	Robert Andrew Boyd.
Certain improvements in machinery for cutting or mincing meat and stuffing the same into skins or intestines, for forming sausages. (Communicated by Parcher Miles.)	2437	23rd Sept. 1865	Joseph Donnell.
Construction of vessels for preserving food and liquids.	2473	27th Sept. 1865	Louis Henri Gillet.
Improvements in treating meat and in obtaining products therefrom.	2558	5th Oct. 1865	Robert Morean.
Preparation of meat for food	2677	17th Oct. 1865	Arthur Hill Hassall, M.D.
Improvements in preserving provisions and in the apparatus connected therewith.	2812	1st Nov. 1865	Isham Baggs.
Preservation of meat and the concentration of its juices.	2899	10th Nov. 1865	Theophilus Redwood.
Preserving meat and other articles for food	2919	13th Nov. 1865	Wilson Fox.
Improvements in preserving animal and vegetable substances, and in means or apparatus employed therein.	2953	16th Nov. 1865	Richard Jones.
An improved machine or apparatus for cleaning or dressing currants and other fruits.	2978	20th Nov. 1865	Arthur Biskett.

Subject-matter of Patent.	Number of Patent.	Date.	Name of Patentee.

PRESERVING FOOD, &c. —continued.

An improved trap or liquid sealing to the covers of cisterns, pans, jars, tubs and other vessels or chambers - - - - - - - (for preserving meat, &c.)	8886	20th Nov. 1865	George Putland Humming. Henry Coyle.
Improvements in the preservation of animal substances, such improvements being especially useful when those substances are intended for use as food.	8009	23rd Nov. 1865	Theophilus Redwood.
Mode of and means for preserving fruit and other perishable substances. (Communicated by Benjamin Markley Nyce.)	8043	27th Nov. 1865	William Robert Lake.
An improved machine for dressing, sifting, cleaning and polishing fruit, coffee, grain and other matter, parts of which are applicable to coffee sifting, roasting, cooling and cleaning, and other purposes.	8183	6th Dec. 1865	Edwin Whele.
An improved method of and apparatus for making mortars, bowls, spill pots, jelly cans, galvanic troughs and other similar articles - - -	8169	8th Dec. 1865	William Houlton. Joseph Worthington.
An improved mode of preserving animal and vegetable substances. (Communicated by Francis Stabler.)	3172	9th Dec. 1865	Alfred Vincent Newton.
A new and improved compound to be employed as a drinking beverage. (Communicated by Edward Dorn.)	8203	12th Dec. 1865	Joachim Kaspary.
Improvements in the treatment of animals intended for human food, and in the preservation of meat.	3298	20th Dec. 1865	John Gamgee.

PRESSES, COMPRESSING, PACKING.

Improvements in producing and finishing photographs and photographic transparencies on paper and other suitable substances, and in the machinery employed therein - - -	56	7th Jan. 1865	Barrowclough Wright Bentley. William Henry Bailey.
Machinery for the manufacture of "cavendish," "negrohead" and other tobacco.	68	9th Jan. 1865	William Davies.
Machinery or apparatus for the manufacture of compressed bricks.	77	10th Jan. 1865	Humphrey Chamberlain.
Machinery for pressing and cutting tobacco - (Communicated by William Woodman Haw.)	123	14th Jan. 1865	Alfred Vincent Newton.
Presses for the expression of fluids from substances containing the same.	134	16th Jan. 1865	John Marshall.
Improvements in the packings of pistons and piston rods of pumps and steam and other engines, which improvements are also applicable to hydraulic presses.	155	18th Jan. 1865	William Robert Foster.
Facing woollen cloth and other textile fabrics -	175	20th Jan. 1865	John Snell. William Renton.
Fly or embossing presses - - - - - -	206	24th Jan. 1865	James Bailey.
Machinery or apparatus for folding fabrics on to cardboards, for the purpose of hot pressing.	276	1st Feb. 1865	Arthur Freeman.

Subject-matter of Patent.	Number of Patent.	Date.	Name of Patentee.

Presses, &c.—continued.

Improvements in the manufacture of ordnance and other like castings and in the apparatus employed therein, also in carriages or moulds for the same. (cylinders of hydraulic presses.) (Communicated by William Jones.)	296	2nd Feb. 1865	John Henry Johnson.
Improvements in the ventilation of pressing irons heated by gas, and for preventing the condensation of the vapour in the tubes or flues leading therefrom.	850	7th Feb. 1865	Samuel Egan Rosser.
Hydraulic presses - - - - - .	417	14th Feb. 1865	George Whitton.
Machinery for making and pressing bricks -	480	21st Feb. 1865	Charles William Homer.
Apparatus for extracting liquid from solid substances. (Communicated by Lyman Smith.)	486	21st Feb. 1865	William Edward Newton.
Certain improvements in hydraulic pumps in connection with engines of motive-power.	541	24th Feb. 1865	William Orme.
Presses for blocking the tyres of railway and other wheels.	573	1st March 1865	William Holiday.
Hooping or binding bales - - - -	696	6th March 1865	William Riddle.
Certain improvements in the method of securing the extremities of bands or hoops used in packing bales, and in the means employed for such purpose. (Communicated by Edward Taylor Bellhouse.)	663	9th March 1865	William John Dorning.
Improvements in securing low and uniform temperatures, applicable to public and private buildings, also to refrigerators, coolers and condensers, and to ships and other vessels, and in the apparatus employed therein. (for packing-houses.) (Communicated by Daniel Sauer.)	719	14th March 1865	Alfred Vincent Newton.
Presses for cotton and wool - - - .	848	25th March 1865	William Miller.
Vessels or apparatus for melting sealing wax, glue or other substances. (for sealing packets.) (Communicated by Frederick Kuhrmann.)	931	3rd April 1865	William Binger.
Improvements in steam and atmospheric hammers and presses, which improvements are also applicable to steam-engines.	953	4th April 1865	Joseph Vaughan.
Improved apparatus for expressing liquids from pulpy and semi-fluid substances. (Communicated by Louis Pierre Robert de Massy.)	955	4th April 1865	William Edward Newton.
Machinery for finishing yarns or threads - -	1019	10th April 1865	{ Robert Fergusson. Walter Ralston.
Machinery for folding fabrics for pressing - -	1087	13th April 1865	William Speakman Yates.
Improvements in embossing presses to facilitate the operation of relief coloring on envelopes, note paper and other similar articles of stationery.	1294	2nd May 1865	Best Fenner.
Hydraulic presses for compressing cotton and other substances	1854	5th May 1865	{ George Peel, jun'. Isaac Mason.
Certain improvements in hydraulic presses for packing cotton and other materials or substances, and in the boxes for containing the same.	1880	9th May 1865	{ Edward Taylor Bellhouse. William John Dorning.

Subject-matter of Patent.	Number of Patent.	Date.	Name of Patentee.
Presses, &c.—continued.			
Presses used for pressing cotton, wool, hay and fibrous materials.	1429	24th May 1865	George Ashcroft.
An improved plain or graduated gophering or puffing and pressing machine - -	1444	26th May 1865	Charles Cotton. Francis Anderson. Daniel Booker.
A new or improved artificial fuel - - (compressing coal dust for fuel.)	1600	13th June 1865	Charles James Collins.
Improvements in the manufacture of paper and paper stock, and in the utilization of certain waste products resulting therefrom - -	1602	13th June 1865	Thomas Routledge. William Henry Richardson.
Improved machinery for compressing and solidifying coal and other analogous substances.	1606	14th June 1865	Henry George Fairburn.
Copying presses - - - - -	1694	15th June 1865	Phineas Lawrence. George Jefferys.
Improvements in envelopes or wrappers for covering, packing and protecting bottles, jars or other fragile articles, and in apparatus for manufacturing the same.	1680	20th June 1865	George Clark.
An improved hydraulic apparatus for producing motive-power.	1701	26th June 1865	James Egide Spanoghe.
An improved pulping and compressing machine, for the treatment of peat as a fuel, and gas for illuminating purposes - - -	1703	26th June 1865	Charles Wormam. George Evans.
Circular pressing machines for finishing woven fabrics.	1717	25th June 1865	William Ingham.
Improvements in the preparation of amalgams of quicksilver or mercury, and in the application of such amalgams to various purposes in the arts. (working and transporting quicksilver.) (Communicated by Henry Wurtz.)	1719	24th June 1865	William Edward Newton.
An improved mode of pressing and moulding clay, sand, or cement, for making bricks and for other purposes. (Communicated by John Storie.)	1748	1st July 1865	William Robert Lake.
Presses - - - - - - (Communicated by Charles Hughes.)	1850	15th July 1865	William Hughes.
Machinery or apparatus for folding fabrics on to cardboards or metallic plates, for the purpose of hot pressing - - - - -	1909	21st July 1865	William Spenlume Yates. Arthur Freeman.
An improved cotton press - - -	1916	22nd July 1865	Samuel Boyd.
Packing cases or boxes for holding or packing bottles or bottled liquids - - -	2141	14th Aug. 1865	John Hope.
Improvements in lithographic and copper plate printing, and in the machinery or apparatus connected therewith.	2170	23rd Aug. 1865	Donald McKellar.
Copying presses for copying letters and other written documents.	2195	25th Aug. 1865	George Owen.
Construction of presses for the compression of elastic substances. (Communicated by Joseph Wohl.)	2205	24th Aug. 1865	Henri Adrien Bonneville.
Construction of hydrostatic presses - -	2304	9th Sept. 1865	John Weems. William Weems.

Subject-matter of Patent.	Number of Patent.	Date.	Name of Patentee.
PRESSES, &c.—continued.			
Improvements in the manufacture of bricks, blocks, tiles covers and tiles, and in the machinery and apparatus employed therefor. (by compression.)	8383	19th Sept. 1865	James Gillespie.
Hydraulic pressure engines	8445	23rd Sept. 1865	Jacob Dreisörner.
Presses worked by steam and hydraulic power	8447	25th Sept. 1865	William Routledge. Frederick Francis Ommanney.
Construction of presses for hay, cotton, hemp and other substances. (Communicated by Thomas Gennon and Thomas Bolton Webster.)	8454	25th Sept. 1865	Alfred Vincent Newton.
Tools for securing tubes in tube plates, and for other purposes where concentrated power or adjustment is necessary. (for moving stamps for compressing.)	8455	26th Sept. 1865	Richard Taylor Nelson Howry.
A new composition of Indian-rubber mastic or cement, made in a more or less fluid state according to the use to be made of it, and the process or contrivance for applying the same. (cover for packing yards.)	8530	12th Oct. 1865	Auguste Aimé Lennard.
Improvements in hydraulic presses and in apparatus connected therewith	8686	19th Oct. 1865	Thomas Routledge. Daniel Huntley. John Brood Jackson.
Cotton presses. (Communicated by Samuel Boyd.)	8723	21st Oct. 1865	Clotworthy Boyd.
Improvements in calendering and finishing woven fabrics, and in apparatus employed therein.	8766	27th Oct. 1865	Edwin Heyward.
Driving or actuating machinery (printing presses.)	8773	27th Oct. 1865	John Garnett.
Packing and labelling bottles, jars and other fragile articles.	8776	28th Oct. 1865	George Clark.
Improvements in machinery for compressing cotton, wool and other materials, for the economy of transit, which said improvements more particularly relate to the more expeditious filling of the box of the press and fastenings for bales.	8887	3rd Nov. 1865	James Jennings M'Conh.
Making amalgams or alloys of metals (packing by pouring into quicksilver flasks.) (Communicated by Henry Wurts.)	8903	11th Nov. 1865	William Edward Newton.
Apparatus for raising, lowering and moving heavy bodies, and for transmitting and arresting motion for various purposes. (extracting presses.)	5093	2nd Dec. 1865	Thomas Aldridge Weston.
A new or improved press for pressing shawls, clothes, table linen, and various other fabrics, manufactured articles and substances requiring pressure.	8184	5th Dec. 1865	William Bryan Masters.
Waterproof linings of cases, boxes, and apparatus in which articles are desired to be packed waterproof.	8801	11th Dec. 1865	John Jones.
Improved machinery for compressing and solidifying coal, clay and other analogous substances.	8342	14th Dec. 1865	Henry George Fairburn.
Machinery for raising or forming articles of sheet metal. (Communicated by Mellen Bray.)	8319	22nd Dec. 1865	George Tomlinson Bousfield.

Subject-matter of Patent.	Number of Patent.	Date.	Name of Patentee.
PRESSES, &c.—continued.			
An improved cotton bale tie or hoop lock - (*Communicated by Edward Victor Fosman.*)	3061	29th Dec. 1865	William Edward Newton.
Obtaining and employing continuous lengths of tanned leather for various useful purposes (*ropes for packing-cases.*)	3334	23rd Dec. 1865	George Horn. Daniel Horn.
PRINTING AND TRANSFERRING ; TYPE AND OTHER SURFACES FOR PRINTING ; COMPOSING AND DISTRIBUTING TYPE.			
Improvements in producing and finishing photographs and photographic transparencies on paper and other suitable substances, and in the machinery employed therein	56	7th Jan. 1865	Barrowclough Wright Bentley. William Henry Bailey.
Colouring hempy wool and hair - - -	237	26th Jan. 1865	Henry William Ripley.
A new typographic ink - - - -	330	6th Feb. 1865	Anatole Auguste Hulot.
Improvements in colour printing and in apparatus connected therewith.	721	14th March 1865	Isham Baggs.
Preparing, fixing and mordanting cloth and yarns -	762	16th March 1865	Thomas Kenyon the younger.
Dyeing and printing cotton or linen fabrics or yarns.	804	22nd March 1865	Alfred Paraf.
Engraving on metal - - - - (*for printing on stuffs, paper, &c.*) (*Communicated by Narcisse Goilbot and Pierre Heritier.*)	807	22nd March 1865	Richard Archibald Brooman.
Machinery or apparatus for feeding paper to printing machines, and for taking off or removing and piling the same after printing - -	812	23rd March 1865	Edward Field. Francis Wise.
Improvements relating to apparatus for printing ornamental fabrics - - -	870	28th March 1865	James Millar. John Laing.
An improved manufacture of inking rollers - (*Communicated by Lewis Francis and Cyrus Loutrel.*)	914	31st March 1865	Alfred Vincent Newton.
Certain improvements in dyeing or printing upon the fabric known as "sail cloth."	1006	8th April 1865	James Isherwood.
Means of ornamenting linen cuffs and collars -	1010	8th April 1865	Joseph Debnam.
Printing machinery - - - -	1038	11th April 1865	David Payne.
Manufacture of a compound or material to be used as a substitute for india-rubber. (*for coating rollers.*) (*Communicated by Henry Lorverobery and Emile Grossier.*)	1068	15th April 1865	William Clark.
Improvements in taking impressions from the grain of wood, and in transferring the same on to various surfaces - - -	1117	21st April 1865	William Scarratt. William Dean.
Improved means or apparatus for printing felts, floor cloths, carpets and woven fabrics.	1155	25th April 1865	John Wilkinson the younger.

Subject-matter of Patent.	Number of Patent.	Date.	Name of Patentee.

PRINTING, &c.—continued.

Manufacture of flock fabrics . . . (printing, &c.) (Communicated by The American Waterproof Cloth Company.)	1819	1st May 1865	William Edward Newton.
An improved manufacture of waterproof fabric (Communicated by The American Waterproof Cloth Company.)	1819	1st May 1865	William Edward Newton.
Improvements in embossing presses to facilitate the operation of relief coloring on envelopes, note paper and other similar articles of stationery.	1224	2nd May 1865	Root Fenner.
Paper hangings	1243	4th May 1866	Gustave Jonet.
Machinery for distributing printing type . .	1252	4th May 1865	Alexander Mackie. Henry Garside. James Salmon.
Manufacture or treatment of India-rubber or gutta-percha, or compounds thereof, applicable to the production of stereotype plates and other forms.	1257	5th May 1865	Thomas Jeffreys Mayall.
Certain improvements in machinery for setting and distributing printing types. (Communicated by Abiel Abbot Low, Josiah Orne Low, Edward Hotchkiss Robbins Lyman, Charles Frederick Livermore, Augustus Corey Richards and Charles Carroll Yeaton.)	1271	6th May 1865	William Clark.
Machines for drawing and finishing printers' types	1277	9th May 1865	Patrick Welch.
Ornamenting candles . . . . (transferring designs.)	1290	10th May 1865	Peter Brush. Robert Irving.
Improvements in the means and method of producing lithographic impressions, and in the apparatus connected therewith . . .	1295	12th May 1865	George Simmons. George Walter Simmons.
Printing-machines	1344	15th May 1865	Robert Harrild. Horton Harrild.
Stamping or signing letters, papers or other objects	1366	18th May 1865	Carl Fischer. Johann Carl Wilhelm Maas.
Improvements in the treatment of clays and other materials with which they are mixed when used in the manufacture of china, porcelain, earthenware and other like wares, and in ornamenting or decorating china, porcelain, earthenware and other like wares.	1414	23rd May 1865	Alexander Hett.
Calico and linen printing	1420	24th May 1865	John Dale. Alfred Paraf.
Applying coal-tar colors to cottons and linen	1423	25th May 1865	Robert Maxwell.
Improvements in ornamenting japanned surfaces and in machinery or apparatus for that purpose.	1464	27th May 1865	Leonard Brierley.
An improved process for producing printing surfaces	1582	2nd June 1865	Francis John Bolton. Henry Matheson.
An improved hand stamp for printing letters, numerals and other figures.	1636	5th June 1865	Alfred Johnson Aspinall.
An improved photo-electrotyping process . . (Communicated by William Augustus Leggo and George Edward Desbarats.)	1641	5th June 1865	William Edward Newton.
Certain improvements in the manufacture and production of chromates and bichromates of potash employed in dyeing and printing woven fabrics.	1679	10th June 1865	Joseph Mayer Dentith.

Subject-matter of Patent.	Number of Patent.	Date.	Name of Patentee.
PRINTING, &c.—*continued.*			
Apparatus for printing wool, worsted, or other fibrous materials.	1590	10th June 1865	John Henderson.
Improvements in the manufacture of naphthalic acid and chlorosynapthalic acid, and in dyeing and printing - - - - -	1605	13th July 1865	François Alexandre Laurent. John Castheln.
Apparatus for typographic and lithographic printing (*Communicated by Auguste Hippolyte Marianni and François Noel Chaudré.*)	1665	21st June 1865	William Clark.
Apparatus for polishing, smoothing or facing, especially applicable to lithographic stones.	1688	21st June 1865	Charles Henry Gardam.
An improved composition for the manufacture of printers' rollers.	1694	24th June 1865	Frederic Germain David.
Machinery for printing in colors - - - (*Communicated by Martin Margue.*)	1702	26th June 1865	Richard Archibald Brooman.
Printing threads employed in weaving - - - (*Communicated by Stanislas Vigouroux.*)	1780	29th June 1865	Richard Archibald Brooman.
An improved combination of materials for the manufacture of carpets, floor cloths, felt, wall paper, fireproof flexible roofing, ship and boat building, and for other similar purposes (*elastic printing rollers.*)	1775	5th July 1865	John Loughman. Abram Loughman.
Improvements in the production of printing surfaces by photographic agency, and in obtaining prints therefrom.	1791	6th July 1865	Joseph Wilson Swan.
Apparatus for "setting up" or composing type for printing - - - - -	1845	13th July 1865	Alexander Mackie. James Procter James.
Mandrils for rollers such as are used for printing or embossing - - - - -	1860	14th July 1865	David Fulton. John Fulton.
Certain improvements in envelope machines (*Communicated by Thomas Fearie Waymoth, Henry Clay Berlin and George Jones.*)	1898	20th July 1865	Alfred Vincent Newton.
An improved system of manufacturing salts, sulphates and acetates of chrome, and of applying them as mordants, in dyeing and printing textile substances both animal and vegetable.	1905	21st July 1865	Jean Henri Chaudet.
Instruments for marking or impressing railway tickets.	1948	27th July 1865	Russell Mortimer.
Machinery for printing in colors - - -	1978	31st July 1865	Augustus Applegath.
Checking or controlling the payment of fares in cabs and other public vehicles. (*Communicated by Léon Becker and Joseph Leib.*)	2028	4th Aug. 1865	Henri Adrien Bonneville.
Improvements in the ornamentation of glass and in the applications of glass so ornamented. (*Communicated by The Society Roedal Cromwell, Alfred Tavernier and Edouard Dodé.*)	2038	5th Aug. 1865	John Henry Johnson.
Printing and dyeing yarns and fabrics of cotton or other vegetable materials - - - -	2053	8th Aug. 1865	James Fraebea, jun'. Robert Boyd.
Printing-machines - - - - -	2056	8th Aug. 1865	William Rock.
Production of violet colours from magenta, for dyeing and printing.	2070	9th Aug. 1865	Ludwig Schad.
Treating and printing threads employed in weaving (*Communicated by Stanislas Vigouroux.*)	2085	11th Aug. 1866	Richard Archibald Brooman.
Production of surfaces by means of photography - printing surfaces.) (*Communicated by Henry Arel.*)	2110	15th Aug. 1865	Michael Henry.

Subject-matter of Patent.	Number of Patent.	Date.	Name of Patentee.
PRINTING, &c.—continued.			
A new and improved application of imitating embroidery to be employed for the ornamentation of crinolines. (printing.)	8131	18th Aug. 1865	Richard Clarke.
Type distributing and composing machines	2188	18th Aug. 1865	Arthur Young. William Young.
Improvements in lithographic and copper plate printing, and in the machinery or apparatus connected therewith.	2170	23rd Aug. 1865	Donald M'Kellar.
Dyeing and printing woollen or silk fabrics and yarns.	2201	24th Aug. 1865	Alfred Paraf.
Improved machinery for mixing or grinding ointments, paints, drugs and other substances.	2290	6th Sept. 1865	Thomas Charles Gibson.
Certain improvements in machinery or apparatus for "composing" or setting type for printing	2308	8th Sept. 1865	Alexander Mackie. James Procter Jones.
Dyeing and printing fabrics and yarns, and animal or mixed animal and vegetable substances.	2397	11th Sept. 1866	John Lightfoot.
Magnetic telegraphs (making the types.) (Communicated by Robert Kirk Boyle and Guiseppe Tagliabue.)	2356	14th Sept. 1865	William Clark.
Engraving on metal (Communicated by Narcisse Guilbat and Pierre Hérisier.)	2388	19th Sept. 1866	Richard Archibald Brooman.
Improvements in the manufacture of coloring matter, and in the application thereof to dyeing and printing.	2424	22nd Sept. 1865	Alexandre Schalks.
Printing or impressing and dyeing fabrics and tissues. (Communicated by Félix Dehaut.)	2701	19th Oct. 1865	William Clark.
Manufacture of covers applicable to drawing or printing rollers and as rodless blankets	2716	20th Oct. 1865	Manuel Leopold Jouas Lavater. John Kershaw.
An improved method or mode of indicating the names of streets and other places. (printing.)	2759	23rd Oct. 1865	John Murray.
Driving or actuating machinery (printing presses.)	2773	27th Oct. 1865	John Garnett.
Transparent slides for magic lanterns and other similar purpose. (printing.)	2816	1st Nov. 1865	Samuel Solomons.
Printing and dyeing textile fabrics and yarns	2859	6th Nov. 1865	Alfred Paraf.
Preparing the surfaces of paper, leather, woven and other fabrics and substances, for receiving photographic pictures, engravings, lithographs and prints, and for rendering such substances fire and water proof. (Communicated by William Gibson.)	2891	9th Nov. 1865	William Edward Newton.
Means of producing from rosaniline blue and violet colouring matters. (and applying.) (Communicated by Prosper Monnet.)	2894	10th Nov. 1865	Edward Thomas Hughes.
Application of photography to the obtaining of printed proofs or impressions or engravings	2954	17th Nov. 1865	Edward Bullock. James Bullock.

Subject-matter of Patent.	Number of Patent.	Date.	Name of Patentee.
PRINTING, &c.—*continued.*			
Improvements in and adaptation of cylinder printing machines to the double purpose of letter press and lithography, also a new mode of damping litho stones, and a new mode of registering and painting in such machines.	2989	22nd Nov. 1865	Thomas William, Nicholson.
Machinery or apparatus for stamping or impressing railway or other tickets. (*see* "STAMPS.")	3005	22nd Nov. 1865	Alfred Larncfield.
An improved mode of obtaining printing surfaces by photography. (*Communicated by Frederick Von Egloffstein.*)	3058	29th Nov. 1865	Alfred Vincent Newton.
Treatment of matter for dyeing and printing -	3089	30th Nov. 1865	Alexander Campbell Duncan.
An improved mode of applying photographic paper pictures to glass. (*producing transparencies.*)	3092	2nd Dec. 1865	Anna Josephine Wright.
Certain improvements in machinery or apparatus for "composing" or setting type, and also "distributing" type.	3104	4th Dec. 1865	Alexander Markie.
Dyeing, printing and other operations based on chemical reactions. (*Communicated by Mathias Paraf-Javal.*)	3110	4th Dec. 1865	Richard Archibald Brooman.
A new method of and apparatus for regulating the tension of threads in weaving and other operations. (*printing.*) (*Communicated by Stanislas Figuerras.*)	3226	14th Dec. 1865	Richard Archibald Brooman.
Manufacture of stays or corsets - - - (*of printed fabric.*)	3238	14th Dec. 1865	William Pretty.
Manufacture of bed quilts, table and toilet covers - (*printing.*)	3285	16th Dec. 1865	{ Thomas Jones. { Joseph Berkley.
Dyeing and printing - - - -	3290	19th Dec. 1865	Louis Durand.
Preparation of glue or gelatine so as to render it insoluble in water, and applicable by the admixture of other substances, to various purposes for which common glue or gelatine cannot now be used. (*for printers' inking rollers.*) (*Communicated by Henry Wirtz.*)	3325	23rd Dec. 1865	William Edward Newton

For Engraving Cylinders, *see* "ENGRAVING."
For Telegraphic Printing, *see* "TELEGRAPHS."
For Printing-colours, *see* "DYES."

PROPELLING, DRIVING, WORKING; TRANSMITTING POWER AND MOTION; CONVERTING MOVEMENTS.

1.—Propelling Ships; Locomotion on Water; Propellers, Paddle Wheels and Screws.

Subject-matter of Patent.	Number of Patent.	Date.	Name of Patentee.
Apparatus for propelling vessels - - -	29	5th Jan. 1865	William Watson.
Apparatus for transmitting and converting reciprocating motion into rotary motion applicable to various useful purposes.	145	17th Jan. 1865	William John Cunningham.

Subject-matter of Patent.	Number of Patent.	Date.	Name of Patentee.
PROPELLING, &c.—continued.			
Improvements in cars and in the modes of securing them.	161	19th Jan. 1865	Emmanuel Denis Farcot.
Machinery for propelling vessels	239	26th Jan. 1865	John Hamilton, jun'.
Improved machinery or apparatus for propelling boats, ships, vessels or other floating craft and objects.	368	9th Feb. 1865	Moses Birt.
Construction, arrangement and mode of applying paddle wheels for propelling boats or other vessels. (Communicated by Hippolyto Salmon.)	405	13th Feb. 1865	John Garrett Tongue.
An improved screw propeller and an improved application of the motive-power to the propelling of boats and steam ships, applicable also to other purposes. (Communicated by Christopher Edward Dempier.)	510	23rd Feb. 1865	John George Hughes.
Side propellers for ocean and river vessels	602	4th March 1865	Luke Thomas.
Dredgers . } (propelling.)	838	24th March 1865	William Simons. Andrew Brown.
Improvements in paddle wheels, parts of which are applicable to other purposes.	935	3rd April 1865	William Cantrill Gollings.
A new method of obtaining and applying water as a motive-power for propelling ships, boats and other vessels.	1063	13th April 1865	George Romulet.
Apparatus for feeding boilers, raising water and propelling vessels. (Communicated by Pierre Samain.)	1062	13th April 1865	Richard Archibald Brennan.
Construction of ships or vessels or cars to float on water.	1083	18th April 1865	William Redder.
Screw propelling apparatus	1118	21st April 1865	Robert Griffiths.
Paddle wheel propellers adapted for propelling vessels in water.	1138	24th April 1865	Richard Henry Dart.
Propelling vessels	1216	1st May 1865	Morris West Ruthven.
Apparatus for receiving the thrust of screw propeller and other revolving shafts }	1334	3rd May 1865	Edward Thornton Read. John Brough Fyfe.
Paddle wheels (Communicated by Matthew Augustus Crooke.)	1288	9th May 1865	Charles Stuart Baker.
Apparatus for propelling and steering vessels	1451	30th May 1865	Jonathan Jopling.
Propelling vessels	1562	10th June 1865	Daniel Spink.
Propellers for ships and other vessels	1645	19th June 1865	Charles Hook. Alfred Prace.
Oars, paddles, rowlocks, seats and fittings for boats and vessels.	1781	29th June 1865	John Cox.
Apparatus for propelling ships and other vessels	1752	1st July 1865	John Calvert.
Motive-power by capillary attraction	1874	19th July 1865	Johann Ernst Friedrich Lüdeke.
Apparatus for propelling vessels	1890	20th July 1865	Cortland Herbert Simpson.
Improvements in the propulsion of ships and in machinery or apparatus connected therewith. (Communicated by Thomas Craig.)	1899	21st July 1865	Saint John Vincent Day.
Apparatus for obtaining and applying motive-power to various useful purposes }	2060	11th Aug. 1865	William Thomas Cole. Henry Spink Swift. Augusto Suarez.
Apparatus for propelling vessels (Communicated by Ambrose Rapkin.)	2223	29th Aug. 1865	William Clark.

Subject-matter of Patent.	Number of Patent	Date.	Name of Patentee.
PROPELLING, &c.—*continued.*			
Obtaining and employing continuous lengths of tanned leather for various useful purposes (*for rudder lines.*)	8354	23rd Dec. 1865	George Horn, Daniel Horn.
Construction of side propellers for navigable vessels	3373	29th Dec. 1865	Benedict Burchall.
XI.—Propelling Carriages; Locomotion on Land.			
Apparatus for effecting locomotion or propelling on land. (*Communicated by Auguste Bernier and Hyppolite Louis Godard Desmaret.*)	271	31st Jan. 1865	Michael Henry.
A new method for removing or destroying the momentum of heavy bodies by means of an elastic machine or machines, so as to prevent injury and damage from concussion, applicable to ship cables, ship and fort armour, railway trains, tenders to pier heads, and floating piers, gangways, breakwaters and other similar structures, also as a motive-power. (*for propelling carriages.*) (*Communicated by William Graham M'Iver.*)	321	6th Feb. 1865	Clements Robert Markham.
Apparatus for propulsion by atmospheric pressure	606	3rd March 1865	Sir John Scott Lillie, Knight.
Locomotive engines and carriages for common roads and tramways, and also for agricultural and other purposes.	730	20th March 1865	Alexander Richard Mackenzie.
Improved mechanism or apparatus for propelling carriages and other road vehicles, by hand power.	766	22nd March 1865	William Lane.
A new or improved arrangement of mechanism for propelling waggons in connection with railway points.	896	30th March 1865	George Greenish.
An improved application of steam power to locomotion on ordinary roads. (*Communicated by Alfred Trillraubeau.*)	1002	8th April 1865	William Edward Gedge.
An improved method of and apparatus for laying single line articulated railways, and a method of propelling thereon, particularly applicable for agricultural purposes.	1221	12th May 1865	Richard Winder.
Means and apparatus for effecting traction on railways and roads where traction is used.	1222	12th May 1865	Richard Edward Donovan, Daniel O'Brien.
Mass-motive carriages	1288	19th May 1865	George Rowl.
Apparatus for facilitating the traction of public and other vehicles. (*Communicated by Joseph François D'Artron.*)	1626	15th June 1865	Henri Adrien Bonneville.
An improved method of training guns. (*moving the carriages.*)	1706	7th July 1865	Henry Duncan Preston Cunningham.
Traction engines. (*Communicated by Alexander Kame Richards.*)	1668	11th July 1865	Morris Harvey Keene.
Apparatus for the locomotion of trains on railways, by atmospheric pressure.	1852	14th July 1865	William Padmore Boylan.
Motive-power by capillary attraction	1874	19th July 1865	Johann Ernst Friedrich Lüdeke.

Subject-matter of Patent.	Number of Patent.	Date.	Name of Patentee.
PROPELLING, &c.—continued.			
Apparatus for obtaining and applying motive-power to various useful purposes	2080	11th Aug. 1865	William Thomas Cole. Henry Spink Bird. Augusto Henra.
Improvements in propelling vehicles and ships, and to apparatus for the same.	2498	28th Sept. 1865	Daniel Spink.
Machinery or apparatus for preparing and supplying food for cattle. (moving the waggon.)	2514	30th Sept. 1865	Robert Willacy.
Railway carriages and locomotives (Communicated by Henry Giffard.)	2681	11th Oct. 1865	Michael Henry.
Carriages propelled by manual power	2625	11th Oct. 1865	Thomas De Bonley.
A new appliance of an electro-magnetic apparatus to increase the adherence of locomotive engine wheels to the rails.	2977	20th Nov. 1865	Angelo Vacaroli.
Improvements in constructing atmospheric railways and carriages, and in working the same, parts of which are applicable to exhausting and condensing air for other purposes.	3178	9th Dec. 1865	Alexander Dewl.
Boilers or apparatus for generating steam - (for road steam-carriages.) (Communicated by John Belleville.)	3269	18th Dec. 1865	Richard Archibald Brooman.
XII.—Driving Machinery, Ploughs and Pumps; Feed Motions, Guides, Adjustments and Traverses; Transmitting Power and Motion; Cranks and Gearing.			
Sewing-machines and apparatus belonging thereto -	3	2nd Jan. 1865	Thomas Antony Mumby.
Machinery for smoothing or finishing paper	5	2nd Jan. 1865	James Roger Crompton.
Manufacturing paper (Communicated by Jules Joseph Mancey.)	15	3rd Jan. 1865	Leopold D'Aubriville.
Drilling apparatus for hand or steam power, adaptable also as a vice and for lifting purposes	16	3rd Jan. 1865	George Hodgson. James Pitt.
Certain improvements in mules for spinning -	21	4th Jan. 1865	John Knowles. James Banks.
Certain improvements in sewing-machines and mechanism for driving the same. (Communicated by Jacob Zackerman.)	36	5th Jan. 1865	Alfred Vincent Newton
Jack and slubbing frames	63	9th Jan. 1865	Ashworth Barlow.
Improvements in steam hammers and in apparatus employed in combination with steam hammers.	89	11th Jan. 1866	John Ramsbottom.
Machinery for opening and carding cotton and other fibrous materials.	90	11th Jan. 1865	Robert Tempest.
Machinery or apparatus for cleaning and decorticating grain.	115	13th Jan. 1865	Wilson Ager.
Machinery for preparing, spinning, doubling and winding wool, mohair, alpaca, silk, flax, cotton or other fibrous substances	130	16th Jan. 1865	James Banting Farre. John Hurst.
Mules for spinning and doubling -	133	16th Jan. 1865	William Rowbottom.
Improvements in driving rolls for rolling metals, and in apparatus employed therein. (Communicated by Antoine François Marret.)	155	16th Jan. 1865	Richard Archibald Brooman.
Machinery or apparatus for planing and moulding or otherwise shaping wood	142	17th Jan. 1865	John Robinson. John Smith.

Subject-matter of Patent.	Number of Patent.	Date.		Name of Patentee.

PROPELLING, &c.—continued.

Subject-matter of Patent.	Number of Patent.	Date.		Name of Patentee.
Apparatus for transmitting and converting reciprocating motion into rotary motion, applicable to various useful purposes.	146	17th Jan.	1865	William John Cunningham.
Machinery for mowing and reaping . . . (Communicated by Valerius Ironsmith Kirchner.)	200	23rd Jan.	1865	William Edward Newton.
Improvements in the grinding and feeding apparatus of mills for grinding corn and other substances, and in the combination of such mills with flour-dressing machines . . . (adjustments.)	205	24th Jan.	1865	Richard Robert Riches. Charles James Watts.
Throstle spinning frames . . . (obtaining variable drag.) (Communicated by Charles Leykerr.)	239	27th Jan.	1865	Charles Denton Abel.
Construction of pumps for lifting and forcing liquids.	237	27th Jan.	1865	James Hind.
Action and arrangement of drilling machines, turning lathes, and other machines tools in which a variable speed is required.	241	27th Jan.	1865	John Combe.
Applying power to the working of ships' windlasses, winches, capstans, pumps and other ships' gear.	242	27th Jan.	1865	Handel Moore.
Apparatus for effecting locomotion or propelling on land. (Communicated by Auguste Bernier and Hyppolite Louis Godard Desmarest.)	271	31st Jan.	1865	Michael Henry.
Improved mechanism for giving intermittent or continuous revolving motion of different velocities, without the use of change wheels . . .	278	31st Jan.	1865	Thomas Hall. Samuel Henary.
Working ships' pumps	303	3rd Feb.	1865	Matthew Blank.
A new method for removing or destroying the momentum of heavy bodies by means of an elastic machine or machines, so as to prevent injury and damage from concussion, applicable to ship cables, ship and fort armour, railway trains, tenders to pier heads and floating piers, gangways, breakwaters and other similar structures, also as a motive-power. (for driving machinery.) (Communicated by William Graham M'Ivor.)	331	6th Feb.	1865	Clements Robert Markham.
Machinery for breaking the stems of and preparing flax, hemp and other fibrous substances. (Communicated by Auguste Henri Leron.)	339	7th Feb.	1865	Henry Bernoulli Barlow.
Mode of ploughing and performing other like operations upon the land by steam power.	366	9th Feb.	1865	Richard Winder.
Improved mechanism for operating the working parts of sewing-machines. (Communicated by Elias Howe, jun'.)	370	9th Feb.	1865	Alfred Vincent Newton.
Machinery for preparing cotton and other fibrous substances. ("shortening motion.")	378	10th Feb.	1865	Edward Lord.
Looms for weaving	377	10th Feb.	1865	Rowland Gibson Hazard.
Manufacture of flies . . . . (Communicated by Moers Griffin Crane.)	412	14th Feb.	1865	William Boase Newbery.
Sewing-machines . . . . (Communicated by Elias Howe, jun'.)	430	15th Feb.	1865	Alfred Vincent Newton.

Subject-matter of Patent.	Number of Patent.	Date.	Name of Patentee.

PROPELLING, &c.—continued.

Subject-matter of Patent.	Number of Patent.	Date.	Name of Patentee.
Pumps and apparatus for working the same	486	15th Feb. 1865	George Tyrril Humpkin.
Shifting wrenches (Communicated by Pierre Augustin Somail.)	487	17th Feb. 1865	William Clark.
Machinery for sewing or uniting leather and other hard substances, particularly applicable to the manufacture of boots and shoes.	494	21st Feb. 1865	Charles Beakh.
An improved apparatus for shearing and burling all sorts of woven fabrics. (Communicated by Calixte Hippolyte Jean Pierre Dromay and Jean Compagnair.)	517	24th Feb. 1865	William Edward Gedge.
Machinery for sawing wood	522	24th Feb. 1865	Nacquel William Worms.
Sewing-machines	527	24th Feb. 1865	William Winter.
Sewing-machines	551	27th Feb. 1865	Robert Barclay.
Machinery for mining coal and other substances (Communicated by William Watson Orier and Robert H. Boyd.)	556	28th Feb. 1865	George Louder.
Improvements in the manufacture of textile fabrics and in the machinery or apparatus employed therefor. (carrying traverse in cop winding.)	562	24th Feb. 1865	David Chalmers.
An improved machine for pointing or drawing down railway spikes, and which said improved machine is also applicable for forming or drawing down the shanks of ordinary spikes and other articles of irregular shape.	575	1st March 1865	Mouro Baylise.
Reaping machinery	576	1st March 1865	Nicholas Henwood.
Mules for spinning and doubling	577	1st March 1865	John Dodd.
Apparatus for operating engineers' and carpenters' tools by hand or other power. (adjusting.) (Communicated by Henry Wismar.)	600	3rd March 1865	James Spence.
Binding attachments for sewing-machines	601	4th March 1865	Henry Everard Cliffee. Abraham Hoffoung.
An improved machine for shaping file or other "blanks" by means of dies fitted into vibrating jaws.	616	4th March 1865	Thomas Turton.
Improvements in machinery for grinding corn and other substances, and in horse gear or apparatus for driving the same, which horse gear is also applicable for driving other machinery.	652	6th March 1865	Frederick William Tarar.
Machinery for preparing flax, hemp and other fibrous materials requiring like treatment	680	10th March 1865	Joseph Samuel. Samuel Millbourn.
Improved machinery or apparatus for scouring stones, marbles, slates and bricks	686	11th March 1865	Jonas Hird. Joshua Walker.
Machinery or apparatus to be employed in the bleaching and dyeing of hanks or skeins of yarns and threads. (producing compound motion.)	718	14th March 1865	Longin Gantert.
Machinery for rolling and shaping metals	736	16th March 1865	John Ramsbottom.
Machinery and apparatus for mining or working coal and other minerals	737	16th March 1865	James Farrar. Edwin Booth.
Differential wheel gearing	744	17th March 1865	John Standfield.
Sewing-machines	766	18th March 1865	Owen Robinson.
Improved machinery for manufacturing paper and cloth-lined paper collars for gentlemen and ladies.	789	20th March 1865	Solomon Sally Grey.

Subject-matter of Patent.	Number of Patent.	Date.	Name of Patentee.
PROPELLING, &c.—continued.			
Machinery for working puddled balls or blooms of iron and steel.	779	20th March 1865	William Menelaus.
Locomotive engines and carriages for common roads and tramways, and also for agricultural and other purposes.	780	20th March 1865	Alexander Richard Mackenzie.
Apparatus for cutting pasteboard and other like boards. (Communicated by Elisur Ely Clerk.)	789	21st March 1865	William Clark.
Machinery for threshing and rubbing barley and other grain.	793	21st March 1865	Bernard James Webber.
A new or improved machine for dressing and rounding the inner surfaces of felloes.	794	22nd March 1865	Hiram Smith Jacobs.
Machinery and apparatus for indicating, selecting and reading in such cards of designs or patterns as are transferred and perforated on cards, papers or their substitutes, and for reproducing and repeating duplicates of such operations on such materials, for jacquard machines.	815	23rd March 1865	Duncan Mackenzie.
Machinery for sewing and stitching	818	23rd March 1865	Robert Wilson Morrell.
Sewing-machines	820	24th March 1865	Alfred Haillot.
Improvements in sewing-machines, which improvements also involve or comprise a new mode of manipulating the threads of the needle and shuttle in forming the "lock-stitch."	848	25th March 1865	Earle Harry Smith.
Machines for planing and shaping metals	858	27th March 1865	John Todd.
Improvements relating to apparatus for printing ornamental fabrics (applying guides.)	870	29th March 1865	James Millar. John Laing.
Forging machines	861	28th March 1865	Joseph Wright.
Sewing-machines	863	29th March 1865	William Newton Wilson.
Cranes	864	29th March 1865	William Irlam.
File cutting machinery (Communicated by Alfred Wood.)	865	29th March 1865	William Brookes.
Improvements in machinery for the cutting of nails, brads or spikes, and in the conformation of some of such nails and spikes.	866	29th March 1865	Richard Cardwell Robinson.
Certain improvements in machinery or apparatus used in carding cotton or other fibrous substances	867	29th March 1865	Evan Leigh. Frederick Allen Leigh.
Improvements in wringing machines, parts of which are applicable to the construction of rollers. (Communicated by Stephen Wing and Henry Holly.)	882	1st April 1865	Henry Lewis.
Looms for weaving	828	1st April 1865	Alfred William Pearce.
An improved machine for rounding and polishing shot, shell and other balls or spheres. (Communicated by William Davis Weaver.)	862	4th April 1865	William Clark.
Improvements in certain electric telegraphs, part of which invention is applicable to other purposes.	880	5th April 1865	Adam Millar.
Traction engines (driving gear.)	889	5th April 1865	John Guy Newton Alleyne.

Y

Subject-matter of Patent.	Number of Patent.	Date.	Name of Patentee.
PROPELLING, &c.—*continued.*			
Spools or bobbins to be used in certain frames for preparing fibrous materials for spinning.	1127	22nd April 1865	Joshua Henry Wilson.
Improvements in the fitting of surface condensery tubes, and in the tools to be used therein, and in the means of retarding corrosion in steam-boilers. (*Communicated by William Judson.*)	1132	22nd April 1865	Alfred Vincent Newton.
Improvements in motive-power machinery for cultivating land, part of which improvements is applicable to driving machinery generally -	1134	22nd April 1865	James Howard, Edward Tenney Bousfield.
Improvements in means or apparatus for measuring the flow or passage of liquids, which improvements are also applicable in obtaining motive-power.	1150	25th April 1865	Thomas Walker.
Sewing-machines - - - - -	1160	26th April 1865	John Fairweather. William Fairweather.
Machinery for sewing and embroidering - -	1167	26th April 1865	George Mumby.
File cutting machines - - - -	1172	26th April 1865	James Dodge.
Machinery for reducing friable substances to powder.	1173	27th April 1865	Henry Walker Wood.
Machinery for cutting or shaping masts, spars and other beams and articles of wood.	1179	27th April 1865	Samuel Harvey.
Machinery or apparatus for working or cutting coal or minerals, and for compressing or exhausting air to be employed therein or for other purposes, some parts of which apparatus are also applicable to upright shafts, and other parts for regulating the flow or discharge of steam or other elastic fluids.	1202	29th April 1865	William Leatham.
Machinery or apparatus employed in breweries and distilleries.	1204	29th April 1865	Francis Gregory.
Mangles - - - - - -	1217	1st May 1865	William Watts. John Joseph Cooper.
Straight line dividing engines and tools for regulating distances.	1245	4th May 1865	William Ford Stanley.
Ploughs - - - - - -	1246	4th May 1865	John Stalkartt.
Improvements in the preparation of jute, hemp, flax and other fibrous materials, and in the machinery or apparatus employed therein.	1262	5th May 1865	James M'Gleshan.
Certain improvements in machinery for setting and distributing printing types. (*Communicated by Abiel Abbot Low, Josiah Orne Low, Edward Hutchinson Robbins Lyman, Charles Frederick Livermore, Augustus Carey Richards and Charles Carroll Yreton.*)	1271	8th May 1865	William Clark.
Ploughs - - - - - -	1280	12th May 1865	John Eddy.
Machinery for the manufacture of hinges - (*Communicated by Jean Baptiste Evrard and Jean Pierre Boyer.*)	1285	13th May 1865	William Clark.
Steam cranes - - - - -	1343	15th May 1865	Charles James Appleby.
Printing-machines - - - -	1344	15th May 1865	Robert Harrild. Horton Harrild.
Reaping and mowing machines - - -	1371	18th May 1865	William Manwaring.
Sewing-machines - - - - -	1377	18th May 1865	James Laing.
Machinery for driving piles - - -	1376	18th May 1865	William Essnie.
An improved mangle - - - -	1418	24th May 1865	Henry Nunn.

Subject-matter of Patent.	Number of Patent.	Date.	Name of Patentee.
PROPELLING, &c.—continued.			
Machinery for printing in colours - - - (Communicated by Martin Morgira.)	1708	26th June 1865	Richard Archibald Brooman.
Cotton gins - - - - - (Communicated by Frederick Tudor Ackland, Henry George Mitchell and Mustapha Mustapha.)	1714	27th June 1865	John Henry Johnson.
Twist lace machines - - - - -	1723	29th June 1866	{ Richard Bool. John Cozan.
Machinery or apparatus for cutting, punching and bending sheet metal. (Communicated by Nathan Harper.)	1729	29th June 1865	Robert Henry Lamb.
Knitting-machines - - - - - (Communicated by William Williams Clay.)	1747	1st July 1865	George Davies.
Machines for making paper board - - -	1756	3rd July 1865	John Franklin Jones.
Certain improvements in machinery or apparatus for turning and cutting wood and other substances, to be employed in the manufacture of spools or bobbins or other similar articles.	1773	5th July 1865	John Braithwaite.
Improved machinery for boring rocks and hard substances.	1778	5th July 1865	George Low.
Machinery for the manufacture of paper board and paper.	1787	6th July 1865	John Franklin Jones.
Certain improvements in machinery or apparatus to be employed in the manufacture of metallic bolts, rivets and spikes.	1796	7th July 1865	Eric Hugo Waldenström.
Improved apparatus for gauging and marking the width of tucks and pleats on fabrics under operation in sewing-machines.	1811	8th July 1865	George Baldwin Woodruff.
Machinery for washing, wringing, mangling and drying domestic clothes or other fabrics and fibrous substances.	1827	10th July 1865	{ Henry Fearnley. Christopher Smith.
Regulating or controlling the power employed in actuating sewing and other machines of a light nature.	1828	11th July 1865	Benjamin Fothergill.
Straight eye clearing guides or cleaners, for winding silk, cotton or other fibrous substances.	1873	19th July 1865	{ John Batkin Whitehall. Thomas Pillings.
Motive-power by capillary attraction - -	1874	19th July 1865	Johann Ernst Friedrich Ledrke.
Processes and machinery for producing fibres suitable for being spun, from rags or remnants of woven or other textile fabrics made of silk, wool, cotton or other fibrous materials.	1881	19th July 1865	Henry Ernest Gillet.
Improved mechanism for propelling, driving and forcing purposes.	1898	20th July 1865	Thomas Swinburne.
Sewing-machines - - - - -	1904	21st July 1865	Alfred Smith.
Means of and apparatus for raising water for agricultural and other useful and ornamental purposes. (Communicated by Jean Louis Célestin Ackard.)	1919	22nd July 1865	William Edward Gedge.
Machinery for planing metals - - - (Communicated by William Sellers.)	1949	26th July 1865	William Edward Newton
Applying and utilising water power - - (driving mills.)	1967	29th July 1865	Valentine Baker.
Preparing machinery for flax, tow, jute and other fibrous materials - - - - - }	1977	31st July 1865	{ John Lawson. Edward Gerrard Fison.

Subject-matter of Patent.	Number of Patent.	Date.	Name of Person.
PROPELLING, &c.—continued.			
Improvements in and apparatus for treating peat in bogs and obtaining it therefrom, also applicable to tilling and cultivating land.	2004	2nd Aug. 1865	Charles Hodgson.
Apparatus used in rolling leather	2007	2nd Aug. 1865	John Henry Tyler.
An improved method of working guns	2014	3rd Aug. 1865	Henry Duncan Preston Cunningham.
Apparatus applicable as a motive-power engine, a pump or fluid meter. (Communicated by Francis Bernard de Kererrancs.)	2021	4th Aug. 1865	William Clark.
Machinery or apparatus for sizing, drying and beaming yarns of cotton or other fibrous substances	2022	4th Aug. 1865	{ John Oxenhryrr. John Dodgson.
Machinery for manufacturing cigars (Communicated by John Prentice.)	2032	4th Aug. 1865	Alfred Vincent Newton
Construction of binders for sewing-machines	2033	4th Aug. 1865	George Baldwin Windsel
Apparatus for washing yarns	2044	7th Aug. 1865	{ William Pollock. John Statin.
Printing-machines	2066	8th Aug. 1865	William Bock.
Improvements in the lubricating of spindles, the necks or bolsters in which the said spindles revolve having a traversing motion in the said neck or bolster.	2069	9th Aug. 1865	Jacob Henry Radcliffe.
Construction of steam-engines	2062	9th Aug. 1865	Henry Cartwright.
Construction of sewing-machines particularly adapted for sewing socks and bags	2067	9th Aug. 1865	{ Barnabas Rau. Edward Goodall the younger. John Ingham.
Looms for weaving	2078	10th Aug. 1865	{ Henry Ingham. James Brindley.
Machinery or apparatus for the manufacture of needles.	2074	10th Aug. 1865	Chauncey Orrin Crosby.
Process of and machinery for cleaning china grass and flax, and removing therefrom the resinous and woody matters that adhere to the useful fibres of the plant.	2078	10th Aug. 1865	Joseph Faron.
Machines for making eyelets (Communicated by James Lewis Harlow and Theodore Laverne Payne.)	2079	10th Aug. 1865	William Edward Newton
Apparatus for obtaining and applying motive-power to various useful purposes	2080	11th Aug. 1865	{ William Thomas Cole. Henry Spink Swift. Augusto Suarez.
Machinery for preparing cotton, wool and other fibrous materials	2088	12th Aug. 1865	{ Jonas Tatham. John Smith.
Certain improvements in looms for weaving	2091	12th Aug. 1865	William Bullough.
Machinery or apparatus for the manufacture of paper bags. (Communicated by Delevan Clerk.)	2116	16th Aug. 1865	John Henry Johnson.
Lawn mowing machines	2118	16th Aug. 1865	James Bryce Brown.
Certain improvements in machinery for making bricks. (Communicated by Egbert Cox Bradford and James Henry Renick.)	2148	19th Aug. 1865	William Edward Newton.
Improvements in lithographic and copper plate printing, and in the machinery or apparatus connected therewith.	2170	23rd Aug. 1865	Donald McKellOr.

Subject-matter of Patent.	Number of Patent.	Date.	Name of Patentee.

PROPELLING, &c.—continued.

Steam hammers	2174	24th Aug. 1865	David Davies.
Improvements in apparatus by means of which certain liquids, common air, and certain elastic fluids are made available in the production of light, and their quantity regulated and measured, parts of which improvements are applicable for other purposes. *(propelling through tubes.)*	2194	25th Aug. 1865	Edwin Augustus Curley.
Improvements in the manufacture of velvet and in the apparatus employed therein. *(regulating height of pile.)* *(Communicated by Messieurs Fraisse-Brossard fils jeunes.)*	2204	26th Aug. 1865	Henri Adrien Bonneville.
Applying motive-power to sewing-machines, for the purpose of rendering them self-acting.	2218	29th Aug. 1865	Geminiano Zanni.
Sewing or stitching machines	2257	6th Sept. 1865	Robert Allen Parkin. George Callaway.
Machinery for winding yarn cops	2297	7th Sept. 1865	William Oldham.
Machinery or apparatus for hulling and winnowing grain. *(Communicated by Friedrich Henchel and Wilhelm Serk.)*	2300	7th Sept. 1865	William Lloyd Wise.
An improved wheel feed for sewing-machines	2315	9th Sept. 1865	John Ilem.
Reaping-machines	2324	11th Sept. 1865	Charles Thomas Burgess.
Clothes wringing machines, the mode of communicating rotary motion in which is also applicable to other machines having similarly rotating parts. *(Partly communicated by James Pease and David Lyman.)*	2336	12th Sept. 1865	Thomas Drew Stetson.
Machinery for the manufacture of rivets	2355	14th Sept. 1865	John Wakefield.
Improved machinery for cutting stone *(Communicated by George Jeffords Wardwell.)*	2365	15th Sept. 1865	Alfred Vincent Newton.
Machinery or apparatus for shaping metal articles *(Communicated by Robert Heapy Butcher.)*	2371	16th Sept. 1865	John Henry Johnson.
Machinery for cutting and shaping cork, with apparatus for registering the manufacture.	2393	20th Sept. 1865	Leon Villette.
Mills for crushing and grinding wheat and other grain.	2399	20th Sept. 1865	John Tye.
Machinery for excavating earth *(guiding, varying depth of cut.)*	2403	21st Sept. 1865	John Bostock Hulme.
Machinery for grinding, dressing, smoothing or polishing flags and stones, without the use of the ordinary cutting tools	2411	21st Sept. 1865	Benjamin Claffer. James Thompson. Charles Thompson.
Hoisting machines *(Communicated by William Miller.)*	2414	21st Sept. 1865	William Robert Lake.
Construction of presses for hay, cotton, hemp and other substances. *(Communicated by Thomas Gennon and Thomas Bolton Webster.)*	2454	25th Sept. 1865	Alfred Vincent Newton.
Tools for securing tubes in tube plates, and for other purposes where concentrated power or adjustment is necessary.	2455	26th Sept. 1865	Richard Taylor Nelson Howry.
Machinery for tempering and preparing peat for fuel. *(Communicated by Nathaniel Frothingham Potter.)*	2459	26th Sept. 1865	George Tomlinson Bousfield.

Subject-matter of Patent.	Number of Patent.	Date.	Name of Patentee.
PROFILING, &c.—*continued.*			
Washing and wringing machines - - - (*Communicated by Thomas Blotcher.*)	2478	27th Sept. 1865	Richard Archibald Brooman.
Improved self-centering and tightening chucks for drilling-machines, lathes, and other machines in which chucks are used. (*Communicated by John Edwin Earle.*)	2491	24th Sept. 1865	Edward Thomas Hughes.
Sewing-machines - - - - (*Communicated by John Nathaniel Turbus.*)	2496	24th Sept. 1865	Richard Archibald Brooman.
Apparatus for grinding cards of carding-engines - (*traversing.*)	2518	30th Sept. 1865	Samuel Faulkner.
Weft winding-machines both for winding on bobbins and cops, also for a shuttle to hold the cop when weaving. (*driving the spindles.*)	2519	30th Sept. 1865	William Longbottom.
Travelling cranes - - - - -	2524	2nd Oct. 1865	{ David Orrig. Robert Barton.
An improved sewing-machine - - - (*Communicated by Henry Hudson.*)	2533	3rd Oct. 1865	William Robert Lake.
File cutting machines - - - - (*adjusting and guiding.*)	2548	4th Oct. 1865	John Dodge.
Machinery for folding fabrics and inserting cardboard or other substances between the folds - (*guiding the fabric.*)	2550	5th Oct. 1865	Richard Tonge.
Sewing-machines - - - - (*Communicated by Joseph Louis Kieffer and Charles Nicolas Eray.*)	2551	5th Oct. 1865	Michael Henry.
Machinery for shaping metal and other substances -	2552	6th Oct. 1865	Beckwith Hughes.
Improvements in and applicable to machines for opening and cleaning cotton and other fibrous materials - - - - - (*driving the feed rollers.*)	2557	5th Oct. 1865	{ Edward Marsland. Peter Williams.
Double or single action pumps - - (*Communicated by Claude Gonin.*)	2583	11th Oct. 1865	William Edward Gedge.
An improved method of working windlasses -	2635	12th Oct. 1865	{ George Deslandes. Albert Deslandes.
Machinery employed for crushing, amalgamating and washing gold quartz and other minerals or matters containing gold or other metal. (*Communicated by James Hart.*)	2643	13th Oct. 1865	William Halen Getty Jones.
Apparatus for finishing textile fabrics - -	2647	13th Oct. 1865	{ William Robertson. James Guthrie Orchar.
Sewing-machines - - - - -	2649	13th Oct. 1865	George Baldwin Woodruff.
Certain improvements in machinery or apparatus for preparing and spinning cotton and other fibrous substances.	2651	14th Oct. 1865	Godfrey Anthony Krass.
Machinery for cutting screws - - -	2652	14th Oct. 1865	Joseph Tangye.
Apparatus for polishing and crushing - -	2655	14th Oct. 1865	James Lamb Hancock.
Construction of ships for raising ballast, ores, coal, minerals and other matters in bulk.	2663	16th Oct. 1865	Charles Henry Murray.
Sewing-machines - - - - -	2666	16th Oct. 1865	Joseph Buchanan Robertson.
Improvements in wheels for common road carriages, in tyres for the same, and in machinery for bending the tyres.	2669	16th Oct. 1865	James Lamb Hancock.
Certain improvements in looms for weaving -	2672	17th Oct. 1865	Edward Lord.

Subject-matter of Patent.	Number of Patent.	Date.	Name of Patentee.
PROPELLING, &c.—continued.			
Machinery for the manufacture of fish hooks	2673	17th Oct. 1865	Albert Fenton.
Machinery for weaving the covering of hand-cord and other tubular fabrics. (Communicated by Isaac Emerson Palmer.)	8661	17th Oct. 1865	Henry Edward Newton.
Machinery for hanging fabrics in stores or chambers	8685	18th Oct. 1865	{ William Schofield. John Smith.
Improvements in block matches and in machinery for making the same	8690	18th Oct. 1865	{ James Whitford Truman. Henry Lori.
An improved method of hanging or suspending blinds from blind rollers, and improvements in the manufacture of such rollers. (adjusting the rollers.)	2729	21st Oct. 1865	Samuel Parkes Matthews.
Sewing-machines (Communicated by Charles Rhodes Goodwin.)	8740	23rd Oct. 1866	William Clark.
Improvements in sewing machinery for using waxed thread. (Communicated by Thomas John Halligan.)	8748	24th Oct. 1865	Alfred Vincent Newton.
Mules for spinning and doubling (Communicated by Ernest Sturm.)	2769	26th Oct. 1865	Henry Bernoulli Barlow.
Driving or actuating machinery	8778	27th Oct. 1865	John Garnett.
Apparatus for producing accelerated motion for driving purposes	8779	29th Oct. 1865	{ John Hawthorn Kitson. John Kirby.
Improvements in the construction and arrangement of sewing-machines, and in the apparatus employed therein	2784	29th Oct. 1865	{ William Westmoreland. Edwin Westmoreland.
Transmitting motion to propelling shafts (Communicated by James Buchanan Eads.)	2807	31st Oct. 1865	William Edward Newton.
Machinery for dressing millstones (Communicated by Eleazer A. Paine.)	2817	1st Nov. 1865	Alfred Vincent Newton.
Machinery or apparatus for reeling silk, cotton or other fibrous threads in the form of skeins. (self-acting guider.)	2830	2nd Nov. 1865	Enoch Rushton.
Improvements in machinery for compressing cotton, wool and other materials, for the economy of transit, which said improvements more particularly relate to the more expeditious filling of the box of the press and fastenings for bales.	2857	3rd Nov. 1865	James Jennings M'Comb.
Mounting and driving millstones	2858	3rd Nov. 1865	Richard Smith, jun'.
A new thrashing machine worked directly on the thrashing floor by oxen or horses.	2868	9th Nov. 1865	Theophilus Berrow.
Machines for fret cutting or sawing	2890	10th Nov. 1865	William Middleton.
Machinery for rolling shafts and axles (Communicated by Thomas Cooper.)	2904	11th Nov. 1865	Alfred Vincent Newton.
Crank axles of locomotives for railroads (Communicated by Dyer Williams.)	2906	11th Nov. 1865	William Robert Lake.
Railway steam-engines and carriages (transmitting the driving power.)	2926	14th Nov. 1865	Joseph Alphonse Loubat.
Apparatus for raising, lowering, moving or transporting heavy bodies	2931	14th Nov. 1865	{ Thomas Aldridge Weston. James Tangye. Richard Chapman.
Means of connecting drums or pulleys with their shafts or drivers. (Communicated by Leverett Homer Olmsted.)	2963	14th Nov. 1865	William Clark.

Subject-matter of Patent.	Number of Patent.	Date.	Name of Patentee.

PROPELLING, &c.—continued.

Subject-matter of Patent.	Number of Patent.	Date.	Name of Patentee.

PROPELLING, &c.—continued.

Certain improvements in looms for weaving	3368	29th Dec. 1865	Thomas Watson.
Machinery for spooling cotton and other yarns and threads.	2276	30th Dec. 1865	Robert Smith.

For Driving-bands, see " Straps."
For adjusting Fire-arms, see " Fire-arms."

PUMPS; PUMPING AND RAISING WATER AND OTHER LIQUIDS; PUMP PISTONS AND PACKINGS; SHIPS' PUMPS; TURBINES; BEER ENGINES.

An improvement in ordinary lift and force pumps	11	3rd Jan. 1865	Martin Benson.
Improvements in the manufacture of elastic packings for pistons, and in lubricating compositions therefor.	10	4th Jan. 1865	Edward Kelrby.
Improvements in the packings of pistons and piston rods of pumps and steam and other engines, which improvements are also applicable to hydraulic presses.	155	19th Jan. 1865	William Robert Foster.
Improved arrangements for coupling steam-engines, turbines or other apparatus employed as motive-power. (see " Water-wheels.") (Communicated by Lesbeiy August Rärdinger.)	159	19th Jan. 1865	Adolf Wilhelm Prager.
Steam-engines (or pumps.)	168	19th Jan. 1865	William Cleveland Hicks.
An improved machine for raising and carrying earth, sand, stones or other similar solid or liquid materials for dredging, ventilating, or winnowing grain or other analogous purposes. (for raising water.)	174	20th Jan. 1865	Louis Rahm.
Improvements applicable to pumps	186	21st Jan. 1865	John Hays Wilson.
Construction of pumps for lifting and forcing liquids.	237	27th Jan. 1865	James Hind.
Applying power to the working of ships' windlasses, winches, capstans, pumps and other ships' gear.	242	27th Jan. 1865	Handel Moore.
Working ships' pumps	308	3rd Feb. 1865	Matthew Blank.
An improved combustion pump (Communicated by Thomas John Linton.)	314	4th Feb. 1866	William Clark.
A new method for removing or destroying the momentum of heavy bodies by means of an elastic machine or machines, so as to prevent injury and damage from concussion, applicable to ship cables, ship and fort armour, railway trains, buffers to pier heads and floating piers, gangways, breakwaters and other similar structures, also as a motive-power. (working pumps.) (Communicated by William Graham M'Ivor.)	391	6th Feb. 1866	Clements Robert Markham.

Subject-matter of Patent.	Number of Patent.	Date.	Name of Patentee.
Pumps, &c.—continued.			
Improvements in and applicable to that and similar apparatus for raising and forcing fluids and feeding steam-boilers, known as "Giffard's Injector."	410	14th Feb. 1865	James Gresham.
Pumps and apparatus for working the same	438	15th Feb. 1865	George Tyrrell Humphry.
Beam engines	463	16th Feb. 1865	James Grafton Jones.
Certain improvements in hydraulic pumps in connection with engines of motive-power.	521	24th Feb. 1865	William Oram.
Pumps	620	6th March 1865	Richard Archibald Brooman.
(Communicated by Howard Meury.)			
Improved combinations of direct acting steam-engines with single or double acting pumps, for pumping water, air or gases.	781	17th March 1865	Jacob Goodfellow.
An improved arrangement of valves and other appliances for a new description of hydraulic engine for raising water and other fluids above their common level, the fluids so raised to be used as a motive-power	791	21st March 1865	{ James Smith. Sydney Arthur Chane.
Obtaining motive-power	802	22nd March 1865	Valentine Baker.
Certain improvements in non-conducting composition for preventing the radiation or transmission of heat or cold.	864	27th March 1865	Ferdinand Le Roy.
(for cooling pumps.)			
Improvements in paddle wheels, parts of which are applicable to other purposes.	935	3rd April 1865	William Cantrill Collings.
(to pumps.)			
Double acting lift and force pumps	943	4th April 1865	Charles Denman Young.
Suction and force pumps	951	4th April 1865	Robert Bayram.
Apparatus for feeding boilers, raising water and propelling vessels.	1062	13th April 1865	Richard Archibald Brooman.
(Communicated by Pierre Samain.)			
Certain improvements in pumps	1099	20th April 1865	Maynardlitch Hounsipin.
(Communicated by Didren Demanlion.)			
Improvements in apparatus for raising water and other fluids, and in raising and lowering such apparatus.	1191	29th April 1865	Julian Bernard.
Certain improvements in pumps	1310	1st May 1865	Charles Edward Herpst.
(Communicated by Messieurs Armand Labarre and Aine Bellel Dussard.)			
Construction of pumps for raising water and other liquids	1360	15th May 1865	{ William Easton, Edward Moore. William Gillies.
Apparatus for raising oil and other liquids from deep wells	1393	20th May 1865	William Edward Newton.
(Communicated by Francis Stebbins Pease.)			
A new system of rotative machines to be used as steam-engines and water pumps.	1447	26th May 1865	Jean Alphonse Heinrich.
A new or improved machine for obtaining motive-power and other useful purposes.	1466	29th May 1865	Henry Moseley.
(for raising or projecting water.)			
Certain improvements in the formation and construction of metallic vessels, chambers or hollow cylinders used in hydraulic apparatus, cannon or heavy guns, and for like purposes.	1505	1st June 1865	Herbert Adams.

Subject-matter of Patent.	Number of Patent.	Date.	Name of Patentee.

PUMPS, &c. —continued.

Subject-matter of Patent.	Number of Patent.	Date.	Name of Patentee.
Turbines - - - - -	1654	5th June 1865	{ Thomas Gentle. Joseph Allmark.
An improved apparatus for separating the whey from the curd in the manufacture of cheese.	1655	5th June 1865	Philip Coombes.
An improved metallic stuffing box - -	1656	7th June 1865	Victor Duterne.
Hydraulic motive-power machinery - -	1642	17th June 1865	Valentine Baker.
Apparatus for the decantation and raising of petroleum and other oils.	1784	24th June 1865	Paul Jacovaco.
Steam pumping machines or engines - -	1780	3rd July 1865	Martin Benson.
Pumps - - - - - - (Communicated by Jean Pierre Tejan.)	1864	17th July 1865	Richard Archibald Brooman.
Obtaining motive-power when heated air or aeriform fluid is employed.	1915	22nd July 1865	Matthew Piers Watt Boulton.
Means of and apparatus for raising water for agricultural and other useful and ornamental purposes. (Communicated by Jean Louis Celestin Ackard.)	1919	22nd July 1865	William Edward Gedge.
Fire engines and hydraulic machines - -	1953	24th July 1865	Leon Paul Larocke.
Applying and utilising water power - - (driving turbines, pumping.)	1967	29th July 1865	Valentine Baker.
Improvements in the raising, lifting or drawing and forcing of water and other liquids, and in the apparatus and means employed therefor - (steam liquid raiser.)	1996	2nd Aug. 1865	{ James McEwan. William Neilson.
Apparatus applicable as a motive-power engine, a pump or fluid meter. (Communicated by Francis Bernard de Kivrereaux.)	2031	4th Aug. 1865	William Clark.
Slaking and manufacturing pumps for use in ships and other purposes.	2107	15th Aug. 1865	Abel Mills.
Hydropults and hydrostatic pumps - - -	2205	5th Sept. 1865	James Webster.
An improved construction of engine which can be used either as a motor or for pumping. (Communicated by John Benjamin Root and William Benjamin.)	2455	25th Sept. 1865	William Edward Newton.
Centrifugal pumps and fans - - -	2480	28th Sept. 1865	Arthur Rigg, jun'.
Apparatus for administering injections and douches to the human body.	2555	5th Oct. 1865	William Robert Barker.
Improvements in apparatus and means for extinguishing fires, part of such improvements being applicable for other purposes.	2559	5th Oct. 1865	William Henry Phillips.
Rotary engines and pumps - - - (Communicated by Public Chairday.)	2667	6th Oct. 1865	Richard Archibald Brooman.
Double or single action pumps - - - (Communicated by Claude Goain.)	2622	11th Oct. 1865	William Edward Gedge.
Apparatus for raising liquids - - -	2632	12th Oct. 1865	Jean Urain Bartier.
Improvements in hydraulic presses and in apparatus connected therewith - - }	2666	19th Oct. 1865	{ Thomas Routledge. Daniel Bentley. John Broad Jackson.
Rotary pumps - - - - - (Communicated by Edward Rorach.)	2706	20th Oct. 1865	Charles Denton Abel.
Construction of pumps for raising or forcing water or other liquids or fluids - - }	2745	21th Oct. 1865	{ Hyde Bateman. Edward Gooch Garrard.

Subject-matter of Patent.	Number of Patent.	Date.	Name of Patentee.
Pumps, &c.—continued.			
An improved non-conducting composition for preventing the radiation or transmission of heat or cold. (*for protecting pumps from frost.*)	2858	4th Nov. 1865	James Thyr.
Construction of pumps for raising water and other liquids.	2940	15th Nov. 1865	William Easton.
Improvements in means or apparatus for conveying the passage or flow of liquids, for raising and forcing fluids, and for obtaining motive-power, also in means for the manufacture of parts of such apparatus.	2968	17th Nov. 1865	Walter Payton.
Improvements in the hulls and tackle of navigable vessels, and in the gear for propelling the same by wind and steam or other motive-power engine, and clearing the same from water, and in apparatus connected therewith to enable the said vessels to be converted in floating graving docks, or lifts for raising vessels and other submerged or partially submerged heavy bodies to or above the surface of the water.	3031	25th Nov. 1865	John Ferrier.
Certain apparatus for injecting and ejecting fluids and liquids. (*lifting liquids from great depths.*)	3179	9th Dec. 1865	Andrew Barclay.
Turbines for obtaining motive-power, applicable also to raising and forcing fluids, and to propelling ships or vessels. (*Communicated by Joseph Denis Forest, Jean Joseph Lion Forest, Michel Basile Abel Forest, Joseph Etienne Elei Choiron and Emmanuel Denis Forest.*)	3232	13th Dec. 1865	William Bromken.
An improved construction of rotary engine - - (*or pump.*)	3225	13th Dec. 1865	Peter Gardner.
Pumps - - - - - (*ships' pumps, beer engines.*)	3315	22nd Dec. 1865	William Jackson.
Pumps - - - - -	3330	23rd Dec. 1865	{ Henry Davis Hoxhold. William Blanch Brain.
Purses and Fastenings.			
An improved system of closing spatter-dashes, applicable also to boots, portemonnaies and other similar articles.	658	9th March 1865	Emile Carchon.
An improved fastening for purses and other like articles - - - - - (*Communicated by Carl Poser, Jacob Poser and Ludwig Pohl.*)	2347	13th Sept. 1865	{ David Hyam. { John Hyam.
Adaptation of elastic material to articles requiring a bellows arrangement, or a partially rigid and partially expansible arrangement. (*for purses.*)	2433	22nd Sept. 1865	Matthew Cartwright.
An improvement in clasps or fastenings - - (*for purses.*)	2525	2nd Oct. 1865	Frederic Jenner.

Subject-matter of Patent.	Number of Patent.	Date.	Name of Patentee.
PURSES, &c.—continued.			
Improvements in satchels and in the manufacture of the gussets of leather satchels, bags and purses and of the gussets of other articles made of leather.	2707	20th Oct. 1865	Frederick Thompson.
Locks or catches for portmonnaies, portfolios or other articles - - - - - - -	2959	15th Nov. 1865	George Chambers. George Gregory.
RAGS AND WASTE; SEPARATING FIBRES FROM FABRICS.			
Certain improvements in the manufacture of lint -	73	10th Jan. 1865	Samuel Shaw Brown.
Machinery for opening and carding cotton and other fibrous materials. (*tearing rags.*)	90	11th Jan. 1865	Robert Temperst.
Means or apparatus for extracting or expressing oil or grease from the greasy waste of fibrous substances or other substances containing oil or grease - - - - - -	361	20th Jan. 1865	William Trall. Abraham Naylor.
Improved machinery for cutting, sifting, separating, bruising, sacking and preparing straw and other vegetable fibrous substances to be employed in the manufacture of various kinds of paper, and also for preparing food for cattle - - -	340	7th Feb. 1865	John Comes. William Nimpson.
Separating wool from refuse mixed fabrics and materials.	511	23rd Feb. 1865	Samuel Narille.
An improved method of treating, cleaning or preparing painted or other canvas, tarpaulins and dirty cotton waste, so as to render the same suitable to be used for household and other purposes for which they may be applicable.	752	17th March 1865	William Maurice Williams.
Manufacture of yarn so as to render same applicable as a substitute for woollen yarn, for manufacturing into shawls and other textile fabrics. (*waste hemp and flax.*)	774	20th March 1865	Isidor Phillppsthel.
An improved process for reducing or preparing waste animal matters, for the purpose of employing the same in the preparation of manures or fertilising compounds.	883	29th March 1865	William Moxon Foller.
Improvements in the manufacture of paper and paper stock, and in the utilization of certain waste products resulting therefrom - -	1602	13th June 1865	Thomas Routledge. William Henry Richardson.
(*treating rags.*)			
Process and machinery for producing fibres suitable for being spun, from rags or remnants of woven or other textile fabrics made of silk, wool, cotton or other fibrous materials.	1881	19th July 1865	Henry Ernest Gilles.
Means of and apparatus for treating animal and vegetable fibrous materials, which apparatus is also applicable to various useful purposes.	1958	27th July 1865	Henry Sherwood.
Improvements in reducing vegetable fibre to pulp, and in machinery employed therein.	2002	2nd Aug. 1865	William Wharton Bardon.

Subject-matter of Patent.	Number of Patent.	Date.	Name of Patentee.
Rags, &c.— *continued.*			
Apparatus for steeping or treating paper pulp and other matters subjected to the action of alkalies. (rags.) (*Communicated by Messieurs Negret, Orioli and Fredel.*)	2574	6th Oct. 1865	William Clark.
A means or method of and apparatus to be employed for utilising waste braids for weaving	3257	16th Dec. 1865	Francis Johnson. William Astley.
Machinery used in tearing silk and other fabrics and rags	3386	29th Dec. 1865	Sidney Collum. Charles Collum.
Means or apparatus for extracting wool from cotton and other vegetable substances contained in mixed fabrics	3379	30th Dec. 1865	Arthur Knowles. James Knowles. Joshua Barraclough.

Railways and Railway Carriages.

I.—Permanent Way, Rails, Rail-joints, Chairs and Sleepers; Portable Railways, Atmospheric Railways, Tramways.

Improvements in the permanent way of railways and in buckled plates to be used therein, the same being applicable to the construction of fire-proof buildings, bridges and other like structures, also in the machinery or apparatus for producing such improved plates.	164	19th Jan. 1865	Robert Mallet.
Apparatus for taking up and delivering mails and other parcels in railway trains while in motion. (*Communicated by Julius Kopfer Carior.*)	177	20th Jan. 1865	William Clark.
Construction of permanent way for railroads	184	21st Jan. 1865	James Godfrey Wilson.
Improved apparatus for transmitting letter bags and parcels to and from railway trains whilst in motion. (*Communicated by Charles Louis Ferdinand Vareilhes-Laplotte.*)	187	21st Jan. 1865	Charles Denton Abel.
Improvements in rail and tramways, in laying electric telegraph wires, and in compositions for insulating the same. (*Communicated by Jean Armand Emile Lalombre.*)	269	31st Jan. 1865	Richard Archibald Brooman.
Permanent way of railways	275	31st Jan. 1865	Ewing Pye Colquhoun. John Pardoe Ferris.
Railway chairs, fastenings and sleepers	318	4th Feb. 1865	Robert Richardson.
A new method for removing or destroying the momentum of heavy bodies by means of an elastic machine or machines, so as to prevent injury and damage from concussion, applicable to ship cables, ship and fort armour, railway trains, tenders to pier heads, and floating piers, gangways, breakwaters and other similar structures, also as a motive-power. (*Communicated by William Graham M'Iver.*)	321	6th Feb. 1866	Clements Robert Markham.
Permanent way of railways	388	11th Feb. 1865	John Porter. James Porter.
Railway rails	434	16th Feb. 1865	Denison Chauncey Fiske.

Subject-matter of Patent.	Number of Patent.	Date.	Name of Patentee.
RAILWAYS, &c.—continued.			
Permanent way and rolling stock of railways	620	24th Feb. 1865	John Kennedy Donald.
Railway chairs, fastenings and sleepers	644	27th Feb. 1865	Henry Hennon Heacon.
An improved process and apparatus for impregnating wood with chemical solutions. (railway sleepers.) (Communicated by Ernest Bario and Jules Henory.)	690	2nd March 1865	William Edward Newton.
Apparatus for propulsion by atmospheric pressure	696	3rd March 1865	Sir John Scott Lillie, Knight.
Improvements in the construction of railway plant to ensure the safety of passengers' lives in the event of accident or collision	699	11th March 1865	Charles Middleton Bernot. Nathaniel Symons.
Improvements in the means and apparatus employed for treating timber with antiseptic or preservative fluids, also applicable to other purposes. (for railway sleepers.)	734	16th March 1865	Samuel Bagster Boulton.
Permanent way of railways (Communicated by Gabriel Dümler.)	758	16th March 1865	William Lorder.
Manufacture or construction of rails for railways (Communicated by Gabriel Dümler.)	832	24th March 1865	William Lorder.
Street railways (Communicated by William Drummond O'Brien.)	823	1st April 1865	Richard Archibald Brooman.
Machinery for the manufacture of railway bolts and spikes and other like articles.	978	7th April 1865	Thomas Wilkes.
Construction of the permanent way of railways (Communicated by Moritz Hill.)	1151	22nd April 1865	William Bünger.
Construction of railway rails and wheels	1158	25th April 1865	John Townsend Bucknill.
Improvements in railway chairs and in the mode of securing rails thereto. (Communicated by Charles W. Stafford.)	1169	26th April 1865	Richard Eccles.
Improvements in the manufacture of pig iron or foundry metal, and in making and treating castings of such metal. (for railway chairs.)	1209	1st May 1865	Henry Bessemer.
Securing the rails of the permanent way of railways	1806	11th May 1865	William Tyou.
An improved method of and apparatus for laying single line articulated railways, and a method of propelling thereon, particularly applicable for agricultural purposes.	1321	12th May 1865	Richard Winder.
Construction of the permanent way of railways	1511	1st June 1865	Thomas Hunt.
An improved method of and machinery for cutting and excavating rock for railway tunnels and other purposes. (Communicated by Thelm Lindsley.)	1567	12th June 1865	George Hazeltine.
Improvements in the permanent way of railways and in locomotives applicable thereto.	1568	12th June 1865	William James Hixon.
Improved sanitary apparatus or arrangements for preventing noxious exhalations such as arise when coating or treating iron or other articles. (tarring railway gauge bars.)	1690	24th June 1865	Matthew Andrew Muir. James M'Ilwham.
Forming the permanent ways of railways	1705	26th June 1865	John Whittle.
Securing the rails of railways	1718	27th June 1865	John Kirkham.
An improved circular endless railway (Communicated by Ernest Michaux.)	1771	5th July 1865	William Edward Gedge.

2

Subject-matter of Patent.	Number of Patent.	Date.	Name of Patentee.
RAILWAYS, &c.—*continued.*			
Permanent ways of railways - - -	1842	12th July 1865	James Edwards Wilson
Apparatus for the locomotion of trains on railways, by atmospheric pressure.	1852	14th July 1865	William Podmore Baylis
Mode of connecting rails for railways and tramways	1878	19th July 1865	Constantine Henderson
Construction and working of furnaces for puddling, balling, heating and melting metals. *(and for forming a tramway for trucks to receive ashes, &c.)*	1883	19th July 1865	David Caddick.
Manufacture of iron and steel - - - *(rolling rails.)* *(Communicated by Martin Diraddeuf Henrwas.)*	1904	29th July 1865	Ephraim Sabel.
Manufacture of iron rails and girders - - - *(Communicated by Martin Diraddeuf Henvons.)*	1976	31st July 1865	Ephraim Sabel.
Improvements in the construction of atmospheric railways and carriages, and in working the same.	1997	1st Aug. 1865	Alexander Doull.
Improvements in and apparatus for treating peat in bogs and obtaining it therefrom, also applicable to tilling and cultivating land.	2004	2nd Aug. 1865	Charles Hodgson.
Improved means or apparatus for retarding or stopping railway carriages and trains.	2045	7th Aug. 1865	John Mead.
Apparatus and fittings to be used in ships, for facilitating the loading, unloading and stowage of their cargoes. *(Communicated by Gilbert Auguste Fournier des Curels.)*	2046	7th Aug. 1865	William Clark.
An improved mode of and apparatus for facilitating the transportation and delivery of letters, newspapers and other freight. *(Communicated by Alfred Ely Beach.)*	2049	7th Aug. 1865	Alfred Vincent Newton.
Railway chairs - - -	2099	14th Aug. 1865	William Frederick Reeves
Railway chairs, fastenings and sleepers - -	2162	25th Aug. 1865	Henry Henson Henson.
Construction of the permanent way of railways -	2163	25th Aug. 1865	William Rogers.
Improvements in apparatus by means of which certain liquids, common air, and certain elastic fluids are made available in the production of light, and their quantity regulated and measured, parts of which improvements are applicable for other purposes. *(atmospheric pressure railway.)*	2164	25th Aug. 1865	Edwin Augustus Cowley.
The improvement of the permanent way of railways and carriages for the same.	2227	30th Aug. 1865	James Cole Green.
Permanent way of railways - - - *(Communicated by Jules Voutherin.)*	2256	1st Sept. 1865	William Clark.
Treating, working or manipulating cast steel, for the manufacture of wheel-tires, armour plates, or other articles requiring great hardness and tensile strength. *(rails.)*	2377	5th Sept. 1865	Julius Omed.
Machinery for excavating earth - - -	2403	21st Sept. 1865	John Rowlark Hulme.
Improvements in railways and in the wheels for railways. *(Communicated by Alexander Skelton.)*	2405	21st Sept. 1865	Alfred Vincent Newton.
Improvements in the construction of railway plant to ensure the safety of passengers' lives in the event of accident or collision	2422	26th Sept. 1865	Charles Middleton Kernot. Nathaniel Symons.

Subject-matter of Patent.	Number of Patent.	Date.	Name of Patentee.
RAILWAYS, &c.—continued.			
Pneumatic ways for the transmission of letters, merchandise and passengers. (Communicated by Elias Parkman Needham.)	2557	3rd Oct. 1865	William Edward Newton.
Permanent way of railways - - - -	2694	11th Oct. 1865	Demian Chauncey Pierce.
A new self-adjusting apparatus for railway signals, applicable also to other purposes. (working level crossing gates.)	2718	20th Oct. 1865	George Mussell.
Railway chairs - - - - -	2724	21st Oct. 1865	John Durrant Fraser.
Obtaining sliding surfaces by the interposition and circulation of a liquid or gaseous fluid between the frictional surfaces. (sliding railways.)	2729	21st Oct. 1865	Louis Dominique Girard.
Means or apparatus for distributing sand or other suitable matter on the rails of railways, to promote adhesion of the locomotive wheels thereto.	2798	31st Oct. 1865	David Perfitt Griffiths Matthews.
Permanent way of railways - - -	2952	14th Nov. 1865	Thomas Dobie.
Improved machinery for cutting tunnels and sinking shafts - - - - - (cutting levels.)	3040	15th Nov. 1865	{ Alexander Alison, Henry Hoskings.
Improvements in the construction of railways and in spikes for securing the rails in position. (Communicated by John M'Murtry.)	3054	24th Nov. 1865	Alfred Vincent Newton.
Improvements in the manufacture and treatment of railway bars, tyres and axles, also in the construction of furnaces, machinery and apparatus connected therewith.	3084	1st Dec. 1865	Thomas Weatherburn Dodds.
Carriages, and endless tracks on and with which they run.	3100	2nd Dec. 1865	Adolphe Nicole.
Certain improvements in the manufacture of railway chairs and in the manner of securing rails thereto.	3121	6th Dec. 1865	Joseph Taylor.
Permanent way of railroads - - - (Communicated by Achille Cyprien Legrand.)	3168	9th Dec. 1865	Henri Adrien Bonneville.
Improvements in constructing atmospheric railways and carriages, and in working the same, parts of which are applicable to exhausting and condensing air for other purposes.	3173	9th Dec. 1865	Alexander Doull.
Permanent way of railways - - - (Communicated by Henry Warren Warner.)	3199	11th Dec. 1865	William Robert Lake.
Manufacture of railway bars - - -	3224	13th Dec. 1865	John Sanderson.
Permanent way and wheels of railways - - (Communicated by Mr. Gerard Christiaan Heyning.)	3352	23rd Dec. 1865	Hector Auguste Dufrené.
22.—Railways, Switches, Points, Crossings and Turntables.			
Machinery or apparatus for working switches and signals of railways.	147	18th Jan. 1865	William Jeffreys.
Apparatus for working and controlling railway switches, points and signals.	422	15th Feb. 1865	Michael Lane.
An improved apparatus for shifting points on railways from an engine or train in motion.	474	20th Feb. 1865	George Henry Hibbert Ware.

Subject-matter of Patent.	Number of Patent.	Date.	Name of Patentee.
RAILWAYS, &c.—continued.			
Improvements in and connected with levers for railway switches and signals.	709	14th March 1865	James Done.
Railway points and switches - - -	844	25th March 1865	Henry Columbus Harry.
Improvements in the manufacture of crossings for the permanent way of railways, and also in tyres for wheels.	1090	20th May 1865	Joseph Armstrong.
Turntables - - - - -	1671	23rd June 1865	Candido Bavelli.
Points and crossings of railways - - -	1751	1st July 1865	William M'Gregor.
Railway switches - - - - (Communicated by William Wharton, jun'.)	1786	6th July 1865	John Henry Johnson.
Apparatus and fittings to be used in ships, for facilitating the loading, unloading and stowage of their cargoes. (Communicated by Gilbert Auguste Fournier des Corats.)	2045	7th Aug. 1865	William Clark.
The improvement of the permanent way of railways and carriages for the same. (elevated switch point.)	2237	30th Aug. 1865	James Cole Green.
Apparatus for working railway switches, points and signals.	2659	16th Oct. 1865	Henry Skinner.
Certain improvements in "crossings" to be employed on railways or tramways.	2760	26th Oct. 1865	James Johnson.
A new or improved method of and apparatus for locking and unlocking gates, turnstiles and stiles, on railway crossings.	3188	6th Dec. 1865	George Daws.
Improvements in the construction and manufacture of steel crossings for railways, and in the moulds for casting the same, all or part of which said improvements in moulds are applicable for casting other articles.	3339	23rd Dec. 1865	Francis William Webb.
III.—Railway Carriages; Coupling, Uncoupling and altering positions of Carriages and Engines.			
Improvements in locomotive engines and in the springs of railway carriages.	85	5th Jan. 1865	James Edwards Wilson.
Construction of railway carriages - -	95	11th Jan. 1865	Rork Chidley.
Apparatus for taking up and delivering mails and other parcels in railway trains while in motion. (Communicated by Jules Kopler Curier.)	177	20th Jan. 1865	William Clark.
Improved apparatus for transmitting letter bags and parcels to and from railway trains whilst in motion. (Communicated by Charles Louis Ferdinand Vercillon-Lafitalie.)	187	21st Jan. 1865	Charles Denton Abel.
Improved apparatus for adjusting the weight of railway carriages and engines. (Communicated by Johann Heinrich Ehrhardt.)	216	24th Jan. 1865	Otto Gümell.
Bogie trucks used for supporting railway locomotive engines, carriages and waggons.	404	13th Feb. 1865	William Adams.
An improved means of securing the safety of railway passengers.	454	17th Feb. 1865	Coleman Defries.
Permanent way and rolling stock of railways -	520	24th Feb. 1865	John Kennedy Donald.

Subject matter of Patent.	Number of Patent.	Date.	Name of Patentee.
RAILWAYS, &c.—continued.			
Apparatus for coupling and uncoupling railway waggons or carriages - - - -	609	4th March 1865	Daniel Morris. Joseph Morris. James Morris.
Improvements in carriage ways and in carriages for the same.	641	9th March 1865	William Henry James.
Apparatus for enabling the passengers in a railway train to communicate with the guard.	679	10th March 1865	Albert Westhead.
Improvements in the construction of railway plant to ensure the safety of passengers' lives in the event of accident or collision - - -	688	11th March 1865	Charles Middleton Kernot. Nathaniel Symons.
Locomotive engines and carriages for common roads and tramways, and also for agricultural and other purposes.	780	20th March 1866	Alexander Richard Mackenzie.
Improvements in the construction of railway carriages, to facilitate the passage of the guard or other person from end to end of the train whilst it is travelling.	866	27th March 1865	John Calvin Thompson. John James Malbourne Green.
A new or improved arrangement of mechanism for propelling waggons in connection with railway horses.	895	30th March 1865	George Greenish.
Improvements in the construction of locomotive engines and railway carriages, for facilitating their passage round curves - - - (Communicated by George John Horner.)	916	31st March 1865	George Robert Stephenson. George Henry Phipps.
Means for communicating between the passengers and guards of railway trains or between two or more different situations. (Communicated by Thomas Hunt.)	1030	11th April 1865	John Henry Johnson.
Couplings for railway carriages, waggons, trucks and other vehicles.	1035	11th April 1865	Josiah Dudley.
Apparatus for signalling on railway trains - -	1055	13th April 1865	Albert Westhead.
Apparatus for covering railway trucks or vans and other carriages - - - - -	1075	17th April 1865	Edward Morgan. George Henry Morgan.
Means of communicating and signalling between the passengers, guards and drivers of railway trains.	1076	17th April 1865	George William Garrood.
Means of covering railway trucks, vans and other carriages.	1090	19th April 1865	William Riddell.
Apparatus for communicating and signalling between passengers, guards and drivers of railway trains, by day or by night - - -	1097	20th April 1865	David Hancock. Thomas Evans.
Wheels and the manner of applying the same to railway carriages for passengers' and goods' traffic as also the leading wheels for locomotives.	1114	21st April 1865	William Day.
A new mail catching apparatus for bags or packages, without stopping the express trains or others.	1369	16th May 1865	André Charanne.
An improved method of testing railway and other springs - - - - - - -	1374	16th May 1865	Joseph Mitchell. George Tilfourd.
Apparatus for increasing the safety of railway passengers and trains, signalling, lighting and forming a communication between all parts of such trains, also for securing the carriage doors.	1462	31st May 1865	Richard Howarth.
Construction of vans, waggons or carts employed for transporting furniture and other goods, on common roads and railways.	1466	31st May 1865	Frederick Haseldine.

Subject-matter of Patent.	Number of Patent.	Date.	Name of Patentee.
RAILWAYS, &c.—continued.			
An improved system of telegraphic communication on railways, parts of which invention are also applicable to other telegraphic purposes.	1542	5th June 1865	Alice Isabel Lucas Gordon.
Improvements in lamps for railway and other carriages, and in connecting lamps to carriages, a part of which improvements may also be applied to handles for carriages	1637	17th June 1865	Walter Howes. William Barley.
Enabling the guards of railway trains to pass from one part of a railway train to another.	1643	19th June 1865	Henry Defries.
Locomotive engines and railway carriages	1646	19th June 1865	George Smith the younger.
Improvements in or applicable to railway and other carriage windows.	1718	28th June 1865	John Kay Farnworth.
Improvements in railway carriages, which improvements are intended to neutralize the destructive effects arising from the collision of trains.	1746	30th June 1865	Louis Favre.
Improvements in locomotive engines and in springs of railway carriages.	1769	4th July 1865	James Edwards Wilson.
An improved combination of materials for the manufacture of carpets, floor cloth, felt, wall paper, fireproof flexible roofing, ship and boat building and for other similar purposes. (lining for railway carriages.)	1776	5th July 1865	John Longbottom. Abram Longbottom.
Construction of springs for railroad and other carriages.	1860	15th July 1865	John Crawford Walker.
Construction of railway carriages	1924	25th July 1865	John Rigg.
Improvements in the construction of atmospheric railways and carriages and in working the same.	1987	1st Aug. 1865	Alexander Doull.
Improvements in the construction of railway carriages and in railway breaks and signals, part of which is applicable to marine purposes	2005	2nd Aug. 1865	William Henry Petitjean. Edward M'Nally.
Improvements in the sackings of metallic and other bedsteads, sofas, couches and other like articles, which said improvements may also be applied to the seats of chairs, railway carriages and other articles. (Communicated by Thomas Trausington.)	2026	5th Aug. 1865	Henry Geering.
A self-acting coupling for railway carriages and wagons	2037	5th Aug. 1865	Thomas Smith. John Brook.
An improved mode of and apparatus for facilitating the transportation and delivery of letters, newspapers and other freight. (Communicated by Alfred Ely Beach.)	2019	7th Aug. 1865	Alfred Vincent Newton.
Couplings or fastenings of railway carriages or trucks.	2082	11th Aug. 1865	Richard Douglas Morgan.
Improvements in and applicable to railway carriages to enable passengers to pass from one compartment to another, and to give signals on trains in motion.	2088	11th Aug. 1865	Thomas English Stephens.
Improved safety couplings for railway carriages	2159	22nd Aug. 1865	Frederick Charles Reynolds.
Construction of vans, waggons or carts employed for transporting furniture and other goods on common roads and railways.	2192	26th Aug. 1865	Frederick Hazeldine.

Subject-matter of Patent.	Number of Patent.	Date.	Name of Patentee.
RAILWAYS, &c.—continued.			
The improvement of the permanent way of railways and carriages for the same.	2187	30th Aug. 1865	James Cole Green.
An improved mode of retaining and preventing the vibration of sliding windows used in dwellings and in railway and other vehicles, and for an improved apparatus for effecting the said purposes - - -	2232	30th Aug. 1865	{ Thomas Wrigley. Marcus Brown Westhead.
Improvements in the means of fixing or attaching the bobbins of winding and other machines on to their spindles, which improvements are also applicable to other similar or analogous purposes, and to the detaching of railway carriages from trains whilst in motion.	2250	31st Aug. 1865	John Ward.
A new shackle or coupling for connecting railway carriages, wagons and other vehicles used on railroads, whereby going between the carriages, wagons or other vehicles, to couple or uncouple, is rendered totally unnecessary - -	2288	4th Sept. 1865	{ Samuel Richards Freeman. Abraham Greedy.
Apparatus used in opening and closing carriage and other windows.	2319	9th Sept. 1865	John Pennington.
A locomotive car - - - - -	2344	13th Sept. 1865	Joseph Page Woodbury.
Improvements in locomotive engines, parts of which improvements are also applicable to railway carriages.	2370	16th Sept. 1865	Russel Aitken.
Railway carriages and other vehicles - (Communicated by Henry Harlem Trevor.)	2394	20th Sept. 1865	John Henry Johnson.
An improved apparatus or mechanism for locking and unlocking railway carriage doors, and for making signals with reference thereto.	2442	23rd Sept. 1865	John Hawkins Simpson.
Improvements in the construction of railway plant to ensure the safety of passengers' lives in the event of accident or collision - -	2469	26th Sept. 1865	{ Charles Middleton Kernot. Nathaniel Symons.
Construction of railway carriages, wagons and trucks, and other road vehicles.	2561	7th Oct. 1865	Henry Griffith Craig.
Railway carriages and locomotives - - (Communicated by Henry Clifford.)	2621	11th Oct. 1865	Michael Henry.
Apparatus for raising and lowering the windows of railway and other carriages and other windows.	2816	1st Nov. 1865	John Kay Farnworth.
Formation of railway carriages - -	2848	6th Nov. 1865	{ Reuben Sims. Robert Burns.
Railway steam-engines and carriages - -	2923	14th Nov. 1865	Joseph Alphonse Loubat.
Apparatus for increasing the safety of railway passengers and trains, signalling and forming a communication externally and internally between all parts of such trains, lighting, warming and securing the doors of the carriages, and indicating therein and at the stations the names of the places at which the train stops.	3049	29th Nov. 1865	Richard Howarth.
Improvements in constructing atmospheric railways and carriages, and in working the same, parts of which are applicable to exhausting and condensing air for other purposes.	3173	9th Dec. 1865	Alexander Doull.

Subject-matter of Patent.	Number of Patent.	Date.	Name of Patentee.
RAILWAYS, &c.—*continued*.			
Construction and arrangement of railway carriages, for the purpose of obviating or diminishing the bad consequences of collisions of or accidents to railway trains - - - -	3244	14th Dec. 1865	Henry Negretti. Joseph Warren Zambra.
See also "WHEELS FOR CARRIAGES." *See also* "AXLES." For Ventilating Railway Carriages, *see* "VENTILATION." For Lighting Railway Carriages, *see* "LAMPS."			
IV.—**Railway Buffers and Breaks; Retarding and Stopping Trains; Preventing Collisions, &c.**			
Improvements in furnaces and boilers and parts connected with them, for generating steam and heating fluids, and also for improved apparatus for reducing and shutting off steam and regulating the speed of steam-engines.	395	11th Feb. 1865	John Cass.
Machinery for stopping railway trains - - (*Communicated by Candido Ravelli.*)	487	22nd Feb. 1865	Eugenio Jverzen.
Construction of buffers for railway carriages	513	23rd Feb. 1865	William Rowe.
An improved means of securing and protecting the india-rubber rings of buffer springs of railway carriages, which invention is also applicable to air-pump and valve seatings, and bds faced with india-rubber.	620	6th March 1865	William John Oliver.
Railway breaks - - - - - (*Communicated by Charles Louis Joseph Félix Jorquot.*)	748	17th March 1865	Henri Adrien Bonneval.
Improved mechanical arrangements for stopping or retarding railway carriages, waggons and trucks.	1091	10th April 1865	George Voigt.
Certain improvements in brakes for railway carriages.	1491	25th May 1865	Jules Xavier Joseph Barbaix.
An improved break applicable to various descriptions of steam-engines and also to railway purposes. (*Communicated by Eugène Dulbrill.*)	1542	5th June 1865	Frederick Tolhausen.
An improved force dispeller or spring buffing apparatus.	1590	12th June 1865	William Jeffrey Hopkins.
An improved self-acting break for four-wheeled carriages.	1604	13th June 1865	James Griffiths.
Apparatus for preventing collisions and other accidents on railways. (*see* "SIGNALS.") (*Communicated by Eugène Vincenzi.*)	1621	15th June 1865	William Clark.
An improved apparatus for stopping railway trains	1684	23rd June 1865	William Jeremiah Murphy.
Means of and apparatus for retarding the velocity of the wheels of railway and other carriages when in motion.	1710	27th June 1865	Henry Shaw.
Means applied for arresting and stopping the motion of locomotive engines, trains, carriages and other rolling stock of railways.	1738	30th June 1865	Patrick Denis Finnigan.

Subject matter of Patent.	Number of Patent.	Date.	Name of Patentee.
RAILWAYS, &c.—*continued.*			
Improvements in railway carriages, which improvements are intended to neutralize the destructive effects arising from the collision of trains.	1748	30th June 1865	Louis Faure.
Locomotive engines (Communicated by Auguste De Bergue.)	1754	3rd July 1865	Charles De Bergue.
Apparatus for stopping and retarding railway carriages and locomotive engines.	1759	3rd July 1865	Joseph Navenn.
Railway signals	1856	14th July 1865	{ Augustus De Metz. Thomas Wickens Fry.
Signal and alarm apparatus for railways and railway trains.	1880	19th July 1865	Joseph Grimlley Rowe.
Apparatus for preventing accidents on railways (see "SIGNALS.")	1845	26th July 1865	{ Jean Jacques Namael Wenk. Alexandre Alphonse Mathieu.
Apparatus for retarding the progress of railway carriages and trains.	1964	24th July 1865	William King.
An improved break for railway and other wheeled carriages.	1959	24th July 1865	Robert Brightmore Mitchell.
Means or apparatus for stopping or retarding railway carriages	1969	29th July 1865	{ John Swinburne. James Laming.
Improvements in the construction of railway carriages and in railway breaks and signals, part of which is applicable to marine purposes	2005	2nd Aug. 1865	{ William Henry Pritchen. Edward McNally.
Signals for railways	2009	3rd Aug. 1865	Edward Samuel Horridge.
Railway electrical signal apparatus	2013	3rd Aug. 1865	William Henry Preece.
Improved means or apparatus for retarding or stopping railway carriages and trains.	2045	7th Aug. 1865	John Mead.
Apparatus or mechanism for stopping or retarding railway trains.	2154	21st Aug. 1865	William Shakespear.
A new or improved method of and apparatus for applying electro-magnetism as a break power on railways	2329	31st Aug. 1865	{ Edward Coupe. David Hancock.
An improved hydraulic break for railway and other purposes.	2537	12th Sept. 1865	William Jeremiah Murphy.
Railway breaks (Communicated by Eugène Etienne Berthonieux, Jean Maarien and Louis Durrediot.)	2576	19th Sept. 1865	Michael Henry.
Railway carriages and other vehicles (operating the breaks.) (Communicated by Henry Hudson Trewe.)	2584	20th Sept. 1865	John Henry Johnson.
Atmospheric buffing apparatus	2590	2nd Oct. 1865	Thomas Williams.
Mechanical arrangements for stopping or retarding railway carriages, waggons and trucks.	2595	9th Oct. 1865	George Voight.
An improved arrangement of buffing and drawing apparatus for railway carriages	2840	3rd Nov. 1865	{ George Wilson. William Kuebing Hyden.
Breaks	2957	11th Nov. 1865	{ Joseph Williamson. James Lindley. James Coleman.
An improved arrangement of mechanism for stopping or retarding railway carriages, waggons, trucks or other rail or tram road vehicles	2943	15th Nov. 1865	{ Louis Alexis Velu. François Eugène Foue. Louis Eugène Alphonse Foue.

Subject-matter of Patent.	Number of Patent.	Date.	Name of Patentee.

RAILWAYS, &c.—continued.

Breaks or apparatus for stopping or retarding railway trains. — 3368 30th Dec. 1865 David William Thomas

(*See also* "SIGNALS.")

REAPING, MOWING, MAKING HAY.

Machinery for mowing and reaping (Communicated by Valérian Ivanovitch Kirchner.)	200	23rd Jan. 1865	William Edward Newton
Improvements in reaping-machines, parts of which improvements are also applicable to mowing-machines.	884	11th Feb. 1865	David Henry Barber.
Lawn-mowing machines - - - -	468	17th Feb. 1865	James Bryce Brown.
Reaping machinery - - - -	576	1st March 1865	Nicholas Heawood.
Reaping and mowing machines - -	1371	18th May 1865	William Manwaring.
Reaping and mowing machines - -	1503	1st June 1865	William Jones Boyne.
Reaping and mowing machines - -	1690	28th June 1865	Mark Anderwood the younger.
Heating chisels, knives, plane irons, gouges, augers, steels, shears, scythes and saws.	1715	27th June 1865	William Brooks.
Reaping and mowing machines - - -	1815	8th July 1865	Joseph Byford.
Reaping machines - - - -	1834	11th July 1865	William Scott Cubitt. Arthur Hopkins Curtis. John Corden.
Lawn-mowing machines - - - -	2119	16th Aug. 1865	James Bryce Brown.
Reaping and mowing machines - - -	2310	9th Sept. 1865	John Brigham. Richard Buckerton.
Reaping machines - - - - -	2524	11th Sept. 1865	Charles Thomas Boyne
An improvement in machines for binding grain (Communicated by Albert Goodyear.)	2453	22nd Sept. 1865	Joseph Shelden.
Construction of reaping and mowing machines -	2875	14th Nov. 1865	William Manwaring.
Improvements in reaping and mowing machines, part of which is applicable to machinery in general.	3142	6th Dec. 1865	Adam Carlisle Bambr.
Obtaining and employing continuous lengths of tanned leather for various useful purposes (*for tackle for grass mowers.*)	3334	23rd Dec. 1865	George Hurn. Daniel Hurn.

REFLECTORS FOR LAMPS; REFLECTION OF LIGHT.

An improved reflecting apparatus for street and other lamps.	643	7th Feb. 1865	Romain De Bruy.
Apparatus for holding and regulating the position of lamp shades or reflectors. (Communicated by Guillaume Pascal.)	704	13th March 1865	William Clark.

Subject-matter of Patent.	Number of Patent.	Date.	Name of Patentee.
REFLECTORS, &c.—continued.			
Manufacture of reflectors for lamps and of surfaces for reflecting light generally.	697	30th March 1865	Benjamin Bough.
Means of communicating and signalling between the passengers, guards and drivers of railway trains.	1079	17th April 1865	George William Garrood.
Reflecting lamps	1268	8th May 1865	William Charles Cropp.
Certain improvements in apparatus for illuminating (Communicated by Monsieur Louis Joseph Amélie de Monnerville.)	1269	8th May 1865	Peter Armand Le Comte de Fontaine Moreau.
A new or improved instrument to be employed in examining and facilitating operations on the throat. (Instrument with reflector.) (Communicated by Philippe Othon de Clermont.)	1921	24th July 1865	Richard Archibald Brennan.
Improvements in the construction of railway carriages and in railway breaks and signals, part of which is applicable to marine purposes - -	2005	2nd Aug. 1865	{ William Henry Petitjean. Edward M'Nally.
An improved apparatus for and method of ascertaining the state of sewers, tunnels, drifts or other subterraneous works, without descending thereinto, by means of the natural, artificial or magnesium light, part of which apparatus is applicable to levelling purposes.	2449	25th Sept. 1865	Richard William Barons.
Preparation of glue or gelatine so as to render it insoluble in water, and applicable by the admixture of other substances to various purposes for which common glue or gelatine cannot now be used. (Transparencies for reflectors.) (Communicated by Henry Wurtz.)	3226	23rd Dec. 1865	William Edward Newton.

RETORTS AND CRUCIBLES.

Apparatus for charging and drawing gas retorts and for other purposes - - - -	142	17th Jan. 1865	{ Healy James Reed. James John Holden.
Apparatus for distilling petroleum and other volatile liquids and for making gas. (Communicated by George Hughes Sinclair Duffus.)	447	16th Feb. 1865	William Edward Newton.
Manufacture of crucibles and pots in which metals or other substances may be melted. (from plumbago.)	620	6th March 1865	George Skinner.
Apparatus for distilling oils and other liquids from coal and other substances. (Communicated by William George Washington Jaeger.)	737	15th March 1865	William Edward Newton.
Apparatus for the distillation of coal and peat, and such other substances as are or may be used for the manufacture of solid and liquid volatile hydrocarbons, or for the manufacture of the said hydrocarbons and coke.	799	22nd March 1865	William Mattieu Williams.
Apparatus for distilling hydrocarbons from coal, schists and other minerals.	1079	17th April 1865	Joseph Dougan.
Apparatus used in distilling hydrocarbons - -	1361	16th May 1865	George Walton.

Subject-matter of Patent.	Number of Patent.	Date.	Name of Patentee.
RETORTS, &c.—continued.			
Improvements in the retorts used in the manufacture of gas and in other distillations, which improvements are adaptable to evaporating vessels.	1494	25th May 1865	John Ambrose Coffey.
Annealing pots and saucers for annealing iron and steel wire, sheet metal and other articles.	1460	30th May 1865	John Hibell.
An improved method and apparatus for distilling coal shale and other carbonaceous substances. *(Communicated by John Howarth.)*	1553	7th June 1865	James Howarth, M.D.
Improvements in the manufacture of gas retorts and other articles made of fire-clay, and in furnaces for burning the same and for other purposes.	1737	30th June 1865	William Richardd.
Manufacture of pots and crucibles wherein metals and other materials may be heated or melted.	1884	19th July 1865	George Nimmo.
Moulds for casting metallic pipes, retorts and other articles.	2216	29th Aug. 1865	George Robinson.
Improvements in moulding crucibles and other hollow articles of plastic materials, and in apparatus employed therein. *(Communicated by Howard Maynard.)*	2464	26th Sept. 1865	Richard Archibald Brooman.
An improved mode of decarbonizing retorts. *(Communicated by George Washington Edge.)*	2465	26th Sept. 1865	Alfred Vincent Newton.
Improvements in producing and combining gases to be used for heating purposes, and in the construction of retorts for producing and combining such gases.	2527	2nd Oct. 1865	Silas Covell Salisbury.
Improvements in the distillation of coal and shale, and in the apparatus employed therein.	2793	30th Oct. 1865	Edward Meldrum.
Improvements in the production or manufacture of gas for heating or illuminating, and in the retorts and apparatus employed in such manufacture.	2985	17th Nov. 1865	James Harbart.
A new or improved cement or composition, applicable to the agglomeration or moulding of various materials, and to other useful and decorative purposes. *(for making crucibles.)* *(Communicated by Stanislas Sorel and Emile Justin Menier.)*	3119	5th Dec. 1865	Richard Archibald Brooman.
A new and improved fire pot and retort for stoves, ranges and furnaces in which steam is generated and superheated.	3140	6th Dec. 1865	William Essie.
An improved retort for distilling or extracting products from cannel, coal, shale or schist, and more especially from the small coal or dust technically known as "slack."	3285	20th Dec. 1865	John Gibbon.
Improvements in the manufacture of steel and purified iron, and in the apparatus employed therein. *(Communicated by Antoine Goly-Caroini.)*	3300	21st Dec. 1865	Henri Adrien Bonneville.
Improvements applicable to steam-boilers, iron, steel, retort and other furnaces.	3356	26th Dec. 1865	Joshua Fisher.

Subject-matter of Patent.	Number of Patent.	Date.	Name of Patentee.
ROCKETS ; FIREWORKS.			
Rocket guns and rocket harpoons and apparatus to be used therewith, for the capture of whales and other purposes - - - -	880	27th Feb. 1865	Thomas Welcome Roys, Gustavus Adolphus Lilliendahl.
Rockets - - - - - -	1103	20th April 1865	William Hale.
A new firework producing instantaneously the forms of serpents and other forms of a like nature. (Communicated by Frederic Barnett and Charles Albert Roussille.)	2283	7th Sept. 1865	Frederick Tolhausen.
An improved pyrotechnic toy - - -	6186	11th Dec. 1865	Thomas King.
A new kind of fireworks of a non-explosible and non-offensive nature, fit to be used in drawing rooms. (Communicated by Jean Baptiste Ferdinand Fredureau and Henri de Chatenaes.)	3387	24th Dec. 1865	Ernest Oppenheim.
ROPES, CORDAGE, TWINE, OAKUM, WIRE ROPES.			
A new method for removing or destroying the momentum of heavy bodies by means of an elastic machine or machines, so as to prevent injury and damage from concussion, applicable to ship cables, ship and fort armour, railway trains, fenders to pier heads, and floating piers, gangways, breakwaters and other similar structures, also as a motive-power. (Communicated by William Graham M'Iver.)	321	6th Feb. 1865	Clements Robert Markham.
Separating fibre from vegetable materials containing the same. (Communicated by Antonio Mecci.)	968	4th April 1865	George Tomlinson Bousfield.
Compounds for waterproofing and insulating purposes. (protecting ropes or cables.)	1982	25th July 1865	Frederick Augustus Abel.
Improvements in the manufacture of rope, cordage, yarn, wire rope, and other such like twisted and plaited fabrics, and in the machinery employed therein - - - - -	2225	30th Aug. 1865	Thomas Cope, William Garst.
Mode of treating the roots of the lucerne plant, for the purpose of manufacturing paper, pasteboard, fabrics and ropes therefrom. (Communicated by John Peter Caminade.)	2523	2nd Oct. 1865	Charles Denton Abel.
Improvements in the manufacture of yarns, string and paper, and in the preparation of dyes, and in dyeing fabrics, by the application of vegetable substances not hitherto used for such purposes.	3318	22nd Dec. 1865	John Alexander Cooper.
Obtaining and employing continuous lengths of tanned leather for various useful purposes (making ropes, cords, &c.)	3326	23rd Dec. 1865	George Horn, Daniel Horn.
For Telegraphic Cables—see "TELEGRAPHS."			

Subject-matter of Patent.	Number of Patent.	Date.	Name of Patentee.
Sewing, &c—continued.			
Sewing-machines	551	27th Feb. 1865	Robert Bamby.
Binding attachments for sewing-machines . .	601	4th March 1865	{ Henry Everard Clifton. { Abraham Hoffnung.
Sewing-machines	708	14th March 1865	Owen Robinson.
Sewing-machinery . . . . . (Communicated by David Wood Grove Humphrey.)	776	20th March 1865	Alfred Vincent Newton.
Machinery for sewing and stitching . .	812	23rd March 1865	Robert Wilson Morrell.
Sewing-machines	830	24th March 1865	Alfred Haillot.
Improvements in sewing-machines, which improvements also involve or comprise a new mode of manipulating the threads of the needle and shuttle in forming the " lock-stitch."	848	25th March 1865	Earle Harry Smith.
Sewing-machines	963	29th March 1865	William Newton Wilson.
An improved guide applicable to sewing-machines -	1047	17th April 1865	{ Frederic Bapty. { Edward Brydges Nayers.
Sewing-machines	1106	26th April 1865	{ John Fairweather. { William Fairweather.
Machinery for sewing and embroidering -	1187	26th April 1865	George Munby.
Manufacture of boots and shoes . . . (Communicated by William Emerson Baker.)	1818	12th May 1865	George Hamblim.
Sewing-machines	1831	13th May 1865	James Key Caird.
Sewing-machines	1877	14th May 1865	James Laing.
Sewing-machines	1884	19th May 1865	Henry de Mornay.
Sewing-machines	1407	22nd May 1865	James Moore Clements.
Ornamenting table cloths and other articles with embroidery.	1429	23th May 1865	William Madders.
An improvement in sewing-machines, which improvement is also applicable to other machines driven by a strap or band.	1506	9th June 1865	John Draper.
Sewing-machines . . . . . (Communicated by Lewis Plener.)	1578	9th June 1865	George Hawkins.
Sewing-machines	1584	12th June 1865	{ John Glasbrook. { Mark Nield Mills. { Benjamin Riley Mills.
An improved construction of sewing-machine -	1592	12th June 1865	James Hayes.
Sewing-machines	1611	14th June 1865	{ George Edward Keats. { John Keats.
Improved sewing-machinery and stitch formed by the same. (Communicated by John Jay Sibley.)	1641	17th June 1865	George Hawkins.
Improvements in sewing-machines and in the machinery or apparatus connected therewith.	1661	20th June 1865	Duncan M'Glashan, jun'.
Sewing-machines . . . . . (Communicated by Thaddeus Hiram Walter.)	1670	22nd June 1865	George Hawkins.
Improved apparatus for gauging and marking the width of tucks and pleats on fabrics under operation in sewing-machines.	1811	8th July 1865	George Baldwin Woodruff.
Regulating or controlling the power employed in actuating sewing and other machines of a light nature.	1838	11th July 1865	Benjamin Fothergill.
Sewing-machines . . . . . (Communicated by John Turton.)	1803	21st July 1865	Richard Mott Wanzer.
Sewing-machines	1804	21st July 1865	Alfred Smith.

Subject-matter of Patent.	Number of Patent.	Date.	Name of Person.
SEWING, &c.—*continued.*			
Certain improvements in sewing-machinery (*Communicated by Isaac Merritt Singer.*)	1941	26th July 1865	Alfred Vincent Newton
Construction of binders for sewing-machines -	2039	4th Aug. 1865	George Baldwin Woodruff
Construction of sewing-machines particularly adapted for sewing sacks and bags -	2067	9th Aug. 1865	Hermalus Ross. Edward Gandell the younger.
A new and improved application of imitation embroidery to be employed for the ornamentation of crinolines. (*see* "PRINTING.")	2131	19th Aug. 1865	Richard Clarke.
Improvements in sewing-machines and in winders for sewing-machines -	2165	23rd Aug. 1865	Henry Willis. George Ross.
Sewing-machines -	2169	23rd Aug. 1865	Daniel Macpherson.
Applying motive-power to sewing-machines, for the purpose of rendering them self-acting.	2218	29th Aug. 1865	Geruladano Zansi.
Ornamenting and protecting the edges of bed-quilts, counterpanes, toilet covers, carriage rugs and other similar coverings, by edging, binding or fringing by machinery -	2258	1st Sept. 1865	Robert Kaweles. Joseph Lindley.
Sewing or stitching machines -	2297	6th Sept. 1865	Robert Allee Parkis. George Callaway.
An improved wheel feed for sewing machines -	2313	9th Sept. 1865	John How.
Sewing-machines - (*Communicated by Jean Louis Thowen.*)	2451	23rd Sept. 1865	Edward Thomas Hughes.
Sewing-machines - (*Communicated by John Nathaniel Turton.*)	2496	28th Sept. 1865	Richard Archibald Brooman.
An improved sewing-machine - (*Communicated by Henry Hadman.*)	2539	3rd Oct. 1865	William Robert Lake.
Sewing-machines - (*for making button holes.*) (*Communicated by Joseph Louis Kieffer and Charles Nicolas Eroy.*)	2551	5th Oct. 1865	Michael Henry.
Improvements in ruffles or frills composed of strips of fabrics, and in the machinery or apparatus employed for their manufacture.	2579	6th Oct. 1865	Chauncey Orris Crosby.
Sewing-machines -	2649	13th Oct. 1865	George Baldwin Woodruff.
Sewing-machines -	2668	16th Oct. 1865	Joseph Buchanan Robertson.
Sewing-machines - (*Communicated by Charles Rhodes Goodwin.*)	2740	23rd Oct. 1865	William Clark.
Improvements in sewing machinery for using waxed thread. (*Communicated by Thomas John Halligan.*)	2748	24th Oct. 1865	Alfred Vincent Newton
Improvements in the construction and arrangement of sewing-machines, and in the apparatus employed therein -	2784	28th Oct. 1865	William Westmacott. Edwin Westmacott.
Cabinet furniture - (*sewing-machine cabinets.*)	2901	11th Nov. 1865	Daniel Slater.
Apparatus for threading needles - (*Communicated by Frederick Emile Tesier and Victor Tesier.*)	2925	14th Nov. 1865	Henri Adrien Bonneville
Sewing-machines - (*Partly communicated by George Sairder.*)	2974	18th Nov. 1865	Henry Clifton.
Sewing-machines -	2968	20th Nov. 1865	James Pitt.

Sewing, &c.—continued.

ments in sewing-machines and in sewing braidering.	3079	1st Dec.	1865	Isaac Merritt Singer.
machines - - - - -	3088	1st Dec.	1865	{ Henry Hedley. / George Ainsley. }
d machinery for manufacturing sewing-needles - - - - . , (by communicated by Joseph Thorn.)	3143	6th Dec.	1865	{ Nahum Salamon. / William John Lawrence / Davids. }
d arrangement of the parts in sewing-tus, for using wax thread for sewing on the of boots and shoes.	3170	9th Dec.	1865	William Jackson.
ments in sewing-machine shuttles, and in nding or reeling of the thread employed hem.	3208	12th Dec.	1865	Marc Klots.
machines - - - - -	3317	13th Dec.	1865	James Henry Smith.
oved method of applying wax to the threads n sewing-machines. communicated by Jed Dawley and John Blocher.)	3340	14th Dec.	1865	William Robert Lake.

AND BOAT BUILDING, SHEATHING, AIRING, WORKING, LOADING AND LOADING; MASTS, SPARS, &c.

us for containing, cleansing and repairing nchos and sides of ships while afloat, which atus is also applicable for other purposes.	105	12th Jan.	1865	Rudolph Frederick Mell.
ilding - - - - -	157	16th Jan.	1865	Joseph Betterley.
roved machine for raising and carrying earth, stones or other similar solid or liquid mate-for dredging, ventilating, or winnowing , or other analogous purposes. ending ships.)	174	20th Jan.	1865	Louis Bahno.
ments in cleansing ships' bottoms at sea, in the machinery, apparatus or means con-d therewith.	225	20th Jan.	1865	John Harrison.
g power to the working of ships' windlasses, ses, capstans, pumps and other ships' gear.	242	27th Jan.	1865	Handel Moore.
g the bottoms and sides of ships and other erged structures, to prevent fouling and '.	264	1st Feb.	1865	John Moyusy.
ction of armour plated ships, forts and other structures.	266	1st Feb.	1865	John Hughes.
ments in armour plated ships, forts, gun ges and works of defence, and in fastenings	273	2nd Feb.	1865	Charles Langley.

Subject-matter of Patent.	Number of Patent.	Date.	Name of Patentee.
SHIP-BUILDING, &c.—continued.			
A new method for removing or destroying the momentum of heavy bodies by means of an elastic machine or machines, so as to prevent injury and damage from concussion, applicable to ship cables, ship and fort armour, railway trains, tenders to pier heads, and floating piers, gangways, breakwaters and other similar structures, also as a motive-power. (Communicated by William Graham M'Iver.)	321	6th Feb. 1865	Clemens Robert Meibaum.
Ships and vessels - - - - -	337	7th Feb. 1865	Raymond Brown. Français Alexandre le Mat.
Improvements in apparatus for discharging coals and other cargo from ships' holds, applicable also to the raising and transferring of weights from one point to another - - - -	359	8th Feb. 1865	George Elliot. Henry Coase.
Protecting wooden surfaces from the fouling and injury to which they are ordinarily liable in sea water. (ships' bottoms.)	363	9th Feb. 1865	John Cornelius Onge Halbert.
Improvements in buoys, beacons, floats or pontoons, which improvements are also applicable to floating bodies generally - - -	387	11th Feb. 1865	Charles Atherton. Amherst Hawkes Rous.
Apparatus for giving alarms - - - (of leakage in ships.)	392	11th Feb. 1865	Charles West.
An improved blowing apparatus - (for ship builders.)	427	15th Feb. 1865	Samuel Richards Freeman. Abraham Grundy.
Construction of armour plated ships - (Communicated by Charles Otis Halpole.)	428	16th Feb. 1865	George Tomlinson Bonfield.
Armour plates for vessels of war and for other similar purposes.	455	17th Feb. 1865	John Brown.
Improvements in ships of war, partly applicable to ships designed for the merchant service. (Communicated by Augustus Walker.)	509	23rd Feb. 1865	George Hamilton.
Improvements in the construction of beams or supports applicable to the building of bridges, viaducts, roofs, arches and ships, and in instruments to be used therein.	576	1st March 1865	William Edward Lyle.
Improvements in coatings for the prevention of the fouling to which iron and other ships and structures are ordinarily liable in sea water.	624	6th March 1865	Francis Cruickshank.
Improvements in coating the bottoms of iron ships and other surfaces, to prevent oxidation, the adhesion of marine animals and plants, and in compositions to be therein employed.	681	10th March 1865	Richard Perry Roberts.
Differential wheel gearing - - - (for capstans.)	744	17th March 1865	John Standfield.
Improvements in vessels of war and in ordnance -	783	21st March 1865	William Vincent Crum.
Certain improvements in machinery and appliances for the manufacture of nails, pins and rivets - (boat nails.)	785	21st March 1865	Charles Parnet. Thomas Turner.
Cabin furniture for ships and other vessels - (see " FURNITURE.")	830	24th March 1865	Charles Heron.
Construction of ships' yards and spars - -	872	29th March 1865	Turret Glover, jun.

matter of Patent.	Number of Patent.	Date.	Name of Patentee.
10, &c.—continued.			
kin for raising and lowering	837	3rd April 1865	Pierre Joseph Jannet.
and other vessels - -	904	6th April 1865	John Bethell.
and other submerged structural corrosion.	970	6th April 1865	Edward Ritherdon.
low for preventing the fouling veerh. William Baker Davis.)	1008	8th April 1865	George Davis.
proved mode of constructing a navigable vessel.	1057	15th April 1865	Charles Robinson Fisher.
r vessels or cars to float on	1063	19th April 1865	William Badder.
construction of ships of war , part of which improvements i fortifications.	1107	20th April 1865	Henry Cantwell.
r wooden planking to iron vessels, and also to the outside	1149	25th April 1865	William Husband.
or shaping masts, spars and cles of wood.	1170	27th April 1865	Samuel Harvey.
fortifications, such improvable to the construction and ad floating batteries.	1309	1st May 1865	George Johnson.
hing shields of steel, iron or ups, fortifications and other	1326	2nd May 1865	Thomas Hay Campbell.
ion for coating iron or other similar purposes.	1370	5th May 1865	John Cornelius Craig's Halketa.
tion of electricity - - fouling of ships' bottoms.)	1412	23rd May 1865	Henry Wilde.
for loading and discharging } other vessels - }	1648	26th May 1865	{ George Elliot. Robert Pattison Clark.
ufacture of paints applicable ships' bottoms, and for other	1680	31st May 1865	Thomas Spencer.
and other tarry and coal pile	1690	31st May 1865	William Edward Newton.
tv or deck covers.) he American Waterproof Cloth			
s bottoms of ships or vessels	1547	6th June 1865	Barnet Solomon Cohen.
pparatus for the purpose of drains on ships' cables when	1609	14th June 1865	Charles du Vendrevre.
- - - - -	1612	14th June 1865	William Robinson Malley.
- - - - -	1689	24th June 1865	Henri Adrien Bonneville.
anis Prosper Reynaud.) tation and raising of petro-	1724	26th June 1865	Paul Jacroveson.
ing ships.) , masts and fittings for boats	1731	29th June 1865	John Cox.
as structures rendering them r ships' masts and buildings	1755	3rd July 1865	Edward Deane.

A A 2

Subject-matter of Patent.	Number of Patent.	Date.	Name of Patentee.
SHIP-BUILDING, &c.—continued.			
An improved combination of materials for the manufacture of carpets, floor cloth, felt, wall paper, fireproof flexible roofing, ship and boat building, and for other similar purposes - -	1778	5th July 1865	John Longbottom. Abram Longbottom.
Preparation of paints (used for coating ships' bottoms.)	1807	7th July 1865	George Fraissan.
Constructing ships and vessels - - -	1817	8th July 1865	Christopher Oswald Pengouth.
A new and improved mode of elevating ships or boats in the water, to enable them to pass over mud bars, shallows and the like, and for raising sunken vessels and docks.	1838	12th July 1865	Thomas Cato M'Ken.
An improved composition for coating ships' bottoms, and the surfaces of other vessels or structures which are exposed to the action of sea water - - - - -	1943	26th July 1865	Frederick Pullman. Richard Gunnan.
Applying and utilising water power - - (for discharging cargoes.)	1987	29th July 1865	Valentine Baker.
An improvement in ejectors for discharging bilge water and for other purposes. (Communicated by Nathan Lefflayvell Chappell and Blase Lavillard.)	1981	31st July 1865	Alfred Vincent Newton.
An improved composition for coating the bottoms of iron and wooden ships, by which the same are preserved from fouling and the iron from corrosion, whether internally or externally, by sea or other water or moisture, which is applicable to iron of any kind exposed to the action of moisture.	1988	1st Aug. 1865	William Le Prentis.
Iron knees and riders for ships' fastenings, and iron frames for wood and iron ships.	2010	3rd Aug. 1865	Peter Cato.
Apparatus and fittings to be used in ships, for facilitating the loading, unloading and stowage of their cargoes. (Communicated by Gilbert Auguste Fournier des Cerets.)	2049	7th Aug. 1865	William Clark.
A new or improved composition for coating iron or wooden ships' bottoms.	2190	16th Aug. 1865	Samuel Parry.
An improved apparatus to facilitate the cleaning and examination of the bottoms of ships and other submerged structures.	2162	22nd Aug. 1865	Darcus Oven Jones.
Floating lights, beacons, floating batteries and other vessels.	2178	24th Aug. 1865	John Moody.
Life rafts and surf boats - - - - (Communicated by Edward Livingston Perry.)	2278	4th Sept. 1865	Alfred Vincent Newton.
Machinery or apparatus for raising and lowering heavy bodies - - - - (discharging cargoes.)	2276	5th Sept. 1865	John Campbell Esau. William Fairlie.
Treating, working or manipulating cast steel, for the manufacture of wheel tires, armour plates, or other articles requiring great hardness and tensile strength.	2277	5th Sept. 1865	Julien Grand.
Floating vessels, and apparatus used for unloading vessels containing coals, corn or grain - -	2302	7th Sept. 1865	William Cory. John Henry Adam, C1
Mounting and working guns in ships, forts and batteries.	2306	8th Sept. 1865	John Walker.

Improvements in cleansing and coating the bottoms of ships and other submerged surfaces, to prevent oxidation and the adhesion of marine animals and plants, also in compositions to be employed for these purposes.	2310	9th Sept. 1865	Richard Percy Roberts.
casting dry docks	2387	19th Sept. 1865	Edwin Clark.
fe-rafts	2510	30th Sept. 1865	John Witherden Hurst.
ships' water-closets	2540	4th Oct. 1866	Edwin William De Bacril. Richard Farrell Dale.
manufacture of bricks and other analogous materials. (for naval construction.)	2571	6th Oct. 1865	Victor Jean Baptiste Germaix.
means employed for cleansing the bottoms of ships or vessels.	2559	7th Oct. 1865	Thomas Matthew Gisborne.
new composition of india-rubber mastic or cement, made in a more or less fluid state according to the use to be made of it, and the process or contrivance for applying the same. (coating hulls of ships.)	2680	12th Oct. 1865	Auguste Aimé Leyssard.
certain composition having anti-corrosive and anti-fouling properties, for the preservation of and keeping clean the bottoms of iron vessels, and also for the preservation of iron submerged and iron structures exposed to the action of the atmosphere or water	2653	14th Oct. 1865	William Jardine Combe MacMillan. James Mason. John Vickers Scarborough.
new or improved means and apparatus for destroying ships and such like floating bodies, parts of which said apparatus are also applicable to saving life and property at sea. (Communicated by Monsieur Stanislas Sorel.)	2756	26th Oct. 1865	Hector Auguste Dufrend.
an improved coating for covering the bottoms of iron and steel ships and other navigable vessels and marine works, to prevent oxidation and the adhesion of animal and vegetable matter thereto.	2791	30th Oct. 1865	Robert Doyne Dwyer.
an improved method of sheathing iron vessels	2838	2nd Nov. 1865	Edwin Clark.
mode of preventing vessels from sinking, which means are also applicable for raising sunken vessels.	2851	4th Nov. 1865	Thomas Page
new and improved cement . . } (for lining iron vessels.)	2963	7th Nov. 1865	Thomas Grann. James O'Donoghue.
construction of ships	2982	20th Nov. 1865	John Wayne.
protecting the bottoms and sides of ships and other structures exposed to the action of sea water.	3000	22nd Nov. 1865	Cowper Phipps Coles.
sinking or sheathing iron ships and iron framed ships.	3012	23rd Nov. 1865	William Robinson Mulley.
improvements in the hulls and tackle of navigable vessels, and in the gear for propelling the same by wind and steam or other motive-power engine, and clearing the same from water, and in apparatus connected therewith to enable the said vessels to be converted in floating graving docks, or lifts for raising vessels and other submerged or partially submerged heavy bodies to or above the surface of the water.	3091	25th Nov. 1865	John Ferrier.
construction of ships' parrels . . . (see " Ships' Rigging.")	3089	27th Nov. 1865	John Manifold.

Subject-matter of Patent.	Number of Patent.	Date.	Name of Patentee.
SHIP-BUILDING, &c.—*continued.*			
Construction of ocean steamers and paddle wheels for propelling the same, which paddle wheels are also applicable to the propulsion of other steam vessels.	3090	2nd Dec. 1865	Isaac Merritt Singer.
Apparatus for cleansing ships' bottoms - -	3230	13th Dec. 1865	Henry Frederick M‘Killop.
Constructing and mooring floating structures -	3265	18th Dec. 1865	{ Charles Liddell. Robert Stirling Newall.
Apparatus to facilitate the cleansing, examination and repair of the bottoms of ships and other submerged structures.	3313	22nd Dec. 1865	James Anderson.
Pipes, tubular columns and hollow structures, for masts, oars, shear legs, life boats and ordinary boats, for water, gas and waste water pipes, and for other similar constructions where great strength is required.	3314	22nd Dec. 1865	Edward Deane.
Obtaining and employing continuous lengths of tanned leather for various useful purposes (*for fender lines.*)	3334	23rd Dec. 1865	{ George Hurn. Daniel Hurn.
Means of applying copper or alloys of copper to the bottoms and sides of navigable vessels built of iron, steel or homogeneous metal.	3339	26th Dec. 1865	William Francis Deane.
Construction of sea going vessels - - -	3356	28th Dec. 1865	Norman Willis Wheeler.
For Ships' Logs, see "MEASURING PROCESS." For Sounding Apparatus, see "Do." For Ships' Pumps, see "PUMPS." For Graving Docks, see "DOCKS." For Rudders, see "STEERING." For Anchoring Ships, see "SHIPS." For Ventilating Ships, see "VENTILATION." For Lighting Ships, see "LAMPS." For Ships' Compasses, see "COMPASSES."			
SHIPS' BOATS (*Lowering and Disengaging*).			
Apparatus for lowering boats and disengaging them from their tackle.	210	25th Jan. 1865	Thomas Steel.
Improved apparatus for the instantaneous lowering and detaching of ships' boats.	890	29th March 1865	Alexander Chaplin.
Apparatus for sustaining and lowering ships' boats -	2041	5th Aug. 1865	Cortland Herbert Simpson.
SHIPS' RIGGING AND SAILS; REEFING AND FURLING SAILS; SHIPS' RIG.			
Reefing and furling sails - - - -	62	11th Jan. 1865	Henry Coutanche.
Reefing and furling sails - - - -	148	18th Jan. 1865	Anders Boborn Bäll.

Subject-matter of Patent.	Number of Patent.	Date.	Name of Patentee.
Ships' Rigging, &c.—continued.			
Sewing-machines - - - - (for making sails.) (Communicated by Edmond Philippe and Dominique Gence.)	304	3rd Feb. 1865	William Clark.
A new and useful or improved mode of connecting a gaff to the mast of a navigable vessel.	1087	18th April 1865	Charles Robinson Fisher.
Manufacture of malleable iron sheaves and bushes for pulley blocks - - - -	1086	19th April 1865	Joseph Gardner. Richard Lee. George Henry Webb. Samuel Hargrove. Charles Hargrove. Samuel Hargrove, jun'.
Rigging of sailing boats and vessels - -	1670	21st June 1865	William Charles Rickman.
Construction of sewing-machines particularly adapted for sewing sacks and bags - - (and for sewing sails.)	2087	9th Aug. 1865	Barnabas Russ. Edward Gandell the younger.
Means of attaching and detaching the sails of navigable vessels to and from the stays, yards and other fittings connected therewith.	2777	26th Oct. 1865	James Murray. Charles Wells.
Ships' and pulley blocks for general purposes -	2864	8th Nov. 1865	Thomas Westley. Walter Bibby.
Construction of ships' parrels - - -	3089	27th Nov. 1865	John Manifold.
Obtaining and employing continuous lengths of tanned leather for various useful purposes - (for rigging sails, cables, halyards, &c.)	3334	23rd Dec. 1865	George Hare. Daniel Hare.

Shirts, Collars, Wristbands, Neck-ties, Cravats, Scarfs, Drawers, Hose.			
Apparatus for securing studs in shirt fronts and similar garments.	176	20th Jan. 1865	Charles Searle.
Machinery and tools for making collars, cuffs, wristbands and other articles of dress, also adapted for cutting metal blanks - -	369	13th Feb. 1865	David Barr. William Henry Page. James Clement Newry.
Paper and cloth-lined paper collars for ladies and gentlemen.	656	24th Feb. 1865	Solomon Sally Oray.
Manufacture of stockings and other articles of hosiery.	725	15th March 1865	Henry Owen.
Improved machinery for manufacturing paper and cloth-lined paper collars for gentlemen and ladies.	769	20th March 1865	Solomon Sally Gray.
Gentlemen's scarves - - - -	778	20th March 1865	Matthew Eley.
Manufacture of yarn so as to render same applicable as a substitute for woollen yarn, for manufacturing into shawls and other textile fabrics.	774	20th March 1865	Isidor Philippstal.
Means of ornamenting linen cuffs and collars -	1010	8th April 1865	Joseph Dobson.
Manufacture of dress shirts and drawers made by means of the stocking frame.	1188	28th April 1865	Edward Moore.
A new and improved kind of shirt - -	1468	29th May 1865	Henry Tipper.
Improvements in paper or cloth-lined paper collars, and in the machinery for manufacturing the same.	1537	6th June 1865	James Atkins Woodbury.

Subject-matter of Patent.	Number of Patent.	Date.	Name of Patentee.
Shirts, &c.—continued.			
An improved machine for curling or curving collars and cuffs.	1569	12th June 1863	George Speight.
An improved arrangement for fastening shirts, collars and other articles of wearing apparel, by which the ordinary button or stud is dispensed with. (see "Buttons.")	1615	15th June 1866	Stanislaus Beloms.
An improved description of stud for fastening shirts, cuffs, waistcoats and other articles of wearing apparel. (see "Buttons.")	1616	15th June 1866	Stanislaus Beloms.
An improved shirt front (Communicated by Emile Froard.)	1785	29th June 1866	William Edward Newton.
Manufacture of collars and cuffs (Communicated by Henri Lacroix Girard.)	1741	30th June 1865	Richard Archibald Brooman.
An improved manufacture of scarfs, cravats and ties	2046	7th Aug. 1863	{ William Crosher. George Crosher.
Stockings	2177	24th Aug. 1865	Frederick Aychbourn.
Shirts and other like garments	2254	1st Sept. 1865	John Money Cate.
Articles of wearing apparel (collars.)	2317	9th Sept. 1863	Richard Charles Nevins
Improvements in ruffles or frills composed of strips of fabrics, and in the machinery or apparatus employed for their manufacture.	2576	6th Oct. 1865	Chauncey Osgin Canby.
Certain new and useful improvements in shirt collars and bosoms (Communicated by Celina Edgar Richards.)	2637	12th Oct. 1863	{ Vernon Augustus Remington. Virgil Jackson Maninger
Bows or ties for articles of dress	2976	18th Nov. 1865	Isaac Lazarus.
Certain improvements having reference to shirt collars, and mechanism for manufacturing the same.	3068	29th Nov. 1863	George Knowles Saer.
Obtaining and employing continuous length of tanned leather for various useful purposes (for stockings, drawers, shirts, neckties, scarfs, &c.)	3334	23rd Dec. 1865	{ George Herz. Daniel Herz.
Shot, Shell, Bullets and other Projectiles; Torpedoes.			
Improvements in the construction of shells, and in the explosive powder and fuse to be used therewith and for other purposes.	136	16th Jan. 1866	John Berkeley Cate.
Projectiles	171	20th Jan. 1865	George Adams Cock.
Improvements in fire-arms and in ammunition for the same.	188	21st Jan. 1865	Jacob Snider, jun'.
A self adjusting lever powder and shot charger for fire-arms.	302	3rd Feb. 1865	William Burton.
Cannon shot and shells	346	7th Feb. 1865	Raphael Brandon.
An improvement in the manufacture of patched balls for fire-arms.	367	9th Feb. 1863	Milo Peck.

matter of Patent.	Number of Patent.	Date.	Name of Patentee.
C.—continued.			
guns for central fire breech-loading ordnance.	989	3rd April 1865	Johann von der Poppenburg.
for rounding and polishing balls or spheres. William Davis Winsor.)	968	4th April 1865	William Clark.
sh-loading fire-arms and ordlikes.	1177	27th April 1865	James Carr.
niting the fuses of shells. Thomas Taylor.)	1211	1st May 1865	John Blackie, jun'.
mode of rifling muzzle-loading rtiles for the same. John Seipel.)	1283	13th May 1865	William Spence.
or rifled ordnance. Benjamin Berkley Hotchkiss.)	1552	6th June 1865	George Hamline.
lunate. Frederike Schrall.)	1595	13th June 1865	George Haseltine.
ch-loading fire-arms and in artiles to be used therewith.	1894	20th July 1865	William Le Pensière.
" " "	1989	1st Aug. 1865	Andrew Noble.
ving fire-arms, in projectiles	2100	15th Aug. 1865	James Brown.
ion of projectile. Irwin Legs.)	2361	19th Sept. 1865	Alfred Vincent Newton.
ng fire-arms, and in missiles with, and in the machinery these improvements.	2498	28th Sept. 1865	William Ellis Metford.
ch-loading guns and in pro- s.	2512	30th Sept. 1865	Edward Lindner.
	2623	12th Oct. 1865	Henry Woadby Williams.
ral fire breech-loading fire- inition for the same	2709	20th Oct. 1865	{ Joseph Needham. { George Henry Needham.
in projectiles	2787	26th Oct. 1865	Alfred Krupp.
" " "	2831	2nd Nov. 1865	Charles Frederic Henwood.
itions or charges for rifled fire-arms.	2886	4th Nov. 1865	Joseph Whitworth.
" " " "	2909	11th Nov. 1865	Charles William Jones.
ing iron and steel and in for this purpose.	3018	24th Nov. 1865	Joseph Whitworth.
pplications of electricity for charge of torpedo mines, ara, and in the apparatus	3154	9th Dec. 1865	Nathaniel John Holmes.
ted by Matthew Fontaine			
ch-loading fire-arms and in ams. ")	3243	15th Dec. 1865	James Aston.
lar projectiles	3275	19th Dec. 1865	Charles Ambrose M'Evoy.
ile for rifled cannon or	3276	19th Dec. 1865	Edward Augustus Dana.

Subject-matter of Patent.	Number of Patent.	Date.	Name of Patentee.
SHOW-CASES, EXHIBITING GOODS FOR SALE, SHOP SAFES, FRONTS AND COUNTERS; NAME PLATES, STREET NAME INDICATORS.			
Window sales for the protection of property	395	6th Feb. 1865	Robert Shaw.
Certain improved means for holding, attaching or suspending fancy articles as exposed in bazaars, show rooms or shop windows, for sale, as well as the providing of means for portably fitting or holding the price ticket to such articles, a modification of which arrangement is also applicable for holding and filing papers, or other purposes	505	23rd Feb. 1865	William Westbury. Thomas Wathen.
Shop and other counters and surfaces on which money is placed in passing it from one person to another.	567	24th Feb. 1865	Sydney Whiting.
Protecting letters, numerals and ornamental designs on glass.	1111	21st April 1865	David Simeon Buchanan.
Improvements in the manufacture and application of devices and representations to tombstones, and in other public or exposed situations, for various purposes (for placards.)	1130	22nd April 1865	Alfred Grainger. Charles Michael Girdler.
Construction of shop fronts and other similar parts of buildings.	2054	8th Aug. 1865	William Reid Corson.
An improved method or mode of indicating the names of streets and other places.	2759	23rd Oct. 1865	John Murray.
Apparatus for increasing the safety of railway passengers and trains, signalling and forming a communication externally and internally between all parts of each train, lighting, warming and securing the doors of the carriages, and indicating therein and at the station the names of the places at which the train stops.	3068	29th Nov. 1865	Richard Howarth.
Construction of show-cases, picture-frames, house and shop furniture and fittings, and other similar articles.	3364	29th Dec. 1865	David Vogl.

SIFTING, SORTING, SEPARATING.

Apparatus for hulling grain and for reducing granular substances.	89	5th Jan. 1865	Gustav Adolph Buchholz.
Improved machinery for cutting, sifting, separating, bruising, washing and preparing straw and other vegetable fibrous substances to be employed in the manufacture of various kinds of paper, and also for preparing food for cattle	340	7th Feb. 1865	John Cowen. William Simpson.
An improved apparatus for separating grain (Communicated by Henry Francis Hart.)	348	7th Feb. 1865	William Edward Newton.
Separating wool from refuse mixed fabrics and materials.	511	23rd Feb. 1865	Samuel Saville.

Subject-matter of Patent.	Number of Patent.	Date.	Name of Person.

SIFTING, &c.—continued.

Subject-matter of Patent.	Number of Patent.	Date.	Name of Person.
An improved method of and apparatus for separating ashes from cinders.	2667	16th Oct. 1865	James Leigh Barnes.
Preparation of meal for food - - - (sifting powdered dry meal.)	2677	17th Oct. 1865	Archer Hai Bana?. V.
A new or improved sifter for sifting cinders, slack and gravel, and for other like purposes.	2669	18th Oct. 1865	Charles Henry Cox.
Machinery for screening, tempering and moulding clays and earths into bricks, tiles, and other articles.	2726	21st Oct. 1865	Isaac Reburn.
Improved machinery to be used in the manufacture of paper. (a new.) (Communicated by Heinrich Vockler.)	3061	27th Nov. 1865	William Edward Newton.
Improvements in machinery employed when wearing hair, and in preparing and treating hair for wearing. (asserting.) (Communicated by Charles Bradley.)	3066	29th Nov. 1865	George Tomlinson Bonfield.
An improved machine for dressing, sifting, cleaning and polishing fruit, coffee, grain and other matter, parts of which are applicable to coffee sifting, roasting, cooling and cleaning, and other purposes.	3165	6th Dec. 1865	Edwin Wkele.
Apparatus for screening grain, seed, rice, tea and other materials.	3239	14th Dec. 1865	Henry William Mile.
Obtaining and employing continuous lengths of tanned leather for various useful purposes (for screens, sieves and strainers.)	3384	23rd Dec. 1865	{ George Horn. Daniel Horn. }
An improved method of and apparatus for preserving, purifying, mixing, separating, cooling, aerating, reading and otherwise treating grain, corn, and various other matters.	3341	27th Dec. 1865	Gaston Charles Jer Marquis D'Auy. .

SIGNALS, ALARMS, COMMUNICATING APPARATUS.

Subject-matter of Patent.	Number of Patent.	Date.	Name of Person.
Improved means of communication between the passengers and guard, and between the guard and driver of a railway train in motion.	50	5th Jan. 1865	Charles Pickwork.
Apparatus used in train signalling on railways -	52	6th Jan. 1865	Edward Tyer.
Motive-power and means of communication between passengers while travelling, and appliances connected therewith.	55	7th Jan. 1865	George Bell Gallery.
An improved apparatus for communication between railway passengers and guards.	67	12th Jan. 1865	Isaac Goodlad.
Improvements in tills and the means of securing and checking money taken by servants.	101	12th Jan. 1865	George Gem.
A new or improved kind of signal for communicating between persons travelling in railway carriages and the guards or conductors or other officials in charge for the time of the train of which such carriages form part.	107	12th Jan. 1865	John Bird Hill.

matter of Patent.	Number of Patent.	Date.	Name of Patentee.
&c.,—continued.			
o be employed for commodi- passengers and guard of a	121	14th Jan. 1865	Richard Lea.
, buoys and spindles . - William Smith Sampson.)	126	14th Jan. 1865	Theodore Bourne.
n for working switches and	147	18th Jan. 1865	William Jeffreys.
ting communications between and drivers in railway trains.	179	20th Jan. 1865	William Mather.
ed means for giving alarm in le in part as improvements in correlly.	267	31st Jan. 1865	Matthew Cartwright.
paratus for effecting com- : the passengers, guards and nilway trains, by night or by	289	2nd Feb. 1865	John William Gray.
se in railway carriages to give a guard and engine driver, in couny.	290	2nd Feb. 1865	Edwin Whittaker.
ignal applicable to railways, other such like purposes.	357	8th Feb. 1865	Alfred Warn Banks.
unicating between the pas- engine driver of a railway	378	10th Feb. 1865	Arthur Cordy Edwards.
durms - - -	393	11th Feb. 1865	Charles West.
g and controlling railway signals.	453	15th Feb. 1865	Michael Lane.
or the prevention of collisions canals, or on land - -	445	16th Feb. 1865	{ Henry Clifton Cleaver. Joseph Cleaver.
tinating apparatus for the ray passengers, buildings, er objects - - -	472	18th Feb. 1865	{ Leicester William Glen Rowe. Adolphe Barb.
ro-magnetic apparatus for id other purposes - -	488	22nd Feb. 1865	{ Charles Vincent Walker. Alfred Owen Walker.
ssengers and guard or driver	504	23rd Feb. 1865	Godfrey Sinclair.
the guard of a railway train g foot board.	530	24th Feb. 1865	George Scott.
- - - -	539	25th Feb. 1865	William Calvert.
arms to facilitate the com- passengers and guards of h said apparatus to equally rrants and other signals	545	27th Feb. 1865	Ferdinand Dancart.
valling apparatus specially ing on board ship. John Blackie.)	559	27th Feb. 1865	John Blackie, jun'.
or the protection of houses irglars, parts of the invention other purposes.	819	6th March 1865	Cromwell Fleetwood Var- ley.
alarms - - -	884	9th March 1865	William Henry Hudson.
f and apparatus for ascer- ng the presence of explosive	885	9th March 1865	George Frederick Ansell.

Subject-matter of Patent.	Number of Patent.	Date.	Name of Patentee.

matter of Patent.	Number of Patent.	Date.	Name of Patentee.
&c.—continued.			
tion between the passengers guard and driver of railway	1395	6th May 1865	Sanders Trotman.
vo regulator, pressure gauge, m and "blow off" for steam	1305	11th May 1866	John Henry Johnson.
Peter Riordan.)			
f effecting communication, guard and engine driver list in motion - - .)	1333	12th May 1866	William Chubb. Solomon Fry.
r facilitating communication different parts of a railway	1353	16th May 1865	Mons Defrise.
in lamps for burning mineral d.) Mounier Louis Theodore	1410	22nd May 1865	Peter Armand Le Comte de Fontaine Moreau.
ng the safety of railway pas-t, signalling, lighting, and ication between all parts of securing the carriage doors.	1492	31st May 1865	Richard Howarth.
r signalling on railway trains nication between passengers a in charge of each train.	1495	31st May 1865	Isaac Rogers.
ing the pressure of steam or ad for signalling.	1497	31st May 1865	Frederic Newton Gisborne.
ing on railway trains and for ation between parts of each	1502	1st June 1865	Henry Martin.
f telegraphic communication of which invention are also elegraphic purposes.	1543	5th June 1865	Allen Imhul Lucas Gordon.
ls in railway trains - -	1603	13th June 1865	Edward Samuel Horridge.
conducting electric currents us, and of actuating signals	1609	14th June 1865	Andrew Edward Brus.
sting collisions and other t. Sophie Vincent.)	1621	15th June 1865	William Clark.
tus for effecting and recording ications. Sarah Martha Bucknell.)	1633	16th June 1865	Michael Henry.
tion between passengers and aim.	1640	17th June 1865	Edwin Bywley.
f railway trains to pass from r train to another.)	1643	19th June 1865	Henry Defries.
railway carriages to enable s train to communicate with engine driver thereof.	1650	20th June 1865	William Henson.
of passengers and others for y trains.	1676	22nd June 1865	Michel Ségrin.
apparatus for producing the	1696	24th June 1865	Charles Ross Bamber.

Subject-matter of Patent.	Number of Patent.	Date.	Name of Patentee.

SIGNALS, &c.—continued.

Subject-matter of Patent.	Number	Date	Name of Patentee.
Means or apparatus for communicating signals on railway trains in motion.	1689	26th June 1865	John Nugent.
Improvements in apparatus for giving signals on board ships, and which are also applicable for other purposes.	1772	5th July 1865	Frederic Newton Gisborne.
Means of obtaining or producing oxygen applicable to various useful purposes. (light for signals.)	1780	6th July 1865	Hermann Beigel.
Improvements in apparatus and components used by persons employed under water, part of the improvements being also applicable for the use of persons employed where noxious gases or vapours prevail.	1840	12th July 1865	Auguste Denayrouse.
Railway signals	1866	14th July 1865	Augustus De Metz. Thomas Wickens Fry.
Signal and alarm apparatus for railways and railway trains.	1880	19th July 1865	Joseph Grindley Rowe.
An improved apparatus for producing sound for signals, calls and alarms, adapted to use on vessels, railway trains, buoys, roads, lighthouses, and in other places of danger. (Communicated by The Incorporated Marine Signal Company.)	1898	20th July 1865	John Harkness Wray.
Construction of railway carriages (with communication along the train.)	1924	25th July 1865	John Rigg.
Apparatus for preventing accidents on railways	1945	26th July 1865	Jean Jacques Samuel Wenk. Alexandre Alphonse Mathieu.
Means of and apparatus for treating animal and vegetable fibrous materials, which apparatus is also applicable to various useful purposes. (producing steam for fog signals.)	1952	27th July 1865	Henry Sherwood.
Improved means of communication by signals between passengers, guards and drivers of railway trains.	1955	29th July 1865	Isaac Gregory.
Improved apparatus for communication between passengers and guards in railway trains.	1997	2nd Aug. 1865	John Groves Teal.
Apparatus and means for giving alarm in case of fire	1998	2nd Aug. 1865	John Cross. Charles Joseph Barr.
Means of communication between the passengers and guard and driver of a railway train.	1999	2nd Aug. 1865	Frederick Charles Dear.
An improved method of and apparatus for signalling and giving alarm on railways	2000	2nd Aug. 1865	Joseph Pirkin. Richard Bailey.
Improvements in the construction of railway carriages and in railway breaks and signals, part of which is applicable to marine purposes	2006	2nd Aug. 1865	William Henry Petit-jean. Edward McNally.
Signals for railways	2009	3rd Aug. 1865	Edward Samuel Herridge.
Means of fastening or securing the tongues or rods of fog horns.	2011	3rd Aug. 1865	William Henry Brookes
Railway electrical signal apparatus	2016	3rd Aug. 1865	William Henry Preece.
Apparatus for communicating and signalling between passengers, guards and drivers of railway trains	2058	9th Aug. 1865	Horatio Fletcher. George Gore.

Subject of Patent.	Number of Patent.	Date.	Name of Patentee.
&c.—continued.			
immediate warning of undue sound by fire, spontaneous other causes, of leakage in sddue irruption of water, and of choke damp in mines.	2004	9th Aug. 1865	Charles West.
applicable to railway carriages re to pass from one compart-d to give signals on trains in	2088	11th Aug. 1865	Thomas English Stepham.
for extinguishing fire and }	2109	15th Aug. 1865	{ William Oldfield Wilson. Joseph Wilson.
galvanic batteries for giving } a case of fire, and any other }	2144	19th Aug. 1865	{ John Samuel Watson. Albert Horwood. Charles Brumit.
stric telegraph cables, and in therethrough.	2218	24th Aug. 1865	William Peter Piggott.
in the method of lighting } s connected therewith }	2208	9th Sept. 1865	{ Alexander Markie. James Paterson.
ng and indicating on railways	2309	9th Sept. 1865	John Anderson.
ting between the occupants drivers or other attendants	2400	20th Sept. 1865	Ernest Patita.
for electric bells, and a new combined, for ringing electric als.	2421	22nd Sept. 1865	Walker Motcley.
s or mechanism for locking way carriage doors, and for reference thereto.	2442	23rd Sept. 1865	John Hawkins Simpson.
in signalling on railways -	2474	27th Sept. 1865	Alfred Moore.
. . . . -	2528	2nd Oct. 1865	Henry Gilbert James.
ing by means of combined	2575	6th Oct. 1865	William Arena Martin.
in telegraphic communication idicating danger.	2584	7th Oct. 1865	Charles Harman Meliey.
les	2588	7th Oct. 1865	John Hancock.
railway switches, points and	2689	16th Oct. 1865	Henry Skinner.
apparatus for railway signals, her purposes.	2715	20th Oct. 1865	George Maxsall.
s signals being made by pneu-mics.	2755	25th Oct. 1865	Alexander Brewcks Black-burn.
tting and receiving signals - Count Ambjorn Piotro Sperrr.)	2841	3rd Nov. 1865	Alexander Hamea Bras-des.
ng communications between rd and engine driver in rail-giving notice to engine drivers	2845	4th Nov. 1865	Henry Redcliff.
Samuel Cornwallis Assabury.)			
i tell-tales - - } iructions.) }	2864	7th Nov. 1865	{ Charles Julian Vinhoff. James Adolphe Matthie-sen.

Subject-matter of Patent.	Number of Patent.	Date.	Name of Patentee.
SIGNALS, &c.—continued.			
Railway signals - - - - -	2907	11th Nov. 1865	{ Samuel Head. James Slater.
Safety apparatus for the prevention of accidents upon railways, by working signals or alarms in order to attract the attention of the guard or driver of the train. (*Communicated by Pierre François Rorke.*)	2980	14th Nov. 1865	William Edward Newton.
Improved apparatus for effecting a communication between the passengers of a railway train and the guard or driver or both.	3003	22nd Nov. 1865	Samuel Alexander Bell.
Apparatus for signalling on railways - -	3032	25th Nov. 1865	Charles Frederick Whitworth.
Apparatus for increasing the safety of railway passengers and trains, signalling and forming a communication externally and internally between all parts of such trains, lighting, warming and securing the doors of the carriages, and indicating therein and at the stations the names of the places at which the train stops.	3048	29th Nov. 1865	Richard Howarth.
An improved apparatus for signalling between passengers, guards and engine drivers of railway trains, which said apparatus is applicable also for other purposes	3173	9th Dec. 1866	{ Robert Pickup. John Heald.
Apparatus for the use of passengers and others in signalling on railway trains.	3291	23th Dec. 1865	Michal Siégrist.
Steering indicators and tell-tales - -	3341	26th Dec. 1865	{ Charles Jullien Vinball. James Adolphe Mambenam.
Apparatus by which motion can be communicated or transmitted from one place to another, and between different parts of a ship or other structure, to exhibit orders and messages, and to give signals.	3361	30th Dec. 1865	John Sacheverell Glaborn.

SIZING, WARPING, BEAMING AND PREPARING YARNS FOR WEAVING.

Improved mechanism for giving intermittent or continuous revolving motion of different velocities, without the use of change wheels - - (*taking up beams of sizing-machines.*)	279	31st Jan. 1865	{ Thomas Hall. Samuel Bonser.
Certain improvements in mechanism or apparatus for lubricating the cylinders of "slashing" and "tapering" machines, such machinery being employed in the sizing of cotton and other yarns.	466	16th Feb. 1865	Thomas Ogden.
An improved method of treating yarns or threads previously to the processes of dyeing or dressing.	490	22nd Feb. 1865	James Mallison.
Certain improvements in machinery or apparatus for drying "warps" of cotton and other fibrous substances - - - - (*after sizing.*)	929	29th March 1865	{ Richard Holroyd. Joseph Holroyd Bolton.
Dyeing and sizing cotton, silk, woollen and other yarns - - - -	1418	23rd May 1866	{ Isaac Holt. William Holt. James Holt. Joseph Mando.

SIZING, &c.—continued.

machines for sizing yarns, beams or warps woven	1729	29th June 1865	David Mercer. Thomas Mercer. Jonathan Mercer. Joseph Mercer.
roved sizing material to be employed for or dressing yarns preparatory to weaving. ...icated by *John Urie Bilbedlie*.)	1906	21st July 1865	Edward Schmidt.
ry or apparatus for sizing, drying and ing yarns of cotton or other fibrous atter	2022	4th Aug. 1865	John Gaukroger. John Dodgson.
g and printing threads employed in weaving ...municated by *Stanislas Vigouroux*.)	2069	11th Aug. 1865	Richard Archibald Brooman.
...ments in the means of fixing or attaching obbins of winding and other machinery on to spindles, which improvements are also able to other similar or analogous purposes. to the detaching of railway carriages from whilst in motion. ...ful in warp machines.)	2250	31st Aug. 1865	John Ward.
...cture of artificial gum, size or stiffening r.	2810	1st Nov. 1865	John Sellers.
...ry or apparatus employed for sizing yarns	2868	6th Nov. 1865	James Eastwood.
...improvements in sizing and dressing yarns	3010	23rd Nov. 1865	Nathaniel Greenhalgh. James Mallison.
...vements in machinery employed when weav- air, and in preparing and treating hair for ...ng. ...wtop.) ...municated by *Charles Bradley*.)	3066	29th Nov. 1865	George Tomlinson Bousfield.
...or improved method of preparing esparto, or mogador grasses or other similar veg- substances, for spinning, weaving, and for ...tuting the hair and for other fibres now in "Sossusia.")	3166	8th Dec. 1865	Oliver Mayne. George Hodgcombe Smith.
...method of and apparatus for regulating the ...m of threads in weaving and other operations. ...ping.) ...municated by *Stanislas Vigouroux*.)	3289	14th Dec. 1865	Richard Archibald Brooman.

: PREVENTION; BURNING AND CON-
DENSING SMOKE; SAVING FUEL.

Subject-matter of Patent.	Number of Patent.	Date.	Name of Patentee.
SMOKE PREVENTION, &c.—continued.			
Improvements in puddling, heating and other reverberatory furnaces used in the manufacture of iron and steel and for other purposes, which improvements may also be applied to steam-boiler furnaces.	179	20th Jan. 1865	John Brown.
Improvements in furnaces and boilers and parts connected with them, for generating steam and heating fluids, and also for improved apparatus for reducing and shutting off steam and regulating the speed of steam-engines.	385	11th Feb. 1865	John Coe.
Smoke consuming apparatus	564	2nd March 1865	{ Samuel Hopkins. Edwin Hopkins.
An improved process of and apparatus for making caustic liquor or caustic lees.	620	6th March 1865	Thomas Nelson.
An improvement in the construction of hot air stoves for blast furnaces.	646	9th March 1865	Joseph Cliff.
Steam-boilers and the furnaces thereof	695	11th March 1865	{ Edward Bryce Wise. James Bowden.
Manufacture of iron and steel	849	11th March 1865	James Henderson.
Stoves or fire-places, ash pans and fenders	880	23rd March 1865	James Clifford Mapes.
Means and apparatus for utilising the heat of steam (saving fuel.)	854	25th March 1865	David Ecder Birch.
Improvements in the construction of furnaces for the consumption of smoke	862	27th March 1865	{ Charles Meldrum. John Pernly.
Steam-boilers	908	31st March 1865	{ John Swinlaird. David Swinlaird. Benjamin Swinlaird. Ormond Swinlaird.
Means or method of curing or preventing smoky chimneys.	911	31st March 1865	Benjamin Greenwood.
Improvements in the mode of and apparatus for purifying smoke, which improvements are also applicable to other purposes in which gas or vapour is to be separated from substances combined therewith or held in suspension therein. (Communicated by Joseph Bourgeois and John Mathew.)	1002	7th April 1865	Michael Henry.
Arrangement of furnaces used for puddling and reheating iron, the generation of steam and other similar purposes.	1084	13th April 1865	William Burdman.
Construction of ships or vessels or cars to float on water.	1082	18th April 1865	William Boddie.
Smoke consuming furnaces (Communicated by Etienne Smart and Eugene de Fleury.)	1168	25th April 1865	Richard Archibald Brooman.
Furnaces	1190	27th April 1865	Dundas Simpson.
Improvements in steam generators and engines, and in apparatus for feeding steam generators. (communicating fuel.) (Communicated by George Bailey Brayton.)	1340	3rd May 1865	John Henry Johnson.
Mode of and apparatus for obtaining and applying motive power. (consuming fuel.)	1809	10th May 1865	{ Stanislas Pokrzywki. Michel Myszobi.
Construction of furnaces or fire-places (Communicated by Lewis Philip Cohen.)	1451	29th May 1865	Mylins Cohen.

Matter of Patent.	Number of Patent.	Date.	Name of Patentee.
ריזוו, &c.—continued.			
■	1459	25th May 1865	Peter Young.
employed for preventing chimneys, facilitating the refracm, and for ventilating ...	1471	29th May 1865	{ Edward Myers. James Stodart.
-	1499	31st May 1865	Thomas Semmerson.
. . . .	1521	2nd June 1865	Henry Edward Newton.
brom Samuel Mitchell.)			
aratus or arrangements for exhalations such as arise ing iron or other articles -	1690	2th June 1865	{ Matthew Andrew Muir. James Mellerham.
r consuming smoke - François Augustus Fouché and	1697	24th June 1865	William Clark.
a-boilers, furnaces and connected therewith.	1745	30th June 1865	Edwin Elliott.
production of gases from in the application thereof to	1841	12th July 1865	Harrison Blair.
as for treating animal and aterials, which apparatus is iron useful purposes. s of smoke.)	1668	27th July 1865	Henry Sherwood.
promoting the combustion of steam-boilers, dyers' or or furnaces, whereby smoke economised - -	1972	31st July 1865	{ Benjamin Robinson. Joseph Varley.
abular boilers - -	1990	1st Aug. 1865	Louis Emile Constant Martin.
n the manufacture of plate l. artin Direnband Heureur.)	2018	3rd Aug. 1865	Ephraim Sabal.
snnected with the manufac-	2100	14th Aug. 1865	James Thomas Larkey.
ו the manufacture of glass d for other like purposes. reming Bertini.)	2108	15th Aug. 1865	John Frederick Bertini.
icrs	2189	25th Aug. 1865	William Edward Newton.
ry Clark Sargeant.)			
leading and utilising gal- vapours, and in apparatus urpose.	2219	29th Aug. 1865	Adolf Garht.
ι apparatus - -	2255	1st Sept. 1865	Alfred Vincent Newton.
ry Ballby.)			
ng incrustation in steam- resting explosions of such and water, and containing ...	2272	4th Sept. 1865	{ James Howard. William Stafford. William Porter M'Callam.
rs and furnaces, and in roof - - - -	2291	6th Sept. 1865	{ Edward Green. Edward Green the younger.
s for consuming smoke in	2292	19th Sept. 1865	Charles Worssam.

Subject-matter of Patent.	Number of Patent.	Date.	Name of Patentee.
SMOKE PREVENTION, &c.—*continued.*			
Improvements in and applicable to furnaces for the consumption of smoke.	2405	21st Sept. 1865	William Watkin.
Apparatus for ventilating and for preventing down draught in flues.	2467	26th Sept. 1865	John Hillier.
Collecting or drawing off the gases from blast furnaces -	2507	29th Sept. 1865	John Addenbrooke. George Addenbrooke. Philip Anthony Millward.
Improvements in apparatus for the regulation of the up and down currents of air, and for the prevention and cure of smoky chimneys.	2600	10th Oct. 1866	William Cooke.
An improved ventilating apparatus for use in steam boats, vessels and other places requiring to be ventilated.	2609	10th Oct. 1865	John Garrison Woodward.
Manufacture of gas - - - - (saving fuel.)	2620	11th Oct. 1865	James Crutchett.
Improvements in steam-boilers and other apparatus applicable to the heating and evaporation of liquids, parts of which improvements are applicable also to other purposes - -	2651	16th Oct. 1865	Francis Wise. Edward Field. Enoch Harrison Ayde.
A new or improved steam containing apparatus, or an apparatus intended to make available as fuel all or part of the steam actually evolving from engines into the atmosphere, and also to absorb the smoke resulting from the combustion.	2675	17th Oct. 1865	François Georges Sicard.
Furnaces - - - - -	2682	17th Oct. 1865	William Beardmore.
Steam-boilers - - - - -	2709	23rd Oct. 1865	Alexander Chaplin.
Construction of furnaces and boilers for the consumption of smoke - - - }	2746	24th Oct. 1865	Charles Matthews. Henry Scotch Southwick. John Feveday.
Furnaces - - - - -	2808	31st Oct. 1865	Robert Camels. Thomas Morton.
An improved apparatus for increasing draught in and preventing or curing smoky chimneys, and economising heat. (Communicated by François Perruphon.)	2822	2nd Nov. 1865	William Edward Gedge.
Apparatus for separating dust from the gases evolved from blast furnaces.	2955	8th Nov. 1865	Charles Cochrane.
Furnaces - - - - -	2953	17th Nov. 1865	Thomas Maxwell Teuten
An improved chimney cowl - - - (Communicated by Victor Etienne Antoine Brou and Jean Victorine Corulio.)	3052	24th Nov. 1865	Henry Edward Newton.
Means or apparatus for economising and inducing more perfect combustion of fuel in furnaces.	3072	29th Nov. 1865	Thomas Lancaster.
An improved mode of applying the compression of air for ventilating purposes, and the compression of any gas for hurrying along elastic fluids in converting pipes (expelling smoke)	3153	4th Dec. 1865	Pierron de Mondésir. Paul Lebaitre. Augustin Julliaume.
Construction of fire-places and furnaces - (diminishing consumption of fuel.)	3247	15th Dec. 1865	George Warriner.
Certain improvements in the means of collecting waste gases arising from blast furnaces - - }	3391	1st Dec. 1865	Samuel Whitehouse the elder. Samuel Whitehouse the younger. Jeremiah Whitehouse. William Whitehouse.

Subject-matter of Patent.	Number of Patent.	Date.	Name of Patentee.
SMOKE PREVENTION, &c.—*continued*.			
Improvements in smelting copper and in obtaining products from the gases and vapours given off during the said smelting.	3207	18th Dec. 1865	Henry Cossey Edsell.
SOAP.			
Improvements in the manufacture of oxygen gas and in treating and economising the residual products of the said manufacture (*residuum for soap makers*.)	8	2nd Jan. 1865	John Frederick Parker. Joseph Tanner.
An improved method of treating fatty matters	892	29th March 1865	Harmel Childs, jun'.
Improvements in treating fibrous materials and textile fabrics and in producing soap. (*Communicated by Léon Pasquier and Alphonsine Julie Dumont.*)	1443	25th May 1865	Michael Henry.
A new method of manufacturing oil from fatty matters or the residuum arising from the distillation of fatty matters, the manufacture of stearic acid, soap and purification of oils. (*Communicated by Pierre Réné Brownant.*)	1456	27th May 1865	Richard Archibald Brooman.
Improvements in the manufacture of soap and in apparatus employed therein. (*Communicated by Jacob Betts Bennett and James Sidney Gibbs.*)	1540	6th June 1865	Richard Archibald Brooman.
Manufacturing grease from soapsuds (*see "OILS FROM SEEDS."*)	1787	7th July 1865	Isaac Peel. William Hargreaves.
Certain improvements in soap	2140	18th Aug. 1865	Alexander Watt.
Manufacture of soap	3007	22nd Nov. 1865	James John Field.
Improvements in the mode of applying mineral soda to the scouring and lubrication of textile matters and machinery and in the manufacture of soap.	3107	4th Dec. 1865	Leopold Joseph Bouchart.
SOWING SEEDS AND DISTRIBUTING MANURE.			
Improved apparatus for distributing liquid manure	100	12th Jan. 1865	William Russ.
An improvement in lever horse hoe and lever corn drills, for the hoeing and sowing of wheat and turnips and all other seed and root crops.	279	1st Feb. 1865	John Hainty.
An improved corn, seed and manure drill, parts of which invention are also applicable to other similar agricultural implements.	1345	16th May 1865	Henry Benley.
Improved apparatus for distributing liquid manure	1389	19th May 1865	Christopher Smith Billups.
Horse hoe and drills	1569	9th June 1865	James Holmes. George Thomas Holmes. Frederick Robert Holmes.
Drills for sowing seeds and depositing manure	1857	14th July 1865	James Armitage.

Subject-matter of Patent.	Number of Patent.	Date.	Name of Patentee.
Sowing, &c.—continued.			
A new or improved detergent solution to be used in the washing or cleansing of wool and woollen fabrics. (Communicated by Charles Dyonis Reinfold.)	1882	25th July 1865	John Henry Johnes.
An improved apparatus for scattering lime, guano or other artificial manures, either in a dry or liquid state or for scattering disinfectants.	2846	4th Nov. 1865	Alexander Jamson.
Spindles; Spindles and Flyers.			
Flyers for preparing cotton and other fibrous materials for spinning - - - -	66	9th Jan. 1865	{ Richard Ashton Lightoller, George Henry Lightoller.
Throstle spinning frames - - - (form of flyers.) (Communicated by Charles Leyherr.)	236	27th Jan. 1865	Charles Denton Abel
Improvements in steam hammers applicable to the manufacture of files, to welding flyers of cotton machinery and to other purposes.	641	7th March 1865	James Dodge.
Improved means or apparatus for lubricating vertical or diagonal spindles and shafts.	782	31st March 1865	James Waterhouse Mabley.
Improvements in locks and in fixing knobs and spindles to doors and latches.	844	4th April 1865	Richard Noble.
Apparatus for lubricating spindles, shafts or other frictional surfaces. (Communicated by William Francis Rippon.)	1090	13th April 1865	James Rippon.
Apparatus for shaping corks - - -	1065	15th April 1865	John M'Dowell
Certain improvements in machinery or apparatus for rolling or shaping metallic articles of irregular form, such as "file-blanks" and similar articles.	1190	24th April 1865	Edward M'Nally.
Improved apparatus for cutting, turning and smoothing metal pipes and the surfaces of bolts, rods or spindles - - - -	1211	11th May 1865	{ George Mansfield, Edward Worrall.
Machinery or apparatus for tapering, pointing or reducing wires or rods for spindles, bobbins' teeth, pins for dressers and similar articles.	1262	16th May 1865	Chauncey Oscia Oad.
Improvements in locks and latches and in staples and spindles for the same.	1762	6th July 1865	George Carter.
Improvements in the lubricating of spindles, the necks or bolsters in which the said spindles revolve having a traversing motion in the said neck or bolster.	2056	9th Aug. 1865	Jacob Henry Radcliffe.
Flyers used in doubling machines - -	2611	10th Oct. 1865	Mark Walker.
Certain improvements in machinery or apparatus for twisting or doubling cotton or other yarns -	2621	12th Oct. 1865	{ James Broughton Edge, Enoch Hirst.
Certain improvements in machinery or apparatus for preparing and spinning cotton and other fibrous substances.	2661	14th Oct. 1865	Godfrey Anthony Exon

Subject-matter of Patent.	Number of Patent.	Date.	Name of Patentee.
SPINDLES, &c.—continued.			
Improvements in machinery or apparatus known as "roving," "intermediate," "slubbing" and "throstle" frames and "doublers" and also in winding machines used for preparing, spinning and winding cotton, wool, flax, silk and other fibrous substances.	2719	20th Oct. 1865	William Sumner.
Means or apparatus for preparing, spinning, twisting, doubling or winding cotton, wool, flax or other fibrous material.	2866	7th Nov. 1865	Martyn John Roberts.
Improvements in the construction of door locks, latches and such like fastenings and in knob and handle spindles and furniture used therewith.	2889	9th Nov. 1865	Benjamin Fid.
Machinery for preparing, spinning and twisting flax, cotton, wool and other fibrous substances. (spindles and flyers.)	3212	19th Dec. 1865	John Campbell. Samuel M'Kinstry. Thomas Wilson.
Construction of parts of machines used in spinning and doubling (flyers.)	3234	14th Dec. 1865	John Elce. Robert Cotton.
Improvements in the manufacture of axles for carriages and spindles for various purposes and in machinery to be employed in the said manufacture, part of which improvements in machinery may also be applied to other purposes.	3336	26th Dec. 1865	Elias Lowe. Joseph Constant Lowe. John Lowe. John Birrtell. Thomas Britell. Charles Vernon.
Throstle machines and dye.	3377	30th Dec. 1865	Thomas Parkinson.

SPINNING AND PREPARING FOR SPINNING.

1.—Opening, Cleaning, Breaking and Cleansing Fibrous Materials.

Subject-matter of Patent.	Number of Patent.	Date.	Name of Patentee.
Machinery for ginning cotton	44	6th Jan. 1865	Benjamin Dobson. William Slater. Robert Halliwell.
Machinery for opening and carding cotton and other fibrous materials.	90	11th Jan. 1865	Robert Tempest.
Machinery or apparatus for ginning and cleaning cotton and other fibrous materials (Partly communicated by Albert Westfold.)	191	23rd Jan. 1865	Christopher Brakell. William Hoxbl. William Günther.
Machinery for threshing, beating and dressing flax	231	26th Jan. 1865	William Cressy.
Cotton gins	245	28th Jan. 1865	Benjamin Dobson. William Slater.
Machinery or apparatus for washing wool and other fibrous materials.	251	28th Jan. 1865	John Petrie, jun'.
Apparatus for breaking and scutching flax or similar fibrous materials.	277	1st Feb. 1865	John Grey.
Machinery for washing and drying wool and other fibrous materials.	281	1st Feb. 1865	John M'Naught. William M'Naught, jun'.
Machinery for breaking the stems of and preparing flax, hemp and other fibrous substances. (Communicated by Auguste Henri Lenus.)	332	7th Feb. 1865	Henry Bertaelli Barlow.

Subject-matter of Patent.	Number of Patent.	Date.	Name of Person.
SPINNING, &c.—continued.			
An improved composition as a substitute for leather or other similar materials — — — (for cotton gin rollers.)	446	16th Feb. 1845	Christopher Bristol, William Houki, William Gunther.
Cotton gins — — — — (Communicated by François Derneil.)	531	24th Feb. 1845	Edmund Paul Le Gentlovin.
Machinery for scutching and refining flax and other vegetable substances.	527	6th March 1845	Andrew Potts.
Cotton gins — — — —	573	10th March 1865	Evan Leigh.
Machinery for preparing flax, hemp and other fibrous materials requiring like treatment —	680	10th March 1845	Joseph Bernal, Samuel Milthorn.
Apparatus for washing wool, hair and other fibre —	808	22nd March 1845	George Edmund Denthorpe.
Cotton gins —	851	25th March 1845	William Richardson
Separating fibre from vegetable materials containing the same. (Communicated by Antonio Bruere.)	858	4th April 1845	George Tomlinson Bonfield.
Preparing, spinning and doubling cotton, flax, wool, silk and other fibrous material — —	1118	21st April 1845	James Champin, John Brnsley Sharda
Machinery for preparing and spinning cotton and other fibrous substances.	1185	22nd April 1845	Edward Lord.
Spools or bobbins to be used in certain frames for preparing fibrous materials for spinning.	1197	22nd April 1845	Joshua Henry Wise.
Improvements applicable to rollers of machinery for preparing and spinning fibrous substances, which improvements are also applicable to other rollers which are pressed towards each other.	1180	25th April 1845	William Oxley.
A new or improved method of conditioning or preparing fibres, threads and fabrics, and apparatus to be employed therein. (Communicated by Stanislas Figuenous.)	1169	26th April 1845	Richard Archibald Brooman.
Apparatus employed in preparing and spinning wool, silk, flax and other fibrous substances	1586	2nd June 1845	Samuel Stell, Thomas Brougham, Francis Hall.
Spinning of cotton and other fibrous materials —	1574	9th June 1845	Jakins De Hemptinne.
Cotton gins — — — — (Communicated by Frederick Tabor Ackland, Henry George Mitchell and Mustapha Mariopha.)	1714	27th June 1845	John Henry Johnson.
Treating and preparing flax for scutching —	1688	10th July 1845	George Firmin.
Means or apparatus for opening and straightening wool, cotton and other fibres.	1880	1st July 1845	Joshua Thornton.
Processes and machinery for producing fibre suitable for being spun, from rags or remnants of woven or other textile fabrics made of silk, wool, cotton or other fibrous materials.	1881	13th July 1845	Henry Ernest Gibb.
Means of and apparatus for treating animal and vegetable fibrous materials, which apparatus is also applicable to various useful purposes.	1862	27th July 1845	Henry Sherwood.
Process of and machinery for cleaning chira grass and flax, and removing therefrom the resinous and woody matters that adhere to the useful fibres of the plant.	2078	10th Aug. 1845	Joseph Fara.
Machinery for preparing cotton, wool and other fibrous materials — — —	2089	12th Aug. 1845	Jesse Tatham, John Smith.

Subject-matter of Patent.	Number of Patent.	Date.	Name of Patentee.
SPINNING, &c.—continued.			
Improved machinery for feeding fibrous substances to preparing, carding and other machinery for working wool and other filamentous substances. (Communicated by Alexandre Dera.)	2517	30th Sept. 1865	William Edward Newton.
Mode of treating the roots of the lucerne plant for the purpose of manufacturing paper, pasteboard, fabrics and ropes therefrom. (extracting the fibres for spinning.) (Communicated by John Peter Cominade.)	6683	2nd Oct. 1865	Charles Denton Abel.
Improvements in and applicable to machines for opening and cleaning cotton and other fibrous materials	8867	5th Oct. 1865	{ Edward Marsland. Peter Williams.
Certain improvements in machinery or apparatus for preparing and spinning cotton and other fibrous substances.	6861	14th Oct. 1865	Godfrey Anthony Ermen.
Process of and machinery for preparing flax, hemp, jute, china grass and other analogous vegetable fibres for spinning.	2715	21st Oct. 1865	James Hill Dickson.
Cotton gins - - - - -	2964	20th Nov. 1865	William James Burgess.
Improvements in the mode of applying mineral oils to the souring and lubrication of textile matters and machinery, and in the manufacture of soap. (wool, &c.)	6107	4th Dec. 1865	Leopold Joseph Bouchart.
An improved method in the production of fibre from various fibrous plants and animal products.	6112	4th Dec. 1865	James Stuart.
Machinery for opening and cleaning cotton and other fibrous substances.	6120	5th Dec. 1865	Nathaniel Wright Wilkinson.
Machinery or apparatus for cleaning and ginning cotton and other fibrous substances.	6157	6th Dec. 1865	George Macdonald.
A new or improved method of preparing esparto, alpha or mongodos grasses or other similar vegetable substances, for spinning, weaving, and for substitution for hair and for other fibres now in use - - - - - - -	3156	8th Dec. 1865	{ Oliver Megge. George Hedgecombe Smith.
Machinery for opening and cleaning cotton and other fibrous substances	6260	14th Dec. 1865	{ Thomas Ridley Hetherington. Samuel Thornton.
Improvements in the manufacture of yarns, string and paper, and in the preparation of dyes, and in dyeing fabrics, by the application of vegetable substances not hitherto used for such purposes.	8316	22nd Dec. 1865	John Alexander Cooper.
III.—Carding, Combing and Doubling Fibrous Materials; Making Cards.			
Machinery for opening and carding cotton and other fibrous materials.	90	11th Jan. 1865	Robert Tempest.
Improved machinery or apparatus for shaping the elastic dents of expanding and contracting combs.	189	21st Jan. 1865	Matthew Robinson.
Improved mechanism for giving intermittent or continuous revolving motion of different velocities, without the use of change wheels - (taking up beams of carding-machines.)	679	31st Jan. 1865	{ Thomas Hall, Samuel Bonser.
Carding-engines - - - - -	693	2nd March 1865	John Macmillan Dunlop.

Subject-matter of Patent.	Number of Patent.	Date.	Name of Patentee.
SPINNING, &c. — continued.			
Machinery or apparatus for combing wool and other fibrous substances - - - -	612	6th March 1865	Samuel Smith. William Smith.
Machinery or apparatus for hackling flax, hemp or other similar fibrous substances - -	690	11th March 1865	Thomas Whitehead. Henry Walton Whitehead.
Worsted carding and preparing machinery -	830	23rd March 1865	Henry Oakes.
Certain improvements in machinery or apparatus used in carding cotton or other fibrous substances - - - - - -	887	29th March 1865	Evan Leigh. Frederick Allen Leigh.
Improvements in preparing wool and other fibrous substances, and in the apparatus employed therein - - - - - -	948	4th April 1865	Alfred Illingworth. Henry Illingworth.
Machinery for carding wool or other fibrous substances - - - - -	983	6th April 1865	Joshua Ellis. Charles Walker. William Preston.
Certain improvements in machinery or apparatus to be employed in preparing cotton and other fibrous substances for spinning.	990	7th April 1865	James Thompson.
An improved metallic preparation or composition for cleaning, sharpening, burnishing and grinding articles of cutlery, edge tools or cutting instruments, and for grinding the cards or rollers of carding-engines and the surfaces of cylinders, and covering rollers for various kinds of woollen and cotton machinery.	1054	13th April 1865	George Mountford.
Machinery for combing, preparing and drawing wool or other fibrous material - - -	1084	19th April 1865	Thomas Whitehead. Nicholas Nussey.
Machinery for carding cotton and other fibrous substances and for doubling yarns - - -	1094	20th April 1865	James Hall. William Dunkerley. Samuel Schofield.
Improvements in door and other mats, part of which improvements is also applicable to brushes and brooms, and in producing cord or tooth surfaces employed in operating on various fibrous substances.	1353	9th May 1865	Thomas Jefferson Mayall.
Machinery or apparatus for tapering, pointing or reducing wires or rods for spindles, hatchel teeth, pins for drums, and similar articles.	1465	16th May 1865	Chauncey Orris Crosby.
Screw gills or hackle frames - - -	1419	24th May 1865	Thompson Braoland.
Machinery for separating or sorting fibres and filaments of different lengths, and forming them into a lap or fleece. (Communicated by Charles Simon.)	1430	25th May 1865	Richard Archibald Brooman.
Machinery for combing wool and other filamentous and textile materials. (Communicated by John Harmel, Ernest Harmel and Léon Harmel.)	1550	6th June 1865	Richard Archibald Brooman.
Machinery for combing and hackling fibrous materials.	1587	7th June 1865	William Tongue.
Improvements in rubbing or rolling woollen or cotton cardings, and in apparatus connected therewith.	1618	15th June 1865	Thomas Rothwell.
Machinery for combing wool and other fibrous materials - - - - - -	1604	21st June 1865	John Barfield. Samuel Bairstow Walmsley.
Machinery for combing cotton, wool and other fibrous materials.	2164	23rd Aug. 1865	George Little.

Subject-matter of Patent.	Number of Patent.	Date.	Name of Patentee.
SPINNING, &c.—continued.			
Machinery for combing wool and other fibrous materials - - - - - - -	2223	29th Aug. 1865	Isaac Bailey. William Henry Bailey.
Machinery for combing wool and other fibrous material.	2299	7th Sept. 1865	Augustin Morel,
Cards used in carding-engines and other similar machinery - - - - - -	2452	23rd Sept. 1865	William Turner. Samuel Shaw. William Halliwell.
Machinery or apparatus for preparing and spinning cotton and other fibrous materials.	2476	27th Sept. 1865	William Tatham.
Improved machinery for feeding fibrous substances to preparing, carding and other machinery for working wool and other filamentous substances. (Communicated by Alexandre Dru.)	2517	30th Sept. 1865	William Edward Newton.
Apparatus for grinding cards of carding-engines -	2518	30th Sept. 1865	Samuel Faulkner.
Machinery for carding wool or other fibrous substances - - - - - - -	2553	3rd Oct. 1865	Charles Walker. William Preston.
Certain improvements in machinery for hackling flax or other fibrous substances.	2761	24th Oct. 1865	Stephen Cotton.
Machinery for combing wool and other fibres -	2797	31st Oct. 1865	George Edmund Donisthorpe.
Apparatus for grinding and pointing the cards on carding-engines.	2876	8th Nov. 1865	Robert Swire.
Screw gill boxes - - - - - -	3039	27th Nov. 1865	William Hodgson.
Means or apparatus for preparing and combing wool and other fibrous substances.	3123	5th Dec. 1865	Isaac Holden, M.P.
Apparatus to be employed in the carding of scribbling and carding engines - - -	3161	8th Dec. 1865	George Wailes. Benjamin Cooper.
Combing silk, flax, wool and other fibrous substances.	3162	9th Dec. 1865	James Warburton.
Holders for hackling machines for jute, hemp, flax and other fibrous substances.	3250	15th Dec. 1865	Charles Blyth.
III.—Roving, Rubbing, Spinning, Twisting, Doubling and Throwing Fibrous Materials.			
Certain improvements in mules for spinning -	31	4th Jan. 1866	John Knowles. James Bents.
Jack and slubbing frames - - - -	63	9th Jan. 1865	Ashworth Barlow.
Flyers for preparing cotton and other fibrous materials for spinning - - - - -	69	9th Jan. 1865	Richard Ashton Lightoller. George Henry Lightoller.
Machinery for preparing, spinning, doubling and winding wool, mohair, alpaca, silk, flax, cotton, or other fibrous substances - - -	100	16th Jan. 1865	Jabez Bunting Farrar. John Hirst.
Mules for spinning and doubling - - -	153	16th Jan. 1865	William Rowbottom.
Machinery or apparatus for preparing cotton and other fibrous materials to be spun.	158	19th Jan. 1865	Thomas Mayor.
Improvements applicable to throstle worsted spinning and doubling frames.	162	19th Jan. 1866	Edward Williams.
The manufacture of a new thread for weaving and other uses. (Communicated by Veras Sabran and Gaston Jean.)	212	25th Jan. 1865	Richard Archibald Brooman.

Subject-matter of Patent.	Number of Patent.	Date.	Name of Patentee.
SPINNING, &c.— continued.			
Throstle spinning frames - - - (Communicated by Charles Loyhrrr.)	520	27th Jan. 1865	Charles Denton Abel
A new method for removing or destroying the momentum of heavy bodies by means of an elastic machine or machines, so as to prevent injury and damage from concussion, applicable to ship cables, ship and fort armour, railway trains, tendant to pier heads and floating piers, gangways, breakwaters and other similar structures, also as a motive-power. (driving spinning frames.) (Communicated by William Graham M'Iver.)	521	6th Feb. 1865	Clemente Robert Martin
Improvements applicable to spinning mules and throstles	535	6th Feb. 1865	Edward Williams. Thomas Williams.
Machinery for preparing cotton and other fibrous substances.	578	10th Feb. 1865	Edward Lord.
Mules for spinning and doubling - -	577	1st March 1865	John Dodd.
Improvements in steam hammers applicable to the manufacture of files, to welding flues of cotton machinery and to other purposes.	641	7th March 1865	James Dodge.
Certain improvements in lap machines employed in preparing cotton and other fibrous substances.	756	18th March 1865	Thomas Ogden.
Manufacture of yarn so as to render suits applicable as a substitute for woollen yarn, for manufacturing into shawls and other textile fabrics.	774	20th March 1865	Isidor Philippsa.
Improved means or apparatus for lubricating vertical or diagonal spindles and shafts.	782	21st March 1865	James Waterhouse Ilsley.
Mules for spinning and doubling - -	850	25th March 1865	John Dodd.
Certain improvements in mules for spinning cotton and other fibrous substances - -	919	1st April 1865	William Moral. John Knott. William Dennis.
Improvements in preparing wool and other fibrous substances, and in the apparatus employed therein	948	4th April 1865	Alfred Illingworth. Henry Illingworth.
Machinery for preparing cotton and other fibrous substances.	988	7th April 1865	Moses Barney Hayward
Apparatus for lubricating spindles, shafts or other frictional surfaces. (Communicated by William Francis Eippen.)	1080	13th April 1865	James Eippen.
Machinery for combing, preparing and drawing wool or other fibrous material - -	1084	19th April 1865	Thomas Whitehead. Nicholas Neary.
Machinery for carding cotton and other fibrous substances and for doubling yarns - -	1094	20th April 1865	James Hall. William Dumberly. Samuel Schofield.
Preparing, spinning, and doubling cotton, flax, wool, silk and other fibrous material - -	1118	21st April 1865	James Champion. John Brimley Sturat
Nozzle or bobbins to be used in certain frames for preparing fibrous materials for spinning.	1127	22nd April 1865	Joshua Henry Wilton.
Certain improvements in apparatus for spinning silk and other fibrous substances. (Communicated by Monsieur Justin Louis Auguste Aubrun.)	1209	29th April 1865	Peter Armand Le Comte de Fontaine Moreau.
Improvements in the preparation of jute, hemp, flax, and other fibrous materials, and in the machinery or apparatus employed therein.	1343	5th May 1865	James M'Ginbie.

Subject-matter of Patent.	Number of Patent.	Date.	Name of Patentee.
SPINNING, &c.—continued.			
Machinery or apparatus for tapering, pointing or reducing wires or rods for spindles, hatchel teeth, pins for dressers, and similar articles.	1342	16th May 1865	Chauncey Orrin Crosby.
Certain improvements in apparatus to be employed in spinning cotton and other fibrous materials.	1363	19th May 1865	Thomas Marsden.
Certain improvements in machinery for spinning and doubling cotton and other fibrous substances. (Communicated by Joseph Slater.)	1391	20th May 1865	Charles Bradley.
An improvement in the drawing and other rollers used in preparing and spinning cotton and other fibrous materials and textile manufactures. (Communicated by Amos Askam Taylor.)	1430	24th May 1865	William Edward Newton.
Certain improvements applicable to spinning, weaving and knitting machines. (Communicated by Charles Arthur Rasiguet and Jean Adolphe Lavène.)	1440	25th May 1865	William Edward Newton.
Spinning machinery (Communicated by Julius Striner.)	1483	30th May 1865	Moritz Meisel.
Improved machinery for putting twist in all fibrous substances.	1529	3rd June 1865	William Holden.
Apparatus for doubling and twisting yarns and threads.	1530	5th June 1865	William Toward.
Machinery or apparatus for spinning, doubling or twisting cotton and other fibrous materials	1541	6th June 1865	Alfred Pemberton, Alfred William Pemberton.
Improvements in silk winding machines, part of the said improvements being also applicable to cleaning and doubling machines.	1632	16th June 1865	William Trevor Wanklyn.
Machinery for twisting, doubling and laying all kinds of yarns.	1644	19th June 1865	Edward Whalley.
Improvements in and applicable to machinery for doubling and drawing cotton and other fibrous substances.	1730	30th June 1865	François Delamare-Debrutteville.
An improved combination of materials for the manufacture of carpets, floor cloth, felt, wall paper, fireproof flexible roofing, ship and boat building, and for other similar purposes (rollers for spinning machinery.)	1775	6th July 1865	John Longbottom, Abram Longbottom.
Straight eye clearing guides or cleaners, for winding silk, cotton or other fibrous substances	1872	19th July 1865	John Raikin Whitehall, Thomas Fillings.
Covers for rollers used in spinning cotton	1901	21st July 1865	George Taylor, Joseph Crosley.
Means or apparatus for producing friction or adhesion between pulleys, rollers and the like, and cords, bands, belts or chains passed over or round them. (for spinning frames.)	1937	25th July 1865	Martyn John Roberts.
An improvement in "cap frames"	1966	29th July 1865	Reuben Worsnop.
Preparing machinery for flax, tow, jute and other fibrous materials	1977	31st July 1865	John Lawson, Edward Gerrard Fitton.
Machinery for the manufacture of linen or other yarns or threads.	1986	1st Aug. 1865	Thomas Bell Paton.

Subject-matter of Patent.	Number of Patent.	Date.	Name of Patentee.
SPINNING, &c.—continued.			
Improvements in the lubricating of spindles, the necks or bolsters in which the said spindles revolve having a traversing motion in the said neck or bolster.	2059	9th Aug. 1865	Jacob Berry Reidth
Machinery for preparing cotton, wool and other fibrous materials -	2082	12th Aug. 1865	{ Josue Tatham. John Smith. }
An improved method of twisting threads - (or "Weaving.") (Communicated by Désiré Sirol and Léon Sirol.)	2147	19th Aug. 1865	Richard Archibald Brooman.
Certain improvements in preparing and spinning cotton and other fibrous materials.	2286	6th Sept. 1865	James Pilkington.
Mules for spinning and doubling - - -	2342	13th Sept. 1865	John Dodd.
Spinning frames - - - - (Communicated by Paul Friedheim.)	2348	13th Sept. 1865	Alfred Vincent Newton
Bobbins or spools used in spinning and winding yarns and threads. (Communicated by Charles Reynolds.)	2368	16th Sept. 1865	Jabial Kerks Boyt.
Bobbin holders - - - - (for spinning machines.)	2406	21st Sept. 1865	John Goskling.
Machinery or apparatus for preparing and spinning cotton and other fibrous materials.	2476	27th Sept. 1865	William Tatham
An improvement in machinery for spinning, twisting, doubling and winding yarns or threads. (Communicated by Arance Laporte and Gaspard Ambieux.)	2535	3rd Oct. 1865	William Edward Newton
Flyers used in doubling machines - -	2611	10th Oct. 1865	Mark Walker.
Certain improvements in machinery or apparatus for twisting or doubling cotton or other yarns -	2682	12th Oct. 1865	{ James Broughton Edge Enoch Hirst. }
Improvements in machinery or apparatus known as "roving," "intermediate," "slubbing" and "throstle" frames and "doublers," and also in winding machines used for preparing, spinning and winding cotton, wool, flax, silk and other fibrous substances.	2713	20th Oct. 1865	William Smurr.
Manufacture of covers applicable to drawing or printing rollers and to endless blankets -	2714	20th Oct. 1865	{ Manuel Leopold Jose Lorette. John Korkow. }
Mules for spinning and doubling - - (Communicated by Ernest Stumm.)	2760	26th Oct. 1865	Henry Barnwell Barr.
Machinery for the preparation and spinning of flax and other fibrous substances.	2776	24th Oct. 1865	James Combe
Means or apparatus for preparing, spinning, twisting, doubling or winding cotton, wool, flax or other fibrous material.	2859	7th Nov. 1865	Martyn John Roberts
Certain improvements in machinery or apparatus for spinning and doubling cotton or other fibrous substances - - - - -	2960	20th Nov. 1865	{ James Broughton Edge Enoch Hirst. }
Application of pressure to the rollers of spinning, preparing and other machinery.	2965	21st Nov. 1865	Thomas Richard Barker
"Top rollers" employed in the manufacture of fibrous substances.	3070	30th Nov. 1865	John Kerkow.
Improvements in winding machinery, which improvements are partly applicable to machinery for spinning and doubling.	3139	5th Dec. 1865	John Jackson Ashworth

Subject-matter of Patent.	Number of Patent.	Date.	Name of Patentee.
SPINNING, &c.—continued.			
Machinery for preparing, spinning and twisting flax, cotton, wool and other fibrous substances -	5212	12th Dec. 1865	John Campbell. Samuel M'Kinstry. Thomas Wilson.
Construction of parts of machines used in spinning and doubling - - - - -	5334	14th Dec. 1865	John Eley. Robert Cotton.
Improvements in caps employed in spinning, and in the manufacture thereof.	5325	23rd Dec. 1865	Edward Clifton.
Obtaining and employing continuous lengths of tanned leather for various useful purposes - (bands for spinning wheels.)	5334	23rd Dec. 1865	George Horn. Daniel Horn.
Throstle machines and flys - - - -	5377	30th Dec. 1865	Thomas Parkinson.
SPRINGS.			
Improvements in locomotive engines and in the springs of railway carriages.	85	5th Jan. 1865	James Edwards Wilson.
Regulating and working the valves of steam and other engines.	63	11th Jan. 1865	John Frederick Spencer.
Permanent way and rolling stock of railways -	520	24th Feb. 1865	John Kennedy Donald.
Machinery or apparatus for rolling, shaping or forging metals. (carriage springs.)	701	13th March 1865	Robert Marsden.
Wheels and the manner of applying the same to railway carriages for passengers' and goods' traffic, as also the leading wheels for locomotives.	1114	21st April 1865	William Day.
Machinery for sewing and embroidering - -	1167	26th April 1865	George Mumby.
A new or improved spring apparatus to be applied to the bearings of the axles of pulleys or drums used in collieries - - - - -	1343	15th May 1865	George Elliot. Samuel Bailey Coxon.
An improved method of testing railway and other springs - - - - - - -	1374	18th May 1865	Joseph Mitchell. George Tilleard.
Locomotive engines and railway carriages - -	1646	19th June 1865	George Smith the younger.
Improvements in locomotive engines and in springs of railway carriages.	1789	4th July 1865	James Edwards Wilson.
Improvements in steam carriages and in adapting wheels for common roads to railways. (Communicated by Joseph Alphonse Lenhai.)	1831	10th July 1865	Richard Archibald Brooman.
Construction of springs for railroad and other carriages.	1880	15th July 1865	John Crawford Walker.
Protecting crinoline steel, stay hooks, springs for leggings or gaiters, and other similar fastenings.	1883	19th July 1865	William Edwards.
Improvements in the construction of railway carriages and in railway breaks and signals, part of which is applicable to marine purposes - -	2005	2nd Aug. 1865	William Henry Petitjean. Edward M'Nally.
Manufacture of cast steel and cast iron, and the manufacture of a mixed metal. (for springs.) (Communicated by Emile Martin and Pierre Emile Martin.)	2157	16th Aug. 1865	Richard Archibald Brooman.

Subject-matter of Patent.	Number of Patent.	Date.	Name of Patentee.
SPRINGS—*continued.*			
Bearing and draw springs, and springs to resist concussion.	2459	26th Sept. 1865	William Henry Brown
File-cutting machine . . . . (*India-rubber springs.*)	2548	4th Oct. 1865	John Dodge.
Railway carriages and locomotives . . . (*Communicated by Henry Gifford.*)	2621	11th Oct. 1865	Michael Henry.
Centrifugal governors . . . . (*applying springs.*) (*Communicated by Thomas Richard Pickering.*)	2639	12th Oct. 1865	William Edward Newton
Bedsteads, seats, couches and other articles for sitting and reclining on. (*springs.*)	2654	14th Oct. 1865	James Lamb Hancock.
Improvements in common road carriages and in breaks for the same.	2687	18th Oct. 1865	James Rock the younger
Machinery for the preparation and spinning of flax and other fibrous substances.	2776	24th Oct. 1865	James Combe.
Door springs	2917	13th Nov. 1865	William Williams.
Improvements in helical or spiral springs for upholstery and other purposes, and in machinery for manufacturing the same. (*Communicated by Frederick Chesbrew Payne and John Spencer Giles.*)	3053	24th Nov. 1865	William Edward Newton
STABLES, HORSE BOXES, FEEDING TROUGHS, CATTLE SHEDS.			
An improvement in fixing sliding partitions in stables and other buildings.	610	4th March 1865	Louis Le Chevalier Cannas.
An improved combination of materials for the manufacture of carpets, floor cloth, felt, wall paper, fireproof flexible roofing, ship and boat building, and for other similar purposes - (*horse boxes.*)	1775	5th July 1865	{ John Longbottom. Abram Longbottom.
Improvements in fittings for stables, cowsheds and piggeries, and in alluvium traps for stables and other places.	2499	28th Sept. 1865	Edward Cotton.
Machinery or apparatus for preparing and supplying food for cattle. (*feeding-trough.*)	2514	30th Sept. 1865	Robert Willey.
Improvements in supplying cattle with food and water on railways, and in the apparatus or means connected therewith.	2909	11th Nov. 1865	William Reid.
Improvements in disinfecting stables and cattle sheds, and in the apparatus employed therein.	3075	30th Nov. 1865	John Gawer.
Manufacture of disinfectants . . . . (*for cattle sheds.*)	3115	4th Dec. 1865	John Thomson.
Manufacture of tanks, baths, troughs and other vessels.	3129	5th Dec. 1865	Edward Hardy.

Subject-matter of Patent.	Number of Patent.	Date.	Name of Patentee.
STAMPS, LABELS AND TICKETS; PERFORATING, DAMPING, FIXING AND OBLITERATING STAMPS; STAMPING AND MARKING.			
Apparatus for affixing postage and other gummed stamps and labels.	879	10th Feb. 1865	Herbert William Hart.
Apparatus for stamping and marking (*Communicated by Alexandre Mathieu.*)	866	27th March 1865	George Bishop.
Vessels or apparatus for melting sealing wax, glue or other substances. (*Communicated by Frederick Kührmann.*)	931	3rd April 1865	William Bünger.
Manufacture of postage and other stamps (*Communicated by Samuel Ward Francis.*)	938	3rd April 1865	John Henry Johnson.
Cases or receptacles for matches, stamps, cards and other articles	1131	21st April 1865	George Betjemann. George William Betjemann. John Betjemann.
Tablets, tickets or instruments to be used when drawing lots and prizes, and for such like purposes.	1196	29th April 1865	Charles Gammon.
Stamping or signing letters, papers or other objects	1369	19th May 1865	Carl Fischer. Johann Carl Wilhelm Maas.
An improved hand stamp for printing letters, numerals and other figures.	1536	5th June 1865	Alfred Johnson Aspinall.
Hammers and other machines actuated by steam or other fluid or vapour (*machines for stamping.*)	1607	14th June 1865	Benjamin Massey. Stephen Massey.
Manufacture of chains, bracelets, necklaces and other articles of jewelry. (*forming by pressure.*)	1794	7th July 1865	Pierre Mathurin Charles Betiel.
Certain improvements in envelope machines (*Communicated by Thomas Verie Weymouth, Henry Clay Berlin and George James.*)	1896	20th July 1865	Alfred Vincent Newton.
Instruments for marking or impressing railway tickets.	1948	27th July 1865	Russell Mortimer.
Vessels or apparatus for melting sealing wax, glue or other substances. (*Communicated by Frederick Kührmann.*)	2281	5th Sept. 1865	William Bünger.
An improved mode of and apparatus for securing the labels of trucks and invoices of goods conveyed on railways.	2407	21st Sept. 1865	Edwin William Collier.
Apparatus for affixing postage stamps and other labels to letters and documents.	2412	21st Sept. 1865	Henry Albert Davis.
Securing or fastening envelopes	2430	23rd Sept. 1865	The Honourable Jane Elizabeth Tuchet.
Apparatus for impressing designs upon biscuits made by machinery.	2508	29th Sept. 1865	George Gillitt.
Manufacture of lozenges, cakes and other similar articles, from plastic substances. (*stamping.*)	2534	3rd Oct. 1865	Charles James Tinker.
Improvements in and adaptation of cylinder printing machines to the double purpose of letter press and lithography, also a new mode of damping litho' stones, and a new mode of registering and printing in such machines.	2999	22nd Nov. 1865	Thomas William Nicholson.

Subject-matter of Patent.	Number of Patent.	Date.	Name of Patentee.
STAMPS, &c.—continued.			
Machinery or apparatus for stamping or impressing railway or other tickets.	3006	23nd Nov. 1865	Alfred Leggefield.
A new method of and apparatus for damping and affixing adhesive stamps	3295	23rd Dec. 1865	William Gill. Buckingham Bird.
Apparatus for damping and gumming labels, stamps, envelopes and sheets of paper	3343	27th Dec. 1866	Joseph Benn. George Oswald Lackman
STARCH, SIZE, GLUE, GUM, GUMALINE.			
A new or improved apparatus and means for ascertaining the quality and condition of grain and seed. (amount of gluten.) (Communicated by Christian Joseph Schmitz.)	622	7th March 1865	William Bünger.
Vessels or apparatus for melting sealing wax, glue or other substances. (Communicated by Frederick Kührmann.)	881	3rd April 1865	William Bünger.
Preparation and treatment of gun cotton	1109	20th April 1865	Frederick Augustus Abel
Improvements in taking impressions from the grain of wood, and in transferring the same on to various surfaces (and in making size for paper.)	1117	21st April 1865	William Scarratt. William Dean.
Improvements in the manufacture of waterproof fabrics and in apparatus to be employed therein	1160	25th April 1865	John Collins Wickham. Augusta Edward Dean.
The manufacture of a new resinous gum or balsam (Communicated by Benjamin Hawkins Dade.)	1173	25th April 1865	George Tomlinson Bonfield.
Treating rice and other grain for the manufacture of starch, also to prepare them for use as food and for other purposes.	1616	12th May 1866	Henry Bansford.
An improved sizing material to be employed for sizing or dressing yarns preparatory to weaving. (Communicated by John Ulric Hillwiller.)	1906	21st July 1865	Edward Schnah.
Manufacture of anti-flammable starch	1946	26th July 1865	Tobiah Pepper.
Apparatus for filtering sugar and other liquid substances	2022	4th Aug. 1865	Jens Adolphus Lenn. George Townsend. John Klamch.
Vessels or apparatus for melting sealing wax, glue or other substances. (Communicated by Frederick Kührmann.)	2281	5th Sept. 1865	William Bünger.
Manufacture of artificial gum, size, or stiffening matter.	2810	1st Nov. 1865	John Sellars.
The conversion of the refuse of starch and gum-aline into useful gumaline.	3263	18th Dec. 1865	William Ebenezer Dobus
Preparation of glue or gelatine so as to render it insoluble in water, and applicable by the admixture of other substances, to various purposes for which common glue or gelatine cannot now be used. (Communicated by Henry Wurts.)	3295	23rd Dec. 1865	William Edward Newton.

Subject-matter of Patent.	Number of Patent.	Date.	Name of Patentee.

STEAM AND OTHER BOILERS; CLEANSING AND PREVENTING INCRUSTATION OF BOILERS; WATER-FEEDING APPARATUS FOR BOILERS.

1.—Constructing Steam and other Boilers; Generating and Superheating Steam; Preventing Boiler Explosions.

Subject-matter of Patent.	Number of Patent.	Date.	Name of Patentee.
An improved jacket or protector for metallic and other vessels and structures containing solid substances, liquids or gases, to prevent radiation of heat from or communication of heat to such vessels and structures - - - - (for steam-boilers.)	4	2nd Jan. 1865	{ Edward Bevan. Abel Fleming.
Means of and apparatus for generating steam and heat.	53	5th Jan. 1865	John Malabury Kirby.
Certain improvements in the construction of tubular boilers and in the means for cleaning the tubes of such boilers - - - -	37	5th Jan. 1865	{ James Chapman Amos. William Anderson.
Motive-power and means of communication between passengers while travelling, and appliances connected therewith.	55	7th Jan. 1865	George Bell Galloway.
Improvements in furnace flues for the consumption of smoke.	94	11th Jan. 1865	Abraham Cooper.
Furnaces - - - - - - - - (Communicated by Dominique Chiesa.)	109	12th Jan. 1865	Michael Henry.
Boilers for generating steam - - -	113	13th Jan. 1865	Richard Lewis.
Furnaces for melting metals and smelting ores -	209	24th Jan. 1865	{ William Woodward. Robert Woodward. John Woodward. Adam Woodward, jun'.
Improvements in steam generators or steam-boilers and furnaces, part of which is also applicable to other heat generating apparatus.	243	27th Jan. 1865	Joseph Twibill.
The application of hydro-electricity to steam for the purpose of increasing its expansion and power, and the machinery or apparatus connected therewith, and also the application of galvano or frictional electricity for the same purpose - - - - - -	273	31st Jan. 1865	{ Joseph Fletcher. Daniel Hames.
Improved apparatus for preventing the explosion of steam-boilers.	305	3rd Feb. 1865	John Westerby.
Steam generators - - - - -	346	7th Feb. 1865	John Lake.
Improvements in furnaces and boilers and parts connected with them, for generating steam and heating fluids, and also for improved apparatus for reducing and shutting off steam and regulating the speed of steam-engines.	396	11th Feb. 1865	John Cass.
Steam-boilers - - - - -	401	13th Feb. 1865	Robert William Thomson.
An improved blowing apparatus - - - } (for boiler makers.)	457	14th Feb. 1865	{ Samuel Richards Freeman. Abraham Grundy.
Improvements in puddling furnaces and in apparatus connected therewith. (and steam-boilers.)	473	16th Feb. 1865	John Gay Newton Alleyne.
Boilers for heating water and delivering it at an equal temperature to any number of flow pipes, and also for the generation of steam.	493	22nd Feb. 1865	Jasper Hulley.

Subject-matter of Patent.	Number of Patent.	Date.	Name of Patentee.

STEAM-BOILERS, &c.—continued.

Subject-matter of Patent.	Number of Patent.	Date.	Name of Patentee.
An improved method of extracting gases from mineral oils, and in employing the same for illuminating and heat producing purposes, and in the machinery or apparatus connected therewith. (for generating steam.)	549	27th Feb. 1865	William Sim.
Making the joints of steam generators and parts connected therewith.	582	2nd March 1865	John Muir Hetherington
Smoke consuming apparatus	584	2nd March 1865	Samuel Hopkinson. Edwin Hopkinson.
Steam generators (Communicated by Henry Brown.)	607	4th March 1865	John Henry Johnson.
Combining marine steam-boilers	612	4th March 1865	Edward Humphrys.
Tubular boilers (Communicated by Lewis Felix Meunier.)	634	7th March 1865	Richard Archibald Brosman.
Steam-boilers and the furnaces thereof	685	11th March 1865	Edward Brown Wilson. James Howden.
Construction of steam generators and evaporators (Communicated by Eli Thayer and Solon Peters Pond.)	743	16th March 1865	Alfred Vincent Newton.
Apparatus for generating steam (Communicated by Peter Corfils Möller.)	771	20th March 1865	Johann Tobias Reminger.
Locomotive engines and carriages for common roads and tramways, and also for agricultural and other purposes.	780	20th March 1865	Alexander Richard Marheine.
Means and apparatus for utilising the heat of steam	854	25th March 1865	David Estler Black.
Certain improvements in non-conducting composition for preventing the radiation or transmission of heat or cold. (for building or stopping up boilers.)	864	27th March 1865	Ferdinand Le Roy.
Steam-boilers	909	31st March 1865	John Scurbrick. David Scurbrick. Benjamin Scurbrick. Ormerod Scurbrick.
Improvements in or applicable to boilers furnished with pipes for the circulation of water for domestic purposes.	974	6th April 1865	John Brown.
Steam-boilers, steam-boiler tubes, sides of steam-boilers' flues and furnaces.	988	7th April 1865	George Sykill.
Improvements in steam generators applicable also to condensers or coolers. (Communicated by Thomas Loders.)	1029	11th April 1865	John Henry Johnson.
Arrangement of furnaces used for puddling and reheating iron, the generation of steam and other similar purposes.	1064	13th April 1865	William Boardmore.
An improved safety apparatus for steam-boilers	1069	18th April 1865	John Minton Courtault.
Apparatus for preventing explosions in steam-boilers	1095	20th April 1865	John Hocking the younger.
Improvements in steam generators and engines, and in apparatus for feeding steam generators. (Communicated by George Bailey Brayton.)	1240	3rd May 1865	John Henry Johnson.
Steam-engines (Communicated by Ebenezer Deaford.)	1294	6th May 1865	William Edward Newton
Improvements in means or apparatus for fixing or tightening the ends of boiler and other tubes, and in cutting the ends or other parts of such tubes.	1303	9th May 1865	Ralph Hart Tweddell.

Subject-matter of Patent.	Number of Patent.	Date.	Name of Patentee.

STEAM-BOILERS, &c.—continued.

Subject-matter of Patent.	Number of Patent.	Date.	Name of Patentee.
Machinery for drilling boiler and other plates of metal, and for rivetting them together.	1291	10th May 1865	Daniel Adamson.
A combined safety valve regulator, pressure gauge, water indicator, alarm and " blow off " for steam generators. (Communicated by Peter Riardon.)	1505	11th May 1865	John Henry Johnson.
An improved economic boiler for hot water apparatus, applicable for the heating of hot houses, churches and other public buildings.	1510	1st June 1865	Frederick Knight.
Steam-boilers - - - - - (Communicated by Abram Samuel Mitchell.)	1521	2nd June 1865	Henry Edward Newton.
Safety apparatus for steam-boilers - -	1526	2nd June 1865	James Shepherd.
An improved method of generating heat, and apparatus or means for effecting the same -	1559	7th June 1865	{ William Nun. { Arthur Harff.
Furnaces - - - - - (Communicated by François Durand.)	1590	12th June 1865	Richard Archibald Brooman.
Multitubular hot water boilers - -	1614	14th June 1865	Henry Ormson.
Generating steam - - - -	1622	15th June 1865	Matthew Piers Watt Boulton.
Improvements in distilling and rectifying, and in the apparatus employed therein, parts of which improvements are applicable to steam generators.	1662	20th June 1865	Evaristo Vignier.
Improvements in steam-boilers, furnaces, and engines, and in parts connected therewith.	1745	30th June 1865	Edwin Elliot.
Means and apparatus for increasing the mechanical power of steam.	1620	10th July 1865	William Alexander Lyttle.
Making skelps for iron or steel tubes direct from the rolls, and for machinery to be used in the same.	1858	15th July 1865	Samuel Illingley.
Steam-boilers or generators - - -	1868	14th July 1865	Andrew Barclay.
Means or method of applying mineral oils for generating steam and heat. (Partly communicated by Alexandre Bryda.)	1878	25th July 1865	Wladislaus Zbyszewski.
Apparatus for burning combustible and volatile liquids for generating steam and similar purposes. (Communicated by Patrick Hayes.)	1938	26th July 1865	George Tomlinson Bousfield.
Construction of cooking stoves and ranges - -	1944	26th July 1865	William Barton.
Means of and apparatus for treating animal and vegetable fibrous materials, which apparatus is also applicable to various useful purposes. (producing steam.)	1952	27th July 1865	Henry Sherwood.
Improvements in the manufacture of hoops and tyres, and in the machinery employed therein. (hoops for making boilers.)	1975	31st July 1865	John Ramsbottom.
Locomotive and other tubular boilers - -	1990	1st Aug. 1865	Louis Emile Constant Martin.
Obtaining motive-power by heat - - - (producing steam.)	1993	1st Aug. 1865	Matthew Piers Watt Boulton.
Machinery to be used in the manufacture of plate or sheet iron and steel. (Communicated by Metin Diosdoni Honneur.)	2012	3rd Aug. 1865	Ephraim Robel.
Improvements in generating steam and in heating steam and artiform fluids.	2051	7th Aug. 1865	Matthew Piers Watt Boulton.

Subject-matter of Patent.	Number of Patent.	Date.	Name of Patentee.
STEAM-BOILERS, &c.—*continued.*			
Improvements in the preparation or production of spongy metals, and in their applications. (for lining steam generators.) (Communicated by François Drivet.)	2105	15th Aug. 1865	John Henry Johnson.
Method of heating the ovens and boilers of kitchen ranges or cooking stoves.	2170	24th Aug. 1865	Frederick Thomas.
Steam-boilers or generators (Communicated by Henry Clark Sargeant.)	2190	25th Aug. 1865	William Edward Newton.
Construction of apparatus for distilling and rectifying alcohols. (steam regulator.) (Communicated by François Desiré Savalle.)	2209	28th Aug. 1865	Henri Adrien Bonneville.
The manufacture of boiler and tea-kettle bottoms, and every other description of die-struck hollow ware.	2257	31st Aug. 1865	Michael Judge.
Tubular steam-boilers or generators for agricultural or other locomotive steam-engines.	2260	1st Sept. 1865	John Lake.
Apparatus for preventing incrustation in steam-boilers, and for preventing explosion of such boilers, heating the feed water, and consuming smoke	2272	4th Sept. 1865	James Howard. William Stafford. William Porter M'Callum
An improved method of fixing and unfixing the tubes of steam-boilers. (Communicated by Daniel M'Dowell.)	2284	6th Sept. 1865	Samuel Santos.
Improvements in boilers and furnaces and in cleansing the flues thereof	2291	6th Sept. 1865	Edward Grove. Edward Grove the younger.
An improved safety valve for steam boilers	2323	11th Sept. 1865	Henry Hackett. Thomas Wrigley. Edmund Pearson.
Apparatus for separating dust from the gases evolved from blast furnaces for smelting iron (for heating boilers.)	2391	19th Sept. 1865	Edward Alfred Cowper. Charles William Siemens
Preparing peat or turf for fire lights and fuel, and for machinery to be employed therein. (for steam boilers.)	2436	23rd Sept. 1865	Thomas Vincent Lee.
Tools for securing tubes in tube plates, and for other purposes where concentrated power or adjustment is necessary.	2455	26th Sept. 1865	Richard Taylor Nelson Howey.
Compositions used for coating metallic surfaces (boilers.)	2480	27th Sept. 1865	John Bolley. Charles William Smith.
Apparatus for heating, evaporating and cooling liquids	2494	28th Sept. 1865	Isaac Smith. William Fothergill Batho.
Improvements in producing and combining gases to be used for heating purposes, and in the construction of retorts for producing and combining such gases. (for generating steam.)	2527	2nd Oct. 1865	Silas Corell Salisbury.
Improvements in the manufacture of sheet iron or steel cylinders for boilers and similar articles, and in the apparatus relating thereto. (Communicated by Benôit Bonnard.)	2529	3rd Oct. 1865	Henri Adrien Bonneville.
An improved mode of generating steam	2604	10th Oct. 1865	John Sturgeon.
An improved ventilating apparatus for use in steam boats, vessels and other places requiring to be ventilated.	2606	10th Oct. 1865	John Garnum Woodward.

Subject-matter of Patent.	Number of Patent.	Date.	Name of Patentee.
STEAM-BOILERS, &c.—continued.			
Improvements in the construction of steam generators, applicable also to the construction of condensers, the heating of water generally, and to the warming of buildings. (Communicated by Joseph Harrison, jun'., and Thomas Luders.)	2510	10th Oct. 1865	John Henry Johnson.
Railway carriages and locomotives . . . (Communicated by Henry Gifford.)	2521	11th Oct. 1865	Michael Henry.
Improvements in steam-boilers and other apparatus applicable to the heating and evaporation of liquids, parts of which improvements are applicable also to other purposes . . .	2561	16th Oct. 1865	Francis Wise. Edward Field. Enoch Harrison Aydon.
Caloric or hot air engines . . . . (Communicated by Ouillaume Reinlein.)	2575	17th Oct. 1865	Richard Archibald Brooman.
A new or improved steam condensing apparatus, or an apparatus intended to make available as fuel all or part of the steam actually evolving from engines into the atmosphere, and also to absorb the smoke resulting from the combustion.	2576	17th Oct. 1865	François Georges Sicardo.
Furnaces	2583	17th Oct. 1865	William Beardmore.
An improved apparatus for forming or repairing the moulds of boiler and other tubes. (Communicated by Edward Clark.)	2607	19th Oct. 1865	George Beverly Ghinelin.
Improvements in the manufacture of inflammable gases and in their application to useful purposes. (for generation of steam.)	2716	21st Oct. 1865	Isham Baggs.
Steam-boilers	2733	23rd Oct. 1865	Alexander Chaplin.
Construction of furnaces and boilers for the consumption of smoke	2746	24th Oct. 1865	Charles Matthews. Henry Booth Southwick. John Fereday.
Generating steam in combined vertical cylinders .	2776	24th Oct. 1865	Thomas Brown Jordan.
Improvements in steam hammers and in means of applying them to the manufacture of boilers and tubes.	2806	31st Oct. 1865	Charles Emmet.
Improvements in generating and applying certain gases, and in apparatus to be employed therein. (heating steam-boilers.)	2833	2nd Nov. 1865	James Webster.
An improved non-conducting composition for preventing the radiation or transmission of heat or cold. (for coating steam-boilers.) .	2853	4th Nov. 1865	James Thyr.
Railway steam-engines and carriages . . (constructing the boiler.)	2925	14th Nov. 1865	Joseph Alphonse Loubat.
An improved method of utilising the waste heat of coke ovens. (requiring water.) (Communicated by Antoine Berhier-Perraton.)	3040	24th Nov. 1865	William Edward Gedge.
Furnaces	3095	2nd Dec. 1865	Edward Brown Wilson.
Improvements in steam-boilers and in the furnaces and grates thereof, the same improvements in furnaces and grates being also applicable to other furnaces and to stoves. (Communicated by Robert Winslow Davis, Daniel Davis and Henry Sheldon Anable.)	3141	6th Dec. 1865	William Edward Newton.
Improvements in steam-boilers and in apparatus adapted for cleaning the flues of boilers.	3194	9th Dec. 1865	Norman Willis Wheeler.

Subject-matter of Patent.	Number of Patent.	Date.	Name of Patentee.

Steam-boilers, &c. — continued.

Improvements in locomotive engines and in the means employed for generating steam therein.	6105	9th Dec. 1866	Robert Francis Fairlie.
Steam-boilers or apparatus for generating steam -	5161	11th Dec. 1865	John Townsend.
An improved construction of tool for cutting tubes. (boiler tubes.) (Communicated by David Mosher Nichols.)	5314	13th Dec. 1866	Alfred Vincent Newton.
An improved boiler for generating steam or vapour	3235	14th Dec. 1865	John Clark Wise.
Improved apparatus for manufacturing paper pulp (arranging a rotating boiler.)	5243	14th Dec. 1866	William Alfred West.
Boilers or apparatus for generating steam -	6200	16th Dec. 1866	Richard Archibald Brooman.
(Communicated by Julien Belleville.)			
Corks or valves (for steam-boilers.) (Communicated by Henry Mouro.)	3383	23rd Dec. 1865	Charles Woodward Harrison.
Steam-boilers or generators -	3369	29th Dec. 1865	Andrew Barclay.

See also " Furnaces."*
See also " Gauges."*

XI.—Cleansing and Preventing Incrustation of Boilers; Purifying the Water.

Certain improvements in the construction of tubular boilers and in the means for cleaning the tubes of such boilers -	57	5th Jan. 1865	James Chapman Ince. William Anderson.
A method of and apparatus for preventing incrustations or calcareous deposits in steam-boilers. (Communicated by Alexander Forbes Porter.)	119	14th Jan. 1865	George Davies.
A new or improved apparatus applicable to steam-boilers for preventing deposits therein. (Communicated by Louis Hippolyte Courtois-Haubert.)	219	26th Jan. 1865	Charles Denton Abel.
Steam-boilers -	401	13th Feb. 1866	Robert William Thomson.
Improvements in the fitting of surface condensory tubes, and in the tools to be used therein, and in the means of retarding corrosion in steam-boilers. (Communicated by William Judson.)	1138	23rd April 1866	Alfred Vincent Newton.
An improved composition for preventing incrustation in steam-boilers.	1334	19th May 1865	William Hewitt.
Instruments or apparatus for cleaning the interior of tubes or hollow cylinders, gas chimneys and other hollow articles. (flues of steam-boilers.)	1479	30th May 1865	James Hart the younger.
Improvements in the manufacture of paper and paper stock, and in the utilisation of certain waste products resulting therefrom. (to prevent incrustation in steam-boilers.)	1602	13th June 1865	Thomas Rumsler. William Henry Robertson.
Generating steam -	1622	15th June 1865	Matthew Piers Watt Boulton.
Preventing the incrustation of steam-boilers (Communicated by Charles James Eames.)	1784	29th June 1865	William Edward Newton.

Subject-matter of Patent.	Number of Patent.	Date.	Name of Patentee.
STEAM-BOILERS, &c. —*continued.*			
Apparatus for preventing incrustation in steam-boilers, and for preventing explosion of such boilers, heating the feed water, and consuming smoke - - - - -	2272	4th Sept. 1865	James Howard. William Stafford. William Porter McCallum.
An improved method of fixing and unfixing the tubes of steam-boilers. (*Communicated by Daniel M'Dowell.*)	2284	6th Sept. 1865	Samuel Rowter.
An improved mode of removing and preventing the incrustation of steam-boilers - -	2321	11th Sept. 1865	William Tyne. Stephen Tyne. Robert Clayton.
An improved composition for preventing incrustation in steam-boilers - - - -	2322	11th Sept. 1865	William Howitt.
Improved apparatus for cleaning the tubes of steam-boilers. (*Communicated by Daniel M'Dowell.*)	2346	13th Sept. 1865	Samuel Rowter.
An improved liquid compound for purifying sea and other waters. (*preventing incrustation.*) (*Communicated by Léandre Denjou.*)	2546	13th Oct. 1865	Richard Archibald Broomen.
Improvements in steam-boilers and other apparatus applicable to the heating and evaporation of liquids, parts of which improvements are applicable also to other purposes - - -	2582	16th Oct. 1865	Francis Wise. Edward Field Enoch Harrison Ayden.
An improved mode of and apparatus for cleaning the tubes of steam-boilers. (*Communicated by Abraham Egraton.*)	2761	26th Oct. 1865	George Davies.
Apparatus for preventing incrustation in steam-boilers.	3182	5th Dec. 1865	Josef Toth.
Boilers or apparatus for generating steam - - (*arising from deposit or incrustation.*) (*Communicated by Julius Belleville.*)	3260	14th Dec. 1865	Richard Archibald Broomen.
XIX.—Water-heating Apparatus for Boilers; Heating Feed-water.			
Improvements in and applicable to that and similar apparatus for raising and forcing fluids and feeding steam-boilers, known as "Giffard's Injector."	410	14th Feb. 1865	James Gresham.
An improved construction of Giffard injector - (*Communicated by William Sellers.*)	1051	12th April 1865	Alfred Vincent Newton.
Apparatus for feeding boilers, raising water and propelling vessels. (*Communicated by Pierre Sennin.*)	1061	13th April 1865	Richard Archibald Broomen.
An improved apparatus for condensing steam and feeding boilers with the product therefrom.	1180	27th April 1865	Anthony Francis.
Improvements in steam generators and engines, and in apparatus for feeding steam generators. (*Communicated by George Bailey Brayton.*)	1240	3rd May 1865	John Henry Johnson.
Improvements in surface condensers for steam-engines, and in feeding boilers therefrom.	1669	21st June 1865	Charles Talbot Porter.
Improved apparatus for supplying boilers with water. (*Communicated by Gustav Adolph Riedel.*)	2211	28th Aug. 1865	Alfred Vincent Newton.

Subject-matter of Patent.	Number of Patent.	Date.	Name of Patentee.
STEAM-BOILERS, &c.—continued.			
Apparatus for preventing incrustation in steam-boilers, and for preventing explosion of such boilers, heating the feed water, and consuming smoke	2278	4th Sept. 1865	James Howard, William Bedford, William Porter & Co.
Furnaces of and means of heating the feed water for steam-boilers.	2712	30th Oct. 1865	John White.
An improved self-acting boiler feeder, or apparatus for supplying steam-boilers with water.	2840	4th Nov. 1865	Patrick Benignus O'Neil
Apparatus for heating the feed water for steam-boilers.	2870	13th Nov. 1865	James Hayward Whitehead.
Certain apparatus for injecting and ejecting fluids and liquids.	3176	9th Dec. 1865	Andrew Barclay.
Pumps (for feeding boilers.)	3320	23rd Dec. 1865	Henry Davis Bedell, William Eburah Brain
Improvements in distilling and in relieving distilled and other liquids from gases mechanically mixed therewith. (used in supplying boilers.)	3361	27th Dec. 1865	Norman Wells Wheeler.
STEAM-ENGINES (Stationary, Locomotive and Marine).			
Improvements in the manufacture of elastic packings for pistons, and in lubricating compositions therefor.	10	4th Jan. 1865	Edward Kirby.
Improvements in locomotive engines and in the springs of railway carriages.	85	5th Jan. 1865	James Edward Wise
Locomotive engines (Communicated by Auguste De Bergue.)	48	6th Jan. 1865	Charles De Bergue.
Regulating and working the valves of steam and other engines.	93	11th Jan. 1865	John Frederick Spencer.
Steam-engines (Communicated by Philibert Vabre.)	113	13th Jan. 1865	William Brooks.
Apparatus for transmitting and converting reciprocating motion into rotary motion, applicable to various useful purposes. (locomotive engines.)	148	17th Jan. 1865	William John Oatway Botham.
Improvements in the packings of pistons and piston rods of pumps and steam and other engines, which improvements are also applicable to hydraulic presses.	155	18th Jan. 1865	William Robert Foster
Improved arrangements for coupling steam-engines, turbines or other apparatus employed as motive-power. (Communicated by Ludwig August Riedinger.)	159	19th Jan. 1865	Adolf Wilhelm Prager
Steam-engines	166	19th Jan. 1865	William Cleveland Birt
Locomotive and other steam-engines	167	19th Jan. 1865	Thomas Charles Dorler
Steam-engines	183	21st Jan. 1865	Thomas Lester.
Improved apparatus for adjusting the weight of railway carriages and engines. (Communicated by Johann Heinrich Ehrhardt.)	216	25th Jan. 1865	Otto Odiwell.

Subject-matter of Patent.	Number of Patent.	Date.	Name of Patentee.
STEAM-ENGINES—*continued.*			
Construction of steam-engines (*Communicated by Pierre Jean Laroste.*)	360	30th Jan. 1865	George Davis.
The application of hydro-electricity to steam for the purpose of increasing its expansion and power, and the machinery or apparatus connected therewith, and also the application of galvano or frictional electricity for the same purpose	373	31st Jan. 1865	{ Joseph Fletcher. Daniel Hamer. }
An improved construction of lubricating apparatus for steam-engine purposes	374	31st Jan. 1865	{ Ewing Pye Colquhoun. John Pardoe Ferris. }
Steam-engines	639	7th Feb. 1865	Charles Langley.
Expansive gear for steam-engines	415	14th Feb. 1865	William Fothergill Batho.
Beam engines	428	18th Feb. 1865	James Grafton Jones.
Steam-engines	465	21st Feb. 1865	John Russell Swann.
A new and improved balanced slide valve (*Communicated by James Rawlin.*)	496	23rd Feb. 1865	William Edward Newton.
Steam-engines applicable to ploughing and other agricultural purposes.	582	24th Feb. 1865	James Howard.
Marine steam-engines	643	9th March 1865	John Dean.
Motive-power engines (*Communicated by Auguste Cerin.*)	651	9th March 1865	William Clark.
Increasing the mechanical value of steam as a motive agent. (*Communicated by Thomas Rowland.*)	745	17th March 1865	Benjamin Lawrence.
Improved combinations of direct acting steam-engines with single or double acting pumps, for pumping water, air or gases.	751	17th March 1865	Jacob Goodfellow.
Locomotive engines and carriages for common roads and tramways, and also for agricultural and other purposes.	780	20th March 1865	Alexander Richard Mackenzie.
Double cylinder steam-engines	860	27th March 1865	Joshua Rooke.
Traction engines	863	27th March 1865	{ John Bruckshaw. William Scott Underhill. }
Improvements in the construction of locomotive engines and railway carriages, for facilitating their passage round curves. (*Communicated by George John Horner.*)	916	31st March 1865	{ George Robert Stephenson. George Henry Phipps. }
Improvements in paddle wheels, parts of which are applicable to other purposes. (*to steam-engines.*)	935	3rd April 1865	William Cantrill Gollings.
Means or apparatus for obtaining motive-power by the aid of steam, gas or other fluids. (*Communicated by Joseph Ferrigault, Marie Joseph Denis Farcot, Jean Joseph Leon Farcot, Michel Basile Abel Farcot, Joseph Etienne Eloi Chaleron and Emmanuel Denis Farcot.*)	949	4th April 1865	William Brookes.
Improvements in steam and atmospheric hammers and presses, which improvements are also applicable to steam-engines.	953	4th April 1865	Joseph Vaughan.
Traction engines	957	4th April 1865	John Guy Newton Alleyne.
Apparatus employed to actuate the valves of engines worked by steam, air or other fluid.	982	6th April 1865	James Grafton Jones.

Subject-matter of Patent.	Number of Patent.	Date.	Name of Patentee.
STEAM-ENGINES—*continued.*			
An improved application of steam power to locomotion on ordinary roads. (*Communicated by Alfred Tailleradeau.*)	1002	9th April 1865	William Edward Gedge
Improvements in steam-engines relating to valve motions governors and drain pipes	1105	25th April 1865	Andrew Wylie, John M'Farlane Gray
Marine steam-engines	1213	1st May 1865	Daniel Rankin
Improvements in steam generators and engines and in apparatus for feeding steam generators. (*Communicated by George Henley Brayton.*)	1240	3rd May 1865	John Henry Johnson
Improvements in or applicable to marine condensing steam-engines.	1253	4th May 1865	Thomas Wood
Steam-engines (*Communicated by Ebenezer Denford.*)	1264	6th May 1865	William Edward Newton
Mode of and apparatus for obtaining and applying motive-power	1603	10th May 1865	Stanislas Painpeyni, Michel Mycahla
Means and apparatus for effecting traction on railways and roads where traction is used	1522	12th May 1865	Richard Edward Donovan, Daniel O'Brien
Locomotive engines	1560	16th May 1865	Walter Montgomery
A new system of rotative machinery to be used as steam-engines and water pumps.	1447	26th May 1865	Jean Alphonse Ransel
A new or improved machine for obtaining motive-power and other useful purposes.	1466	29th May 1865	Henry Manley
Certain improvements in steam hammers, partly applicable to steam-engines.	1431	31st May 1866	Peter Pilkington
Improvements in machinery or apparatus for actuating the slide-valves of marine engines and in the slide-valves thereof.	1528	5th June 1865	John Robertson
An improved break applicable to various descriptions of steam-engines and also to railway purposes. (*Communicated by Baptist Dalbeil.*)	1549	5th June 1865	Frederick Tolhurst
An improved metallic stuffing box	1555	7th June 1865	Victor Delaunt
Improvements in safety valves, which improvements are also applicable to steam-engine and other valves	1575	9th June 1865	Charles Fernne, William Hodrkan
Improvements in the permanent way of railways and in locomotives applicable thereto.	1583	12th June 1865	William James Rent
Locomotive engines and railway carriages	1646	19th June 1865	George Smith younger.
Improvements in surface condensers for steam-engines and in feeding boilers therefrom.	1669	21st June 1865	Charles Talbot Ascott
Surface condensers (*Communicated by Albon Cracker Stimers.*)	1677	22nd June 1865	William Edward Kent
Improvements in steam-boilers, furnaces and engines, and in parts connected therewith.	1745	30th June 1865	Edwin Elliot
Locomotive engines (*Communicated by Augusto de Bergue.*)	1754	3rd July 1865	Charles De Bergue
Steam pumping machines or engines	1760	3rd July 1865	Martin Bassett
Improvements in locomotive engines and in springs of railway carriages.	1769	4th July 1865	James Edward Wise
Means and apparatus for increasing the mechanical power of steam.	1880	10th July 1865	William Alexander Lyon

Subject-matter of Patent.	Number of Patent.	Date.	Name of Patentee.
AR-ENGINES—*continued.*			
in steam carriages and in adapting common roads to railways. *sed by Joseph Alphonse Lambot.)*	1821	10th July 1865	Richard Archibald Brooman.
ive-power . . . . - *tted by Monsieur Charles Tellier.)*	1822	11th July 1865	Hector Auguste Dufresť.
et valves -	1834	11th July 1865	Nathaniel Jenkins.
es . . . . . - *sed by Alexander Kevan Richards.)*	1886	11th July 1865	Morris Harvey Kuron.
- . . . . . -	1893	20th July 1865	Richard Clark Bristol.
paratus for steam-engines . -	1897	20th July 1865	Morgan Lawrence Parry.
f valves for steam and other engines - *tted by Thomas Shrimton Davis.)*	1913	22nd July 1865	William Edward Newton.
eam valves - . . . -	1966	24th July 1865	William Edward Newton.
tted by John Wraley Corbett.)			
ter motor, which may be employed learn or gas engine. *ted by Henry Isham.)*	1968	24th July 1865	William Edward Newton.
ive-power by heat . - -	1992	1st Aug. 1865	Matthew Piers Watt Boulton.
in and apparatus for treating peat in taining it therefrom, also applicable l cultivating and - -	2004	2nd Aug. 1865	Charles Hodgson.
licable as a motive-power engine, a d motor. *ted by Francis Bernard de Kerausnes.)*	2021	4th Aug. 1865	William Clark.
f steam-engines - - -	2067	9th Aug. 1865	Henry Cartwright.
ode of relieving slide-valves of back	2069	9th Aug. 1865	James William Longstaff.
btaining and applying motive-power } cful purposes . . }	2080	11th Aug. 1865	William Thomas Cole. Henry Spink Swift. Augusto Soares.
- . . . . - *ted by Giovanni Batista Vrasens.)*	2180	14th Aug. 1865	James Stevenson.
ments in rotatory engines - -	2202	24th Aug. 1865	William Graham. John Broughton. Thomas Corkhill.
s and other vehicles . -	2254	20th Aug. 1865	Samuel Lawrence James.
rments in steam-engines and valves - *ted by George Ichabod Washburn.)*	2296	6th Sept. 1865	William Clark.
of and apparatus for condensing the m-engines.	2378	18th Sept. 1865	Francesco Dalne.
n locomotive engines, parts of which s are also applicable to railway car-	2379	19th Sept. 1865	Russel Aitken.
abricating machinery - - *es.)* *ted by Joseph Bonillon.)*	2429	23rd Sept. 1865	Henri Adrien Bonneville.
unstruction of engine which can be - a motor or for pumping. *ed by John Benjamin Root and enjamin.)*	2453	25th Sept. 1865	William Edward Newton.
ring tubes in tube plates, and for rs where concentrated power or necessary. *ng piston packing rings.)*	2465	26th Sept. 1865	Richard Taylor Nelson Howey.

See also "GUAGES,"
See also "GOVERNORS."

Subject-matter of Patent.	Number of Patent.	Date.	Name of Patentee.
STEERING OR GUIDING SHIPS, CARRIAGES, PLOUGHS, &c.			
A new or improved hydraulic steering apparatus and rudder break . . . . }	115	14th Jan. 1865	{ Alfred Paul. Edwin Paul.
Differential wheel gearing . . . (for steering.)	744	17th March 1865	John Standfield.
Traction engines . . . . } (apparatus for steering.)	803	27th March 1865	John Brockshaw. William Hoyet Underhill.
Navigable balloons	630	1st April 1865	Paul Hærnlein.
A new apparatus or mechanism for flying through the air.	1037	12th April 1865	Gustave Wilhelm Rothleb.
Machinery for cultivating land . . . (Partly communicated by Max Eyth.)	1104	20th April 1865	David Greig.
Improvements in the construction of ships of war and floating batteries, part of which improvements are applicable to land fortifications.	1107	20th April 1865	Henry Caudwell.
Improvements in steering ships or vessels, and in the machinery or apparatus connected therewith.	1187	25th April 1865	William Elder.
Apparatus for steering ships, steamboats and other sailing vessels.	1804	20th May 1865	John Martin.
Apparatus for propelling and steering vessels .	1461	30th May 1865	Jonathan Jopling.
Improved mechanical arrangements for steering ships and other navigable vessels.	1499	31st May 1865	William Augustus Brown.
Apparatus for steering ships and vessels . .	1577	9th June 1865	William Horatio Harfield.
Improvements in the permanent way of railways and in locomotives applicable thereto.	1598	12th June 1865	William James Hixon.
Improvements in steam carriages and in adapting wheels for common roads to railways. (Communicated by Joseph Alphonse Loubat.)	1691	10th July 1865	Richard Archibald Brockman.
Traction engines . . . . (Communicated by Alexander Kevse Richards.)	1820	11th July 1865	Morris Horwry Kerns.
Rudders for steering ships or vessels . .	1919	24th July 1865	John M'Grigor Croft.
Traction engines and other vehicles . . (steering wheels.)	2234	30th Aug. 1865	Samuel Lawrence James.
Improvements in the propelling and steering of steam ships or other vessels, and in the machinery or apparatus employed therefor.	2563	5th Oct. 1865	Robert William Fraser.
Carriages propelled by manual power . . (and guiding carriages.)	2625	11th Oct. 1865	Thomas Du Boulay.
Steering indicators and tell-tales . .	2884	7th Nov. 1865	Charles Jullien Viehoff. James Adolphe Matthiessen.
Steering gear for navigable vessels . . } (Hydraulic gear.)	2885	7th Nov. 1865	{ William Esplen. James Clarke.
Means of and apparatus for steering ships and other floating bodies . . . . }	2938	13th Nov. 1865	Charles Atherton. Amherst Hawker Renton.
An improved construction of steering apparatus .	3171	9th Dec. 1865	Samuel Clark.
Steering indicators and tell-tales . . .	3341	26th Dec. 1865	Charles Jullien Viehoff. James Adolphe Matthiessen.

Subject-matter of Patent.	Number of Patent.	Date.	Name of Patentee.

STEELING, &c.——continued.

| Rudders · · · · · · | 3297 | 25th Dec. 1865 | James Robert Napier. William John Macquorn Rankine. |

For Ships' Compasses, see "COMPASSES."

STONE AND SLATE, ARTIFICIAL STONE AND MARBLE; GRINDSTONE AND MILLSTONE.

Improved means or apparatus for facing flags or smoothing the surface of stones - - -	154	18th Jan. 1865	James Comley. Herbert Haynes.
Improvements in the grinding and feeding apparatus of mills for grinding corn and other substances, and in the combination of such mills with flour dressing machines - - -	206	24th Jan. 1865	Richard Robert Ecles. Charles James Watts.
An improvement in the manufacture of artificial stone for building and other purposes.	441	16th Feb. 1865	William Savage.
Improved machinery or apparatus for squaring slabs, marbles, slates and bricks - - -	688	11th March 1865	Joseph Hurd. Joshua Wallet.
Machinery for cutting and dressing stones and other hard substances. (Communicated by Gustavus Clappers.)	1083	19th April 1865	Maurice Vogl.
Manufacture of slabs, brasses and other articles of artificial stone where great strength is required.	1287	13th May 1865	Frederick Ransome.
Apparatus for polishing, smoothing or facing, especially applicable to lithographic stones.	1668	21st June 1865	Charles Henry Gurber.
Manufacture of terra-cotta or vitreous stone - -	2071	10th Aug. 1865	Mark Henry Blanchard.
Saws for moving and cutting marble and other analogous substances.	2188	25th Aug. 1865	Edward Henry Woodard.
Improved machinery for cutting stone - - - (Communicated by George Jeffords Wardwell.)	2282	15th Sept. 1865	Alfred Vincent Newton.
Machinery for grinding, dressing, smoothing or polishing flags and stones, without the use of the ordinary cutting tools - - -	2412	21st Sept. 1865	Benjamin Chaffer. James Thompson. Charles Thompson.
An improved liquid composition for cleansing, scouring and bleaching textile animal, mineral and vegetable substances - - - (cleansing stone and marble.)	2440	23rd Sept. 1865	Gustave Emile Rolland. Emile Léon Rolland.
Constructing and mounting or hanging mill-stones	2592	18th Oct. 1865	William Henry Parker.
Machinery for dressing mill-stones - - - (Communicated by Eleazer A. Paine.)	2817	1st Nov. 1865	Alfred Vincent Newton.
Mounting and driving mill-stones - - -	2830	3rd Nov. 1865	Richard Smith, jun.
Manufacture of bricks and artificial stone and marble.	2847	7th Nov. 1865	David Barker.
An improved mode of ventilating mill-stones - (Communicated by Alexandre Désiré Lespagnou.)	2924	13th Nov. 1865	Henry Edward Newton.
An improved system of pavement to supersede the macadamised system used in the main streets of large cities and causeways subject to a great circulation of vehicles. (fictitious flagstone.)	3035	25th Nov. 1865	Theophilus Barrow.

Subject-matter of Patent.	Number of Patent.	Date.	Name of Patentee.
STONE, &c.—continued.			
An improved composition for enamel, paint, varnish, cement or plaster. *(for artificial stone or marble.)* *(Communicated by William Barney Watkins.)*	3042	27th Nov. 1865	William Robert Lake.
A new or improved cement or composition, applicable to the agglomeration or moulding of various materials, and to other useful and decorative purposes. *(ashlar stone.)* *(Communicated by Stanislas Sorel and Emile Justin Mercier.)*	3119	5th Dec. 1865	Richard Archibald Brooman.
For Preserving stone, see "PRESERVING WOOD." For Breaking Stones, see "GRINDING MINERALS."			
STRAPS, DRIVING-BANDS AND BELTS.			
Manufacture of boots, shoes, saddlery, harness and other articles. *(driving straps.)* *(Communicated by Toussaint Landrin.)*	160	19th Jan. 1865	William Clark.
Manufacture of driving bands or belts for machinery and other purposes	300	3rd Feb. 1865	{ George Hern. Daniel Hern.
Waterproofing skins, hides and leather . . . *(bands for steam-engines.)*	415	14th Feb. 1865	George Harton.
Apparatus used for bracing the ends of walking sticks, and the skirts or handles of umbrellas and parasols . . .	682	10th March 1865	{ Jonhas Jones. Richard Daniel Jones.
Fasteners for driving-bands, straps, belts, harness or other such like purposes . . .	1282	1st May 1865	{ Joseph Felix Allender. Thomas Frederick Coshan.
Means or apparatus for producing friction or adhesion between pulleys, rollers and the like, and cords, bands, belts or chains passed over or round them.	1927	25th July 1865	Martyn John Roberts.
An improved mode of lacing boots, shoes and other articles united by laces. *(driving belts.)* *(Communicated by Von Hoyener.)*	1981	26th July 1865	John Henry Johnson.
Apparatus for elongating and contracting waist and other belts, which apparatus is also applicable for other purposes . . . *(driving-bands.)*	2236	25th Aug. 1865	{ George Frederick White. Harvey Chamberlain.
Tanning or treating hides applicable for machine bands and other purposes.	2601	7th Oct. 1865	William Harris.
Manufacture of bands, belts, or straps for harness, for driving machinery or for other purposes.	2619	11th Oct. 1865	James Cratchett.
A new composition of india-rubber mastic or cement, made in a more or less fluid state according to the use to be made of it, and the process or contrivance for applying the same. *(cutting straps for machinery.)*	2630	12th Oct. 1865	Auguste Aimé Lervaard.

Subject-matter of Patent.	Number of Patent.	Date.	Name of Patentee.
STRAPS, &c. — continued.			
Fasteners for driving bands, straps, belts, harness or other such like purposes - -	2802	31st Oct. 1865	Thomas Frederick Cashin. Joseph Felix Allender.
Manufacture of leather driving-belts - -	3149	7th Dec. 1865	Charle Duchenne Hitchcock. John Khimmxn.
Certain improvements in the method of attaching and securing together the ends of strapping employed in machinery.	3309	21st Dec. 1865	William Barnsley.
Obtaining and employing continuous lengths of tanned leather for various useful purposes - (*for driving-bands.*)	3334	23rd Dec. 1865	George Horn. Daniel Horn.
SUGAR AND SYRUPS.			
A new system of boiling grain sugar in vacuo -	43	6th Jan. 1865	John Lehundy.
Construction of vacuum pans - - -	67	7th Jan. 1865	Edward Reeves. Conrad William Fiegel.
A new process of manufacturing syrup and sugar from maize and other cereal grains. (*Communicated by Frederick William Gormling.*)	221	26th Jan. 1865	George Haseltine.
An improved process of manufacturing syrup and sugar from maize starch and other cereal grain starch. (*Communicated by Frederick William Gormling.*)	240	24th Jan. 1865	George Haseltine.
Filtering apparatus - - - (*for saccharine solutions.*)	249	24th Jan. 1865	Victor Burq.
Improvements in the mode of treating for evaporating and concentrating purposes, saccharine juice and machinse and other solutions and liquids, and also in machinery or apparatus for the concentration of cane juice and saccharine and other solutions, and for the evaporation of liquids.	418	14th Feb. 1865	Alfred Fryer.
Improvements in refining sugar and in apparatus employed therein. (*Communicated by Alfred Guillou.*)	599	3rd March 1865	Richard Archibald Brosman.
Improved apparatus for expressing liquids from pulpy and semi-fluid substances. (*from beet root for sugar making.*) (*Communicated by Louis Pierre Robert de Massy.*)	988	4th April 1865	William Edward Newton.
Preparation of materials to be used as substitutes for animal charcoal - - (*for sugar refining.*)	1409	22nd May 1865	Richard Müller. Arthur Thomas Wild. John Folliott Powell.
Obtaining jellies, syrups, drinks and other products from the tree Arbutus Uordo, known as the Arbutus.	1640	20th June 1865	Philippe Mingaud.
Improvements in the raising, lifting or drawing and forcing of water and other liquids, and in the apparatus and means employed therefor - (*for sugar houses.*)	1996	2nd Aug. 1865	James M'Ewan. William Nelson.

Subject-matter of Patent.	Number of Patent.	Date.	Name of Patentee.
SUGAR, &c.—continued.			
Apparatus for filtering sugar and other liquid solutions	2082	4th Aug. 1865	Jean Adolphe Leon. George Trairmond. John Kissock.
Improvements in supplying charcoal to sugar decolorising vessels, and in apparatus therefor.	2296	7th Sept. 1865	James Davies.
Improvements in the machinery or apparatus and in the process for the treatment and manufacture of sugar.	2365	19th Sept. 1865	John Fletcher.
Manufacture of materials for decoloring sugar and other saccharine and liquid matters. (Communicated by Christian Jean Goode.)	2402	21st Sept. 1865	William Clark.
Improvements in evaporating and distilling liquids, and in the apparatus employed therein. (making sugar.)	2500	7th Oct. 1865	Tomlin Campbell.
Means and apparatus to be employed in the manufacture of sugar. (Partly communicated by Absalom Hippolyte Lepley.)	2606	10th Oct. 1865	Jean Adolphe Leon.
Improved means and apparatus for the cleansing or bleaching of sugar, which said means and apparatus are also applicable for other useful purposes of a like character.	2872	7th Nov. 1865	Gustavus Adolphus Jasper
An improved manufacture of caramel ("burnt sugar.") (Communicated by Thaddeus Hyatt.)	2960	16th Nov. 1865	Alfred Vincent Newton.
Manufacture of materials for decoloring sugar and other saccharine matters. (Communicated by Christian Jean Goode.)	3078	30th Nov. 1865	William Clark.
SULPHUR.			
Obtaining certain compounds of nitrogen and of sulphur . . . . . (see "ACIDS.")	1366	19th May 1865	Thomas Richardson. Martin Frederick Röcker.
Improvements in condensing and utilising sulphurous smokes and vapours, and in apparatus to be used for that purpose. (obtaining flowers of sulphur.)	2216	29th Aug. 1865	Adolf Gurlt.
Apparatus used for calcining and roasting copper and other ores and substances containing sulphur. (see "ACIDS.")	2350	11th Sept. 1865	Thomas Bell. Thomas Leslie Gregson Bell.
Treating soda waste to obtain sulphur therefrom -	2443	23rd Sept. 1865	Max Schaffner.
Means of securing the handles of table knives and forks and other similar articles. (with sulphur.)	2571	16th Oct. 1865	Thomas M'Grah.
Improvements in the manufacture of sulphur by the reduction of the sulphurous acid accruing from the roasting of sulphuretted ores, and in apparatus for the same.	2896	21st Nov. 1865	Alexandre Calley St. Paul de Sincay.
Treating the oxide of iron residues of gas purifying, in order principally to extract sulphur therefrom.	6099	2nd Dec. 1865	Thomas Bell.

Subject-matter of Patent.	Number of Patent.	Date.	Name of Patentee.
SULPHUR—*continued.*			
Treatment of sulphurous and arsenical pyrites containing copper and tin.	3250	16th Dec. 1865	Charles Petapilly.
Improvements in smelting copper and in obtaining products from the gases and vapours given off during the said smelting. (*ordinary sulphur.*)	3287	19th Dec. 1865	Henry Caesar Ezml
SURGERY, SURGICAL INSTRUMENTS, SPLINTS, AND BANDAGES, TRUSSES FOR HERNIA; ARTIFICIAL LIMBS, INVALID FURNITURE.			
An improved portable pneumatic apparatus applicable in surgery and medicine for all purposes as a douche, for affusion, irrigation, injection, and for enemas.	19	3rd Jan. 1865	Thomas John Ashton
Certain improvements in the manufacture of lint	75	10th Jan. 1865	Samuel Shaw Brown
Portable invalid or bed-tables	625	24th Feb. 1865	Charles James Row.
Construction of a portable vehicle for teaching children to walk and giving assistance to invalids	657	25th Feb. 1865	John Ashew.
An improved instrument for concentrating light, applicable to dental, surgical and other operations.	591	2nd March 1865	Charles Rahn.
An improved abdominal and scrotal bandage	1016	10th April 1865	Allen Stewart.
A new or improved table and support for invalids	1088	15th April 1865	Thomas Edward Hastie
Invalid carriages (*Communicated by Auguste Quidron.*)	1130	21st April 1865	Henry Edward Newton
An improved pessary (*Communicated by Louis Auguste Rigaux.*)	1161	24th April 1865	William Edward Gedge
Artificial arms and hands (*Communicated by Thomas Urve.*)	1185	27th April 1865	William Edward Newton
An improved cased splint for fractures	1587	13th June 1865	Charles Alfred Flemingworth
A new or improved instrument to be employed in examining and facilitating operations in the throat. (*Communicated by Philippe Othon de Clermont.*)	1921	24th July 1865	Richard Archibald Brennan.
Apparatus for elongating and contracting waist and other hales, which apparatus is also applicable for other purposes (*surgical bandages.*)	2234	29th Aug. 1865	George Frederick Winn Harvey Chamberlain.
Improvements in rules for measuring, and in other instruments or articles requiring to be adjusted or disposed at various angles. (*surgical instruments.*)	2615	10th Oct. 1865	Arthur Nicholls.
Artificial eyes	2815	1st Nov. 1865	Auguste Boissonneau.
An improved splint for surgical purposes	2871	7th Nov. 1865	Henry Hide.
Apparatus for facilitating the walking of invalids	2873	7th Nov. 1865	Francis Graham Brown M.R.C.S.
A new or improved elastic belt or band truss	3017	24th Nov. 1865	Charles Bonbor.

Subject-matter of Patent.	Number of Patent.	Date.	Name of Patentee.

SURGERY, &c.—continued.

Improvements in the manufacture or production of stays, corsets and bodices and other similar articles of dress, and in the fastenings for same. (applicable to knee caps.)	3072	24th Nov. 1865	Stephen Dixon.
Construction of artificial arms - - - (Communicated by Thomas Urre.)	3114	4th Dec. 1865	William Edward Newton.
An improved truss - - - -	3203	12th Dec. 1865	Christopher Eaaby.

TAR AND RESIN.

An improved method of treating apatite and other mineral phosphates. (obtaining phosphorus.) (Communicated by Mr. John Oliver.)	8	2nd Jan. 1865	Montagus Richard Leverson.
Treating the pitch obtained in or resulting from the distillation of palm oil and other fats, in candle making.	9	2nd Jan. 1865	Robert Irvine.
Extracting turpentine and tar from resinous wood -	405	13th Feb. 1865	Jean Antoine Pastorelly.
A new or improved method of dissolving pitch - (Communicated by François Colestin Armelin.)	1770	4th July 1865	Richard Archibald Brooman.
An improvement in the treatment of tar and other substances suitable to be used in the manufacture of paint and for other purposes.	2191	25th Aug. 1865	John Moule.
Obtaining spirits of turpentine, resin, pitch, tar, pyroligneous acid and other products, from wood. (Communicated by Albert Hamilton Emery.)	2247	31st Aug. 1865	William Edward Newton.

TELEGRAPHS (Electric); TELEGRAPHIC PRINTING APPARATUS.

Electro-magnets and their application to telegraphic and other purposes. (Communicated by Charles Frédéric Carlier.)	22	4th Jan. 1865	William Clark.
Apparatus used in train signalling on railways -	52	6th Jan. 1865	Edward Tyer.
Coverings of telegraphic conductors and cables -	96	12th Jan. 1865	John Fuller.
An improved system and apparatus for facilitating the working of submarine cables and other conductors of electricity.	156	19th Jan. 1865	Silvanus Frederick Van Choate.
Improvements in rail and tramways, in laying electric telegraph wires, and in compositions for insulating the same. (Communicated by Jean Armand Émile Lahoublère.)	389	31st Jan. 1865	Richard Archibald Brooman.
A new or improved insulating material for telegraphic and other purposes, together with an improvement in protecting telegraph wires, especially applicable to submarine and subterranean telegraphs. (Communicated by John Erdmann.)	369	9th Feb. 1865	William Alfred Marshall.

Subject-matter of Patent.	Number of Patent.	Date.	Name of Patentee.
TELEGRAPHS, &c. —continued.			
Improved apparatus for the protection of houses and property from burglars, parts of the invention being applicable for other purposes.	519	6th March 1865	Cromwell Fleetwood Varley.
Electric telegraphs - - - - (Communicated by Gaetano Bonelli.)	678	10th March 1865	Harry Whinside Cock.
Apparatus for protecting telegraphic instruments from injury from atmospheric or static electricity.	718	14th March 1865	Augustus Bartsch.
Posts or supports for telegraph wires, also applicable to posts or supports employed for other purposes - - - - -	748	17th March 1865	{ George Dibley. Frederick Braby.
An improved socket for fencing and telegraph posts	773	20th March 1865	Arthur Gerard Brown.
Machinery or apparatus for paying-out and for raising electric telegraph cables in deep waters.	828	23rd March 1865	Robert Tidman.
Telegraphic apparatus - - - - (Communicated by Albert Auguste Denairie de Nelisse.)	910	31st March 1865	Henri Adrien Bonnevik.
Improvements in certain electric telegraphs, part of which invention is applicable to other purposes.	990	5th April 1865	Adam Miller.
Improvements in the construction of submarine telegraph cables, and in the mode of submerging or laying them in the water. (Communicated by Jean Lorien, frame.)	1031	11th April 1865	William Edward Newton.
Improvements in and apparatus for communicating intelligence by means of electricity - -	1088	19th April 1865	{ Ralph Augustus Jane. Joseph Hedges.
Means and apparatus for regulating the power and velocity of machinery or apparatus in general. (applicable to telegraphic apparatus.)	1290	2nd May 1865	Charles William Siemens.
Manufacture of parkesine or compounds of pyroxyline, and also mixtures of pyroxyline known as collodion. (for coating telegraph wire.)	1319	11th May 1865	Alexander Parkes.
Insulation of electric telegraph wires - -	1379	19th May 1865	Samuel Alfred Varley.
Telegraph supports, parts of the invention being applicable to other purposes - - -	1380	20th May 1865	{ Cornelius Varley. Samuel Alfred Varley.
Improvements in reproducing or producing copies of writings, drawings, graphs and other characters, and in preparing originals to be transmitted by electric telegraph. (Communicated by Jacques Paul Lambrigot.)	1437	27th May 1865	Richard Archibald Brooman.
An improved system of telegraphic communication on railways, parts of which invention are also applicable to other telegraphic purposes.	1543	5th June 1865	Alice Isabel Lucas Garbo.
An improved method of submerging telegraphic cables	1544	6th June 1865	James Kennedy.
Method of and apparatus for effecting and recording telegraphic communication. (Communicated by Sarah Martha Bartwell.)	1599	16th June 1865	Michael Henry.
Electric telegraph instruments and relays -	1694	30th June 1865	Isham Baggs.
Improvements in submarine telegraphy, which improvements are also applicable in some cases to land telegraphy.	1758	3rd July 1865	Isham Baggs.
Electric telegraphs - - - -	1794	6th July 1865	{ William Thomas. Cromwell Fleetwood Varley.

Subject-matter of Patent.	Number of Patent.	Date.	Name of Patentee.
TELEGRAPHS, &c.—continued.			
Compounds for waterproofing and insulating purposes. (protecting telegraph wires.)	1963	29th July 1865	Frederick Augustus Abel.
Improvements in the mode or method of preparing materials for, and in the manufacture of submarine telegraphic cables, the same being generally applicable for other purposes.	2025	4th Aug. 1865	Frederick George Mulholland.
Electric telegraphic apparatus - (Communicated by Louis Breguet.)	2047	7th Aug. 1865	Louis John Crossley.
Construction of submarine telegraph cables	2088	11th Aug. 1865	Henry Robert Guy.
Apparatus for raising and recovering submerged telegraph cables.	2134	14th Aug. 1865	Josiah Latimer Clark.
Constructing constant galvanic batteries for giving a signal or alarm in case of fire, and any other telegraphic purposes	2144	19th Aug. 1865	John Samuel Watson. Albert Horwood, Charles Brunah.
Machinery to be used in the manufacture of telegraph cables.	2155	21st Aug. 1865	Fleeming Jenkin.
Improvements in the construction of electric telegraph cables and in the preparation of telegraph wires.	2161	22nd Aug. 1865	Charles Marsden.
Floating lights, beacons, floating batteries and other vessels. (for supporting telegraph cables.)	2175	24th Aug. 1865	John Moody.
Submarine electric telegraph cables	2209	24th Aug. 1865	Stopford Thomas Jones.
Improvements in electric telegraph cables, and in transmitting signals therethrough.	2219	24th Aug. 1865	William Peter Piggott.
Electrical telegraphy	2217	29th Aug. 1865	Richard Laming.
Improvements in the manufacture of rope, cordage, yarn, wire rope, and other such like twisted and plaited fabrics, and in the machinery employed therein - (covering telegraph cables.)	2225	30th Aug. 1865	Thomas Cope. William Garvit.
Improvements in laying and maintaining submarine telegraph cables, and in apparatus connected therewith. (Communicated by Amédée Mathurin Gabriel Sebillot.)	2257	1st Sept. 1865	William Clark.
An improved method of laying or submerging ocean telegraph cables.	2261	2nd Sept. 1865	Joseph Sproul.
Improved means or apparatus to be used in laying telegraph cables in the sea or other deep waters.	2262	2nd Sept. 1865	Kirwan Joyce Perceval.
Improvements in covering submarine telegraph cables, and in the machinery and means employed for paying out or hauling in the same.	2320	11th Sept. 1865	Samuel Inkpen.
Improvements in constructing and insulating telegraphic conductors, and in apparatus connected therewith.	2332	12th Sept. 1866	John Macintosh.
Construction of submarine telegraph cables	2341	13th Sept. 1865	John Oliver Chapman Phillips.
Magnetic telegraphs - (Communicated by Robert Kirk Boyle and Guiseppe Toplinker.)	2350	14th Sept. 1865	William Clark.
Manufacturing wire conductors for electro-telegraphic purposes.	2410	22nd Sept. 1865	William Bogarvit.

Subject-matter of Patent.	Number of Patent.	Date.	Name of Patentee.
TELEGRAPHS, &c.—continued.			
An improved indicator for electric bells and a new battery manipulator combined, for ringing electric bells and other signals.	2421	22nd Sept. 1865	Walker Mowley.
Certain improvements in telegraphic cables - -	2509	30th Sept. 1865	James Anson Mee.
Construction of submarine telegraph cables - - (Communicated by Claude Ernest Lami de Nerva.)	2530	3rd Oct. 1865	Henri Adrien Bonnerêt.
Apparatus for laying telegraphic cables in deep water.	2570	6th Oct. 1865	Frederick William Gardiner.
Certain improvements in telegraphic communication for the purpose of indicating danger.	2584	7th Oct. 1865	Charles Hamm Mellor.
Improvements in submarine electric telegraph cables and in apparatus connected therewith.	2605	10th Oct. 1865	François Thiery Bohot.
Submarine telegraphy - - - -	2612	10th Oct. 1865	John Fletcher Wilm.
The improvement of the means of and apparatus for laying submarine electrical telegraphic wires, lines, cables or other contrivances of a like sort.	2670	16th Oct. 1865	Reinhold Edward Karlbach.
An improved method of laying submarine telegraphic cables or wires.	2705	20th Oct. 1865	Empson Edward Middleton.
Electric telegraph conductors - - - -	2723	21st Oct. 1865	Alexander Parkes.
Improvements in the construction and working of electric telegraphs and in apparatus connected therewith, partly applicable to other purposes.	2762	26th Oct. 1865	Henry Wilde.
Testing and working submarine electric telegraph wires.	2766	26th Oct. 1865	Willoughby Smith.
An improvement in electric telegraphy - -	2914	13th Nov. 1865	Walker Mowley.
Improvements in submarine electric telegraph cables and in machinery employed in the manufacture and submergence thereof - - - -	2941	15th Nov. 1865	{ Arthur Wells. Walter Hall.
Improvements in the construction of and in the method of laying submarine electric cables.	2942	16th Nov. 1865	John De La Haye.
Telegraph taking and marking instruments -	3006	23rd Nov. 1865	Charles Henry Cludlam.
Certain improvements in insulators for electrical purposes - - -	3191	5th Dec. 1865	{ John Prout. Henry Harrison. Bernhard Barber.
Improvements in the application of electricity for the testing and discharge of torpedo mines, either on land or at sea, and in the apparatus connected therewith. (and speaking through the mine.) (Partly communicated by Matthew Fontaine Maury.)	3164	8th Dec. 1865	Nathaniel John Holms
Construction of wire conductors for electro-telegraphic purposes.	3180	9th Dec. 1865	William Boggett.
Manufacturing and laying down submarine telegraphic cables.	3192	11th Dec. 1865	Theophilus Berron.
Construction of wire conductors for electro-telegraphic purposes.	3299	21st Dec. 1865	William Boggett.
Obtaining and employing continuous lengths of tanned leather for various useful purposes (for telegrapher uses.)	3334	23rd Dec. 1865	{ George Hare. Daniel Hare.
Machinery for paying out and hauling in or picking up, part solely applicable to paying out and hauling in telegraph cables.	3346	27th Dec. 1865	Samuel Griffith.

Subject-matter of Patent.	Number of Patent.	Date.	Name of Patentee.
TELEGRAPHS, &c.—continued.			
Manufacture of electric conductors insulated with india-rubber.	8347	27th Dec. 1865	Hugh Adams Silver.
Improvements in the construction of general electric typo-comitelegraphic machines, and in the mode of working them.	5354	24th Dec. 1865	François Thierry Hubert.
Construction of telegraphic cables or conductors	8357	29th Dec. 1865	Cromwell Fleetwood Varley.
TESTING THE STRENGTH AND QUALITY OF MATERIALS.			
A new or improved apparatus and means for ascertaining the quality and condition of grain and seed. (Communicated by Christian Joseph Schmitz.)	632	7th March 1865	William Blinger.
A new apparatus for ascertaining the degree of torsion and resistance in the threads of textile substances. (Communicated by Monsieur Biraviael Felix Bruart.)	1285	3rd May 1865	Peter Armand Le Comte de Fontaine Moreau.
Machines for testing the strength of chains and cables and for other like purposes.	1347	15th May 1865	James Tangye.
An improved method of testing railway and other springs - - - - - - -	1374	16th May 1865	Joseph Mitchell. George Tilford.
Improved means of testing alloys of gold - .	1994	3rd Aug. 1865	Henry Lery.
Apparatus or means for ascertaining the quality and condition of grain and seed. (Communicated by Christian Joseph Schmitz.)	2088	14th Aug. 1865	William Blinger.
Apparatus for ascertaining specific gravities and the bulk of solids, and also for other similar uses.	2480	29th Sept. 1865	Alfred Manley Bennett.
Improvements in the construction of billiard tables and improved apparatus for ascertaining the degree of elasticity of the cushions and the strength of the cloth. (Communicated by Eugene Pannier, jun'.)	2609	10th Oct. 1865	William Edward Gedge.
An improved apparatus for ascertaining the degree of torsion and resistance in the threads of textile substances.	8329	2nd Nov. 1865	Bimaimd Felix Bruart.
THERMOMETERS, BAROMETERS, HYDRO-METERS, LIQUOMETERS, SACCHARO-METERS, ELECTROMETERS ; TESTING THE STRENGTH OF FLUIDS ; WIND REGISTERS.			
Hydrometers - - - - -	75	10th Jan. 1865	Edward Wilds Ladd. Ludwig Oertling.

Subject matter of Patent.	Number of Patent.	Date.	Name of Patentee.
THERMOMETERS, &c. — continued.			
An improved apparatus or liquometer for ascertaining and indicating the strength of liquids. (Communicated by Claude Alphonse Valson.)	182	14th Jan. 1865	Richard Archibald Brooman.
Improved apparatus for measuring the specific gravity of liquids. (hydrometer and saccharometer.) (Communicated by Edward Payne.)	446	16th Feb. 1865	John Fullock Heaney.
Improvements in ascertaining the presence of "fixing" agents in photographic productions, in removing the said fixing agents therefrom, and in apparatus connected therewith. (Communicated by Wilhelm Reissig.)	677	10th March 1865	Theodor Reissig.
Improvements in self-acting alarms for indicating excess of heat or cold, parts of which improvements are applicable to the transmission of messages. (Communicated by Charles Diem.)	1229	2nd May 1865	John Henry Johnson.
Hydrometers for ascertaining the strength of spirits and the specific gravity of fluids. (Communicated by Claude Alphonse Valson.)	1349	15th May 1865	Henri Adrien Bonneville.
Apparatus for indicating the pressure of steam or liquids in gauges, and for signalling.	1497	31st May 1865	Frederic Newton Gisborne.
An improved method of submerging telegraphic cables. (or testing during submersion.)	1544	5th June 1865	James Kennedy.
An improvement in apparatus for indicating the hygrometric condition of the atmosphere.	1610	14th June 1865	William Edson.
Electric telegraph instruments and relays - (electrometers.)	1654	20th June 1865	Isham Baggs.
A new instrument or anemograph for delineating and registering the direction and force of the winds.	1859	12th July 1865	Samuel Burt Howlett.
An improved instrument for indicating atmospheric changes.	1891	20th July 1865	Henry Augustus Chun.
Apparatus for regulating the passage or flow of steam, water and other fluids.	2042	7th Aug. 1865	Adrienne Anastasie Faubert.
Aneroid barometers.	2714	20th Oct. 1865	Thomas Cooke.
Testing and working submarine electric telegraph wires.	2768	26th Oct. 1865	Willoughby Smith.
Apparatus for indicating and registering high temperatures.	2780	28th Oct. 1865	Frederick Herbert Gossage.
Improvements in the applications of electricity for the testing and discharge of torpedo mines, either on land or at sea, and in the apparatus connected therewith. (Partly communicated by Matthew Fontaine Maury.)	3154	6th Dec. 1865	Nathaniel John Holmes.
Construction of barometers - - - (Communicated by Antoine Michel Fabre.)	3187	9th Dec. 1865	Henri Adrien Bonneville.
Apparatus for regulating heat obtained by the combustion of gas. (by expansion and contraction of mercury.)	3269	16th Dec. 1865	Henry Planch.

Subject-matter of Patent.	Number of Patent.	Date.	Name of Patentee.
THRASHING, WINNOWING, HULLING, DECORTICATING, DRESSING, CLEANING, DRYING, STORING AND PRESERVING CORN, GRAIN, SEEDS AND RICE.			
Apparatus for hulling grain and for reducing granular substances.	32	5th Jan. 1865	Gustav Adolph Buchbols.
Machinery or apparatus for cleaning rice, coffee and other grains or seeds having an outer hull or inner pellicle. (Communicated by Nathaniel Greene and Walter Clement Key.)	64	9th Jan. 1865	John Henry Johnson.
Machinery or apparatus for cleaning and decorticating grain.	115	13th Jan. 1865	Wilson Ager.
An improved machine for raising and carrying earth, sand, stones or other similar solid or liquid materials for dredging, ventilating, or winnowing grain, or other analogous purposes.	174	20th Jan. 1865	Louis Balma.
Machinery for thrashing, beating and dressing flax.	231	26th Jan. 1865	William Crosty.
A new method for removing or destroying the momentum of heavy bodies by means of an elastic machine or machines, so as to prevent injury and damage from concussion, applicable to ship rudders, ship and fort armour, railway trains, tenders to piers, and floating piers, gangways, breakwaters and other similar structures, also as a motive-power. (driving winnowing machines.) (Communicated by William Graham M'Iver.)	321	6th Feb. 1865	Clemmens Robert Markham.
An improved apparatus for separating grain. (Communicated by Henry Francis Hart.)	348	7th Feb. 1865	William Edward Newton.
Improvements in the means of decorticating grain and other seeds, and in apparatus for the same. (Communicated by Gustave Lataste, Christophe Ours Ballet and Clément Montville.)	661	24th Feb. 1865	William Clark.
A new or improved apparatus and means for ascertaining the quality and condition of grain and seed. (Communicated by Christian Joseph Schmidt.)	632	7th March 1865	William Blinger.
Machinery or apparatus for thrashing grain or seed. (Communicated by Isidor Pintos.)	736	16th March 1865	Moritz Meisel.
Combined apparatus for threshing, dressing and grinding grain and other agricultural produce.	742	16th March 1865	James Marshall.
A new or improved machine for peeling or skinning almonds.	790	18th March 1865	James Henry Walker.
Machinery for thrashing and rubbing barley and other grain.	788	21st March 1865	Bernard James Webber.
Treatment of rice. (Communicated by Robert Pfeifer.)	842	31th March 1865	John Henry Johnson.
Rolling or forging steel or wrought iron in bars, to be used as beaters or beating bars upon the drum concaves or beater plates of concaves in thrashing machines.	925	1st April 1865	William Gray.
Improved apparatus for reducing wheat and other straw.	965	6th April 1865	Richard Garrett, jun'.

Subject-matter of Patent.	Number of Patent.	Date.	Name of Patentee.
THRASHING, &c.—continued.			
Apparatus for winnowing, sifting or riddling corn, grain and seed.	1108	20th April 1865	William Bourne.
An improved fan or exhaust for thrashing-machines (Communicated by Hyppolyte Halté and Auguste Harté.)	1241	3rd May 1865	William Edward Gedge.
An improved apparatus for shelling peas and beans, stoning fruit and other similar purposes.	1244	4th May 1865	Edward Greninger Smith.
Improvements in drying malt and grain, and in the machinery or apparatus connected therewith.	1277	10th May 1865	John Forbes.
An improved apparatus for sifting flour and other substances. (Communicated by Howard Tilden.)	1569	9th June 1865	George Haseltine.
Corn screens	1625	15th June 1865	John Hartley.
Machinery for cleaning and decorticating rice and other grains and seeds.	1777	5th July 1865	Joseph Wren Gray.
Improvements in drying grass, hay and other substances, and in the machinery for effecting the same (corn, &c.)	1948	29th July 1865	Baldwin Latham. Robert Campbell.
Applying and utilising water power (driving thrashing machines.)	1957	29th July 1865	Valentine Baker.
Apparatus or means for ascertaining the quality and condition of grain and seed. (Communicated by Christian Joseph Schmitz.)	2098	14th Aug. 1865	William Bänger.
An improved mode of and apparatus for drying timber, grain and other marketable products. (Communicated by Henry Bulkley.)	2187	17th Aug. 1865	Alfred Vincent Newton.
Machinery for treating cotton seeds in order to remove the cotton therefrom, and to prepare the seeds for crushing.	2198	26th Aug. 1865	François Antoine Edmund Guiramand de Manor
Machinery or apparatus for hulling and winnowing grain. (Communicated by Friedrich Henckel, and Wilhelm Seeb.)	2300	7th Sept. 1865	William Lloyd Wise.
Improvements in grinding wheat and other grain, and in apparatus for drying and improving the condition of damp wheat or other grain.	2485	24th Sept. 1865	Benjamin Wren.
Cleaning cotton seeds (Communicated by Etienne Laporte.)	2564	5th Oct. 1865	John Charles Scovin.
Construction of ships for raising ballast, corn, coal, minerals and other matters in bulk.	2663	16th Oct. 1865	Charles Henry Murray
A new thrashing machine worked directly on the thrashing floor by oxen or horses.	2889	9th Nov. 1865	Theophilus Bertram.
An improved machine for taking off the fibre from cotton seed and cleaning it.	2969	17th Nov. 1865	William Henry Cape.
Manufacture of beaters for thrashing machines	3071	31st Nov. 1865	William Gray. Edward Gray. John Gray.
An improved machine for dressing, sifting, cleaning and polishing fruit, coffee, grain and other matter, parts of which are applicable to coffee sifting, roasting, cooling and cleaning, and other purposes.	3123	6th Dec. 1865	Edwin Whale.
An improvement in apparatus for elevating bar, grass or similar materials, and discharging the same from the said apparatus.	3186	11th Dec. 1865	Edward Livingston Wacker

Subject-matter of Patent.	Number of Patent.	Date.	Name of Patentee.

THRASHING, &c.—continued.

Subject-matter of Patent.	Number of Patent.	Date.	Name of Patentee.
Apparatus for scouring grain, seed, rice, tea, and other materials.	3229	14th Dec. 1865	Henry William Miller.
Machinery for drying and bleaching grain and other materials.	3270	19th Dec. 1865	William Cressy.
An improved method of and apparatus for preserving, purifying, mixing, separating, cooling, aerating, roasting and otherwise treating grain, ores and various other matters.	3344	27th Dec. 1865	Gaston Charles Ange Marquis D'Ausy.

THREADS AND YARNS.

Subject-matter of Patent.	Number of Patent.	Date.	Name of Patentee.
The manufacture of a new thread for weaving and other uses. (Communicated by Verax Salron and Gaston Jessé.)	212	25th Jan. 1865	Richard Archibald Brooman.
Machinery or apparatus to be employed in the bleaching and dyeing of hanks or skeins of yarns and threads. (finishing threads.)	710	14th March 1865	Longin Gantert.
Manufacture of yarn so as to render same applicable as a substitute for woollen yarn, for manufacturing into shawls and other textile fabrics.	774	20th March 1865	Isidor Philippsthal.
A new or improved method of conditioning or preparing fibres, threads and fabrics, and apparatus to be employed therein. (Communicated by Stanislas Figuerras.)	1169	25th April 1865	Richard Archibald Brooman.
A new apparatus for ascertaining the degree of torsion and resistance in the threads of textile substances. (Communicated by Monsieur Bénagué Frère Bromer.)	1236	3rd May 1865	Peter Armand Le Comte de Fontaine Moreau.
Processes and machinery for producing fibres suitable for being spun, from rags or remnants of woven or other textile fabrics made of silk, wool, cotton or other fibrous materials.	1831	19th July 1865	Henry Ernest Gillen.
Machinery for the manufacture of linen or other yarns or threads. (See "Spinning.")	1965	1st Aug. 1865	Thomas Bell Paton.
An improved method of twisting threads (See "Weaving.") (Communicated by Désiré Sicel and Léon Sicel.)	2147	19th Aug. 1865	Richard Archibald Brooman.
Improvements in the manufacture of rope, cordage, yarn, wire rope, and other such like twisted and plaited fabrics, and in the machinery employed therein	2225	30th Aug. 1865	{ Thomas Cope, William Gorret.

Subject-matter of Patent.	Number of Patent.	Date.	Name of Patentee.
TOBACCO AND SNUFF ; CIGARS, CIGAR-HOLDERS, PIPES AND CIGAR LIGHTERS ; SMOKING PIPES ; TOBACCO POUCHES.			
Machinery for the manufacture of "cavendish," "negrohead" and other tobacco.	69	9th Jan. 1865	William Davies.
Machinery for pressing and cutting tobacco (Communicated by William Woodman Huer.)	152	14th Jan. 1865	Alfred Vincent Newton.
A chemical combustible substance and apparatus to which it is applicable. (as a cigar light.) (Communicated by François Stoker.)	477	20th Feb. 1865	William Edward Gedge.
An improvement in cigars - - - -	565	2nd March 1865	Charles Lewis Roberts.
An improvement in putting up tobacco for smoking, and in the implements or pipes for smoking the same, and in making tobacco paper. (Communicated by Luther Hobson Hale.)	615	4th March 1865	William Edward Newton.
An improved top or mouth piece for cigars or cheroots - - - - -	770	24th March 1865	{ Thomas Oliver, Joseph William Mann.
Spittoons (Communicated by Emile Gabriel Aubry and Claude Joseph Barral.)	882	23th March 1865	John Henry Johnson.
An improved cigar cutter - - -	1180	24th April 1865	Henry Charles Butcher.
Clay tobacco pipes - - -	1452	23rd June 1865	Lesley White.
Utilizing the stalks, smalls and waste of tobacco for certain purposes - - -	1844	13th July 1865	{ George Clayton Colye. Charles Lewis Roberts.
An improved pouch or receptacle for holding tobacco and other similar purposes.	1871	14th July 1865	William Antil Richards.
Machinery for manufacturing cigars (Communicated by John Prentice.)	2003	4th Aug. 1865	Alfred Vincent Newton.
Machinery for making cigarettes - -	2160	22nd Aug. 1865	Manuel Joad Lopez Y Mênca.
Pipes used for smoking - - -	2326	11th Sept. 1865	Charles Ambrose M'Evoy
Apparatus for cutting tobacco - -	2340	15th Sept. 1865	Edward Thornton Reed.
Smoking-pipes and cigar holders, and an improved tobacco cartridge to be used with the same. (Communicated by Elijah Morse.)	2369	15th Sept. 1865	Noal Myers.
An improvement in cheops or instrulings (for cigar cases.)	2445	2nd Oct. 1865	Frederic Jerneer.
Machinery or apparatus for the manufacture of wooden spills.	2677	6th Oct. 1865	Thomas Manbin.
An improved apparatus for igniting cigars or tobacco.	2869	7th Nov. 1865	Hyde Bateman.
An improved tray or holder for cigars or pipes and the ashes therefrom. (Communicated by Louis Gilles Gallien.)	3102	2nd Dec. 1865	Richard Archibald Brooman.
A new method of preparing plants of the eucalyptus family and myrtaceous plants, and the application thereof to the purposes of tobacco and snuff. (Communicated by Prosper Vincent Rameit.)	3174	9th Dec. 1865	Richard Archibald Brooman.
An improved mode of igniting cigars, cigarettes and other similar articles.	3280	24th Dec. 1865	Charles Louriston Wilyams Kindler.

Subject-matter of Patent.	Number of Patent.	Date.	Name of Patentee.
TOYS.			
Manufacture of a compound or material to be used as a substitute for India-rubber. (Communicated by Henry Loravabery and Emile Gresier.)	1069	16th April 1865	William Clark.
Rotatory aërial swings - - - - -	1072	17th April 1865	James John Matthewson. Heinrich Louis Rudolph Nehler.
A new or improved composed spherical rest for ornamental turning lathes. (forming cups and balls.)	1441	25th May 1865	Thomas Hallam Hohlyn.
An improved combination of materials, for the manufacture of carpets, floor cloth, felt, wall paper, fireproof flexible roofing, ship and boat building, and for other similar purposes - (dolls and toys.)	1776	6th July 1865	John Longbottom. Abram Longbottom.
An improved method of forming India-rubber, gutta-percha or such like balls.	1998	2nd Aug. 1865	Alfred Ford.
A toy or game called flying fish - - -	2145	19th Aug. 1865	George Whitford.
Improvements in the construction of flying toys, also applicable to other purposes. (Communicated by Charles Edmond François Couturier.)	2206	26th Aug. 1865	Henri Adrien Bonneville.
A new mechanical propelling screw toy - -	2572	6th Oct. 1865	Louis Alexandre Isidore Daumesnil.
Manufacture of chemical toys known as Pharaoh's serpents.	2694	18th Oct. 1865	Thomas King.
An improved pyrotechnic toy - - -	3196	11th Dec. 1865	Thomas King.
Preparation of glue or gelatine so as to render it insoluble in water, and applicable by the admixture of other substances to various purposes for which common glue or gelatine cannot now be used. (for toys.) (Communicated by Henry Werts.)	3295	23rd Dec. 1865	William Edward Newton.
TURNING; LATHES FOR TURNING.			
Apparatus for transmitting and converting reciprocating motion into rotary motion, applicable to various useful purposes. (rotating lathes.)	166	17th Jan. 1865	William John Canningham.
Action and arrangement of drilling machines, turning lathes, and other machine tools in which a variable speed is required.	241	27th Jan. 1865	John Combe.
Improved machinery for shaping hat and bonnet blocks.	255	24th Jan. 1865	William Hiram Higgins.
An improved machine for rounding and polishing shot, shell and other balls or spheres. (Communicated by William Davis Winow.)	982	4th April 1865	William Clark.

H H

Subject-matter of Patent.	Number of Patent.	Date.	Name of Patentee.
TURNING, &c.—continued.			
Improved apparatus for cutting, turning and smoothing metal pipes, and the surfaces of bolts, rods or spindles	1211	11th May 1865	George Mountford. Edward Worrell.
Certain improvements in apparatus for cutting or forming screws, which is also applicable for cutting pipes or tubes.	1411	23rd May 1865	Edward M'Nally.
A new or improved compound spherical rest for ornamental turning lathes.	1441	25th May 1865	Thomas Hallam Hoblyn.
Machinery for turning and finishing bodies of a spherical form. (Communicated by Robert Carsley.)	1468	27th May 1865	Thomas Bourne.
Machinery or tools for cutting metals or other materials.	1571	9th June 1865	William Wilson Huler.
Certain improvements in machinery or apparatus for turning and cutting wood and other substances, to be employed in the manufacture of spools or bobbins or other similar articles.	1773	5th July 1865	John Braithwaite.
Improved self-centering and tightening chucks for drilling-machines, lathes, and other machines in which chucks are used. (Communicated by John Edwin Earle.)	2491	26th Sept. 1865	Edward Thomas Hughes
Chucks for turning lathes	2660	17th Oct. 1865	Robert Burley.
Apparatus for producing accelerated motion for driving purposes. (for lathes.)	2770	28th Oct. 1865	John Hawthorn Kitson. John Kirby.
Lathe chucks (Partly communicated by Charles Churchill.)	2782	30th Oct. 1865	James Buckingham.
Means of connecting drums or pulleys with their shafts or drivers. (for rogue lathes.) (Communicated by Leverett Homer Olmsted.)	2903	14th Nov. 1865	William Clark.
Improvements in the manufacture of axles for carriages and spindles for various purposes, and in machinery to be employed in the said manufacture, part of which improvements in machinery may also be applied to other purposes (axles and spindles for lathes.)	3328	26th Dec. 1865	Elias Lomn. Joseph Constant Loren. John Loure. John Brettell. Thomas Brettell. Charles Vernon.
Machinery for boring, turning and shaping articles of metal	3369	29th Dec. 1865	William Harrisson. Thomas Walker.
UMBRELLAS, PARASOLS, UMBRELLA FURNITURE; WALKING-STICKS.			
Umbrellas and other like articles	114	13th Jan. 1865	John Weeks.
Apparatus used for binding the ends of walking sticks, and the sticks or handles of umbrellas and parasols	672	10th March 1865	Joshua Jones. Richard Daniel Jones.
Umbrella and parasol tip fasteners	829	24th March 1865	Robert Leblanch.
Fixed bands or rib holders for umbrellas and parasols, and which said band is also applicable as an ornamental appendage to walking-sticks and other purposes.	910	31st March 1865	Thomas Kemp Mace.

Subject-matter of Patent.	Number of Patent.	Date.	Name of Patentee.
UMBRELLAS, &c.—continued.			
Metal ribs for umbrellas and parasols - - -	1802	10th May 1865	{ Robert Hadfield. Jabez Shipman.
Umbrellas, parasols and sunshades - - -	1529	5th June 1865	John Stephenson.
Umbrellas and parasols - - - -	1678	22nd June 1865	Nicholas de Barkey.
New or improved compositions in imitation of ivory and wood, to be employed in the manufacture of umbrella tips, umbrella and walking stick handles, and other useful and ornamental purposes - - - - -	1663	23rd June 1865	{ Michael Dietrich Rosenthal. Solomon Gradenwitz.
Improvements in the manufacture of umbrellas and parasols, and in apparatus employed therein.	2345	13th Sept. 1865	Samuel Fox.
Sun-shades or canopies for perambulators and other wheeled carriages.	8389	19th Sept. 1865	Henry Lloyd.
Adaptation of elastic material to articles requiring a hollow arrangement, or a partially rigid and partially expansible arrangement. (for umbrellas.)	2425	22nd Sept. 1865	Matthew Cartwright.
A mode or modes of inserting glass or other transparent plates in the fabric of umbrellas or in other pliant fabrics. (Communicated by Erasmus Allington Pond, Mark Staples Richardson and Edmund Alonzo Morse.)	2880	9th Nov. 1865	John Henry Johnson.
An improved stretcher for umbrellas and parasols -	8097	2nd Dec. 1865	Richard Cook.
New or improved compositions in imitation of ivory and wood, to be employed in the manufacture of umbrella tips, umbrella and walking-stick handles, and other useful and ornamental purposes - - - - -	8810	22nd Dec. 1865	{ Michael Dietrich Rosenthal. Solomon Gradenwitz.
Preparation of glue or gelatine so as to render it insoluble in water, and applicable by the admixture of other substances to various purposes for which common glue or gelatine cannot now be used. (for parasol sticks.) (Communicated by Henry Wurtz.)	8825	23rd Dec. 1865	William Edward Newton
Obtaining and employing continuous lengths of tanned leather for various useful purposes - (for umbrellas, sun shades, &c.)	8834	23rd Dec. 1865	{ George Hurn. Daniel Hurn.
UPHOLSTERY (Mattresses, Beds, Cushions, Curtains, Curtain and Stair Rods, Cornice Poles) ; **RUGS, MATS AND MATTING.**			
The application and use of certain materials to be employed in the manufacture of carpets and hearth rugs - - - - -	7	2nd Jan. 1865	{ John Spencer. Noah Broomhead.
Construction of spring mattrasses and palliasses -	24	4th Jan. 1865	Dionisio Verrechio.
An improved elastic mattrass or bedstead - (Communicated by François Carré.)	67	11th Jan. 1865	William Edward Gedge.

Subject-matter of Patent.	Number of Patent.	Date.	Name of Patentee.
UPHOLSTERY, &c.—continued.			
Elastic mattresses and bedding (Communicated by Madame Jeanne Lelarge.)	92	12th Jan. 1865	Edward Thomas Hughes.
An improved method for the suspension of curtains	195	23rd Jan. 1865	James Radcock.
Improvements applicable to air cushions, mattresses, portable baths, and other like air inflated articles.	317	4th Feb. 1865	Arthur Henry Robinson.
Manufacture of cornice pole and other rings	977	6th April 1865	Charles Horton Williams.
Manufacture of Goth fabrics (for carpets.) (Communicated by The American Waterproof Cloth Company.)	1319	1st May 1865	William Edward Newton.
An improved manufacture of waterproof fabric (for carpets, rugs, mats, &c.) (Communicated by The American Waterproof Cloth Company.)	1319	1st May 1865	William Edward Newton.
Improvements in door and other mats, part of which improvements is also applicable to brushes and brooms, and to producing cord or tooth surfaces employed in operating on various fibrous substances.	1283	9th May 1865	Thomas Jefferson Mayall.
Manufacture of carpets and other terry and cut pile fabrics. (Communicated by The American Waterproof Cloth Company.)	1490	31st May 1865	William Edward Newton.
Manufacture of mats, matting and brushes	1758	3rd July 1865	{ George Haro. { Daniel Haro.
An improved combination of materials for the manufacture of carpets, floor cloth, felt, wall paper, fireproof flexible roofing, ship and boat building, and for other similar purposes (stair cloths, mats, &c.)	1778	5th July 1865	{ John Longbottom. { Abram Longbottom.
An improved material for stuffing seats, cushions, mattresses and other articles. (Communicated by Emile Rousseau.)	1800	7th July 1865	Thomas Frederick Henley.
An improved mattress and palliasse for the use of the nursery, invalids or hospitals.	1888	17th July 1865	Stephen Demmmore.
Improvements in the makings of metallic and other bedsteads, sofas, couches and other like articles, which said improvements may also be applied to the seats of chairs, railway carriages and other articles. (Communicated by Thomas Thawington.)	2036	5th Aug. 1865	Henry Gerring.
Machinery to be used in the manufacture of stair rods.	2077	10th Aug. 1865	Thomas Allcock.
Manufacture and ornamenting of carpets, rugs and other fabrics. (curtains.)	2191	25th Aug. 1865	Lemuel Clayton.
A new or improved ventilating spring mattress	2511	30th Sept. 1865	Joseph Edwin Townshend
A new composition of India-rubber mastic or cement, made in a mass or less fluid state according to the use to be made of it, and the process or contrivance for applying the same. (see "OIL-CLOTHS.")	2630	17th Oct. 1865	Auguste Aimé Lervaard.
Bedsteads, seats, couches and other articles for sitting and reclining on.	2636	14th Oct. 1865	James Lamb Hancock.
A new kind of double faced carpet or tapestry with similar or different patterns on each face.	2702	30th Oct. 1865	Alexander Braquenié.

Subject-matter of Patent.	Number of Patent.	Date.	Name of Patentee.
UPHOLSTERY, &c.—*continued.*			
Improvements in helical or spiral springs for upholstery and other purposes, and in machinery for manufacturing the same. (*Communicated by Frederick Chreabrow Payne and John Spencer Giles.*)	3023	24th Nov. 1866	William Edward Newton.
Construction of floor mats, flesh and bath brushes made principally of india-rubber.	3216	13th Dec. 1865	George Barber.
Obtaining and employing continuous lengths of tanned leather for various useful purposes (*for making matting, for window curtains, &c.*)	6334	23rd Dec. 1866	{ George Hern. Daniel Hern.

VALVES, TAPS, STOP-COCKS, PLUGS; REGULATING THE FLOW AND PRESSURE OF FLUIDS.			
Taps	67	9th Jan. 1865	Joseph Calkin.
Regulating and working the valves of steam and other engines	82	11th Jan. 1865	John Frederick Spencer.
Street and other lamps and lanterns	151	16th Jan. 1865	John William Gregg.
Steam-engines	188	19th Jan. 1865	William Cleveland Hicks.
Steam-engines	182	21st Jan. 1866	Thomas Lester.
An improved elastic valve and high pressure and general tap	213	26th Jan. 1865	{ Stephen Sharp. Daniel Smith.
Improved apparatus for preventing the explosion of steam-boilers	205	3rd Feb. 1865	John Westerby.
An improved combustion pump (*Communicated by Thomas John Linton.*)	814	4th Feb. 1865	William Clark.
Certain improvements in breech-loading ordnance	272	10th Feb. 1865	Alfred Krupp.
Improvements in furnaces and boilers and parts connected with them, for generating steam and heating fluids, and also for improved apparatus for reducing and shutting off steam and regulating the speed of steam-engines. (*regulating valve.*)	290	11th Feb. 1865	John Cass.
Expansion gear for steam-engines	415	14th Feb. 1865	William Fothergill Batho.
Hydraulic presses	417	14th Feb. 1865	George Whittee.
An improved method of stopping bottles	464	14th Feb. 1865	John James Chidley.
Improvements in washing-machines and in apparatus connected therewith.	481	21st Feb. 1865	Robert Willison.
Steam-engines	485	21st Feb. 1865	John Russell Scram.
A new and improved balanced slide valve (*Communicated by James Rankin.*)	496	22nd Feb. 1865	William Edward Newton.
An improved fluid valve	547	27th Feb. 1865	Comyn Ching.
An improved means of securing and protecting the india-rubber rings of buffer springs of railway carriages, which invention is also applicable to air pump and valve seatings and lids faced with india-rubber.	628	6th March 1865	William John Oliver.
Water-closet apparatus	648	9th March 1865	John Shanks.

Subject-matter of Patent.	Number of Patent.	Date.	Name of Patentee.
VALVES, &c.—continued.			
An improved combined tea-price and valve	684	11th March 1865	Charles Johnson.
Apparatus for supplying regulated or measured quantities of water and other fluids.	707	13th March 1865	Robert Gordon Rattray.
Improvements in the means and apparatus employed for treating timber with antiseptic or preservative fluids, also applicable to other purposes.	724	16th March 1865	Samuel Bagster Boulton
Corks or valves	734	17th March 1865	William Roberts.
Improved arrangements and apparatus for drawing off liquors or liquids from casks and other vessels, without the aid of pumps.	781	16th March 1865	Joseph Wells.
An improved arrangement of valves and other appliances for a new description of hydraulic engine for raising water and other fluids above their common level, the fluids so raised to be used as a motive-power	791	21st March 1865	{ James Smith. Sydney Arthur Chums
Stoves or fire-places, ash pans and fenders	826	23rd March 1865	James Clifford Morgan.
Obtaining motive-power from airiform fluids and from liquids.	827	23rd March 1865	Matthew Piers Watt Boulton.
Double cylinder steam-engines	860	27th March 1865	Joshua Rooke.
Improvements in gas-meters and in the machinery or apparatus connected therewith.	917	31st March 1865	James Bathgate.
Double acting lift and force pumps	943	4th April 1865	Charles Denman Young.
Apparatus employed to actuate the valves of engines worked by steam, air or other fluid. (See "STEAM-ENGINES.")	942	6th April 1865	James Grafton Jones.
Certain improvements in gas-engines	988	6th April 1865	Pierre Hugon.
Apparatus for preventing explosions in steam-boilers.	1026	20th April 1865	John Horbling the younger.
Taps or stop cocks (Communicated by Oscar Pionel.)	1101	20th April 1865	William Clark.
Gas regulators and valves for the same (Communicated by Charles Money Crumm.)	1109	20th April 1865	Francis Wise.
Improvements in steam-engines, relating to valve motions, governor and drain pipes	1186	29th April 1865	{ Andrew Wyllie. John M'Farlane Gray.
Machinery or apparatus for working or cutting coal or minerals, and for compressing or exhausting air to be employed therein or for other purposes, some parts of which apparatus are also applicable to upright shafts, and other parts for regulating the flow or discharge of steam or other elastic fluids.	1202	29th April 1865	William Leathum.
Valves for liquids, steam and gases	1286	2nd May 1865	Thomas Russell.
Improvements in steam generators and engines, and in apparatus for feeding steam generators. (Communicated by George Bailey Brayton.)	1340	3rd May 1865	John Henry Johnson.
Steam engines (Communicated by Ebenezer Denford.)	1364	6th May 1865	William Edward Newton.
Apparatus for measuring spirits (Communicated by John Hutchings Car, John Murphy and William Murphy.)	1373	6th May 1865	John Henry Johnson.
A combined safety valve regulator, pressure gauge, water indicator, alarm and "blow off" for steam generators (Communicated by Peter Riordan.)	1505	11th May 1865	John Henry Johnson.

Subject-matter of Patent.	Number of Patent.	Date.	Name of Patentee.

Valves, &c—continued.

Subject-matter of Patent.	Number of Patent.	Date.	Name of Patentee.
Water gauges and cocks	1520	13th May 1865	Alexander Weir.
Wet gas-meters	1595	20th May 1865	William Smith. George Browne Smith.
A new or improved method of obtaining motive-power, together with certain machinery or apparatus for applying the same	1504	1st June 1865	David Hancock. Frederick Barnes.
Valves for steam and other fluids and liquids	1510	2nd June 1865	John Nuttall.
Safety apparatus for steam-boilers	1529	2nd June 1865	James Shepherd.
Improvements in machinery or apparatus for actuating the slide-valves of marine engines, and in the slide-valves thereof.	1538	5th June 1865	John Robertson.
Dry gas-meters	1548	6th June 1865	Henry Herrman Kronschroeder. John Frederick Gustav Kronschroeder.
Improvements in safety valves, which improvements are also applicable to steam-engine and other valves	1575	9th June 1865	Charles Vernon. Wilham Hodgkins.
Hammers and other machines actuated by steam or other fluid or vapour	1607	14th June 1865	Benjamin Massey. Stephen Massey.
Construction of taps or valves (Communicated by Ernest Alexander Ribert.)	1645	20th June 1865	Edward Griffith Brewer.
Certain improvements in apparatus for measuring and indicating the flow of liquids.	1674	22nd June 1865	Edward Kenworthy Dutton.
A new and improved food or fluid regulator for feeding bottle and other tubes.	1797	29th June 1865	William Botham.
Locomotive engines (Communicated by Auguste De Bergue.)	1764	3rd July 1865	Charles De Bergue.
Steam pumping machines or engines	1760	3rd July 1865	Martin Benson.
Steam and water valves	1834	11th July 1865	Nathaniel Jenkins.
Improvements in apparatus and equipments used by persons employed under water, part of the improvements being also applicable for the use of persons employed where noxious gases or vapours prevail.	1840	12th July 1865	Auguste Deneyrouse.
Slide valves	1893	20th July 1865	Richard Clark Bristol.
Construction of valves for steam and other engines (Communicated by Thomas Shrimton Doris.)	1913	22nd July 1865	William Edward Newton.
An improved portable chamber or receptacle to contain aerated liquids, and the apparatus connected therewith by which the flow of such liquid is regulated and measured.	1928	25th July 1865	Max Benjamin Schumann.
Conical plug steam valves (Communicated by John Wesley Corbett.)	1966	28th July 1865	William Edward Newton.
Improvements in the construction of atmospheric railways and carriages, and in working the same.	1987	1st Aug. 1865	Alexander Deull.
Apparatus applicable as a motive-power engine, a pump or fluid meter. (Communicated by Francis Bernard de Kertervonet.)	3021	4th Aug. 1865	William Clark.
Apparatus for filtering sugar and other liquid solutions	3032	4th Aug. 1865	Jean Adolphe Leon. George Townsend. John Kinnick.
Apparatus for regulating the passage or flow of steam, water and other fluids.	2043	7th Aug. 1865	Adrienne Anastasie Foubert.

Subject-matter of Patent	Number of Patent	Date	Name of Patentee
VALVES, &c.—*continued.*			
An improved mode of relieving slide valves of back pressure.	2C88	9th Aug. 1865	James William Langstaff.
Gas-burners	8094	12th Aug. 1865	Henry Woodward.
Steam hammers	8174	24th Aug. 1865	David Davies.
Improvements in apparatus by means of which certain liquids, common air, and certain elastic fluids are made available in the production of light, and their quantity regulated and measured, parts of which improvements are applicable for other purposes.	8184	25th Aug. 1865	Edwin Augustus Carley.
Apparatus for supplying regulated or measured quantities of water.	8189	26th Aug. 1865	Robert Gordon Rattray.
Improved apparatus for supplying boilers with water. *(actuating the lifting valves.)* *(Communicated by Gustav Adolph Riedel.)*	8211	29th Aug. 1865	Alfred Vincent Newton.
Certain improvements in steam-engines and valves *(Communicated by George Ichabod Washburn.)*	8286	6th Sept. 1865	William Clark.
An improved safety valve for steam-boilers	8823	11th Sept. 1865	Henry Hackett. Thomas Wrigley. Edmund Pearson.
Vent pegs for casks or vessels from which beer or other liquid is drawn off from time to time.	8266	13th Sept. 1865	Robert Mann Lowne.
A new and improved machine for the collecting and diffusing of water or other fluids.	8419	22nd Sept. 1865	Charles Wyatt Orford.
Apparatus for lubricating machinery *(slide valves.)* *(Communicated by Joseph Banillon.)*	8489	23rd Sept. 1865	Henri Adrien Bonneville.
Hydraulic pressure engines	8445	23rd Sept. 1865	Jacob Dreinigant.
Steam-engines *(valve motion.)*	8470	27th Sept. 1865	John Rodger Arnaldi.
Improved self-centering and tightening chucks for drilling-machines, lathes, and other machines in which chucks are used. *(taps.)* *(Communicated by John Edwin Earle.)*	8491	28th Sept. 1865	Edward Thomas Hughes.
Machinery and apparatus for bleaching, steeping, cleaning and washing fibrous and other materials, yarns and fabrics	8501	29th Sept. 1865	William Schofield. John Smith.
Pneumatic ways for the transmission of letters, merchandise and passengers. *(Communicated by Elias Perkman Needham.)*	8537	3rd Oct. 1865	William Edward Newton.
Double or single action pumps *(Communicated by Claude Genin.)*	8622	11th Oct. 1865	William Edward Gedge.
Improvements in and applicable to slide valves, pistons and glands	8700	19th Oct. 1865	Thomas Adams. George John Parnum.
An improved apparatus for regulating the supply of water to tanks, water butts or cisterns, applicable also to other purposes *(valve tap and regulator.)*	8710	21st Oct. 1865	Richard Fell. Davy Hammand.
Steam-engines	8760	26th Oct. 1865	Edmund Hunt.
Looms for weaving *(opening the air valve.)*	8943	3rd Nov. 1865	Arthur Heald.

Subject-matter of Patent.	Number of Patent.	Date.	Name of Patentee.
VALVES, &c.—*continued.*			
Regulating the flow of water and other fluids in pipes and valves, and determining the quantity passing through the same.	2905	11th Nov. 1865	Joseph Alfred Nicholson.
Method and means of securing and discharging the contents of pipes and vessels.	2926	14th Nov. 1865	Samuel Middleton.
Improvements in cocks for steam, water, air and gases at high pressure, and also in gauge cocks and water gauges for boilers, and sediment tubes for cocks and pipes.	2990	21st Nov. 1865	Samuel Barnett.
An improvement in ejectors for discharging bilge water and for other purposes. (Communicated by *Nathan Leffingwell Chappell.*)	3001	22nd Nov. 1865	Alfred Vincent Newton.
Apparatus for increasing the safety of railway passengers and trains, signalling and forming a communication externally and internally between all parts of such trains, lighting, warming and securing the doors of the carriages, and indicating therein and at the stations the names of the places at which the train stops. (*form and packing of spherical taps.*)	3048	29th Nov. 1865	Richard Howarth.
Certain apparatus for injecting and ejecting fluids and liquids.	3170	9th Dec. 1865	Andrew Barclay.
Producing and applying rotating motion by means of an apparatus to be worked by fluids, steam, compressed air, or by water or by gas.	3272	19th Dec. 1865	John Wright Carr.
Improved apparatus for burning combustible vapor (such as that from naphtha or coal oil) for heating, cooking and lighting purposes. (Communicated by *James Stratton.*)	3317	22nd Dec. 1865	George Davies.
Cocks or valves . . . . . (Communicated by *Henry Moore.*)	3359	23rd Dec. 1865	Charles Woodward Moore.
VENTILATION ; SUPPLYING AND PURIFYING AIR FOR BUILDINGS, MINES, SHIPS, CARRIAGES, &c.			
Construction of railway carriages . . (and ventilating.)	95	11th Jan. 1866	Rock Chidley.
An improved machine for raising and carrying earth, mud, stones or other similar solid or liquid materials for dredging, ventilating, or winnowing grain, or other analogous purposes.	174	20th Jan. 1866	Louis Belem.
Boots and shoes	190	23rd Jan. 1865	John Kadir.
Improvements in armour plated and other ships or vessels, also applicable to fortifications generally. (*tubes for ventilation.*)	296	2nd Feb. 1865	Julius Saunders Jeffreys.
A new method for removing or destroying the momentum of heavy bodies by means of an elastic machine or mechanism, so as to prevent injury and damage from concussion, applicable to ship cables, ship and fort armour, railway trains, tenders to part heads and floating piers, gangways, breakwaters and other similar structures, also as a motive-power. (*saving products.*) (Communicated by *William Graham M'Ivor.*)	321	5th Feb. 1866	Clements Robert Markham.

Subject-matter of Patent.	Number of Patent.	Date.	Name of Patentee.
VENTILATION, &c.—*continued.*			
Apparatus for ventilating horticultural and other buildings.	323	6th Feb. 1865	Charles Beard.
Improvements in ventilating blinds or screens, and in means of ventilating ships and vessels.	450	15th Feb. 1865	Charles Langley.
Improvements in treating sewage and in arranging apparatus in sewers and culverts to facilitate the ventilation of such structures.	451	16th Feb. 1865	Richard Smith.
Apparatus for ventilating hats	455	22nd Feb. 1865	John Carter.
Improvements in ships of war, partly applicable to ships designed for the merchant service. (Communicated by Augustus Walker.)	508	23rd Feb. 1865	George Hawkins.
Apparatus for heating and cooling atmospheric air and other uniform bodies, and for heating ovens and for heating and ventilating buildings.	636	7th March 1865	Loftus Perkins.
Furnaces and fire-places	692	11th March 1865	Edward Brown Wilson.
Improvements in securing low and uniform temperatures, applicable to public and private buildings, also to refrigerators, coolers and condensers, and to ships and other vessels, and in the apparatus employed therein. (Communicated by Daniel Sutton.)	720	14th March 1865	Alfred Vincent Newton.
Improved means of ventilation by the use of perforated tubular cornices and centre-pieces.	818	23rd March 1865	Thomas Harvey Saunders.
Ventilating blinds	879	24th March 1865	Henry Welchman King.
Improved apparatus for collecting or receiving pulverised flint or dust.	908	31st March 1865	Eliza Leah.
An improved hot ventilator	951	5th April 1865	Robert Standley.
Improvements in machinery or apparatus for drilling or boring rocks and other hard substances, in tunnelling, mining and other like operations, parts of which improvements are also applicable to the ventilating of the workings in mines and similar places. (Communicated by Herman Haupt.)	981	6th April 1865	John Henry Johnson.
Fire-places and flues and apparatus connected therewith.	990	7th April 1865	Edward Walch.
Improvements in apparatus for lighting and ventilating ships, part of which is also applicable for producing fresh water at sea.	996	7th April 1865	Henry Edmunds.
Means and apparatus employed for preventing downward draft in chimneys, facilitating the escape of smoke therefrom, and for ventilating apartments or buildings.	1471	29th May 1865	{ Edward Myers. James Stodart. }
An improved method of and machinery for cutting and excavating rock for railway tunnels and other purposes. (Communicated by Thales Lindsley.)	1557	12th June 1865	George Hawkins.
Method of constructing partitions, walls, floors and roofs of buildings.	1585	13th June 1865	John James Rochester.
Improvements in ventilating railway carriages and in the apparatus to be employed therefor.	1616	17th June 1865	William Clay.
Improved sanitary apparatus or arrangements for preventing noxious exhalations such as arise during ... or treating iron or other articles	1690	24th June 1865	{ Matthew Andrew Muir. James M'Ilwham. }

Subject-matter of Patent.	Number of Patent.	Date.	Name of Patentee.
VENTILATION, &c.—continued.			
Improvements in tubular structures rendering them specially applicable for ships' masts and building purposes. (shafts for ventilation.)	1755	3rd July 1865	Edward Deane.
Means of obtaining or producing oxygen applicable to various useful purposes. (for purifying air in ships, mines, &c.)	1780	6th July 1865	Hermann Brigel.
A diving apparatus for submarine purposes - -	1837	12th July 1865	Thomas Cato McKean.
Improvements in apparatus and equipments used by persons employed under water, part of the improvements being also applicable for the use of persons employed where noxious gases or vapours prevail.	1840	13th July 1865	Auguste Denayrouse.
Ventilators - . . . . . -	1866	18th July 1865	John Paul Baugh Le Patourel.
Fire engines and hydraulic machines - - (or reservoired ventilators.)	1965	29th July 1865	Leon Paul Laroche.
Roofing-tiles and slabs . . . . (ensuring ventilation.)	1991	1st Aug. 1865	Frederick Ransome.
Ventilators	2111	16th Aug. 1865	James Billings.
Punkahs	2148	19th Aug. 1865	John Edwin Marsh.
An improved arrangement of apparatus and materials to be employed for effecting the deodorizing of the noxious gases arising from sewers and drains, and for the more effectual ventilation and inspection of such sewers and drains.	2451	25th Sept. 1865	Edward Brooks the younger.
Apparatus for ventilating and for preventing down draught in flues.	2467	26th Sept. 1865	John Hillier.
A new or improved ventilating spring mattress -	2511	30th Sept. 1865	Joseph Edwin Townshend.
Certain improvements in window fittings - -	2803	10th Oct. 1865	William Cooke.
An improved ventilating apparatus for use in steam boats, vessels and other places requiring to be ventilated.	2809	10th Oct. 1865	John Harrison Woodward.
Trapping and ventilating sewers - . -	2814	10th Oct. 1865	Richard Abell.
Greenhouses	2884	18th Oct. 1865	Thomas Humgate Preston Dennis.
Ventilators for windows and other like openings -	2790	31st Oct. 1865	David Blair White.
Improvements in apparatus for obtaining fresh water from salt and impure water, also applicable for ventilating purposes.	2958	17th Nov. 1865	Samuel Hazard Huntly.
Apparatus for preventing draughts of air between the door and the lower part of doors.	3050	24th Nov. 1865	Louis Desiré Carbonnier.
An improved mode of applying the compression of air for ventilating purpose, and the compression of any gas for hurrying along elastic fluids in conveying pipes . . . -	3168	8th Dec. 1865	Platron de Moudrin. Paul Lebatre. Augustin Jullienne.
Improvements in constructing atmospheric railways and carriages, and in working the same, parts of which are applicable to exhausting and condensing air for other purposes. (for ventilation.)	3178	9th Dec. 1865	Alexander Doull.
An improved mode of and apparatus for purifying and deodorizing impure air, whether in buildings, ships, mines or sewers, which improvement is also applicable for ventilating purposes - -	3287	30th Dec. 1865	Joseph John Harrison. Edward Harrison.

Subject-matter of Patent.	Number of Patent.	Date.	Name of Patentee.

VENTILATION, &c.—continued.

A new and improved apparatus for cooling and purifying air in rooms or compartments, and ventilating the same.
(*Communicated by Levi Stevens Lyman.*) — 3282 — 30th Dec. 1865 — William Clark.

Pipes, tubular columns and hollow structures, for masts, cars, shear legs, life boats and ordinary boats, for water, gas and waste water pipes, and for other similar constructions where great strength is required.
(*shafts for ventilation.* — 3314 — 22nd Dec. 1865 — Edward Dunn.

VICES, PINCERS, WRENCHES, DRILL-BRACES, SCREWSTOCKS AND SCREW-DRIVERS.

Drilling apparatus for hand or steam power adaptable also as a vice and for lifting purposes — 10 — 3rd Jan. 1865 — { George Hodgson. James Pim.

Improved pincers for gas and other pipes
(*Communicated by Jules Chevrière.*) — 88 — 11th Jan. 1865 — William Edward Gedge.

Machinery for opening and carding cotton and other fibrous materials.
(*vice for holding the legs of spiked drums.*) — 90 — 11th Jan. 1865 — Robert Tempest.

Shifting wrenches
(*Communicated by Pierre Augustin Semall.*) — 437 — 17th Feb. 1865 — William Clark.

Apparatus used for bending the ends of walking sticks, and the sticks or handles of umbrellas and parasols — 628 — 10th March 1865 — { Joshua Jones. Richard Dassel Jones.

Construction of screws and screw drivers
(*Communicated by Jared Augustus Ayres.*) — 1367 — 19th May 1865 — Alfred Vincent Newton.

Vices — 1473 — 29th May 1865 — William Johnson.

Tube cutters and screw stocks — 1527 — 3rd June 1865 — Charles Taylor.

Vices — 1781 — 3rd July 1865 — { Lamb Henry. Gustavus Richards.

An improved combination drill brace — 2312 — 28th Aug. 1865 — { Edward Davies. Richard Hobbs Tumrian.

Screw wrenches
(*Communicated by Monsieur Charles Bourguin.*) — 2396 — 30th Sept. 1865 — Hector Augusto Dufresal.

Screw wrenches
(*Communicated by Charles Churchill.*) — 2789 — 28th Oct. 1865 — James Buckingham.

A combined adjustable spanner, tube cutter and pipe wrench.
(*Communicated by Henry Hitchings Bourguemoth and Martin Van Wisher.*) — 3036 — 27th Nov. 1865 — John Phillips Bar agrumash.

Subject-matter of Patent.	Number of Patent.	Date.	Name of Patentee.

WASHING, CLEANSING AND WRINGING FABRICS, YARNS AND MATERIALS.

Subject-matter of Patent.	Number of Patent.	Date.	Name of Patentee.
Washing, squeezing and mangling machinery	22	5th Jan. 1865	John William Branford.
Machinery or apparatus for washing wool and other fibrous materials.	251	24th Jan. 1865	John Petrie, jun'.
Machinery for washing and drying wool and other fibrous materials	321	1st Feb. 1865	John M'Naught. William M'Naught, jun'.
A new method for removing or destroying the momentum of heavy bodies by means of an elastic machine or machines, so as to prevent injury and damage from concussion, applicable to ship cables, ship and fort armour, railway trains, tenders to piers heads, and floating piers, gangways, breakwaters and other similar structures, also as a motive-power. (driving washing-machines.) (Communicated by William Graham M'Ivor.)	331	6th Feb. 1865	Clements Robert Markham.
Apparatus for rinsing and drying by centrifugal force. (Communicated by Félix Moreau and Auguste Rariasé.)	604	4th March 1865	Henri Adrien Bonneville.
Washing machines (Communicated by Félix Moreau and Auguste Rariasé.)	605	4th March 1865	Henri Adrien Bonneville.
Machinery or apparatus to be employed in the bleaching and dyeing of hanks or skeins of yarns and threads. (apparatus for washing.)	718	14th March 1865	Longin Cantert.
Apparatus for washing wool, hair and other fibre	808	22nd March 1865	George Edmund Donisthorpe.
An improved machine for washing, wringing and mangling.	837	24th March 1865	James Andrew Nenney.
Improvements in wringing machines, parts of which are applicable to the construction of rollers. (Communicated by Stephen Wing and Henry Holly.)	929	1st April 1865	Henry Lewis.
Treating wool in order to cleanse it from burrs, seeds and other foreign matters	1042	12th April 1865	Henry Riker. George Jermain.
Washing or steeping and bleaching textile or fibrous materials. (Communicated by Messieurs Negret, Oriol and Predal.)	1144	24th April 1865	William Clark.
Improvements in treating fibrous materials and textile fabrics, and in producing soap. (Communicated by Leon Pasquier and Alphonsine Julie Dumont.)	1448	25th May 1865	Michael Henry.
A new or improved machine for washing raw materials, worked out or overworked, to be employed in the manufacture of fabrics, and specially of fabrics made into pieces.	1484	29th May 1865	Jean Alphonse Heinrich.
Machinery or apparatus for washing wool and other fibrous materials.	1500	31st May 1865	John Petrie, jun'.
Washing-machines	1744	30th June 1865	William Hook Davey.

Subject-matter of Patent.	Number of Patent.	Date.	Name of Patentee.
WASHING, &c.—_continued._			
An improved self-acting apparatus for obtaining a circulation of volatile liquids. (applied to cleaning linen.) (Communicated by Messieurs François Mennet and Auguste Joquin.)	1818	7th July 1865	Hector Auguste Dufrené.
Machinery for washing, wringing, mangling and drying domestic clothes or other fabrics and fibrous substances	1827	10th July 1865	Henry Fearnly. Christopher Smith.
An improved apparatus for cooking, a portion of the same being applicable for washing and ironing.	1917	22nd July 1865	William Wapshare.
A new or improved detergent solution to be used in the washing or cleaning of wool and woollen fabrics. (Communicated by Charles Dyonise Reinfeld.)	1982	25th July 1865	John Henry Johnson.
Machinery or apparatus for washing wool and other fibrous materials.	2039	5th Aug. 1865	John Petrie, jun'.
Apparatus for washing yarns	2044	7th Aug. 1865	William Pollock. John Stoba.
Machinery used in washing, bleaching and dyeing yarns and textile fabrics, in the hank	2115	16th Aug. 1865	John Smith. William Schofield.
Improvements in washing fabrics and threads, and in machinery employed therein. (Communicated by Stanislas Vigoureux.)	2129	17th Aug. 1865	Richard Archibald Brewman.
Clothes wringing machines, the mode of communicating rotary motion in which is also applicable to other machines having similarly rotating parts. (Partly communicated by James Praw and Daniel Lyons.)	2336	12th Sept. 1865	Thomas Drew Stetson.
An improved arrangement and combination of the working parts of machinery or apparatus employed for washing, wringing and mangling clothes and fabrics.	2450	25th Sept. 1865	George Frederic Smucker.
Construction of washing-machines and churns	2471	27th Sept. 1865	John Taylor.
Washing and wringing machines. (Communicated by Thomas Bletcher.)	2478	27th Sept. 1865	Richard Archibald Brewman.
Machinery and apparatus for bleaching, scoping, clearing and washing fibrous and other materials, yarns and fabrics	2501	29th Sept. 1865	William Schofield. John Smith.
Improved machinery for feeding fibrous substances to preparing, carding and other machinery for working wool and other filamentous substances. (washing-machines.) (Communicated by Alexander Dere.)	2517	30th Sept. 1865	William Edward Newton.
An improved washing or cleansing liquor or solution.	2548	7th Oct. 1865	James Roddy.
Rollers for washing yarns and fabrics and for other purposes	2686	18th Oct. 1865	William Schofield. John Smith.
Improvements in the mode of applying mineral oils to the scouring and lubrication of textile textiles and machinery, and in the manufacture of soap.	3107	4th Dec. 1865	Leopold Joseph Bouchart.

Subject-matter of Patent.	Number of Patent.	Date.	Name of Patentee.
WASHING, &c.—continued.			
Means or apparatus for the fulling, scouring and cleansing of woollen yarns and cloths - - -	3521	13th Dec. 1865	{ Benjamin Forrest. William Prestley. }
For Washing Ores, see "METALS." For Washing Bottles, see "BOTTLES." For Washing Casks, see "CASKS." For Washing Coals, see "FUEL." For Washing Potatoes, see "PRESERVING FOOD." For Washing Corn see "THRASHING." For Washing Clay, see "BRICKS."			
WATER-CLOSETS, URINALS AND COMMODES.			
Water-closet apparatus - - - -	642	8th March 1865	John Shanks.
Apparatus for supplying regulated or measured quantities of water and other fluids. (to urinals, &c.)	707	13th March 1865	Robert Gordon Rattray.
Seats of water-closets - - - -	887	5th April 1865	Jean Isidore Darribet.
Indicators and fastenings for water-closets and other purposes.	1098	20th April 1865	Henry Kindon Taylor.
Water-closets - - - - -	1364	17th May 1865	Fielding Fletcher.
Mechanical arrangement of water-closets for ships -	1740	30th June 1865	Henry William Ronore.
A new or improved apparatus for supplying disinfecting liquids to water-closets, urinals and other places requiring the same.	1879	19th July 1865	Charles Nicholas.
Water-closet apparatus, urinals and the like, and appliances thereto.	2270	4th Sept. 1865	Stephen Kettle.
Ships' water-closets - - - -	2546	4th Oct. 1865	{ Edwin William de Russett. Richard Farrell Dale. }
An improved description of water-closet - -	2918	13th Nov. 1865	Peter Ellis.
An improved mode of applying the compression of air for ventilating purposes, and the compression of any gas for hurrying along elastic fluids in conveying pipes - - - - (purifying cesspools.)	3155	8th Dec. 1865	{ Pierron de Mondésir. Paul Lebaitre. Augustin Jullirane. }
WATERING; SUPPLYING AND DISTRIBUTING WATER; FOUNTAINS AND WELLS.			
An improved portable pneumatic apparatus applicable to surgery and medicine for all purposes as a douche, for affusion, irrigation, injection, and for enemas. (see "MEDICINE.")	18	3rd Jan. 1865	Thomas John Ashton.

Subject-matter of Patent.	Number of Patent.	Date.	Name of Patentee.
WATERING, &c.—continued.			
An improved machine for raising and carrying earth, sand, stones or other similar solid or liquid materials for dredging, ventilating or winnowing grain, or other analogous purposes. (for agricultural irrigation.)	174	20th Jan. 1865	Louis Balme.
Filtering apparatus (for supply of towns)	248	28th Jan. 1865	Victor Burg.
An improved method of propelling agricultural implements. (for irrigation.)	1616	15th June 1865	Virgile Poitevin.
Steam pumping machines or engines	1780	3rd July 1865	Martin Browne.
Fountains	1612	10th July 1865	Frederick Taylor.
Means of and apparatus for raising water for agricultural and other useful and ornamental purposes. (Communicated by Jean Louis Crétin Achard.)	1916	22nd July 1865	William Edward Gedge.
Fire engines and hydraulic machines	1955	24th July 1865	Leon Paul Laroche.
Well sinking tubes (Communicated by Hiram John Messenger, Stephen Brewer and Byron Mudge.)	2176	24th Aug. 1865	William Edward Newton.
Apparatus for supplying regulated or measured quantities of water.	2160	25th Aug. 1865	Robert Gordon Rattray.
Improved apparatus for supplying boilers with water. (Communicated by Gustav Adolph Riviel.)	2211	28th Aug. 1865	Alfred Vincent Newton.
Hydropults and hydrostatic pumps	2305	9th Sept. 1865	James Webster.
A new and improved machine for the collecting and diffusing of water or other fluids.	2416	22nd Sept. 1865	Charles Wyatt Orford.
Improvements in apparatus and means for extinguishing fires, part of such improvements being applicable for other purposes. (for watering gardens.)	2559	5th Oct. 1865	William Henry Phillips.
Double or single action pumps (Communicated by Claude Genin.)	2623	11th Oct. 1865	William Edward Gedge.
An improved apparatus for regulating the supply of water to tanks, water butts or cisterns, applicable also to other purposes	2710	20th Oct. 1865	{ Richard Fell. Davy Hammond.
Improvements in sinking and operating wells, and in the apparatus employed therein. (Communicated by James Suggett.)	3074	30th Nov. 1865	John Henry Johnson.
Pumps (for waterworks.) }	3280	23rd Dec. 1865	{ Henry Davis Hoskold. William Blanch Brain.
See also " VALVES." *For Water Pipes, see "* PIPES."			
WATERPROOF, FIREPROOF AND AIRPROOF FABRICS, BUILDINGS, &c.; WATERPROOFING, FIREPROOFING AND AIRPROOFING.			
Vulcanizing compounds and vulcanized fabrics (Communicated by Simon Stevens.)	179	20th Jan. 1865	Benjamin Franklin Stevens.

Subject-matter of Patent.	Number of Patent.	Date.	Name of Patentee.
WATERPROOFING, &c.—continued.			
Improvements in the treatment of oils obtained from the distillation of tar, and in the application of the same to the purposes for which ordinary drying oils are applicable. (for waterproofing,) (Communicated by Claudius Cordier and Vincent Cordier.)	244	27th Jan. 1865	John Henry Johnson.
Certain improvements in rendering uninflammable cotton, silk and other textile fabrics.	313	4th Feb. 1865	Edmund Hottin.
Waterproofing skins, hides and leather	413	14th Feb. 1865	George Harton.
Waterproof and other coats and capes	471	18th Feb. 1865	{ Charles Désiré Barge. / Alexandre Hermant.
Improved means of preventing the leakage of barrels, and of rendering packages and fabrics impervious to air and gases. (Communicated by Lewis Francis and Cyrus Lambert.)	913	31st March 1865	Alfred Vincent Newton.
Manufacture of a compound or material to be used as a substitute for india-rubber. (Communicated by Henry Lorenberry and Emile Granier.)	1068	15th April 1865	William Clark.
Improvements in the manufacture of waterproof fabrics and in apparatus to be employed therein	1160	25th April 1865	{ John Collier Wickham. / Auguste Edward Heine.
An improved manufacture of waterproof fabric (Communicated by The American Waterproof Cloth Company.)	1219	1st May 1865	William Edward Newton.
Manufacture of parkesine or compounds of pyroxyline and also solutions of pyroxyline known as collodion. (for waterproofing cloth.)	1313	11th May 1865	Alexander Parkes.
Umbrellas, parasols and sunshades	1589	5th June 1865	John Stephenson.
An improved combination of materials for the manufacture of carpets, floor cloth, felt, wall paper, fireproof flexible roofing, ship and boat building and for other similar purposes (fireproof.)	1775	5th July 1865	{ John Longbottom. / Abram Longbottom.
An improved process for applying airproof solutions to the interior of casks and barrels. (Communicated by Edward Deloran Woodruff.)	1957	24th July 1865	William Edward Newton.
Compounds for waterproofing and insulating purposes.	1982	29th July 1865	Frederick Augustus Abel.
Preparing charges for fire-arms and for blasting (waterproofing the charges.)	2286	2nd Sept. 1865	Constant Reichen.
Cricket, racket, tennis and foot balls	2328	11th Sept. 1865	Charles Huntley.
An improvement in the manufacture of waterproof soles for boots and shoes.	2449	25th Sept. 1865	John Wiggins Coburn.
Manufacture of knickerbockers and such like coverings for the legs.	2460	26th Sept. 1865	William Ambler.
An improved process for preparing skins and hides or leather, so as to render such substances waterproof and more durable than heretofore.	2516	30th Sept. 1865	John William Moore Miller.
Cartridges for breech-loading fire-arms	2543	4th Oct. 1865	{ Joseph Jones. / Frederick James Jones.
An improved composition or material to be employed in waterproofing or rendering woven fabrics impervious to moisture.	2560	6th Oct. 1865	Henry Francis Smith.

Subject-matter of Patent.	Number of Patent.	Date.	Name of Patentee.
WATERPROOFING, &c.—continued.			
Rendering wood for building and other purposes non-combustible or non-inflammable.	2826	11th Oct. 1865	William Ball.
A new composition of india-rubber mastic or cement, made in a more or less fluid state according to the use to be made of it, and the process or contrivance for applying the same.	2630	17th Oct. 1865	Auguste Aimé Larousse.
Preparing the surfaces of paper, leather, woven and other fabrics and substances, for receiving photographic pictures, engravings, lithographs and prints, and for rendering such substances fire and water proof. (Communicated by William Gilmer.)	2891	9th Nov. 1865	William Edward Newton.
Waterproof linings of cases, boxes and apparatus in which articles are desired to be packed water-proof.	3201	11th Dec. 1865	John Jones.
Improvements in the manufacture of boots and shoes for rendering them waterproof.	3270	19th Dec. 1865	James Belton.
Preparation of glue or gelatine so as to render it insoluble in water, and applicable by the admixture of other substances to various purposes for which common glue or gelatine cannot now be used. (as a waterproof sizing.) (Communicated by Henry Wurtz.)	3325	23rd Dec. 1866	William Edward Newton.
WATERWHEELS AND ENGINES; HYDRAULIC MOTIVE-POWER.			
Motive-power and means of communication between passengers while travelling and applicances connected therewith.	55	7th Jan. 1865	George Hall Galloway.
Improved arrangements for coupling steam-engines, turbines or other apparatus employed as motive-power. (Communicated by Ludwig August Riedinger.)	159	19th Jan. 1865	Adolf Wilhelm Prager.
Steam-engines - - - - (or water engines.)	168	19th Jan. 1865	William Cleveland Hicks.
Steam engines - - - -	435	14th Feb. 1865	James Grafton Jones.
An improved mercuro-hydraulic motor (Communicated by Pierre Eugene Lourier.)	492	22nd Feb. 1865	Richard Archibald Brooman.
Obtaining motive-power from aëriform fluids and from liquids.	501	22nd Feb. 1865	Matthew Piers Watt Boulton.
An improved arrangement of valves and other appliances for a new description of hydraulic engine for raising water and other fluids above their common level, the fluids so raised to be used as a motive-power - - -	791	21st March 1865	James Smith. Sydney Arthur Chase.
Obtaining motive-power - - - -	802	22nd March 1865	Valentine Baker.
Improvements in obtaining motive-power, parts of which improvements are applicable to the compressing of air and gases.	840	24th March 1865	Valentine Baker.

Subject-matter of Patent.	Number of Patent.	Date.	Name of Patentee.
WATERWHEELS, &c.—continued.			
Improvements in paddle wheels, parts of which are applicable to other purposes. (To *water-engines*.)	985	3rd April 1865	William Cantrill Gollings.
Means or apparatus for obtaining motive-power by the aid of steam, gas or other fluids. (Communicated by Joseph Perrigault, Marie Joseph Denis Farcot, Jean Joseph Léon Farcot, Michel Basile Abel Farcot, Joseph Etienne Eloi Chéfron and Emmanuel Denis Farcot.)	949	4th April 1865	William Brookes.
A new motive-power engine - - -	1052	12th April 1865	Herman Leonhardt.
A new method of obtaining and applying water as a motive-power for propelling ships, boats and other vessels.	1083	13th April 1865	George Rommelet.
Improvements in means or apparatus for measuring the flow or passage of liquids, which improvements are also applicable in obtaining motive-power.	1150	25th April 1865	Thomas Walker.
Improved means or apparatus for gaining or acquiring motive-power.	1166	25th April 1865	Claude Jacquelin, jun'.
Certain improvements in water wheels - - (Communicated by Espéras Romestin.)	1189	26th April 1865	Arthur Charles Henderson.
A new or improved method of obtaining motive-power, together with certain machinery or apparatus for applying the same - - -	1504	1st June 1865	David Hancock. Frederick Barnes.
Machinery for obtaining power when fluid pressure is employed.	1578	9th June 1865	Lieutenant-Colonel James Baker.
Hydraulic motive-power machinery - -	1642	17th June 1865	Valentine Baker.
An improved hydraulic apparatus for producing motive-power.	1701	26th June 1865	Jean Egide Spanoghe.
Construction or arrangement of sluices or dams -	1870	14th July 1865	Timothy Ward Wood.
Certain improvements in the method of obtaining motive-power and in apparatus connected therewith.	1910	22nd July 1865	Edmund Perré.
Means of and apparatus for raising water for agricultural and other useful and ornamental purposes. (Communicated by Jean Louis Crüstin Achard.)	1915	22nd July 1865	William Edward Gedge.
An improved water meter, which may be employed as a water, steam or gas engine. (Communicated by Henry Adam.)	1956	24th July 1865	William Edward Newton.
Applying and utilising water power - -	1967	29th July 1865	Valentine Baker.
Means of and mechanism for obtaining motive-power.	2020	4th Aug. 1865	Adderley Sleigh.
Apparatus for obtaining motive-power - -	2425	22nd Sept. 1865	George Binnie M'Nicol.
Hydraulic pressure engines - - - -	2448	23rd Sept. 1865	Jacob Dreissörner.
A new method of obtaining and applying water as a motive-power, for propelling ships by means of paddle wheels, inside and outside.	2641	13th Oct. 1866	George Rommlet.
Improvements in means or apparatus for measuring the passage or flow of liquids, for raising and forcing fluids, and for obtaining motive-power, also in means for the manufacture of parts of such apparatus.	2966	17th Nov. 1865	Walter Payton.

Subject-matter of Patent.	Number of Patent.	Date	Name of Patentee.
WATER-WHEELS, &c.—continued.			
Turbines for obtaining motive-power, applicable also to raising and forcing fluids, and to propelling ships or vessels. (Communicated by Joseph Denis Ferrat, Jean Joseph Léon Ferrat, Michel Basile Abel Ferrat, Joseph Etienne Elie Chatean and Emmanuel Denis Ferrat.)	3332	13th Dec. 1865	William Branch.
Producing and applying rotating motion by means of an apparatus to be worked by fluids, steam, compressed air, or by water or by gas.	3279	19th Dec. 1865	John Wright Carr.
A new or improved method of and apparatus or machinery for applying water or other fluid as a motive-power	3290	23rd Dec. 1865	{ Edmund Dwyer. Henry Mann.
See also "GOVERNORS."			
WEARING-APPAREL, MILITARY OUTFITS; TAILORS' TRIMMINGS.			
An "improved clothes fastener" that may also be used as a letter clip. (See "DRYING.")	309	31st Jan. 1865	James William Gill.
Garments for ladies', gentlemen's and children's wear.	353	9th Feb. 1865	Julius Singer.
Manufacture of shirt borderings and linings to be applied to wearing apparel. (Communicated by Carl Spennempel.)	351	9th Feb. 1865	William Stants.
Machinery and tools for making collars, cuffs, wristbands and other articles of dress, also adapted for cutting metal blanks	399	13th Feb. 1865	{ David Karr. William Henry Page. James Clement Newry.
A new or improved combined garments	420	14th Feb. 1865	Robert Pasco Barrett.
Waterproof and other coats and capes	471	18th Feb. 1865	{ Charles Désiré Barge. Alexandre Hermant.
Certain improvements in scarfs and in the manufacture of the same. (Communicated by Leon de Mours Poirate.)	491	22nd Feb. 1865	Isaac Parkcato.
Gaiters, spatterdashes and other similar articles	599	1st March 1865	Jean Baptiste Toumaine.
An improved method of and means or apparatus for measuring the human body. (for coats.)	636	7th March 1865	John Hemhgrave Wilson.
An improved machine for cutting button holes (Communicated by George Rehfus.)	657	11th March 1865	Julius Garelly.
An improved method of treating, cleaning or preparing painted or other canvas, tarpaulins and dirty cotton waste, so as to render the same suitable to be used for household and other purposes for which they may be applicable. (for cutting up into garments.)	732	17th March 1865	William Maurice Williams.
Mode of forming and making clothing (Communicated by Thomas Scott Lambert, M.D., and Theodore Bartos.)	736	18th March 1865	Gerard Ralston.

Subject-matter of Patent.	Number of Patent.	Date.	Name of Patentee.
WEARING-APPAREL, &c.—continued.			
Mechanism for attaching buttons to fabrics (Communicated by George Belfast.)	762	18th March 1865	Francis Wise.
Improvements applicable to capes, paletôts, overcoats and other such like garments.	1120	22nd April 1865	John Emary.
Improved apparatus for securing buttons to fabrics (Communicated by William James Gordon and Edmund David Gilbert.)	1151	25th April 1865	George Davies.
Manufacture of flock fabrics (for robe linings, clothing, &c.) (Communicated by The American Waterproof Cloth Company.)	1218	1st May 1865	William Edward Newton.
An improvement in buttons and means of attaching the same.	1294	11th May 1865	Herbert William Hart.
Apparatus for measuring the button figure for garments.	1528	3rd June 1865	Edward Eastman.
An improved description of stud for fastening shirts, cuffs, waistcoats and other articles of wearing apparel. (see " Buttons.")	1616	15th June 1865	Stanislaus Helman.
Under vests	1721	24th June 1865	James Webster.
Manufacture or " making up " of trousers	1825	10th July 1865	John Jones.
Improvements in apparatus and equipments used by persons employed under water, part of the improvements being also applicable for the use of persons employed where noxious gases or vapours prevail.	1840	12th July 1865	Auguste Denayrouze.
Parts of military and other outfits	1936	25th July 1865	Thomas Jefferson Mayall.
Apparatus for taking measurements (Communicated by George Beard.)	2112	16th Aug. 1865	William Clark.
Apparatus for elongating and contracting waist and other belts, which apparatus is also applicable for other purposes (fastenings for trousers, &c.)	2234	29th Aug. 1865	George Frederick White. Harvey Chamberlain.
Apparatus applied to pockets to ensure the safety of their contents	2260	30th Aug. 1865	Charles Francis Anderson. David Durant.
Ornamentation of fringes and trimmings	2260	5th Sept. 1865	Thomas Hird Bailey.
Articles of wearing apparel (see " Hoists.")	2317	9th Sept. 1865	Richard Charles Newbery.
Improvements in buttons and in attaching buttons to garments or fabrics.	2753	25th Oct. 1865	George Augustus Huddart.
An improved method of draughting patterns for coats, waistcoats and other close fitting garments, and apparatus to be used in obtaining the measurements for the same	2955	17th Nov. 1865	John Henry Smith. George Robert Smith.
Improvements in sewing-machines and in sewing or embroidering. (making button holes.)	3070	1st Dec. 1865	Isaac Merritt Singer.
Improvements applicable to coats, cloaks and other like outer garments	3157	8th Dec. 1865	William Calvert. John Stewart Robertson.
Improvements in buttons and in the method of attaching buttons and ornaments to garments and other articles. (Communicated by Frederic Ingersoll Palmer.)	3164	8th Dec. 1865	George Tomlinson Bousfield.

Subject-matter of Patent.	Number of Patent.	Date.	Name of Proprietor.

WEARING-APPAREL, &c.—continued.

| Obtaining and employing continuous lengths of tanned leather for various useful purposes (for trousers, coats, &c.) | 3534 | 23rd Dec. 1866 | { George Hurn, Daniel Hurn. |

See also "BUTTONS."
See also "GLOVES."
See also "HATS."
See also "SHIRTS."
See also "PETTICOATS."

WEAVING, BRAIDING, PLATTING; PREPARING FOR WEAVING.

1. Sizing, Warping, Beaming and Preparing Yarns for Weaving.

Improved mechanism for giving intermittent or continuous revolving motion of different velocities, without the use of change wheels (taking up beams of sizing-machines.)	272	31st Jan. 1865	{ Thomas Hall, Bernard Bonner.
Certain improvements in mechanism or apparatus for saturating the cylinders of "slashing" and "tapering" machines, such machinery being employed in the sizing of cotton and other yarns.	405	16th Feb. 1865	Thomas Ogden.
An improved method of treating yarns or threads previously to the processes of dyeing or dressing.	490	22nd Feb. 1865	James McKinⸯⸯⸯ.
Certain improvements in machinery or apparatus for drying "warps" of cotton and other fibrous substances (after sizing.)	889	29th March 1866	{ Richard Holroyd, Joseph Holroyd Ralton.
Dyeing and sizing cotton, silk, woollen and other yarns	1413	23rd May 1865	{ Isaac Holt, William Holt, James Holt, Joseph Maude.
Sizing machines for sizing yarns, beams or warps to be woven	1789	29th June 1865	{ David Mercer, Thomas Mercer, Jonathan Mercer, Joseph Mercer.
An improved sizing material to be employed for sizing or dressing yarns preparatory to weaving. (Communicated by John L'Ève Hilleiller.)	1908	21st July 1866	Edward Nelmesh.
Machinery or apparatus for sizing, drying and beaming yarns of cotton or other fibrous substances	2022	4th Aug. 1866	{ John Omukreger, John Dealgven.
Treating and printing threads employed in weaving (Communicated by Stanislas Figourras.)	2063	11th Aug. 1865	Richard Archibald Brooⸯⸯⸯ.
Improvements in the means of fixing or attaching the bobbins of winding and other machines on to their spindles, which improvements are also applicable to other similar or analogous purposes, and to the detaching of railway carriages from trains whilst in motion. (useful in warp machines.)	2250	31st Aug. 1865	John Ward.
Manufacture of artificial gum, size or stiffening matter.	2810	1st Nov. 1865	John Sellers.

Subject-matter of Patent.	Number of Patent.	Date.	Name of Patentee.
WEAVING, &c.—continued.			
Machinery or apparatus employed for sizing yarns	3083	14th Nov. 1865	James Eastwood.
Certain improvements in sizing and dressing yarns	3010	23rd Nov. 1865	Nathaniel Greenhalgh. James Mallison.
Improvements in machinery employed when weaving hair, and in preparing and treating hair for weaving. (dressing.) (Communicated by Charles Bradley.)	3066	29th Nov. 1865	George Tomlinson Bousfield.
A new or improved method of preparing esparto, alpha or megasdor grasses or other similar vegetable substances, for spinning, weaving, and for substitution for hair and for other fibres now in use. (see "SPINNING.")	3156	4th Dec. 1865	Oliver Maggs. George Hedgcumbe Nesmith.
A new method of and apparatus for regulating the tension of threads in weaving and other operations. (warping.) (Communicated by Stanislas Vigourous.)	3239	14th Dec. 1865	Richard Archibald Brooman.
III.—Weaving Plain, Figured and Double Fabrics; Jacquards and Looms; Woven Fabrics.			
Looms for weaving	43	5th Jan. 1865	John Alfred Castree.
Weaving ornamental fabrics	45	6th Jan. 1865	John Crow. James Mornaley.
The manufacture of a new thread for weaving and other uses. (see "SPINNING.") (Communicated by Yves Sabrox and Gaston Jrod.)	212	25th Jan. 1865	Richard Archibald Brooman.
Certain improvements in looms for weaving	293	2nd Feb. 1865	John Maynes.
A new method for removing or destroying the momentum of heavy bodies by means of an elastic machine or machines, so as to prevent injury and damage from concussion, applicable to ship cables, ship and fort armour, railway trains, tenders to perthmds, and floating piers, gangways, breakwaters and other similar structures, also as a motive-power. (driving looms.) (Communicated by William Graham M'Ivor.)	321	6th Feb. 1865	Clements Robert Markham.
Improvements in and connected with jacquard apparatus for weaving.	329	6th Feb. 1865	William Cockburn
Looms for weaving	377	10th Feb. 1865	Rowland Gibson Hayard.
An improved protector for the needles and cards used in jacquard machines.	409	13th Feb. 1865	William Collinson Ridlings, sen'.
An improved manufacture of barège stuffs (Communicated by Edmond Dirson.)	440	16th Feb. 1865	William Edward Gedge.
Circular box looms	459	22nd Feb. 1865	John Keighley. Richard Narphard.
Certain improvements in scarfs and in the manufacture of the same. (Communicated by Leon de Mave Parients.)	491	22nd Feb. 1865	Isaac Parients.

Subject-matter of Patent.	Number of Patent.	Date.	Name of Patentee.
WEAVING, &c.—continued.			
Looms for weaving - - - -	454	22nd Feb. 1865	John Hodgson. John Godfrey. William Shackleton.
Certain improvements in looms for weaving -	608	23rd Feb. 1865	Aaron Barker.
Improvements in the manufacture of textile fabrics and in the machinery or apparatus employed therefor. (broad looms.)	649	28th Feb. 1865	David Chalmers.
Certain improvements in and applicable to looms weaving.	662	2nd March 1865	Samuel Brooks.
Looms for weaving - - -	750	17th March 1865	James Bullough.
Weft stop motions for looms - - -	769	18th March 1865	Edwin Pilling. John Harper.
Weaving ornamental fabrics - - - } (shawls.)	810	23rd March 1865	James Macaulay. Robert Watson.
Machinery and apparatus for indicating, selecting and reading in such cards of designs or patterns as are transferred and perforated on cards, papers or their substitutes, and for reproducing and repeating duplicates of such operations on such materials, for Jacquard machines.	816	23rd March 1865	Duncan Mackenzie.
Machinery or apparatus employed in the manufacture of cloth and other fabrics - - }	821	23rd March 1865	Joseph Last. Munn Mellor.
Looms for weaving - - - -	824	23rd March 1865	George Henry Castree. John Alfred Castree.
Looms for weaving - - - -	845	25th March 1865	James Milton.
Looms for weaving - - - -	907	31st March 1865	Lang Bridge.
Looms for weaving - - - -	936	1st April 1865	Alfred William Pearce.
Looms for weaving - - - -	1002	11th April 1865	Archibald Turner.
Certain improvements in looms for weaving -	1051	13th April 1865	Christopher Turner. Thomas Roon.
Certain improvements in looms for weaving -	1070	17th April 1865	Mark Smith.
Certain improvements in looms for weaving -	1089	19th April 1865	James Edward Hyde Andrew.
Jacquard and indexing machines - -	1361	5th May 1865	Joseph Wadsworth. Henry Dussart. James M'Murdo.
Manufacture of a certain description of woven fabric called "turkish towelling."	1381	9th May 1865	James Gorton.
Jacquard machines - - - -	1396	10th May 1865	James Melvin.
Improvements in power looms for weaving and in apparatus connected therewith.	1507	11th May 1865	William Jamieson.
Apparatus employed in weaving brocaded and ornamental fabrics - - - }	1512	11th May 1865	Dennis Ellis. Matthew Hollas.
An improved woven fabric - - -	1516	12th May 1865	Thomas Smith. Henry James.
Certain improvements in looms for weaving -	1417	24th May 1865	Thomas Calvert. David Montgomery.
Looms for weaving - - - -	1437	25th May 1865	David Walsh.
Certain improvements applicable to spinning, weaving and knitting machines. (Communicated by Charles Arthur Radiguet and Jean Adolphe Lartur.)	1440	25th May 1865	William Edward Newton.
Looms for weaving - - - -	1524	3rd June 1865	Thomas Forster. James Eckersley.

Subject-matter of Patent.	Number of Patent.	Date.	Name of Patentee.
WEAVING, &c.—*continued.*			
Printing threads employed in weaving (*Communicated by Stanislas Vignoreus.*)	1730	29th June 1865	Richard Archibald Brooman.
Looms for weaving	1743	30th June 1865	John Keighley.
Looms for weaving	1876	19th July 1865	Mark Knowles.
Weaving ornamental fabrics	1960	24th July 1865	William Cockburn.
Certain improvements in looms for weaving	1961	25th July 1865	Robert Clayton. James Roper. John Goulding.
Certain improvements in looms for weaving	2061	9th Aug. 1865	Thomas Ramsden Shaw.
Looms for weaving	2078	10th Aug. 1865	John Ingham. Henry Ingham. James Broadley.
Certain improvements in looms for weaving	2081	12th Aug. 1865	William Follough.
Looms for weaving	2116	16th Aug. 1865	William Gadd. John Moore.
Improvements in the manufacture of textile fabrics and in the machinery or apparatus connected therewith. (*winding cops.*) (*Communicated by David Chalmers.*)	2117	16th Aug. 1865	Flora M'Dougall Chalmers
Looms for weaving	2286	7th Sept. 1865	John Smith.
Looms for weaving	2385	20th Sept. 1865	Joseph Edmondson.
Certain improvements in looms for weaving	2566	9th Oct. 1865	Peter Todd. Joseph Holding.
Certain improvements in looms for weaving	2672	17th Oct. 1865	Edward Lord.
Looms for weaving	2811	1st Nov. 1865	Adrien Jackson. James Clough. Charles Ashley.
Shuttle motion for looms (*Communicated by Julius Schottenfels.*)	2826	3rd Nov. 1865	Frederic Tothamore.
Looms for weaving	2843	3rd Nov. 1865	Arthur Heald.
Power looms for weaving	2947	16th Nov. 1865	Matthew Caton. Henry Holden.
Manufacture of shawls (*Communicated by Pierre Howard Maillard.*)	2961	17th Nov. 1865	Richard Archibald Brooman.
Manufacture of endless cloths	2966	17th Nov. 1865	James Heywood Whitehead.
Improvements in machinery employed when weaving hair, and in preparing and treating hair for weaving. (*Communicated by Charles Bradley.*)	3066	29th Nov. 1865	George Tomlinson Bousfield.
Certain improvements in looms for weaving (*Communicated by Wilhelm Gminder.*)	3091	2nd Dec. 1865	Edward Beott.
Manufacture of shawls and similar ornamental weavings.	3145	6th Dec. 1865	William Houghton Clabburn.
Machinery or apparatus in looms for weaving	3152	7th Dec. 1865	Joseph Wordlatt.
A new method of and apparatus for regulating the tension of threads in weaving and other operations. (*Communicated by Stanislas Vignoreus.*)	3256	14th Dec. 1865	Richard Archibald Brooman.
Looms for weaving	3307	21st Dec. 1865	William Edward Laycock.

Subject-matter of Patent.	Number of Patent.	Date.	Name of Patentee.
WEAVING, &c.— *continued.*			
An improved method of and apparatus for simultaneously manufacturing or weaving two separate cloths at one and the same operation, on a common head or power loom slightly modified for the purpose. (Communicated by Gerbrecht'Irick.)	3211	22nd Dec. 1865	Léopold D'Aubreville.
Preparation of glue or gelatine so as to render it insoluble in water, and applicable by the admixture of other substances, to various purposes for which common glue or gelatine cannot now be used. (material for weaving their hottoms.) (Communicated by Henry Wirtz.)	3325	23rd Dec. 1865	William Edward Newton.
Obtaining and employing continuous lengths of tanned leather for various useful purposes (for weaving matting, soils, &c.)	3384	27rd Dec. 1865	{ George Horn. { Daniel Horn.
Machinery for boring, turning and shaping articles of metal (crank axles of looms.)	3372	29th Dec. 1865	{ William Harrison. { Thomas Walker.
Certain improvements in looms for weaving	3366	29th Dec. 1865	{ Joseph John Harrison. { Edward Harrison.
Certain improvements in looms for weaving	3386	29th Dec. 1865	Thomas Watson.
III.—Weaving Carpets, Velvets and other Pile and Terry Fabrics; Carpet Looms.			
The application and use of certain materials to be employed in the manufacture of carpets and hearth rugs	7	3rd Jan. 1865	{ John Spencer. { Noah Brummhead.
Certain improvements in looms and apparatus for weaving velvet-pile and terry-faced fabrics, and a certain mode of producing designs on such like fabrics.	162	19th Jan. 1865	Joseph Barth.
Manufacture of carpets and other terry and cut pile fabrics. (see "CRIMIXTED FABRICS.") (Communicated by The American Waterproof Cloth Company.)	1409	31st May 1865	William Edward Newton.
Manufacture of pile fabrics	1510	2nd June 1865	{ William Gadd. { John Moore.
Improvements in the manufacture of velvets, plushes and other pile fabrics, and in the machinery or apparatus connected therewith.	1937	25th July 1865	Jules Béhimard the younger.
Manufacture and ornamenting of carpets, rugs and other fabrics.	2151	25th Aug. 1865	Lemuel Clayton.
Improvements in the manufacture of velvet and in the apparatus employed therein. (Communicated by Messieurs Fraisse-Brossard fils jeune.)	2204	29th Aug. 1865	Henri Adrien Bonneville.
A new kind of double faced carpet or tapestry with similar or different patterns on each face.	2792	30th Oct. 1865	Alexander Bouquernié.
Power looms for weaving pile fabrics, such as "patent Axminster" carpeting.	3109	4th Dec. 1865	John Stewart Templeton.

Subject-matter of Patent.	Number of Patent.	Date.	Name of Patentee.
WEAVING, &c.—continued.			
IV.—Knitting; Lace Making; Stocking Frames; Warp Fabrics; Nets and Knotted Fabrics.			
Manufacture of looped fabrics in warp machinery	117	13th Jan. 1865	William Wilkins.
New or improved machinery for the manufacture of wire and other netting. (netting of threads.) (Communicated by Edmund Paul Henri Gondmin.)	360	9th Feb. 1865	Richard Archibald Brooman.
Manufacture of lace in twist lace machines	588	24th Feb. 1865	James Hartshorn. William Redgate.
Improvements in the manufacture of lace or other fabrics made on bobbin net or twist lace machines, and in the machinery or apparatus employed therein.	606	4th March 1865	Henry Taylor.
Manufacture of lace or net in twist lace machines	716	14th March 1865	John Wilkie.
Manufacture of stockings and other articles of hosiery.	725	15th March 1865	Henry Owen.
Manufacture of fabrics in lace machinery	601	22nd March 1865	William Clarke.
Manufacture of lace in twist lace machines	871	5th April 1865	Frederic Rainford Keane.
Machinery for the manufacture of lace (Communicated by Désiré Siraï and Léon Siraï.)	1087	19th April 1865	Richard Archibald Brooman.
Manufacture of articles of lace or net fabric	1189	22nd April 1865	Charles James Kerman. John Alexander Kerman.
Manufacture of dress shirts and drawers made by means of the stocking frame.	1199	24th April 1865	Edward Moore.
Manufacture of elastic knitted or looped fabrics	1575	9th May 1865	Robert Barlow Cooley.
Machinery or apparatus employed in circular knitting machines	1597	20th May 1865	Edwin Attenborough. Samuel Mellor. George Blackburn.
Certain improvements applicable to spinning, weaving and knitting machines. (Communicated by Charles Arthur Radiguet and Jean Adolphe Levine.)	1440	25th May 1865	William Edward Newton.
Knitting-machines (Communicated by Isaac William Lamb.)	1445	26th May 1865	William Clark.
Manufacture of lace in twist lace machines	1512	1st June 1865	Henry Mallet.
Twist lace machines	1725	29th June 1865	Richard Hoot. John Cowe.
Knitting-machines (Communicated by William Williams Clay.)	1747	1st July 1865	George Davis.
Manufacture or production of bobbin net or twist lace made on bobbin net or twist lace machines.	1787	3rd July 1865	Stephen Fairn.
Machinery for making lace (Communicated by Alfred Masson.)	2219	9th Sept. 1865	William Edward Newton.
Improvements in certain knitted fabrics and in the means for producing the same.	2719	21st Oct. 1865	Thomas Webb.
Knitting-machine needles (Communicated by Isaac William Lamb.)	2960	17th Nov. 1865	William Clark.
Knitting-machines (Communicated by Asa Sessions.)	2965	20th Nov. 1865	Samuel Norris.
Manufacture of ornamental laces and fabrics in twist lace machinery.	3109	4th Dec. 1865	William Clarke.

Subject-matter of Patent.	Number of Patent.	Date.	Name of Patentee.
WEAVING, &c.—continued.			
V.—Weaving Fringes, Ribbons, Trimmings, Braid, Plaiting.			
Manufacture of driving bands or belts for machinery and other purposes - - -	500	3rd Feb. 1865	George Hare. Daniel Hare.
Manufacture of shirt borderings and linings to be applied to wearing apparel. (Communicated by Carl Spannagel.)	551	7th Feb. 1865	William Staats.
Improvements in covered steel for crinoline shirts, and in the machinery for covering and uniting the same. (Communicated by Olivre Rogers Burnham.)	559	2nd March 1865	William Sparks Thomson.
An improved method of twisting threads - (Communicated by Désiré Sirol and Léon Sirol.)	2147	19th Aug. 1865	Richard Archibald Brooman.
Ornamenting and protecting the edges of bedquilts, counterpanes, toilet covers, carriage rugs and other similar coverings, by edging, banding or fringing by machinery - - -	2285	1st Sept. 1865	Robert Knowles. Joseph Lindley.
Ornamentation of fringes and trimmings - (or " Cemented Fabrics.")	2960	5th Sept. 1865	Thomas Bird Bailey.
Machinery for weaving the covering of blind-cord and other tubular fabrics. (Communicated by Isaac Emerson Palmer.)	2661	17th Oct. 1865	Henry Edward Newton.
Shuttle motion for looms - - - (ribbon and brace looms.) (Communicated by Julius Schottenfels.)	2828	3rd Nov. 1865	Frederic Tolhausen.
Manufacture of shawls - - - (Communicated by Pierre Honoré Maillard.)	2961	17th Nov. 1865	Richard Archibald Brooman.
Manufacture of ornamental laces and fabrics in twist lace machinery. (" progren.")	3108	4th Dec. 1865	William Clarke.
Improvements in the manufacture of trimmings and in the machinery employed therein.	3320	23rd Dec. 1865	William Smith.
VI.—Shuttles.			
Looms for weaving - - - -	1039	11th April 1865	Archibald Turner.
Certain improvements in looms for weaving -	2061	9th Aug. 1865	Thomas Ramsden Shaw.
Shuttles for weaving purposes - - -	2129	17th Aug. 1865	Abraham Akroyd. Jonathan Lister.
Weft-winding machines both for winding on bobbins and cops, also for a shuttle to hold the cop when weaving.	2419	30th Sept. 1865	William Longbottom.
Machinery for weaving the covering of blind-cord and other tubular fabrics. (Communicated by Isaac Emerson Palmer.)	2661	17th Oct. 1865	Henry Edward Newton.
VII.—Temples, Pickers, Healds and Reeds.			
Improvements in healds for looms, and in machinery or apparatus for manufacturing and winding the same upon " shafts."	347	7th Feb. 1865	Alfred Augustus Larmuth.
Certain improvements in and applicable to looms for weaving.	552	2nd March 1865	Samuel Brooks.

Subject-matter of Patent.	Number of Patent.	Date.	Name of Patentee.
WEAVING, &c.—continued.			
Self-acting temples for looms - - -	1142	24th April 1865	Charles Eastwood. George Eastwood.
Pickers for looms - - - - -	1800	29th April 1865	George Pomeroy Dodge.
Looms for weaving - - - - -	2073	10th Aug. 1865	John Ingham. Henry Ingham. James Broadley.
Certain improvements in looms for weaving - -	2091	12th Aug. 1865	William Bullough.
Certain improvements in looms for weaving - -	2678	17th Oct. 1865	Edward Lord.
Reeds for weaving cross-net, jute and other fibres	2693	19th Oct. 1865	Thomas Catchpole.
Machinery for the manufacture of healds for looms for weaving - - - - -	3038	25th Nov. 1865	Richard Thomas Heathersall. Samuel Cook. William Henry Hocking.
Pickers used in looms for weaving - - -	3094	2nd Dec. 1865	Richard Edmondson.
A means or method of and apparatus to be employed for utilising waste healds for weaving -	3257	16th Dec. 1865	Francis Johnston. William Anley.
VIII.—Moving off and Taking-up Motion; Stopping Looms.			
Improved mechanism for giving intermittent or continuous revolving motion of different velocities, without the use of change wheels (taking-up motion.)	272	31st Jan. 1865	Thomas Hall. Samuel Booner.
Certain improvements in looms for weaving (stopping the take-up motion.)	293	2nd Feb. 1865	John Maynes.
Looms for weaving - - - - (letting off motion.)	494	22nd Feb. 1865	John Dodgeon. John Gaukroger. William Shackleton.
Weft stop motions for looms - - -	769	19th March 1865	Edwin Pilling. John Harper.
Looms for weaving - - - - -	848	25th March 1865	James Milton.
Looms for weaving - - - - -	907	31st March 1865	Lang Bridge.
Certain improvements in looms for weaving - -	1081	13th April 1865	Christopher Turner. Thomas Room.
Certain improvements in looms for weaving - -	1070	17th April 1865	Mark Smith.
Improvements in power looms for weaving and in apparatus connected therewith.	1307	11th May 1865	William Jamieson.
Certain improvements applicable to spinning, weaving and knitting machines. (stopping.) (Communicated by Charles Arthur Radiquet and Jean Adolphe Lavier.)	1440	25th May 1865	William Edward Newton.
Looms for weaving - - - - -	1524	3rd June 1865	Thomas Forster. James Eckersley.
Looms for weaving - - - - -	1803	7th July 1865	James Bullough.
Looms for weaving - - - - -	2073	10th Aug. 1865	John Ingham. Henry Ingham. James Broadley.
Certain improvements in looms for weaving -	2091	12th Aug. 1865	William Bullough.
Taking up motions of looms for weaving - -	2843	4th Oct. 1865	James Wadsworth. Thomas Hall. Samuel Booner.

Subject-matter of Patent.	Number of Patent.	Date.	Name of Patentee.
WEIGHING-MACHINES, SCALES, INDICATING WEIGHT.			
Improved apparatus for adjusting the weight of railway carriages and engines. (Communicated by Johann Heinrich Kirchardt.)	219	25th Jan. 1865	Otto Günnell.
Improved apparatus for measuring the specific gravity of liquids. (Communicated by Edward Payer.)	449	16th Feb. 1865	John Fulleck Heanrey.
Certain improvements in platform weighing-machines.	787	14th March 1865	James M'Connell.
An improved system of continuous self-acting and self-registering machinery for weighing grain, flour and other ponderable matters	832	23rd March 1865	{ Thomas Roberts. Louis Lau. }
An improved balance with index for weighing railway passengers' luggage.	1115	21st April 1865	Abraham Cahn Herrman.
Hydrometers for ascertaining the strength of spirits and the specific gravity of fluids. (Communicated by Claude Alphonse Valson.)	1348	15th May 1865	Henri Adrien Bonneville.
Apparatus or means for ascertaining the quality and condition of grain and seed. (Communicated by Christian Joseph Schmitz.)	2029	14th Aug. 1865	William Bangor.
Apparatus for ascertaining specific gravities and the bulk of solids, and also for other similar uses.	2490	29th Sept. 1865	Alfred Mosley Brunett.
WHEELS FOR CARRIAGES, RAILWAY WHEELS; WHEEL TIRES, &c.			
A new method for removing or destroying the momentum of heavy bodies by means of an elastic machine or machines, so as to prevent injury and damage from concussion, applicable to ship cables, ship and fort armour, railway trains, tenders to piers and floating piers, gangways, breakwaters and other similar structures, also as a motive-power. (Communicated by William Graham M'Ivor.)	321	6th Feb. 1865	Clements Robert Markham.
Case hardening or converting partially into steel, articles of wrought or malleable iron. (facts of malleable iron wheels.) (Partly communicated by Anthony Leonard Fleury.)	395	11th Feb. 1865	Edwin Henry Newly.
Process for blacking the tyres of railway and other wheels.	572	1st March 1865	William Holiday.
Casting steel railway-wheel tyres	614	4th March 1865	Joseph Whitley.
Improvements in the manufacture of railway wheel tyres, and in the implements or tools employed in such manufacture.	695	9th March 1865	William Daniel Allen.
An improved rotary spader or digging machine for tilling land (Communicated by Cicero Comstock.)	671	10th March 1865	Edwin Addison Phillips.

Subject-matter of Patent.	Number of Patent.	Date.	Name of Patentee.

WHEELS, &c.—continued.

Improvements in the construction of railway plant to ensure the safety of passengers' lives in the event of accident or collision - - -	666	11th March 1865	{ Charles Middleton Kernot. Nathaniel Symons.
A new or improved machine for dressing and rounding the inner surfaces of fellies.	794	22nd March 1865	Hiram Smith Jacobs.
Traction engines - - - - } (travelling wheels.)	863	27th March 1865	{ John Brockshaw. William Scutt Underhill.
Manufacture of steel tires for railway wheels - -	978	28th March 1865	Francis William Webb.
An improved application of steam power to locomotion on ordinary roads. (Communicated by Alfred Tuilleradeau.)	1002	8th April 1865	William Edward Gedge.
A new or improved compensating wheel to be used with locomotives, carriages and other vehicles on railway and tram roads, in conjunction with or without the wheels now used, in order to obtain at curves and other parts of the road a rolling instead of a sledging motion now effected by wheels in present use on railway and other tram roads.	1022	11th April 1865	James John Myers.
Improvements in carriage and other wheels and in connecting or fixing the said wheels to their axle-boxes.	1034	11th April 1865	Stephen Wright.
Wheels and the manner of applying the same to railway carriages for passengers' and goods' traffic, as also the lending wheels for locomotives.	1114	21st April 1865	William Day.
Construction of railway rails and wheels - -	1158	25th April 1865	John Townsend Bucknall.
Improvements in the manufacture of crossings for the permanent way of railways, and also in tyres for wheels.	1396	20th May 1865	Joseph Armstrong.
Machinery employed in the manufacture of hoops and tyres.	1425	25th May 1865	John Ramsbottom.
Manufacture of cast-steel railway tires - -	1428	25th May 1865	John Firth.
Improvements in making cast-steel railway tires, and in apparatus therefor.	1455	27th May 1865	John Martin Rowan.
Wheels for locomotive engines, railway carriages and other purposes. (Communicated by Robert Elsdon.)	1601	13th June 1865	John Henry Johnson.
Locomotive engines and railway carriages - -	1646	19th June 1865	George Smith the younger.
An improved system of wheels for railway carriages	1653	20th June 1865	Emile Dupuat.
Improvements in steam carriages and in adapting wheels for common roads to railways. (Communicated by Joseph Alphonse Lawbat.)	1691	10th July 1865	Richard Archibald Brooman.
Traction engines - - - - - (Communicated by Alexander Kerse Richards.)	1836	11th July 1865	Morris Harvey Kerne.
Manufacture of iron and steel - - - - (rolling wheel tire.) (Communicated by Martin Dieudonné Hrutnau.)	1964	29th July 1865	Ephraim Habel.
Improvements in the manufacture of hoops and tyres and in the machinery employed therein.	1975	31st July 1865	John Ramsbottom.
The improvement of the permanent way of railways and carriages for the same.	2227	30th Aug. 1865	James Cole Green.
Traction engines and other vehicles - - -	2264	30th Aug. 1865	Samuel Lawrence James.
Apparatus used for removing axle-boxes from wheels.	2269	4th Sept. 1865	Joseph Drabble.

Subject-matter of Patent.	Number of Patent.	Date.	Name of Patentee.
WHEELS, &c.—continued.			
Treating, working or manipulating cast steel, for the manufacture of wheel-tires, armour plates or other articles requiring great hardness and tensile strength.	2277	5th Sept. 1865	Julian Gaund.
A locomotive car	2344	13th Sept. 1865	Joseph Page Woodbury.
Improvements in railways and in the wheels for railways. (Communicated by Alexander Slirken.)	2409	21st Sept. 1865	Alfred Vincent Newton.
Improvements in the construction of railway plant to ensure the safety of passengers' lives in the event of accident or collision	2463	28th Sept. 1865	Charles Middleton Kernot. Nathaniel Nymous.
Railway carriages and locomotives (Communicated by Henry Giffard.)	2621	11th Oct. 1865	Michael Henry.
Manufacture of tyres for railway wheels	2654	14th Oct. 1865	William James Armitage-Fairfax Wrailey, John Hodgren.
Improvements in wheels for common road carriages, in tyres for the same, and in machinery for heading the tyre.	2696	16th Oct. 1865	James Lamb Hancock.
Improvements in forging and swaging steel and iron wheel tyres, and in the apparatus or tools employed for that purpose.	2688	19th Oct. 1865	Josiah Fenton.
Wheels for carriages and other vehicles	2708	20th Oct. 1865	Samuel Richard Rowe.
Improvements in the manufacture of wheels for railway carriages, and in the machinery to be employed therein.	2771	27th Oct. 1865	Thomas Greenwood.
Construction of wheels for engines and vehicles used on railways.	2960	6th Nov. 1865	Richard Christopher Mansell.
Casting hoops of steel suitable for making tyres	2968	8th Nov. 1865	William Daniel Allen.
Improvements in the manufacture and treatment of railway bars, tyres and axles, also in the construction of furnaces, machinery and apparatus connected therewith.	3084	1st Dec. 1865	Thomas Weatherburn Dodds.
Certain improvements in the manufacture of tyres for railway wheels and the apparatus connected therewith.	3186	8th Dec. 1865	Richard Evan Price.
Naves and axletree boxes of carriage wheels	3210	12th Dec. 1865	Levi Lamson Sovereign.
Permanent way and wheels of railways (Communicated by Mr. Gerard Christian Bruning.)	3322	23rd Dec. 1865	Hector Augustus Dufrend.

WHEELS FOR MACHINERY; COG-WHEELS, PULLEYS, CAMS, &c.			
Construction, arrangement and mode of applying paddle-wheels for propelling boats or other vessels. (Communicated by Hippolyte Salmon.)	408	13th Feb. 1865	John Garrett Tongue.
An improved rotary spader or digging machine for tilling land. (Communicated by Cicero Comstock.)	671	10th March 1865	Edwin Addison Phillips.

Subject-matter of Patent.	Number of Patent.	Date.	Name of Patentee.
WEELS, &c.—*continued.*			
Apparatus for cutting pasteboard and other like boards. (*Communicated by Elisur Ely Clark.*)	789	21st March 1865	William Clark.
Mechanism applicable to frame-filling machines for wooden matches, trellis and ramwriam.	1003	8th April 1865	Henry Joseph Remlick.
Machinery for cutting files - - - -	1015	8th April 1865	Thomas Turton.
Printing machinery - - - - - -	1028	11th April 1865	David Payne.
Certain improvements in looms for weaving - -	1061	13th April 1865	{Christopher Turner. Thomas Roota.
Apparatus for shaping corks - - - -	1065	15th April 1865	John M'Dowall.
Certain improvements in looms for weaving	1070	17th April 1865	Mark Smith.
" Pulleys " used by brewers and others for lifting and lowering weights into and out of carts, waggons or trucks.	1091	19th April 1865	Fredric William Gilbert.
Machinery for cutting and dressing stones and other hard substances. (*Communicated by Gustavus Coppers.*)	1098	19th April 1865	Maurice Vogl.
Machinery for moulding and making cores for moulding or casting metals.	1122	21st April 1865	Richard Cunham.
Engines, machinery and implements employed in ploughing and tilling land.	1123	21st April 1865	Collion Hall.
Digging machinery - - - - -	1124	22nd April 1865	Ormrod Coffeen Evans.
Improvements in motive-power machinery for cultivating land, part of which improvements is applicable to driving machinery generally	1134	22nd April 1865	{James Howard. Edward Tracey Bousfield.
Improvements in the manufacture of pig iron or foundry metal, and in making and treating castings of such metal. (*for wheels.*)	1203	1st May 1865	Henry Bessemer.
Straight line dividing engines and tools for regulating distances. (*detent wheel.*)	1345	4th May 1865	William Ford Stanley.
An improved method of and apparatus for moulding wheels. (*fly wheels, &c.*)	1488	30th May 1865	Luke Martin.
An improvement in steam-engine governors - (*Communicated by Estus Jarad and Henry Stephen Mansfield and Lyman Arnold Cool.*)	1561	7th June 1865	William Edward Newton.
Sewing-machines - - - - - - (*Communicated by Louis Pierne.*)	1878	9th June 1865	George Hamilton.
Lifts for transferring passengers, goods and heavy weights, from the lower to the upper floor of hotels, club houses and other buildings, with greater safety than heretofore.	1822	10th July 1865	David Cowan.
An improvement in the mode of uniting different metals, such as iron and copper or alloys, to form compound metallic castings. (*adapted to wheels, frames, &c.*)	1885	19th July 1865	George Nemmo.
Means or apparatus for producing friction or adhesion between pulleys, rollers and the like, and cords, bands, belts or chains passed over or round them.	1927	25th July 1865	Martyn John Roberts.
Construction of steam-engines - - -	2053	9th Aug. 1865	Henry Cartwright.
Pulleys for raising and lowering heavy bodies -	2329	12th Sept. 1865	{George Tangye. Joseph Jewsbury.

Subject-matter of Patent.	Number of Patent.	Date.	Name of Patentee.
WHEELS, &c.—continued.			
Construction of presses for hay, cotton, hemp and other substances. (gear wheels.) (Communicated by Thomas Grounds and Thomas Bolton Webster.)	2454	25th Sept. 1865	Alfred Vincent Newton.
Apparatus for raising liquids · · ·	2573	12th Oct. 1865	Jean Urcin Bastier.
Clod crushers and chain harrows · ·	2634	17th Oct. 1865	William Collcurne Cambridge.
Improvements in sewing machinery for using waxed thread. (constructing feed wheels.) (Communicated by Thomas John Halligan.)	2748	24th Oct. 1865	Alfred Vincent Newton.
Apparatus for moulding toothed or other wheels or pullies or portions of circles, for casting.	2751	25th Oct. 1865	George Leach Scott.
Ships' and pulley blocks for general purposes ·	2884	8th Nov. 1865	Thomas Worsley. Walter Bibby.
Apparatus for raising, lowering, moving or transporting heavy bodies. (pulley blocks.)	2903	14th Nov. 1865	Thomas Aldridge Weston. James Tongye. Richard Chapman.
Means of connecting drums or pulleys with their shafts or drivers. (Communicated by Leverett Hamer Olmsted.)	2933	14th Nov. 1865	William Clark.
Machinery for the manufacture of moulds for casting metallic wheels. (toothed wheels and pulleys.)	2959	17th Nov. 1865	Thomas Joseph Perry.
Improvements in the bearings of certain wheels and pulleys applicable to various kinds of machinery.	3221	14th Dec. 1865	William Winter.
WINDING, REELING AND BALLING YARN AND THREAD.			
Machinery for preparing, spinning, doubling and winding wool, mohair, alpaca, silk, flax, cotton or other fibrous substances · · ·	130	16th Jan. 1865	John Bunting Farrar. John Hirst.
Improvements in the manufacture of textile fabrics and in the machinery or apparatus employed therefor. (winding cops for weaving.)	563	24th Feb. 1865	David Chalmers.
Machinery for winding yarns or threads on to quills, spools and bobbins.	901	30th March 1865	Archibald Turner.
Apparatus used in the winding and rewinding of silk and other fabrics. (see "FINISHING.")	931	1st April 1865	William Kilby.
Improvements in silk winding machines, part of the said improvements being also applicable to cleaning and doubling machines.	1638	16th June 1865	William Trevor Wanklyn.
Straight eye clearing guides or clearers, for winding silk, cotton or other fibrous substances · ·	1878	19th July 1865	John Bethin Whitehall. Thomas Pillings.

Subject-matter of Patent.	Number of Patent.	Date.	Name of Patentee.
WINDING, &c.—continued.			
Improvements in the manufacture of textile fabrics and in the machinery or apparatus connected therewith. (winding cops; weaving.) (Communicated by David Chalmers.)	2117	16th Aug. 1865	Flora M'Dougall Chalmers.
Improvements in sewing-machines and in winders for sewing-machines - - - -	2168	23rd Aug. 1865	Henry Willis. George Rice.
Improvements in the means of fixing or attaching the bobbins of winding and other machines on to their spindles, which improvements are also applicable to other similar or analogous purposes, and to the detaching of railway carriages from trains whilst in motion.	2250	31st Aug. 1865	John Ward.
Machinery for winding yarn cops - - -	2297	7th Sept. 1865	William Oldham.
Improvements in the winding of knitting cotton and in the apparatus employed therefor.	2311	9th Sept. 1865	Henry Shanks.
Bobbins or spools used in spinning and winding yarns and threads. (Communicated by Charles Reynolds.)	2388	16th Sept. 1865	Jehiel Keeler Hoyt.
Weft winding machines both for winding on bobbins and cops, also for a shuttle to hold the cop when weaving.	2519	30th Sept. 1865	William Longbottom.
An improvement in machinery for spinning, twisting, doubling and winding yarns or threads. (Communicated by Aroust Laysson and Gaspard Andrieux.)	2538	3rd Oct. 1865	William Edward Newton.
" Firm " winding machines for winding flax, cotton and other fibrous materials.	2585	7th Oct. 1865	Joseph Kirby.
Improvements in machinery or apparatus known as "roving," "intermediate," "slubbing" and "throstle" frames and "doublers," and also in winding machines used for preparing, spinning and winding cotton, wool, flax, silk and other fibrous substances.	2715	24th Oct. 1865	William Sumner.
Machinery or apparatus for reeling silk, cotton or other fibrous threads in the form of skeins.	2823	2nd Nov. 1865	Enoch Bushton.
Means or apparatus for preparing, spinning, twisting, doubling or winding cotton, wool, flax or other material.	2869	7th Nov. 1865	Martyn John Roberts.
Improvements in winding machinery, which improvements are partly applicable to machinery for spinning and doubling.	3119	5th Dec. 1865	John Jackson Ashworth.
Improvements in sewing-machine shuttles, and in the winding or reeling of the thread employed with them.	3205	12th Dec. 1865	Marc Kolts.
Machinery for spooling cotton and other yarns and threads.	3376	30th Dec. 1865	Robert Smith.

Subject-matter of Patent.	Number of Patent.	Date.	Name of Patentee.
WINDOW BLINDS, SUN BLINDS, FIRE-SCREENS.			
Apparatus for painting venetian blinds and similar articles - - - - - - -	170	20th Jan. 1865	Donald Munro. Thomas Wright.
An improved window-blind cord check - -	196	23rd Jan. 1865	Elton Templemore.
Improvements in ventilating blinds or screens, and in the use of ventilating ships and vessels.	422	15th Feb. 1865	Charles Langley.
Certain improvements in venetian blinds for carriages, and which said improvements are also applicable to certain blinds or screens for other purposes.	678	10th March 1865	Thomas Startin.
Ventilating blinds - - - - -	679	29th March 1865	Henry Welshman King.
Manufacture of wire gauze dish covers, plate covers, window blinds, fire guards and meat safes -	1401	22nd May 1865	David Poole. Henry Brittain the younger.
Improvements in the construction of rollers for window blinds and in apparatus connected therewith.	1847	14th July 1865	William Meddowcroft.
The use and application of paper, printed or otherwise ornamented with water colors, for covering floors and other analogous purposes, as a substitute for carpets and oil cloths, and of an improved coating or varnish to be applied to the same, to protect its surface from injury and wear. (and for covering window blinds.)	1878	19th July 1865	Anson Henry Platt.
Means or apparatus for producing friction or adhesion between pulleys, rollers and the like, and cords, bands, belts or chains passed over or round them. (for roller blinds.)	1987	25th July 1865	Martyn John Roberts.
Improvements in the ornamentation of glass and in the applications of glass so ornamented. (Communicated by The Society Rendal Cromwell, Alfred Terreuer and Edward Dodd.)	2036	5th Aug. 1866	John Henry Johnson.
Sun-shades or canopies for perambulators and other wheeled carriages. (the "UMBRELLAS.")	2359	19th Sept. 1865	Henry Lloyd.
Certain improvements in window fittings - -	2503	10th Oct. 1865	William Cooke.
Machinery for weaving the covering of blind-cord and other tubular fabrics. (Communicated by Isaac Emerson Palmer.)	2581	17th Oct. 1865	Henry Edward Newton.
Improvements in rollers for roller blinds, and in roller-blind furniture, and in fixing roller blinds at any required height.	2586	19th Oct. 1865	Joseph Everard.
Window-blinds and screens - - - -	2609	19th Oct. 1865	John Ballard.
An improved method of hanging or suspending blinds from blind rollers, and improvements in the manufacture of such rollers.	2732	21st Oct. 1865	Samuel Parkes Matthews.
Preparation of glue or gelatine so as to render it insoluble in water, and applicable by the admixture of other substances, to various purposes for which common glue or gelatine cannot now be used. (transparencies for fire screens.) (Communicated by Henry Wirth.)	3283	23rd Dec. 1865	William Edward Newton.

Subject-matter of Patent.	Number of Patent.	Date.	Name of Patentee.
WINDOW BLINDS, &c.—continued.			
Retaining and employing continuous lengths of tanned leather for various useful purposes (cords for roller blinds.)	3334	23rd Dec. 1865	{ George Hurn. / Daniel Hurn.
WINDOWS AND SASHES; WINDOW-FRAMES AND SHUTTERS.			
Improvements in producing and finishing photographs and photographic transparencies on paper and other suitable substances, and in the machinery employed therein (for windows.)	56	7th Jan. 1865	{ Barrowclough Wright Hensley; / William Henry Bailey.
Window safes for the protection of property	330	6th Feb. 1865	Robert Nier.
Fastenings for doors, windows, drawers and other like purposes	389	9th Feb. 1865	{ George Edward Meek. / William Howe Howen.
Certain improvements in sash fastenings, and which said fastenings are also applicable to other useful purposes.	482	21st Feb. 1865	William Hitchin.
Construction of fastenings or bolts for window sashes and other purposes.	672	10th March 1865	William Smith.
Improvements in the manufacture of metallic bedsteads, which improvements are also applicable to the manufacture of other metallic articles. (window bars.)	699	13th March 1865	James Atkins.
Means of covering railway trucks, vans and other carriages.	1090	19th April 1865	William Riddell.
Indicators and fastenings for water-closets and other purposes.	1099	20th April 1865	Henry Kindon Taylor.
Invalid carriages (Communicated by Auguste Quétron.)	1120	21st April 1865	Henry Edward Newton.
Certain improvements in window sashes and frames, whereby the sashes may be removed and applied at pleasure, part of which improvements are also applicable to sashes as ordinarily constructed.	1278	4th May 1865	John Casey.
An improved system of telegraphic communication on railways, parts of which invention are also applicable to other telegraphic purposes.	1545	5th June 1865	Alice Isabel Loran Gordon.
Fastenings for doors, windows, drawers and other like purposes	1576	9th June 1865	{ George Edward Meek. / William Howe Howen.
Improved means or apparatus to be applied to doors and windows for the purpose of supporting or maintaining them in any required position when open, and in securing them when shut.	1561	10th June 1865	Arthur Hamilton Gilmore.
Improved arrangements for opening and shutting carriage windows	1618	14th June 1865	{ Sidney Courtauld. / Charles Wilkins Atkinson.
Improvements in or applicable to railway and other carriage windows.	1718	24th June 1865	John Kay Farnworth.
Apparatus for preventing the opening of sash windows from the outside, and for the secure fastening thereof.	1726	24th June 1865	Edwin Reynolds.

Subject-matter of Patent.	Number of Patent.	Date.	Name of Patentee.
Windows, &c.—continued.			
Apparatus for cleaning windows	1807	21st July 1865	Charles Gardner.
An improved fastening or lock	2003	2nd Aug. 1865	Richard Bailey. Joseph England.
Improvements in the construction of railway carriages and in railway breaks and signals, part of which is applicable to marine purposes	2006	2nd Aug. 1865	William Henry Petit-jean. Edward M'Nally.
An improved mode of retaining and preventing the vibration of sliding windows used in dwellings and in railway and other vehicles, and for an improved apparatus for effecting the said purposes	2159	3th Aug. 1865	Thomas Wrigley. Marcus Brown Wrax-head.
Apparatus for cleaning the outsides of windows from the interior.	2243	31st Aug. 1865	George Nurnton.
Apparatus used in opening and closing carriage and other windows.	2319	9th Sept. 1865	John Pennington.
An invention having reference to windows or the sashes thereof.	2349	13th Sept. 1865	Sigourney Wales.
Certain improvements in window fittings	2603	10th Oct. 1865	William Cooke.
Improvements in rules for measuring, and in other instruments or articles requiring to be adjusted or disposed at various angles. (shutters.)	2618	10th Oct. 1865	Arthur Nicholls.
Greenhouses	2684	19th Oct. 1865	Thomas Hungate Preston Dennis.
Improved apparatus to be fitted to windows when cleaning, painting or otherwise.	2737	21st Oct. 1865	Joseph William Lee.
Suspending or supporting window sashes and sliding shutters.	2754	23rd Oct. 1865	Henry Newman.
Ventilators for windows and other like openings.	2799	31st Oct. 1865	David Blair White.
Apparatus for raising and lowering the windows of railway and other carriages and other windows.	2810	1st Nov. 1865	John Kay Farnworth.
Improved means or apparatus to be applied to doors and windows, for the purpose of supporting or maintaining them in any required position when open, and in securing them when shut.	2819	1st Nov. 1865	Arthur Hamilton Gilmore.
A mode or modes of inserting glass or other transparent plates in the fabric of umbrellas or in other pliant fabrics. (Communicated by Erasmus Althington Pond, Mark Staples Richardson and Edmund Alonzo Morse.)	2890	4th Nov. 1865	John Henry Johnson.
An improved sash fastening for windows	2947	21st Nov. 1865	William Parsons.
Certain improvements in the manufacture of folding shutters.	3194	11th Dec. 1865	John Goddard.
Construction and mode of hanging window-sashes	3320	23rd Dec. 1865	Richard May Marigold. Samuel Fitzjohn.
Obtaining and employing continuous lengths of tanned leather for various useful purposes (window and shutter lines.)	3334	23rd Dec. 1865	George Harn. Daniel Harn.

Subject-matter of Patent.	Number of Patent.	Date.	Name of Patentee.
WIRE-WORKING; WIRE-ROPES; TELEGRAPH CABLES.			
Coverings of telegraphic conductors and cables	98	12th Jan. 1865	John Fuller.
Manufacture of crinoline skirts - - -	108	13th Jan. 1865	Joseph Knight.
Improvements in rail and tramways, in laying electric telegraph wires, and in composition for insulating the same. (Communicated by Jean Armand Émile Lainébre.)	199	31st Jan. 1865	Richard Archibald Brooman.
Improvements in heddles for looms, and in machinery or apparatus for manufacturing and winding the same upon "shafts."	347	7th Feb. 1865	Alfred Augustus Larsenth.
New or improved machinery for the manufacture of wire and other netting. (Communicated by Edmund Paul Henri Gondin.)	390	8th Feb. 1865	Richard Archibald Brooman.
A new or improved insulating material for telegraphic and other purposes, together with an improvement in protecting telegraph wires, especially applicable to submarine and subterranean telegraphs. (Communicated by Jules Erckmann.)	503	9th Feb. 1865	William Alfred Marshall.
Improvements in covered steel for crinoline skirts, and in the machinery for covering and uniting the same. (Communicated by Oliver Rogers Burnham.)	649	2nd March 1865	William Sparks Thomson.
Constructing strained wire fences - - -	647	2nd March 1865	Robert Johnson.
An improvement in covered springs for clothing and in means for manufacturing the same, applicable also to other purposes.	682	6th March 1865	Timothy Sheldon Sperry.
An improved mode of pointing or tapering the ends of metallic rods or wires, applicable to the manufacture of pins, needles, and other articles where points or tapered ends are required. (Communicated by Henri Conderay.)	976	6th April 1865	Edwin Henry Newby.
Improvements in the construction of submarine telegraph cables, and in the mode of submerging or laying them in the water. (Communicated by Jean Lucien Armen.)	1081	11th April 1865	William Edward Newton.
Machinery or apparatus for tapering, pointing, or reducing wires or rods for spindles, hatchel teeth, pins for drums, and similar articles.	1098	10th May 1865	Chauncey Orrin Crosby.
Manufacture of wire gauze dish covers, plate covers, window blinds, fire guards, and meat safes.	1401	22nd May 1865	David Powis. Henry Brittain the younger.
Annealing pots and muffles for annealing iron and steel wire, sheet metal and other articles.	1480	30th May 1865	John Hiltell.
An improved method of submerging telegraphic cables.	1544	5th June 1865	James Kennedy.
Compounds for waterproofing and insulating purposes. (protecting wires.)	1889	29th July 1865	Frederick Augustus Abel.
Improvements in the mode or method of preparing materials for, and in the manufacture of submarine telegraphic cables, the same being generally applicable for other purposes.	2026	4th Aug. 1865	Frederick George Mulholland.

Subject-matter of Patent.	Number of Patent.	Date.	Name of Patentee.
WIRE, &c. — *continued.*			
Construction of submarine telegraph cables	2080	11th Aug. 1865	Henry Robert Guy.
Machinery to be used in the manufacture of telegraph cables.	2156	21st Aug. 1865	Fleeming Jenkin.
Improvements in the construction of electric telegraph cables and in the preparation of telegraph wires.	2161	22nd Aug. 1865	Charles Marsden.
An improved furnace for annealing iron and steel wire or rods.	2166	23rd Aug. 1865	John Howard Scott.
Submarine electric telegraph cables	2209	24th Aug. 1865	Stopford Thomas Jones.
Improvements in electric telegraph cables, and in transmitting signals therethrough.	2213	24th Aug. 1865	William Peter Piggott.
Improvements in the manufacture of rope, cordage, yarn, wire rope, and other such like twisted and plaited fabric, and in the machinery employed therein	2225	30th Aug. 1865	{ Thomas Copr. William Grant.
Improvements in covering submarine telegraph cables, and in the machinery and means employed for paying out or hauling in the same.	2396	11th Sept. 1865	Samuel Inkpen.
Improvements in constructing and insulating telegraph conductors, and in apparatus connected therewith.	2332	12th Sept. 1865	John Macintosh.
Construction of submarine telegraph cables	2341	13th Sept. 1865	John Oliver Chapman Phillips.
Manufacturing wire conductors for electro-telegraphic purposes.	2416	22nd Sept. 1865	William Boggett.
Certain improvements in telegraphic cables	2502	30th Sept. 1865	James Austin Mee.
Construction of submarine telegraph cables (*Communicated by Claude Ernest Lami de Nozan.*)	2590	3rd Oct. 1865	Henri Adrien Bonneville.
Improvements in submarine electric telegraph cables and in apparatus connected therewith.	2606	10th Oct. 1865	François Thierry Hubert.
Submarine telegraphy	2612	10th Oct. 1865	John Fletcher Wiles.
The improvement of the means of and apparatus for laying submarine electrical telegraphic wires, lines, cables or other contrivances of a like sort.	2670	16th Oct. 1865	Reinhold Edward Kaalbach.
Machinery for the manufacture of fish hooks	2675	17th Oct. 1865	Albert Penton.
Testing and working submarine electric telegraph wires.	2765	26th Oct. 1865	Willoughby Smith.
Plating or combining gold, platinum and other metals or their alloys. (*plating wire.*)	2848	3rd Nov. 1865	Edward John Northwood.
Improvements in submarine electric telegraph cables, and in machinery employed in the manufacture and submergence thereof	2941	15th Nov. 1865	{ Arthur Wells. Walter Hall.
Improvements in the construction of and in the method of laying submarine electric cables.	2948	16th Nov. 1865	John De la Haye.
Construction of wire conductors for electro-telegraphic purposes.	3180	9th Dec. 1865	William Boggett.
Manufacturing and laying down submarine telegraphic cables.	3192	11th Dec. 1865	Theophilus Barrens.
Construction of wire conductors for electro-telegraphic purposes.	3299	21st Dec. 1865	William Boggett.

Subject-matter of Patent.	Number of Patent.	Date.	Name of Patentee.
WIRE, &c.—continued.			
Preparation of glue or gelatine so as to render it insoluble in water, and applicable by the admixture of other substances to various purposes for which common glue or gelatine cannot now be used. (for coating wire and ribbon.) (Communicated by Henry Wurtz.)	5295	23rd Dec. 1865	William Edward Newton.
Manufacture of electric conductors insulated with India-rubber.	5347	27th Dec. 1865	Hugh Adams Silver.
Construction of telegraphic cables or conductors	5387	30th Dec. 1865	Cromwell Fleetwood Varley.
WOOD AND VENEERS; ARTIFICIAL WOOD.			
Preparing or treating wood and other vegetable fibrous materials for the manufacture of pulp for paper. (Communicated by Zéphirin Gaspard Alexandre Nathan Pétrone Oriol, Amable Alfred Fredet and Pierre Amable Henri Matussière.)	80	10th Jan. 1865	William Clark.
Machinery or apparatus for planing and moulding or otherwise shaping wood	143	17th Jan. 1865	{ John Robinson. John Smith.
Bark, soles of feet protectors, to be used loose in boots and shoes, or affixed thereto (of wood.)	608	31st March 1865	{ John Poole. Thomas Brown.
Machinery or apparatus for cutting scrolls, frets and filigree work.	929	1st April 1865	James Keenan.
Improvements in taking impressions from the grain of wood, and in transferring the same on to various surfaces (and for decorating wood.)	1117	21st April 1865	{ William Scarratt. William Dean.
Machinery for cutting dovetails for joiners' work	1671	21st June 1865	William Roberts.
New or improved compositions in imitation of ivory and woods, to be employed in the manufacture of umbrella tips, umbrella and walking stick handles, and other useful and ornamental purposes	1692	23rd June 1865	{ Michael Dietrich Rosenthal. Solomon Grademwitz.
Staining and graining woods	1851	14th July 1865	{ John Morrough Murphy. James Morrough Murphy.
An improved process for rendering wood incombustible.	1900	21st July 1865	Louis Alphonse Maurice Claudin.
An improved mode of and apparatus for drying timber, grain and other marketable products. (Communicated by Henry Bulkley.)	2127	17th Aug. 1865	Alfred Vincent Newton.
An improved method or process for ornamenting walls and other surfaces of buildings. (carving with cramps.) (Communicated by Carl Friedrich Günther.)	2158	18th Aug. 1865	George Howard.
Ornamenting and surfacing veneers and other articles of wood.	2279	5th Sept. 1865	Thomas Thompson Ponsonby.

Subject-matter of Patent.	Number of Patent.	Date.	Name of Patentee.

Wood, &c.—continued.

Machinery for making casks, barrels and other wooden vessels of capacity. — 2438 — 22nd Sept. 1865 — James Davidson.

An improved liquid composition for cleansing, scouring and bleaching textile animal, mineral and vegetable substances (cleansing wood.) — 2440 — 23rd Sept. 1865 — { Gustave Emile Rolland. Emile Léon Rolland.

Machinery or apparatus for the manufacture of wooden spills. — 2577 — 6th Oct. 1865 — Thomas Machin.

Rendering wood for building and other purposes non-combustible or non-inflammable. — 2620 — 11th Oct. 1865 — William Hall.

Apparatus for splitting and preparing cane. — 2717 — 20th Oct. 1865 — Rémy Bissey.

An improved process for bending or arching wood. (Communicated by Lewis Porrohère.) — 2723 — 21st Oct. 1865 — William Edward Gedge.

Preparing the surfaces of paper, leather, woven and other fabrics and substances, for receiving photographic pictures, engravings, lithographs and prints, and for rendering such substances fire and water-proof. (surfacing wood.) (Communicated by William Gibson.) — 2801 — 9th Nov. 1865 — William Edward Newton.

Manufacture of embossed wood. (Communicated by Henry May and Henry Taylor Blake.) — 2896 — 10th Nov. 1865 — Alfred Vincent Newton.

An improved method or process for producing paper makers' pulp from cane, bamboo and other analogous substances. (Communicated by Charles Heaton.) — 2922 — 13th Nov. 1865 — William Robert Lake.

Machinery for cutting mouldings in wood. (Communicated by John Bartlett Winslow.) — 3040 — 27th Nov. 1865 — William Edward Newton.

Improved machinery to be used in the manufacture of paper. (from wood.) (Communicated by Heinrich Voelter.) — 3041 — 27th Nov. 1865 — William Edward Newton.

Machinery or tools for cutting wood or other substances. (moulding-machines.) — 3188 — 9th Dec. 1865 — William Wilson Hulse.

New or improved compositions in imitation of ivory and wood, to be employed in the manufacture of umbrella tips, umbrella and walking-stick handles, and other useful and ornamental purposes — 3310 — 22nd Dec. 1865 — { Michael Dietrich Boerm- thal. Solomon Gradenwitz.

Preparation of glue or gelatine so as to render it insoluble in water, and applicable by the admission of other substances to various purposes for which common glue or gelatine cannot now be used. (for preserving.) (Communicated by Henry Warts.) — 3345 — 23rd Dec. 1865 — William Edward Newton.

For Sawing Wood, see "Cutting."
For Preserving Timber, see "Preserving Wood."

www.ingramcontent.com/pod-product-compliance
Lightning Source LLC
Chambersburg PA
CBHW031932220326
41598CB00062BA/1684

* 9 7 8 3 7 4 1 1 7 0 3 4 8 *